TAKING SIDES

Clashing Views in

Special Education

FIFTH EDITION

D0769566

TAKING↻SIDES

Clashing Views in

Special Education

FIFTH EDITION

Selected, Edited, and with Introductions by

MaryAnn Byrnes
University of Massachusetts—Boston

The **McGraw·Hill** Companies

TAKING SIDES: CLASHING VIEWS IN SPECIAL EDUCATION, FIFTH EDITION

Published by McGraw-Hill, a business unit of The McGraw-Hill Companies, Inc., 1221 Avenue of the Americas, New York, NY 10020. Copyright © 2011 by The McGraw-Hill Companies, Inc. All rights reserved. Previous edition(s) © 2009, 2008, and 2005. No part of this publication may be reproduced or distributed in any form or by any means, or stored in a database or retrieval system, without the prior written consent of The McGraw-Hill Companies, Inc., including, but not limited to, in any network or other electronic storage or transmission, or broadcast for distance learning.

Some ancillaries, including electronic and print components, may not be available to customers outside the United States.

Taking Sides® is a registered trademark of the McGraw-Hill Companies, Inc.
Taking Sides is published by the **Contemporary Learning Series** group within the McGraw-Hill Higher Education division.

2 3 4 5 6 7 8 9 0 DOC/DOC 1 0 9 8 7 6 5 4 3 2 1

MHID: 0-07-805003-0
ISBN: 978-0-07-805003-9
ISSN: 1537-0739

Managing Editor: *Larry Loeppke*
Senior Developmental Editor: *Jade Benedict*
Senior Permissions Coordinator: *Shirley Lanners*
Marketing Specialist: *Alice Link*
Senior Project Manager: *Jane Mohr*
Design Coordinator: *Brenda A. Rolwes*
Cover Graphics: *Rick D. Noel*
Buyer: *Nicole Baumgartner*
Media Project Manager: *Sridevi Palani*

Compositor: MPS Limited, a Macmillan Company
Cover Image: © Getty Images/RF

Library of Congress Cataloging-in-Publication Data

Main entry under title:
    Taking sides: clashing views in special education/selected, edited, and with introductions by MaryAnn Byrnes.—5th ed.

    Includes bibliographical references and index.
    1. Special education, I. Byrnes, MaryAnn, *ed.* II. Series.
                                    371.9

Editors/Academic Advisory Board

Members of the Academic Advisory Board are instrumental in the final selection of articles for each edition of TAKING SIDES. Their review of articles for content, level, and appropriateness provides critical direction to the editors and staff. We think that you will find their careful consideration well reflected in this volume.

TAKING SIDES: Clashing Views in SPECIAL EDUCATION
Fifth Edition

EDITOR

MaryAnn Byrnes
University of Massachusetts—Boston

ACADEMIC ADVISORY BOARD MEMBERS

Mary Bay
*University
of Illinois—Chicago*

Todd Fletcher
University of Arizona

Maria Reyes
*University of Central
Florida*

Lusa Lo
*University of
Massachusetts—Boston*

Preface

Special education is full of questions, emotions, and opinions. Public responsibility for the education of children with disabilities is a relatively new endeavor that is still exploring its identity and boundaries. Sometimes it seems that just as one set of issues is resolved (such as the creation of a range of services in public schools) a host of new challenges (such as leaving no child behind) arises. Other issues, including appropriate funding and inclusion, all but defy resolution. Through *Taking Sides: Clashing Views in Special Education,* I invite you to consider several current issues in this volatile and rewarding field.

Taking Sides: Clashing Views in Special Education has two major goals. First, to introduce key questions in special education, so readers can learn from authors who have thought extensively about educational policy and practice. Second, to encourage thinking and discussion, so readers can explore possibilities and debate the consequences of positions and actions. I hope you will find yourselves engaged and enlivened by the conversations these topics begin. Most of all, I trust your deliberations will contribute to constructive solutions to puzzles that demand careful thinking and dedication to all our children.

Some basic principles guided the choice of selections for this book. Each reading needed to represent a widely held point of view on the question at hand. Other opinions surely exist, but the ones presented needed to be broadly held. Each had to employ solid reasoning; its position could not be easily refuted because of faulty logic. Finally, each selection needed to be interesting to read. If an article did not captivate my attention—and that of my students—I did not want it included.

This book includes 20 issues, addressing active debates in the field. There are three sections. Unit 1, Special Education and Society, introduces questions of social policy and practice. Unit 2, Access and Accountability, highlights perspectives on educational expectations and outcomes. Unit 3, Exceptionalities, presents critical considerations about atypical learners and the treatments suggested for their benefit.

Each issue is framed as a question and begins with an *Introduction,* designed to set the stage. Two readings, presenting contrasting points of view, come next. Each issue closes with a *Postscript,* summarizing the expressed points of view, suggesting others, and presenting additional readings on the topic. The *Introductions* and *Postscripts* also feature questions to stimulate your thinking as you weigh the topic at hand and its relationship to schools. Each question represents challenges to be resolved in the policy and practice of educating children with disabilities.

Due to page constraints, most selections have been edited. Use the heading citations to locate the entire article, along with its bibliography.

To further expand your thinking, you may want to reference the *Internet References* pages that precede each section. These contain a sampling of Internet site addresses (URLs) that represent varied points of view and offer resources as well as links to related sites and bibliographies.

The YES and NO positions on every issue express strongly held opinions. You may agree or disagree with the authors, or you may find your own view lies somewhere in between. Perhaps you will identify additional perspectives as you study the issues more thoroughly. You will certainly find connections between issues. Class discussions may lead you to formulate a fresh response to the issue question. Doubtless, as you continue in your professional and personal life, your thinking will change and develop. What is critical as you read this book is that you reflect on positions, possibilities, and emotions so you can form opinions to guide your actions and decisions.

A word to the instructor   An *Instructor's Manual with Test Questions* (multiple-choice and essay) is available through The McGraw-Hill Contemporary Learning Series for the instructor using *Taking Sides* in the classroom. Also available is *Using Taking Sides in the Classroom,* a general guidebook that presents strategies and examples of using the pro-con method in classroom settings. Faculty members using this text also have access to an online version of *Using Taking Sides in the Classroom* and a correspondence service, located at http://www.mhcls.com/usingts/.

Taking Sides: Clashing View in Special Education is only one title in the *Taking Sides* series. The table of contents for any of the other titles can be found at the Taking Sides Web site at http://www.mhcls.com/takingsides/.

Changes to this edition   This fifth edition includes eight completely new issues: Are Labels Good for Kids? (Issue 1); Are Charter School Doors Open to Students with Disabilities (Issue 5); Should Insurance Cover Treatments and Services for Autism? (Issue 6); Should Special Education and General Education Merge? (Issue 9); Should Colleges Be More Accommodating to Students with Disabilities? (Issue 14); Is ADHD a Real Disorder? (Issue 18); Are There Scientifically Effective Treatments for Autism? (Issue 19); and Does Working with Parents Have to Be Contentious? (Issue 20). The *Introduction* as well as several Issue *introductions and postscripts* have been revised with updated research references. Finally, this edition begins with a unique section titled *Emerging Issues: Impending Changes in NCLB and IDEA*. This section introduces readers to controversies surrounding the reauthorization of the Elementary and Secondary Education Act (ESEA) and Individuals with Disabilities Education Improvement Act (IDEA).

Acknowledgments   Spirited debate about "the right thing to do" has been part of my life since I became a teacher. So long as we keep children in mind, debating possibilities is exhilarating. First, and most importantly, I thank the children, educators, and parents who frame the questions and continually teach me almost anything is possible—not always easy, but possible. Many thanks to my graduate assistant, Jenny Amaral, whose curiosity and background in journalism uncovered more than one bit of surprising information. Additionally, I have appreciated the helpfulness of Jade Benedict and all the supporting staff at McGraw-Hill. And, of course, Joe.

MaryAnn Byrnes
University of Massachusetts—Boston

Contents in Brief

Contents

UNIT 1   SPECIAL EDUCATION AND SOCIETY   1

Issue 1.   Are Labels Good for Kids?   2

Gwyn W. Senokossoff, an instructor in childhood education and literacy, and Kim Stoddard, associate professor in special education (both at the University of South Florida St. Petersburg), describe the first author's struggles to find a diagnosis, appropriate intervention, and support for her son with childhood bipolar disorder. Scott M. Shannon, psychiatrist and former president of the American Holistic Medical Association, explains why he believes it is advantageous to look for ways to relieve stressors in a child's environment rather than seek a label, which might do more harm than good.

Issue 2.   Does IDEA 2004 Contain Substantial Changes?   22

H. Rutherford Turnbull III, cofounder and codirector of the Beach Center on Disability at the University of Kansas, sees major changes in IDEA 2004. In line with the Bush administration's priorities, Turnbull identifies a shift toward requiring parents and students to take more responsibility for their own behavior and for relationships with schools. Tom E. C. Smith, professor at the University of Arkansas, focuses his research on disability law and inclusion. Reflecting on IDEA 2004, Smith believes that although some changes seem significant, they will make little difference in the daily practice of special education teachers.

Issue 3.   Is Eliminating Minority Overrepresentation Beyond the Scope of Public Schools?   45

M. Suzanne Donovan and Christopher T. Cross, researchers representing the findings of a National Research Council (NRC) study on minority students in special and gifted education, believe overrepresentation issues are complex and not easily resolvable. While teachers can make a difference, environmental factors and poverty have a large impact and require interventions beyond schools. Daniel J. Losen and Gary Orfield, both policy experts, present the results of research commissioned by the Civil Rights Project (CRP) of Harvard University. While agreeing with some of the NRC recommendations, these findings suggest that patterns will change with stricter enforcement of federal and state regulations.

Issue 4. Can Whole-School Reform Reduce Discipline Problems? 75

Howard S. Adelman and Linda Taylor, codirectors of the UCLA School Mental Health Project, based in the Center for Mental Health in Schools, believe that many discipline problems could be eliminated by whole-school initiatives that create and sustain an environment that addresses positive social and emotional development as well as academics. William C. Frick and Susan C. Faircloth, assistant professors at the University of Oklahoma and The Pennsylvania State University, respectively, present dilemmas faced by principals torn between balancing the needs of one particular student who exhibits disruptive behavior with those of the rest of the student body whose learning is affected by the single student's actions.

Issue 5. Are Charter School Doors Open to Students with Disabilities? 95

The Center for Education Reform (CER) advocates for school change, emphasizing charter schools. Through gathering and disseminating information on charters, CER shares promising instructional options. The 2008 Annual Survey illustrates how charters successfully educate a range of students, including those who might be eligible for special education. Thomas Hehir, prominent educational policy maker, agrees that charter schools can offer desirable options. Testifying before Congress, Hehir expresses his strong concern that the doors of charter schools are often closed to students with disabilities. He cautions that these closed doors might constitute a denial of civil rights.

Autism Speaks, the nation's largest autism science and advocacy organization founded by Suzanne and Bob Wright (former vice chairman of General Electric and CEO of NBC and NBC Universal), presents eight arguments in support of legislation mandating health insurance coverage of autism services. Writing for the Council for Affordable Health Insurance, an organization that promotes the affordable health care access for all Americans, Victoria C. Bunce and J.P. Wieske discuss national trends in state-mandated health care benefits for children with autism, arguing that responsibility for these costs belongs elsewhere.

John Hockenberry, an award-winning television commentator, a radio host, and a foreign correspondent, who happens to use a wheelchair, celebrates the increased access brought about by implementation of the Americans with Disabilities Act (ADA). Lynda A. Price, Paul J. Gerber (university faculty members and researchers), and Robert Mulligan (a district special education administrator) contend that the opportunities for ADA-mandated access are underused by individuals with learning disabilities.

Rachel Brown-Chidsey and Mark W. Steege, faculty members at the University of Southern Maine, who have conducted extensive research in the area of student assessment, describe Response to Intervention (RTI) as a systematic way for educators to help all children experience appropriate educational practices. Douglas Fuchs and Donald D. Deshler, professors at Vanderbilt University and the University of Kansas, respectively, prolific scholars, and co-directors of the National Research Center on Learning Disabilities, urge educators to identify and explore unresolved aspects of RTI before wholesale implementation.

Mary T. Brownell, Paul T. Sindelar, and Mary T. Kiely, policy scholars from the University of Florida, Gainesville, and Louis C. Danielson at the American Institutes for Research (Danielson) link political changes with special education teacher preparation. They conclude that the future of special education rests within content-rich Response to Intervention (RTI) practices. Margaret J. McLaughlin, policy architect and analyst from the University of Maryland, sees a disconnect between the singular academic outcomes of No Child Left Behind (NCLB) Act/Elementary and Secondary Education Act (ESEA) and the individualized needs of students with disabilities. Merging is not wise when some students with disabilities are treated unjustly if held to unitary academic outcomes.

Samuel L. Odom, Ellen Brantlinger, Russell Gersten, Robert H. Horner, Bruce Thompson, and Karen R. Harris, all college faculty members and educational researchers, begin their article with definitive support for research-based methodology. They herald proposals for quality indicators, to establish rigor in an array of research methods that can identify effective educational practices. Frederick J. Brigham, associate professor at the University of Virginia, Charlottesville, William E. Gustashaw III and Andrew L. Wiley, both doctoral candidates at the University of Virginia, Charlottesville, and Michele St. Peter Brigham, a special education practitioner, believe that disagreement, mistrust, and the shifting general education environment preclude the usefulness of scientifically based research to guide daily instruction.

Jennifer Booher-Jennings, a doctoral candidate at Columbia University, finds the accountability pressures of No Child Left Behind (NCLB) are leading some administrators to advise teachers to focus only on those children who will improve their school's scores; other students don't count much. The U.S. Department of Education FAQ Sheet on IDEA and NCLB advises readers that the link between these two statutes is sound, emphasizing how they work together to ensure that every student's performance and needs receive appropriate attention.

Kevin S. McGrew, educational researcher and director of the Institute for Applied Psychometrics (IAP), and Jeffrey Evans, consultant and educational researcher for IAP, are wary that stereotypes of individuals with cognitive disabilities are used to form limited (and limiting) expectations and self-fulfilling prophecies. James M. Kauffman, professor emeritus of education at the University of Virginia, Charlottesville, and special education philosopher/ researcher, believes that educators and parents must acknowledge that some students with cognitive disabilities cannot reach high academic standards and are best served by programs that develop other skills.

Rosalind and Joe Vargo, parents of Ro, use their voices to tell a powerful story of their daughter's success in fully inclusive educational programs, from kindergarten through college. Amy D. Marcus, staff reporter at *The Wall Street Journal,* records the voices of Eli's parents and teachers as they react to his message to leave a fully inclusive program in favor of a separate special education class.

Hazel Denhart, who lectures at Portland State University, uses disability theory perspective to analyze the perceptions of students with learning disabilities about their experiences in higher education. Her interviewees identify social barriers that make college a less-than-welcome experience, and she recommends steps to reduce institutional intolerance. Melana Z. Vickers, an editorial writer for *USA Today,* uses information from interviews with on-campus experts, professors, and students to raise serious questions about the legitimacy of accommodations and disability services. Many of her interviewees think disabilities leading to accommodations can be purchased, to the detriment of everyone's experience.

UNIT 3   EXCEPTIONALITIES   313

John Cloud, a staff writer for *Time Magazine* since 1997, profiles a number of extraordinarily gifted young people challenged for the first time in a specialized school that pushes them to reach their potential in a way that public schools could not. Susan Winebrenner and Dina Brulles work with educators to design and deliver cluster-based programs that address the needs of the gifted within their neighborhood school and provide options for a range of students to reach their potential.

Lynn S. Fuchs, a prolific scholar in the area of learning disabilities and one of the several researchers in the National Research Center for Learning Disabilities, explains how Response to Intervention (RTI) strategies can separate a struggling learner from one with specific learning disability (SLD). Cathy G. Litty (Western Carolina University) and J. Amos Hatch (University of Tennessee) discuss the increasing academic pressures for kindergarten children; they believe special education services should be provided as soon as possible to students who will eventually be found eligible.

Nathaniel S. Lehrman, clinical director (retired) of the Kingsboro (NY) Psychiatric Center, warns that new mental health screening requirements, heralded as a way to increase the health of the nation, will intrude on basic freedoms, lead to inappropriate labels, and increase revenue for pharmaceutical companies. Mark D. Weist, Marcia Rubin, Elizabeth Moore, Steven Adelshiem, and Gordon Wrobel, consultants and researchers in mental health, see this screening as a way to identify those who need early intervention in order to prevent the development of debilitating mental illnesses.

Evelyn B. Kelly, a science writer, journalist, and adjunct professor at the College of Education, St. Leo University, presents an encyclopedia of characteristics, causes, and interventions for the several conditions that are all very real attention deficit hyperactivity disorders. Hara E. Marano, also an author and journalist, frequently writing for *Psychology Today* and other popular publications, believes that "hothouse parenting" and "overparenting" have created children who overreact to life events because they have not been allowed to develop naturally.

James B. Adams (Arizona State University), Stephen Edelson (Center for the Study of Autism), Temple Grandin (Colorado State University), and Bernard Rimland (Director of the Autism Research Institute) recommend to parents of young children with autism an array of effective treatment options, many of them biomedical based. The Committee on Educational Interventions, chaired by Catherine Lord, director of the University of Michigan's Autism and Communication Disorders Center, summarizing their examination of research studies of educational treatments for children with autism, found little consistent evidence to support the efficacy claims made by their proponents.

Jenna Goudreau relates the compelling story of parents who have to fight with school systems and battle legal complexities to get the free appropriate public education they feel is right for their children with disabilities. Jennifer Krumins, a special education teacher and mother of a child with autism, advises parents to ease tension, stress, and pressure by finding an advocate who can serve as an "interpreter" in a complex educational system and teach them how to secure the necessary supports with a positive approach.

Correlation Guide

The *Taking Sides* series presents current issues in a debate-style format designed to stimulate student interest and develop critical thinking skills. Each issue is thoughtfully framed with an issue summary, an issue introduction, and a postscript. The pro and con essays—selected for their liveliness and substance—represent the arguments of leading scholars and commentators in their fields.

Taking Sides: Clashing Views in Special Education, 5/e is an easy-to-use reader that presents issues on important topics such as *social interaction, stratification, inequality,* and *deviance*. For more information on *Taking Sides* and other *McGraw-Hill Contemporary Learning Series* titles, visit www.mhcls.com.

This convenient guide matches the issues in *Taking Sides: Clashing Views in Special Education*, 5/e with the corresponding chapters in our best-selling McGraw-Hill Special Education textbook by Taylor et al.

Taking Sides: Special Education, 5/e	Exceptional Students: Preparing Teachers for the 21st Century by Taylor et al.
Issue 1: Are Labels Good for Kids?	**Chapter 2:** The Special Education Process: From Initial Identification to the Delivery of Services
Issue 2: Does IDEA 2004 Contain Substantial Changes?	**Chapter 4:** Students with Learning Disabilities
Issue 3: Is Eliminating Minority Overrepresentation Beyond the Scope of Public Schools?	**Chapter 1:** An Overview of Special Education
Issue 4: Can Whole School Reform Reduce Discipline Problems?	**Chapter 3:** School, Family, and Community Collaboration **Chapter 4:** Students with Learning Disabilities
Issue 5: Are Charter School Doors Open to Students with Disabilities?	**Chapter 4:** Students with Learning Disabilities
Issue 6: Should Insurance Cover Treatments and Services for Autism?	**Chapter 2:** The Special Education Process: From Initial Identification to the Delivery of Services **Chapter 11:** Students with Autism Spectrum Disorders
Issue 7: Has the ADA Accomplished Its Goals?	**Chapter 1:** An Overview of Special Education
Issue 8: Is Response to Intervention (RTI) Ready for Implementation?	**Chapter 4:** Students with Learning Disabilities
Issue 9: Should Special Education and General Education Merge?	**Chapter 1:** An Overview of Special Education **Chapter 3:** School, Family, and Community Collaboration
Issue 10: Can Scientifically Based Research Guide Instructional Practice?	**Chapter 2:** The Special Education Process: From Initial Identification to the Delivery of Services

Taking Sides: Special Education, 5/e	Exceptional Students: Preparing Teachers for the 21st Century by Taylor et al.
Issue 11: Does NCLB Leave Some Students Behind?	**Chapter 2:** The Special Education Process: From Initial Identification to the Delivery of Services **Chapter 4:** Students with Learning Disabilities
Issue 12: Should Students with Cognitive Disabilities Be Expected to Demonstrate Academic Proficiency?	**Chapter 4:** Students with Learning Disabilities
Issue 13: Is Full Inclusion the Least Restrictive Environment?	**Chapter 3:** School, Family, and Community Collaboration
Issue 14: Should Colleges Be More Accommodating to Students with Disabilities?	**Chapter 3:** School, Family, and Community Collaboration
Issue 15: Do Gifted and Talented Students Need Special Schools?	**Chapter 15:** Students Who Are Gifted and Talented
Issue 16: Can RTI Reduce the Numbers of Children Identified with Specific Learning Disability (SLD)?	**Chapter 13:** Students Who Are At Risk: Early Identification and Intervention
Issue 17: Is Mental Health Screening an Unwarranted Intrusion?	**Chapter 2:** The Special Education Process: From Initial Identification to the Delivery of Services
Issue 18: Is ADHD a Real Disorder?	**Chapter 14:** Students with Attention Deficit/Hyperactivity Disorders
Issue 19: Are There Scientifically Effective Treatments for Autism?	**Chapter 11:** Students with Autism Spectrum Disorders
Issue 20: Does Working with Parents Have to be Contentious?	**Chapter 3:** School, Family, and Community Collaboration

Introduction

"I introduce . . . a bill . . . to ensure equal opportunities for the handicapped by prohibiting needless discrimination in programs receiving federal financial assistance. . . . The time has come when we can no longer tolerate the invisibility of the handicapped in America. . . . These people have the right to live, to work to the best of their ability—to know the dignity to which every human being is entitled. But too often we keep children whom we regard as 'different' or a 'disturbing influence' out of our schools and community altogether. . . . Where is the cost-effectiveness in consigning them to . . . 'terminal' care in an institution?"

—Senator Hubert H. Humphrey (D-Minnesota), January 20, 1972, on introducing to Congress a bill mandating education for children with disabilities (as quoted in *Back to School on Civil Rights,* National Council on Disability, 2000).

"Unfortunately, this bill promises more than the federal government can deliver, and its good intentions could be thwarted by the many unwise provisions it contains. . . . Even the strongest supporters of this measure know as well as I that they are falsely raising the expectations of the groups affected by claiming authorization levels which are excessive and unrealistic. . . . [This bill also contains a] vast array of detailed complex and costly administrative requirements which would unnecessarily assert federal control over traditional state and local government functions."

—President Gerald Ford, November 29, 1975, upon signing federal legislation to mandate education for children with disabilities (as quoted in *Congress and the Nation, IV*).

Special education was born of controversy about who belongs in schools and how far schools need to stretch to meet student needs. The debate continues.

Think hard about your school experience. When was the first time you saw someone with a disability? What do you remember? Compare your recollections with those of someone one generation older—and one younger. The differences will be startling.

Who remembered The Room? Usually it was in the basement of the school. Hardly anyone went into The Room. Hardly anyone came out. The kids in The Room never seemed to be part of recess or assemblies or lunch or gym. The teachers were also invisible. Sometimes the windows of The Room were covered with paper. Usually the shades were drawn. Kids whispered about The Room, but no one really knew what happened *in there*.

Likely, the students who went to school in The Room seemed older, bigger, and not as smart as most of the other kids in the school. They had few books to learn from and rarely studied any but the most basic academic subjects. No one really knew what happened to the kids in The Room once they left elementary school. There never seemed to be a Room at the high school. Difficult as it is to believe, those who made it inside The Room may have been the lucky ones.

In 1970, not all that long ago, if you were the parent of a child with a disability, your neighborhood school could say your child was not welcome—that there was no place in the school for your child. Choices were limited. You could teach your child at home (or just have him spend his days there); you could try to find a space in a school run by dedicated religious people; or you send your child to live in a faceless institution. Try looking at Burton Blatt's *Christmas in Purgatory: A Photographic Essay on Mental Retardation* (Human Policy Press, 1974) for a view of some of the worst options.

I remember The Room in the elementary schools I attended, but I never knew much about its students. I also remember the Catholic school for girls with Down syndrome, where I volunteered as a Girl Scout. The residents learned cooking and sewing while I was getting ready for high school and college. I never saw the girls outside the school and didn't know what they did when they grew into adults.

There were also the boys who sat in the back row of my classes and tried to avoid the attention of adults. The teachers hoped these boys would just be quiet and behave. The boys dropped out of school as soon as they could.

Years later, in the early 1970s, after teaching fourth grade for 2 years, I entered special education because I was intrigued with unlocking the puzzles that made learning so hard for some of my students. One of my early jobs was as a teacher in an updated version of The Room. It was my first experience in a small district. The day before school began, all the teachers and their students were listed in the local newspaper, along with their bus routes. I eagerly looked for my name, but instead of Mrs. Byrnes, I read "Emotionally Disturbed Classroom." For the entire time I worked at that school, I was the *emotionally disturbed teacher.*

Times had changed somewhat since I attended elementary school. My classroom was on the main floor, next door to the third grade; we had some academic books and we had lunch and recess with everyone else. But we were still different. Each day, my students and I needed to leave our room from 11:30 to 1:30 so it could be used by the gym teacher while the gym was used as a cafeteria. Since there were only 10 of us, taking our classroom space seemed an easy solution. No one appeared to care where we went or what we did during that time. Plenty of people were surprised to see us camp out in the library, tackling *real* schoolwork.

In contrast, think about the schools of today. Children with learning problems significant enough to be disabilities are the focus of concentrated attention. Skilled professionals and researchers strive to understand disabilities and address them with specific teaching methods and approaches. Parents and teachers actively consider ways to adapt instruction. Program options seem limitless. Many children with disabilities grow into adults who hold jobs and contribute to society instead of spending their lives in isolation at home, in institutions, or on the streets.

Despite this progress, I still know schools in which classes for students with disabilities are located in sections of the school where no one else ever goes. There are still districts where people must be reminded to include students with disabilities when counting up the number of new math books that need to be ordered. And once formal schooling ends, there are still many young adults who sit at home without jobs because there is no employment support.

Has the promise of special education been met, fallen short, or been exceeded? Has society done too much or not enough? Despite what feels like progress, arguments about special education continue. Many of them are included in this book.

As you consider the controversial issues in this volume, think about the people with disabilities you first remember. How did today's special education shaped their lives? What about the young adults with visible disabilities working in your community? Where might they be without special education? How have the dreams of Hubert Humphrey and the cautions of Gerald Ford been realized?

Recent History and Legal Foundations

The history of special education in American public schools is brief and defined by legislation. Private or religious schools have long offered specialized options for students who were blind, or deaf, or had mental retardation. Until the last quarter of the twentieth century, public options were largely limited to residential institutions and a few *Opportunity Classes* in public schools.

After the civil rights struggles of the 1960s came the realization that another significant segment of our children—those with disabilities—were not offered a quality education. Although a few states instituted their own policies and regulations regarding education of children with disabilities, districts could still refuse to admit these students.

Successful state court cases established that children with disabilities had rights to an education. This led to the 1975 passage of federal Public Law 94-142 that offered federal funds to every public school district delivering a free and appropriate public education to all children with disabilities. Renamed the Individuals with Disabilities Education Improvement Act (IDEA) in subsequent reauthorizations, the regulations connected to these statutes form the foundation of special education. Individual states constructed legislation to clarify federal language or to extend commitments beyond the federal standard.

Elements of the No Child Left Behind Act of 2001 (NCLB) are reflected in the 2004 IDEA reauthorization. This linkage holds schools accountable for student performance, sets exacting standards for teacher qualifications, and requires that educators implement research-based instructional practices. NCLB includes accountability provisions for students with disabilities; IDEA describes intervention strategies that must take place in general education classrooms. There is much discussion about the interconnectedness of NCLB (a general education-based law) and IDEA (with its focus on special education).

Some wonder if the two will eventually merge—and ponder the impact on children and teachers.

Additional legislation affects the lives of individuals with disabilities: Section 504 and the Americans with Disabilities Act (ADA). Section 504 of the Rehabilitation Act of 1973 is a civil rights statute prohibiting organizations that receive federal funds from discriminating against any individual based on a disability that substantially limits a major life activity. Reasonable accommodations must be implemented so individuals with disabilities have equal access to the activities of such organizations. Curb cuts, lowered water fountains, and signs in Braille increased in use in response to Section 504. Since school districts receive federal funds, Section 504 forbids the exclusion of students with disabilities, although it does not address education with the detail of IDEA. You may encounter students on 504 plans. These students do not require specially designed instruction, but they might need accommodations or related services to have access to education.

The ADA, passed in 1990, extended the protections of Section 504 to the private sector. The ADA forbids businesses, governmental agencies, or public accommodations (other than churches or private clubs) from discriminating against any individual who has a disability that substantially limits a major life activity. The ADA carries the same responsibility for accommodations as Section 504, impacting the practices of almost every employer.

Aspects of these laws are sometimes vague and undefined. Terms are interpreted differently across the states, and businesses struggle with the range of accommodations, the meaning of "reasonable," and conflicting research results. Clarity is often achieved through the resolution of legal challenges, some of which have reached the Supreme Court. A single court decision can radically alter the obligations of an employer.

Court decisions can cause the ground to shift for schools as well. For example, as you proceed through the readings, you will encounter the debate between *least restrictive environment and free* and *appropriate public education.* Each term is critical to the development of a school's special education program, but each is also fluid in meaning. Federal law does not provide precise, operational definitions. Schools do their best to apply these terms to individual children with widely varying needs. As with businesses and the ADA, court cases about individual children continue to define what is *restrictive* and what is *appropriate.* Medical advances refine the meaning of *education.*

Essential Terms and Concepts

Special education has its own unique vocabulary and terms, just as any other field. Being familiar with the concepts discussed below will increase your understanding of the issues ahead.

Disabilities: IDEA 2004 lists the following disabilities: autism, deaf-blindness, deafness, developmental delay, emotional disturbance, hearing impairment, mental retardation, orthopedic impairment, other health impairment, specific learning disability, speech or language impairment, traumatic brain injury, and visual impairment. Autism and traumatic brain injury were added to this list relatively recently, as a result of lobbying and research developments. Be alert for changing terminology. Congress is moving to replace the term "mental retardation" with "intellectual disability," signaling respect and a sensitivity to negative connotations.

States may use unique names for disabilities, but all must be encompassed by the federal legislation. Additionally, state laws frequently augment the federal definitions of each disability with particular diagnostic criteria, satisfied through the administration of appropriate assessment tools in the "language and form most likely to yield accurate information about what the child knows and can do academically and functionally" (IDEA 2004).

Note that the list of disabilities does not include children who need instructional assistance solely because of language differences, cultural differences, or lack of instruction. In order for a child to be considered eligible for special education, the school's educational team must determine that a disability exists.

Federal definition of a child eligible for special education: According to IDEA, this is a child with a disability who is not making effective progress in school because of that disability and who requires specially designed instruction and/ or related services in order to make progress in school. Federal legislation applies to individuals from birth to the receipt of a high school diploma or age 22. In most states, public schools are charged with educational responsibility beginning on a child's third birthday.

Individualized Education Program (IEP): IDEA requires each child's educational team, including parents, to meet at least annually to formulate this agreement that describes the education of a child with a disability. The IEP outlines the impact of the student's disability, current educational status, necessary accommodations, the nature and amount of services to be provided to the child, and target goals for each year. All educators are bound to abide by the terms of an approved IEP. Services cannot be delivered—nor can they be ended—without signed parental approval. Parents who disagree with evaluations or services have the right to seek redress through administrative hearing and/or legal suit.

Related services: These supportive, noneducational services enable a child with a disability to access the general curriculum. Related services can include, but are not limited to the following: transportation, various therapies, mobility instruction, social work, and medical services for diagnostic or evaluation purposes.

Free and appropriate public education (FAPE): This cornerstone of IDEA guarantees that special education and related services are provided at no cost to parents. The word *appropriate,* never clearly defined, has been the source of much controversy and litigation. The impact of the word *free* has strained many town budgets.

Continuum of services: Special education services take many forms and are delivered in varied settings. Inside classrooms, these can range from consulting with a teacher on the format of a test, to team teaching between a special educator and an English teacher, to 1:1 services from a paraprofessional. Outside the general education class, specially designed instruction might be delivered to small groups of children with disabilities. A few children are taught in separate classes or schools (day, residential, or hospital) that enroll only children with disabilities. The entire spectrum of options, known as the continuum of services, must be considered when designing individualized special education programs.

Least Restrictive Environment (LRE): Another key element of IDEA, this phrase refers to each school's responsibility to ensure that "to the maximum extent appropriate, children with disabilities . . . are educated with children who are nondisabled; and that . . . removal from the regular educational environment occurs only if the nature or severity of the disability is such that education in regular classes with the use of supplementary aids and services cannot be achieved satisfactorily." Here, too, differing interpretations of undefined terms can lead to disagreement and litigation.

Inclusion: This word may be one of the first that comes to mind when special education is mentioned. Surprisingly, the term *inclusion* does not appear in any federal legislation. Its meaning differs across states, districts, and even within schools, and can change from year to year. Defining and applying this term has resulted in inspiration as well as confusion, frustration as well as opportunity, creativity as well as litigation. The common element in all definitions involves increasing the participation of children with disabilities in general education classes.

Differing Orientations

Underlying the controversies in this *Taking Sides: Clashing Views in Special Education* are four distinct perspectives, each of which affects the way people envision a solid special education program. Although disagreements cannot always be reduced to one of these, it is likely that people who support differing sides of an issue question will also be on opposite sides of the following dynamics.

Medical or Educational Model?

The medical model of special education views disabilities as conditions that can be improved, remedied, remediated, perhaps prevented. Medical model adherents seek a specific treatment or therapy to address the physical, psychological, or cognitive issues that result in school problems.

Those who follow an educational model aim to address the impact of a disability on school performance directly. Proponents focus on improving educational success through teaching skills or particular strategies that compensate for areas of difficulty. Is it wiser to deliver occupational therapy to improve the penmanship of a child with cerebral palsy or to teach the child how to use voice-activated software to enable his or her words to become print?

Special Need or Disability?

Children can have a special need, but not a disability. Laws about special education specifically exclude children whose learning difficulties are solely due to language differences, cultural differences, poverty, or lack of instruction. Neither do they include students who are gifted and talented. Almost everyone can remember struggling with learning at one point in life. Children in each of these groups may not have their needs met without extra attention from someone.

Special education is about the education of children who have a disability rather than those who struggle. This delineation causes controversy. If we know children whose lives place them at risk for failure, should we wait till that failure occurs before we give help or should we expand special education to include them? If we expand special education by including these children, are we helping them or burdening them with a stigmatizing label?

General Education or Special Education Responsibilities?

In the early 1970s, millions of children with disability were excluded from school. Federal laws mandated their education, which initially occurred mostly in secluded locations by specialized teachers. Seeing these students progress, teachers and parents began to seek out special education services. In many districts, special education ceased being a stigma and became a desired resource, particularly when budget stress increased class sizes and reduced overall supports.

As the number of children receiving services increased, resistance rose to the expansion and costs of special education and to its separation from the overall school curriculum. This backlash resulted in tighter definitions, restricting services to those who are truly disabled and increasing expectations that classroom teachers assume responsibility for a wider range of children.

NCLB took these deliberations one step further, introducing the idea that students should not be considered for special education if it can be determined that they have not experienced research-based classroom instruction. Interventions by the general education teacher are required as a part of the evaluation process. IDEA 2004 encourages teachers to adopt Response to Intervention strategies before seeking special education. Will schools initiate and sustain general education supports for all children, lessening the pressure for special education?

Academics or Functional Skills?

The accountability provisions of NCLB redefined the connection between general and special education personnel. Because schools must be answerable for the academic achievement of students in special education, *where* students learn has become less important than the knowledge they acquire.

Learning priorities must be considered. The majority of students with disabilities can make good academic progress, with appropriate support. Sometimes teams determine that functional skills to support success in daily living are a higher priority. In the past, students with both emphases could receive a high school diploma. With the advent of high-stakes testing, this is often no longer possible. Will heightened standards result in better outcomes for students with disabilities? Will students be equally prepared for adulthood?

Understanding Controversy

Precisely because the issues surrounding special education are so powerful, and the stakes for children so high, it is vital that we engage actively in their resolution.

To achieve this end, it is essential to recognize differences and collaborate to reach common ground.

Disagreements about Applying the Law

Parents and teachers must come to agreement about the best way to meet the needs of a child with a disability. Honorable people may be equally committed to the goal of a free and appropriate public education in the least restrictive environment, but differ on the definition and application of these terms. Although few argue about the meaning of *free*, some parents and teachers prefer focused instruction in small groups of children with similar learning needs, whereas other parents and educators feel the letter and spirit of the law can only be met when all children (regardless of individual need) are taught solely within the general education classroom.

Two children may be very similar, but have dramatically different special education programs because the preferences and reasoning of their educational teams differ. Since each child is unique, and can experience only one option at a time, it is impossible to guarantee which choice will lead to the best outcome. In fact, the best option may change as the child grows and develops.

Sometimes the differing views of parents and teachers lead to heated arguments. Everyone wants to help; often the disagreement is about which path to take. Because we see children as individuals—as our future—these controversies often reach to our core.

The keys to coming to consensus involve listening, learning, and being open to new information and fresh perspectives. Equally important is evaluating each source of information, and each course of action, in a measured, careful way, even if it differs substantially from what you feel is right. Often, putting yourself in the other person's place helps. What would I do if this were my child? What would I do if I were the teacher?

It helps to focus on the child in the middle of this discussion. As with most issues regarding children, the best solution is achieved when the adults involved put aside attitudes, emotions, and pride and strive to understand what the other person wants and why they want it. This can be very difficult to do.

Disagreements about Interpreting Facts and Figures

While some of the questions in this *Taking Sides* address decision making about individual children, others require the interpretation of objective facts. Analyzing these controversies requires a different approach.

For example, educators and legislators often argue about the significant increase in special education numbers and costs. Although this is a debate that deserves examination, it is also one that highlights the importance of evaluating information carefully. Meaning often depends on the context used for interpretation.

Consider the following statement: "Federal law first insisted in 1975 that public schools educate disabled students. Since then, the portion of students receiving special education services has increased 64%. Today, 13.5% of all public school students have been diagnosed with a disability. Special education, it turns out, is no longer particularly special at all" (Winters and Greene, www.forbes.com, 2009).

How could the number of children in special education more than double? There must be a way to slow this trend. At this rate there won't be any money to buy books. Perhaps the law is poorly written. Perhaps districts are not evaluated closely enough. Perhaps parents are too unreasonable or administrators too ready to provide any service requested. Which is it?

Additional information might affect the interpretation. The cited enrollment statistics begin with 1976, the first year after federal law called for a free and appropriate public education for all children with disabilities. In 1973, the Senate Labor and Public Welfare Committee documented "more than seven million deaf, blind, retarded, speech-impaired, emotionally disturbed or otherwise handicapped children in the United States . . . only 40 percent were receiving an adequate education, and many were not in school at all" (*Congress and the Nation IV,* 1973).

Millions of children with disabilities were not *in* school in 1976, so their addition to the rolls made a big impact. Many children were in institutions, which declined in size and scope as school doors opened. Many underserved children became identified as having a disability and entered the special education count. How should we consider these?

Background information about statistics or seemingly objective facts can affect your understanding of their meaning and, with it, your position on the issue. Bringing to light the assumptions made by others may do the same.

Some believe special education enrollments have risen due to *invisible disabilities* invented by those looking for a cause, an excuse for poor performance, or any way to get extra help for their children. Some believe teachers seek special education to mask their own inability to teach students whose language and/or culture does not match their own. Still others contend science is becoming more adept at understanding learning and behavior; in doing so, researchers discover evidence explaining why some students struggle and productive strategies to facilitate learning.

Some maintain that society has become looser and more permissive. Drugs and alcohol are more available. Children are not supervised the way they used to be and are influenced heavily by exposure to media representations of violent behavior. Others point to statistics on poverty, one-parent homes, three-job parents, and the disintegration of family and community supports to explain increasing numbers of students who push the limits of courtesy, tolerance, and the law.

Some are proud that medicine is making remarkable strides, sustaining one-pound babies and victims of tragic accidents or chronic illnesses, who survive, returning to school ready to learn. Others are concerned that these miracles of life require extensive support and extraordinary methods beyond the scope of schools. Many contend that vaccines invented to sustain health actually lead to disabilities.

Each perspective puts a different spin on the analysis of enrollment figures in special education. The interpretation you choose to accept depends on the argument you find most compelling. Careful deliberation of all information helps you formulate your own opinion and understand the opinions of others.

Being Aware of Bias

Each of us brings to every discussion our own background and inclinations. We cannot help but apply these to the issues in this book. In fact, those individual experiences may very well lead to creative options that change the course of a debate. As you begin to tackle your first issue, I offer the following reflections, gathered from students, parents, and colleagues.

Acknowledge and be mindful of your own experiences. If you, or a family member, encountered special education (or the lack of it), you may have formed strong opinions about its worth. If you have not had direct experience, your community's media coverage of special education may have shaped your thoughts. Recognize the impact of your experience and consider its influence as you debate the issues.

Be cautious of solutions that claim to apply equally to every situation. Two children with Down syndrome can be as different from each other as two *typical* seventh grade children. Urban and suburban elementary schools pose very different sets of possibilities and limitations. Appropriate strategies in kindergarten usually transfer poorly to 10th grade.

Think of possibilities rather than limitations. It is easy to say "That can't be done," and be constrained by what you have already observed. Creative solutions emerge from asking "How could we do this?"

Consider the impact of roles, motivations, and perspectives. Teachers come to their work because they want to help children grow and learn. Special education professionals believe in the ability to help children with disabilities become productive learners and adults. Parents seek educators who are dedicated to helping children reach their potential. District administrators serve two masters. First, they believe in the power of education and want to clear financial and legal hurdles so teachers can focus on children as much as possible. Second, they understand that they are entrusted with the finite resources of a community and must be answerable for their decisions in a way that will sustain the confidence of the citizens. Finally, legislators are committed to ensuring equal treatment and benefit to constituents whose lives span a wide range of circumstances.

All of these roles demand responsibility and accountability. The tasks of each role shape opinions and decisions. The outlook of people holding each role can lead to distinctly different perspectives, powerful arguments, and creative solutions. Consider the background of each of the authors you read as you evaluate their viewpoint. What in their backgrounds led them to their respective conclusions?

Final Words

As you read the selections in this book and discuss them with your colleagues, your challenge is to sort through competing arguments and information to form your own opinions about the education of children with disabilities.

Perhaps you will have opportunities to apply your point of view to an issue within your community or school. Perhaps you will discover practices in those schools that will change your opinion on an issue.

Controversies in special education will likely endure. The topics will change, but there will always be arguments about the right thing to do for children who seem to need so much.

Your own contributions will reflect the way you use experience and new knowledge. You might be tempted to search for global answers. You might find yourself frustrated by limited options. You might devise a unique solution that works perfectly for your district and your school.

As a special education administrator, especially in the spring, I often woke up in the middle of the night with a seemingly irresolvable problem running and running and running through my brain. Usually it involved balancing competing views of how to help a child. None of the options seemed totally satisfactory. A wise friend suggested I let go of the feeling that I needed to solve the problem alone and, instead, ask others to discuss together the pros and cons of each avenue. This suggestion has always served me well as I struggle over issues of doing the right thing for children; I have been comforted by knowing my colleagues were awake too. I hope the issues in this *Taking Sides* keep you thinking at night and that my friend's suggestion helps you come to your own conclusions about educating children with disabilities.

Emerging Issues: Impending Changes in NCLB and IDEA

As this fifth edition of *Taking Sides: Clashing Views in Special Education* goes to print, new controversies are emerging about two laws that affect children with disabilities: No Child Left Behind (NCLB) Act and the Individuals with Disabilities Education Improvement Act (IDEA). Both are due for reauthorization. This section outlines the status of the process and some of the topics to be addressed by federal legislators and the Obama administration. In keeping with the focus of this *Taking Sides*, elements affecting students with disabilities are emphasized. Several of these are treated in more depth in the following Issues: Does IDEA 2004 Contain Substantial Changes? (Issue 2); Is Response to Intervention (RTI) Ready for Implementation? (Issue 8); Should Special Education and General Education Merge? (Issue 9); Can Scientifically Based Research Guide Instructional Practice? (Issue 10); Does NCLB Leave Some Students Behind? (Issue 11); Should Students with Cognitive Disabilities Be Expected to Demonstrate Academic Proficiency? (Issue 12); and Can RTI Reduce the Number of Children Identified with Specific Learning Disability (SLD)? (Issue 16).

Reauthorization Process

Every 5 years, federal statutes undergo a lengthy reauthorization process. Constituent groups identify areas of satisfaction and concern. Professional associations convey their observations and recommend changes. Policy analysts reflect on how the statute aligns with the current administration's goals and priorities. Legislators pour over data, searching for patterns of performance, achievement, and financial expenditure to determine whether the intent of the legislation is being realized.

Once input is received, the House and Senate create separate reauthorization bills, which are debated and amended. When passed, a joint conference committee undertakes the daunting task of combining the two versions into one document acceptable to both houses. The approved bill proceeds to the President for signature. Regulations are promulgated and sent out for comment. Finally, the new version moves to states for implementation.

Perspectives on NCLB's Impact on Students with Disabilities

NCLB was signed into legislation in 2001 by the second President Bush. With the latest reauthorization of the Elementary and Secondary Education Act of 1965, educators may be familiar with its more pedestrian name: Title I. This statute provides funds for supplemental instruction to students characterized as disadvantaged. Although a bipartisan effort, NCLB focused on improving achievement for all students and reducing the achievement gap between disadvantaged students and those with more advantage. NCLB was due for reauthorization in 2007.

Numerous criticisms have been leveled at NCLB, which is sometimes called one of the most intrusive federal laws to have been visited on school districts. The Commission on No Child Left Behind was established "to move beyond the often heated and uninformed rhetoric about the No Child Left Behind Act and examine the evidence about the law's effects through a dispassionate bipartisan process" (*Beyond NCLB: Fulfilling the Promise to Our Nation's Children,* www.aspeninstitute.org, 2008). After gathering information "from those all over the country who live with the law every day," the Commission reported that the changes wrought by NCLB "have not been enough" to prepare students for college and work. Relative to students with disabilities, the Commission recommended improvements in the quality of assessments and increased emphasis on teacher effectiveness and supports.

Policy analysts who once championed NCLB as the key to education reform have turned away. Chester Finn (*The End of the Education Debate,* www.nationalaffairs.com, 2009) observes that consensus has eroded and that the unified goals of NCLB do not match the demands of today's diverse society. Diane Ravitch (*The Death and Life of the Great American School System,* 2010) now believes the federal government was "dictating ineffectual remedies which had no track record of success."

Perspectives on IDEA

Although reauthorization of IDEA '97 was due in 2002, the final bill was not ready for President Bush's signature until 2004. The next reauthorization date was set for 2011. This extended time might be in response to the 2004 reauthorization experience. On the other hand, it might reflect a desire to consider NCLB's reauthorization first. Currently, no formal timeline for review has been announced.

Several elements of IDEA 2004 are connected with NCLB. Accountability for student performance and highly qualified teachers are but two. Response to Intervention (RTI), a tiered general education approach, is contained in IDEA, not NCLB. Will reauthorization bring these two laws further together—perhaps even merging them?

A Blueprint for Reform

In March 2010, President Obama released his plan for reauthorizing NCLB. *A Blueprint for Reform* (www2.ed.gov/policy/elsec/leg/blueprint/blueprint.pdf, 2010) signaled its departure from NCLB with a very different name. This *Blueprint* contains several substantive changes. As before, issues related to students with disabilities are highlighted below.

Proficiency for All

The NCLB target required every child in America to be academically proficient by 2013–2014. Authors of *The Proficiency Illusion* (Cronin, Dahlin, Adkins, and Kingsbury, 2007) observed that some states were lowering their standards in order to reach progress targets. Diane Ravitch (2010), once a proponent, now calls this goal "an aspiration" that is "utterly out of reach." Arne Duncan, secretary of education, described full proficiency as "utopian."

President Obama's *Blueprint* sets a new goal. By 2020, every student will graduate from high school, ready for college or a career. What level of college? What kind of career?

Highly Effective Teachers

The Administration's *Blueprint* broadens the focus from NCLB's training and licensure requirements (Highly Qualified Teachers) to outcomes (Highly Effective Teachers). Student performance and classroom observations will be two of the effectiveness determiners. Will teacher effectiveness reflect IEP goals, academic standards, or both? How should the diversity of students with disabilities be considered? Can teacher effectiveness be measured while students are in school, or must it also consider eventual performance in college and/or career?

Accountability for Results

Given the goal of full proficiency by 2014, NCLB held schools accountable for the Adequate Yearly Progress (AYP) of all students, including those with disabilities. Some states dodged accountability by identifying large subgroup sizes—others by using separate standards for students with disabilities. The accountability mechanism could be affected by the fluid nature of this subgroup. Students exit special education when their skills improve; students who have just been found eligible enter the subgroup.

The Obama *Blueprint* considers student progress rather than an absolute target. Common curriculum standards are being encouraged. What will happen as districts move from one standard to the other? How long will this take? Will individual growth models help students with disabilities or hide them under lowered expectations? What effect will growth models have on teacher interest in inclusion?

In Closing

As you absorb the reauthorization complexities of NCLB and IDEA, weigh their influence. What differences will come from the reauthorization changes? How will they affect your life as an educator? How will they impact the future of your students? What changes do you think would best support educational growth for all students?

Internet References . . .

Individuals with Disabilities Education Improvement Act of 2004

The final Individuals with Disabilities Education Act (IDEA) regulations are over 1700 pages long. Should you want to consult them as a primary source, they can be found at this site:

http://www.ed.gov/policy/speced/guid/idea/idea2004.html

The School Mental Health Project

Based at the University of California Los Angeles, The School Mental Health Project (SMHP) was created in 1986 to pursue theory, research, practice, and training addressing mental health and psychosocial concerns through school-based interventions. SMHP works closely with districts, agencies, and organizations across the country to develop and disseminate effective resources and practices. The Web site contains an array of resources about controversial topics, positive programs, and research-based recommendations.

http://smhp.psych.ucla.edu

OSEP Technical Assistance Center on Positive Behavioral Interventions and Supports

This federally funded technical assistance center maintains an extensive Web site dedicated to informing educators and school systems about an array of schoolwide behavioral interventions. Examples of positive practice are available for use with families, entire schools, classrooms, and individuals. The Web site includes links to practicing schools, a newsletter, and online information and supports.

http://www.pbis.org

Thomas B. Fordham Foundation

Affiliated with the Manhattan Institute for Policy Research, the Thomas B. Fordham Foundation supports research, publications, and action projects, with a special interest in education reform. This site contains a link to Rethinking Education for a New Century, a compilation of thought-provoking essays about the status of special education in today's schools.

http://www.edexcellence.net/foundation/global/index.cfm

Special Education and Society

It seems simple enough. All students—including those with a disability—have a right to education. Unfortunately, society needed to be compelled by force of law to provide that education. The boundaries of required services are interpreted as frequently by the words of litigation as by the decisions of educators. Opportunities for some are interpreted as limitations for others. Recent education reform laws stress the benefits of schoolwide models, rather than reliance on special education as the only source of student support. At the same time, the line separating medical and educational needs becomes increasingly blurry. The cost of society's commitment to include everyone becomes increasingly contentious with strained finances. The spirit and the letter of the laws need to be interpreted as each educational dimension changes.

- Are Labels Good for Kids?

- Does IDEA 2004 Contain Substantial Changes?

- Is Eliminating Minority Overrepresentation Beyond the Scope of Public Schools?

- Can Whole-School Reform Reduce Discipline Problems?

- Are Charter School Doors Open to Students with Disabilities?

- Should Insurance Cover Treatments and Services for Autism?

ISSUE 1

Are Labels Good for Kids?

YES: Gwyn W. Senokossoff and Kim Stoddard, from "Swimming in Deep Water: Childhood Bipolar Disorder," *Preventing School Failure* (vol. 53, no. 4, pp. 89–93, Winter 2009).

NO: Scott M. Shannon, from *Please Don't Label My Child: Break the Doctor-Diagnosis-Drug Cycle and Discover Safe, Effective Choices for Your Child's Emotional Health* (Rodale, 2007).

ISSUE SUMMARY

YES: Gwyn W. Senokossoff, an instructor in childhood education and literacy, and Kim Stoddard, associate professor in special education (both at the University of South Florida St. Petersburg), describe the first author's struggles to find a diagnosis, appropriate intervention, and support for her son with childhood bipolar disorder.

NO: Scott M. Shannon, psychiatrist and former president of the American Holistic Medical Association, explains why he believes it is advantageous to look for ways to relieve stressors in a child's environment rather than seek a label, which might do more harm than good.

Your child has changed. Her activity level is way up; she sleeps fitfully and very little. Without sleep, her schoolwork declines and her temper flares at home and on the playground. You cannot sleep when she is restless, nor can your spouse or younger children, so you all have less patience. Her school calls frequently, interrupting your focus at work. Nothing you or your partner does makes a difference—not punishment, not reasoning, not rewards. Everyone has suggestions for you; none seems to work. Can't you feel the stress?

In this issue's first selection, Gwyn W. Senokossoff and Kim Stoddard describe how hopeless the first author felt when her youngest son, Matthew, began to exhibit unusual and extreme behaviors after moving to a new home. As his mother, Senokossoff could not understand what was causing Matthew's behavior. Worse, she did not know how to help him or his teachers. While reading a book on childhood bipolar disorder, Matthew's mother recognized her son. Finding this label helped her understand Matthew, explain him to others, and identify appropriate medications and interventions.

In the second selection, Scott M. Shannon acknowledges the pressures parents feel when they see their child suffering. Through his own practice as a psychiatrist working with children and adolescents, and his own experience as a parent, Shannon understands that it is natural for parents to want to relieve their child's distress. He expresses concern, however, that finding a label for the child's difficulties all too often leads to medications—sometimes several. Although these drugs might relieve the symptom, he cautions that they may have unintended consequences, including masking the real reason for the child's distress.

Ros Krasny (*Reuters.com*, 2010) reported results of a recent study revealing that the number of preschool children diagnosed with bipolar disorder "has doubled over the last decade." The number of children whose difficulties have been diagnosed as serious mental disorders has more than tripled in the last 15 years (Benedict Carey, *New York Times*, 2006). This may have coincided with the 1994 revision of the *DSM-IV*, which greatly increased the number of disorders described. Perhaps this correlates with the rising number of pharmaceutical interventions available. Carey also wonders whether people are becoming more open about discussing their problems, seeing diagnostic labels (often more than one) as a way to get services.

Discussing the puzzles of children who struggle with some academics although they show gifts in other areas, Jeffrey W. Gilger and George W. Hynd (*Roeper Review*, 2008) present the concept of atypical brain development. This theory posits that individuals develop uniquely, with an individual set of strengths and weaknesses. In this model, labels are less necessary because variability, itself, is *normal*.

Thomas Knestrict (*EP Magazine*, 2009) studied families who identified their children as having severe disabilities. He relied on parent perception and did not require confirmation of severity by doctors or schools. His parents said that one way they became more resilient was to move beyond a label to consider the child's changes and growth without constant reference to what others define as *normal*.

As you read these articles, consider reasons for the changes in the child described in the first paragraph. Her activity level could signify attention-deficit hyperactivity disorder (ADHD), infected tonsils that disrupt her breathing (and thus her sleep), sensitivity to the crying of her new baby sister, worries about school performance, or one of the disorders discussed in this issue's articles. If you were her parent, would you seek a label? What would influence your decision?

YES

Gwyn W. Senokossoff and
Kim Stoddard

Swimming in Deep Water: Childhood Bipolar Disorder

Several years ago on Oprah Winfrey's booklist, there was a book called *The Deep End of the Ocean*. This book was later made into a movie starring Michelle Pfeiffer. In the book, a woman loses her 3-year-old son in a hotel in Chicago, and he is missing for over 10 years before he is reunited with his family. Throughout this mother's journey, she must find the courage to go on with her life and raise her other two children. At times, she feels like she is swimming in the deep end of the ocean.

That is exactly how I (G. W. Senokossoff) felt 2 years ago when my youngest son, Matthew, began to struggle and exhibit extreme—and sometimes unusual—behaviors in school and home. I have always loved children and waited a long time to have my own. Being an educator, I am supposed to be good with kids, yet I did not know how to fix Matthew's problems. I hope that sharing our story will help other children, parents, and teachers who are dealing with similar situations to get the support that they desperately need.

Also, 2 years ago, my sons and I moved into our new home, at which time they enrolled in new schools. Matthew was starting first grade and his teacher was my friend and former colleague. As the year progressed, I began to receive notes about Matthew's work and behavior. His teacher indicated that he was often off-task, did not complete his work, and wandered around the classroom disturbing the other children. When the teacher asked him to return to his seat or when his classmates complained, he would roar like his favorite dinosaur. At other times, Matthew would sit at his desk and destroy school supplies or draw on himself. When the teacher confronted him, according to Matthew, it was always someone else's fault. He often said that his classmates were bothering or teasing him. Also, Matthew is very sensitive to and stimulated by noise. When his teacher raised her voice or the classroom became noisy, he would become agitated.

At the first parent–teacher conference, Matthew was given an academic instructional plan because he was not performing on grade level. He refused to complete the writing assessment. My son, who learned to read during the first few months of kindergarten and absorbed facts and could repeat them at will, was struggling in the first grade.

At the same time, we were dealing with unusual behaviors at home. Matthew was getting up at all hours of the night. Sometimes, he would wake me

From *Preventing School Failure*, vol. 53, no. 4, Winter 2009, pp. 89–93 (Notes omitted). Copyright © 2009 by Routledge/Taylor & Francis Group. Reprinted by permission via Rightslink.

up; at other times, I would hear him and check on him. A few times, he climbed out of his bedroom window to wander around or look for things such as bats. Also, Matthew was fascinated by fire. One morning, my other son and I awoke to the fire alarm. Matthew had taken out the grill lighter from the top shelf of a closet where I had hidden it, and he had set his behavior chart on fire.

In addition to his sleeplessness, Matthew became angry when he made a poor choice and was given consequences or when he felt misunderstood. His temper tantrums grew; he became increasingly aggressive and went into rages that often lasted hours.

In September, a psychiatrist diagnosed Matthew with Attention Deficit with Hyperactivity Disorder (ADHD) and prescribed a stimulant and eventually an antidepressant to combat his anger; however, the tantrums continued. Also, Matthew had trouble making and keeping friends in our neighborhood and at school. Several times, I had to apologize to other parents for his behavior. Although Matthew's tantrums started at home with his family, he soon began to act out in public and at school. During this time, I could not figure out what was wrong. My child was out of control and I did not know how to help him. Then, during one session with our therapist, she asked me if I had read the book *The Bipolar Child*. I had not, so I bought the book and, after reading the first few chapters, knew that my son had childhood bipolar disorder (CBD).

As the year progressed, Matthew continued to have trouble at school, especially during less structured times, such as physical education and lunch. Although he was reading on a fourth-grade level and able to complete all of his assessments successfully, he was still off-task for a large part of the day. Then, in April, we found a pediatric psychiatrist who specialized in ADHD and bipolar disorder. During our first meeting, he gave us the diagnosis that we needed to get the proper medication for Matthew. Since then, Matthew qualified for the gifted program, which he attends once a week. He is currently in a third-grade inclusion classroom. With his current medication, Matthew's behavior has stabilized and I continue to work with a therapist on various behavior intervention strategies.

Bipolar Disorder

The challenges that Matthew and his family face because of his bipolar disorder affect more than 750,000 children a year. Unfortunately, many children go undiagnosed or misdiagnosed as ADHD, conduct disordered, oppositionally defiant, and depressed. As many as 80% of children with bipolar condition are undiagnosed for up to 10 years before receiving appropriate services to treat it. The discipline strategies that most schools use—repeated detentions with a final result of suspension—are ineffective for most children, especially for those with bipolar condition. Many school personnel lack an understanding of the condition, whereas the child and family continue to feel the stigma and guilt associated with the child's behavior problems.

Researchers first identified bipolar disorder in the early 1800s. Although bipolar disorder is the most prevalent psychotic disorder in adults, most professionals consider the onset of the condition to rarely occur before puberty. The research for CBD is in its infancy. The first diagnostic criteria for CBD occurred in the early 1960s with the use of adult criteria. As professionals began to apply the same diagnostic criteria and treatment for children, they realized adult onset and CBD manifest themselves in different ways. In addition, researchers found that treatment that is considered effective for adults can actually exacerbate the condition in children, which has prompted more specific investigation into childhood and adolescent bipolar disorder as separate conditions from adult onset.

CBD

CBD occurs before adolescence and, in many cases, results in more severe behavior problems. Although CBD is considered a low-incidence disability, it occurs more often than the combined incidence of common childhood illnesses such as juvenile diabetes, cancer, AIDS, and epilepsy. Furthermore, the disorder is more difficult to diagnose in children because of the infancy of the field and overlap of other mitigating conditions such as ADHD.

Those who manifest early-age onset often have mood changes that shift from manic to depressive (referred to as *rapid cycling*), which often result in irritable behavior and frustrating tantrums. Also, delusions and hallucinations occur more frequently in childhood onset than in adult or adolescent onset. Misdiagnosis of CBD often occurs because the overt behaviors of the student are so disruptive that educators view it as a behavioral rather than medical issue. In addition, 70–90% of children with CBD also have ADHD, whereas 19% of children with ADHD are also identified as having CBD. Both conditions may result in hyperactivity, irritability, and distractibility. However, the child with CBD may also exhibit behaviors such as grandiosity, flight of ideas, racing thoughts, and a decreased need for sleep. The stimulant medication prescribed for children with ADHD often exacerbates the bipolar condition, which results in an acceleration of the cycling behavior. Unfortunately, professionals often look at the children's environment and blame poor parenting skills and a lack of discipline in the home. Among parents of adopted children, behavioral problems sometimes are attributed to attachment disorder and researchers have suggested psychotherapy for treatment. Unfortunately, the probability of recovery from CBD also diminishes when there is too much time between the first symptoms and the actual treatment.

The likelihood that a child will recover from CBD increases when educators and other professionals are knowledgeable of the condition and various variables that may affect a student with a predisposition for the disorder. Children with bipolar disorder may appear outgoing, personable, highly energetic, and goal directed in the manic phase. Often, parents and teachers value and reinforce these characteristics during the early school years. The difference between appropriate and manic behaviors is the intensity and frequency of the behaviors. Children in the manic phase may not be able to stop their behavior. They must constantly be doing something and believe that they can do just about anything well. They also require little sleep. Children with ADHD seem to be in constant motion, involved in undirected behavior, and sleep through the night. Children with CBD need only 3–4 hr of sleep and when awake routinely perform multiple tasks that are all goal directed. When the depressive episode appears, an astute teacher may notice the change and begin to investigate why such a drastic change has occurred in the student. The depressive episode may include the following: lack of enjoyment in life, change in appetite, fatigue, feelings of worthlessness or guilt, poor concentration, and thoughts of death and suicide. Over 50% of individuals are diagnosed with bipolar disorder during a depressive episode. Because most children exhibit rapid cycling, it may be difficult for teachers, parents, or other professionals to see a discrete completion of one phase and the beginning of the next. Most adults with bipolar disorder have episodes that last 1–3 months, followed by normal day-to-day functioning behavior between phases.

The quick interepisode recovery for children with bipolar disorder often results in disruptive behavior because of their irritability and frustration with the rapid changes in their mind and body. Children themselves refer to it as the inability to shut off their brain. It is a roller-coaster ride in which they have no control, so they act out because of frustration and anxiety over the situation. In most classrooms in which a child is disruptive, the teacher imposes consequences for inappropriate behavior. Therefore, a child who has CBD does not seem to have control over his or her behavior, so the consequences add further frustration and may escalate the acting out behavior to a more significant degree.

Because of the frenzied and erratic behavior of children with CBD, many are socially rejected by their peers. Reports on children with bipolar disorder indicate that more than 50% of them have no friends, are made fun of by others, and have poor relationships with their siblings. Furthermore, they may face academic challenges because of the increased risk for learning disabilities and a higher likelihood of deficits in cognitive functioning, math, and verbal memory. When children with CBD experience stress, their episodic behavior increases. Across the elementary grades, the stress that accompanies the increased academic demands seems to play a role in the increase in episodic behaviors or the triggering of bipolar behaviors.

Adolescent Onset Bipolar Disorder

Although concerns for adolescent bipolar disorder are similar to adults, there are differences in the manifestation of the disorder. Adolescents with bipolar disorder have similar manic characteristics as children; however, the manifestation of the behavior may be slightly altered. Adolescents with bipolar disorder often feel a sense of grandeur and importance in life, believe that rules are for others and do not apply to them, and manifest cockiness in the classroom. They may continually question a teacher's skills in the classroom and even extend this point by failing a class to prove that the teacher was incompetent. Adolescents show longer episodic behavior but still may cycle as in childhood onset. The challenges that adolescents with bipolar disorder face are similar to the challenges that all adolescents face, but with an increase in the intensity and severity of the problems. In addition, adolescents with bipolar disorder face a greater risk for drugs and alcohol abuse, as well as a higher rate of suicide. Also, 30% of adolescents with bipolar disorder attempt suicide by the age of 18, and many of them turn to drugs and alcohol to cope. Drug and alcohol addiction occurs in approximately 39% of adolescents with bipolar disorder. The hypersexuality of adolescents with bipolar disorder can have serious consequences that include increased risk of communicable diseases and pregnancy. Accordingly, it is important to develop a treatment plan that enables adolescents to maintain a degree of stability in overall emotional development.

Treatment and Services

In the beginning, the treatment for children and adolescents with bipolar disorder followed the same treatment plan as adult onset. However, as researchers studied the effects of pharmacological intervention, concerns arose over the effectiveness of the drugs, especially the exacerbation of manic behavior. Most experts believe the best long-term intervention includes a multimodal treatment plan involving psychosocial therapy, educational training, and maintenance medication. Most professionals support the practice of stabilizing the mood swings before treating other mitigating disorders such as ADHD, OCD, or depression. In addition, most professionals contend that each new disability should be treated in a sequential manner to determine interactive factors of multiple medications.

The key to long-term effective treatment of CBD is monitoring the effects of each medication and the mix of multiple drug interactions; this monitoring must occur at home and in school. Teachers must report changes in students' mood and overt behaviors. It is useful if teachers keep anecdotal charts to record the date, time of behavior, and duration of behaviors. In addition, the inclusion of a mood chart helps students and teachers identify the mood of students at particular times of the day. Also, a mood chart may help professionals to identify any correlations between behaviors and moods that occur throughout the school day.

Researchers have not established any clear guidelines on the maximum length of pharmacological treatment for children and adolescents. For adults, the recommendation is to begin to taper drug use after 18 months when possible. In some cases, drug intervention is needed for a much longer period of time.

The unintended side effects of medication often hinder successful treatment of children and adolescents. For example, weight gain is a concern for all individuals, and some female adolescents refuse the medication despite the effectiveness of mood stabilization drugs. In addition, with medication, there can be increased difficulty with cognitive functioning, including problems with word retrieval and memory. Thus, it is important to monitor the effectiveness of the drug on the child's mood and how the drug affects the child. A proper diet and exercise may help to reduce the negative side effects of the medication. Also, researchers have found that exercise assists with mood elevation in individuals who have been diagnosed with bipolar conditions.

Teachers' Role

Teachers play a critical role in understanding students with bipolar disorder and assisting them in being successful in school. School personnel should have some knowledge on the characteristics that a child with bipolar behavior may convey, such as inappropriate emotional response (e.g., laughing hysterically, crying for no reason), inappropriate or precocious sexual behavior, rapidly changing moods in a short period of time, defiance of authority, daredevil behavior, excessive involvement in multiple projects, delusions and hallucinations, sleeping too little, extreme sadness or loneliness, and racing thoughts and speech patterns.

The distinguishing difference between bipolar disorder and situational behavior problems that are due to extenuating circumstances is the intensity and duration of the behavior. It would be normal for an individual to be extremely sad because of the loss of a loved one. However, it would be abnormal for an individual to be extremely sad because of being asked to sit at his or her desk to begin class.

After a student is diagnosed with bipolar disorder, an individual education plan (IEP) should be written under the *other health impaired* category. The IEP should cover accommodations for the student and a means to assess progress throughout the year. The following accommodations provide a student with the support to be successful in the classroom: (a) consistent scheduling of courses, (b) area for debriefing when emotions overwhelm the student, (c) notice of changes in the schedule beforehand, (d) a staff member in the school to talk with when emotions are overwhelming, and (e) flexibility in the length and difficulty of assignments when needed because of cycling of behavior.

A student with bipolar disorder is no different from a student with diabetes, asthma, or epilepsy. The overt behavior of a student with a bipolar disorder is often beyond his or her control even with medication. Assuring the student that he or she is a welcome part of the school community—as well as establishing an understanding of the needs of the child—will provide a stabilizer for the student and assist him or her in succeeding in the classroom.

At-Home Support for a Child with Bipolar Disorder

There are several useful strategies that parents of children with bipolar disorder may use at home. Flexibility, patience, conflict-resolution skills, and consistency are essential. Flexibility, or the ability to adjust the schedule to the child's needs, is important. For instance, if the parents are entertaining guests at home or going out to attend an event and the child becomes agitated or irritable, it is advantageous to have a quiet place at home where he or she can go to calm down. However, the parents may need to leave the event early to care for their child. The ability to exercise patience is essential, as is ignoring minor negative behaviors and focusing on more positive responses.

Also, strong conflict-resolution skills are important. Being able to deflate a growing tantrum is crucial. Often, parents deal with many stresses concurrently and lose patience with misbehavior; however, negative, loud behavior only stimulates and escalates the child's behavior. Although people don't want to excuse poor behavior, they have to de-escalate the situation first. After the child is calm again, they should discuss the consequences of his or her actions.

The final, most important strategy is consistency, which children with bipolar disorder need in addition to structure. Routines are critical. Parents should have a morning routine that the child follows and set a timer. Also, parents should have a homework and bedtime routine. In the 2 years that the doctors were diagnosing and stabilizing Matthew, he was frequently late to school and our mornings were often a battle. Matthew is very rigid, or black-and-white, in his thinking, and he has difficulty making quick transitions. Setting up routines has helped him to know exactly what to expect.

In addition to routines, I helped Matthew set goals, and he earned rewards for meeting his goals. Many times, his rewards centered around time spent doing a favorite task. Also, Matthew has strategies that he used when he began to feel frustrated or stressed. These strategies include taking deep breaths, unclenching his fists, and moving to a quiet area to regain control. These strategies have significantly helped Matthew learn to cope.

Family dynamics are also affected. Matthew has a teenage brother who has learned how to remain calm and be helpful to him. It has been difficult for his brother, though, because of the focus and constant care that is required for Matthew. I have tried to support our older son in other ways.

Conclusion

The first doctor that we worked with hesitated to diagnose Matthew. Many psychiatrists are reluctant to diagnose children. After many struggles, I found a pediatric psychiatrist who was willing and able to help Matthew. We were also working with a highly skilled therapist. Matthew's rages have greatly diminished and he is learning to control his behavior and accept responsibility for his actions.

Current research suggests that many children are born with bipolar disorder and may not be diagnosed until adolescence. Also, children with bipolar disorder may not exhibit severe behaviors until they experience a traumatic event that triggers the symptoms. With Matthew, it may have been our move. When I look back at Matthew's behavior over the years, it is clear that he was always an active and headstrong child. As a baby, he often did not sleep through the night, and, as a toddler, he had tantrums. However, many toddlers go through similar stages, and Matthew did not display severe behavior problems until we moved to a new home.

Because CBD is not a well-known problem, there is limited support for children with a bipolar disorder and each family's story may differ. Parents should seek medical treatment and academic support for their children. Many professionals are not well informed on how to deal with these children. Yet, the incidence of pediatric bipolar disorder has been increasing steadily since World War II, and schools will need to learn to support these children and their families.

Remember the voice of one child with bipolar disorder:

> Hi, I'm Matthew. I'm going to tell you what it feels like to have Bipolar disorder. I've been made fun of by other children. If you have this problem don't attempt to fix it yourself. Instead go find an adult and tell them what happened. When I'm angry I feel like I want to hurt the person who made fun of me but I don't. School was the hardest. Almost everyone in my class was making fun of me. At P. E. my classmate was making fun of me. Then he ran off laughing. It was hard to listen to my teacher I was off task and thinking about other things then I wouldn't hear the teacher. Well . . . I'm on Summer Break and I'm out of school so I don't need that much medicine oh! Did I mention that I took medicine? Nope guess not. The medicine helps me focus, calm down a little and go to sleep. Well that's it for me. [*sic*].

Please Don't Label My Child: Break the Doctor-Diagnosis-Drug Cycle and Discover Safe, Effective Choices for Your Child's Emotional Health

Lost to a Label

Labeling is what happens when our children show signs of distress and trouble and we, the well-meaning adults in their lives, intervene. On the face of it, we do the right thing when we are able to identify the symptoms of "dis-ease" in our children and turn to experts for help. But something curious happens when we defer—with the best of intentions—to doctors, psychologists, health care providers, educators, and other "experts" in order to help our children. Too often, the *relief of symptoms* becomes the sole goal of treatment, and our children wind up labeled and medicated but feeling no better.

I don't mean to be the voice of doom and gloom about this, and of course, it can be useful—even crucial—to first aggressively treat the symptoms a child exhibits. What does alarm me, however, is how many of our children are being treated *only* on a symptomatic level and thus become lost to their labels. When this happens, the true source of the upset often remains unidentified and unaddressed. . . . [O]ne of the most frightening aspects of overlabeling [is that] more and more kids are on two or more psychiatric drugs at a time. This is true despite there being little or no research on what the effects of combining such drugs has on children.

. . . How did we get into this situation of overlabeling our kids? I believe it's a problem of well-intentioned parenting colliding head-on with a rigid and label-oriented medical culture. Parents have kids who are suffering, and they want to find relief for them. They turn to a medical system that rewards quick diagnosis over thoughtful and reflective care and prizes the myth of "silver bullet" treatment over accurate understanding. . . . Labels, to many parents, appear at first glance to be a kind of lifeboat. Who wouldn't be relieved and hopeful when whatever ails their child is quickly and succinctly identified? But the long-term cost of labeling outweighs any short-term relief of symptoms.

From *Please Don't Label My Child: Break the Doctor-Diagnosis-Drug Cycle and Discover Safe, Effective Choices for Your Child's Emotional Health,* by Scott Shannon, MD (Rodale, 2007), pp. 1–2, 3, 5–11, 12–13, 14–20, 24. Copyright © 2007 by Scott M. Shannon. Reprinted by permission of Rodale Press. All rights reserved.

Instead of stopping to contemplate what brain stressors might be undermining a child's ability to enjoy emotional and mental well-being, we parents have a tendency to panic at the signs of upset in our children, to become fearful in the face of serious symptoms. When this happens, our good parental intentions go bad.

How do I know this? First, I am a parent who has had to resist the urge to label my own kids whenever the going gets tough for them—or for me. Second, I am a child psychiatrist whose practice is bursting at the seams with children who have been aggressively (and often erroneously) diagnosed with and treated for major psychiatric problems but who are not getting better. Third, I speak to professional groups around the country, and I hear firsthand how frustrated and concerned my colleagues are with the current situation. Labeling our children often cripples them instead of liberating them. The very labels that we turn to in order to help our children can actually do more harm than good.

Psychiatric Labels: Hard Science?

. . . [P]sychiatry [is] . . . not a hard science. There is no blood test or brain scan we can use to diagnose a condition like ADHD. Psychiatric diagnosis is based on the personal observation and judgment of the practitioner, which are colored by temperament, interest, skill, level of knowledge, degree of training, and innumerable other factors. . . .

Psychiatry does very little research into the reliability of our diagnostic system in actual clinical practice. One reason may be that the results are so embarrassing and destructive to psychiatry that no one wants to consider them. In one such example, reported in May 2006 in *Clinical Psychiatry News*. In this study 376 patients at a large psychiatric hospital in Tucson, Arizona, were readmitted within 30 days of their initial discharge, and very few received the same diagnosis. Fewer than half of the patients with bipolar disorder were given the same diagnosis. Ninety percent of patients with schizoaffective disorder got a new and different diagnosis. In this study 255 people had two admissions; only 50 of these (less than 20 percent) were given the same diagnosis. If they had three admissions, only 7 of 82 patients (9 percent) received the same label. When they were readmitted four times, only 2 of 27 (7 percent) got the same tag. The poor souls who were sick enough to be admitted more than four times batted zero for 12. The researcher who did this study gave this advice: "Take the prior diagnosis with a grain of salt because other diagnosticians may not be as careful as you." I don't think I could have said it better. Can you imagine what the diagnostic reliability would have been if these patients had been children? Everyone in the field of psychiatry knows that kids are much harder to diagnose, simply because they are "moving targets" as they constantly grow, change, and mature.

We psychiatrists have some understanding of how the human brain functions, but we have very little understanding of what causes the brain to malfunction in ways that cause emotional or mental disorders. In order to organize and "codify" the way we think about mental disruptions, psychiatry has evolved around an ever-expanding encyclopedia of terminology that gives a diagnostic name to a symptom or cluster of symptoms. These psychiatric terms are the labels I've been referring to, and they can be found in the *DSM*-IV (*Diagnostic and Statistical Manual of Mental Disorders*), . . . the official handbook created by and for psychiatrists that names and defines mental disorders.

[When] [t]he *DSM* . . . was first published in 1952, [it] contained 106 mental disorders.When it was updated in 1968, there were 182. . . . [In] the most current edition . . . edited in 1994, there are more than 300 mental disorders identified . . . : Could the numbers of serious mental and emotional disorders really have *tripled* in 42 years? The answer is no. I believe the proliferation of mental and emotional disorders . . . reflects our tendency toward "diagnosis creep," toward our willingness to find illness where there may be simply difference.

The labels we most frequently give to kids include the acronyms for and names of some complex and serious mental, emotional, and social disorders. These disorders, though once thought to be very rare in children, are being diagnosed (and misdiagnosed) at alarming rates. (In the 1970s, ADHD was considered quite rare, and only about 150,000 American children were thought to have it. Today, nearly four million American kids are labeled with ADHD, and most of them are also being given very powerful drugs to "control" it.) . . .

The Advantages of Labels

Diagnostic labels were designed to facilitate healing. There is no doubt about this. Using such labels is not only crucial to guiding appropriate treatment, it also provides a source of much-needed relief for the parents of any child who is suffering. Once a diagnosis is made, parents experience an immediate sense of reassurance that the problems that plague their child are understood and will be addressed. With a diagnostic label in hand, parents can often break out of the isolation that comes with having a seriously troubled child. They can then find support among parents with kids who have been similarly diagnosed. They can also do research and learn more about the diagnosis, which, one hopes, will help them learn more about their child.

As a physician, finding a suitable diagnosis gives me a departure point, an entrée into treating a child, and this is a crucial first step in any good treatment. I turn to diagnostic labels daily in my own practice and use them to get a handle on the symptoms that may be debilitating a child under my care. I use these labels cautiously, however, as I'm aware of the tendency (even in myself) to become persuaded that the diagnosis—or the label—is the end point of treatment.

The Disadvantages of Labeling

Of course, there are negative consequences of diagnostic labeling, even when the diagnosis is correct.

For one, a physician who has chosen a diagnosis may stop looking for other causes of a child's symptoms. For example, when a child is labeled

ADHD, the adults around him may then miss the fact that his symptoms indicate a stress reaction to some traumatic experience or signal the stress brought on by an undetected learning disability. The kind of myopic thinking that an overreliance on labels promotes can have terrible consequences, including prolonged and unnecessary suffering for our kids. . . . Once a diagnostic label is applied, it is often understood so rigidly that many potentially helpful treatment options are ignored (or disallowed by insurers), much to the detriment of the child in question.

Of course, the greatest cost of labeling is the effect on our children. Children who are labeled in some way (however well-intentioned and therapeutically appropriate that label may be) feel separated from their peers, which takes a terrible toll on their self-esteem. Children have difficulty distinguishing a label from who they are; they also believe that because they have earned a label, they are somehow "less than," "broken," or "sick."

This tendency toward labeling is dangerous because it fractures and fragments the way we look at things, particularly how we view our kids. Instead of seeing robust, complicated, three-dimensional people, we start to see our kids as being one-dimensional. When we begin to identify and know our kids only by the symptoms they exhibit, we have, however inadvertently, abandoned them.

Even when a good diagnosis is made and a child is relieved of terrible symptoms, the stigma surrounding the initial diagnostic label may prompt the child to view himself as being somehow defective or "bad." He may come to see himself as nothing more than a problem to be solved rather than as the lovable and breathtakingly complex human being he is. Putting a label on him distorts his—and our—perception of who he is.

There is also social stigma that comes with diagnostic labeling. I find the ADHD label to be particularly noxious for kids. Take Johnny, a pleasant and playful 9-year-old. . . . His parents, who were very concerned about him, wanted to know if he indeed had ADHD, as diagnosed by his pediatrician. I actually did confirm the diagnosis and agreed with the use of stimulants to treat Johnny's symptoms. The drugs worked wonders in terms of allowing him to focus and concentrate, but it wasn't until I spent some time with Johnny in therapy and worked with him on the self-esteem issues brought on by the diagnosis that his performance in school began to improve. After a term of school under my care, Johnny brought home passing grades for the first time—even in math, his most difficult subject. I asked him what he thought had changed. "I used to think my brain was broken—isn't that what ADHD means?" he said. "Now I know it isn't, and so I can enjoy my schoolwork, even math."

Although labeling Johnny brought him symptomatic relief, he needed to refuse to identify himself with that label in order to thrive. . . .

Multiple Labels

One of the true travesties of the epidemic of labeling is co-morbidity, which, in plain English, means the application of more than one diagnosis. On average, every child who is seen by a child psychiatrist comes away with not one but three different diagnoses. This means that children who are identified as being ADHD are also tagged as being depressed. Or a child who has OCD may also be diagnosed as having mild bipolar disorder. Although one may find reassurance in this, thinking that our children are being looked at comprehensively, what co-morbidity indicates to me, more than anything else, is how profoundly complex our children are and how poorly our diagnostic system serves them. . . .

Incorrect Labels

Sometimes, kids are diagnosed with the wrong condition entirely. When this happens, you have a serious problem on your hands. Not only will the child not get the treatment she needs, she will continue to suffer—and so will her parents. The off-target treatment she does receive may not help at all, and it may even aggravate her symptoms. This happens very frequently with ADHD; I see kids all the time who are dealing with the effects of terrible, unacknowledged brain stressors. Instead of identifying the problem, someone slaps an ADHD tag onto these kids, and they continue to suffer, legitimately. If a child is anxious— and stress causes great anxiety in all of us—being given stimulants may make him more so. If he has endured an unspoken trauma, he will continue to suffer unless that trauma is acknowledged and addressed by the caregivers around him. All doctors—myself included—make this mistake at times. . . . Here's an example of how damaging an inaccurate diagnosis can be.

Nick

When Nick was 6, he lived with his mother, who struggled to manage a busy job . . . while raising three children on her own. Nick's father, a bright but underachieving computer programmer who liked to drink, had finally left his wife—and their kids—in the rural small town he had taken them to. . . . Not long after the divorce, Nick's first-grade teacher called his mother to complain that the boy would not sit still and pay attention and that he was seriously disrupting the class.

Nick's mother took him to see their family doctor, who immediately became annoyed with Nick because he refused to sit still and insisted on rummaging through the doctor's supplies. The doctor promptly diagnosed ADHD and prescribed Ritalin. The medication seemed to help Nick to sit still and focus—for a few days. Then things got worse. His mother . . . became too depressed to be emotionally available to her children. Nick began to further act out at home and at school. The doctor upped the Ritalin dose, and after Nick failed to improve over the next few weeks, he raised it again. Nick began to hit kids at school and his siblings at home. When his teachers or his mother asked him to do something, he did the opposite, or he threw things and screamed. He became a tempest of a boy. In response, his doctor added the antipsychotic drug Risperdal . . . to control the aggressive behavior.

On high doses of Ritalin and Risperdal, Nick was somewhat more manageable, although he became lethargic and began to gain weight. Because of his severe behavior and aggression, the school moved him into a classroom with other "high-needs" kids, most of whom had learning difficulties and poor social skills.

In the meantime, Nick's mother sought help for herself [and]. . . decided to move back home. . . .

When I met him, Nick was 9 years old and obese (although his mother told me he had been thin most of his life). His clothes and hair were disheveled. He didn't seem to care how he looked; he didn't seem to care much about anything. To my astonishment, he related to me on the intellectual level of a teen. . . . He compensated for an overall lack of social skills with a sharp and sarcastic sense of humor. . . . He was observant, intelligent, and a bit eccentric but clearly his own person. . . .

As we talked and I had the chance to watch Nick, I saw that he had some mildly compulsive traits. Specifically, he liked to order and count some of his possessions. I decided to taper his medications and do some testing. His IQ was over 140 for analytic skills, which is higher than all but about 1 percent of the population. Although he lagged in some academic areas, his greatest shortfall was in his social skills. The bottom line was that Nick didn't have ADHD at all. He was bored by school and had been extremely stressed by his family's turmoil. . . .

Off medication, Nick was a handful: He was energetic, talkative, sarcastic, curious, testy, and stubborn. However, his mother, who now had more psychological ballast and generally felt better . . . realized that his "hyperactivity" surfaced mainly when he was bored or upset. At my urging, she agreed to put Nick into an educational program specifically designed for kids with two areas of uniqueness. . . . His teachers encouraged his curiosity and intellect while providing special instruction in developing stronger social skills. They were also tolerant of his need for stimulation and movement.

Nick is now 11. He has lost some weight and makes more effort with his appearance and personal hygiene. The only medication he takes is a very low dose of a drug called Luvox . . . to help him with his compulsions. Relaxation training and calming herbs have helped him feel on more of an even keel. He enjoys his family and his home life and is loved by his mother, brother, and sister.

Nick is the perfect example of a child who became lost in a label. In his case, his hyperactive and frustrated behavior blinded the adults around him to his high intelligence and his thirst for knowledge. . . .

Minimizing the Harmful Effects of Labeling: A Holistic Approach

. . . [I]t's our responsibility to minimize the harm these labels do. . . . We must be willing to look at any and all aspects of a child's life that seem to be off-kilter and not just focus on the symptoms that are most apparent to adults. . . . I sometimes find that I can do the most good if I don't apply any diagnostic label at all. That's what I did when Melanie's parents came to see me.

Melanie

I spent two sessions trying to understand 9-year-old Melanie, but I made little headway until I had the chance to spend some time with her parents. Both are engineers who work long hours, but they're devoted to their only child. The family came to me because Melanie was struggling with anxiety, sad moods, and a volatile temper. . . . She had already been . . . given two very different diagnostic labels (depression, from the family doctor, and intermittent explosive disorder, from a psychologist). Melanie's parents were hoping I could resolve this diagnostic confusion for them.

After seeing the girl three times, I told her parents that she was somewhat fragile emotionally, which meant she needed a lot of support and attention from them. Then I outlined a very rich and holistic treatment plan for her. They seemed pleased by how comprehensive all this was, but I sensed some hesitation. . . . Finally, Melanie's mother spoke up: "But what is her diagnosis, Doctor?"

I believed that Melanie was feeling great stress due to the lack of a steady, consistent emotional connection with her busy and distracted though well-meaning parents. Of course, I couldn't say this out loud, so instead I told them that I would need their help in making a diagnosis. "Melanie . . . is suffering from either a mood disorder, an anxiety disorder, oppositional defiant disorder, intermittent explosive disorder, or parent-child conflict." I asked both parents to watch her very closely and at the end of each day, to sit down with her and together decide which category she fell into on that day. . . . I sent them out the door with the symptom checklist for each of the five disorders and a firm commitment to work hard on this assignment until we met the following week.

After five more sessions, this strategy bore amazing fruit. Melanie's parents were spending so much time with her—really connecting with her—that they declared that she really didn't fit into any of the five categories. They had given Melanie such high-quality attention and time over the 6 weeks that she had become much more relaxed and happy. She had also shed much of her anger. A bonus of this "treatment plan" was that her parents were working less and spending more time focused on their child and their home life. Both parents remarked about how . . . much happier they had all become.

. . . I could have taken the easy route with Melanie and diagnosed her as having a mood disorder. I would have then prescribed antidepressant medication, which would have cleared up her symptoms. But the label—and the treatment—wouldn't have touched the true stress at the heart of Melanie's problem: her lack of connection with her overworked and emotionally unavailable parents. . . . [R]esisting the urge to label her allowed her parents to look at her in new ways. They began to address the stress that was at the root of her problem. By doing this—without the aid of drugs or labels—they began a healing process that will strengthen Melanie's mental and emotional health for the long haul.

How We Can Avoid Labels and Drugs and Heal Our Kids

Everyday, I see kids who are labeled, and everyday, their parents ask me questions like these: "Does Johnny have ADHD?" "I was told Mary has bipolar disorder—will this ruin her life?" "My insurance company will pay for treatment only if Billy's diagnosis fits into one of these five categories. Do any of them fit him?" "My son wants to enlist in the Marines, but they say that since he was diagnosed with bipolar disorder, he can't. Why is this?"

These are important questions, but to my mind, the parents are not asking quite the right ones. Instead, they should be wondering: "Why is my child being labeled with such a serious disorder?" "Why has my child gone from being many things (a son, a student, a friend, an athlete) to being only this?" And finally, "What is keeping my child from enjoying the kind of mental and emotional health that she should have?"

. . . Our kids, given the chance, can tell us (even in nonverbal ways) what's bothering them. It's our job to listen to them attentively and openly, to resist labeling them, and to work to remove the stressors from their lives that are blocking their mental and emotional health.

POSTSCRIPT

Are Labels Good for Kids?

People have different views of how difficult it is to obtain a label for a child's behavior and/or learning problems. Matthew's mother, Gwyn W. Senokossoff, notes that some professionals focus on the family and environment and are unwilling to consider medical possibilities. Senokossoff saw a number of reluctant doctors before finding one who was "willing and able" to provide the diagnosis needed for specific medication. That doctor, and others, identified overlapping conditions and additional medications, all of which helped Matthew "focus" and "calm down." Scott M. Shannon cited numerous examples of physicians and other professionals who are quick to provide a label but reluctant to look beyond a symptom to consider the whole individual and his/her environment.

Labels can serve a purpose. Describing a set of behaviors with a term helps people discuss conditions and behaviors. Medically, we can differentiate between flu symptoms versus those of a cold. In his compelling narrative (*Unstrange Minds*, 2007), Roy Richard Grinker expresses his pleasure that a label exists to talk about autism and his daughter's experiences. According to Grinker, the label opens doors to research, services, and supports. In his opinion, a particular set of behavior exists. The behaviors do not disappear if there is no label, but there might not be understanding and targeted services. Matthew was angry when he was punished for behavior that people did not understand was beyond his control.

Labels can have negative consequences. Shannon mentions Johnny, who thought his attention-deficit hyperactivity disorder (ADHD) label meant his "brain was broken"; this affected his confidence in attempting school tasks. Tom Hehir (*Educational Leadership*, 2007) has no problem with labels but does oppose "ableism," an attitude that views people through stereotyped lenses of what someone with a disability supposedly cannot accomplish.

The familiar bumper sticker "Jars Should Be Labeled, Not People" is distributed by PeopleFirst (www.peoplefirst.org.uk), a British organization that promotes the practice of seeing people as individuals rather than disabilities: a child who has autism rather than an autistic boy. Seeing the person first focuses on the individual, not the label.

In 2006, the 130-year-old American Association on Mental Retardation renamed itself as the American Association on Intellectual and Developmental Disabilities. In response to its community, the new name communicates a progressive approach and moves beyond a diagnostic term that is all-too-often used as an insult.

Over 25 years ago, Stainback and Stainback (1984) recommended that the medical model of naming behavior and learning patterns be discarded because "deviant labels" are hurtful and create bureaucracies and artificial barriers. They recommended a world in which every child is provided with a unique education. Schools would be flexible and help would be available to every child who needs it. Would costly special education services exist if there were no labels and focused laws? Is a label-free education possible in these days of high standards and shrinking budgets? Perhaps, this is the goal of Response to Intervention techniques.

Senokossoff sought assistance through a medical model that identifies overlapping disorders and uses medication as a key to treatment. She remembers Matthew as an active, headstrong baby and wonders if the trauma of their move might have triggered latent medically based symptoms. Shannon likely would have preferred to explore the family's move rather than prescribe medication as a first intervention. What do you think would have happened if these intelligent, well-intentioned, concerned people had come together over Matthew?

ISSUE 2

Does IDEA 2004 Contain Substantial Changes?

YES: H. Rutherford Turnbull III, from "Individuals with Disabilities Education Act Reauthorization: Accountability and Personal Responsibility," *Remedial and Special Education* (November/December 2005), 320–326

NO: Tom E. C. Smith, from "IDEA 2004: Another Round in the Reauthorization Process," *Remedial and Special Education* (November/December 2005) 314–319

ISSUE SUMMARY

YES: H. Rutherford Turnbull III, cofounder and codirector of the Beach Center on Disability at the University of Kansas, sees major changes in IDEA 2004. In line with the Bush administration's priorities, Turnbull identifies a shift toward requiring parents and students to take more responsibility for their own behavior and for relationships with schools.

NO: Tom E. C. Smith, professor at the University of Arkansas, focuses his research on disability law and inclusion. Reflecting on IDEA 2004, Smith believes that although some changes seem significant, they will make little difference in the daily practice of special education teachers.

The first federal special education statute (The Education of All Handicapped Children Act) was passed in 1975. It opened school doors for millions of excluded children with disabilities.

IDEA 97 made some landmark changes to special education law. Perhaps the most earthshaking was the requirement that all students with disabilities participate in state and local assessment systems. Not only were students with disabilities placed into schools, but also they now must have access to the general curriculum.

The fifth reauthorization of IDEA began in 2001. It was expected to move quickly. Despite good intentions, the new Individuals with Disabilities Education Improvement Act (still called IDEA) was not signed by President Bush until 2004.

The process to formalize regulations was also expected to move quickly. However, these were not posted in *The Federal Register* until mid-August 2006, after the Education Department considered more than 5500 comments. Regulations became official 60 days after posting. Final regulations, over 1700 pages in length, can be found at http://www.ed.gov/policy/speced/guid/idea/idea2004.html.

Next, state governments aligned federal regulations with their unique state laws. The latter can exceed, but not fall below, federal standards. Not until state regulations are formulated do educators and parents know what they must do to comply with any reauthorization. Current IDEA information is available through your state department of education and/or the federal Web site: http://www.ed.gov/policy/speced/guid/idea/idea2004.html.

This reauthorization was conducted in a highly charged atmosphere. No Child Left Behind (NCLB), holding districts accountable for the progress of all children (including those with disabilities), was impacting schools. The Fordham Foundation had just released a comprehensive analysis of the accomplishments and shortcomings of IDEA (*Rethinking Special Education for a New Century*, 2001) as had the President's Commission on Excellence in Special Education (PCESE) (2002). Both called for substantial changes to increase accountability, reduce paperwork, and reign in what each perceived as rampant litigation.

The major changes in IDEA 2004 addressed many of the criticisms that had been levied. Substantial differences can be found in the following areas:

- Increased alignment with NCLB, including the definition of highly qualified teachers and the requirement to use research-based instruction
- Use of Response to Intervention, as a general education process and as an alternative means of identifying students with specific learning disabilities
- Flexibility of team practices, including the "excusal" of some participants
- Elimination of short-term objectives, except for students with significant cognitive needs
- Heightened emphasis on transition
- More administrative latitude in disciplinary proceedings, including manifestation determination

The two articles in this issue consider the changes in IDEA 2004. They differ dramatically in their interpretation of the significance of these elements.

H. Rutherford Turnbull III believes IDEA 2004 is substantially altered. He finds the new provisions substantially increase the responsibilities of parents and students, echoing the Welfare Reform Act of 1996.

Tom Smith predicts that although a number of new elements of IDEA 2004 appear substantial, they will have little real impact on the daily practices of schools. He sees that the core element of IDEA—providing free and appropriate public education—remains unchanged.

As you read these articles, consider the impact of IDEA 2004 on several constituencies. How has IDEA 2004 affected your life as an educator? As a parent? As an administrator?

YES    H. Rutherford Turnbull III

Individuals with Disabilities Education Act Reauthorization: Accountability and Personal Responsibility

It is important at the outset to recognize that law is a form of behavior modification. It regulates the behaviors between the government and the governed, and it shapes the behavior of both. In this respect, the law plays its traditional role of social engineering—shaping the ways that society operates.

Seen in this light, the reauthorized Individuals with Disabilities Education Act (IDEA; 2004) engineers society and shapes behavior in three basic ways. First, it authorizes the expenditure of federal funds and shapes how those funds and the complementary state and local educational agencies' funds are spent, and it aligns those funds and their expenditure patterns with the earlier IDEA (1997) and with the No Child Left Behind Act of 2001 (NCLB). It continues to be—but becomes more like—a *school reform* law. Second, IDEA grants rights to students and their parents: It continues to be a *civil rights* law. Third, IDEA particularizes the relationships that students and their parents have with local and state educational agencies. It partakes of social reform on a large scale—more like a *"welfare state"* reform law than a civil rights or school reform law.

Taking these three approaches to social engineering as a whole, and based on a close analysis of IDEA's text, it becomes clear that IDEA is more consistent than ever with other federal policies that impose accountability standards and procedures on the beneficiaries of federal largesse. The accountability that IDEA (1997) and NCLB imposed on the schools is now imposed on the students and their parents as well. To support this argument, it is appropriate to begin with analyzing IDEA as an education law, then showing how IDEA retains its basic nature as a civil rights statute, and finally discussing its new accountability and responsibilities provisions, their origins, their relationships to other disability laws, and their implications as welfare law reform.

From *Remedial and Special Education*, vol. 26, no. 6, November/December 2005, pp. 320–326. Copyright © 2005 by Hammill Institute on Disabilities and Sage in association with American Rehabilitation Counseling Association (ARCA). Reprinted by permission via Rightslink.

IDEA as Education Law

When Congress reauthorized IDEA in 2004, it aligned IDEA with the Elementary and Secondary Education Act (ESEA; 1965), as amended by the . . . NCLB. To understand how this is so, it is helpful to describe the six principles that underlie NCLB (Erwin & Soodak, 2005) and show how IDEA connects to them.

The most obvious and, therefore, the first to be mentioned principle of NCLB is *accountability* for the outcomes (results) of education. NCLB's provisions for the mandatory assessment of student proficiency during the elementary school years are its principal means for ensuring accountability. In 1997, IDEA provided that students with disabilities will have a right to participate in state and district assessments. In 2004, IDEA provides that students will participate, with accommodations and sometimes by alternate assessments, in the NCLB assessments. . . . The significant change is not that the students will engage in the state and district assessments, but that IDEA now references and therefore aligns with NCLB.

To support its accountability principle, NCLB adopts a second principle, the *highly qualified teacher* principle. Without a qualified teacher corps, improved student outcomes will be elusive, and accountability for those outcomes difficult to achieve. Accordingly, IDEA (2004) requires special education staff to be highly qualified. . . . The second principle is a means to achieve the first.

NCLB's third principle is also a means to achieve its ends: The highly qualified teachers will use *scientifically based instruction* (SBI; sometimes called *evidence-based instruction*). IDEA reiterates the SBI requirement through several different provisions:

1. It disqualifies a student from IDEA benefits if the student's educational needs or deficiencies result from "a lack of appropriate instruction in reading, including the essential components of reading instruction," as defined in . . . the Elementary and Secondary Education Act of 1965, as amended by NCLB. . . .
2. It restricts a student from being classified as having a specific learning disability by authorizing an LEA to "use a process that determines if the child responds to scientific, research-based intervention as part of the evaluation procedures.". . .
3. It requires a student's special education, related services, and supplementary aids and services (as set out in the student's . . . IEP) to be "based on peer-reviewed research to the extent practicable." . . .
4. It authorizes the SEA and LEAs to support preservice and professional development (inservice) activities that train educators to use "scientifically based instructional practices.". . .
5. It authorizes "whole-school approaches, scientifically based early reading programs, positive behavioral interventions and supports, and early intervening services" that can prevent students from being classified into special education. . . .
6. It defines "highly qualified" teachers in terms that originate in NCLB. . . .

7. It authorizes the SEA and LEAs to expend Part B money for "early intervening services" that are coordinated with their NCLB activities. . . .
8. It sponsors research, training, demonstration, and other programs that align with NCLB. . . .

NCLB's fourth principle is *local flexibility,* the theory being that too many restrictions are imposed on SEAs and LEAs by too many federal laws and that if the SEAs and LEAs have more flexibility to use their federal funds as suitable to meet their particular needs, they will achieve more acceptable outcomes. Thus, fiscal and programmatic flexibility advances agency accountability, and site-based management is sanctioned. Similarly, IDEA recognizes that SEAs and LEAs have the primary responsibility for educating students with disabilities and that there is a limited role for the federal government (Sec. 601)(c)(6). It is appropriate, then, for IDEA to seek to reduce federal paperwork requirements . . . and to grant SEAs and LEAs more discretion in how they use Part B funds. . . .

NCLB's fifth principle relates to *safe schools,* the theory being that agency accountability and student proficiency are unlikely to be realized when the teaching and learning environment is unsafe. To advance the safe school and acceptable outcome approach, IDEA retains the 1997 provision that allows an LEA to put a student into an interim alternative educational setting for a maximum of 45 days if the student carries weapons or drugs to school or injures others, but it now allows the LEA to take into account any "unique circumstances" relative to that student and his or her conduct. This vague provision is consistent with the flexibility principle, but it targets the discipline issue, not the expenditure issue: The LEA needs to be able to exercise its discretion to carry out the safety principle and thereby advance the accountability principle.

Moreover, IDEA (2004) also makes it more difficult for a student to prove that his or her behavior and disability are causally connected. . . . Under the 1997 law, the student's IEP team had discretion (the statute used the word "may") to conclude that the student's behavior was not a manifestation of his or her disability if (a) the student's IEP and placement were "appropriate," and special education services, supplementary aids and services, and behavior intervention strategies "were provided consistent with" the student's IEP; (b) the student's disability did not "impair" the student's ability to understand "the impact and consequences" of his or her behavior; and (c) the student's disability did not "impair" his or her ability "to control the behavior" for which the school would be disciplining the student.

Under the 2004 reauthorization, however, the discretionary "may" has been deleted. In its place, IDEA (2004) provides that the student's "conduct shall be determined to be a manifestation" of his or her disability under certain conditions. Furthermore, those conditions are more stringent. Instead of the original three conditions, there are now only two, and each is itself more exacting. One is that the student's conduct "was caused by, or had a direct and substantial relationship to" the student's disability. Note the change; "caused" and "direct and substantial relationship" are more immediately connected to the conduct than the two 1997 standards of "did not know" and "could not control." The other condition is that the student's conduct was "the direct result" of the LEA's "failure to implement" the student's IEP. Note again the change: Gone is the 1997 language about services not being provided "consistent with" the student's IEP and placement. "Causation" and "direct relationships" are now clearly more connected to conduct than "consistency" or fidelity of implementation.

NCLB's sixth principle is *parent participation and choice*. This has always been one of IDEA's six principles: the right to be involved in a nondiscriminatory evaluation, to be on the IEP team, to have access to and control over the release of records, and to be eligible for membership on various SEA or LEA advisory boards.

The new IDEA (2004) retains these provisions but clarifies that parents have responsibilities as well. Section 612(a)(10) limits tuition reimbursement and conditions it on the parents' giving an LEA notice and opportunity to cure alleged violations of the student's right to FAPE. Section 614(a)(1)(D) imposes duties on parents with respect to the initial evaluation, and Section 614(c)(3) does the same with respect to reevaluations. Sections 615(b)(5) and (e) make mediation available and create premediation meetings. Section 615(b)(6) creates a 2-year statute of limitations and thus requires parents to complain in a timely way. Section 615(a)(7) obligates parents to notify the LEA concerning "the nature of the problem of the child" and the "proposed resolution" of the problem of the child (not "of the school") and thus imposes on them the duty to specify what is wrong with their child and what the LEA should do for their child. Section 615(c)(E) restricts the parents' (and LEA's) right to amend their due process hearing complaint: The parents have to get their complaint right the first time around, or else the school cannot respond, because it would always be subject to being caught off guard by another and different complaint. Section 615(d)(1)(A) provides that parents may receive the procedural safeguards notice only once a year (with some exceptions), rather than on demand as often as they want it. Section 615(f)(1) requires parents and the LEA to hold a prehearing "resolution session" and to provide sufficient final notice so that the parents' complaint might be resolved before the hearing. Section 615(f)(2) requires the parents to disclose all evaluations and recommendations that they intend to use in the hearing. Section 615(f)(3)(C) creates a 2-year statute of limitations, counting from the time when a parent knew or reasonably should have known that a local educational agency violated IDEA, thus putting the parents to the task of regularly monitoring their child's education. Section 615(i)(3) regulates that award of parents' attorneys' fees and allows a court to charge the LEA's fees to the parents' attorneys if the parents' complaint is frivolous or if the parents do not proceed in good faith during the pendency of any hearing, trial, or appeal.

In summary, the reauthorized IDEA (2004) imposes many new duties on students and their parents, giving them the message that they are personally responsible for their conduct—a point that the following discussion expands.

IDEA as Civil Rights Law

IDEA is still a civil rights law. Section 612(c) parrots the Americans with Disabilities Act (1990; the disability community's civil rights law) by proclaiming that the nation's disability policy consists of ensuring equal opportunity, full participation, independent living, and economic self-sufficiency. The very term *equal opportunity* derives from the equal protection clause of the 14th Amendment (prohibiting a state from denying anyone in its jurisdiction the "equal protection" of the law), and the 14th Amendment itself was the basis on which students with disabilities first gained access to the schools as a matter of constitutional right. More than this, however, IDEA retains the original six principles that endow it as a civil rights law.

Section 612 codifies the *zero rejection* principle by continuing to require that the state plan to provide for the education of *all* students with disabilities and by retaining the "no cessation" provision. Moreover, the Section 615 discipline provisions ensure that students with disabilities will have procedural and substantive protection against discipline that might terminate their right to an education or alter the nature of FAPE for them.

Sections 614(a)–(c) continue the *nondiscriminatory evaluation* principle by retaining the safeguards for nondiscriminatory evaluation. The requirement that the evaluation now must attend to the student's academic, developmental, and functional characteristics simply makes the evaluation more specific. Moreover, the evaluation team still needs to determine the "relative contribution" of "cognitive, behavioral, physical, and developmental factors" to a student's educational needs. Thus, three characteristics, or domains, become the focus of an evaluation under the IEP: academic (consistent with NCLB), developmental, and functional (consistent with the "alternate assessment" provisions of IDEA). The four contributing factors—cognitive (a surrogate for academic), behavioral, physical, and developmental—must be evaluated and taken into account, separately and collectively.

Section 614(d) retains the *appropriate education* principle by setting out the required content of a student's IEP—the theory being that if the content standard is met, the student's education will "benefit" the student and thus meet the *Rowley* definition of "appropriate."

Section 615(f), however, minimizes the "process" component of the *Rowley* definition by providing that a procedural violation constitutes the denial of a free, appropriate public education only if it impedes the student's right to such an education, significantly impedes the parents' opportunity to participate in decision making, or causes a deprivation of educational benefits. This provision seems to codify case law: no significant procedural harm, no substantive foul.

Several sections of the 2004 IDEA restate the *least restrictive environment* principle. Section 612(a)(5) and Sections 614(b)(2)(A) and (c)(1)(B)(iv) continue to ensure that the student may participate and have the opportunity to make progress in the general curriculum. They also retain the requirement that the student's IEP must advance the student's participation in the general curriculum, extracurricular, and other school activities, consistent with the principle of the least restrictive environment.

Likewise, two sections of IDEA (2004) retain the *procedural due process* principle. Section 614 retains the procedural safeguards related to evaluation, program, and placement, and Section 615 retains the procedural due process protections related to grievances, although, as noted earlier, it adds new provisions regarding dispute resolution and mediation and makes it more difficult for a student to resist unilateral placement (see the "unique circumstances" provision) and to prove manifestation of a disability.

Finally, Sections 614 and 615 retain the *parent participation* principle by conferring opportunities on the parents to participate in decisions affecting their child's education.

By retaining its original six principles, IDEA remains a foundation for the 18 core concepts and the related nine overarching principles of disability policy. For example, the zero rejection principle reflects the core concept of *antidiscrimination*. The nondiscriminatory evaluation principle reflects the core concept of *classification*. The appropriate education principle reflects the core concept of *individualized appropriate services*. The least restrictive environment principle reflects the core concept of *integration*. The procedural due process principle reflects the core concept of *accountability*. The parent participation principle reflects the core concept of *empowerment and participatory decision making*.

These core concepts reflect constitutional principles (*life, liberty,* and *equality*) and ethical principles (*dignity, family as foundation,* and *community*). Thus, for example, the NCLB principles of accountability, highly qualified teachers, and scientifically based instruction reflect the core concepts of accountability, professional and system capacity development, and individualized appropriate services, respectively. The principle of local flexibility reflects the core concept of accountability. The principle of safety reflects the core concept of protection from harm. The principle of parental participation and choice reflects the core concept of empowerment and participatory decision making.

The fact that NCLB reflects some of the same core concepts of disability policy as IDEA is significant: It shows how very universalistic and less exceptionalistic IDEA has become. It is "mainstream" disability policy, of course, but it also has become part of the mainstream of education policy.

Two Preludes to IDEA as Accountability Policy

Two reports predicted that the reauthorized IDEA would focus far more on student and parental accountability than it had in the past. The first was *Rethinking Special Education for a New Century*. The second was the report of the President's Commission on Excellence in Special Education (2002). Both reports made similar critiques of special education, and both sought similar improvements to IDEA. Both focused on outcome rather than process, on a model of prevention rather than failure, and on children with disabilities as "general education children first" (President's Commission, 2002). Both reports paid attention to IDEA as an education law but less attention to IDEA as a civil rights law. Most significantly, both reports argued that IDEA leads students with disabilities to have unacceptable outcomes, low expectations, and a diminished sense of personal responsibility.

The point about personal responsibility was made most directly in *Rethinking*, in the chapter by Horn and Tynan, who argued that one of IDEA's "unintended negative consequences" included the "application of an accommodation philosophy to populations better served with prevention or intervention strategies." The "accommodation model," when applied to some "low- and under-achieving students," replaces a goal of "independence" with one of "lifetime dependence on special accommodations, often at tax-payers' expense." The accommodations, and especially the discipline provisions, have been "teaching students in special education that they are entitled to operate under a different set of rules than everyone else." These accommodations constitute "encouragement for special education students to see their disability as rationale for a life-time entitlement to special accommodations." The consequence of these accommodations is that the "end game" of independence has been forgotten: "special education in far too many instances serves to separate, not integrate, through the use of special rules and procedures not available to non-disabled students." Special education "seems focused on encouraging a lifetime entitlement to special accommodations." The "true victims" are the students themselves; they learn that there are "two standards" and they are "encouraged to rely upon special accommodations rather than being challenged to achieve at high levels."

Horn and Tynan's critique has a basic message: IDEA creates dependency. That message is consonant with the messages given by welfare law reform during the last decade, as the following discussion makes clear.

IDEA as Welfare Law

By analyzing the messages that Congress and the Supreme Court have been giving in welfare and disability policy during the past decade, and by bearing in mind Horn and Tynan's critique, it becomes obvious that IDEA extends the basic message of personal responsibility that was the core of welfare reform. This message also relates as much to personal responsibility as it does to social obligations and the social contract.

Congress, the Supreme Court, and the Principle of Personal Responsibility

Congress reformed welfare programs in 1996 by enacting the Personal Responsibility and Work Opportunity Reconciliation Act (PRWORA). This law targeted a subpopulation that allegedly had "learned" to be dependent—namely, families who had been supported by aid-to-dependent-families programs. PRWORA authorized time-limited and conditional cash grants, requiring the head of family to enroll in some educational program or work and entitling the family to receive the grants for only 2 years.

In a nutshell, PRWORA declared an end to learned dependency and imposed responsibilities on heads of families; it taught welfare beneficiaries that they should not continue to expect different treatment from other citizens. It signaled that people should expect less from their government and more from themselves. It proclaimed the renaissance of self-reliance and a work-ethic policy that asserts that everyone has a responsibility to contribute to society.

Similarly, IDEA reflects the theory that special education "teaches" students with disabilities to expect "different" treatment in society. This is a fundamental premise of the Finn et al. report and the Horn and Tynan chapter: The discipline provisions "teach" students with disabilities that they are different, can behave in different (and less acceptable, less conforming) ways and still expect to be treated differently ("no cessation" under Section 612, and special procedural safeguards, including manifestation determinations, under Section 615). The reauthorized IDEA sent a different message, as the many provisions cited earlier demonstrate.

In PRWORA and IDEA, Congress did more than restate the "responsibility" principle. Fundamentally, it restated the quid pro quo of the social contract: Society will do something for you if you cannot do it for yourself, but you first must be responsible for yourself. Self-reliance precedes social support. Personal responsibility precedes social dependency.

The Supreme Court also has advanced the principle of personal responsibility, principally (in its disability-law cases) in *Sutton v. United Air Lines* (1999). In this case, the court held that in determining whether the ADA protects a person, it is permissible to take into account whether the person can or does mitigate his or her disability. If a person's impairment is or can be mitigated, that person does not have a disability. *Sutton's* message and subtext is clear: If you can mitigate your disability, you should, and if you do not, ADA will not cover you.

Following *Sutton,* the Supreme Court made a deliberate effort to reduce the number of people that the ADA covers. The best example is its decision in *Williams v. Toyota.* There, the court declared that the "major life activities" that a person's impairment must significantly limit are performing household chores, bathing, and brushing one's teeth; those activities do not include being able, with accommodations, to perform a particular job. By reducing the number of people who are entitled to accommodations because they have disabilities, the court adopted the premise of *Rethinking* and the President's Commission (2002), namely, that too many people have been included as "disabled" and that it is better social policy to restrict admission to disability entitlements than to allow people to enter the disability category easily. . . .

The Supreme Court's message, then, is congruent with Finn et al., the report of the President's Commission (2002), and the reauthorized IDEA (2004): Disability policy and law should benefit fewer, not more people, and it should teach those who do qualify and those who seek to qualify as having a disability that they have obligations as well as rights and entitlements.

IDEA and the Principle of Personal Responsibility

The reauthorized IDEA (2004) restates the principle of personal responsibility in at least two ways. In this respect, IDEA is consistent with the message that Congress sent in PRWORA and the Supreme Court sent in the ADA employment cases.

First, as noted earlier, IDEA grants a variety of rights to students' parents to participate in decisions about their child's education, but it also imposes duties on them as they do participate. Moreover, IDEA also makes the personal responsibility theme explicit, . . . with respect to the students themselves. Here, Congress declares that students' education can be made more effective when educators have "high expectations" of them and enable them to "meet their developmental goals," to meet the "challenging expectations that have been set for all children," and to "be prepared to lead productive . . . adult lives." . . . Under an analysis of IDEA as welfare law, the provisions about meeting "developmental goals" arguably refer to students' behavior, not just to their academic achievement. Likewise, under the same analysis, the provisions about "lead[ing] productive . . . adult lives" arguably refer to being economically self-sufficient, working and contributing to the nation's economy, or making other socially valued contributions.

Second, as also explained earlier, IDEA allows LEAs to take into account "any unique circumstances on a case-by-case basis" when determining whether to order a change in a student's placement because of conduct that violates school rules. . . . This provision is a Damoclean sword: The "unique circumstances" are a thin hair that can protect the student or, if it is cut, cause the sword of discipline to strike the student. In either event, it permits LEAs to take into account whether the student chose to act responsibly or was incapable of making that choice.

The reauthorized IDEA (2004) also makes it more difficult for students to defend themselves against a disciplinary sanction by alleging "manifestation." As pointed out above, the reauthorized law requires students to prove that their conduct was "caused by" or had a "direct and substantial relationship" to their disability. It also removes the lax standard that the student's services were not delivered "consistent" with the IEP and replaces it with the standard that the LEA must fail to implement the student's IEP and thereby directly cause the student's conduct.

Rights and Responsibilities Within IDEA: Teaching New Lessons

The changes in IDEA's parent participation and student discipline provisions impose a duty of responsibility on parents and students alike. These beneficiaries must either follow new, highly specific procedures and standards or justify why they do not.

The new IDEA, then, teaches parents and students that they have responsibility for their own actions. It intends to shape their behavior by causing them to unlearn their alleged sense of entitlement to act in certain ways. It seeks to reduce their dependency on the schools and to increase their dependency on themselves. It calls on them to be more self-reliant and self-governing. It bears repeating: Section 601(c)(5)(A) proclaims that students' education can be made more "effective" if there are "high expectations" for them (including both behavioral expectations and academic expectations) and ways of "strengthening the role and responsibility of parents." . . .

IDEA, Title I of ESEA, and the New Morbidity

It is not just in its parent and student rights provisions that IDEA reveals that it is a welfare law. There is also a clear line between (a) IDEA and its concern with student outcomes, especially outcomes for ethnically and linguistically diverse students . . . (b) NCLB and the special provisions for Title I schools (i.e., for "poor students" in school); and (c) the "new morbidity." The term *new morbidity* refers to evidence that disability has a positive correlation with poverty and other demographic factors, such as family structure, ethnicity/ culture, language, and geography.

IDEA and NCLB focus especially on students whom the new morbidity affects—under IDEA, students from minority populations (Sec. 601(c)(10)– (13)), and under NCLB, the Title I eligible ("poor") students. PRWORA and welfare reform focused on these students' families. Together, IDEA and NCLB continue the PRWORA welfare reform policies passed nearly a decade ago and the *Sutton* line of cases.

Conclusion

It seems unseemly to argue that the reauthorized IDEA is, at its core, part of the reforms that PRWORA and *Sutton* launched more than half a decade before Congress turned its attention to IDEA. Somehow, the notion that students' and parents' rights were sacrosanct had become the conventional wisdom. Yet the transitory nature of "conventional wisdom" is apparent in the very terms that define the concept itself: *Conventional* refers to the conventions, the mores, of a certain time, place, and culture. As our country's history shows, conventions and mores change; the underlying principles (the so-called six principles of IDEA and the so-called core concepts of disability policy) may not have changed, but the ways in which they are expressed in practice and codified in law do.

So it seems to be with the reauthorized IDEA. The conventional notion that rights are paramount now seems to be descendant, not ascendant. At the same time, the notion that rights entail responsibilities is ascendant; this notion does not supersede the importance of rights, but it does assert that, in our society, rights and responsibilities go hand in hand. This is a message of paramount importance to the special education and disability communities. Whether these communities will hear that message—which is sure to be repeated in debates about Social Security, Medicaid, and ADA—and how they will respond to it if they hear it are the stuff of the future.

 **NO**

IDEA 2004: Another Round in the Reauthorization Process

The Individuals with Disabilities Education Act (IDEA; 1997) has once again been reauthorized. Although the reauthorization was thought to be on a fast track when it was initially begun in 2001, the law was finally passed in November 2004 and signed by President Bush in December 2004. The Individuals with Disabilities Education Improvement Act (2004), still to be referred to as IDEA, contains some significant changes; however, after careful review, the changes may not be as significant as first thought.

Certainly, the lives of children with disabilities in this country have been forever altered as a result of federal legislation. Beginning with the passage of Public Law 94-142, the Education for All Handicapped Children Act, in 1975, federal policies and federal dollars have been an integral component of special education. Overall, there is no doubt that the lives of children with disabilities have improved significantly. Let us review some of the major changes that have resulted from this law; some of the changes made in previous reauthorizations; and finally, some of the major changes associated with IDEA 2004.

Public Law 94-142

When Public Law 94-142 (the Education for All Handicapped Children Act) was passed in 1975, the state of special education was vastly different from what it is today. Prior to its passage, Congress found that up to 1 million of the estimated 8 million children with disabilities in the United States were excluded from public school services, and another 3 million were being served inappropriately. The original four purposes of P.L. 94-142 included

- to assure that all children with disabilities have available to them . . . a free appropriate public education which emphasizes special education and related services designed to meet their unique needs
- to assure that the rights of children with disabilities and their parents . . . are protected
- to assist States and localities to provide for the education of all children with disabilities
- to assess and assure the effectiveness of efforts to educate all children with disabilities

From *Remedial and Special Education*, vol. 26, no. 6, November/December 2005, pp. 314–319. Copyright © 2005 by Hammill Institute on Disabilities and Sage in association with American Rehabilitation Counseling Association (ARCA). Reprinted by permission via Rightslink.

Public Law 94-142 resulted in many changes in the way children with disabilities were identified and provided with services. Prior to its passage, special education was a mere footnote in U.S. educational statistics. There were fewer than 3.5 million children with disabilities served in public schools, mostly in isolated, self-contained settings; and teacher preparation for special education was a minor activity. Some of the major requirements of P.L. 94-142 included the following:

- Child Find. Schools were required to locate children with disabilities and initiate the referral process to determine their eligibility for services under this act.
- Individualized Education Program (IEP). Every child served in special education must have an IEP. Although not intending to do so, the IEP requirement resulted in massive amounts of paperwork for special education teachers.
- Least Restrictive Environment (LRE). To the maximum extent appropriate, children with disabilities should be educated with their nondisabled peers. This resulted in "mainstreaming" and the practice of including many students with disabilities in general education settings.
- Nondiscriminatory Assessment. All children must be given a comprehensive assessment prior to determining their eligibility for special education, and this assessment must be administered in such a way as not to discriminate against individuals from different cultural/language groups.
- Related Services. Services that are necessary for a child to benefit from special education, such as physical therapy or transportation, must also be provided.
- Due Process Rights. Children with disabilities, and their parents, must be afforded certain due process rights, including the right of notice and consent prior to actions affecting their child and the right to a due process hearing to resolve complaints and disagreements between parents and the school.
- Funding. Congress said that the federal government would eventually fund up to 40% of the excess costs of educating students with disabilities. Although Congress still has not come close to the 40% level, hundreds of millions of dollars have supported programs under this legislation.
- Free, appropriate public education (FAPE). Schools were required to provide a free, appropriate public education to all students with disabilities. This includes determining the eligibility of children and developing and implementing an IEP for each child. All of the services to children under this act must be provided without cost to the parents.

Although there were many other provisions in the original P.L. 94-142, these were the ones having the greatest impact.

Since P.L. 94-142 was passed, there have been several reauthorizations that have made changes in the law. Although some of these changes have been significant, they have not altered the basic requirements of the original legislation. All children with disabilities must be referred, evaluated, and determined to be eligible or not; all eligible students must have IEPs; and all must be provided with a free, appropriate public education, meaning they must be

Table 1

Key Components of Reauthorizations of P.L. 94-142/IDEA

Reauthorization	Key components
1983 (P.L. 98-199)	1. Provided incentives for states to serve preschool children with disabilities.
	2. Required states to collect information and address issues related to students transitioning from school to post-school.
(P.L. 101-457)	1. Mandated services for children 3-5 lowering all of the requirements of P.L. 94-142 to include 3-5 year old children.
	2. Provided for attorney's fees in due process or court cases where parents prevailed.
(P.L. 101-476)	1. Added autism and traumatic brain injury to the list of disabilities covered under IDEA.
	2. Changed the name of the act from the Education for All Handicapped Children Act to the Individuals with Disabilities Education Act.
	3. Required schools to initiate transition services no later than age 16.
1997 (P.L. 105-17)	1. Required schools to initiate transition planning no later than age 14.
	2. Required schools to include behavior intervention plans for students with behavior problems.

served in the least restrictive environment. Some of the major changes associated with successive reauthorizations up to 1997 are included in Table 1.

IDEA 2004

The reauthorization of IDEA in 2004 included a name change: The word "improvement" was inserted, making the official title of the legislation the "Individuals with Disabilities Education Improvement Act." However, the law is still referred to as IDEA. Several significant changes were included in the reauthorization. The following section will describe these changes and discuss the actual implications of the changes.

Highly Qualified Teachers

IDEA 2004 includes a requirement that special education teachers meet the "highly qualified" mandate introduced in the No Child Left Behind Act (NCLB; 2001) legislation. This is the first reauthorization of IDEA that includes any specific requirements related to teacher qualifications. Until this act, determining the qualifications of teachers had always been left to the states. IDEA 2004 now requires teachers to be "highly qualified." Highly qualified means that

1. All special education teachers must be highly qualified under the NCLB definition; also, special education teachers must have a state special education certification; not hold an emergency, temporary, or provisional certification; and have at least a bachelor's degree.

2. Special education teachers who teach content courses and are the teachers of record for those courses must meet the NCLB *highly qualified* requirements. This means that they must be licensed in the subjects taught, similar to general classroom teachers under NCLB.

The ramifications of this addition to the legislation are just now being understood. The Council for Exceptional Children (CEC) has referred to this component of the law as "an extraordinary federal intrusion into what has been the domain of States and the profession." CEC has added that these requirements are bureaucratic, impractical, unsound, and intrusive. Many special education teachers have been involved in providing instruction and support to students in subject areas, especially in middle and high schools. Getting these teachers licensed in these content areas will undoubtedly cause many problems. Teachers are allowed to become licensed through state high objective state standard of evaluation (HOUSSE) options, which is a way states can license teachers under NCLB; however, for the immediate future, these requirements will create problems for many teachers, local districts, and states.

Funding

Finally, more than 30 years since the passage of P.L. 94-142, Congress appears to be ready to meet its promise of full funding for IDEA. P.L. 94-142 said that Congress would fund special education programs under the law at a rate up to 40% of excess costs for educating children with disabilities. Congress has never come close to the 40% level. In fact, federal funding for IDEA has never reached the 20% level. IDEA 2004 lays out a path for full funding. The law authorizes Congress to fund IDEA for $12.36 billion for fiscal year 2005 and an additional $2.3 billion each year through 2011, when full funding will be achieved.

Individualized Education Programs

The level of paperwork associated with special education has increased significantly since the passage of P.L. 94-142. In some cases, special education professionals seem to spend as much time on paperwork as on programs for their students. Excessive paperwork has actually been cited by some teachers as their primary reason for leaving the teaching profession. The 2004 reauthorization has made some changes directly targeting a reduction in paperwork. One of the changes incorporated in IDEA 2004 is deleting the requirement that IEPs include short-term objectives, except for students who are assessed using alternative assessment procedures that are aligned with alternate achievement standards. Eliminating short-term objectives hopefully will not have a negative impact on appropriate programming but will result in a reduction of paperwork.

Another change in IEPs relates to transition requirements. Whereas IDEA 1997 required schools to include transition planning in IEPs when the child reached 14 years of age, IDEA 2004 only requires schools to include a statement of transition goals based on age-appropriate transition assessments beginning with the first IEP that will be in effect when the child reaches 16 years of age.

IDEA 2004 also provides some flexibility in attendance at IEP meetings by permitting team members not to attend if their area of expertise is not needed, as agreed by other team members, and not to attend if they provide written information related to the IEP meeting prior to the meeting, again with team approval. IEPs can also be modified during the year without the entire team being present if the school and parents agree to a written amendment after the original IEP is developed. These provisions should help limit the number of times that complete teams have to get together to develop and modify IEPs. It also keeps some school personnel from having to attend meetings when their expertise is really not needed.

Finally, relative to the IEP, IDEA 2004 has established a 15-state pilot program for multiyear IEPs. States can apply for participation in the pilot program. Under the pilot program, states can develop IEPs for up to 3 years on a trial basis. Whereas students' progress toward achieving their 3-year goals would have to be measured annually, IEPs would not have to be rewritten on an annual basis. This pilot program, advocated by many professionals and some professional organizations, will determine if students can receive FAPE using multiyear IEPs, just as they receive FAPE using annual IEPs. If the results of the pilot program are positive, it is likely that all states will be able to move to multiyear IEPs.

Due Process Requirements

The original P.L. 94-142 included specific due process requirements, including the right to notice and consent and the right to a due process hearing. Parents must give consent prior to the initial evaluation and placement of their child in special education, and they must be notified prior to other actions dealing with their child. IDEA 2004 continues to require that schools obtain consent prior to initial evaluation and placement. If parents refuse their consent for initial evaluation, schools may pursue this denial through due process. However, parental refusal of consent to special education placement may not be pursued by the school through due process. In this situation, the child is not considered a child with a disability under IDEA, and the school district is not responsible for ensuring FAPE for the child.

IDEA 2004 also includes some significant changes related to due process hearings. Parents have been able to recoup attorney fees in situations where they prevailed in due process hearings and court cases, but the schools have not been able to recoup attorney fees in situations where they prevailed. IDEA 2004 enables schools to recoup costs in certain situations from the parents and parents' attorneys.

Specifically, IDEA 2004 says that the court may award fees to the prevailing state education agency (SEA) or local education agency (LEA) against parents' attorneys who (a) file a complaint or other cause of action that is frivolous, unreasonable, or without foundation or (b) continue to litigate after litigation clearly has become frivolous, unreasonable, or without foundation. The prevailing SEA or LEA may also be awarded fees by the courts against the parents' attorney or against the parents if the complaint or subsequent cause of action was presented for any improper purpose (e.g., to harass, cause delay, or increase the cost of litigation).

It is hoped that these provisions will reduce the number of complaints, due process hearing requests, and court actions, unless the situation truly merits those actions. Schools have complained in the past that some parents are filing complaints to retaliate against a school or school personnel and that often parents or their attorneys continue the litigation process to enhance the level of attorney fees. The fact that parents and their attorneys can be held accountable for these fees in situations where the courts think their actions are unwarranted may reduce the level of complaints.

Expulsion and Suspension

Disciplinary procedures for students with disabilities have been a highly debated topic for many years. In fact, disagreements on disciplining students with disabilities have been a major stumbling block in successfully reauthorizing IDEA on several previous occasions. Advocates for children with disabilities have resolutely supported students and opposed disciplinary procedures for this group of children that did not take the effect of the child's disability into consideration. This has resulted, correctly, in schools having to consider the impact of the disability on the behavior. If a suspension was for fewer than 10 days, and the student did not already have a series of suspensions that might add up to 10 days, then the school could suspend the student, similar to suspending any other student. However, if the suspension or expulsion added up to more than 10 days, the schools had to conduct a manifestation determination to determine the relationship, if any, between the disability and the inappropriate behavior. If a relationship was found to exist, then the school could not remove the student. If no relationship was found, the child could be removed from the school but the school had to continue to provide FAPE.

IDEA 2004 makes some changes to the disciplinary procedures for children with disabilities. Similar to IDEA 1997, prior to any suspension or expulsion for more than 10 days, a manifestation determination must be made. If no relationship is found, then the school may suspend or expel the student, similar to a student without disabilities. In this case, however, the school must continue to provide FAPE to the student. If there is a relationship between the disability and the behavior, then the school may not expel or suspend the student. A relationship is found if the behavior was caused by or had a *direct and substantial* relationship to the child's disability, or if the school had failed to implement the child's IEP. IDEA 2004 adds the *direct and substantial* language, possibly making it more difficult to determine that the behavior is related to the disability. If the manifestation determination concludes that there is a relationship between the disability and the behavior, then a functional behavior assessment is conducted and a behavior intervention plan is developed.

The child is returned to the original placement unless both parties agree to a change of placement. The parents or the school may appeal a decision. In this case, the student will remain in the alternative placement until appeals are exhausted. An expedited hearing process is held.

In certain instances (e.g., the child has a weapon, is using or in possession of drugs, or inflicts serious bodily injury on someone), the child may be removed for up to 45 school days without regard to whether the behavior is a manifestation of the disability. This action can be taken without a hearing officer's involvement. IDEA 1997 said that a child could be removed for 45 days; by changing this to 45 *school* days, IDEA 2004 in effect allows a substantial increase in the period of time the child can be removed. Again, parents may appeal this decision and have an expedited hearing. While under appeal, the student remains in the placement that resulted from the inappropriate behavior, not the student's placement before the behavior occurred.

Eligibility for Students Classified as Having LD

Overidentification of students as having learning disabilities (LD) has been a concern for many years. Indeed, with more than 50% of all students with disabilities in this classification, many professionals have long been concerned about the use of a discrepancy formula to determine eligibility. Some have agreed that the use of this formula, which requires a severe discrepancy between IQ and achievement scores, has led to overidentification. Although IDEA has never required a discrepancy formula, many states and local education agencies have adopted this model of LD.

IDEA 2004 makes a point that a discrepancy between achievement and aptitude is not required to classify a student as having LD. It further states that schools may use a child's response to intervention as part of their eligibility process. Therefore, a school may choose to implement intervention programs, such as reading programs, and, if a child responds positively to the program, determine that a child is not eligible under IDEA. IDEA 2004 gives schools this flexibility. This language was added to IDEA 2004 in an attempt to limit the number of students identified as eligible for special education services who may simply be experiencing difficulties resulting from inappropriate instruction. If interventions are successful, there is no reason to identify the child as having LD and being eligible for special education.

Other Changes

In addition to the aforementioned changes in IDEA 2004, there are many other changes that schools will be implementing. These include

- changing definitions of *assistive technology device*
- optional establishment of a risk pool with up to 10% of IDEA funds reserved for state-level activities for high-cost activities and supports
- allowing up to 15% of a school's IDEA funds for prereferral interventions
- flexibility in using Part C funds

- including homeless children in child-find activities
- allowing reevaluations of students not more than once each year and not more than every 3 years, unless school and parents agree it is not necessary
- conducting evaluations in the language or form most likely to yield accurate results, not necessarily in the child's native language

Conclusions

IDEA 2004 includes some significant changes to IDEA 1997; however, in many instances, practices will remain relatively similar. The basic requirement of IDEA—to provide a free, appropriate public education to children with disabilities—has not changed. There are numerous changes, but some of the notable ones include (a) adding NCLB language related to highly qualified special education teachers; (b) increasing funding to the authorized 40% level over a period of years through 2011; (c) changing eligibility for classification as having LD; (d) adding flexibility to attendance at IEP meetings; (e) creating a pilot demonstration for multiyear IEPs; (f) deleting the requirement for short-term objectives on the IEP; and (g) modifying suspension and expulsion requirements.

These notable changes may or may not have a significant impact on schools. Obviously, one change that could negatively affect schools is the requirement that special education teachers meet the NCLB *highly qualified* standard. With special education teachers already in short supply, adding this bureaucratic requirement could only exacerbate the situation, without improving educational opportunities for children with disabilities. Only time will determine the impact of this requirement, as school personnel and professional organizations lobby for a change. Increasing funding for special education could have a dramatic impact on services. However, the first budget proposal from the White House after the passage of IDEA 2004 added only $500 million to the IDEA budget, as opposed to the more than $2 billion called for in the legislation. Therefore, although it initially looked like a movement toward full funding would be made, reality has already set in that the likelihood of such an increase is low.

Changes made in the IEP requirements appear to be major. However, it is unlikely that, previously, all individuals participated in IEP development and changes at every meeting. In practice, IEPs were often developed by one individual or a small number of individuals and were likely changed without a formal IEP meeting. The changes in IDEA 2004 only legitimize those actions. Not having to include objectives might reduce some of the paperwork associated with IEPs; however, there still must be ongoing efforts to ensure that adequate progress is being made toward the student's annual goals. Finally, the multiyear IEP seems to be an idea that could significantly reduce paperwork. However, this is only a pilot program for up to 15 states, and even in schools that participate in the program, school personnel must determine if progress is being made toward the multiyear goals on at least an annual basis.

So, finally, IDEA has been reauthorized once again. Although the 3 years of debate focused on many of the same issues that have been dealt with in each reauthorization—discipline, due process rights, attorney fees, overidentification—the result is similar in many ways to the "old" law. As always, the changes do not satisfy everyone and, in fact, may not satisfy anyone. Hopefully, however, with each reauthorization of IDEA, realizing the original intent of P.L. 94-142 becomes more likely: meeting the needs of each child with a disability in the most appropriate way.

POSTSCRIPT

Does IDEA 2004 Contain Substantial Changes?

Contemplate IDEA 2004 in light of the recommendations of *Rethinking Special Education (Rethinking)* and the PCESE. As noted, these pre-reauthorization documents called for substantial changes to increase accountability, reduce paperwork, and reign in what each perceived as rampant litigation.

In today's climate of standards-based assessment, accountability is defined by whether students demonstrate increased academic performance. Writing on IDEA's 25th anniversary, Katsiyannis, Yell, and Bradley (*Remedial and Special Education*, 2001) declared that IDEA had met its initial goal of providing access to education for students with disabilities. They predicted that future reauthorizations needed to secure increased educational quality to improve achievement. Clearly, IDEA 2004 embraces a results-driven philosophy.

Not everyone is happy with this change. Writing earlier, Turnbull and Turnbull (*Education Next*, 2002) comment that special education encompasses more than academics, including efforts to help students succeed in the larger arenas of work, communication, and socialization. They worry that parents might lose confidence in a system that ignores these domains.

Two *Rethinking* papers (Horn and Tynan, 2001; Lanigan, 2001) maintained that confidence and accountability must be reciprocal. Parents desiring supports from IDEA must assume personal responsibility in the educational process. According to Turnbull's selection, IDEA 2004 "makes accountability a bilateral concept." Parents and students (as well as schools) must now be more accountable for their actions.

Reactions to these changes are mixed. Some feel the regulations are overly complicated, asking parents to waive rights that help their children (Cleveland, www.thearc.org, 2005; Sabia, www.ndss.org, 2005). Others, like Peter Wright (www.wrightslaw.com/idea/art/goodlaw.optimist.pw.htm, 2005), a high-profile advocate, express no concern about the changes. Wright was actually surprised by his positive response.

Paperwork is the bane of everyone's existence, especially if you would prefer to spend your time teaching. Several contributors to *Rethinking* noted that special education has become consumed with documenting compliance with reams of paper.

IDEA 2004 seems to take paperwork reduction seriously. Meetings are streamlined, short-term objectives have been eliminated for most students, and pilot projects for multiyear IEPs will be funded.

Smith holds out hope that elimination of objectives will stem the paperwork tide. However, he maintains that many other provisions sound more dramatic than they are, and will make little difference in the daily lives of teachers. He is not alone.

Looking at IEP changes, Gartin and Murdick (*Journal of Special Education Leadership,* 2005) feel the elimination of objectives for most students responds to paperwork complaints from both parents and teachers. Simultaneously, they are haunted by the possibility that paperwork may actually increase as teachers document other aspects of IDEA 2004, including agreements for excusing colleagues from team meetings.

Smith's predictions seem fulfilled in other arenas. The heralded multi-year paperwork reduction pilots have hit a snag. Apparently, documenting the efforts of these projects demands a workforce exceeding the capacity of any state (Samuels, *Education Week,* 2006). Furthermore, districts must submit "massive" amounts of data documenting progress on issues such as parent involvement and disproportional representation (Samuels, *Education Week,* 2005). If the paperwork burden is shifted from teachers to administrators, not much will have changed (Weatherly, *In CASE,* 2005) and administrators will have even less time to help teachers meet student needs.

Two final contrasting views complement the main selections: one from parents and the other from teachers. From the standpoint of the Center for Law and Education, IDEA 2004 "undermines" hard-won rights, reduces school accountability, and punishes parents for seeking the best for their child (Boundy, www.cleweb.org, 2006). Reflecting the teacher's perspective, Pardini's interviewees felt the daily practice of teaching is so far removed from the law, they doubt any changes will make a difference (www.rethinkingschools.org, 2002).

Think about the changes in IDEA 2004. Have they, as Turnbull predicts, modified our behavior or, as Smith says, do the alterations "not satisfy everyone and, in fact, may not satisfy anyone?"

ISSUE 3

Is Eliminating Minority Overrepresentation Beyond the Scope of Public Schools?

YES: M. Suzanne Donovan and Christopher T. Cross, eds., from "Executive Summary," in *Minority Students in Special and Gifted Education* (National Academy Press, 2002), pp. 1–14

NO: Daniel J. Losen and Gary Orfield, eds., from "Introduction: Racial Inequity in Special Education," in *Racial Inequity in Special Education* (Harvard Education Press, 2002), pp. XV–XXXVII

ISSUE SUMMARY

YES: M. Suzanne Donovan and Christopher T. Cross, researchers representing the findings of a National Research Council (NRC) study on minority students in special and gifted education, believe overrepresentation issues are complex and not easily resolvable. While teachers can make a difference, environmental factors and poverty have a large impact and require interventions beyond schools.

NO: Daniel J. Losen and Gary Orfield, both policy experts, present the results of research commissioned by the Civil Rights Project (CRP) of Harvard University. While agreeing with some of the NRC recommendations, these findings suggest that patterns will change with stricter enforcement of federal and state regulations.

As far back as 1968, Lloyd M. Dunn *(Exceptional Children,* 1968) examined the developing field of special education and voiced concern that African American children were disproportionately placed in special education, resegregated into substantially separate classes for the mentally retarded.

Accurate analysis is affected by the complexity of both racial designation and disability definitions. Racial designations, reported by individuals, are shaped by the categories provided on official forms. As more people have a multiracial heritage (think of Tiger Woods), choosing one racial "category" may become irrelevant. Additionally, eligibility qualifications for disabilities differ across states. Some use no discrete categories.

Several procedures are used to calculate special education enrollment statistics. Some compare the percentage of each racial group in the overall school population with their proportion in special education. Others study the racial composition of individual disability categories.

Despite varying reporting options and definitional complications, there is overall agreement that children of color are disproportionately represented in special education. This seems so, especially in the socially defined disabilities such as mental retardation, emotional disturbance, and learning disabilities. The challenge is deciding why disproportionality exists and what remedies can reduce it.

Two influential reports were issued in 2002. Because of their depth, their continuing relevance, and contrasting recommendations, these form the readings for this issue.

M. Suzanne Donovan, a researcher in education and public policy, and Christopher T. Cross, who has been active in government and local board of education associations, edited a report representing the work of over a dozen scholars who are members of the National Research Council (NRC) Committee on Minority Representation in Special Education. Directed by NRC and Congress to update NRC's 1982 study of this same issue, their work was expanded to consider racial underrepresentation in gifted and talented programs. The committee reviewed existent research studies to determine why disproportionality exists. Their conclusions and recommendations highlight environmental variables suggesting that there may be reasons for overrepresentation that extend into the classroom.

Daniel J. Losen and Gary Orfield share a professional commitment to studying the impact of law and public policy on the opportunities available for communities of color. Both have been heavily involved in designing and guiding policy formation, with a particular connection to the Civil Rights Project (CRP) at Harvard University. The impetus for their study was provided by the compelling voices of community leaders concerned about children wrongly placed in special education. To broaden the knowledge base, CRP commissioned leading scholars to analyze conditions and contributing factors and to generate solutions. The collective findings led to recommendations that racial disproportionality should become a top school priority, facilitated (if necessary) through federal and state enforcement of school practices.

Federal regulations endeavor to address disproportionality in special education, considering both overrepresentation and underrepresentation. Individuals with Disabilities Education Act (IDEA) '97 mandated that states collect and report special education enrollment information by race and ethnicity. IDEA 2004 requires that states and districts establish policies and procedures to "prevent the inappropriate overidentification or disproportionate representation by race and ethnicity of children as children with disabilities," examine data to determine if disproportionality exists, use federal funds to provide "early intervening services" to reduce overrepresentation, and document their efforts (and results) at reducing disproportionality (*Dialog Guides for IDEA 2004 Regulations*, http://www.ideapartnership.org). Not unexpectedly, states reported confusion when formulating their own definitions of "significant disproportionality" and "inappropriate identification" (Paula Burdette, 2007, http://www.nasdse.org).

As you read these selections, discuss their similarities and differences. How do the findings correspond to your own experiences and observations? Does overrepresentation exist in your district? If so, what steps are in place to reduce it?

YES

**M. Suzanne Donovan and
Christopher T. Cross**

Executive Summary

From the enactment of the 1975 federal law requiring states to provide a free and appropriate education to all students with disabilities, children in some racial/ethnic groups have been identified for services in disproportionately large numbers. Public concern is aroused by the pattern of disproportion. In the low-incidence categories (deaf, blind, orthopedic impairment, etc.) in which the problem is observable outside the school context and is typically diagnosed by medical professionals, no marked disproportion exists. The higher representation of minority students occurs in the high-incidence categories of mild mental retardation (MMR), emotional disturbance (ED), and to a lesser extent learning disabilities (LD), categories in which the problem is often identified first in the school context and the disability diagnosis is typically given without confirmation of an organic cause.

The concern is not new. In 1979 the National Research Council (NRC) was asked to conduct a study to determine the factors accounting for the disproportionate representation of minority students and males in special education programs for students with mental retardation, and to identify placement criteria or practices that do not affect minority students and males disproportionately. Twenty years later, disproportion in special education persists: while about 5 percent of Asian/Pacific Islander students are identified for special education, the rate for Hispanics is 11 percent, for whites 12 percent, for American Indians 13 percent, and for blacks over 14 percent. The NRC, at the request of Congress, has been asked to revisit the issue. In this case, however, the Office for Civil Rights in the U.S. Department of Education extended the committee's charge to include the representation of minority children in gifted and talented programs as well, where racial/ethnic disproportion patterns are, generally speaking, the reverse of those in special education.

Current Context

Since the 1982 NRC report, much has changed in general education as well as in special education. The proportion of minority students in the population of school-age children has risen dramatically—to 35 percent in 2000—increasing the diversity of students and of primary languages spoken in many schools. And state standards have raised the bar for the achievement expected of all

From *Minority Students in Special and Gifted Education* by M. Suzanne Donovan and Christopher T. Cross, eds. (January 14, 2002, pp. 1–14). Copyright © 2002 by the Committee on Minority Representation in Special Education, National Research Council. Reprinted by permission of National Academies Press.

students. More than 1 in 10 students is now identified for special education services: in the past decade alone, there has been a 35 percent increase in the number of children served under the Individuals with Disabilities Education Act (IDEA). And many more of these students are receiving special education and related services in general education classrooms.

The distribution of students across special education categories has changed as well. Identification rates for students with mental retardation today are about a quarter lower than in 1979. While the decline has applied across racial/ethnic groups, disproportionate representation of black students in that category has persisted. Just over 1 percent of white students but 2.6 percent of black students fall into that category.

Two decades ago, fewer than 3 percent of students were identified with learning disabilities (LD). That number approaches 6 percent of all students today. Only American Indian students are represented in disproportionately large numbers in that category. But for all racial/ethnic groups, the LD category accounts both for the largest number of special education students and for the largest growth rate in special education placements.

While these demographic and policy changes create a somewhat different context today from that confronting the earlier NRC committee, the problems are conceptually quite similar. At the outset, both committees confronted a paradox: if IDEA provides extra resources and the right to a more individualized education program, why would one consider disproportionate representation of minority children a problem? The answer, as every parent of a child receiving special education services knows, is that in order to be eligible for the additional resources a child must be labeled as having a disability, a label that signals substandard performance. And while that label is intended to bring additional supports, it may also bring lowered expectations on the part of teachers, other children, and the identified student. When a child cannot learn without the additional supports, and when the supports improve outcomes for the child, that trade-off may well be worth making. But because there is a trade-off, both the need and the benefit should be established before the label and the cost are imposed. This committee, like its predecessor, does not view the desirable end necessarily as one in which no minority group is represented in disproportionate numbers, but rather one in which the children who receive special education or gifted program services are those who truly require them and who benefit from them.

Who requires specialized education? Answering that question has always posed a challenge. The historic notion of a child with an emotional or learning disability or a talent conveys a "fixed-trait" model, in which the observed performance is the consequence of characteristics internal to the child. Assessment processes have been designed as an attempt to isolate those children with internal traits that constitute a "disability" or a "gift." And clearly there can be within-child characteristics that underlie placement in one of the high-incidence categories. Neurobiological investigations, for example, reveal different patterns of brain activity in dyslexic and nondyslexic children while reading.

However, in the past few decades a growing body of research has pointed to the critical role that context can play in achievement and behavior. The same child can perform very differently depending on the level of teacher support, and aggressive behavior can be reversed or exacerbated by effective or ineffective classroom management. In practice, it can be quite difficult to distinguish internal child traits that require the ongoing support of special education from inadequate opportunity or contextual support for learning and behavior.

Committee's Approach

The conceptual framework in which the committee considered the issue of minority disproportion in special education and gifted and talented programs, then, is one in which the achievement or behavior at issue is determined by the interaction of the child, the teacher, and the classroom environment. Internal child characteristics play a clear role: what the child brings to the interaction is a function both of biology and of experience in the family and the community. But the child's achievement and behavior outcomes will also reflect the effectiveness of instruction and the instructional environment.

The committee did not view the problem of disproportionate representation in special education as one of simply eliminating racial/ethnic differences in assignment. If special education services provide genuine individualized instruction and accountability for student learning, we consider it as serious a concern when students who need those supports are passed over (false negatives) as when they are inappropriately identified (false positives). Likewise with respect to gifted and talented programs, we consider it a problem if qualified minority students are overlooked in the identification process, but consider it an undesirable solution if minority students are selected when they are not adequately prepared for the demands of gifted and talented programs. The committee's goal, then, was to understand why disproportion occurs. To address our charge, the committee asked four questions:

1. *Is there reason to believe that there is currently a higher incidence of special needs or giftedness among some racial/ethnic groups? Specifically, are there biological and social or contextual contributors to early development that differ by race or ethnicity?*

Our answer to that question is a definitive "yes." We know that minority children are disproportionately poor, and poverty is associated with higher rates of exposure to harmful toxins, including lead, alcohol, and tobacco, in early stages of development. Poor children are also more likely to be born with low birthweight, to have poorer nutrition, and to have home and child care environments that are less supportive of early cognitive and emotional development than their majority counterparts. When poverty is deep and persistent, the number of risk factors rises, seriously jeopardizing development.

Some risk factors have a disproportionate impact on particular groups that goes beyond the poverty effect. In all income groups, black children are more likely to be born with low birthweight and are more likely to be exposed to harmful levels of lead, while American Indian/Alaskan Native children are more likely to be exposed prenatally to high levels of alcohol and tobacco. While the separate effect of each of these factors on school achievement and performance is difficult to determine, substantial differences by race/ethnicity on a variety of dimensions of school preparedness are documented at kindergarten entry.

2. *Does schooling independently contribute to the incidence of special needs or giftedness among students in different racial/ethnic groups through the opportunities that it provides?*

Again, our answer is: "yes." Schools with higher concentrations of low-income, minority children are less likely to have experienced, well-trained teachers. Per-pupil expenditures in those schools are somewhat lower, while the needs of low-income student populations and the difficulty of attracting teachers to inner-city, urban schools suggest that supporting comparable levels of education would require higher levels of per-pupil expenditures. These schools are less likely to offer advanced courses for their students, providing less support for high academic achievement.

When children come to school from disadvantaged backgrounds, as a disproportionate number of minority students do, high-quality instruction that carefully puts the prerequisites for learning in place, combined with effective classroom management that minimizes chaos, can put students on a path to academic success. While some reform efforts suggest that such an outcome is possible, there are currently no assurances that children will be exposed to effective instruction or classroom management before they are placed in special education programs or are screened for gifted programs.

3. *Does the current referral and assessment process reliably identify students with special needs and gifts? In particular, is there reason to believe that the current process is biased in terms of race or ethnicity?*

The answer here is not as straightforward. The majority of children in special and gifted education are referred by teachers. If a teacher is biased in evaluating student performance and behavior, current procedures provide ample room for those biases to be reflected in referrals. Some experimental research suggests that teachers do hold such biases. But whether bias is maintained when teachers have direct contact with children in the classroom is not clear. For example, research that has compared groups of students who are referred by teachers finds that minority students actually have greater academic and behavior problems than their majority counterparts.

Once students are referred for special education, they must be assessed as eligible or ineligible. Whether the assessment process is biased is as controversial as the referral process. However research shows that context, including familiarity with test taking and the norms and expectations of school, may depress the scores of students whose experiences prepare them less well for the demands of classrooms and standardized tests.

Whether the referral and assessment of students for special and gifted education is racially biased or not, are the right students being identified—

students who need and can benefit from those programs? Here the committee's answer is "no." The subjectivity of the referral process allows for students with significant learning problems to be overlooked for referral, and the conceptual and procedural shortcomings of the assessment process for learning disabilities and emotional disturbance give little confidence that student need has been appropriately identified. Importantly, current procedures result in placements later in the educational process than is most effective or efficient.

4. *Is placement in special education a benefit or a risk? Does the outcome differ by race or ethnic group?*

The data that would allow us to answer these questions adequately do not exist. We do know that some specific special education and gifted and talented interventions have been demonstrated to have positive outcomes for students. But how widely those interventions are employed is not known. Nor do we know whether minority students are less likely to be exposed to those high-quality interventions than majority students. What evidence is available suggests that parent advocacy and teacher quality, both of which would be expected to correlate with higher-quality interventions, are less likely in higher-poverty school districts where minority children are concentrated.

At the core of our study is an observation that unites all four questions: there is substantial evidence with regard to both behavior and achievement that early identification and intervention is more effective than later identification and intervention. This is true for children of any race or ethnic group, and children with or without an identifiable "within-child" problem. Yet the current special education identification process relies on a "wait-to-fail" principle that both increases the likelihood that children will fail because they do not receive early supports and decreases the effectiveness of supports once they are received. Similarly, the practice of identifying gifted learners after several years of schooling is based on the "wait 'til they succeed" philosophy rather than a developmental orientation.

While this principle applies to all students, the impact is likely to be greatest on students from disadvantaged backgrounds because (a) their experience outside the school prepares them less well for the demands of schooling, placing them at greater risk for failure, and (b) the resources available to them in general education are more likely to be substandard. Early efforts to identify and intervene with children at risk for later failure will help all children who need additional supports. But we would expect a disproportionately large number of those students to be from disadvantaged backgrounds.

The vision we offer in the report is one in which general and special education services are more tightly integrated; one in which no child is judged by the school to have a learning or emotional disability or to lack exceptional talent until efforts to provide high-quality instructional and behavioral support in the general education context have been tried without success. The "earlier is better" principle applies even before the K-12 years. The more effective we are at curtailing early biological harms and injuries and providing children with the supports for normal cognitive and behavioral development in the earliest years of life, the fewer children will arrive at school at risk for failure.

Conclusions and Recommendations

. . . Here we give the conclusions we consider key, along with the recommendations. They are organized here in the following major categories: referral and eligibility determination in special education (SE) and gifted and talented education (GT); teacher quality (TQ); biological and early childhood risk factors (EC); data collection (DC); and expanding the research and development base (RD).

Special Education Eligibility

From our review of the current knowledge base, several important conclusions have led the committee to rethink the current approach to special education:

5. Among the most frequent reasons for referral to special education are reading difficulties and behavior problems.
6. In recent years, interventions appropriate for the general education classroom to improve reading instruction and classroom management have been demonstrated to reduce the number of children who fail at reading or are later identified with behavior disorders.
7. There are currently no mechanisms in place to guarantee that students will be exposed to state-of-the-art reading instruction or classroom management before they are identified as having a "within-child" problem.
8. Referral for the high-incidence categories of special education currently requires student failure. However, screening mechanisms exist for early identification of children at risk for later reading and behavior problems. And the effectiveness of early intervention in both areas has been demonstrated to be considerably greater than the effectiveness of later, postfailure intervention.

These findings suggest that schools should be doing more and doing it earlier to ensure that students receive quality general education services to reduce the number of students with pronounced achievement and behavior problems. The committee's proposed alternative would require policy and regulatory changes at both the federal and state levels of government.

Federal-Level Recommendations

Recommendation SE.1: The committee recommends that federal guidelines for special education eligibility be changed in order to encourage better integrated general and special education services. We propose that eligibility ensue when a student exhibits large differences from typical levels of performance in one or more domain(s) and with evidence of insufficient response to high-quality interventions in the relevant domain(s) of functioning in school settings. These domains include achievement (e.g., reading, writing, mathematics), social behavior, and emotional regulation. As is currently the case, eligibility determination would also require a judgment by a multidisciplinary team, including parents, that special education is needed.

The proposed approach would not negate the eligibility of any student who arrives at school with a disability determination, or who has a severe disability, from being served as they are currently. But for children with milder high-incidence disabilities, the implications for referral and assessment are considerable. Assessment for special education eligibility would be focused on gathering information that documents educationally relevant differences from typical levels of performance, and that is relevant to the design, monitoring, and evaluation of treatments.

While eligibility for special education would by law continue to depend on establishment of a disability, in the committee view, noncategorical conceptions and classification criteria that focus on matching a student's specific needs to an intervention strategy would obviate the need for the traditional high-incidence disability labels such as LD and ED. If traditional disability definitions are used, they would need to be revised to focus on characteristics directly related to classroom and school learning and behavior (e.g., reading failure, math failure, persistent inattention and disorganization).

State-Level Recommendations

Regulatory changes would be required in most states for implementation of a reformed special education program that uses functional assessment measures to promote positive outcomes for students with disabilities. Some states have already instituted changes that move in this direction and can serve as examples. These states' rules require a systematic problemsolving process that is centered around quality indicators associated with successful interventions.

> *Recommendation SE.2: The committee recommends that states adopt a universal screening and multitiered intervention strategy in general education to enable early identification and intervention with children at risk for reading problems. For students who continue to have difficulty even after intensive intervention, referral to special education and the development of an individualized education program (IEP) would follow. The data regarding student response to intervention would be used for eligibility determination.*

> *Recommendation SE.3: The committee recommends that states launch largescale pilot programs in conjunction with universities or research centers to test the plausibility and productivity of universal behavior management interventions, early behavior screening, and techniques to work with children at risk for behavior problems. Research results suggest that these interventions can work. However, a large-scale pilot project would provide a firmer foundation of knowledge regarding scaling up the practices involved.*

Federal Support of State Reform Efforts

> *Recommendation SE.4: While the United States has a strong tradition of state control of education, the committee recommends that the federal government support widespread adoption of early screening and intervention in the states.*

Gifted and Talented Eligibility

The research base justifying alternative approaches for the screening, identification, and placement of gifted children is neither as extensive nor as informative as that for special education.

> *Recommendation GT.l: The committee recommends a research program oriented toward the development of a broader knowledge base on early identification and intervention with children who exhibit advanced performance in the verbal or quantitative realm, or who exhibit other advanced abilities.*

This research program should be designed to determine whether there are reliable and valid indicators of current exceptional performance in language, mathematical, or other domains, or indicators of later exceptional performance. Research on classroom practice designed to encourage the early and continued development of gifted behaviors in underrepresented populations should be undertaken so that screening can be followed by effective intervention.

School Context and Student Performance

School resources, class size, and indicators of teacher quality are associated with learning and behavior outcomes. However, their influence is exerted primarily through teacher–student interactions. Moreover, in the prevention and eligibility determination model the committee is recommending, general education assessments and interventions not now in widespread use are proposed as standard practice. Key to our proposals, then, are sustained efforts at capacity building, and sufficient resources, time, and coordination among stakeholders to build that capacity.

State-Level Recommendations
Teacher Quality: General education teachers need improved teacher preparation and professional development to prepare them to address the needs of students with significant underachievement or giftedness.

> *Recommendation TQ.l: State certification or licensure requirements for teachers should systematically require:*
>
> - *competency in understanding and implementing reasonable norms and expectations for students, and core competencies in instructional delivery of academic content;*
> - *coursework and practicum experience in understanding, creating, and modifying an educational environment to meet children's individual needs;*
> - *competency in behavior management in classroom and noninstructional school settings;*
> - *instruction in functional analysis and routine behavioral assessment of students;*

- *instruction in effective intervention strategies for students who fail to meet minimal standards for successful educational performance, or who substantially exceed minimal standards;*
- *coursework and practicum experience to prepare teachers to deliver culturally responsive instruction. More specifically, teachers should be familiar with the beliefs, values, cultural practices, discourse styles, and other features of students' lives that may have an impact on classroom participation and success and be prepared to use this information in designing instruction.*

While a foundational knowledge base can be laid in preservice education, often classroom experience is needed before teachers can make the most of instructional experiences.

- *States should require rigorous professional development for all practicing teachers, administrators, and educational support personnel to assist them in addressing the varied needs of students who differ substantially from the norm in achievement and/or behavior.*
- *The professional development of administrators and educational support personnel should include enhanced capabilities in the improvement and evaluation of teacher instruction with respect to meeting student's individual needs.*

Recommendation TQ.2: State or professional association approval for educator instructional programs should include requirements for faculty competence in the current literature and research on child and adolescent learning and development, and on successful assessment, instructional, and intervention strategies, particularly for atypical learners and students with gifts and disabilities.

Recommendation TQ.3: A credential as a school psychologist or special education teacher should require instruction in classroom observation/assessment and in teacher support to work with a struggling student or with a gifted student. These skills should be considered as critical to their professional role as the administration and interpretation of tests are now considered.

Federal-Level Recommendations

This committee joins many others at the NRC and elsewhere in calling for improved teacher preparation. How to move from widespread agreement that change is needed to system reform is a challenge that will itself require careful study.

Recommendation TQ.4: The committee recommends that a national advisory panel be convened in an institutional environment that is protected from political influence to study the quality and currency of programs that now exist to train teachers for general, special, and gifted education. The panel should address:

- *the mechanisms for keeping instructional programs current and of high quality;*
- *the standards and requirements of those programs;*
- *the applicability of instructional programs to the demands of classroom practice;*

- *the long-term influence of the programs in successfully promoting educational achievement for pre-K, elementary, and secondary students.*

Direct comparison to other professional fields (e.g., medicine, nursing, law, engineering, accounting) may provide insight applicable to education.

Biological and Social Risk Factors in Early Childhood

Existing intervention programs to address early biological harms and injuries have demonstrated the potential to substantially improve developmental outcomes. The committee concludes that the number of children, particularly minority children, who require special education can be reduced if resources are devoted to this end. In particular, the committee calls attention to the recommendation of the President's Task Force on Environmental Health Risks and Safety Risks to Children to eliminate lead from the housing stock by 2010.

Federal-Level Recommendations

The committee also looked at social and environmental influences on development with no clear biological basis that might differ by race or ethnicity. Because there is evidence that early intervention on multiple fronts, if *it is of high quality,* can improve the school prospects for children with multiple risk factors and reduce the likelihood that they will require special education, the committee recommends a substantial expansion and improvement of current early intervention efforts. Our recommendation is addressed to federal and state governments, both of whom currently play a major role in early childhood education.

> *Recommendation EC.l: The committee recommends that all high-risk children have access to high-quality early childhood interventions.*

> - *For the children at highest risk, these interventions should include family support, health services, and sustained, high-quality care and cognitive stimulation right from birth.*
> - *Preschool children (ages 4 and 5) who are eligible for Head Start should have access to a Head Start or another publicly funded preschool program. These programs should provide exposure to learning opportunities that will prepare them for success in school. Intervention should target services to the level of individual need, including high cognitive challenge for the child who exceeds normative performance.*
> - *The proposed expansion should better coordinate existing federal programs, such as Head Start and Early Head Start, and IDEA parts C and B, as well as state-initiated programs that meet equal or higher standards.*

While much is known about the types of experiences young children need for healthy development, improving the quality of early childhood programs will require refinement of the knowledge base in ways that are directly useful to practice, and bridging the chasm between what is known from research and best practice and is done in common practice. This will require a sustained vision and a rigorous research and development effort that transforms knowledge about what works and what does not work into field-tested program content, supporting materials, and professional development.

> *Recommendation EC.2: The committee recommends that the federal govern-ment launch a large-scale, rigorous, sustained research and development pro-gram in an institutional environment that has the capacity to bring together excellent professionals in research, program development, professional devel-opment, and child care/preschool practice for students from all backgrounds and at all levels of exceptional performance.*

Improving Data Collection and Expanding the Research Base

The data documenting disproportionate representation are difficult to inter-pret in a variety of respects that make them a weak foundation on which to build public policy. Moreover, the data provide little if any insight into factors that contribute to placement or services that students receive.

Federal-Level Recommendations

> *Recommendation DC.1: The committee recommends that the Department of Education conduct a single, well-designed data collection effort to monitor both the number of children receiving services through the Individuals with Disabilities Education Act or through programs for the gifted and talented, and the characteristics of those children of concern to civil rights enforcement efforts. A unified effort would eliminate the considerable redundancy, and the burden it places on schools, in the current data collection efforts of the Office for Civil Rights and the Office of Special Education Programs.*

While a more careful data collection effort of the sort outlined here would improve the understanding of who is being assigned to special education and gifted and talented programs, it would do little to further understanding of the reasons for placement, the appropriateness of placement (or nonplacement), the services provided, or the consequences that ensue.

> *Recommendation DC.2: The committee recommends that a national advi-sory panel be convened to design the collection of nationally representative longitudinal data that would allow for more informed study of minority dis-proportion in special education and gifted and talented programs. The panel should include scholars in special education research as well as researchers experienced in national longitudinal data collection and analysts in a variety of allied fields, including anthropology, psychology, and sociology.*

In our study of the issues related to the representation of minority chil-dren in special education and gifted and talented programs, the existing knowledge base revealed the potential for substantial progress. We know much about the kinds of experiences that promote children's early health, cognitive, and behavioral development and set them on a more positive trajectory for school success. We know intervention strategies that have demonstrated success with some of the key problems that end in referral to special education. And we know some features of programs that are correlated with successful outcomes for students in special education.

Between the articulation of what we know from research and best practice, and a change in everyday practice, lies a wide chasm. It is the distance between demonstrating that vocabulary development is key to later success in reading, and having every Head Start teacher trained and equipped with materials that will promote vocabulary development among Head Start children. It is the distance between knowing that classroom management affects a child's behavior, and the school psychologist knowing how to help a specific teacher work with a specific child in the classroom context. It is the distance between those who are most knowledgeable and experienced agreeing on what teachers need to know, and every school of education changing its curriculum. Bridging the chasm will require that we become better at accumulating knowledge, extending it in promising areas, incorporating the best of what is known in teacher training efforts and education curricula and materials, and rigorously testing effectiveness. It will require public policies that are aligned with the knowledge base and that provide the support for its widespread application.

> *Recommendation RD.1: We recommend that education research and development, including that related to special and gifted education, be substantially expanded to carry promising findings and validated practices through to classroom applicability. This includes research on scaling up promising practices from research sites to widespread use.*

For medical problems like cancer, federal research programs create a vision, focus research efforts on areas with promise for improving treatments, conduct extensive field tests to determine what works, and facilitate the movement of research findings into practice. If the nation is serious about reducing the number of children who are on a trajectory that leads to school failure and disability identification as well as increasing the number of minority students who are achieving at high levels, we will need to devote the minds and resources to that effort commensurate with the size and the importance of the enterprise.

Introduction: Racial Inequity in Special Education

Before Congress passed the Education for All Handicapped Children Act—now known as the Individuals with Disabilities Education Act (IDEA)—nearly half of the nation's approximately four million children with disabilities were not receiving a public education. Of the children who were being educated in public schools, many were relegated to a ghetto-like existence in isolated, often run-down classrooms located in the least desirable places within the school building, or sent to entirely separate facilities. Since its passage in 1975, the IDEA has brought tremendous benefits: today, approximately six million children with disabilities enjoy their right to a free appropriate public education. IDEA's substantive rights and procedural protections have produced significant and measurable outcomes for students with disabilities: their graduation rates have increased dramatically, and the number of these students who go on to college has almost tripled since 1978 (though it is still quite low).

Despite these improvements, the benefits of special education have not been equitably distributed. Minority children with disabilities all too often experience inadequate services, low-quality curriculum and instruction, and unnecessary isolation from their nondisabled peers. Moreover, inappropriate practices in both general and special education classrooms have resulted in overrepresentation, misclassification, and hardship for minority students, particularly black children.

A flood of concerns expressed by community leaders about minority children being misplaced in special education prompted The Civil Rights Project at Harvard University to commission the research for [our] book. Since the early 1970s, national surveys by the Office for Civil Rights (OCR) of the U.S. Department of Education have revealed persistent overrepresentation of minority children in certain disability categories. The most pronounced disparities then were black children who, while only 16 percent of the total school enrollment, represented 38 percent of the students in classes for the educationally mentally retarded. After more than twenty years, black children constitute 17 percent of the total school enrollment and 33 percent of those labeled mentally retarded—only a marginal improvement. During this same period, however, disproportionality in the area of emotional disturbance (ED) and the rate of

From *Racial Inequity in Special Education* by Daniel J. Losen and Gary Orfield (Harvard Education Press, 2002, pp. XV–XXXVII). Copyright © 2002 by the President and Fellows of Harvard College. All rights reserved. For more information, please visit www.harvardeducationpress.org.

identification for both ED and specific learning disabilities (SLD) grew significantly for blacks.

To better understand this persistent overrepresentation trend, as well as growing reports of profound inequities in the quality of special education, The Civil Rights Project set out to find the best research available. In the original call for papers we asked leading scholars from around the country to document and clarify the issues for minority students with regard to special education. As researchers pursued this task and analyzed possible contributing factors, our fears about the persistence of these problems, the complexities of the contributing factors, and the lack of proven solutions were confirmed.

Our primary purpose in presenting this information is to identify and solve the problem, not to assign blame. This research is intended to inform the debate on special education and racial justice and to provide educators, researchers, advocates, and policymakers with a deeper understanding of the issues as they renew their efforts to find workable solutions. Using national-, state-, district-, and school-level data, these studies document the current trends for minority students regarding identification and restrictiveness of placement. They explore some of the most likely causes, dispel some myths and oversimplified explanations, and highlight the complex interplay of variables within the control of educators at all levels of government. Recognizing the critical role that advocacy has played in securing the rights of all children to educational opportunity, [our] book also provides analysis of the evolving role of the law in stopping inappropriate practices that harm children of color, and in guaranteeing equitable benefits from special education.

The findings [here] point to areas where much improvement is needed and offer an array of ideas for remedies and suggestions for continued research. It is important to recognize that concerns about special education are nested in concerns about inequities in education generally. Special education overrepresentation often mirrors overrepresentation in many undesirable categories—including dropping out, low-track placements, suspensions, and involvement with juvenile justice—and underrepresentation in desirable categories such as gifted and talented. Because special education inequities are often tied to general education issues, remedies should address shortcomings in both special and general education. The recommendations, which are aimed at improving policy and practice, were developed through extensive analysis of the efforts and experiences of educators, policymakers, attorneys, and civil rights enforcement agents. We hope the recommendations will help prevent harmful misidentification and inappropriate placements of minority students, and encourage effective and equitable leadership, enforcement, and distribution of resources to ensure that all children who need special education support receive appropriate and high-quality services.

Issues Explored and Findings

Much of the empirical research . . . explores patterns of overrepresentation of minority children by disability category and whether, once identified, they experience relatively less access to the general education classroom than similarly situated white children. The evidence suggests that black overrepresentation is substantial in state after state. The studies reveal wide differences in disability identification between blacks and Hispanics and between black boys and black girls that cannot be explained in terms of social background or measured ability.

Both the statistical and qualitative analyses . . . suggest that these racial, ethnic, and gender differences are due to many complex and interacting factors, including unconscious racial bias on the part of school authorities, large resource inequalities that run along lines of race and class, unjustifiable reliance on IQ and other evaluation tools, educators' inappropriate responses to the pressures of high-stakes testing, and power differentials between minority parents and school officials.

[We] . . . examine whether the numerous causes of overrepresentation are likely race linked, which is a distinctly different inquiry from whether intentional racial discrimination is the primary cause. Absent a blatantly discriminatory (i.e., illegal as written) policy or practice, to establish that different treatment is purposeful and racist requires specific proof of intent, which is usually discovered through legal enforcement proceedings. The research [here] is obviously not specific enough to explore questions of intent.

Overidentification

On October 4, 2001, the U.S. House of Representatives Committee on Education and the Workforce convened hearings about the overidentification of minority students in special education. In his testimony, Representative Chaka Fattah concluded with the following story of Billy Hawkins:

> For the first fifteen years of his life Billy Hawkins was labeled by his teachers as "educable mentally retarded." Billy was backup quarterback for his high school football team. One night he was called off the bench and rallied his team from far behind. In doing so, he ran complicated plays and clearly demonstrated a gift for the game. The school principal, who was in the stands, recognized that the "retarded boy" could play, and soon after had Billy enrolled in regular classes and instructed his teachers to give him extra help. Billy Hawkins went on to complete a Ph.D. and is now Associate Dean at Michigan's Ferris State University.

Students like Billy Hawkins seldom get the "call off the bench" and an opportunity to shine in front of their principal. Instead, they are removed from the mainstream and never realize their talent. Unfortunately, some in Congress responded to findings we released in earlier reports and to stories like Dr. Hawkins' by opposing efforts to guarantee and fully fund special education at the level Congress originally intended, claiming a need to "fix" special education before providing more funds. [We address] discrete areas of deep racial inequity within a much larger system of special education. It would be wrong to restrict or withhold promised expenditures for all students with disabilities in every state of the nation based on the issues identified in this research.

Of the inequalities in education experienced by minority schoolchil-dren, those in special education are better documented than most. In 1998, approximately 1.5 million minority children were identified as having mental retardation, emotional disturbance, or a specific learning disability. More than 876,000 of these were black or Native American, and black students were nearly three times as likely as white students to be labeled mentally retarded. Mental retardation diagnoses are relatively rare for all children, and the last twenty years have witnessed a modest decrease in the percentages of students labeled mentally retarded for nearly all racial groups.

Despite this fact, U.S. Department of Education data from 2000–2001 show that in at least thirteen states more than 2.75 percent of all blacks enrolled were labeled mentally retarded. The prevalence of mental retardation for whites nationally was approximately 0.75 percent in 2001, and in no state did the incidence among whites ever rise above 2.32 percent. Moreover, nearly three-quarters of the states with unusually high incidence rates (2.75–5.41%) for blacks were in the South. This is arguably a continuation of the problem as a southern phenomenon that was first observed in the National Research Council's data from 1979, although both then and now many northern states also exhibit remarkably high rates. One positive sign is that southern states exhibited the largest decreases in sheer percentages since 1979.

The data in these studies are generally analyzed in one of three ways. In one, a given minority group's percentage enrollment in the general population is compared to that group's percentage identification in a given disability category. In the second, the actual risk level for a minority group is calculated by dividing the number of students from a given racial group with a given disability by the total enrollment of that racial group. And in the third way, these risk levels are calculated for each minority group and then compared. These comparisons are described as risk ratios and are usually reported in comparison to white children.

. . . Tom Parrish, a senior research analyst with the American Institutes for Research, calculates risk levels using U.S. Department of Education data based on the number of children eligible for special education reported by each state for children between the ages of six and twenty-one in 1998, and compares that with census estimates of children of the same age for each state for the same year. Parrish then calculates the risk ratios for each minority group by cognitive disability category for every state and for the nation.

He finds that black children are 2.88 times more likely than whites to be labeled mentally retarded and 1.92 times more likely to be labeled emotionally disturbed.

Blacks are the most overrepresented minority group in every category and in nearly every state. The gross racial disparities that exist between many minority groups and whites in terms of mental retardation also exist in other cognitive disability categories, but are less pronounced. Nationwide, blacks and Native Americans are less often overidentified for specific learning dis-abilities (i.e., black children are more than twice as likely as white children to be found to have a specific learning disability in only nine states).

Parrish also shows the extent of overidentification of other minorities in the ED and SLD categories. In the SLD category, for example, only in Hawaii are Asian Americans/Pacific Islanders identified at nearly twice the rate of whites. On the other hand, Native American children in six states are identified at more than twice the rate of whites.

Latinos and Asian Americans are generally underidentified compared to whites in most states and in most categories, raising the possibility of inadequate attention to their special needs; however, the state-level data may underreport the problem for some groups. According to a 1982 National Research Council (NRC) report, district-level data on Hispanics from 1979 suggested that a wide variety of both over- and underrepresentation tended to cancel each other out in aggregate state-level data. Neither the 2002 NRC report, "Minority Students in Special and Gifted Education," nor the studies [here] conducted a district-level analysis with national data comparable to that contained in the 1982 study of Hispanic identification rates. However, Alfredo Artiles, Robert Rueda, Jesus Jose Salazar, and Ignacio Higareda, in their analysis of large urban school districts in California, reveal that disproportionate representation in special education is far more likely for (predominantly Latino) English-language learners in secondary school than in elementary school. Thus, the problem may even be hidden when elementary and secondary school data are aggregated at the district level.

Edward Fierros and James Conroy's research . . . , which does examine district-level data from throughout Connecticut and from selected U.S. cities, suggests that the state data may miss disturbing trends for minority overrepresentation in a given category or educational setting. Generally speaking, the most serious racial disparities (both under- and overrepresentation) become apparent when data on minority children are disaggregated by race/ethnicity subgroups, cognitive disability category, gender, and placement—at least down to the district level.

Educational Placement

Readers should not forget that students with disabilities are entitled to receive supports and services in a setting best suited to their individual needs, and not to be automatically assigned to a separate place, subjected to low expectations, or excluded from educational opportunities. While substantially separate educational environments are certainly best for some individuals, it is equally well established in research that students with disabilities benefit most when they are educated with their general education peers to the maximum extent appropriate, and this is reflected in the law.

Fierros and Conroy's work demonstrates that, once identified as eligible for special education services, both Latinos and blacks are far less likely than whites to be educated in a fully inclusive general education classroom and far more likely to be educated in a substantially separate setting. The data Fierros and Conroy explore show a consistent trend toward less inclusion for minority children at the national, state, and district levels. The relationship between race and greater exclusion, also not examined in the NRC's 2002 report, suggests that, among students with disabilities, black and Latino children with disabilities may be consistently receiving less desirable treatment than white children. Fierros and Conroy further disaggregate the racial data by disability type for the state of

Connecticut and find a lower level of inclusion for blacks and Hispanics compared to whites among each of the three disability types examined (students with mental retardation, emotional disturbance, and specific learning disabilities).

The concern with the overrepresentation of minorities would be mitigated if the evidence suggested that minority children reaped benefits from more frequent identification and isolation. But as government officials acknowledge and as data demonstrate, this does not appear to be the case.

Low-Quality Evaluations, Supports, and Services

. . . Many minority children do have disabilities but are at risk of receiving inappropriate and inadequate services and unwarranted isolation. Osher et al. point out that, for some children, receiving inappropriate services may be more harmful than receiving none at all. For others, not receiving help early enough may exacerbate learning and behavior problems. Both problems are reflected in disturbing statistics on outcomes for minority children with disabilities. . . . There are dramatic differences in what happens to minority students with disabilities after high school:

> In the 1998–1999 school year, over 2.2 million children of color in U.S. schools were served by special education (U.S. Department of Education, 2000). Post–high school outcomes for these minority students with disabilities are strikingly inferior. Among high school youth with disabilities, about 75 percent of African American students, as compared to 47 percent of white students, are not employed two years out of school. Slightly more than half (52%) of African Americans, compared to 39 percent of white young adults, are still not employed three to five years out of school. In this same time period, the arrest rate for African Americans with disabilities is 40 percent, as compared to 27 percent for whites (Wagner, D'Amico, Marder, Newman, & Blackorby, 1992).

In addition to these patterns, Osher, Woodruff, and Sims provide new data depicting substantially higher rates of disciplinary action and placement in correctional facilities for minority students with disabilities still in school. Based on their review of the data and other research, they suggest that investments in high-quality special education and early intervention are sorely needed and could reduce the likelihood that minority students with disabilities will develop serious discipline problems or eventually wind up in correctional facilities.

Racial Discrimination and Other Contributing Factors

In a society where race is so strongly related to individual, family, and community conditions, it is extremely difficult to know what part of the inequalities are caused by discrimination within the school. These studies, however, do uncover correlations with race that cannot be explained by factors such as poverty or exposure to environmental hazards alone. While the scope of this research does not attempt to depict a definitive causal link to racial discrimination, the research does suggest that unconscious racial bias, stereotypes, and other race-linked factors have a significant impact on the patterns of identification, placement, and quality of services for minority children, and particularly for African American children.

The researchers recognize that factors such as poverty and environmental influences outside of school contribute to a heightened incidence of disability in significant ways. All analysts who attempt to sort out the causes of inequality in U.S. institutions of course face the dilemma that some of the differences in subtracted control variables are themselves products of other forms of racial discrimination. For example, if a researcher determined that 40 percent of the association between race and shorter life expectancy could be explained by poverty, we have to understand that the poverty in question may be influenced by employment discrimination or be due in part to a second-generational effect of segregated schooling. Therefore, despite the importance of statistical controls, it is well established that many controls will lower the estimates of the effect of race when race is examined as an isolated variable. What happens in school is only a subset of the far more pervasive impact of racial discrimination that affects minority families and their children.

Even when researchers assume that poverty is independent of race and subtract race and other background variables, many of the trends highlighted by this research appear to contradict the theory that poverty is primarily to blame and that race is not a significant factor. Those trends include the following: (a) pronounced and persistent racial disparities in identification between white and black children in the categories of mental retardation and emotional disturbance, compared with far less disparity in the category of specific learning disabilities; (b) a minimal degree of racial disparity in medically diagnosed disabilities as compared with subjective cognitive disabilities; (c) dramatic differences in the incidence of disability from one state to the next; and (d) gross disparities between blacks and Hispanics, and between black boys and girls, in identification rates for the categories of mentally retarded and emotionally disturbed.

The data on disproportionate representation is compatible with the theory that systemic racial discrimination is a contributing factor where disparities are substantial. Moreover, the trends revealed in [our] book are consistent with the theory that different racial groups, facing different kinds of stereotypes and bias, would experience racial disparities differently. States with a history of racial apartheid under de jure segregation, for example, account for five of the seven states with the highest overrepresentation of African Americans labeled mentally retarded—Mississippi, South Carolina, North Carolina, Florida, and Alabama. This trend suggests that the "soft bigotry of low expectations" may have replaced the undeniable intentional racial discrimination in education against blacks that once pervaded the South. In contrast, no southern state was among the top seven states where Hispanic children deemed mentally retarded were most heavily overrepresented.

The effects of poverty cannot satisfactorily explain racial disparities in identification for mental retardation or emotional disturbance. Regression analysis suggests that race, gender, and poverty are all significant factors. Oswald, Coutinho, and Best specifically asked whether, "taking into account the effects of social, demographic, and school-related variables, gender and ethnicity are significantly associated with the risk of being identified for special education." Their examination of each factor at the district level (based on all of the districts surveyed in OCR's database combined with the National Center for Education Statistics, Common Core of Data) finds that, although disability incidence often increases with poverty, when poverty- and wealth-linked factors are controlled for, ethnicity and gender remain significant predictors of cognitive disability identification by schools. Specifically, wealth-linked factors included per pupil expenditure, median housing value, median income for households with children, percentage of children in households below the poverty level, and percentage of adults in the community who have a twelfth-grade education or less and no diploma.

Most disturbing, was that in wealthier districts, contrary to the expected trend, black children, especially males, were *more likely to be labeled* mentally retarded. Moreover, the sharp gender differences in identification within racial groups, also described in the 2002 NRC report, are not explained by the poverty theory.

Large demographic differences among minority groups are also discussed by Parrish and by Fierros and Conroy, and each confirms that the influence of race and ethnicity is significant, and apparently distinct from that of poverty. For example, Parrish reviews the data for each racial group across all fifty states and finds that, in comparison to whites, each minority group is at greater risk of being labeled mentally retarded as their percentage of the total enrolled population increases.

That poverty does account for some of the observed racial disproportions in disability identification comes as no surprise. Certain minority groups are disproportionately poor. Logically, one would expect poverty to cause a higher incidence of "hard" disabilities (e.g., blindness and deafness) among members of low-wealth minority groups, due to the impact of poor nutrition and inadequate prenatal care. But the most recent research shows that blacks in any given state are substantially less likely to be overrepresented in these hard categories.

Finally, the theory that poverty and socioeconomic factors can explain all or most of the observed racial disparities fails to account for the extreme differences between black overrepresentation and Hispanic underrepresentation, differences that are even more significant in many states than disparities between blacks and whites. For example, blacks in Alabama and Arkansas are more than seven to nine times as likely as Hispanics to be labeled mentally retarded. Moreover, nationally and in many other states, the disparity in identification rates for mental retardation and emotional disturbance between blacks and Hispanics is greater than the disparity between blacks and whites. Yet Hispanics, like blacks, are at far greater risk than whites for poverty, exposure to environmental toxins in impoverished neighborhoods, and low-level academic achievement in reading and math. Thus, the high variation in identification rates among minority groups with similar levels of poverty and academic failure casts serious doubt on assertions by some researchers that it is primarily poverty and not bias that creates these deep racial disparities.

Multiple Contributing Factors

Most students with disabilities enter school undiagnosed and are referred by regular classroom teachers for evaluations that may lead to special education identification and placement. Therefore, the cause of the observed racial disparity is rooted not only in the system of special education itself, but also in the system of regular education as it encompasses special education. Most students referred for evaluation for special education are deemed in need of services. If differential referral is a key element, then the perceptions and decisions of classroom teachers, as well as school-level policies and practices that have an impact on students in regular classrooms, are, likewise, key elements.

Based on years of research, Beth Harry, Janette Klingner, Keith Sturges, and Robert Moore conclude in their chapter that "[t]he point at which differences [in measured performance and ability] result in one child being labeled disabled and another not are totally matters of social decisionmaking." Special education evaluations are often presented to parents as a set of discrete decisions based on scientific analysis and assessment, but even test-driven decisions are inescapably subjective in nature. The existence of some bias in test *content* is not the primary concern. Harry et al.'s research, for example, describes how subjective decisions creep into all elements of the evaluation *process,* including whom to test, what test to use, when to use alternative tests, how to interpret student responses, and what weight to give results from specific tests. All of these alter the outcomes. As Harry et al. point out, "a penstroke of the American Association on Mental Retardation (AAMR)" lowered the IQ score cutoff point for mental retardation from 85 to 70, "swiftly curing thousands of previously disabled children."

School politics, power relationships between school authorities and minority parents, the quality of regular education, and the classroom management skills of the referring teacher also introduce important elements of subjectivity that often go unrecognized. Other race-linked forces at work include poorly trained teachers who are disproportionately employed in minority schools (some of whom use special education as a disciplinary tool), other resource inequalities correlated to race, beliefs in African American and Latino inferiority and the low expectations that accompany these beliefs, cultural insensitivity, praise differentials, fear and misunderstanding of black males, and overcrowded schools and classrooms that are disproportionately located in school districts with high percentages of minority students. Add to these forces the general phenomenon of white parents' activism, efficaciousness, and high social capital exercised on behalf of their children compared to the relative lack of parent power among minority parents, and one can understand how the combination of regular education problems and the special education identification process has had a disparate impact on students of different races and ethnicities.

Sweeping reforms may also trigger harmful outcomes. For example, Artiles et al.'s preliminary examination of the "Unz Initiative," which eliminated bilingual education in California, suggests that English-language learners whose access to language supports is limited are more likely to be placed in restrictive special education settings. And as Jay Heubert describes in detail in his chapter, over the last ten years the use of high-stakes testing may have disproportionately punished poor and minority students, students with disabilities, and English-language learners: "There is evidence that states with high minority enrollments in special education are also likely to have high-stakes testing policies." Heubert goes on to cite evidence that "promotion testing is . . . likely to increase, perhaps significantly, the numbers of students with disabilities and minority students who suffer the serious consequences of dropping out." He points out that the National Research Council has described simple retention in grade as "an ineffective intervention." The aspirational benefits of raising standards aside, Heubert concludes that minority students with disabilities are at "great risk . . . especially in states that administer high-stakes promotion and graduation tests. . . ."

The Status of the Law and Enforcement Policy

Beginning with *Brown v. Board of Education*, litigation and enforcement under civil rights law has been essential to improving racial equity in education. Title VI of the Civil Rights Act of 1964 provided an important lever for racial justice in education that was especially effective when the federal government made enforcement a high priority. Critically important was that, under the Title VI regulations, plaintiffs could use statistical evidence to prove that even a policy that was race neutral on its face had an adverse and unjustifiably disparate impact on children of color in violation of the law. As Daniel Losen and Kevin Welner describe in their chapter, the legal landscape shifted dramatically following the U.S. Supreme Court's 2001 ruling in *Alexander v. Sandoval* which declared that there is no implied private right of action to bring legal challenges under "disparate-impact" theory. Therefore, court challenges that would rely on serious statistical disparities to prove allegations of discrimination are nearly extinguished today. Although the government and individuals filing complaints with government agencies may still use the Title VI regulations to redress the racially disparate impact of neutral policies, enforcement of disparate impact regulations is more vulnerable to an administration's enforcement policy preferences than ever before.

Untouched by *Sandoval* is the potential to challenge policies or practices where the racial disparities in special education identification or placement arise in the context of hearings on school desegregation. For example, in Alabama in 2000, a court review of consent decrees in that state resulted in a settlement yielding comprehensive state- and district-level remedies for overidentification of minorities.

Losen and Welner point out that disability law is becoming a relatively stronger basis for leveraging remedies from states and school districts where overidentification, underservicing, or unnecessarily restrictive placements are an issue. They explain further how systemic legal actions are better suited for seeking effective comprehensive remedies that could address contributing factors in both regular and special education. In her chapter, Theresa Glennon closely examines and evaluates the Office for Civil Rights' enforcement efforts where disability law and Tide VI converge. Glennon's recommendations include better coordinated investigations and interagency information sharing, clearer guidance for schools, and more comprehensive compliance reviews by well-trained investigators.

Sharon Soltman and Donald Moore provide an extensive analysis of how to fashion a remedy through litigation in a case known as *Corey H*. Their thorough chapter combines many years of research on effective practices with models of school improvement. They set forth a roadmap for school district reform to ensure that children with disabilities in Illinois be educated in the least restrictive environment as required by law. The multitiered *Corey H.* remedy entails a ten-year process for change, in one set of schools each year. The plaintiffs also won a large infusion of state funding to make implementing the *Corey H.* requirements a fully funded mandate. Further research on the efficacy of the court-ordered remedy should prove extremely useful to policymakers and others seeking to guarantee that minority children with disabilities have appropriate educational opportunities.

The only study in this volume that explores restricting federal funds as a remedy does so in the context of analyzing the viability of the Department of Education's Office for Special Education Programs' (OSEP) enforcement mechanisms for redressing racial disproportionality. In that study, Thomas Hehir argues forcefully for more frequent exercise of partial withholding by enforcement agents that is narrowly targeted to leverage compliance by specific states or districts in certain areas. As Hehir points out, partial withholding would allow OSEP to ratchet up its enforcement efforts without wholesale withdrawal of federal funds, which would heighten the risk of political backlash and have a negative impact on students in properly run programs. Likewise, federal policymakers should improve IDEA implementation and civil rights enforcement without imposing wholesale limitations on federal special education funding, which would have a negative impact on children with disabilities nationwide. Of course, there may be extreme cases in noncompliant districts where the only way to end serious violations is to cut off general funds, which proved very effective in spurring the desegregation of southern schools.

Moreover, Tom Parrish's research suggests that some state funding formulas are contributing to problems of overidentification. Some of these formulas fail to follow the federal model, which relies on U.S. Census data to determine allocations. The most problematic state formulas instead channel funds by disability identification and/or program and are suspected of creating incentives for overidentification.

Recommendations

Theses studies and the NRC's 2002 report both suggest that special education issues faced by minority children often begin with shortcomings in the realm of general education well before teachers or parents seek an evaluation for special education eligibility. Therefore, policy solutions that fail to consider the connection with general education classrooms will unlikely bring about significant change.

A New Federal Initiative with Implications for State Accountability

Our nation's education policy is at a crossroads. Leaders demand an end to the "soft bigotry of low expectations" and our government has promised to improve the achievement of all children in 2002 through the new education reform act, known as the No Child Left Behind Act. Racial equity is rooted in the commitment to teach all children well, with particular attention to meeting the needs of minority children.

To tackle racial disparities in achievement and graduation rates, the president and Congress embraced three reform approaches: public reporting, accountability at all levels (school, district, and state), and mandatory enforcement. These three reform approaches could be used to address the gross racial disparities in special education identification, restrictiveness of placement, and quality of services.

For policymakers, there is no need to pinpoint a specific cause or allege race discrimination in order to achieve racial equity. Scholars report that many schools today still operate under a deficit model, where school authorities regard students with disabilities as the embodiments of their particular disability and ask only *what the special educators are required to do in order to accommodate the student's problem.* A universal commitment to equity in special education would help erode this deficit model by shifting the focus to *what all public educators should do to improve educational opportunities and outcomes for all children.*

There is bipartisan acknowledgement that special education issues faced by minority children need a federal legislative response. This apparent consensus holds promise for effective federal reform. Reform attempts in the recent past can be improved upon. In 1997 the IDEA was amended to require states to collect and review data on racial disproportionality in both identification and placement and to intervene where disproportionality is significant. Before that, in 1995, the Office for Civil Rights made racial disproportionality in special education a top priority. The persistence of this problem suggests that states' legal obligations under IDEA and our civil rights enforcement priorities have not been met.

OCR was once a major force in the effort to desegregate our nation's schools, suggesting that the agency's efficacy is related to political will as much as it is to resources. It is apparent that there is a glaring need for stepped-up enforcement and oversight by both federal and state agencies. These actions must be geared toward encouraging the active participation of educators at all levels if there is to be any hope of meaningful and lasting improvement. Most important, aggressive efforts to remedy these issues are only the starting point. The efficacy of enforcement interventions and attempted reforms must be evaluated in terms of the outcomes for minority children.

Both general and special education teachers and administrators need better training to deliver effective instruction in the least restrictive, most inclusive environment appropriate. Meeting this need, along with the need for better data collection on racial and ethnic disparities and enhanced civil rights enforcement, would require an infusion of special education funds, which could be expected to result in net gains in education outcomes and savings in juvenile justice expenditures in the long term. By increasing federal oversight and by encouraging states to intervene where appropriate, the federal government could help improve the quality of instruction, supports, and services received by minority students in both regular and special education.

Although OCR still does not collect national data to determine racial disparities in the educational environment, the 1997 IDEA amendments obligate the states to collect sampled data. If the government required every state and school district to collect disaggregated data by race with disability category and educational setting (all three together), research on overrepresentation would benefit tremendously.

Moreover, much general education reform law is predicated on the concept that public pressure at the local level from parents and community stakeholders will stimulate meaningful improvements. To generate local reform pressure, the Bush education program requires public reporting of test achievement by a number of student subgroups, including disability status and major racial and ethnic subgroups. Policymakers could likewise stimulate meaningful improvements in special education by amending the IDEA to require public reporting of racial disparities in special education identification and placement.

IDEA should also require states to intervene under specified circumstances (they now have complete discretion) and to provide technical assistance to effect reforms. Such required intervention and assistance would likely foster greater self-reflection and improvement at the district level. While adopting mandatory interventions would be helpful, given the context of shrinking state education budgets, an emphasis on rewards and continued supports to foster successful efforts must be an integral part of any new enforcement efforts.

Finally, new mechanisms for minority children to exercise their rights under IDEA, including legal services support, would help considerably.

Toward Comprehensive Solutions to Systemic Problems at the District Level

The research and analysis presented in [the] volume are intended to serve educators, advocates, and policymakers alike. In addition to raising awareness of the issues, suggesting changes in legislation, and improving the enforcement of existing requirements, much can be accomplished with greater determination by school leadership.

For communities of color, disproportionate representation in special education is just one facet of the denial of access to educational opportunity. Denial begins in the regular education setting with school segregation, low tracking, test-based diploma denial and retention, overly harsh discipline, less access to programs for the gifted, and resource inequalities that have a distinctly racial dimension. Education leaders who suspect a problem at their school can accomplish a great deal by clearly stating that this problem is one that they and their staff can do something about, and that it has a racial dimension. By squarely shouldering responsibility and resolving to improve outcomes for all children as they tackle the racial disparities, school leaders can also reduce racial tensions among staff and in their school community and recover lives and talents that would otherwise be wasted. Tackling these issues should be a shared responsibility, not the duty of the principal or special education administrator alone. Furthermore, technical assistance can be sought from state and federal agencies, including OCR and OSEP, without triggering legal action. School leaders concerned with the issues raised above can also renew their efforts to involve parents and community in innovative ways. Some suggested methods include entering into partnerships with community organizations in order to boost minority parent involvement, and engaging school-based councils that would share decisionmaking power, working more closely with social service agencies to ensure that at-risk students receive high-quality services and that social workers and teachers are collaborating effectively, and increasing direct outreach to families.

Moreover, teachers need support to change their practice and improve classroom outcomes. In many cases regular classroom teachers have received little or no training in working with students from diverse backgrounds or with special education students, or have had little practicum experience in inclusive classrooms. Similarly, many special education teachers have not had the degree of training in the core curriculum or on how to work in a full-inclusion setting. Without both academic and multicultural training and time for special education and regular education teachers to collaborate, it is unrealistic to expect significant improvement.

Protecting the civil rights of all students benefits society at large. Obviously, it is much better if this problem is solved within the school than through external enforcement. Strong leadership at all levels could make an important difference. There is a great deal of work that can and should be done by schools, by districts, by states, and by federal lawmakers and enforcement agents that would improve educational opportunities for minority children in general, and make tremendous progress in solving the specific problems highlighted [here].

There are no quick fixes. The problems [we explore] have many roots, and creating better outcomes requires difficult changes at many levels. Far more research is needed on the practices that produce inequality and the reforms that can successfully correct them. We need to reach the point at which every child is treated as if he or she were our own child, with the same tirelessly defended and protected life possibilities. In schools where we can predict the racial makeup of a special education class before we open the door, we must have leadership, if possible, and enforcement, if necessary, to ensure that each child receives the quality academic support and special services he or she truly needs without diminishing any of the opportunities that are any child's right in American society. We hope [our] book will contribute to that dream.

POSTSCRIPT

Is Eliminating Minority Overrepresentation Beyond the Scope of Public Schools?

These selections provide only a glimpse into the projects they represent. Reading both reports in their entirety delivers a much more textured appreciation of their extensive treatment of disproportionality.

The studies share common concerns about the issues surrounding overrepresentation. Their opening words, however, signal their differences. M. Suzanne Donovan and Christopher T. Cross do not necessarily want to end disproportionate representation, if it delivers a benefit. Daniel J. Losen and Gary Orfield would like schools to end disproportionality, asserting that minority children in special education have not received that hoped-for benefit.

In their literature review, Donovan and Cross find that there may be external reasons for overrepresentation. Citing risks inherent in poverty, including environmental hazards, they conclude that children who have encountered these conditions come to school at a greater risk. There are actual differences in school readiness. Schools can address student performance, but environmental issues are matters of "political priority."

Losen and Orfield agree that environmental circumstances affect school readiness and performance but raise two compelling puzzles. First, if environmental issues are causal, why is there no overrepresentation in every disability category? Second, why do Hispanic children, who generally share economic status with African Americans, experience less overrepresentation?

Racial bias is hard to evaluate, say all the authors. The NRC study notes that the effects of prejudice are often subtle and intangible. Losen and Orfield comment that it is difficult to determine whether disproportionality results from intentional, biased behaviors but describe what happens in schools as a "subset" of racial impacts in society. Both sets of researchers agree that educators must reexamine an evaluation process that can be subjective and influenced by cultural differences.

John P. Manning and William Gaudelli (*Teacher Education and Special Education*, 2007) speak passionately about "modern myths of poverty and special education." Asserting that the origins of the achievement gap reside neither in schools nor in students, the authors say that holding schools responsible masks the "history of negligence that has plagued poor children in our society." The current expectation for uniform academic achievement exacerbates the problem. To resolve overrepresentation, the authors urge special education teachers to openly challenge elementary teachers and administrators about their referrals.

Both studies agree that responsive general education programs are critical. To what extent is overrepresentation affected by poor schools with inexperienced teachers and principals?

Although doctors identify the most visible disabilities, approximately 90 percent of referrals to special education are made by general education teachers: 73–90 percent of those referred are found eligible (Harry & Klingner, *Why Are So Many Minority Students in Special Education?*, 2007). Dismayed that special education is often redefined as the appropriate option for any children whom the regular education system finds too difficult to serve, the authors ask if it would not make more sense to simply help struggling learners, rather than seek a disability label.

First-year teachers remarked that they were overwhelmed by the diversity in their new classrooms, even though they gave high marks to their preparation programs (*Lessons Learned,* http://www.publicagenda.org, 2008). Novices had the same reaction to the number of students with special needs. The report notes that these responses might be related to the fact that new teachers are often assigned the "hardest-to-reach" students. Could new teachers be reaching out for any available assistance?

Is disproportionality an issue for schools to solve or a broader societal challenge? If poverty and environmental problems were alleviated, what differences would we see? Will the uniform expectations from NCLB ensure general education attention to the needs of all children or motivate educators to seek assistance through special education? Will stricter governmental oversight relieve disproportionality? These challenging questions must be raised and addressed for the benefit of all children.

ISSUE 4

Can Whole-School Reform Reduce Discipline Problems?

YES: Howard S. Adelman and Linda Taylor, from "Rethinking How Schools Address Student Misbehavior and Disengagement," *Addressing Barriers to Learning* (vol. 13, no. 2, Spring 2008)

NO: William C. Frick and Susan C. Faircloth, from "Acting in the Collective and Individual 'Best Interest of Students': When Ethical Imperatives Clash with Administrative Demands," *Journal of Special Education Leadership* (vol. 20, no. 1, pp. 21–32, March 2007)

ISSUE SUMMARY

YES: Howard S. Adelman and Linda Taylor, codirectors of the UCLA School Mental Health Project, based in the Center for Mental Health in Schools, believe that many discipline problems could be eliminated by whole-school initiatives that create and sustain an environment that addresses positive social and emotional development as well as academics.

NO: William C. Frick and Susan C. Faircloth, assistant professors at the University of Oklahoma and The Pennsylvania State University, respectively, present dilemmas faced by principals torn between balancing the needs of one particular student who exhibits disruptive behavior with those of the rest of the student body whose learning is affected by the single student's actions.

Individuals with Disabilities Education Act (IDEA) ensures a free and appropriate public education for students with disabilities. Students with emotional/behavioral disabilities are among those accorded this right. These students typically experience difficulty complying with general school rules and social conventions. Some may internalize conflict, withdrawing and perhaps hurting themselves. Others react aggressively, externalizing their conflict. While both types of behavior must be addressed, externalizing behavior is usually the most visible and therefore the most problematic for teachers.

Educators encounter a dilemma when students with a disability violate school norms. The behavior (e.g., starting a fight) breaks the rules, but the student starting the fight has a disability that prevents him from restraining his impulses. Repeated suspensions for the same behavior could effectively expel the student, depriving him of his legally protected education and services, constituting a change of placement.

In its early authorizations, IDEA emphasized academic access; there was no mention of "the troublesome topic of discipline" (Osborne & Russo, *ELA Notes*, 2007). IDEA 97 remedied that oversight by stipulating that students should not be removed from school for behavior that was a manifestation of their disability or the result of an inappropriate Individualized Education Program (IEP). Behavior unrelated to the disability could receive the standard consequence. Unfortunately, IDEA 97 contained no precise definition of the term manifestation (Osborne & Russo, 2007). Often the appropriateness of the IEP became the primary focus of discussion, removing or delaying disciplinary consequences.

IDEA 2004 tightened legal requirements regarding manifestation determination, making it easier to discipline students with disabilities (Zirkel, *Journal of Special Education Leadership*, 2006). The emphasis has shifted from whether the IEP was appropriate to whether it has been implemented. A tougher standard exists for finding specific behavior directly related to the disability. Schools have broader latitude to send students with disabilities to short-term alternate facilities for longer periods of time. Parents now bear the burden of proof if they disagree with the school's determination regarding manifestation.

Boyd (*Children's Rights*, 2006) voices concern about the impact of these changes, especially on students with mild/moderate disabilities. She notes that some might act out in frustration as they struggle with tasks that are confusing or beyond their current capabilities. Observing that teachers may impose disciplinary consequences without recognizing the impact of a mild/moderate disability, she worries that these students will become "isolated and left with nothing but frustration and an inability to learn."

Howard Adelman and Linda Taylor agree that disciplined students might become disengaged, and unmotivated to continue learning. Acknowledging the pressures on teachers, Adelman and Taylor advocate school improvement efforts that seek to identify the reasons for difficult behavior, incorporate positive behavioral supports to minimize the occurrence of undesirable behavior, and re-engage troubling students, whether or not they have a disability.

William Frick and Susan Faircloth analyze the words of high school principals struggling to balance the needs of the whole student body with those of individual students with disabilities. These leaders are comfortable providing instructional accommodations and adaptations to meet student needs, but unsettled by the ethical dilemmas they face when trying to be fair to everyone in disciplinary matters.

As you read these articles, think about how your school approaches behavior and discipline. Are there consistently applied schoolwide standards and expectations? How do educators work to understand the reasons behind inappropriate behavior? How is inappropriate behavior addressed? Are all students treated fairly?

YES

Howard S. Adelman
and Linda Taylor

Rethinking How Schools Address Student Misbehavior and Disengagement

The essence of good classroom teaching is the ability to create an environment that first can mobilize the learner to pursue the curriculum and then can maintain that mobilization, while effectively facilitating learning. The process, of course, is meant not only to teach academics but [also] to turn out good citizens. While many terms are used, this societal aim requires that a fundamental focus of school improvement be on facilitating positive social and emotional development/learning.

Behavior problems clearly get in the way of all this. Misbehavior disrupts. In some forms, such as bullying and intimidating others, it is hurtful. And, observing such behavior may disinhibit others. Because of this, discipline and classroom management are daily topics at every school.

Concern about responding to behavior problems and promoting social and emotional learning are related and are embedded into the six arenas we frame to encompass the content of student/learning supports. How these concerns are addressed is critical to the type of school and classroom climate that emerges and to student engagement and re-engagement in classroom learning. As such, they need to be fully integrated into school improvement efforts.

Disengaged Students, Misbehavior, and Social Control

After an extensive review of the literature, Fredricks, Blumenfeld, and Paris conclude: *Engagement is associated with positive academic outcomes, including achievement and persistence in school; and it is higher in classrooms with supportive teachers and peers, challenging and authentic tasks, opportunities for choice, and sufficient structure.* Conversely, for many students, disengagement is associated with behavior and learning problems and eventual dropout. The degree of concern about student engagement varies depending on school population.

In general, teachers focus on content to be taught and knowledge and skills to be acquired—with a mild amount of attention given to the process

From *Addressing Barriers to Learning*, vol. 13, no. 2, Spring 2008, pp. 1–2, 4–6. Copyright © 2008 by UCLA Center for Mental Health in Schools. Reprinted by permission. http://smhp.psych.ucla.edu

of engaging students. All this works fine in schools where most students come each day ready and able to deal with what the teacher is ready and able to teach. Indeed, teachers are fortunate when they have a classroom where the majority of students show up and are receptive to the planned lessons. In schools that are the greatest focus of public criticism, this certainly is not the case.

What most of us realize, at least at some level, is that teachers in such settings are confronted with an entirely different teaching situation. Among the various supports they absolutely must have are ways to re-engage students who have become disengaged and often resistant to broadband (nonpersonalized) teaching approaches. To the dismay of most teachers, however, strategies for re-engaging students in *learning* rarely are a prominent part of pre- or inservice preparation and seldom are the focus of interventions pursued by professionals whose role is to support teachers and students. As a result, they learn more about *socialization* and *social control* as classroom management strategies than about how to engage and re-engage students in classroom learning, which is the key to enhancing and sustaining good behavior.

Reacting to Misbehavior

When a student misbehaves, a natural reaction is to want that youngster to experience and other students to see the consequences of misbehaving. One hope is that public awareness of consequences will deter subsequent problems. As a result, a considerable amount of time at schools is devoted to discipline and classroom management.

An often stated assumption is that stopping a student's misbehavior will make her or him amenable to teaching. In a few cases, this may be so. However, the assumption ignores all the research that has led to understanding *psychological reactance* and the need for individuals to maintain and restore a sense of self-determination. Moreover, it belies two painful realities: the number of students who continue to manifest poor academic achievement and the staggering dropout rate in too many schools.

Unfortunately, in their efforts to deal with deviant and devious behavior and to create safe environments, too many schools overrely on negative consequences and plan only for social control. Such practices model behavior that can foster rather than counter the development of negative values and often produce other forms of undesired behavior. Moreover, the tactics often make schools look and feel more like prisons than community treasures.

In schools, short of suspending a student, punishment essentially takes the form of a decision to do something that the student does not want done. In addition, a demand for future compliance usually is made, along with threats of harsher punishment if compliance is not forthcoming. The discipline may be administered in ways that suggest the student is seen as an undesirable person. As students get older, suspension increasingly comes into play. Indeed, suspension remains one of the most common disciplinary responses for the transgressions of secondary students.

As with many emergency procedures, the benefits of using punishment may be offset by many negative consequences. These include increased negative attitudes toward school and school personnel. These attitudes often lead to more behavior problems, anti-social acts, and various mental health problems. Because disciplinary procedures also are associated with dropping out of school, it is not surprising that some concerned professionals refer to extreme disciplinary practices as "pushout" strategies.

In general, specific discipline practices should be developed with the aim of leaving no child behind. That is, *stopping misbehavior must be accomplished in ways that maximize the likelihood that the teacher can engage/re-engage the student in instruction and positive learning.*

The growing emphasis on positive approaches to reducing misbehavior and enhancing support for positive behavior in and out-of-the-classroom is a step in the right direction. So is the emphasis in school guidelines stressing that discipline should be reasonable, fair, and non-denigrating (e.g., should be experienced by recipients as legitimate reactions that neither denigrate one's sense of worth nor reduce one's sense of autonomy).

Moreover, in recognizing that the application of consequences is an insufficient step in preventing future misbehavior, there is growing awareness that school improvements that engage and re-engage students reduce behavior (and learning) problems significantly. That is why school improvement efforts need to delineate

- efforts to prevent and anticipate misbehavior
- actions to be taken during misbehavior that do minimal harm to engagement in classroom learning
- steps to be taken afterwards that include a focus on enhancing engagement. . . .

Focusing on Underlying Motivation to Address Concerns About Engagement

Moving beyond socialization, social control, and behavior modification and with an emphasis on engagement, there is a need to address the roots of misbehavior, especially underlying motivational bases. Consider students who spend most of the day trying to avoid all or part of the instructional program. An *intrinsic* motivational interpretation of the avoidance behavior of many of these youngsters is that it reflects their perception that school is not a place where they experience a sense of competence, autonomy, and/or relatedness to others. Over time, these perceptions develop into strong motivational dispositions and related patterns of misbehavior.

Misbehavior Can Reflect Proactive (Approach) or Reactive (Avoidance) Motivation

Noncooperative, disruptive, and aggressive behavior patterns that are *proactive* tend to be rewarding and satisfying to an individual because the behavior itself is exciting or because the behavior leads to desired outcomes (e.g., peer recognition [and] feelings of competence or autonomy). Intentional negative behavior stemming from such approach motivation can be viewed as pursuit of deviance.

Misbehavior in the classroom may also be *reactive*, stemming from avoidance motivation. This behavior can be viewed as protective reactions. Students with learning problems can be seen as motivated to avoid and to protest against being forced into situations in which they cannot cope effectively. For such students, many teaching situations are perceived in this way. Under such circumstances, individuals can be expected to react by trying to protect themselves from the unpleasant thoughts and feelings that the situations stimulate (e.g., feelings of incompetence, loss of autonomy, [and] negative relationships). In effect, the misbehavior reflects efforts to cope and defend against aversive experiences. The actions may be direct or indirect and include defiance, physical and psychological withdrawal, and diversionary tactics.

Interventions for Reactive and Proactive Behavior Problems Begin with Major Program Changes

From a motivational perspective, the aims are to (a) prevent and overcome negative attitudes toward school and learning, (b) enhance motivational readiness for learning and overcoming problems, (c) maintain intrinsic motivation throughout learning and problem solving, and (d) nurture the type of continuing motivation that results in students engaging in activities away from school that foster maintenance, generalization, and expansion of learning and problem solving. Failure to attend to motivational concerns in a comprehensive, normative way results in approaching passive and often hostile students with practices that instigate and exacerbate problems.

After making broad programmatic changes to the degree feasible, intervention with a misbehaving student involves remedial steps directed at underlying factors. For instance, with intrinsic motivation in mind, the following assessment questions arise:

- Is the misbehavior unintentional or intentional?
- If it is intentional, is it reactive or proactive?
- If the misbehavior is reactive, is it a reaction to threats to self-determination, competence, or relatedness?
- If it is proactive, are there other interests that might successfully compete with satisfaction derived from deviant behavior?

In general, intrinsic motivation theory suggests that corrective interventions for those misbehaving reactively requires steps designed to reduce reactance and enhance positive motivation for participation. For youngsters highly motivated to pursue deviance (e.g., those who proactively engage in criminal acts), even more is needed. Intervention might focus on helping these youngsters identify and follow through on a range of valued, socially appropriate alternatives to deviant activity. Such alternatives must be capable of producing greater feelings of self-determination, competence, and relatedness than usually result from the youngster's deviant actions. To these ends, motivational analyses of the problem can point to corrective steps for implementation by teachers, clinicians, parents, or students themselves.

Promoting Social and Emotional Learning

One facet of addressing misbehavior proactively is the focus on promoting healthy social and emotional development. This emphasis meshes well with a school's goals related to enhancing students' personal and social well being. And, it is essential to creating an atmosphere of "caring," "cooperative learning," and a "sense of community" (including greater home involvement).

In some form or another, every school has goals that emphasize a desire to enhance students' personal and social functioning. Such goals reflect an understanding that social and emotional growth plays an important role in

- enhancing the daily smooth functioning of schools and the emergence of a safe, caring, and supportive school climate
- facilitating students' holistic development
- enabling student motivation and capability for academic learning
- optimizing life beyond schooling.

An agenda for promoting social and emotional learning encourages family-centered orientation. It stresses practices that increase positive engagement in learning at school and that enhance personal responsibility (social and moral), integrity, self-regulation (self-discipline), a work ethic, diverse talents, and positive feelings about self and others.

It should be stressed at this point that, for most individuals, learning social skills and emotional regulation are part of normal development and socialization. Thus, social and emotional learning is not primarily a formal training process. This can be true even for some individuals who are seen as having behavior and emotional problems. (While poor social skills are identified as a symptom and contributing factor in a wide range of educational, psychosocial, and mental health problems, it is important to remember that symptoms are correlates.)

What Is Social and Emotional Learning?

As formulated by the Collaborative for Academic, Social, and Emotional Learning (CASEL), social and emotional learning (SEL) "is a process for helping children and even adults develop the fundamental skills for life effectiveness. SEL teaches the skills we all need to handle ourselves, our relationships, and our work, effectively and ethically. These skills include recognizing and managing our emotions, developing caring and concern for others, establishing positive relationships, making responsible decisions, and handling challenging situations constructively and ethically. They are the skills that allow children to calm themselves when angry, make friends, resolve conflicts respectfully, and make ethical and safe choices."

CASEL also views SEL as "providing a framework for school improvement. Teaching SEL skills helps create and maintain safe, caring learning environments. The most beneficial programs provide sequential and developmentally appropriate instruction in SEL skills. They are implemented in a coordinated manner, school-wide, from preschool through high school.

Lessons are reinforced in the classroom, during out-of-school activities, and at home. Educators receive ongoing professional development in SEL. And families and schools work together to promote children's social, emotional, and academic success."

Because of the scope of SEL programming, the work is conceived as multi-year. The process stresses adult modeling and coaching and student practice to solidify learning related to social and emotional awareness of self and others, self-management, responsible decision making, and relationship skills.

Natural Opportunities to Promote Social and Emotional Learning

Sometimes the agenda for promoting social and emotional learning takes the form of a special curriculum (e.g., social skills training, character education, [and] assets development) or is incorporated into the regular curricula. However, classroom and school-wide practices can and need to do much more to (a) capitalize on *natural* opportunities at schools to promote social and emotional development and (b) minimize transactions that interfere with positive growth in these areas. Natural opportunities are one of the most authentic examples of "teachable moments."

An appreciation of what needs more attention can be garnered readily by looking at the school day and school year through the lens of goals for personal and social functioning. Is instruction carried out in ways that strengthen or hinder development of interpersonal skills and connections and student understanding of self and others? Is cooperative learning and sharing promoted? Is counterproductive competition minimized? Are interpersonal conflicts mainly suppressed or are they used as learning opportunities? Are roles provided for all students to be positive helpers throughout the school and community?

The Center's website offers specific examples of natural opportunities and how to respond to them in ways that promote personal and social growth. . . .

The Promise of Promoting Social and Emotional Learning

Programs to improve social skills and interpersonal problem solving are described as having promise both for prevention and correction. However, reviewers tend to be cautiously optimistic because so many studies have found the range of skills acquired are quite limited and so is the generalizability and maintenance of outcomes. This is the case for training of specific skills (e.g., what to say and do in a specific situation), general strategies (e.g., how to generate a wider range of interpersonal problem-solving options), as well as efforts to develop cognitive-affective orientations, such as empathy training. Reviews of social skills training over several decades conclude that individual studies show effectiveness, but outcome studies often have shown lack of generalizability and social validity. However, the focus has been mainly on social skills training for students with emotional and behavior disorders.

Recent analyses by researchers involved with the Collaborative for Academic, Social, and Emotional Learning (CASEL) suggest that "students who receive SEL programming academically outperform their peers, compared to those who do not receive SEL. Those students also get better grades and graduate at higher rates. Effective SEL programming drives academic learning, and it also drives social outcomes such as positive peer relationships, caring and empathy, and social engagement. Social and emotional instruction also leads to reductions in problem behavior such as drug use, violence, and delinquency."

Promotion of Mental Health

Promotion of mental health encompasses efforts to enhance knowledge, skills, and attitudes in order to foster social and emotional development, a healthy lifestyle, and personal well-being. Promoting healthy development, well-being, and a value-based life are important ends unto themselves and overlap primary, secondary, and tertiary interventions to prevent mental health and psychosocial problems.

Interventions to promote mental health encompass not only strengthening individuals but also enhancing nurturing and supportive conditions at school, at home, and in the neighborhood. All this includes a particular emphasis on increasing opportunities for personal development and empowerment by promoting conditions that foster and strengthen positive attitudes and behaviors (e.g., enhancing motivation and capability to pursue positive goals, resist negative influences, and overcome barriers). It also includes efforts to maintain and enhance physical health and safety and *inoculate* against problems (e.g., providing positive and negative information, skill instruction, and fostering attitudes that build resistance and resilience).

While schools alone are not responsible for this, they do play a significant role, albeit sometimes not a positive one, in social and emotional development. School improvement plans need to encompass ways the school will (1) *directly facilitate* social and emotional (as well as physical) development and (2) *minimize threats* to positive development (see references at end of this article). In doing so, appreciation of differences in levels of development and developmental demands at different ages is fundamental, and personalized implementation to account for individual differences is essential.

From a mental health perspective, helpful guidelines are found in research clarifying normal trends for school-age youngsters' efforts to feel *competent, self-determining,* and *connected with significant others.* And, measurement of such feelings can provide indicators of the impact of a school on mental health. Positive findings can be expected to correlate with school engagement and academic progress. Negative findings can be expected to correlate with student anxiety, fear, anger, alienation, a sense of losing control, a sense of hopelessness and powerlessness. In turn, these negative thoughts, feelings, and attitudes can lead to externalizing (aggressive, "acting out") or internalizing (withdrawal, self-punishing, delusional) behaviors.

Clearly, promoting mental health has payoffs both academically and for reducing problems at schools. Therefore, it seems evident that an enhanced commitment to mental health promotion must be a key facet of the renewed emphasis on the whole child by education leaders.

Concluding Comments

Responding to behavior problems and promoting social and emotional development and learning can and should be done in the context of a comprehensive system designed to address barriers to learning and (re)engage students in classroom learning. In this respect, the developmental trend in thinking about how to respond to misbehavior must be toward practices that embrace an expanded view of engagement and human motivation and that includes a focus on social and emotional learning.

Relatedly, motivational research and theory are guiding the development of interventions designed to enhance student's motivation and counter disengagement. And, there is growing appreciation of the power of intrinsic motivation.

Now, it is time for school improvement decision makers and planners to fully address these matters.

William C. Frick and
Susan C. Faircloth

 **NO**

Acting in the Collective and Individual "Best Interest of Students": When Ethical Imperatives Clash with Administrative Demands

The focus of this investigation was on how secondary principles interpret the experience of leadership decision making as a moral activity in relation to a specific ethical lens, the Ethic of the Profession, and its associated Model for Promoting Students' Best Interests. This ethical framework elevates the profession of educational leadership by positing a central moral ideal in the form of an injunction of special duty: "serve the best interests of the student" whereby "promoting the success of all students" by focusing on the individual needs of children. The Ethic of the Profession is an eclectic framework incorporating established ethical paradigms of justice, care, critique, and community not as totally distinct, incommensurable moral reasoning, but as complementary—a "tapestry of ethical perspectives that encourage . . . rich human response to . . . many uncertain ethical situations." The Ethic of the Profession indicates that a disparity exists between diverse ethical perspectives related to the education of students, professional codes meant to inform decision making and conduct, and the personal moral values of administrators that influence their judgment and behavior. When reflective school leaders attempt to integrate established ethical paradigms and professional and personal codes of ethics, the result is often moral dissonance, or a "clashing of codes." In responding to this inevitable discord, the Ethic of the Profession is grounded in a reasoned consideration of the educational shibboleth "serve the best interests of the students."

The student's best interests are the focal point of the Ethic of the Profession. A model for determining the best interests of the student consists of a robust focus on the essential nature of individual rights, the duty of responsibility to others for a common interest, and respect as mutual acknowledgment of others as having worth, value, and dignity unto themselves.

An important consideration for this investigation was the distinction practicing secondary school administrators make between the best interests of the student (one) and the best interests of the students (all or most). In reviewing the literature on the best interests of students, Walker indicates

From *Journal of Special Education Leadership*, 20(1), March 2007, pp. 21–22, 23, 24, 25–29 (excerpts). Copyright © 2007 by Council of Administrators of Special Education (CASE). Reprinted by permission.

that "the interests of children supersede the interests of all other interests." Walker argues, however, that it may be very difficult to know with precision and appositeness what the best interests of students might be. The Ethic of the Profession and its Model for Promoting Students' Best Interests clearly and intentionally refer to the best interests of the student (one) as opposed to the best interests of students (group, many, or all). This ethical frame does not recognize a difference between the two perspectives and purports that

> if the individual student is treated with fairness, justice, and caring, then a strong message is sent to all students that they will be treated with similar justice and caring and that they should treat others similarly. Thus, rights carry with them responsibilities, so much so that the rights of one individual should not bring harm to the group.

The (individual) student's best interests are at the center of the Ethic of the Profession and, according to this decision-making framework, individuals (particularly students) possess inherent worth and dignity unto themselves and they need not strive to maintain their value. With this said, educational leaders must first decide if the individual is acting responsibly in asserting his or her rights. If not, there are opportunities to teach responsibility, which is challenging and requires vigilance, but the potential is great for students to share responsibility for their own development.

Purpose of the Study

. . . [The] primary intent in this study was to pilot the use of this frame in the field of education leadership to test the explanations and definitions of what professional moral practice entails, the defined by the Ethic of the Profession and its Model for Promoting Student's Best Interests, compared to the explanations and definitions practitioners use. The focus was on practicing administrators' understanding of the expression "the best interests of the student" and additional aspects of moral practice and reasoning removed from classroom or seminar settings.

Method

As part of the overall study from which this specific research is derived, verification was sought as to whether or not educational leaders could relate experiences of discord between organizational policies and professional expectations meant to inform judgment, decision making, and conduct and their own personal moral values (whether held privately or expressed publicly). In addition, this research investigation sought to know and understand how the expression "the best interests of the student" was defined and used in decision making. . . .

Participants

. . . A range of people occupying the position of secondary school principal were sought as participants for this research. Secondary principals were selected because of their work in managing the size, scale, and level of problems associated with a complex and often bureaucratic service organization. This range of participants constituted a broad variety of individual and contextual factors and backgrounds. . . . Three female and eight male principals participated in this study. One male and one female were black and the other nine were white. Participants ranged in age from 35 to 55 years old and had worked in their administrative role from 2 to 19 years. The size of student enrollment in participants' respective schools ranged from 80 to 2200, with two principals serving in rural schools, three serving in suburban schools, three serving in suburban/metro schools, and three in urban schools. . . .

Findings

As a result of the focus and stamina required to lead an entire school organization, each participant in this study indicated in some fashion a sharp distinction and clear difference between the best interests of individual students and the best interests of students as a group. The distinction administrators made was markedly different from the conceptual framework guiding this study. They viewed the work of deciding and acting in the best interests of the student body as being qualitatively different from working with individual students. Participants indicated that balancing the two priorities was difficult, but essential, within the confines of a bureaucratic institution.

In their daily work, most principals thought about the best interests of students in general, as a corporate body, and when specific student-related issues came to their attention they would alter their perspective on students' best interests and focus on unique, individual student needs. This pattern of thought was prevalent and consistent across participants in terms of their interpretation of the expression "the best interest of the student." . . .

A young, male high school principal put it this way: "You look at each situation, and I think [about] a decision: How many kids can I impact versus how many may I not impact, across the board?" A similar attitude was expressed by a veteran high school administrator who said:

> I think there are times when you have to do things in the collective best interests. There is no question you have to do things sometimes that a student may have to have an issue sacrificed for the benefit of the entire student body, or for the safety of the student body, or for a variety of reasons. And because we do work within a system, we're not working in a private setting where we can handle each student individually: we're working in a system where we have to handle the entire global group. So yeah, people are sometimes, I hate to say people are sacrificed, but their issue may be sacrificed for the benefit of all. That's a bureaucratic issue.

Another principal communicated the view of focusing primarily on individual student needs and best interests as specified in the Model for Promoting Students' Best Interests when he explained, "Given certain circumstances, you can send a message to the entire student body based on what happens to an individual." Although he believed focusing on a case by case treatment of individual students can have some effect on the best interests of the entire student body, this level of individual interaction was not sufficient for ensuring a complete consideration of the best interests of all students under his supervision.

Although the principals' first order of business was considering, deciding, and acting in the best interests of students as a group, they were cognizant of the potential danger of the distinction, especially when, according to one participant, "you just give people what they need" at an individual rather than a group level. The perspectives participants held about balancing what was in the best interests of one student as opposed to an entire group were diverse. Most believed that public schooling was becoming increasingly individualized and student centered, with planning and interventions designed to address the needs and talents of every student, whereas other principals expressed their frustration with public education and organizational life where "political correctness" and a "one size fits all approach" dictated how to respond when addressing students' needs or seeking to serve their best interests.

The majority of the principals focused on special education policy to illustrate the qualitative difference, in their view, between the best interests of the student (one) and the best interests of the students (all or most). It was difficult for principals to address the best interests of the student (one), although they would have liked to, because of policies and protections for groups of students. One aspect (instructional) of the policies and protections resonated with their moral notions of equity, fairness, and social justice whereas the other aspect (discipline) was morally troubling and restrictive and did not address the best interest of the individual student.

The two contrasting views, one of student-centered discretion and the other a one size fits all way of doing business, were fueled by the same source—special education mandates and the provisions of the Individuals with Disabilities Education Improvement Act (IDEIA) and the No Child Left Behind Act (NCLB). Most principals fully supported IDEIA and the current direction of public education. For example, a female high school principal indicated that "what's best for all is not necessarily what's best for the individual. Education these days is working toward the needs of each child, [such as] differentiation of instruction and curriculum in the classroom. This is a good thing." This view was also held by a young, male, rural high school principal who imagined that public education will eventually remake itself into an endeavor centered on serving individual student needs, promoting each student's success, and attending to "best interests" at an individual/personal level. He said:

> I think we're always going to make [decisions for] the best interests
> of the whole. That's been the direction of education, but then we are
> prescribing more of what is in the individual best interests of certain
> students, and it's likely to continue on that track. I think we're going to
> be doing more of that now. . . . Every day we think about our services
> for special education; what we're doing in special education. I think
> we've got to service kids. I think we're obligated to do that, [but] I think
> we're overprotective of special education. I think it's a copout when we
> put the responsibility to work with low achieving or special needs kids

on special education teachers. I think it's everybody's responsibility to work with those special needs kids. . . . I think there'll be a point where, I mean people keep laughing about this, and they've been laughing about this 10, 15, 20 years ago when they said, "Every kid is going to have an IEP. I think we're headed that way, I really do. We're headed in a direction where we're really individualizing a lot of decision making and the way things are being done."

Other principals took a completely different perspective on the "direction education was headed." One middle school principal believed that the balance between the individual and the group was skewed more toward the group, particularly in instructional matters. He was deeply disturbed by this type of attitude and indicated that uniform treatment of all students did not achieve the goals and purposes of public education. He said:

> I think we have a philosophy in education today that we believe that one size fits all. . . . There needs to be more recognition of the uniqueness of mankind and individual needs in that one size doesn't fit all—people haven't sensed that uniqueness or that specialness in a sea of numbers. And I think that sometimes we lose masses because that's not occurring.

Expressing this position in a more critical tone, a veteran high school principal did not mince words about his viewpoints when it came to the restrictions placed on him by special education policy when desiring to make decisions in, what he believed to be, the best interests of students. He spoke primarily about student discipline and how the balance between individual and group is skewed because of the standards of uniform treatment he must comply with based on federal, state, and district policy. His frustration was about treating every student in a protected class the same way, or within the parameters of restrictive policy mandates, without being granted the administrative discretion and decision making necessary to respond to students in their best interests. . . . He indicated:

> Public education dictates to you what you can and can't say, or do, or feel, or be; because you are all things to all people—that's the nature of public education. And a result of that, being all things to all people . . . my own personal positions are inconsequential for the most part, unless it's a major philosophical issue. There are many things that are [a major philosophical issue], but because we live in a politically correct world, we cannot deal with things that are actual . . . and so as a result of that, we cannot act on what we know to be true, we have to act on what the public perceives to be acceptable, so that is a dilemma sometimes.

The same principal illustrated the tension he feels when complying with special class protections and his desire to respond morally, decide and act ethically, and deal with students as individuals. The extended quote that follows illustrates the importance, for this principal, of engaging and responding to students on a personal and individual level rather than being forced to decide and act in the best interests of students as a group. According to this participant, there is a moral danger in dictated and uniform prescriptions for attending to and managing students as a group that essentially ignore or do away with administrative discretion.

> I have special education questions every single day. What's best for the child? Well in this building we have 470 special education students. So there's a large group, and I think the moral questions come every day: What's right for those particular students? I think, in weighing that out [it] combines with What's right then for regular education students? You look at them as separate tracks. Clearly the moral dilemma is there: 'How can I treat two people who do the same thing totally differently and still acquire some integrity of fairness?' The answer is you can't. So you do the best you can. Knowing the fact that if I have a special education student sitting here, he has a knife on him; he's OK to have that knife on him because he is a special education student. And I have a regular education student with the same knife on him, and I have to expel him for a year and this [special education] kid doesn't get anything because it's OK—that's a moral dilemma for me. It's a moral dilemma for me when I have a special education student extort money from a student in the hallway, and I have a regular education student extort money in the hallway, and I have to suspend one or expel one and not the other. It's a moral dilemma when . . . I have a special education student punch a teacher in a fight and a regular education student punch a teacher in a fight [and] one's expelled for assaulting staff, the other one gets nothing because the parent won't agree to a suspension. That's a moral dilemma for me—that's a problem for me, because that's wrong. No matter how you cut that up in my mind that's wrong. I know there's somebody . . . somewhere that could cut that up in their own mind and make that right. I can't do that, and I've not been able to do that over 32 years' time. Pretty sure it won't change in the next five or ten.

More than half of the principals in this study focused on special education policy to illustrate the qualitative difference, in their view, between the best interest of the student (one) and the best interests of the students (all or most). Results of this study, specific to handling special education student issues, indicate that it is difficult to address the best interests of the student (one), although the participants would have liked to, because of educational policies and protection for groups of students. Although the instructional aspects of the policies and protections resonated with participants' moral notions of equity, fairness, and social justice, the disciplinary aspects of the same policies and protections were morally troubling and restrictive and did not address the best interest of the individual student.

Discussion

The turbulent intersection of education policy, professional ethics, and personal morality became evident as participants talked about working with students on an individual basis. . . . Serving the best interests of the student meant being fair and acting fairly, and in the eyes of participants who talked about fairness as a principle or virtue, the rule or quality was immensely important. However, fairness required responding with personal investment to each student based on their unique needs, not being inextricably tied to formulaic procedures or regulations that did not allow for reasonable distinctions between equality and equity. As one respondent indicated, "You just give people [students] what they need" at an individual level. It seems that participants would not want to be questioned about why they were not doling out the same treatment or responding and acting in the same, uniform manner toward every student.

. . . The principals in this study described the difficulties they experienced, both externally by way of publicly defending their decisions and actions to others and internally as a moral struggle between their own sense of fairness as equity and the uniform procedures and policies that were to be applied equally to all students.

Principals expressed, in a variety of ways, the importance of treating students equitably. . . . Another principal put the matter this way:

> I think we struggle with what is fair and consistent. We have to treat everybody as an individual, but we have to be consistent with our discipline. I know sometimes we have to weigh it. How is it going to be looked at by the rest of the kids or the faculty if one thing happens to this kid who did the same behavior as another kid? See, they don't get the background information. . . . You definitely have to keep your faculty happy; you have to be supportive and let them know you're backing them up, but they don't know that we can't treat everybody the same sometimes for the same behavior because there's circumstances out there. I wish some people would just understand that and even parents too.

Implications

Implications for Practice

This study raises important questions regarding . . . preparing building-level administrators, to respond to the dilemmas that arise when the best interests of the individual student clash with the best interests of students as a whole. The potential for such dilemma is clearly illustrated by the increasing demand on school leaders to meet the individual needs of children with special educational needs as mandated by the IDEIA and the often competing demands of NCLBA, which may be described as being directed toward the more collective interests of students as a group rather than individual students.

Implications for Policy

To assist school leaders in navigating these potential ethical and administrative dilemmas, policy makers must give increased attention to the ways in which the implementation of current and future policies affects school leaders' abilities to respond to individual student needs as well as fosters and sustains inclusive learning environments for all students. An example such action includes recent federal policy discussions pertaining to the use of the Response to Intervention (RTI) model, which may have the potential to assist educators in more effectively addressing student academic and learning needs as well as disciplinary and behavioral issues. Using the RTI model may assist building-level principals and their staff in mitigating what principals, such as those in this study, identify and experience as qualitative differences between respond-ing to the best interests of the student (one) and responding to the best inter-ests of the students (all or most). As noted earlier in the findings, in addition to the instructional aspects of special education policies and protections, it may be easier for some school leaders to equate the provision of instructional accommodations and adaptations with the moral notions of equity, fairness, and social justice, whereas the disciplinary aspects may be viewed as morally troubling, restrictive, and at odds with the practice of meeting the best interest of the individual student. Again, this illustrates the potential for both admin-istrative and ethical dilemmas for school leaders. . . .

Conclusion

As discussed, principals in this investigation expressed satisfaction in their press for equitable responses to student learning needs, particularly for those students identified as requiring special instructional services. In contrast, par-ticipants reported a significant unsettledness with special class protections that dismiss, and thereby limit, the principal's ability to take fair and just dis-ciplinary actions. These findings suggest that secondary principals, who play a significant role in special education leadership in their respective building assignments, experience a moral tension between serving the best instruc-tional interests of each identified student under their supervision and care and the disciplinary policies and procedural regulations that limit, according to participants' perspectives, moral discretion, ethical judgment, and reasonable retributive justice pertaining to student disciplinary matters. Although special education disciplinary policies and procedural regulations were created and enforced to preserve students' rights to a free and appropriate education as a protected class, some principals ironically view these policies and regulations as morally and ethically inadequate in addressing individual student needs.

Given the complexity of today's educational system, it is imperative that school leaders be skilled in balancing the competing demands that emerge from the challenge to meet the best interests of the students as well as the best inter-ests of all students. According to Donaldson, leadership that builds commit-ment to mutual moral purposes positions school leaders to respond justly and equitably to "increasingly diverse student needs and increasingly demanding societal needs . . . as agents of a 'free, appropriate education' for every American child" (pp. 49–50). Building such a commitment in the face of "pluralistic pres-sures" from a wide range of constituencies is one matter (Gardner, 1990), but attending to the best interests of the student in face-to-face encounters must be the first order of the day for school administrators. Before building broad and lasting collective commitment to moral purposes, principals need to find ethi-cal satisfaction in the decisions they make, about individual students.

POSTSCRIPT

Can Whole-School Reform Reduce Discipline Problems?

Arter *(Teaching Exceptional Children,* 2007) agrees with Frick and Faircloth's principles: traditionally schools have treated behavioral and academic difficulties differently. However, student misbehavior may be a reaction to academic difficulties; the time students spend out of class for discipline causes them to fall further behind academically. Unless the cycle is broken, the spiral continues downward. The behavior becomes increasingly unacceptable.

In the full text of their article, Adelman and Taylor present an exhibit on positive behavioral interventions and support (PBIS). Like Response to Intervention (RTI), PBIS encompasses a range of interventions designed to model and support positive behavior rather than focus on punishing negative behavior. Trussell *(Intervention in Schools and Clinic,* 2008) comments that PBIS schools create environments that support both social and learning outcomes, preventing the emergence of problem behaviors.

Two key resources support educators interested in pursuing a PBIS model. The federally funded technical assistance Web site (www.pbis.org) contains extensive resources and links to state PBIS contacts. Second is a comprehensive guide to mental health and school improvement, developed by Adelman and Taylor (http://smhp.psych.ucla.edu/mhbook/mhbookintro.htm, 2008). The authors emphasize the importance of including counselors, psychologists, and school social workers in school reform to create an array of proactive practices that do not depend on a disability label for access. This vision of school reform is rare, but promising.

A driving force for this type of reform might be the reality that some students just do not thrive in traditional schools, exceeding the tolerance level of teachers and administrators (Quinn, Poirier, Fuller, Gable, & Tonelson, *Preventing School Failure,* 2006). These students often flourish in alternative learning environments, which provide a unique blend of structure, support, and flexibility.

Alternative schools have seen a dramatic increase recently, perhaps due to mismatches between today's expectations and student performance. Students with disabilities account for 12–19% of alternative school enrollment (Bullock, *Preventing School Failure,* 2006). There is no one definition of an alternative school, but Tissington *(Preventing School Failure,* 2006) identified three varieties. Type I schools focus on educational specialties, such as magnet schools; Type II schools address disciplinary issues and are sometimes seen as the last chance before expulsion; Type III alternatives are therapeutic, delivering specialized treatment for students with disabilities.

The specialized focus of alternative schools helps students become re-engaged with academics while simultaneously working with their families to improve social and emotional skills (Hughes & Adera, 2006). Although alternatives strike a balance between safe schools and keeping troubling children in school, Van Acker (*Preventing School Failure*, 2007) cautions that grouping children with behavioral issues in one place eliminates role models and could exacerbate negative behavior.

Troubling, aggressive, unacceptable behavior might begin with bullying—playground pushing, shoving, and rude language. This behavior is often overlooked. It is stressful for teachers and more difficult to address than instructional challenges. Unfortunately, without intervention, bullies can become increasingly aggressive and antisocial (Crothers & Kolbert, *Intervention in School and Clinic*, 2008).

Quinn and Poirier (in Rutherford, Quinn, & Mathur, 2004) highlight the cost of not addressing unacceptable behavior. Without intervention, delinquent behavior leads to substance abuse, school failure, and criminal activity. Prisons are expensive. Lost happiness and productivity also come with a substantial cost.

Several options to address troubling behavior exist. Doing nothing is not one of them. What will your school do to develop and support positive behavior? Are alternative schools part of these options?

ISSUE 5

Are Charter School Doors Open to Students with Disabilities?

YES: **Center for Education Reform,** from "Annual Survey of America's Charter Schools" (Center for Education Reform, July 2008)

NO: **Thomas Hehir,** from Hearing on "The All Students Achieving through Reform Act of 2009, H.R. 4330," Testimony before the House Committee on Education and Labor (February 24, 2010)

ISSUE SUMMARY

YES: The Center for Education Reform (CER) advocates for school change, emphasizing charter schools. Through gathering and disseminating information on charters, CER shares promising instructional options. The 2008 Annual Survey illustrates how charters successfully educate a range of students, including those who might be eligible for special education.

NO: Thomas Hehir, prominent educational policy maker, agrees that charter schools can offer desirable options. Testifying before Congress, Hehir expresses his strong concern that the doors of charter schools are often closed to students with disabilities. He cautions that these closed doors might constitute a denial of civil rights.

School choice, a major component of education reform, offers parents alternatives to their neighborhood school. States determine the breadth of choice available. Intradistrict options range from open-enrollment programs to magnet schools focusing on thematic education. Depending on state law, charter schools may be considered part of a school district or a distinct district unto themselves. A few states prohibit the existence of charters.

States determine the regulations governing charter schools, which must be approved by an authorizer to gain existence. Proposers present a charter that contains a mission statement, performance goals, and accountability procedures. States may designate local school districts to review, approve, and monitor charter schools or delegate this responsibility to private agencies. The National Association of Charter School Authorizers (www.qualitycharters.org) supports and represents member agencies.

Charter schools are funded by direct transfers of funds from public schools. When a child moves from a public school to a charter, a certain amount of money, intended to cover per pupil operating costs, is transferred from the public school to the charter.

States may also establish voucher programs as another element of school choice. In these, parents can receive an amount of money (a voucher) to use across district lines to enroll in their chosen program, even in a private (including religious) school. Vouchers are sometimes funded by tax credits to businesses.

Charter and private schools are exempt from many of the rules that structure (some say bind) public schools. Charters have the latitude to create unique and innovative curricula. They do not need to hire licensed teachers. Union contracts are rare, although some are beginning to appear. This range of flexibility is intended to create more desirable alternatives for all children than those found in bureaucracy-laden neighborhood public schools.

School choice is intended to change public schools. The possibilities offered through charter schools and vouchers are meant to be competition for scarce funding dollars, motivating public schools to move beyond their traditions.

Education Secretary Arne Duncan likes charter schools because they "think differently" (Duncan, 2010). Signaling the administration's belief that charters make a significant contribution to student learning, criteria for receiving Race to the Top funds included a requirement that states must encourage and support charters, along with other innovative school programs. Additionally, applicants must have provided assurance that low-performing schools might be turned over to a charter-management organization.

Although free from many regulations, privately funded and charter schools must abide by federal laws ensuring equal educational opportunities for students with disabilities. While these regulations prohibit discrimination through the Americans with Disabilities Act, many of IDEA's specific protections are not always available. Charters typically enroll a lower percentage of children with disabilities (CREDO, 2010). Lively discussions have emerged about whether students with disabilities have equal opportunity in the world of school choice.

As you read the following selections, consider the options open to students with disabilities and their parents. Does school choice offer the promise of better education, regardless of setting? Are charter schools providing opportunities to children without the burden of legislative labels? Do children with disabilities have a fair chance to open the same doors as their peers without disabilities?

Annual Survey of America's Charter Schools

Introduction

Great public schools are made, not born.

Great public schools offer the public a wide variety of programs, approaches and learning opportunities.

Great public schools are large enough to have variety, but small enough to create the kind of community culture that has been linked to successful education.

Great public schools work hard to serve those who are most in need, and give no excuses for reasons they cannot.

Great public schools can make decisions on their own about fundamental operational issues; how and when the school day and school year are organized; the skills, responsibilities and pay of teachers; the degree to which all staff participate in activities; and how parents can contribute best to the education of their offspring.

Great public schools are fiscally accountable and their operations are transparent to the public.

Great public schools are not easy to make, but they are increasingly available to children in all states, thanks to the introduction of the charter school idea.

By definition, charter schools are great public schools. Some are already there, some are still working at it, and occasionally, some miss the mark altogether. Like any relatively new innovation, however, the kinks are part of the experience that can make all aspects of schooling better. Mistakes are good to learn from if discovered quickly and corrected.

And that is perhaps the most salient reason that charter schools now serve students in larger percentages than any other single reform of public education to date. This great public education innovation is delivering on the promise of what makes a great public school.

The data reviewed in this year's *Annual Survey of America's Charter Schools,* by the Center for Education Reform, tells that story clearly. The unique results of this survey should be educational for the uninitiated, solace for the skeptics, and fodder for the fans.

See for yourself, and tell us if you agree—or not.

From *America's Charter Schools,* July 2008, pp. 2–6. Copyright © 2008 by The Center for Education Reform, Washington, DC. Reprinted by permission. www.edreform.com

Summary of Key Findings

This survey was sent out to approximately 4,100 schools, with a 20 percent response rate, and presents an intense view into the context for and environment surrounding the operation of the nation's charter schools. The conclusions we draw from the data are consistent with a variety of research and other statistical exercises, which are normally done with a smaller subset. This data provides an overall look at the key factors that influence charter school operations.

The survey is broken out into four sections, designed to get a glimpse into the overall management and environment of charter schools across the country. The four sections detailed in this analysis are Size and Scope, Demographics, Operations and Management. There is a brief introductory summary of each section, followed by an in-depth analysis using statistics and information taken from the charter schools' responses.

This report gives the most comprehensive look to date at the charter school environment. Key findings include:

- States with multiple authorizers create the highest quality and quantity of charter schools.
- Charter schools have grown at a rapid pace over the last ten years, but state caps and moratoriums on new schools are now impeding the necessary growth.
- Even though they are public schools and should receive the same amount of federal, state and local funds, charter schools receive nearly 40 percent less funding than other public schools.
- Despite receiving less money, charter schools are able to offer longer school days, longer school years, and innovative curricula not available in conventional public schools.
- Contrary to what charter school opponents have reported for years, charter schools do serve a majority of at-risk, minority and poor students.
- States with strong charter laws give charter schools freedom and autonomy to manage their own operations. Eighty-five percent of respondents do not participate in a union or collective bargaining unit, and charters are moving towards performance incentives and merit-based pay.

Size and Scope

Steady Growth
In the 2007-08 school year, there were 4,128 charter schools serving over 1.24 million students in 40 states and Washington, D.C. Since the mid-1990s charter schools have experienced double-digit annual growth. This year, however, charter growth dipped by a few percentage points, to nine percent, because of artificial constraints placed on the market in the form of charter school caps and moratoriums on new schools.

Meeting Parent Demands for Smaller Schools
Charter schools tend to be smaller in size, enrolling on average 348 students, nearly 35 percent less than conventional public schools. According to the National Center for Education Statistics, in 2005-06, the average number of

students per public school was 521. Studies have shown that smaller schools can be advantageous for learning, creating an intimate environment to better serve the individual needs of students.

As the number of charter schools across the country continues to grow at a rapid pace, the interest in these innovative schools continues to rise. Fifty-nine percent of schools that responded to the survey said they have significant waiting lists, averaging 198 students in length. That means that over the last year, the average size of a waiting list has increased by 33 percent due to the massive demand for charter schools in the face of slower growth.

The Importance of Multiple Authorizers

As of this survey, 17 states have authorizers other than local school boards that have the ability to approve and manage charter schools. (Georgia added an independent authorizer, the Georgia Charter Schools Commission in spring 2008; it will be operational in the fall). An additional eight states have strong binding appeals processes that allow applicants an open and objective avenue to seek a charter if it initially is denied by an authorizer.

States with multiple chartering authorities have almost four times more charter schools than states that only allow local school board approval. Local boards are also more likely to grant charters when state laws permit multiple authorizers. About 80 percent of the nation's charter schools are in states with multiple authorizers or a strong appeals process. These states are also home to the highest quality charter schools.

Demographics

Reaching Children Most in Need

It has been suggested by some researchers in their analysis of government data that charter schools serve fewer disadvantaged children than conventional public schools in comparable neighborhoods. Using the free and reduced lunch program to inform their demographic analysis, critics have suggested that charter school achievement is lower than that of similar public schools because charter scores must be adjusted for a lower poverty rate. According to the CER survey, 54 percent of all charter school students qualify for free and reduced lunch; however, 38 percent of charters do not participate in these programs for a variety of administrative, financial and political reasons, and not because their students do not qualify.

Therefore, the prime indicator used by statisticians to determine poverty and compare achievement of like students is flawed. The Center for Education Reform offers evidence that puts to rest the notion that charter students are less poor—and therefore achieving less—than students in conventional public schools. As shown in the achievement statistics at the end of this report, despite being poorer, these students are achieving at a higher level.

Increasing Educational Opportunities for Underserved Students

It is a recycled myth that charter schools drain only the best students from the local school district. Charter schools are public schools and cannot select their students based on academic performance. According to the data, they teach students who are largely underserved in the conventional public school environment. The majority of charter school students are minority (52 percent), at-risk (50 percent), or low-income (54 percent).

Charter schools are doing an especially good job of targeting services to students at both ends of the instructional spectrum who are being failed by a "one-size-fits-all" education system: teen parents, special education students, English language learners, and gifted and talented students. Conventional public schools often do not provide the individualized attention and tailored curricula that these students need to ensure their success.

Operations

Academic Accountability

Charter school students are required to take the same state standardized tests as conventional public school students. Eighty-six percent of survey respondents report administering some type of standardized test, most often a state test as well as another academic assessment. Schools where additional testing is not mandatory are often schools that provide alternative learning programs with non-traditional assessments for special populations such as students who have dropped out of school, students with severe disabilities, and students of pre-school age.

Providing Innovative, Quality Choices

Charter schools provide for innovative curricula and options, in response to the demand for more focused curricula that meet the needs of each school's student population. Of the survey respondents, 79 percent said their school has a particular theme or focus. Some schools focus on specific disciplines such as math, science or the arts, others use well-known methods like Core Knowledge or Montessori, and many charters focus on students' future plans to attend college or start a career.

One of the most important, yet simple, values provided by charter schools is increased instructional time. It is rare for a conventional public school student to attend school for more 180 days a year or longer than six and a half hours a day. A majority of charter survey respondents have extended the school day, the school year, or a combination of both.

Management

Doing More with Less

Charter schools receive fewer dollars and spend less than conventional schools. Among reporting charter schools, the average amount of per-pupil funding they received was $6,585, and the average cost per pupil was $7,625. According to a 2008 study by the U.S. Census, conventional public schools received $10,771 per pupil and spent $9,138 per pupil. Nationwide, charter schools, which are public schools and entitled to the same funding, are only receiving 60 percent of what conventional public schools receive. This inequity forces charters to spend their valuable time and resources looking for outside additional funding sources.

Maximizing Resources

Unlike conventional district schools, charter schools generally do not receive funding to cover the cost of securing and maintaining a facility. Of charter schools that responded, only 25 percent receive some funding specifically targeted towards facilities. Charter schools improvise by converting non-traditional school spaces such as retail facilities, former churches, and warehouses into classrooms, cafeterias, auditoriums and gym space. Sixty-five percent of survey respondents rent their school facility, and are spending a significant portion of their already stretched budgets on rental and maintenance costs.

An effective balance between teachers and administrators is key to ensuring schools meet their primary responsibility, to educate children. Charter schools generally maintain high ratios of teachers to administrative personnel, averaging 20 full-time teachers to four full-time noninstructional staff.

Teachers Have More Independence

In certain locales, collective bargaining agreements nullify the freedoms that define most charter schools. In order to offer novel approaches to teaching and deliver results, charter schools need the autonomy to manage their principals, administrators, and teachers. Eighty-five percent of the schools that responded to our survey said their teachers do not participate in a union or collective bargaining unit. Many that do participate are required to do so by weak state charter laws.

Uniform pay guidelines that follow local or state pay levels at least on a minimum level represent the majority of teacher compensation in our survey. We believe this occurs because district rules and regulations stifle charter school autonomy in management and personnel practices. Charters also must remain competitive in the market to attract the best teachers. However, once one begins teaching in a charter school, performance-based pay, contracts based on skills, and other pay incentives, which take considerable work and innovation to develop, are not uncommon in the charter school world. Thirty percent of respondents also said that some of their teachers are certified through alternative programs, which allow charter schools greater flexibility in hiring teachers with specific skills in subjects.

Thomas Hehir  **NO**

Hearing on "The All Students Achieving through Reform Act of 2009, H.R. 4330

Introduction

My name is Thomas Hehir. I am a Professor of Practice at the Harvard Graduate School of Education where I teach courses on educating students with disabilities and federal education policy. I also work as a consultant in the area of special education primarily with large city school districts. My clients have included New York City, Los Angeles, San Diego, and Baltimore among others. I have spent my entire career in the field of special education as a classroom teacher, local administrator in both Boston and Chicago, and as a university professor. I also served as Director of the Office of Special Education Programs for the U.S. Department of Education during the first six years of the Clinton Administration.

In relationship to today's hearings I do not purport to be an expert on all aspects of charter schools. My expertise is primarily in special education. My knowledge of charter schools is based on work I have done in San Diego and Los Angeles assisting these districts to improve their programs for students with disabilities. I have also supervised two doctoral students who have conducted research on the participation of students with disabilities in charters in Massachusetts and New Orleans, reviewed the literature in this area in preparation for teaching my courses. Further I have consulted with faculty colleagues who have done research on charters, and consulted with many of my former students who run charters. I have done research in three charter-like "pilot schools" in Boston that have enrolled a diverse population of students with disabilities that are outperforming their urban counterparts. I have also had the opportunity to speak with numerous parents of children with disabilities who have enrolled their children in charters or have considered the option.

I would like to state from the onset that I am a proponent of charter schools. I believe that parents, particularly those who reside in urban and low-income areas, should have choice within the public system. The need for choice is even greater for families of students with disabilities given the huge variability between schools in implementing the *Individuals with Disabilities Education Act* (IDEA).

From U.S. House of Representatives, H.R. 4330, February 24, 2010.

The Opportunity Charters Present for Special Populations

Charters provide choice to all parents. For parents of students with disabilities, choice is highly valued due to the high degree of variability that exists across public schools in educating their children. Though we have made great strides in improving educational offerings for students with disabilities, noncompliance with IDEA continues in many schools. Affluent parents sometimes move to get their children into schools that welcome their children and provide them with a high-quality education. I have done work with a high school in the Boston suburbs that does a great job including students with disabilities. I have met a number of parents who moved to this community simply to allow their children to attend this school. Poor and middle-class parents do not have that option. Charters can and in some cases do provide this option.

Some charter schools have even been created by activists who are seeking a more inclusive and effective option for children with disabilities. The Mary Lyons School, Boston Arts Academy pilot schools, Democracy Prep Charter in Harlem, and Chime Charter in Los Angeles are examples of schools that from their onset have sought to be inclusive of a diverse population of students with disabilities.

There is also evidence that charters may serve students with disabilities in more inclusive settings than traditional public schools. Chris Wilkens, a doctoral student at Harvard, found that urban charters in Massachusetts were more likely to serve similar students with disabilities in inclusive settings than traditional urban public schools. His research also found that overplacement of African American students in special education was far less of a problem in charters than traditional urban public schools.

Many charters focus intently on individualization that is a central tenet of IDEA. Others such as the KIPP schools focus on explicit direct instruction needed by many students with disabilities and other students who may struggle in school. These approaches may account for some of the lower levels of special education identification in charter schools. To the extent that these practices prevent inappropriate referrals to special education, they should be encouraged.

A similar dynamic exists for English language learners and other special populations. Like students with disabilities, English language learners participate in charters in much smaller numbers than they exist in the population at large. However, some advocates for English language learners have seized upon the opportunity provided by charters to promote better education for these children. For instance, the National Council of La Raza has supported the establishment of over 50 charters in their efforts to expand educational opportunity for this population.

The Problem of Charters and Special Populations

Research on the participation of special populations and charters demonstrates that in most places these students are underrepresented. For instance in the area of disability, charters generally serve fewer children with disabilities than traditional public schools. When one looks at students with more significant or complicated disabilities in general, charters serve far fewer students and in many instances none at all. Research conducted in a number of major cities bears this out. In San Diego, close to 10% of all students now attend charter schools. Though the enrollment of students with disabilities in traditional public schools overall approaches 12%, the average enrollment of students with disabilities in non-conversion (from scratch) charter schools during the 2005–2006 school year was 5.8% (Hehir & Mosqueda, 2008). With respect to students requiring extensive special education services, the imbalance is even more dismal. For example, during the 2005-06 school years, there were only three children with mental retardation in all San Diego non-conversion charter schools *combined*; traditional schools across the district, meanwhile, educated almost one thousand students with mental retardation. That same year, non-conversion charter schools in San Diego educated just two students with autism.

The picture is quite similar in Los Angeles. The enrollment of students in charter schools throughout the city is large (approximately 8%). The enroll-ment of students with disabilities across the district averages over 11%, while the enrollment of students with disabilities in independent charter schools averages fewer than 7% (Independent Monitors Office, 2009). As in San Diego, the distribution of disability types within independent Los Angeles charter schools is skewed; for students with disabilities requiring extensive special education services, the likelihood they will be enrolled in independent charter schools is one-fourth that of traditional public schools.

Similar data emerges for charters serving urban areas in Massachusetts. For the 2006–07 school years, the percentage of enrolled students with disabil-ities in traditional urban schools was 19.9%, while the percentage of enrolled students with disabilities enrolled in urban charter schools was significantly lower, 10.8%. As is the case in Los Angeles and San Diego, significantly fewer students were enrolled in all urban charter schools who had more substantial needs such as mental retardation, emotional disturbance, and autism. Several cities' charter schools enrolled none of these students.

The underenrollment of English language learners in charters mirrors that of students with disabilities in many places. In Boston where approximately 20% of students are English language learners, only one charter school enrolled more than 4%. In NYC a similar pattern emerges where the district enrollment is 15% English language learners and the charters serve approximately 4%.

As for disadvantaged students, there is some evidence that charters in some places may enroll a more advantaged population. However, the vast majority of charters are enrolling large number of disadvantaged students.

Why Is Underrepresentation a Problem?

The underrepresentation of special populations in charter schools is a problem on a number of levels:

   a. First low participation rates raise potential civil rights concerns. Stu-dents with disabilities, English language learners and homeless stu-dents have rights as American citizens both granted to them by the Constitution and within various federal education laws. Anecdotal information suggests that some parents are discouraged from applying to charter schools and that some charter schools "send back" students with complicated needs to traditional public schools. America has opened doors to previously excluded groups through the Civil Rights Act, the IDEA and The Elementary and Secondary Education Act. The federal government needs to assure that discrimination is not occurring within the charter sector.

b. The "experiment" that charters represent is compromised when charters do not serve the same populations as traditional public schools. One of the primary justifications for allowing charters to exist is to demonstrate better approaches for educating students for whom the current education system has failed. If they fail to serve representative populations, their claims to being exemplary are significantly compromised.

c. The failure of charters to enroll representative populations of students from special populations can disadvantage traditional public schools financially. As the San Diego school system demonstrates, the financial responsibility for educating students with disabilities rests with the traditional public schools. Yet, the charters receive roughly the same amount of money per-capita. It should be noted the per-capita cost in most school districts includes the cost of educating special populations and that this cost is higher per pupil. For instance, the cost of providing language supports to English language learners or transportation to homeless students increases the financial burden on school districts. In the case of students with disabilities, this cost can be much higher. The population least represented in charters, students with low incidence and more complex disabilities, are the most expensive for schools to educate.

d. There is financial incentive for charters not to educate students for whom additional costly services may be necessary. Under the current system, many charters receive the same amount of money per student whether they educate students with more complex needs or not. Many charters, like many traditional public schools, encumber most of their money on the first day of school by hiring staff. When an unforeseen need arises during the year, they may not have the resources to address that need. In traditional public schools the central office may step in with needed support or the anticipated needs of students from special populations are budgeted upfront. Some charters have established similar mechanisms but many have not. Therefore, when a child with additional needs becomes apparent the charter may not have the resources to meet this need. I am aware of charters that have not even budgeted for a single special education teacher upfront.

Policy Considerations

In my opinion, it is time for policy makers to directly address the issue of imbalanced enrollment of students from special populations in charter schools. Though some may have argued in the past that charter schools needed time to get established, and to have flexibility to experiment, they are now a well-established segment of our education system. The charter choice should be available to all students and parents. Toward that end I believe the federal government has a role in assuring equity and promoting more effective public school choice for parents of children from special populations. The following recommendations are offered:

> (1) **The federal government should require states to proactively address issues of access involving special populations as a condition for receiving federal funds.**

The US Department of Education historically has played a crucial role in promoting equity in education in the areas of racial desegregation, gender equity and disability access among others. The lack of access for special populations to some charters raises serious equity and civil rights concerns. At a minimum, states should be required to submit their authorizing regulations to their Departments of Education for approval. States should further be required to investigate charters that enroll significantly fewer students from special populations than their surrounding area contains. It is important to emphasize here that states should be allowed flexibility as there should not be an expectation that charters always mirror the population of the surrounding area. Some charters may have lower special education counts simply because they have been successful in eliminating inappropriate referrals to special education. Others may have been established to serve English language learners. These innovations should not be discouraged. The point here is that the state needs to reasonably assure the federal government that special populations' access to charters is not impeded.

States should also be required to assist charter operators in meeting their obligations to provide access to special populations. The vast majority of charter operators I have met want to address the needs of all students. Again, this may take many forms and states should be allowed a good deal of flexibility in meeting this requirement.

> (2) **The federal government should establish a federal technical assistance center focusing on the needs of students from special populations in charter schools.**

This center would primarily serve the states in meeting their obligations detailed above. Such a center could provide states with model authorizing documents as well as information about successful practices in charters serving special populations. This model has worked very effectively in IDEA and the Elementary and Secondary Education Act as a vehicle to promote better practices in the schools.

(3) Fund research on serving special populations in charter schools.

Though I am sure Congress has gotten advice from many quarters on how to address these issues, there is no consensus on the range or extent of the problems concerning special populations and charter schools. I believe this issue is important enough to warrant a National Research Council study. Such a study would provide an objective picture of the current state of charters and special populations and identify promising practices. Congress should also fund a research program to investigate ways in which charters can better serve special populations.

Final Reflections

This past year I assisted my cousin in choosing an elementary school in Boston for her four-year-old twin boys. Having worked in the Boston system from 1977 to 1987, I was pleasantly surprised at how much the system had improved. My cousin is currently considering two public charters and two traditional public schools for the boys. All four are strong choices. This contrasts to the system I left where parents were often given few or no choices and were forced to send their children to underperforming schools. I believe Boston is a far better system for a number of reasons but one is parental choice. Boston outperforms most major cities on the National Assessment of Educational Progress as does the state of Massachusetts. Parental choice is deeply embedded in the state as well. The challenge facing Massachusetts as well as Congress is how we make this choice real for all parents.

Finally, in doing research for this testimony I relied on an old and tested method; Facebook. I posted a request for assistance to my former students many of whom work in charters. They responded well to their old professor. One related that she was working as a psychologist in a major city with troubled youth many of whom are in the foster care system. Many of her students have opted for charters in lieu of large impersonal high schools that had utterly failed them. She found that charters had been particularly effective in serving GLBT youth who felt unsafe in traditional high schools. Another student related how her sister had placed her son in a local charter school and how happy she was that she was not forced to send him to an underperforming elementary school. However, she has another child with disabilities for whom this choice was not an option. For her disabled daughter, she had no choice and was forced to place her in the same underperforming school she avoided for her son. She has been forced to file for a due process hearing in order to get an acceptable choice for her. This will be a huge financial burden on the family. Public school choice is an incomplete option for this family.

It's time for the adults who run charters and for those who authorize them to act. The charter "experiment" has gone on long enough. Access to all must become a priority. When PL 94-142 was passed in 1975 opening up the doors of schools to thousands of previously excluded students with disabilities Congressman Miller stated, "I believe the burden of proof . . . ought to rest with the administrator or teacher who seeks for one reason or another to remove a child from a normal classroom. . . ." We need to provide that same logic to charter schools and special populations. The burden of proof should fall on government officials, charter school operators and charter advocates who need to take proactive responsibility to deal with the very real issues of access for special populations.

I hope Congress leads the way.

Thank you.

POSTSCRIPT

Are Charter School Doors Open to Students with Disabilities?

Today's 5000 charter schools owe their existence to a Minnesota law passed in 1991. Teachers and school districts create and manage some charters. Post-Katrina, the majority of New Orleans children attend charter schools, many of which are operated by the Orleans Parish School Board, which also oversees traditional schools (Weber, http://works.bepress.com, 2009). Some companies coordinate a network of schools. Green Dot (www.greendot.org) focuses its efforts on Los Angeles. KIPP (Knowledge Is Power Program: www.kipp.org) schools are found across the country.

The 2008 Charter School Survey highlights the innovative quality programs its respondents provide. Small group instruction, extended school time, and independent teachers deliver "especially good services" to what CER describes as "children most in need." After reviewing progress in all states, a subsequent CER report (*The 2009 Accountability Report,* www.edreform.com) stated their data "indicates that charter schools are outpacing their conventional public school peers."

While lauding charter schools, Secretary Duncan also expressed concern that these accomplishments are inconsistent. Recent studies by CREDO (http://credo.stanford.edu/home, 2010), a Stanford-based research organization focusing on education reform, presented data calling into question the achievements claimed by charter schools. On average, students in public and charter schools performed equally well. Referring to such findings as "a wake up call," Duncan encouraged charter schools to seek the accountability outlined in their charters.

In his testimony, Thomas Hehir also calls for accountability. Acknowledging that charters may serve students with disabilities in inclusive settings, he voices concern that their numbers are small, and include few children with severe disabilities. To ensure that students with disabilities have equal opportunity, and that charter schools are fairly evaluated, Hehir urged Congress to require equal access as a condition of receiving federal funds.

Access and achievement can be difficult to document and summarize. Averaging special education enrollment across charter schools that enroll few, and those specially designed for students with disabilities, can present distorted data (Miron, Urschel, Mathis, & Tornquist, *Schools without Diversity,* 2010). Average figures mask wide variations. Some parents reported being encouraged not to continue their application.

The Council for Exceptional Children (CEC) (www.cec.sped.org), the largest international professional organization advocating for children with disabilities, emphasizes that charters need to abide by the ADA and Section 504 so that children with disabilities have equitable access. CEC offers an additional perspective. Some children with disabilities and their parents may decide to forfeit their special education status when enrolling in a charter, believing the instructional environment worth the trade-off. When these students move on to higher education or employment, they may encounter barriers if they seek legally allowed accommodations. Since they were not considered to have a disability during school years, establishing that status might be challenging.

Do flexible charter environments provide opportunities beyond the traditional special education model? Can charters claim success without enrolling a full range of students? Can small charter schools provide the kind of specially designed instruction found in public schools? Will creative charter options create unexpected opportunities as these students become adults, or lead to unanticipated challenges?

ISSUE 6

Should Insurance Cover Treatments and Services for Autism?

YES: Autism Speaks Government Relations Department, from "Arguments in Support of Private Insurance Coverage for Autism-Related Services," www.autismspeaks.org (February 2009)

NO: Victoria C. Bunce and J.P. Wieske, from "Health Insurance Mandates in the States 2009," (The Council for Affordable Health Insurance, February 10, 2009); and "The Growing Trend Toward Mandating Autism Coverage *Issues & Answers*," The Council for Affordable Health Insurance's *Issues & Answers* (no. 152, March 27, 2009)

ISSUE SUMMARY

YES: Autism Speaks, the nation's largest autism science and advocacy organization founded by Suzanne and Bob Wright (former vice chairman of General Electric and CEO of NBC and NBC Universal), presents eight arguments in support of legislation mandating health insurance coverage of autism services.

NO: Writing for the Council for Affordable Health Insurance, an organization that promotes the affordable health care access for all Americans, Victoria C. Bunce and J.P. Wieske discuss national trends in state-mandated health care benefits for children with autism, arguing that responsibility for these costs belongs elsewhere.

How many parents can afford $30,000 to educate their child? What about $60,000 or $72,000? Each of these is an estimate of the annual cost for services to a child with autism. The numbers vary as do children with Autism Spectrum Disorders (ASDs). The more severe the autism, the more extensive the services and the higher the cost.

One child in 110 is diagnosed with autism, according to the Centers for Disease Control and Prevention (CDC). Most children are diagnosed before age 3. CDC reported a 57 percent increase between 2002 and 2006 (*Morbidity and Mortality Weekly Report,* December 2009). A number of possible explanations exist: broader interpretation of the category of autism, improved diagnostic tools, increased public awareness, and a shift to autism from other disability categories.

Children with ASDs present with significant difficulties in communication, language, and social interaction. They may also have seizures, gastrointestinal difficulties, and other medical disorders.

Parents are bombarded with alternative treatment options, some of which claim to cure autism. No single treatment has been found universally effective. There is wide agreement that early intervention is essential (Abt Associates, 2008).

Faced with managing treatment expenses long before their child is eligible for school, some parents mortgage their homes, tap into retirement savings, and/or declare bankruptcy (Foden, www.iancommunity.org, 2008). Others tackle complex bureaucracies to secure Medicaid eligibility waivers for their child (Reinke, *EP,* 2009).

Parents also turn to their health insurance. Many find their policies deny coverage of autism-related services because certain treatments are considered "experimental and unproven," and therefore not likely to be helpful (Abramson, *NPR.org,* 2007). Companies may have blanket exclusions for any child with autism: no coverage for anything related to autism, ever (Abt Associates, 2008).

Movements have arisen to force health insurance companies to change their practices. Individual families and organizations focused on autism have lobbied legislators in several states to mandate coverage. Autismcrisis.org describes itself as a grassroots organization focusing energy on identifying potential conflicts of interest between individual legislators and the health care industry.

The Abt Associates report (2008) cited here analyzed evidence submitted to the Pennsylvania legislature as it considered action on an autism mandate. Abt determined that presented evidence supported the need and effectiveness of the bill. Effective in 2009, Pennsylvania's legislation instituted an annual expenditure cap (adjustable for inflation), and no lifetime cap. Funding for medicines, tests, and therapeutic services is included.

This issue's first selection was prepared by Autism Speaks (www.autismspeaks .org), an organization dedicated to improving awareness, advocacy, and life conditions for people with autism and their families. The paper's eight arguments supporting mandated coverage by private health insurance companies have been used across the country as individual state's debate mandates.

The second selection is composed of two short reports from the Council for Affordable Health Insurance (CAHI), written by Victoria C. Bunce and J.P. Wieske. The first introduces a survey of mandates currently in place across the country, highlighting the growing popularity of autism mandates. The second expands on autism mandates. The authors caution that each new mandate leads to increased health care premiums and decreased services for everyone. CAHI argues that health insurance should cover short-term needs, not the long-term care required by children with autism.

As you read these articles, think of the lengthy national health care debates. Although the act precludes dismissing autism as a preexisting condition, not all insurance companies or policies are required to abide by this standard. What is your state's policy? What is your company's policy?

YES

Arguments in Support of Private Insurance Coverage of Autism-Related Services

Executive Summary

Autism is a complex neurobiological disorder and is the fastest growing serious developmental disability in the U.S. The Centers for Disease Control estimates that 1 in 110 children has autism. These children require extensive services from medical professionals. Early intervention is critical to gain maximum benefit from existing therapies. Most private health insurance plans do not provide coverage for Applied Behavior Analysis (ABA) and other autism-related services.

This document contains eight arguments in favor of requiring private health insurance policies to cover the diagnosis and treatment of autism spectrum disorders for individuals under the age of 21. These arguments are based on epidemiological, social, and economic studies of the children and families affected by autism and prove the significant long-term financial and public health benefits of this requirement.

We first point out that children with autism have substantial medical needs and have a difficult time accessing necessary treatments through Medicaid and private health insurance. Most insurance policies contain specific exclusions for autism. This is a hardship for many families, who are often forced to cope with delayed, inadequate, and fragmented care through the Medicaid system. Often, families must pay for costly treatments out-of-pocket or forego them.

We then review some of the many studies and reports that document the effectiveness of intensive behavioral therapies in the treatment of autism. An autism insurance mandate should specifically target coverage of Applied Behavior Analysis (ABA) and other structured behavioral therapies, which are the most effective forms of treatment and have the best outcomes, both in human costs and in long-term economic benefits.

We then comment on the experiences of several states with insurance reform. Their experiences show that the policy holder costs resulting from the passage of legislation requiring comprehensive autism services have been relatively small.

From www.autismspeaks.org, report by Autism Speaks Government Relations Department, February 2009, pp. 4–9, 11–13, 15–20. Copyright © 2009 by Autism Speaks. Reprinted by permission.

Finally, we point out that the mandate offers hope that children with autism will need less intensive care in the future. They will, in short, have a better chance at a normal life. . . .

What Is Autism?

Autism is a complex neurobiological disorder that typically lasts throughout a person's lifetime. It is part of a group of disorders known as autism spectrum disorders (ASD). Today, 1 in 110 individuals is diagnosed with ASD, making it more common than pediatric cancer, diabetes, and AIDS combined. It occurs in all racial, ethnic, and social groups and is four times more likely to strike boys than girls. Autism impairs a person's ability to communicate and relate to others. It is also associated with rigid routines and repetitive behaviors, such as obsessively arranging objects or following very specific routines. Symptoms can range from very mild to quite severe.

Argument 1: **Mandated private health insurance coverage will provide services that are desperately needed by children with autism, who have greater health care needs than children without autism.**

Children with autism have a tremendous need for services from trained medical professionals. These children are at risk for a range of other medical conditions, including behavioral or conduct problems, attention-deficit disorder or attention-deficit/hyperactivity disorder, stuttering, stammering, and other speech problems, depression and anxiety problems, bone, joint, or muscle problems, ear infections, hearing and vision problems, allergies (especially food allergies), and frequent and severe headaches. These problems greatly affect their overall health and their need for and use of health care services.

A . . . study by James G. Guerney and others highlights the broad medical needs of children with autism. Using data from the National Survey of Children's Health, Guerney showed that relative to children without autism, children with autism require more services for physical, occupational, and speech therapy. Children with autism are also much more likely to have poor health, to require medically necessary care for behavioral problems, and to be using medications. [P]arents of children with autism were more likely to report the presence of a variety of concurrent medical conditions and the need for more visits to a range of medical service providers than parents of children without autism.

This reform of private health insurance coverage will address the broad medical needs of children with autism. It will ensure that these children will receive the full range of therapies necessary to ameliorate their condition.

Argument 2: **Treatments for autism are difficult to access, often inadequate, and frequently delayed. Denied coverage by private group health insurance companies, parents are often forced either to pay out-of-pocket or forego the treatments their children need.**

Children with autism face barriers in accessing early intensive behavioral treatments and other therapies. According to the Institute of Medicine, the term "access" is defined as "the timely use of personal health services to achieve the best possible health outcomes." For a child with autism, lack of access to services can be the cause of inconsistent and uncoordinated care. Children with autism often experience barriers to access with even greater frequency than children with other special health care needs. In fact, one study found that "over one-third of the children with autism were reported to have experienced an access problem with respect to specialty care from a medical doctor in the preceding 12 months." A study of the Tennessee Medicaid system, TennCare, found that for children with autism, "the rate of service use was only one tenth what should be expected based on prevalence rates." . . .

Within the Medicaid system, the amount of public money spent for services for developmental disabilities including autism is now eight times the rate of spending just a few decades ago. Medicaid accounts for 75% of all funding for services for the developmentally disabled, making it the largest single public payer of behavioral health services. Children with disabilities comprise a significant portion (15%) of all Medicaid recipients, and an even more significant portion (31%) of disabled children use the Medicaid system as their primary insurer.

Medicaid suffers from very low reimbursement rates that make it difficult for many locations to retain service providers. Moreover, services that can be accessed through the Medicaid system are often inadequate at meeting the specific needs of a child with autism. The system operates as a short-term service provider, tending to push children through treatment as quickly as possible. The success of the Applied Behavior Analysis, however, depends in part, on the amount of time the child with autism spends with the provider of the therapy.

The failings of Medicaid point to the importance of the private health care system in providing services to children with autism. But nationwide there are very few private insurance companies or other employee benefit plans that cover Applied Behavior Analysis and other behavioral therapies. Most insurance companies designate autism as a diagnostic exclusion, "meaning that any services rendered explicitly for the treatment of autism are not covered by the plan, even if those services would be covered if used to treat a different condition." . . .

Families that refuse to allow their children to suffer through the inadequate Medicaid system and are denied coverage by their private health insurance carriers often end up paying for therapies out of their own pockets. For these families, the financial burden is immense. Without the negotiating powers of an insurance company behind them, out-of-pocket prices are extremely high. Parents can often spend upwards of $50,000 per year on autism-related therapies, often being forced to wager their own futures and the futures of their non-autistic children to pay for necessary autism-related therapies. Children whose parents cannot afford to pay for behavioral and other therapies and who cannot access adequate therapies through the Medicaid system simply go without these interventions.

Argument 3: **Mandated private insurance coverage will bring effective autism services within the reach of the children who need them. The efficacy of Applied Behavior Analysis (ABA), the centerpiece of this legislative mandate's benefits, has been established repeatedly.**

Private health insurance coverage of autism services will allow children with autism to access Applied Behavior Analysis (ABA), a proven treatment for their condition. Several studies have shown that as many as 47 percent of the children that undergo early intensive behavioral therapies achieve higher education placement and increased IQ levels. A significant portion of children who receive ABA are placed into mainstream educational settings. Children who begin their treatment with minimal IQ levels end treatment with substantially higher levels of intellectual functioning. These results have been shown to last well beyond the end of treatment. As such, the effectiveness of ABA therapy has allowed many children to forego costly intensive special education in the future. . . .

Argument 4: Government and scientific organizations have endorsed Applied Behavior Analysis (ABA) and other structured behavioral therapies.
ABA is the treatment of choice for autism. Its efficacy has been recognized in a number of prominent reports, including the following:

- **The 2001 U.S. Surgeon General's Report on Mental Health,** which states, "Among the many methods available for treatment and education of people with autism, applied behavior analysis (ABA) has become widely accepted as an effective treatment. Thirty years of research demonstrated the efficacy of applied behavioral methods in reducing inappropriate behavior and in increasing communication, learning, and appropriate social behavior."
- **The New York State Department of Health** assessed interventions for children ages 0-3 with autism, and recommended that "behavioral interventions for reducing maladaptive behaviors be used for young children with autism when such behaviors interfere with the child's learning or socialization or present a hazard to the child or others."
- **The Maine Administrators of Services for Children with Disabilities** notes in their report that "There is a wealth of validated and peer-reviewed studies supporting the efficacy of ABA methods to improve and sustain socially significant behaviors in every domain, in individuals with autism. Importantly, results reported include 'meaningful' outcomes such as increased social skills, communication skills, academic performance, and overall cognitive functioning. These reflect clinically significant quality of life improvements. While studies varied as to the magnitude of gains, all have demonstrated long-term retention of gains made."
- **The National Institute of Mental Health** reports, "The basic research done by Ivar Lovaas and his colleagues at the University of California, Los Angeles, calling for an intensive, one-on-one child–teacher interaction for 40 hours a week, laid a foundation for other educators and researchers in the search for further effective early interventions to help those with ASD attain their potential. The goal of behavioral management is to reinforce desirable behaviors and reduce undesirable ones."
- **The National Institute of Child Health and Human Development** lists Applied Behavior Analysis among the recommended treatment methods for Autism Spectrum Disorders.

- **The National Research Council's** 2001 report on Educating Children with Autism acknowledged, "There is now a large body of empirical support for more contemporary behavioral approaches using naturalistic teaching methods that demonstrate efficacy for teaching not only speech and language, but also communication."
- **The Association for Science in Autism Treatment** recommends ABA-based therapies, stating, "ABA is an effective intervention for many individuals with autism spectrum disorders."

Argument 5: **To combat the difficulty many families face in accessing Applied Behavior Analysis (ABA) and other structured behavioral treatments through public insurance, . . . states have passed autism insurance mandates that specifically require private insurance companies to provide coverage of these therapies, thus creating a public–private partnership for the provision of care.**

While there are several states that have passed autism-specific private insurance mandates, very few states specifically mandate coverage for ABA and other structured behavioral therapy programs. Without coverage of these crucial, medically necessary, evidence-based therapies, the effectiveness of most mandates is severely diminished. . . .

Argument 6: **The costs of the proposed benefit are small and will have very little impact on the cost of health insurance premiums for the individual consumer.**

. . . The Council for Affordable Health Insurance, a research and advocacy association of insurance carriers, released its annual report on state health insurance mandates, *Health Insurance Mandates in the States 2007*. The report defined a mandate as "a requirement that an insurance company or health plan cover (or offer coverage for) common—but sometimes not so common—health care providers, benefits and patient populations." Using this definition, the report identified legislative mandates for autism benefits in ten states: Colorado, Delaware, Georgia, Iowa, Indiana . . . , Kentucky, Maryland, New Jersey, New York, and Tennessee. The report assessed the incremental cost of state-mandated benefits for autism in these ten states *as less than one percent.*

The Council's modest estimate of incremental premium costs is consistent with state government estimates across the country. Prior to enactment of Indiana's sweeping legislation, the Indiana Legislative Services Agency estimated additional premium costs as ranging from $.44 per contract per month to $1.67 per contract per month. In vetoing Ryan's Law in South Carolina, Governor Mark Sanford estimated that the bill, with its $50,000 maximum yearly benefit for behavioral therapy, would add $48 annually to insurance policies. And in Wisconsin, where . . . Assembly Bill 417 would provide the same broad coverage Indiana's statute mandates, the Department of Administration estimates policy increments of between $3.45 and $4.10 per month—about the same as Governor Sanford's estimate for Ryan's Law.

The cost estimates for Indiana, South Carolina, and Wisconsin—all states whose legislation allows a maximum benefit that can be considered high—suggest that an average autism insurance coverage mandate will cost approximately $50 annually per policy holder. For only a modest effect on premium cost, this insurance reform holds the promise of significantly improving the lives of thousands of children.

Argument 7: By improving outcomes for children with autism, mandated private insurance coverage will decrease the lifetime costs of treating and providing services and will actually result in an overall cost savings in the long run.

A . . . study by John W. Jacobson and others titled, *Cost-Benefit Estimates for Early Intensive Behavioral Intervention for Young Children with Autism—General Model and Single State Case,* examined the cost/benefit relationship of early intensive behavioral intervention treatment at varying levels of treatment success. The study used estimates of costs for early intensive behavioral interventions (EIBI) from childhood (age three) through adulthood (age 55) based on prices in the Commonwealth of Pennsylvania and compared these costs with the expected amount of income the child would earn later in life to arrive at an estimated cost savings.

With a success rate of 47 percent for early intensive behavioral intervention therapy (as determined by Lovaas), Jacobson's study found that cost savings per child served are estimated to be from $2,439,710 to $2,816,535 to age 55.

The study also accounts for the initial investment in early intervention by concluding that, with an initial annual cost of $32,820, the total cost-benefit savings of EIBI services per child with autism or PDD for ages 3–55 years average from $1,686,061 to $2,816,535 with inflation.

According to a 2005 Government Accounting Office (GAO) report, "the average per pupil expenditure for educating a child with autism was more than $18,000 in the 1999–2000 school year. This amount was almost three times the average per pupil expenditure of educating a child who does not receive any special education services." With this insurance reform in place, more children would be able to access the early intervention services they need. That investment will, in the long run pay benefits, both economic and social, to the greater population.

Argument 8: Without passage of legislation requiring private health insurance coverage for autism, the costs associated with autism will continue not only to affect families, but will have far-reaching social effects as well.

The cost of autism is borne by everyone. Michael L. Ganz's study of the societal costs of autism, *The Lifetime Distribution of the Incremental Societal Costs of Autism,* examined how the large financial burdens of autism affect not only families with an autistic child but society in general.

Ganz broke down the costs associated with autism into two distinct categories, direct costs and indirect costs. Direct costs include direct medical costs, such as physician, outpatient, clinic services, dental care, prescription medications, complementary and alternative therapies, behavioral therapies, hospital and emergency services, allied health, equipment and supplies, home health, and medically related travel, as well as direct nonmedical costs, such as child care, adult care, respite and family care, home and care modification, special education, and supported employment. Indirect costs include productivity losses for people with autism (calculated by combining standard average work-life expectancies for all men and women with average income and benefits and estimated age- and sex-specific labor force participation rates).

According to Ganz's study, direct medical costs reach their maximum during the first five years of life, averaging around $35,000. As the child ages, direct medical costs begin to decline substantially and continue to decline through the end of life to around $1,000. Ganz goes on to report, "The large direct medical costs early in life are driven primarily by behavioral therapies that cost around $32,000 during the first 5-year age group and decline from about $4,000 in the 8- to 12-year age group to around $1,250 for the 18- to 22-year age group."

In terms of direct medical costs "the typical American spends about $317,000 over his or her lifetime in direct medical costs, incurring 60% of those costs after the age of 65 years. In contrast, people with autism incur about $306,000 in incremental direct medical costs, which suggests that people with autism spend twice as much as the typical American over their lifetimes and spend 60% of those incremental direct medical costs after age 21 years."

The study also found the indirect costs of autism to be significant as well. While in the first 22 years of life, indirect costs are mostly associated with lost productivity for the parents of a child with autism, the costs from age 23 on are associated with lost productivity of the actual individual with autism. . . . The impact of this lost productivity can have enormous ramifications for the tax base of an entire society and the future of the older generation as their children with autism transition into adult care.

Ganz posited that direct medical costs "combined with very limited to non-existent income for their adult children with autism combined with potentially lower levels of savings because of decreased income and benefits while employed, may create a large financial burden affecting not only those families but potentially society in general."

Without the help of private insurance coverage, families affected by autism may never be able to pull their heads above water and provide their children with the medically necessary, evidence-based treatments that they need. It is to the advantage of these families, to the 1 in 150 children affected by autism, and to all of society that private health insurance coverage is provided for these services.

Conclusion

A legislative mandate for coverage of autism asks private insurance companies to make a limited, but significant, contribution to help pay for medically necessary, evidence-based treatments that have been established to be of the greatest impact in fighting this terrible disorder.

Unbelievably, it is not uncommon for insurance carriers to have line-item exclusions for treatment of individuals diagnosed with autism. Across the nation, children with autism are routinely denied insurance benefits for treatment of their disorder. We believe that private insurance companies must contribute their fair share and partner in the financial burdens with these families.

With every new child diagnosed with autism costing an estimated $3 million over his or her lifetime, the current practices are both unfair and not cost effective in the long run for states and their citizens. Autism Speaks is confident that many more state governments will recognize the significant long-term cost benefits found in these legislative measures, will do what is right for their constituents, and will pass legislation requiring private health insurance coverage of autism services.

Victoria C. Bunce
and J.P. Wieske

 **NO**

Health Insurance Mandates in the States 2009

A health insurance "mandate" is a requirement that an insurance company or health plan cover (or offer coverage for) common—but sometimes not so common—health care providers, benefits and patient populations. They include:

- Providers such as chiropractors and podiatrists, but also social workers and massage therapists;
- Benefits such as mammograms, well-child care and even drug and alcohol abuse treatment, but also acupuncture and hair prostheses (wigs); and
- Populations such as adopted and non-custodial children.

For almost every health care product or service, there is someone who wants insurance to cover it so that those who sell the products and services get more business and those who use the products and services don't have to pay out of pocket for them.

The Impact of Mandates. While mandates make health insurance more comprehensive, they also make it more expensive because mandates require insurers to pay for care consumers previously funded out of their own pockets. We estimate that mandated benefits currently increase the cost of basic health coverage from a little less than 20% to perhaps 50%, depending on the number of mandates, the benefit design and the cost of the initial premium. Mandating benefits is like saying to someone in the market for a new car, if you can't afford a Cadillac loaded with options, you have to walk. Having that Cadillac would be nice, as would having a health insurance policy that covers everything one might want. But drivers with less money can find many other affordable car options; whereas when the price of health insurance soars, few other options exist.

Why Is the Number of Mandates Growing? Elected representatives find it difficult to oppose any legislation that promises enhanced care to potentially motivated voters. The sponsors of mandates know this fact of political life. As

From *Health Insurance Mandates in the States* by Victoria Craig Bunce and J.P. Wieske (CAHI, 2008). From *Issues & Answers* by Victoria Craig Bunce and J.P. Wieske, no. 152, March 2009, pp. 1–2. Both Copyright © 2008, 2009 by Council for Affordable Health Insurance (CAHI). Reprinted by permission. www.cahi.org

a result, government interference in and control of the health care system is steadily increasing. So too is the cost of health insurance.

By the late 1960s, state legislatures had passed only a handful of mandated benefits; today, the Council for Affordable Health Insurance (CAHI) has identified **2,133** mandated benefits and providers. And more are on their way.

How do state legislators justify their actions? One way is to deny a mandate is a mandate. For example, legislators may claim that requiring health insurance to cover a type of provider—such as a chiropractor, podiatrist, midwife or naturopath—is not a mandate because they aren't requiring insurance to pay for a particular therapy. But that's a distinction without a difference; if insurance is required to cover the provider, it must pay for the service provided. . .

How Is the Research Compiled?   Since 1992, the Council for Affordable Health Insurance staff has tracked the introduction and passage of health insurance mandates in every state, but not until 2004 did we make this information available to the public. To corroborate our own findings, we survey every department of insurance and talk with other industry experts.

The question is sometimes raised why our mandate count may differ from other groups that identify state mandates. We do not currently differentiate between the individual and small group markets, especially since many states are blurring that traditional distinction by, for example, allowing "groups of one" (i.e., one person is considered a group) to be classified as a small group under federal law. Also, we do not differentiate between a benefit that is mandated and one that must only be offered. Our actuaries advise us that the cost to provide that policy is the same: If the mandate is offered, it is essentially a mandated benefit because only those interested in the mandate will take advantage of it. In addition, states sometimes exempt either the individual or small group markets from specific mandates, or may only apply that mandate to insurance companies that are domiciled in the state (e.g., a Blue Cross policy). Finally, states may pass a mandate in one legislative session only to come back in a later session and either expand or reduce the original bill's scope. That propensity to revise mandate legislation in subsequent years is one of the reasons why we don't include information on when the mandate originally passed.

Mandates and Standard Coverage.   Just because we list something as a mandate doesn't necessarily mean it should be excluded from a standard health insurance policy. Many mandates listed here should be and often are included in comprehensive coverage. The purpose . . . is to tabulate the number of benefits mandated by the states and assess their impact on the cost of insurance—not to make judgments about which mandates should or should not be included in a health insurance policy.

Assessing the Cost of Mandates. . . . . CAHI's independent Actuarial Working Group on State Mandated Benefits analyzed company data and their experience and provided cost-range estimates—less than 1%, 1–3%, 3–5% and

5–10%—if the mandate were added to a policy that did not include the coverage. These estimates are based on real health insurance policies and are not based on theory or modeling. However, mandate legislation differs from bill to bill and from state to state. For example, one state may require insurance to cover a limited number of chiropractor visits per year, while another state may require chiropractors to be covered equally with medical doctors. The second will have a greater impact on the cost of a health insurance policy than the first. It would be impossible to make a detailed assessment of the cost of each state's mandates without evaluating each piece of legislation. Thus, the estimated cost level . . . is considered typical but may not apply to all variations of that mandate. Further, the additional cost of a mandate depends on the benefits of the policy to which it is attached. Example: A prescription drug mandate costs nothing if a policy already covers drugs, but can be very costly if added to a policy that doesn't cover drugs.

A Caution about Comparisons and Cost Estimates.   Because mandates can drive up the cost of health insurance, it would be easy to assume that the states with the most mandates would also have the highest premiums. While that may be true in some states, it is not necessarily so. Some mandates have a much greater impact on the cost of health insurance than others. For example, mental health parity mandates, which require insurers to cover mental health care at the same levels as physical health care, have a much greater impact on the cost of premiums than would mandates for inexpensive procedures which few people need. In addition, mental health mandates often include mini-mandates within them, like coverage for autism diagnosis and treatment.

It may be tempting to think that since a particular mandate doesn't add much to the cost of a health insurance policy, there is no reason for legislators to oppose it. The result of this reasoning is that many states have 40, 50 or more mandates. Although most mandates only increase the cost of a policy by less than 1%, 40 such mandates will price many people out of the market. It is the accumulated impact of dozens of mandates, not just one that makes health insurance unaffordable.

New Mandates to Watch: Federal Mandates.   Historically, Congress deferred health insurance regulation to the states. But with the passage of the Health Insurance Portability and Accountability Act of 1996 (HIPAA), that has begun to change. Congress is increasingly willing and even eager to micromanage health insurance benefits.

[F]ederal health insurance mandates . . . lay out certain requirements that specific state mandates must adopt, because they affect states' health insurance coverage benefits laws. While federal law does not mandate employers of any size offer health insurance coverage, it does require employers who choose to offer insurance that their plans meet certain federal requirements with regard to, for example, mental health, mastectomy and maternity benefits. And states, which still have the primary responsibility for regulating insurers, can require health insurance policies offered by businesses to include certain benefits that must meet the minimum federal requirements. . . .

There are two new federal mandates from 2008: The Mental Health Parity and Addiction Equity Act, which expands the previous federal mental health parity laws to include substance abuse benefits, and Michelle's Law, which requires the continuation of health insurance coverage for full-time college students who take a medical leave of absence (otherwise, they would have become ineligible for dependent-student status under a parent's health insurance plan).

Emerging Mandates. Several mandates are growing in popularity, and we expect to see even more legislative activity in the near future. For example: autism and treatment for its various complications is becoming one of the most discussed mandates.

Autism is a brain disorder that affects three areas of development: communication, social interaction, and creative or imaginative play. In the past, autism has fallen under the broader category of mental health, but one of the latest state legislative trends is to pass a standalone autism mandate separate from mental health benefit mandates. To be clear, health insurance does and should cover physical medical conditions faced by those with autism. In addition, it will usually cover many mental health conditions. However, autism advocates are pushing to have health insurance required to cover areas that would be more accurately described as education. We do not question the benefits of the various educational therapies for autism, and we certainly sympathize with the financial plight of some families faced with significant new care-related expenses, but we do question whether some of the therapies are within the scope of traditional health insurance.

It is also important to point out that federal law plays a role in autism coverage. Under the 2004 Individuals with Disabilities Education Act, or IDEA (PL 108-446), early intervention and special education programs must provide related services and treatments to children with autism. So there could be some overlap with state health insurance mandates. If legislators want to help these families, they could go beyond the IDEA scope and create programs that do just that and fund them from general revenues rather than try to force those costs onto health insurance, which will just increase others' premiums. (For a more in-depth look at the autism issue, see CAHI's "The Growing Trend Toward Mandating Autism Coverage")

In addition, we have reported in the past that several states are trying to extend dependent coverage to people who are clearly past childhood—up to age 30 and even older. The problem is that children between the ages of 2 and 18 are the healthiest segment of the population. Since the vast majority of them don't use many health services, their premiums are very low, which helps young families because they tend to be early in their working careers and so have relatively low incomes. And even though health care costs for young adults are higher, insurers will usually continue to cover them into college and graduate school, if they remain dependents. The important point is that restricting children's coverage to children keeps the premiums low, helping young families. If insurers must start including those who are well into adulthood, premiums for "dependents coverage" will rise, making it unaffordable for many young families.

The question that every legislator needs to ask is: When does one person's or group's need to have some new or traditionally uncovered procedure or therapy paid for by health insurance outweigh the majority's need to keep premiums affordable?

Fortunately, there is evidence that some legislators are getting CAHI's message. At least 30 states now require that a mandate's cost must be assessed before it is implemented. And at least 10 states provide for mandate-lite policies, which allow some individuals to purchase a policy with fewer mandates more tailored to their needs and financial situation.

The Rest of the Story.   The mandates enumerated here don't tell the whole story. States have other ways of adversely affecting the cost of health insurance. For example, several states have adopted legislation that requires health insurers selling in the individual market to accept anyone who applies, regardless of their health status, known as "guaranteed issue." Or they limit insurers' ability to price a policy to accurately reflect the risk an applicant brings to the pool, known as "community rating" or "modified community rating."

Both guaranteed issue and community rating can have a devastating impact on the price of health insurance, especially as younger and healthier people cancel their coverage, leaving the pool smaller and sicker. Thus, in the aggregate, mandates drive up the cost of health insurance. But determining the impact in a particular state requires careful analysis of each piece of mandate legislation, as well as other regulations that have been promulgated. . .

The Growing Trend Toward Mandating Autism Coverage

Autism and treatment for its various complications is becoming one of the most discussed and demanded state benefit mandates. But there is a growing debate over whether, and to what extent, autism is a health-related condition as opposed to a behavioral condition or educational challenge. While health insurance does and should cover health-related aspects of autism, policymakers who want to ensure that families facing the real financial and other challenges posed by autism should develop safety net programs that meet their needs, rather than trying to impose autism-related costs on health insurance.

Mental Health or Habilitative Services?   Currently, health insurance does and should cover physical medical conditions faced by those with autism. In addition, it will often cover many mental health-related conditions. However, autism advocates want to require health insurance to cover therapies more accurately described as educational.

One problem is how to categorize autism treatment: Does it fall under mental health or habilitative services? If autism is a mental health condition, it is more likely to be covered by health insurance. If under habilitative services, then it should be considered long-term care.

A mental health benefit mandate provides for the payment of mental health evaluation and treatment, but sometimes at a higher out-of-pocket cost for the patient, or limitations are imposed on the coverage. Historically, mental health services have higher patient cost-sharing and shorter visit limits than services for physical illness or injury. Mental health parity laws try to minimize or eliminate this difference by requiring the same limitations and cost-sharing for mental health as for traditional medical care.

Habilitative services treatments, by contrast, include occupational, physical and speech therapies for children with a congenital or genetic birth defect, including autism. The goal of such services is to enhance the child's ability to function.

Coverage for Autism.   Under a federal law passed in 2004, the Individuals with Disabilities Education Act, or IDEA, public early intervention and special education programs must provide related services and treatments to children with autism. However, only roughly 3 percent of autistic children's needs are met under IDEA, and President Obama has expressed support for even more comprehensive federal coverage.

State legislatures traditionally have grouped autism in the broader category of mental health, but one of the latest state legislative trends is to pass an autism mandate separately from mental health benefit mandates.

Autism support groups want mandate legislation that provides for evaluation and treatment of autism, as well as specific services such as school mainstreaming.

Which States Cover Autism?   The question of whether autism is a mental health condition covered under health insurance varies from state to state. One of the problems is that scientists and doctors are not certain what causes autism, and so historically treatment differs from one person to the next. Plus autism-coverage advocates often vary in how they interpret existing laws.

- For example, Autism Speaks reports eight states with health insurance autism benefits.
- However, several autism blogs report a higher figure and point to a Connecticut Office of Legislative Research (OLR) report dated December 2006 that says 17 states have some level of coverage for autism, including 10 that require coverage for autism through their laws mandating mental illness coverage. Six of those states have specific autism laws.
- In July 2008, the Connecticut OLR came out with an additional report that broke down the autism mandate differently. Researchers reported that 22 states besides Connecticut mandate some amount of coverage for the treatment of autism—which is consistent with CAHI's own tracking of the autism mandate. Of these, eight require coverage for behavioral treatment services for autism (Arizona, Florida, Indiana, Kentucky, Louisiana, Pennsylvania, South Carolina and Texas) and five plus Connecticut require other coverage related to autism (Colorado, Georgia, Maryland, New York and Tennessee). Nine states and Connecticut include autism in their mental health mandate laws (California, Illinois, Iowa, Kansas, Maine, Montana, New Hampshire, New Jersey and Virginia).

The Autism Society of America is more consistent with the Connecticut OLR report and several autism blogs. The Society's scope is broader than Autism Speaks, and it includes all types of coverage that addresses autism benefits, not just behavioral support.

CAHI has tracked 39 states that have mental health benefit mandates on their books (of which 30 specifically include autism), 47 that have state mental health parity laws and at least three have habilitative services for children.

There was additional autism-mandate activity during the 2008 legislative session. For example, Arizona, Connecticut, Florida, Illinois, Louisiana, Pennsylvania and South Carolina now have state mandate laws. And Hawaii adopted a resolution that requests a study of the social and financial impact of adding an autism mandate to health insurance coverage.

Even so, states are increasingly looking to insurers to cover more—or all—of the costs of caring for autistic children. Not because health insurers have any particular expertise in, or even responsibility for, autism. Legislators want insurers to cover more of the costs simply so the state doesn't have to.

The Push for Expanded Autism Coverage. Autism is a serious problem in the country, and we still don't understand the causes or the cure. The Centers for Disease Control reported in 2007 that one in 150 children has this disorder. And there is a growing recognition that autism should be identified early and treated—hence the American Academy of Pediatrics' recent recommendation that all U.S. children be formally screened for autism twice by the age of two.

We do know these children need significant amounts of care. That's why Wisconsin's approach, which set up the Children's Long-Term Care Community-Based Waiver (or CTLS) to provide a range of services to qualifying individuals, makes the most sense. It provides more integrated care than could possibly be provided by health insurance.

In addition, autism support groups and their families are looking for more financial relief from and coverage for Applied Behavior Analysis and other therapies which, according to proponents, contain some of the most effective forms of treatment, best outcomes and long-term economic benefits. Proponents believe that health insurance companies should assume the financial burden—typically in the range of $50,000 per year per child—for autistic children that families and school districts have borne.

Insurance carriers argue that most medically related treatments are already covered for autism. In addition, they note that autism is an individually based disorder, and so there is often no clear standard of care to determine the appropriate therapy. Further, some see behavioral therapy not as a medical benefit but an educational one. For example, "play therapies" can require up to 10 separate interactions per day, ensuring the child remains focused on the world around him. The therapy may be provided by unlicensed care providers (and/or parents) who can be trained to use the methods very effectively. Some of the other therapies address developmental delays, which are not typically covered under health insurance.

While various educational therapies for autism may be beneficial, and while we recognize that many families struggle under the related financial burdens associated with autism, we question whether some of these therapies are within the scope of traditional health insurance.

The Cost of Autism Coverage. CAHI's actuarial working team estimates that an autism mandate increases the cost of health insurance by about 1 percent. But they caution us that figure may be rising for two reasons. The incidence of autism appears to be growing, and there is a trend to cover more services, which will drive up the cost of each covered individual. If these trends continue, as we expect, the cost of mandating coverage will move into the 1 to 3 percent range.

Conclusion.   Private health insurance, with companies and individuals frequently changing plans or health care networks, doesn't provide the consistent care autistic children need. If legislators want to help these families, they should create programs specifically targeted to meet their needs and properly fund them from general revenues—better than Congress did under the IDEA program—rather than try to force the costs onto health insurance, which will just increase everyone's premiums.

POSTSCRIPT

Should Insurance Cover Treatments and Services for Autism?

Taking a broad view, Ganz (*Archives of Pediatric and Adolescent Medicine*, 2007) projected the lifetime societal costs of *each* person with autism at $3.2 million. Components of this staggering amount include therapies and services, lost parental work productivity, respite care, additional medical complications, and lifetime care and support. Legal fees and the cost of diet foods would raise the total.

If early intervention improved a single child's functioning, the savings would far outweigh the cost. No one questions the efficacy of early intervention services, although there is considerable disagreement about which services make a difference and how much change can be expected. This issue's selections illustrate the heated debate about funding treatments.

Autism Speaks sees services as a health care responsibility. Children with autism have concurrent medical problems, but are denied coverage by many health insurance companies who would cover the same service for children without the diagnosis of autism. The recently revised Mental Health Parity Act requires mental health services (including behavioral therapies) at the same level as physical health, but autism mandates are more specific.

Council for Affordable Health Insurance (CAHI), whose purpose is advocacy for affordable health care for all, projects the financial impact of burgeoning mandates. They state that health insurance companies are increasingly being required to cover services beyond their mission of short-term health care. Legislators are using mandates to avoid providing programmatic options. Schools are skirting their Individuals with Disabilities Education Act (IDEA) responsibilities.

In the midst of Virginia's contemplation of an autism mandate, Rituparna Basu (the-undercurrent.com, 2009) acknowledged the financial stress incurred by parents, but believes the outcomes would either reduce services (in order to contain added costs) or increase premiums for everyone (making coverage unaffordable for some). Basu asks, "If it is unfair to parents of autistic children to have to pay their children's medical bills, how much more unfair is it for other parents to have to pay the same bills?" Basu views mandated coverage as "enforced charity."

The late Dr. Stephen Parker (http://blogs.webmd.com) addresses the "border war between two titans—the health insurance industry and the educational system." Conveying each titan's arguments through imaginary dialogue, Parker thinks it shameful that we are fighting about care for some of our neediest. He decides that "autism is primarily an educational, not a medical, challenge." Unfortunately, he also concludes that schools are "woefully under-funded," and that "she-bear advocates" will be needed to secure services from schools strapped for cash.

In the center are parents trying to do what is best for their child. Financial challenges are far greater than for parents of typical children (Parish et al., *Exceptional Children*, 2008). Work demands must be balanced with the unpredictable needs of their children (Jackson, *The Boston Globe*, 2008). The National Council on Disability (www.ncd.gov, 2009) found limited or nonexistent health insurance for individuals with disabilities throughout their lives.

Few families can afford $50,000 per year to educate one child. Think of the impact of this same amount on a school district, especially a small one. For $50,000, a teacher and paraprofessional could be hired for a class of 25 children. In tight fiscal times, this choice causes pain and anger. Simultaneously, health insurance companies struggle to cover growing demands.

It is ironic that the diagnosis of autism makes children eligible for some intensive services but shuts them out of others. Are autism services the responsibility of the family, health insurance, or schools? What is the cost of avoiding a resolution?

Internet References . . .

Job Accommodations Network

The Job Accommodations Network, operated through the Office of Disability Employment Policy of the U.S. Department of Labor, has as its mission facilitating the employment and retention of workers with disabilities.

http://www.jan.wvu.edu

Reauthorization of the Elementary and Secondary Education Act (ESEA)

This Web site contains up-to-date information on the reauthorization of the Elementary and Secondary Education Act, known as No Child Left Behind in its 2001 version. The government-sponsored site provides text of the legislation, speech video clips and transcripts, and blog responses.

http://www.ed.gov/blog/topic/esea-reauthorization/

What Works Clearinghouse

The What Works Clearinghouse was established in 2002 by the U.S. Department of Education's Institute of Educational Sciences to provide educators, policymakers, researchers, and the public with "a central and trusted source of scientific evidence of what works in education."

http://ies.ed.gov/ncee/wwc/

Intervention Central

Designed and maintained by a New York school psychologist and school administrator, this site contains strategies, publications, and tools to assist in classroom intervention and assessment. A free online newsletter updates readers about additions to the site.

National Dissemination Center for Children with Disabilities (NICHCY) Research Center for Children with Disabilities

A new resource for educators and parents of students with disabilities, this site provides comprehensive information on the research process. One element, The NICHCY Research-to-Practice Database, enables readers to access research about techniques and practices.

http://nichcy.org/

Circle of Inclusion

This Web site, funded by the U.S. Office of Special Education Programs, is targeted at providing information and resources about the effective practices of inclusive educational programs for children from birth through age eight. Links to additional resources and video clips can be found on the home page.

http://www.circleofinclusion.org/

Access and Accountability

*T*hirty years ago, special education was concerned with getting students with disabilities into schools. Next, the conversation turned to opening classroom doors so that students with disabilities had access to typical peers and were included in school experiences. Current deliberations revolve around access to the general curriculum—the real work of schools. With access has come accountability. Now that the doors are open, we all must be accountable for the learning that goes on inside. As this new step in inclusionary practice takes shape, legislators and educators debate whether the next development is a truly seamless system of education, no longer needing the designations, protections, and paperwork of special education.

- Has the ADA Accomplished Its Goals?
- Is Response to Intervention (RTI) Ready for Implementation?
- Should Special Education and General Education Merge?
- Can Scientifically Based Research Guide Instructional Practice?
- Does NCLB Leave Some Students Behind?
- Should Students with Cognitive Disabilities Be Expected to Demonstrate Academic Proficiency?
- Is Full Inclusion the Least Restrictive Environment?
- Should Colleges Be More Accommodating to Students with Disabilities?

ISSUE 7

Has the ADA
Accomplished Its Goals?

YES: John Hockenberry, from "Yes, You Can," *Parade Magazine* (July 24, 2005), pp. 4–5

NO: Lynda A. Price, Paul J. Gerber, and Robert Mulligan, from "Adults with Learning Disabilities and the Underutilization of the Americans with Disabilities Act," *Remedial and Special Education* (November/December 2007), pp. 340–344

ISSUE SUMMARY

YES: John Hockenberry, an award-winning television commentator, a radio host, and a foreign correspondent, who happens to use a wheelchair, celebrates the increased access brought about by implementation of the Americans with Disabilities Act (ADA).

NO: Lynda A. Price, Paul J. Gerber (university faculty members and researchers), and Robert Mulligan (a district special education administrator) contend that the opportunities for ADA-mandated access are underused by individuals with learning disabilities.

As discussed in the "Introduction," three basic federal laws govern the lives of individuals with disabilities: Section 504 of the Rehabilitation Act of 1973, the Individuals with Disabilities Education Act (IDEA), and the Americans with Disabilities Act (ADA).

Section 504 is a civil rights statute prohibiting organizations that receive federal funds from discriminating against any individual based on a disability that substantially limits a major life activity. Reasonable accommodations must be implemented so that individuals with disabilities have equal access to the activities of the organization. Since all school districts receive federal funds, Section 504 covers two groups: students and employees.

Regulations of IDEA form the foundation of special education, upon which individual states base the local legislation to clarify federal language, establish practices, and/or extend commitments beyond the federal standard. Students served under IDEA are automatically covered by Section 504.

Students with disabilities who do not require the specially designed instruction of IDEA are eligible to receive 504 Plans. These outline any accommodations necessary to ensure equal access to educational experience. Holler and Zirkel (*NASSP Bulletin*, 2008) found that the number of students covered by 504 Plans peaked in middle/secondary schools, perhaps as parents sought accommodations for SAT tests.

Finally, the ADA, passed in 1990 by the president George H. W. Bush, extends the protections of Section 504, prohibiting businesses, governmental agencies, or public accommodations (other than churches or private clubs) from discriminating against any individual who has a disability that substantially limits a major life activity. The ADA carries the same responsibility for reasonable accommodations as Section 504, impacting the practices of almost every employer.

John Hockenberry is a prominent journalist and foreign correspondent. At the age of 19, he became a paraplegic in a car accident. He now uses a wheelchair in his daily travel and in his overseas assignments. Reflecting on his experiences under ADA, Hockenberry reminds readers of the increased access that we now take as commonplace. Citing several examples, he observes that ADA-based accommodations have made life more accessible for those who do not have disabilities.

Lynda A. Price and Paul J. Gerber are university professors, whose research focuses on the employment of adults with learning disabilities. Robert Mulligan directs district special education services. These three authors present evidence that adults with specific learning disabilities do not tap into ADA-mandated benefits once they leave public schools. Their findings are a cause for concern, since half the students served by special education are categorized with this disability.

Writing in *Psychology Today*, Hara Marano (2004) thinks disability-related laws may actually have done their job too well. Marano maintains that parents seeking to ensure success for their children embrace "cleverly devised defects" to secure advantages like untimed SATs. This relentless hunt has created a group of fragile children, unable to resolve their own difficulties.

As you read these articles, consider the doors that IDEA has opened for children with disabilities. Access and expectations have greatly increased. Federally, eligible students are covered until they reach the age of 22 or receive their high school diploma. What happens when individuals covered by IDEA leave the schoolhouse and enter adult society—the ultimate inclusionary environment? Does ADA-mandated access depend on disability? Is the subway more accessible than a college classroom?

Yes, You Can

Careful! You might miss the light show. If you surrender to any nervousness or caution and avoid looking at me when I roll by in my wheelchair, you'll miss the fireworks in my front wheels: tiny, colored electric lights that blaze out red, blue and green when they turn. That's right. I have electric scooter wheels on my wheelchair, and the greatest thing about them is how they grab the nervous eyes of some folks and pull them in. "Awesome!" people will say to me as I race across the Brooklyn Bridge. "Hey, that's cool!" I'll hear at an airport as I race to catch a plane. *"Really cool."*

It was two 6-year-old girls who convinced me that high-profile, sparkly wheels were a big improvement over my quiet, in-the-shadows approach to being disabled in public. Those two girls are my oldest twin daughters, Zoe and Olivia. They are almost 7 now, and all of their lives they have ridden on their daddy's lap. Doctors may call me a paraplegic. Strangers might say I am "wheelchair bound." But to my daughters, I have always been a daddy who comes with his own playground apparatus. In their short lives, oblivious of the fears and anxieties of adults, they have known a wheelchair only to represent a warm, safe place.

Going Public

These days, Zoe and Olivia are nearly too big to ride comfortably on my lap anymore, and I will miss them terribly when they stop climbing up altogether. (At least I still have 4-year-old Zach and Regan, our second set of twins!) But I look into the faces of my children and see a sunrise of hope that people with disabilities are experiencing 15 years after the passage of the Americans with Disabilities Act (ADA).

Almost two decades into this landmark civil rights law, people determined to share their distinct talents have begun to take their places in the American mainstream. The signs of their presence go far beyond handicapped parking spaces and wheelchair ramps. Thanks to their persistence, today you are as likely to see a person with a disability on the ski slopes as you are in your workplace. And the momentum is picking up. All across the U.S., people with and without disabilities are bringing about lasting changes in their communities: There are city and state building codes, such as Michigan's, that go

Initially published in *Parade,* July 24, 2005, pp. 4–5. Copyright © 2005 by John Hockenberry. Reprinted by permission of Parade Magazine and John Hockenberry via Watkins/Loomis Literary Agency.

beyond federal law by mandating that doors, passageways and bathrooms be unobstructed. There is the unique federal and civic partnership that designed and built wheelchair access into Boston's venerated Fenway Park, which for decades was off-limits to the disabled. And there is the Center for Creative Play, a universally accessible indoor playspace in Pittsburgh, Pa., for children of all abilities, which projects such a powerful "Welcome, all!" message that families drive hours just to play there. Taken one at a time, these are small changes you might miss unless you modify old assumptions and look at the world with new eyes.

Strength in Numbers

Even the battles today are different. Fifteen years ago, there might have been a debate over whether someone like Tony Sylvester, a young man born with spina bifida, could even go to a public school. Recently, Tony, 19 and a graduate of Wauwatosa West High School in suburban Milwaukee, Wis., waged a tough campaign for his varsity letter. Tony's a forward for the highly ranked Wheelin' Wizards—a wheelchair basketball team that competes with other disabled athletes, independent of their high schools. To appeal the school superintendent's decision to deny the letter, Tony and his mother, Tish, got advice from a powerful ally—IndependenceFirst, a Milwaukee-based organization that helped them pack a school-board meeting with disabled athletes, coaches, parents and the media. As a result, Tony was awarded his letter—a big W, which he wears proudly.

No doubt, there is strength in numbers—and the numbers are growing. IndependenceFirst, the group that helped Tony and Tish, is just one of about 500 Independent Living Centers across the U.S. that have grown up with the ADA. Typically nonresidential, private and nonprofit (though many are state-supported), these community-based centers provide services and act as advocates for people with disabilities. . . . There also are 10 federally funded ADA & information technology centers in the U.S. to help businesses, architects and schools comply with the law by providing information, training and technical assistance. . . .

Clearly, there are fewer excuses today for being inaccessible and indifferent to the disabled. But, in the end, a truly inclusive world will depend on the efforts and courage of those who are not disabled—in a word, society at large. After all, the Civil Rights Act of 1964—which had the backing of the courts, the police and the National Guard—still has not wiped out racism.

It's Up to You, Too

Meanwhile, local victories like Tony Sylvester's boost morale for the bigger struggles that lie ahead. For instance, employment for people with disabilities has not improved significantly since the passage of the ADA. Disabled unemployment has stood near 70% for the past two decades. The ADA itself has suffered setbacks in court decisions and by its own limitations. Businesses can be exempted from the ADA by claiming that compliance is an "undue burden."

And houses of worship do not have to comply at all, even though thousands have because it is the right thing to do. Enforcement of the ADA is left to the courts, where the vast majority of lawsuits are thrown out before they ever reach trial.

Perhaps the most significant accomplishment of the Americans With Disabilities Act is that it has widened the expectation that there ought to be some way in for people with disabilities. One telling example is an incident that occurred a few years ago when I was riding on the New York City subway. The train was declared "out of service" and pulled into a station without an elevator—one of many. The conductor ordered all passengers off the train. With the exception of me and a few women with strollers, everyone got off and trudged up the steps to the sidewalk.

When the conductor offered me no help, my only option was to hop out of my wheelchair and lug myself up the filthy subway stairs on my keister. But then one of the stroller women laid into the conductor: "What's your plan for this man? Is he just supposed to stay down here forever? Is that your plan?" She was riled up on my behalf. "We're not stupid people," she continued. "There's a law that says you have to have a plan. Everybody knows that."

We All Benefit

The conductor went from ignoring a solitary man in a wheelchair to being intimidated by a volunteer SWAT team of Brooklyn moms. He told all of us to stay on the train, then drove us to the next elevator station. The stroller mom looked at me and said with a smile, "You're the guy on TV, right? I love your work." I thanked her and left the train in awe of the anonymous outraged lady who had saved the powerless TV star. Her outrage represented something deeper: an expectation that has grown up with the ADA that disabled people have certain rights that cannot be denied. That's what saved me: her expectation—*our shared expectation*—that there is a place for all in America.

It's not like only the disabled benefit from this. Those ladies with their strollers have me to thank for the sidewalk ramps they love. And do you think that young office workers in the gym realize that it is the deaf they have to thank for the captions on the TV screens that allow them to follow their stocks while they huff and puff? Having a place for all is both the American dream and the engine of our success. We've been working on this freedom thing for the past 229 years. As my daughters might say: It's high time for some awesome, sparkly wheels.

What You Should Know

On July 26, 1990, the Americans With Disabilities Act was signed into law, eliminating discrimination in employment, transportation and public accommodations for the nation's 50 million disabled adults and children. Still, to this day, many with physical and mental disabilities do not get their due. To learn more or for technical-assistance materials, . . . call the ADA Information

Line at 1-800-514-0301. (During business hours, specialists help you apply the law to your own situation.) For TTY, call 1-800-514-0383.

- Employers interested in hiring the disabled can consult the Employer Assistance and Recruiting Network (EARN), a free service of the Department of Labor. . . .

Lynda A. Price, Paul J. Gerber, and Robert Mulligan

 **NO**

Adults with Learning Disabilities and the Underutilization of the Americans with Disabilities Act

At its signing in 1990, then U.S. President George H. W. Bush commented that the Americans with Disabilities Act (ADA) had moved people with disabilities from an era of paternalism to one of empowerment. In essence, the ADA was constructed to markedly change the way that people with disabilities would participate in society. In the ensuing years, the ADA has had a positive effect on people with disabilities, but, when examined more closely, there are questions about whether the ADA has met its potential with all populations of people with disabilities, one of them being learning disabilities (LD).

The part of the ADA that has the most impact on people with learning disabilities is Title 1, which governs practices in the area of competitive employment. Provisions of law are carefully articulated, with precise concepts such as *disability*, *qualified*, *essential functions*, and *reasonable accommodation*. In order for a person with LD to effectively use the ADA, these concepts must be understood. Likewise, some other things need to be mastered pertaining to the learning disability itself. Knowledge of one's challenges, the process of self-disclosure, and monitoring performance under the auspices of the ADA via self-advocacy procedures are most important.

A review of the extant research literature on LD and the ADA is one avenue of discovery. Another is a review of commonly used ADA materials to

1. teach and prepare students with LD during their last years of high school,
2. train professionals about LD and the ADA, and
3. inform consumers (adults with LD and parents) about their rights and prerogatives under the ADA.

. . . This article seeks to uncover the state of the art regarding people with LD and the ADA, especially in terms of preparing for transition.

From *Remedial and Special Education*, vol. 28, no. 6, November/December 2007, pp. 340–344 (excerpts). Copyright © 2007 by Hammill Institute on Disabilities and Sage in association with American Rehabilitation Counseling Association (ARCA). Reprinted by permission via Rightslink.

Review of ADA Research

Business and Industry and the ADA

At the beginning of the ADA era, Gerber probed the knowledge and under-standing of the ADA from executive officers, human resource directors, and personnel managers of nine Virginia companies, some Fortune 500 compa-nies, national companies, and regional companies. It was apparent that the focus of business and industry was on compliance with the ADA, primarily for people with physical and sensory disabilities. At that time, LD were thought of as an enigma or not considered at all. There was even confusion about the true meaning of learning disabilities, which were sometimes equated with mental retardation. Gerber's conclusion indicated a shift in the role and responsibility for people with LD beyond their K–12 school experience:

> It must be remembered that business and industry are not expert when it comes to issues of disability, including learning disabilities. Therefore, the successes of people with learning disabilities will not be contingent upon law and the efforts of business alone. It will be linked to the capabilities and performance of individuals with learning disabilities themselves.

The onus of responsibility had clearly shifted as the expectations of the beyond-school culture set in. People with LD had to be able to effectively advocate for themselves. As adults, they had to be knowledgeable about their "LD profile," know how to self-disclose, and know how to use the provisions of the ADA to their benefit.

In a follow-up study to Gerber's work, Price and Gerber gauged the impact of the ADA. Nine employers . . . were studied to see how people with LD were faring with the ADA in 1998. . . . As in the 1992 study, managers, supervisors, and human resource administrators were interviewed. The results of the study were essentially the same. Moreover, it was very clear that employers were most willing to "work with" employees with LD under the provisions of the ADA. Also, they saw the effectiveness of the ADA being predicated on a part-nership with the employees with LD themselves. In the absence of guidance and expertise in their workplace, employees with LD had to be "experts" in their own right when it came to LD and the ADA.

People with LD and the ADA

A series of investigations were made to discover the realities of the workplace for people with LD in the ADA era. Price, Gerber, and Mulligan studied 25 adults with LD. . . . Five of the 25 respondents mentioned their learning disability while pursuing their job, but they never mentioned the ADA. The remaining 20 adults mentioned neither. None of the adults asked for pre-employment testing accommodations that were allowable under the ADA. Moreover, 19 respondents had no knowledge of the ADA, with many saying that they had never heard of it. Specifically, these adults did not understand how the ADA applied to them or how to use it for their own self-advocacy.

In a pilot study for a larger national study, Gerber, Price, Mulligan, and Williams found that very little was known about the ADA, and thus the ADA was underused. Some of the participants believed that the ADA was solely for people with physical disabilities. Of the 18 adults in the pilot, only 3 participants had learned about the ADA before leaving high school or in a post-secondary setting, with only one receiving any type of secondary transition assistance. . . . Furthermore, this study revealed the importance of a new element within the issue of underutilization—the issue of self-disclosure.

This set of findings foreshadowed what was seen in the national study of 80 adults with LD. . . . The majority of adults with LD in this larger study did not know of the existence of the ADA. If the adults had heard about the ADA, they knew very few details about it. Moreover, they did not see how it applied to them or to their disability.

Interesting enough, the findings of this study paralleled research done on 24 Canadian adults with LD. . . . Canadians have the Charter of Rights and Freedoms that protects individuals with disabilities (including LD) in all facets of society. Even though the Charter is not as focused as the ADA, it guarantees against discrimination in the workplace, including people with disabilities. Despite its existence, it was underused by adults with LD and just played a minor role in employment settings. Many participants in the study did not know how the Charter specifically applied to the workplace. In a comparative study of the American and Canadian data sets, the overall conclusion was that disability laws, whether American or Canadian, were not readily being used by adults with LD. This might be to the disadvantage of employees with LD not only at job entry but also in job advancement.

Reasons for ADA Underutilization

Transition-Oriented Materials

Ever since transition became an important initiative of the federal government in the 1980s, special educators have implemented curricula to prepare students with disabilities for their beyond-school years. Such has been the case for students with LD, although they have generally been grouped in a high-incidence, generic-like category. Curricula have been delivered to students with LD who were going from school to work as well as school to school to work. Granted, when the transition initiative was first proffered to the field, the ADA had not yet become law. It was during the decade of the 1990s that the ADA became part of the conversation regarding transition. Indeed, the ADA was enthusiastically received by the LD community because approximately 85% of people with LD go straight to work in competitive employment settings.

Perhaps one of the reasons for the underutilization of the ADA can be explained by a lack of relevant information on the ADA and LD currently available for the transition planning process. This hypothesis was addressed in a preliminary manner through an examination of widely known transition materials used in secondary schools, taught in personnel preparation courses, and developed for adults with LD. . . .

The 10 transition materials selected were subjectively chosen by the authors as representative of what is currently available in terms of transition ideology and methodology. . . .

[Despite] the best efforts to develop relevant materials for the transition process—some pertaining to students with LD and some not—little or no information is available on the ADA in these materials. Of equal importance, virtually no information is presented on how the ADA and transition specifically apply to individuals with LD. . . .

[The] professional transition literature has not kept up with the challenges of individuals with LD in this critical and frequently neglected area.

The reason for this glaring omission is not entirely certain at this time, but it begs the question: If students do not receive information about the ADA and how to use it effectively in their latter years of school, then when do they ever learn it? Moreover, if the vast majority of students with LD go straight to work, then when will they ever learn about the ADA?

Self-Disclosure in the Workplace

Another issue interwoven with the connections of LD, transition planning, and adulthood is *self-disclosure*. Unlike the school-age special education laws (e.g., IDEA and Section 504), the ADA is predicated on self-disclosure. If people with LD do not self-disclose, then the protections laid out in the ADA are moot. Sadly, this seems to be the case for the vast majority of people with LD in employment settings, as noted in the preceding discussion. . . .

It should be noted that recent work by Gerber et al. has underscored self-disclosure as a significant and complex process in the lives of adults with LD. One component of this process, which is directly relevant to transition and ITPs, is the notion of personal choice. Currently, more than 120 adults with documented LD have reported to the authors that they make new decisions everyday about revealing—and not revealing—their disability. However, such critical decisions are often based on adult-oriented environments (e.g., family, employment, college classroom, [and] church). These choices mirror exactly the five consistent areas of transition planning anticipated by IDEA: postsecondary education, integrated employment, independent living, community participation, and recreation/leisure. Preliminary studies in this area have revealed that most adults with LD are much more comfortable discussing their LD at home with parents or immediate family members, where legislation is not an issue. However, these same individuals are often very reluctant to self-disclose at work—the exact location where the ADA could be a valuable asset for job performance. . . .

Discussion

The underutilization of the ADA is an example of a missed opportunity for individuals with LD. The ADA can make a profound difference in competitive employment settings in job entry, in performance evaluation, and in job advancement. What is highlighted in the examination of the issue of the

ADA vis-à-vis LD is that there is a disconnection between the school-age and beyond-school years. If preparation for the beyond-school years is not sufficient or effective, it has lifelong consequences. In effect, insufficient preparation largely discounts the possibility of accessing the ADA throughout the adult years. Preparation for the adult years is multifaceted. Transition curricula and materials need to be specifically focused on understanding and using the ADA in the most authentic, research-based manner possible. As a result, materials need to be more in-depth, comprehensive, and LD-specific.

This article also suggests the need for greater examination of the ramifications of LD on transition preparation and effective use of the ADA. Clearly, many questions remain to be answered, including the following:

- How do we provide authentic transition training about the ADA for individuals with LD, their parents, teachers, and other related professionals?
- How do we integrate knowledge about the ADA and its consequences in the workplace for individuals with LD into local ITPs?
- How do we provide the most effective preservice and inservice training possible for secondary and postsecondary professionals (high school teachers and counselors, special needs college faculty, etc.) who, in turn, teach others about the transition, LD, and the ADA?

POSTSCRIPT

Has the ADA
Accomplished Its Goals?

John Hockenberry illustrates the successes of the ADA. Twenty years ago, the idea that a human being in a wheelchair could use the subway (much less report from a faraway country) was an unlikely dream. Today, a woman pushing a stroller castigates the subway operator for not considering Hockenberry's needs. The curb cut that makes Hockenberry's travels possible makes life easier for every stroller-pushing adult.

The 2004 National Organization on Disability/Harris Survey of Americans with Disabilities studied changes in quality-of-life indicators. Shockingly, only 35 percent of people with disabilities are employed, compared with 78 percent of typical adults. Still, two-thirds of respondents said the ADA has improved their lives, increasing opportunities in education, income, and employment.

David Morris (*Wall Street Journal,* 2005), CEO of a global company, has hired large numbers of people with disabilities for 20 years. Morris' experience tells him equal employment is sound business practice. Referencing a number of national studies, Morris finds employees with disabilities to be resilient, dedicated, and high performing. Noting that most required accommodations are inexpensive, Morris thinks attitudes are larger barriers to overcome.

Morris' concerns seem on-target. Price, Gerber, and Mulligan note that adults with learning disabilities were uncomfortable with the self-disclosure necessary to gain workplace accommodations. Although these young adults had heard about accomplishments of individuals with disabilities as they attended school fully covered by IDEA's plans and accommodations, they are reticent at work.

The consequences of this silence can be far reaching. Mellard and Lancaster (*Remedial and Special Education,* 2003) observe that while students with less significant disabilities initially work a large number of hours, their overall pay eventually declines because their peers earn more as a result of postsecondary education and training.

Students with disabilities are increasingly enrolling in postsecondary education programs. Most colleges and universities have centers to assist students in obtaining accommodations and communicating with faculty members. As with employment, individuals must self-disclose their disability and request support. Despite the assistance from support centers, colleges can be more isolating than high schools. College faculty are unfamiliar with disabilities or the policies related to student rights and accommodations (Hong, Gonzalez, & Ehrensberger, *Teaching Exceptional Children,* 2007). Frustrated students give up and drop out.

Commissioned by the president George W. Bush, the President's Committee for People with Intellectual Disabilities (2003) acknowledged that many strides have been made through IDEA, including the development of self-advocacy skills. However, the committee expressed grave concerns that "faulty attitudes" held by the general public, especially employers, combined with well-intentioned federal policies, have led to a form of "enforced poverty" for individuals with intellectual disabilities (mental retardation). Finding that approximately 90 percent of adults with intellectual disabilities were unemployed, the committee recommended that schools increase transition services. It also advocated for more flexible federal policies among agencies, to ease the way into employment.

IDEA 2004 increased emphasis on transition planning. Beginning with the IEP in place when the student turns 16, educational teams must consider postsecondary goals related to training, education, employment, and independent living. An action plan must be created for securing postsecondary services to reach these goals. This emphasis may increase attention to the development of self-advocacy skills necessary for successful postsecondary experiences.

What will it take to facilitate access in the workplace or on the campus for those who have experienced it in their earlier education? Does society find it more acceptable to provide equal access to those with physical disabilities and to those whose disabilities are invisible?

ISSUE 8

Is Response to Intervention (RTI) Ready for Implementation?

YES: Rachel Brown-Chidsey and Mark W. Steege, from "What Is Response to Intervention (RTI)?," in *Response to Intervention: Principles and Strategies for Effective Practice* (New York: The Guilford Press, 2005)

NO: Douglas Fuchs and Donald D. Deshler, from "What We Need to Know About Responsiveness to Intervention (and Shouldn't Be Afraid to Ask)," *Learning Disabilities Research & Practice* (May 2007)

ISSUE SUMMARY

YES: Rachel Brown-Chidsey and Mark W. Steege, faculty members at the University of Southern Maine, who have conducted extensive research in the area of student assessment, describe Response to Intervention (RTI) as a systematic way for educators to help all children experience appropriate educational practices.

NO: Douglas Fuchs and Donald D. Deshler, professors at Vanderbilt University and the University of Kansas, respectively, prolific scholars, and co-directors of the National Research Center on Learning Disabilities, urge educators to identify and explore unresolved aspects of RTI before wholesale implementation.

Struggling learners waiting to fail so they could receive special education, rising numbers of children identified as learning disabled, and overrepresentation of minorities in special education—these were among the problems legislators wanted to address when reauthorizing Individuals with Disabilities Education Act (IDEA).

Response to Intervention (RTI) was identified as a remedy that would help more children learn effectively in the general education classroom. Key elements of RTI include the following: an integrated system that uses performance data to drive high-quality instruction, a problem-solving approach to student learning, and a progressive, multitiered system of interventions.

Echoing No Child Left Behind (NCLB), RTI emphasizes a connection between scientifically based instructional practices and continuously monitored student progress. Every student's progress is to be systematically and regularly measured. Careful attention to each child's rate of learning alerts educators to developing difficulties. If a student does not progress, then instruction must change.

Slow progress is viewed as a problem to be addressed by a team of educators who pool their expertise to identify interventions that will help improve the student's learning. Although this sounds like the traditional pre-referral process, there is a key difference. Instead of signaling the prelude to special education referral and services, RTI focuses on documenting a student's responses to significant interventions within general education.

Intervention tiers correspond to instruction and assessment that are increasingly individualized. For the purposes of illustration, three levels are described here; no specific design is specified by IDEA. In Tier 1, children experience effective classroom instruction. All students are screened regularly; teachers are appropriately prepared to use scientifically based teaching methods; educators scrutinize assessment data to identify students who are not progressing adequately. In Tier 2, groups of students showing some difficulty are given additional focused, short-term instruction and assessments. Tier 3 is reserved for individual students who do not respond to Tier 2 and require longer, and more intense, instruction. The tiers are expected to be fluid. As students respond to intervention, they return to a less intense tier.

While there is agreement that instruction in Tiers 1 and 2 is delivered by general education teachers, more variation exists about Tier 3 implementation. Some see Tier 3 as a further level of intensity within general education; others envision it delivered by special education faculty; still others view Tier 3 as the opportunity to evaluate whether a student has a disability (NASDSE, 2006).

Rachel Brown-Chidsey and Mark W. Steege view RTI as a responsive approach to children and a way to ensure that schools deliver the kinds of services that students need. Emphasizing the strength of the problem-solving model, they cite evidence from states that found a reduction in special education numbers after implementing RTI procedures. Even though it is a new solution, Brown-Chidsey and Steege encourage educators to adopt RTI and, in the rest of their book, provide guidance on how to do so.

Douglas Fuchs and Donald D. Deshler are concerned that educators will be pressured to adopt RTI before critical questions are answered. They compare interpretations of many elements, including the problem-solving model, the essentials of appropriate Tier 1 instruction, and the nature of non-responders. Fuchs and Deshler advise educators to thoroughly explore these issues before formulating their own response to this intervention strategy.

As you read these articles, consider your own level of knowledge about RTI. How is RTI being implemented in your neighborhood school? Have educators resolved the questions raised in these selections?

YES

Rachel Brown-Chidsey and Mark W. Steege

What Is Response to Intervention (RTI)?

Consider the case of Sean. Sean is a first grader who has not yet developed important prereading skills that he will need if he wants to succeed in school, graduate, go to college, or get a well-paying job in the future. His parents, his teacher, his principal, and the superintendent of his school district want him to learn how to read. So Sean keeps plugging away in school, sitting attentively when his teacher reads to the class, pointing to pictures in books when his parents read to him at home, and "borrowing" answers from other student's worksheets when completing class assignments. At the end of Sean's first-grade year he takes a test to show what he has learned during the year. The test shows that he knows his colors and shapes, but he still cannot read.

Sean's teacher makes a note about his reading problems in his file before it is sent on to the second-grade teacher. When Sean starts the second grade his teacher is already concerned about his reading difficulties, and she works with him closely for several weeks. At the end of October, his teacher has concluded that Sean must have a learning disability, so she refers him for evaluation. In early January an individualized education plan (IEP) meeting about Sean is held. At the meeting, results from the evaluation are reported. These results show that Sean scored in the low end of the average range on both academic achievement and cognitive (IQ) testing. As a result of these highly consistent scores, Sean's parents are told that their son does not have a learning disability. The parents are relieved to hear that, but then ask, "Who will help our son learn to read?" The assistant principal who is chairing the meeting regretfully tells Sean's parents that, because his school does not have Title I funding and Sean did not qualify for special education, he will have to keep "trying" to learn to read in his current class. Sean's mom starts to cry and his dad stands up and states angrily, "This is crazy! Our son cannot read, but you won't do anything to help him! We're leaving and I'm calling the superintendent."

The foregoing scenario is neither uncommon nor unlikely. In our experience as educators and psychologists we have evaluated and met with the parents of many students who had clear and specific learning needs but could not obtain additional school assistance to meet those needs. The described example is sometimes known as a "waiting-to-fail" model, because Sean may eventually qualify for special education if he continues to lag behind in reading

From *Response to Intervention: Principles and Strategies for Effective Practice* by Rachel Brown-Chidsey and Mark W. Steege (The Guilford Press, 2005), pp. 1–11 (refs. omitted). Copyright © 2005 by The Guilford Press. Reprinted by permission of Guilford Publications.

and cannot engage with or participate in reading-based classroom activities. The tragedy of this model is that by the time Sean meets the criteria for special education eligibility, the best years for teaching him to read will have passed.

The good news for students like Sean is that the instructional methods and educational policies needed to get him the reading (or math, or writing) instruction that he needs are available. The instructional methods and assessment procedures most likely to benefit students like Sean are known as *response to intervention* (RTI). RTI is an assessment–intervention model that allows schools to deliver sound instructional methods to students like Sean who otherwise might fall through the cracks. This book is designed to provide knowledge, skills, and resources for using RTI methods in schools. RTI is a relatively new term for an approach to understanding and addressing students' school difficulties. For the purpose of clarity . . . we developed the following definition. First, let's define the important words in the term:

Response: 1. The act of responding
2. An answer or reply
Intervention: 1. The act of intervening; interposition
2. Any interference that may affect the interests of others, especially of one or more states with the affairs of another; mediation

Essentially, RTI is an objective examination of the cause–effect relationship(s) between academic or behavioral *intervention* and the student's *response* to the intervention. For example, a student's *response* to a specific reading instruction *intervention* can be measured using oral reading fluency indicators. When the core terms *response* and *intervention* are put together, a more general set of educational practices and procedures can be defined. Such practices include providing a specific *intervention* (an interference that affects others) for one or more students and measuring the student(s)' *response* (answer or reply) to the intervention. Put more succinctly, RTI is a systematic and data-based method for identifying, defining, and resolving students' academic and/or behavior difficulties. This definition has certain inherent limitations. For example, it includes only academic and behavior problems. We chose to include only academic interventions because this is an important and emerging application of RTI procedures. Specifically, the most recent version of the Individuals with Disabilities Education Improvement Act included RTI references related to identification of learning disabilities. This use of RTI has widespread implications for many aspects of education . . . Importantly, RTI is designed to take the guesswork out of the assessment and intervention process as it is implemented first in general education, and then, for a small number of students, in special education.

History

The components that make up RTI methods have been used in schools for many years but have not been understood as part of the larger system now known as RTI. For example, teachers have routinely used targeted methods of instruction to help individual students develop certain skills. Likewise, as standard practices, schools have reported on student progress at regular intervals. What makes RTI different from these prior means of helping students is that the assessment and instruction practices are integrated into an objective data-based system with built-in decision stages. This is in contrast to past models of student assessment in which students were assumed to be doing OK unless identified otherwise. In RTI, all students are screened and monitored for specific educational outcomes, and those needing additional assistance are given targeted intervention that is monitored systematically using scientifically based data recording procedures. In essence, RTI integrates high-quality teaching and assessment methods in a systematic way so that students who are not successful when presented with one set of instructional methods can be given the chance to succeed with the use of other practices.

Key Features of RTI

As described in the RTI definition above, there are two main components that distinguish RTI from other teaching and assessment practices. These essential components are *systematic* and *data-based* activities. A conceptual framework of our RTI model . . . reflects three tiers of intervention in RTI. Tier 1 . . . reflects the general education curriculum. This tier is designed for and provided to all students in each grade level. Tier 1 is comprehensive and universal. . . . Tier 1 activities are selected on the basis of effectiveness. Still, not all students will respond to Tier 1 instruction with success. Tier 2 . . . represents those students who need more intensive and specific instruction in order to be successful in school. Importantly, . . . data are the only connecting point, or pathway, between each tier. A student can cross between tiers only when data indicate that it needs to happen. A third tier . . . represents a small subset of students who do not respond to the interventions provided in Tiers 1 and 2. Tier 3 activities include comprehensive assessment to identify whether a student has a specific disability and meets the criteria for special education. Notably, Tier 3 does not include special education services; rather, it is a transition point for those students who have not yet found success in school.

Our model of RTI is built upon previous work related to school assessment and instruction. An early precursor to RTI methods is Deno's "cascade" model of special education service delivery. In this model Deno conceptualized students' educational progress as "developmental capital" that could yield dividends in response to appropriate instruction in the least restrictive environment. Deno's "cascade" features increasingly small instructional groupings matched to the individual student's specific needs. Deno's model was used as a core framework for the implementation of special education regulations during the 1970s and 1980s. While this model helped to make special education a reality for many students, one of the problems seen in special education, starting in the 1980s, was the rapid increase in students identified as having learning disabilities.

In part to address the rapid increase in special education placements, several programs and initiatives have been implemented to address the needs of students before they are given special education services. The first of these attempts was known as the regular education initiative, or REI. This federal policy focused on having as many students as possible remain in "regular" education. Drawing from Deno's cascade model, the idea was to focus on determination of what constituted the least restrictive environment for students with disabilities. Instead of assuming that all students with disabilities would need separate specialized teaching, the REI effort pushed teachers and administrators to keep as many children in their original classrooms as possible.

The REI was criticized from its first days, with concerns ranging from lack of teacher training to violation of student rights. . . . Analysis showed that the REI was not very effective in reducing the number of students receiving special education services. Soon after REI measures were put into place, a second major push to reform special education was begun. Known as "inclusive education," this movement had longer-lasting effects than REI. This effort to change special education policies and practices was focused more on establishing the rights and needs of students with disabilities than reducing the overall number of students receiving special education services. The inclusion movement led to examinations of how special education services were being provided. As with RTI, many researchers suggested that additional training was needed by general education classroom teachers. Most notably, educators were reported to be philosophically supportive of special education but not adequately trained to meet the needs of students with disabilities in inclusive classrooms.

Although the inclusion movement has not totally disappeared, recent efforts to address the large number of students in special education have shifted to using RTI methods as the primary mechanism. Additionally, the reduction efforts are now squarely focused on reducing the number of students identified with learning disabilities rather than reducing special education enrollments overall. Kavale and Forness have suggested that the reason why both REI and inclusion failed to bring about the desired changes in general and special education is that they failed to utilize empirical evidence of effective practices and instead focused on philosophical issues about the moral imperative to educate all children. Of note, Kavale expressed opposition to adoption of RTI policies at the federal level until more evidence was produced that such practices systematically result in desired outcomes. Kavale's criticism of current RTI methods appears to be an extension of the arguments made against REI and inclusion. Kavale and others have argued that until there is clear and substantial evidence that RTI methods produce large-scale improvements in educational outcomes, RTI should not be used at the state or national level.

The problem with waiting to implement RTI on a large scale is that the only way to determine whether it will achieve its promise is to implement it at the state or national level. Such implementation needs to be done with the rights and needs of students uppermost in mind. Importantly, RTI methods include certain "safety net" features that can prevent negative consequences. For example, unlike REI and inclusion, RTI is by definition data-driven, so no decisions are made without evidence to support them. Most importantly, RTI is not simply one intervention or method. It is a set of scientifically based procedures that can be used to make decisions about educational programs. In light of the history of efforts to improve educational outcomes for all students, it is important that current and future such initiatives not get bogged down in rhetoric. . . . [Early] intervention has a huge effect on long-term outcomes. . . .

RTI and Problem Solving

By their nature, RTI methods are problem-solving activities. Although many students and teachers in schools may not perceive their daily experiences as "problems," they do engage in ongoing assessment and reflection. In the course of daily events, teachers (and students) are generally pleased when teaching and learning activities go as expected. Under such circumstances, no major "problems" are evident. When a teacher notices that a student's work is not what was expected, a different reaction is likely to occur. If the teacher finds the student's work to be exemplary, he or she may offer additional praise. If the teacher finds the work to be below expectations, he or she may believe that a learning problem is present. Such a problem could include academic skills such as reading, writing, or math, or it could relate to behavioral expectations such as whether the student is able to stay seated, stand in line, or play with others at recess. Regardless of the event, teachers and students tend not to notice school problems until they occur, and then they are very apparent. As a result of efforts to help all students be successful in school, researchers have developed specific problem-solving methods designed to assist teachers and specialists when school difficulties arise.

RTI methods are closely linked with problem-solving models for school difficulties. . . . Deno's five-part data-based problem-solving model will be used as part of the RTI stages and activities. . . . This model includes (1) problem identification, (2) problem definition, (3) designing intervention plans, (4) implementing the intervention, and (5) problem solution. . . . [Each] of these steps is aligned with specific assessment and instructional activities designed to reduce or eliminate a student's school difficulties. This model is designed to be used continuously and interactively. As one step ends, the next begins. In some cases, not all steps will be implemented. In other cases, each step will be utilized multiple times to help identify the best way to help a student be successful in school. An important feature of this problem-solving model is that it recognizes that schools cannot be problem-free. Instead, it offers a way of dealing with problems when they happen so that the long-term negative impact is minimized.

Problem Identification

The first step begins with problem identification activities. Such activities include any and all moments when a student's school difficulties are initially identified. To help explain this step and the other steps of the model, the metaphor of radar will be used. Problem identification may be likened to the moment when something is first detected on a radar screen. Those monitoring the screen do not know what's causing the "blip" on the screen, but they know it needs to be addressed. A number of different people may participate in problem identification activities. Teachers, parents, students, administrators, bus drivers, and/or cafeteria staff members may help to bring problems to greater attention and put them on the "radar screen." Problem identification is not an end unto itself. Instead, this first step activates a process by which more data about a student's school difficulties can be collected.

Problem Definition

The second step of the problem-solving model is problem definition. This step includes evaluating the nature and magnitude of the problem and determining whether the problem requires an intervention or might resolve itself on its own. This is similar to what sea-farers and aviators must do in order to determine whether the radar signal is from a large attack ship or a small unarmed private vessel. How the pilot responds will be based on the nature of the object identified by the radar. In the same way, educators can help students by defining the nature of the student's problem. Problem definition activities include evaluating the student's skills in certain areas and comparing them to what is expected. Such definitions include measurements such as reading fluency, frequency of on-task behaviors, and rate of homework completion. Only once a student's current behaviors have been identified is it possible to know the magnitude and importance of the problem identified in Step l. Some problems may be very small and likely to resolve on their own over time. Alternatively, other problems may be of immediate concern. If the difference between a student's current performance and what is expected is large, that student is likely to have a serious school problem that needs to be resolved.

Designing Intervention Plans

The third step of the problem-solving model includes putting in place specific activities and procedures designed to reduce significantly the difference between what a student can currently do and what he or she is expected to do. The development of such intervention plans is similar to how a pilot of a boat or plane might respond to information concerning the source of a radar signal. If the captain of a small sailboat is charting a course and finds that he or she is steering toward a much larger vessel, changing course is the prudent thing to do, especially if the larger ship is an aircraft carrier or oil tanker. Educators can help students to chart a new course by designing ways to improve their skills so that they can be successful in school. . . . [All] interventions need to be empirically validated with evidence of effectiveness in school settings. Effective interventions include methods such as direct instruction of specific skills, positive behavior support plans, and peer-assisted learning strategies. . . . A specific time frame and plan for implementing the intervention, what personnel will be involved, and how data will be collected provide crucial links to the next steps of the problem-solving process.

Implementing the Intervention

This step of the model has two major components: implementation and progress monitoring. The intervention should be implemented as planned and intended. If a well-designed intervention is put into action incorrectly, it may be impossible to know whether it could have worked. For this reason, the intervention plan should include some form of treatment integrity check to document whether the plan was implemented as intended. If an intervention is implemented as planned but does not work, it can be changed, but information about initial ineffectiveness is needed in order to design effective alternatives. If some portions of the intervention did work, these might be retained and used with additional new components. The only way to know if an intervention works is to collect data. This is the critical second component of problem-solving step 4. From the very first moment that an intervention is put into place, data concerning the outcomes must be collected. This is no different from a pilot who would monitor the radar screen as well as other sources of information to verify that the threat posed by a larger vessel is reduced as a result of someone changing course. Data collection methods can include recording the frequency, rate, accuracy, duration, and intensity of a behavior or skill. (Determination of what type of data recording procedure to use is based on the specific nature of the problem. Students who are often off-task can be monitored according to the frequency of on-task behaviors. Students with reading difficulties can be monitored by checking and recording oral or silent reading fluency). Progress monitoring also involves ongoing data analysis. Single-case experimental designs are typically used in the analysis of data.

Problem Solution

As mentioned earlier, the problem-solving model is organized in such a way that it can be used to solve a wide range of school problems. It is set up to account for the reality that there will always be problems in schools. Thankfully, many school problems are solvable, and this model has an identifiable end step that documents when a problem is resolved. The specific way that each school problem will be solved will always differ according to the strengths and needs of each child. The important aspect of the fifth, and final, step of the model is that it allows for recognition of school success by noting when certain preset criteria for success are met. Just as the captain of a boat lets out a sign of relief when a new course results in being out of harm's way, students and their support teams can determine a performance level that will mark problem solution and celebrate when it is met. As noted above, the problem-solving model is set up to be used continuously, as needed. For some students, one intervention may be all it takes to achieve problem solution. For others, the problems may be greater in size and number, and multiple problem solution parties will be shared on the pathway to greater success. Importantly, problem solution provides all members of the school team with the chance to identify what has been successful and develop new goals and plans.

RTI and Special Education

As described [earlier], RTI methods share a legacy with prior efforts to improve special education programs. It is impossible to separate RTI completely from special education because RTI activities occur in a sequence along a continuum. When empirically validated interventions are used, it is expected that most students school progress will be appropriate. Still, RTI methods include steps to be taken for students who continue to struggle in school despite attempted interventions. For some students, RTI activities will result in evaluation and eligibility for special education services. Indeed, . . . RTI methods have been included in the most recent reauthorization of the Individuals with Disabilities Education Act. Such methods also fit with other recent education policies such as the No Child Left Behind Act and related state programs. Importantly, RTI methods were developed with the goal of spreading a wide net for identification of students having difficulty in school. This net is designed initially to identify a larger number of students who need help than will end up in special education. The goal is to provide students at risk or already experiencing school difficulties with interventions that prevent additional problems.

An example of the wide-net approach included in RTI is the Texas Primary Reading Instrument (TPRI). This instrument is part of a statewide effort to identify and define the needs of students at risk of reading problems. It is organized such that scores on the TPRI will yield a list of students who may have reading problems. This list is used to design and implement reading interventions that will be monitored over time. It is expected that most students will show reading improvement as a result of the intervention. Those students who do not show improvement are provided with additional intervention that is developed in response to the data collected during the earlier program. Students who consistently struggle to learn to read despite multiple empirically based reading interventions are evaluated to determine whether they are eligible for special education services. Similar programs also have been used in Iowa and Massachusetts. Data from early reading RTI programs in Iowa showed that fewer students were ultimately placed in special education programs after RTI methods were used than before.

RTI and General Education

The success of RTI as a means of reducing the number of students who receive special education services is important for those concerned about too many students being identified as disabled. The more important aspect of RTI data thus far is how many students have found greater school success as a result of data-based educational programming. Yes, fewer students have been labeled as disabled; however, these same students have developed critical basic skills that increase the likelihood they will be successful in school and life. For this reason, RTI is really a general education initiative. RTI activities begin and end in general education. They may serve as a pathway for "child find" activities for some students, but they provide systematic, data-based decision making for far more general education students. Some researchers have noted that general educators are not prepared for the demands that are implicit in RTI methods. Nonetheless, there is emerging evidence that RTI methods are very effective as part of general education, and the U.S. Department of Education's *Reading First* grant program is organized according to several RTI principles.

In order for RTI to become a routine part of general education, teachers, administrators, and specialists will need to learn how to implement and interpret RTI methods and data. Some teachers may not have received much, if any, training in data analysis. Others may worry that RTI is another "add-on" to what they are already doing and fear that there are not enough hours in the school day to incorporate RTI practices. Importantly, RTI does not require "adding on" to what is already being done in the classroom. Instead, it involves reviewing current classroom practices to identify those that yield evidence of effective instruction as well as those that do not. RTI methods call for teachers to *replace* those practices that do not yield student improvement with those that do. When using RTI, general education teachers will remain the most important part of students' school success.

RTI and Public Policy

RTI has already become part of several educational policies and is likely to be incorporated into future programs as well. The rationale for having RTI as a central focus of public education policy is that it is a population-based system for determining which students need more assistance. Population-based decision making comes from the field of public health. Examples of population-based policies already widely in place include mandatory immunization of all school children, review and recall of beef, pork, and poultry by the Department of Agriculture, and warnings about alcohol use on beer, wine, and liquor labels. All of these policies are designed to protect the public health and welfare through systematic procedures, recalls, and warnings. Although population-based decision making has been widely used in health, food, and safety policies for many years, it has been less utilized in school settings. RTI represents a major application of population-based policy in education because it calls for screening of the entire school population for identification of possible school difficulties.

Just as there are many public welfare benefits from immunizations, meat recalls, and alcohols labels, RTI applications in schools are likely to yield important gains for all students. The universal nature of RTI methods mean that all students are reviewed regularly to determine if school problems are present. This prevents students from "slipping through the cracks." Those students who need additional assistance are provided with interventions previously shown to be effective, just as physicians use treatments validated in research studies. The data-driven nature of RTI means that decisions about school practices are derived from students' actual performance in class. New interventions are provided only as needed when data show that existing practices are not working. In the end, RTI is designed to enhance all students' educational outcomes by providing continuous progress monitoring of all students and specialized assistance to those who need it.

Big Ideas About RTI

There are three main components to RTI, high-quality instruction, frequent assessment, and data-based decision making. Each of these components connects to a "big idea" about educational policy. High-quality instruction is based on the idea that all children deserve effective instruction that leads to achieving functional skills. Frequent assessment is based on the idea that continuous assessment leads to skill improvement. Instructional decision making relates to the idea that adjustments to instruction must be based on data. When the three components of RTI are put together with the problem-solving assessment model, decisions about a student's progress toward education goals are much easier to make. . . .

**Douglas Fuchs and
Donald D. Deshler**

 **NO**

What We Need to Know About Responsiveness to Intervention (and Shouldn't Be Afraid to Ask)

In May 2006, David Tilly and seven of his colleagues sent a letter to the Office of Special Education and Rehabilitation Services (OSERS), which was subsequently given to us by one of the authors. The letter writers chided OSERS on several counts, including that, in their view, the agency wrongly promotes a notion that researchers and practitioners need to understand more about responsiveness to intervention (RTI) to ensure its successful implementation. Tilly and associates expressed an opposite belief, claiming that practitioners have all necessary and sufficient information to conduct RTI competently. They wrote, "University- and field-based research strongly supports the use of Problem-Solving/RTI as the service delivery model that results in the most equitable outcomes for the diverse learners in the United States today. . . . RTI implementations have improved outcomes in all students and [have] shown reductions in referrals for special education. . . . The [only remaining] problem is one of scaling, which is a different research question than . . . whether practices like RTI are effective or implementable" [sic].

This "we-know-all-we-need-to-know" message about RTI implementation has also been delivered at conferences and in-service programs across the nation. The obvious intent of the message is to instill confidence among teachers and administrators about RTI implementation and to encourage them to get on with the difficult work of reforming service delivery. A less obvious intent seems to be to characterize those raising questions about RTI as uninformed or (worse) temporizing or (much worse) attempting to obstruct wider use of RTI through passive–aggressive intellectualizing.

We join Tilly and company—and virtually everyone else—in wishing to see stronger and earlier intervening practices in general education. We support a multitiered approach to provide increasingly intensive help to our most academically vulnerable children. We also believe practitioners and researchers know a good deal about how to conduct RTI. Nevertheless, the "we-know-it-all" message strikes us as an exaggeration and counter-productive. It is an exaggeration because the message is factually incorrect. We do not have all necessary technical information to ensure that RTI, to quote Tilly

From *Learning Disabilities Research & Practice*, 22(2), May 2007, pp. 129–135 (refs. omitted). Copyright © 2007 by Council for Exceptional Children. Reprinted by permission of Wiley-Blackwell Publishing.

and colleagues, improves outcomes "in all students"—a fact of which at least some teachers, administrators, and researchers are well aware. The message is counter-productive because practitioners must understand what we collectively do not know so they can avoid costly mistakes. Moreover, by recognizing what we *do not* know, practitioners and researchers can work diligently to find solutions, thereby strengthening our shared capacity to implement RTI successfully on a wide scale.

A case in point is work at the National Research Center on Learning Disabilities (hereafter "LD Center"), which, for the past 5 years, has focused in part on how best to identify nonresponders to Tier 1 instruction who are in need of more intensive and costly instruction at Tier 2. Many advocates of RTI propose use of a one-time universal screen to identify these children. In such an approach, all children in a given school are assessed on a brief measure at the beginning of the school year. Those scoring below a norm-referenced cut point (e.g., 25th percentile on the Woodcock Reading Mastery Tests— Word Identification) or below a performance benchmark associated with poor long-term outcome (e.g., 15 on curriculum-based measurement word identification fluency at the beginning of first grade) enter Tier 2 intervention. The assumption is that low performance relative to the normative cut point or the performance benchmark at the start of the school year constitutes necessary and sufficient evidence that the child has failed to respond to Tier 1 instruction in the previous year and requires more intensive help.

However, in our research at the LD Center, 50 percent of first-grade students identified as nonresponsive to Tier 1 instruction by a one-time universal screen given in early fall "recovered" spontaneously. That is, they made unanticipated satisfactory progress in reading throughout their first-grade year without Tier 2 instruction. The number of these "false positives" (i.e., children who appear at risk but are not) was reduced considerably when, as part of our research, we used data from five weeks of weekly progress monitoring following the universal screen to further specify the nonresponders. On the basis of this research finding, we have been encouraging practitioners to combine the use of a one-time universal screen (to identify at-risk children) with short-term progress monitoring (to identify nonresponders for Tier 2 instruction). We predict that this two-step procedure will save school districts many thousands of dollars by helping them provide Tier 2 instruction to only those students who truly need it. This LD Center research, we believe, illustrates how asking and exploring technical questions can increase our knowledge about RTI implementation and provide practitioners with practical payoffs.

The importance of asking questions—of knowing what we don't know— about RTI implementation is underscored by recently released federal regulations that are bereft of procedural detail. Practitioners across the nation are looking for guidance, and the best they will get will help clarify for them what is known and unknown. It is in this spirit that we wrote this article. Our intent is not to disparage RTI or diminish its value by identifying questions that need answers. Nor is our intent to discourage its implementation. Rather, we wish to say to practitioners, "When implementing RTI, bring as much good knowledge to bear as you can, including the recognition that we don't know everything important about it." Following are a handful of important questions that still need answers. We begin at a general level and move to the more specific.

What's the Purpose of RTI?

Practitioners need to agree on the purpose of RTI—at least practitioners in the same school district or state need to agree. Some who have written about RTI say it should be only about early intervention, while others say "disability identification." Still others say, "both." Those believing RTI should be synonymous with early intervention argue for three or more instructional tiers exclusive of special education.

Implicit in this belief about RTI is a view of education reform that reminds us of the Regular Education Initiative, which emerged in the mid-to-late 1980s. Its leaders had three goals. The first was to merge special and general education into one inclusive system. The second goal was to dramatically increase the number of children with disabilities in mainstream classrooms by use of large-scale, full-time mainstreaming. The third goal, implicit in the first two, was to strengthen the academic achievement of students with high-incidence disabilities, as well as of low-achievers without disabilities. To wit: "Local schools should be encouraged to experiment and evaluate the effectiveness of a variety of educational approaches in solving the widespread persistent problem of how to achieve more productive learning for all students." In short, as general education became better resourced, it would become more resourceful; as it became more "expandable," special education would become more "expendable."

Indeed, this Regular-Education-Initiative-like assumption drives the part of the most recent IDEA reauthorization that gives general education 15 percent of special education monies. The special education law seems to say to practitioners and other stakeholders: "Front load special education dollars into general education to strengthen prevention efforts, and fewer children will require special education on the back end." Notwithstanding the logic and confidence reflected in this message, it is unclear just how preventive and expandable general education can become. Which brings us to the work of Mary Wagner and her colleagues.

Wagner and her associates compared nationally representative high-school students with LD from the mid-1980s to same-age students with LD in 2001–2002. Thus, students in the earlier of the two national studies participated in pre-Regular-Education-Initiative schools; those in the later investigation were more likely to have participated in more inclusive schools. Consonant with our assumption, Wagner, Newman, and Cameto found a greater percentage of the nationally representative 2001–2002 cohort taking more challenging academic courses—courses more frequently conducted in general education settings. Further, whereas only 2 percent of the high schoolers in the mid-1980s earned "mostly As" and only 56 percent graduated, 19 percent in 2001–2002 had "mostly As" and 74 percent graduated.

However, according to Wagner, Newman, Cameto, Levine, and Marder in 2001–2002, class participation of students with LD was much lower than that of their non-disabled peers, and they earned average standard scores of only 86 (20th percentile) and 88 (28th percentile) on the passage comprehension and math calculation subtests, respectively, of the Woodcock–Johnson III Research edition. For passage comprehension, 74 percent of the nationally representative high-school students with LD performed in the bottom quartile; for math calculations, 53 percent were in the bottom quartile. Thus, despite the more inclusive classroom practices apparently engendered by the Regular Education Initiative, the reading and math performance of many high-school students with LD in the 2001–2002 cohort was still poor, raising questions about general education's capacity to accommodate these students' special learning needs.

Wagner and associates' findings are not necessarily cause for pessimism or skepticism about RTI because there are important differences in principle between RTI and the Regular Education Initiative. Rather, results from Wagner and associates' national, longitudinal studies suggest the magnitude of the challenge involved in attempting to make K-12 classrooms substantially more accommodating of greater academic diversity.

Returning to the start of this section, we see RTI as potentially providing both strong early intervention and more valid means of disability identification— not just one or the other. We encourage practitioners and researchers to recognize that assessment and identification are (or should be) inextricably connected to early intervention; to a school district's or school building's capacity to provide more intensive and costly help to its most vulnerable, academically unresponsive children. An assessment and identification process with strong predictive validity is likely to enhance the effectiveness and efficiency of early intervention, as well as strengthen the public's support of it.

What Conditions Support RTI's Successful Implementation?

When practitioners read about effective RTI models in the literature or hear about their successful implementation at professional conferences, they need to understand the conditions, or contextual factors, in the school or district in which RTI was successfully implemented. In other words, educational innovations like RTI gain most traction in settings that provide the necessary conditions to support their use. Less successful implementations elsewhere may be caused by an absence of supporting conditions, rather than because of the particular RTI procedures, per se.

Because RTI consists of numerous components (e.g., multiple instructional tiers, progress monitoring), it must function as a well-orchestrated system to be effective. Effective implementation is dependent upon:

1. Significant and sustained investments in professional development programs to provide teachers with the array of skills required to effectively implement RTI as well as to deal with ongoing staff turnover.
2. Engaged administrators who set expectations for adoption and implementation of RTI, provide the necessary resources, and support the use of procedures that ensure fidelity of implementation.

3. District level support to hire teachers who embrace RTI principles and possess the pre requisite skills to implement it effectively in their classes.
4. A willingness of teaching and ancillary staff (e.g., school psychologists) to have their roles redefined in ways to support effective implementation.
5. The degree to which staff is given sufficient time to "make sense of" and accommodate RTI into their instructional framework, and have their questions and concerns addressed.
6. Whether decisions regarding the adoption of RTI have been influenced by the thoughts and beliefs of practitioners at the grassroots level versus decisions made exclusively by those on high.

In short, failure to ask questions about the factors that surround and support RTI implementation may prevent practitioners from understanding the complete picture. This may lead to adoption of another site's RTI model based on the incorrect assumption that the success of the other site's model (as reported in the literature) is due to what happens in the classroom during the RTI implementation process. In reality, there are many situational factors—inside and outside the classroom—that support and account for its successful implementation. These factors are as important to identify and understand as are the components of the RTI model itself.

What Is the Nature of Tier 1 Instruction?

Practitioners and researchers almost always refer to classroom instruction as Tier 1. Many also describe the importance of classroom teachers using "scientifically validated" instruction. Yet there is widespread uncertainty about what this means. "Scientifically validated" refers to a process of experimentation by which the importance of an instructional procedure or curriculum has been tested. Most rigorous testing involves the use of randomized control trials, whereby students or classrooms, typically, are assigned at random to two or more study groups, including a no-treatment control group or comparison group. Randomized assignment is meant to help prevent or reduce the likelihood of non-treatment forces from influencing findings and complicating their interpretation. Use of randomized control trials, in short, is critically important to program or curriculum development and evaluation.

Randomized control trials or not, there is no instructional program or curriculum that has been validated for use with all children. Hence, when we say that an instructional approach or curriculum is "scientifically validated," we mean it's a "good bet" for many children. It should be considered seriously by practitioners for adoption, but it comes with no guarantees. No instructional program or curriculum is valid for all students or for all time. They must be implemented and evaluated by local practitioners.

The good news here is that there is a large handful of instructional procedures and curricula that have been rigorously tested and that should be considered "good bets" by practitioners for use in Tier 1 settings. Many other instructional procedures and curricula available to practitioners have not been tested rigorously. This doesn't mean that they will be ineffective if used. Rather, there is no scientific basis to know whether they will fail or succeed. They are *not* good bets. All districts or states should establish a vetting process to help teachers and administrators distinguish good bets from bad ones. As we write, few have thought seriously about how to establish such a vetting process.

What Is "Problem Solving" and Does It Promote Academic Achievement Among Children with Severe Learning Problems?

An example of the importance and complexity of understanding the term "scientifically validated" involves "problem solving." Problem solving is an oft-used and sometimes confusing term in the context of RTI. By our count, it is currently used in three ways: first, to describe a process by which differentiated instruction is developed, child-by-child, at Tiers 1 and 2 in general education; second, to signify the data-based, recursive, individualized instruction that special educators should be using with their schools' most difficult-to-teach students; third, to refer to how building-based teams operate to provide support to general educators with academically at-risk students.

Problem solving as a process to develop, implement, and evaluate interventions in general education was conceptualized and first researched by John Bergan and colleagues more than 30 years ago. It is a behavioral approach to school consultation. Its most frequently studied application has been to help teachers of students with conduct problems, such as talking or moving about the classroom without permission, or with "work productivity" problems, including inattentive or undermotivated behavior. Research indicates problem solving can be effective when applied to such student behaviors. Currently, however, some RTI proponents are advancing problem solving as a means of helping classroom teachers deal with students with severe learning problems that go beyond inattention and low motivation despite that it has not been scientifically validated for this purpose.

We need to know whether problem solving in general education identifies or leads to the development of instruction that accelerates the learning of children with severe learning problems not caused by poor attention and motivation. This will require researchers who recognize a need for documenting fidelity of treatment implementation, which will be more challenging than usual because the treatments in a problem-solving process are constructed on a case-by-case basis and often involve the use of combined interventions that have never been tested scientifically. Appropriate measures of fidelity-of-treatment-implementation must be constructed as part of the research process.

Who Are Responders and Nonresponders?

Research on instruction at Tiers 1 and 2 has documented these facts: (a) many students benefit from this instruction, especially when standard treatment protocols (i.e., explicitly scripted activities) drive the activity; (b) there are nonresponders—or students who do not respond to scientifically valid instruction, even when its intensity comes close to that of instruction in a good special education program and is implemented with strong fidelity. Estimates of nonresponders at Tier 2, when the instruction is conducted by researchers, range from 2 to 6 percent of the general school population.

RTI Methods of Identification

Once Tier 2 instruction is delivered, practitioners evaluate student responsiveness. More specifically, performance must be categorized as responsive or nonresponsive. The research literature suggests at least five RTI methods of defining these terms. The first method, which we term "median split," was introduced by Vellutino et al. They measured students on the Woodcock Reading Mastery Tests several times during a multiyear tutoring program and used hierarchical linear modeling to obtain slope of improvement for each child. To derive a cut point for designating responsiveness, the slopes were rank ordered, and the median was determined. Any student whose slope was at or above this median was designated responsive to the tutoring; those whose slopes were below the median were labeled nonresponsive.

Torgesen et al. used an alternative, "normalization" method. He and his colleagues tested students on the Woodcock Reading Mastery Tests at the end of their tutoring intervention and computed standard scores. Those scoring at or above a standard score of 90—the 25th percentile—were designated responsive; those below the 25th percentile, nonresponsive. A third method is also based on performance at the end of tutoring but it employs a criterion-referenced benchmark associated with appropriate future performance. We refer to this as the "final benchmark" method. Good, Simmons, and Kaméenui (2001) followed this approach when they measured students at the end of first-grade intervention with the Dynamic Indicators of Basic Early Literacy Skills (DIBELS) oral reading fluency measure. To define responsiveness, they compared raw scores on this measure against a criterion-referenced benchmark associated with future success on the Oregon highstakes third-grade assessment. First-grade students with final DIBELS scores exceeding 39 were designated responsive. Those with scores below 40 were recognized as unresponsive.

Fuchs and Fuchs developed a fourth method, "dual discrepancy." It is illustrated in the research of Speece and Case, who used curriculum-based measurement passage reading fluency to test students weekly and at treatment's end. "Treatment" was defined as the core reading program in the general classroom. Speece and Case summarized student response in two ways: slope of improvement during treatment and performance level at the end of treatment. Nonresponders were required to demonstrate both slope and performance levels at the end of treatment more than 1 standard deviation (*SD*) below that of classroom peers.

A fifth method of operationalizing responsiveness and nonresponsiveness is based entirely on students' slope, and we refer to it as the "slope discrepancy" method. Students are measured periodically; a slope of academic improvement is computed; students above a normative cut point, referenced to the classroom, school, district, or nation, are deemed responsive, and others are designated nonresponsive. This approach is illustrated in the work of Fuchs, Fuchs, and Compton.

Before proceeding, we wish to point out that alternative RTI methods, measures, testing frequencies, and cut points may be applied in various combinations. For example, recall that Speece and Case used a dual discrepancy method with passage reading fluency determined weekly and at the end of treatment. Their cut point required nonresponders to score 1 *SD* or more below classroom peers on both slope and final level of performance. Alternatively, a school might collect curriculum-based measurement word identification fluency (rather than passage reading fluency) data on a monthly (not weekly) basis, with same-grade school (not classroom) peers providing the normative framework and with a cut point of 0.75 *SD* (rather than 1 *SD*) on slope and final level of performance. The very important question here is, Do different RTI identification methods . . . with alternative measures and testing frequencies, yield the same or different subgroups of responsive and nonresponsive children with similar or dissimilar profiles of disability?

LD Center Research

As part of our LD Center research, we designed a prospective, longitudinal study for which we recruited 42 first-grade teachers who were using the same core reading program. Based on September performance on Woodcock Reading Mastery Tests—Word Identification, Rapid Letter Naming, and teacher judgment, we identified the six lowest-performing first-grade children per class as potentially at-risk for learning disabilities. These 252 children were assigned randomly, within class, to receive tutoring or not. We delivered tutoring in small groups, three times per week for 10 weeks, while monitoring weekly progress on curriculum-based measurement word identification fluency. The children were post-tested at the end of tutoring, at the end of first grade, and at the end of second grade. In first grade, we applied seven traditional and RTI methods for designating reading disabilities: "initial" (beginning of first grade) low achievement, "final" (end of first grade) IQ-achievement discrepancy, median split, final normalization, final benchmark, slope discrepancy, and dual discrepancy. For each of these methods of identification, we considered the impact of using alternate measures.

Our findings indicated that, for our traditional *non-RTI methods*, an initial low achievement definition of reading disabilities, especially in conjunction with the Woodcock Reading Mastery Tests—Word Identification, provided reasonable prevalence estimates, acceptable "specificity" (the degree to which a measure identifies children at low risk for disability status), and good "hit rates" (the proportion of children correctly identified as at risk). But it also produced poor "sensitivity" (how well a measure correctly identifies children at risk for disability status), suggesting that many children appearing at risk but who are not would receive unnecessary first-grade tutoring. By contrast, IQ-achievement discrepancy at the end of first grade, a "traditional" approach to LD identification, provided unrealistically low prevalence estimates and poor sensitivity. It did, however, produce good hit rates and strong specificity. But too many children were not identified at the end of first grade although they showed a need for reading intervention, as revealed by their end-of-second-grade reading disabilities status.

In terms of *RTI methods*, final normalization resulted in an acceptable reading disabilities prevalence rate but produced mixed hit rates, mixed sensitivity, and mixed specificity. Benchmark and median split methods overidentified reading disabilities. Curriculum-based measurement word identification fluency slope and dual discrepancy over-identified reading disabilities but resulted in acceptable hit rates, sensitivity, and specificity.

An important conclusion from our LD Center study was that both traditional methods and RTI methods for defining and distinguishing responsiveness and nonresponsiveness result in different groups of children designated "reading disabled," with each method resulting in varying prevalence rates, severity, and stability. All of this suggests an urgent need for a data-based consensus about what RTI methods of disability identification (in combination with which measures, testing frequencies, and cutpoints) will be most useful. With such consensus, greater consistency in "reading disability" and "learning disability" designations across schools, districts, and states might be achieved.

Is There Need of Formal Testing by Multidisciplinary Teams?

This question creates two camps. The group that answers "no" makes at least two important points. First, it says that a multitiered instructional process will generate all information necessary to understand the learner and her academic needs. Second, the formal testing of working memory, receptive language, processing speed, and the like, will not yield information with strong instructional relevance. Hence it asks why should we measure such cognitive processes? This second point resonates; the first point less so because it reflects a failure to recognize that students chronically unresponsive to multiple tiers of increasingly intensive instruction need something different. That is, implementing "x" instruction or "y" curriculum with greater fidelity, or in groups of three and not five, or providing a token economy instead of verbal praise, is not likely to make learners from chronically nonresponsive students. There is strong need for instructional research that explores whether and how knowing more about cognitive processing leads to more effective teaching and learning.

More of What We Need to Know

1. How relevant is RTI to middle and high schools? If we define RTI's purpose in part as delivering early intervention, then how should we think about RTI for a 10th-grade student reading at a 2nd-grade level? Do we perhaps need a very different model for at-risk students in middle school and high school?

2. Most RTI intervention research has involved early reading. What do we know about effective multitiered instruction that addresses reading comprehension? Writing? Social studies? Science?
3. If classroom teachers implement scientifically validated instruction at Tier 1, who will conduct Tier 2 instruction? If school psychologists, then who will conduct formal evaluations and re-evaluations? If special education teachers, who will work most intensively with chronically nonresponsive children? If para-professionals, who will prepare them?
4. What criteria should practitioners use in school buildings and districts to evaluate the success of their RTI implementation? Student achievement on high-stakes tests? Progress monitoring data? Information on the fidelity with which interventions are implemented? Special education enrollments and costs? In a related way, who should aggregate a school building's data or school district's data, and how should this be accomplished, so practitioners can effectively and responsibly answer the question, "is RTI working?"
5. Where in the RTI process does due process occur?

Conclusion

Like Ed Kaméenui . . . we believe it is constructive and important to think hard about what we know and don't know about RTI, and it is in this spirit that we've written this article. We are not suggesting that there is a paucity of knowledge because, in fact, researchers and practitioners collectively know a good deal about aspects of RTI, like how to monitor student progress accurately and meaningfully. But it is untrue and misleading to claim that we currently have a necessary and sufficient knowledge base to guide the implementation of RTI as a process of early intervention and disability identification across all grades, for all academic skills, in all content areas, and for all children and youth. It behooves teachers, administrators, and researchers to understand what we don't know.

If we were to prioritize areas in which more knowledge is needed, our priorities would be these: First, practitioners need scientifically validated instructional protocols that are likely to accelerate student progress in pivotal skills aside from early reading (e.g., math and writing) and in content areas (e.g., social studies and science). Generally effective instructional protocols are critical because in an RTI framework instruction is the "test" against which student response is measured. Without validated instruction (implemented with fidelity by practitioners), RTI cannot be a valid method of disability identification or early intervention. Second, practitioners require a validated means of determining "responsiveness" and "nonresponsiveness." As indicated, there is a handful of possibilities but no consensus about which are preferable. If practitioners across the nation choose different RTI methods of identification, there may be as much or greater variation in number and type of children identified as having LD than the variation produced by use of IQ-achievement discrepancy.

In part because of the under specification of the most recent federal regulations on RTI, and an absence of necessary and sufficient technical information, we're in a kind of *de facto* de-regulated environment when it comes to RTI. This can mean greater flexibility and discretionary decision making; more room for innovation. At the same time, it contributes to confusion and uncertainty. It also provides opportunity to those who would use this situation for their own purposes. In such circumstances, especially, practitioners must educate themselves by asking tough questions—of themselves and others—as they organize to deliver stronger prevention services and more valid methods of disability identification through RTI implementation.

POSTSCRIPT

Is Response to Intervention (RTI) Ready for Implementation?

Decrying the large numbers of students in special education, one assistant secretary for the Office of Special Education and Rehabilitative Services identified three flaws in the educational system: Many children cannot receive needed help because they do not meet eligibility guidelines; poor school performance is often equated with a disability; and early intervention services are unavailable (Will, *Exceptional Children*, 1986).

Yes, you read the date correctly. 1986. The speaker was Madeline Will, who recommended a partnership between general education and special education to build "a more powerful, more responsive educational system" (Will, 1986). RTI is today's remedy for very similar problems.

It is difficult to find someone completely opposed to RTI (Wright, Dude Publishing, 2007). How can any educator object to using information to make decisions about student learning?

Both selections describe RTI as a significant change in general education. Rachel Brown-Chidsey and Mark W. Steege reassure classroom teachers that RTI will not mean adding extra tasks, just using available information more effectively. Examining student work carefully helps teachers intervene early, rather than waiting until a student fails. Douglas Fuchs and Donald D. Deshler wonder how much prevention can be delivered by a general education teacher, who must balance many compelling priorities.

The scarcity of RTI-related research is frequently mentioned. Most studies have focused on the acquisition of decoding skills in elementary-level children (Gersten & Dimino, *New Directions in Research*, 2006). There is little evidence about the best interventions or the optimal duration of each. Nevertheless, since there is consensus on RTI's basic elements, some see this as part of the process of development rather than a "fatal flaw" (Wright, 2007).

Since RTI is part of existing law, perhaps the question is not whether educators should implement RTI, but how to do so. Although some fret because the U.S. federal government does not specify one model, this gives educators the latitude—and the responsibility—to design RTI programs that respond to their particular community of students (Kame'enui, *Teaching Exceptional Children*, 2007).

One goal of RTI is to reduce the overrepresentation of minorities in special education. Educators must use existing flexibility to consider what RTI means for culturally diverse students, English language learners, and those who live in poverty (NCCRESt, 2005). One essential resource is the National Center for Culturally Responsive Educational Systems (NCCRESt, http://www.nccrest.org), sponsored by the U.S. Department of Education. NCCRESt is dedicated to exploring and disseminating information that helps educators identify and implement "effective literacy and behavioral interventions for students who are culturally and linguistically diverse." The newsletter and Web site are rich sources of technical assistance and professional development. The NCCRESt position statement on RTI cautions that an intervention system that does not consider the complexity of today's students risks being no more than "old wine in a new bottle." Very little will have changed, except the label.

RTI has the potential to be a new way of examining student learning. The outcome could be a comprehensive array of school supports other than special education (Adelman & Taylor, *Addressing Barriers to Learning*, 2006). One thing is certain, the questions about RTI are likely to lead to an array of designs and, perhaps, to the kind of solution Madeline Will envisioned 30 years ago.

As you weigh these perspectives, consider other questions. Does RTI reform special education, or is special education being used as a tool to reform general education practices? If RTI is based in the general education classroom, why isn't it part of NCLB? If RTI does not achieve its goals because of implementation challenges, will special education be held accountable? And, most importantly, what does all this mean for children who struggle?

ISSUE 9

Should Special Education and General Education Merge?

YES: Mary T. Brownell, Paul T. Sindelar, Mary T. Kiely, and Louis C. Danielson, from "Special Education Teacher Quality and Preparation: Exposing Foundations, Constructing a New Model," *Exceptional Children* (Spring 2010), pp. 357–377

NO: Margaret J. McLaughlin, from "Evolving Interpretations of Educational Equity and Students With Disabilities," *Exceptional Children* (Spring 2010), pp. 265–278

ISSUE SUMMARY

YES: Mary T. Brownell, Paul T. Sindelar, and Mary T. Kiely, policy scholars from the University of Florida, Gainesville, and Louis C. Danielson at the American Institutes for Research (Danielson) link political changes with special education teacher preparation. They conclude that the future of special education rests within content-rich Response to Intervention (RTI) practices.

NO: Margaret J. McLaughlin, policy architect and analyst from the University of Maryland, sees a disconnect between the singular academic outcomes of No Child Left Behind (NCLB) Act/Elementary and Secondary Education Act (ESEA) and the individualized needs of students with disabilities. Merging is not wise when some students with disabilities are treated unjustly if held to unitary academic outcomes.

General education and special education have long been engaged in a dance. Sometimes the two have moved separately, sometimes in harmony; rarely in unison. Tension exists between their two fundamental education laws. NCLB Act/ESEA focuses on academic standards; Individuals with Disabilities Education Act (IDEA) on ensuring free appropriate public education for individual students with disabilities. Recently, NCLB Act/ESEA and IDEA have begun to address related topics. The reauthorization of IDEA is on hold, pending that of NCLB Act/ESEA. Many wonder if this sequencing signifies an impending merger of the two laws and educational systems.

Special education legislation first focused on getting students with disabilities into schools. Initially, many received specially designed instruction in small self-contained groups. Over time, some children were enrolled in typical classes, but *pulled out* to receive intensive instruction from specialists. When remediation occurred, students missed the curriculum and activities of the regular classroom.

Inclusionary practices, ranging from co-teaching to full inclusion, attempted to link the two systems. Although bringing students closer together for learning, students with disabilities were often excluded from large-group assessments simply because of the existence of their disability.

IDEA '97 required districts to include students with disabilities in large-scale assessment. Some asserted that access did not "guarantee excellence of educational services and outcomes" (Eisenman & Ferretti, *Exceptional Children*, 2010).

NCLB Act (the 2001 authorization of the ESEA) addressed this concern, holding districts accountable for the academic performance of students with disabilities. The following participation options exist:

- Regular assessment (administered to all students in that grade)
- Regular assessment with accommodations
- Alternate assessment based on grade-level achievement standards
- Alternate assessment based on alternate achievement standards
- Assessment based on modified achievement standards

Striving for consistency with NCLB Act, IDEA 2004 required that the highly qualified special education teacher must demonstrate competence in each core subject area taught. Those providing consultative services or support services must possess at least a bachelor's degree and full state certification in special education.

IDEA 2004 also includes RTI, a construct designed to encourage general education teachers to use data to drive their use of evidence-based practices. Special education teachers play a role in RTI's intervention tiers, although that role differs across schools (Mellard, McKnight, & Woods, *Learning Disabilities Research & Practice*, 2009).

As each of the key law's references topics connected to the mission of the other, it is impossible not to wonder if the federal legislators intend to finally merge special education and general education into one, unified system.

Mary T. Brownell, Paul T. Sindelar, Mary T. Kiely, and Louis C. Danielson note that success in special education has come to mean satisfactory progress in the general education curriculum. In today's accountability "pressure cooker," the authors claim the key to the future is dual licensure of all teachers. Special education and general education teachers must collaborate through RTI to ensure that all students succeed academically.

In contrast, Margaret J. McLaughlin urges legislators and educators to recognize there can be no equity if all students are expected to achieve the same academic outcomes. She believes educators must uphold their legal responsibility to provide appropriate individualized programs focused on what each learner needs to succeed in postschool life.

As you read these articles, consider the future they envision. In one, educators combine talents in service of common curriculum standards designed to lead to college or career readiness. In the other, teachers use their expertise differentially to address unique individual needs for adult life. What are the benefits and drawbacks of each option?

YES ◆ Mary T. Brownell, Paul T. Sindelar, Mary T. Kiely, and Louis C. Danielson

Special Education Teacher Quality and Preparation: Exposing Foundations, Constructing a New Model

Special education teacher preparation has evolved over the past 150 years, since special education teachers were first prepared in residential settings. Shifting perspectives on disabilities, effective practice, and providing services to students with disabilities has led to changes in how special education is conceptualized and organized, and, consequently, how special education preparation programs are structured. Today, special education teacher preparation has lost focus, and there is enormous heterogeneity among programs. Redefining *special education teacher preparation* is difficult, especially when the need to do so occurs as serious questions are being raised about the effectiveness of teacher education generally, and when, for students with disabilities, *successful teaching* has been redefined to mean satisfactory progress in the general education curriculum. These changes occur against a backdrop of high-stakes assessments, rigorous academic standards, and individualized accountability—and persistent shortages of highly qualified special education teachers. . . .

Major Trends in Preparing Special Education Teachers

The first teacher preparation programs in special education emerged in residential facilities and were directed by pioneering clinicians such as Seguin, Gallaudet, and Itard. With the advent of compulsory education and demands to improve the quality of public education, the preparation of special education teachers gradually moved away from these residential settings to teachers' colleges. By the 1960s and early 1970s, a series of public laws designed to increase the provision of high-quality educational services to students with disabilities produced an era of explosive growth in special education teacher education. These early programs were predominantly categorical in focus and, as such, were designed for the purpose of training individuals to teach students with specific disabilities. This categorical orientation dominated special education teacher education well into the 1970s, but by the early 1980s it gave way to a noncategorical approach. Proponents of this approach viewed the learning and behavioral needs of

From *Exceptional Children*, vol. 76, no. 3, Spring 2010, pp. 357–359, 366–374. Copyright © 2010 by Council for Exceptional Children. Reprinted by permission. www.cec.sped.org

students with disabilities on a continuum of severity and questioned the relevance of disability categories to effective planning, instruction, and behavior management. In the 1990s, the push to educate students with disabilities in general education classrooms prompted further reconsideration of special education teachers' roles. Because collaboration figured more prominently in inclusive service delivery than it did when students with disabilities were educated in resource rooms or self-contained classrooms, it became an essential feature of special education teacher preparation. As more students with disabilities were included in general education classrooms, teacher educators designed and implemented programs in which classroom teachers and special education teachers were prepared together.

Today, special education teacher preparation is once again in transition. IDEA has mandated that students with disabilities have access to the general education curriculum. The No Child Left Behind Act of 2001 (NCLB) has mandated that schools are accountable for the performance of these students on assessments aligned with the general education curriculum. In addition to knowing how disability-related problems can derail learning and how research-based strategies can be implemented to intervene, special education teachers must be highly qualified in the core content areas they teach. Yet, conversations about special education teacher preparation have not focused on the knowledge and skills needed to execute content-area instruction for students with disabilities, but rather on traditional views of effective special education practice: knowledge of effective interventions, assessment, and collaboration. The current emphasis on access to the general education curriculum and the need for special education teachers who can facilitate access have raised questions about what "high-quality" special education teachers do and how they are prepared to do it. . . .

Reconceptualizing Special Education Preparation: Thoughts for the Future

. . .

Political Context

The political context for educating students with disabilities has shifted considerably over the past 3 decades. Initial focus on access to educational opportunity has given way to a focus on equitable outcomes. Now, an expectation exists that students with disabilities meet general education standards. This shift has occurred in part as a response to concerns about American children's poor performance on international assessments and the poor performance of students with disabilities on high-stakes assessments. Politicians and political pundits have leveled harsh criticism at teachers and schools that fail to produce desired results in spite of billions of tax dollars being invested in the enterprise. In the special education community, disappointing longitudinal data on the academic performance of students with disabilities, particularly in high-needs schools, have intensified the public outcry. Even parents of students with disabilities are demanding that schools and teachers be held accountable for the performance of their children. The overidentification of students with learning disabilities has compounded concerns about the degree to which students are being educated appropriately. Many scholars and policy makers believe that overidentification results in part from schools' failure to employ effective, evidence-based practices. The use of such practices minimizes the misidentification of students as learning disabled by ruling out the possibility of inadequate instruction. Concern over the failure of public schools to produce results has led to an accountability movement in schools that is unparalleled in any other educational era.

In this accountability pressure cooker, schools and teachers have become targets of reform. The availability of strong scientific evidence that effective practices can mitigate if not prevent learning problems and improve outcomes for all students has led to a strong push for teachers to use such practices in their classrooms. In fact, both NCLB and the Individuals with Disabilities Education Improvement Act (IDEA) speak to the need for schools to provide professional development that will enable teachers to use them. Moreover, that IDEA emphasizes the use of "research-based interventions" such as RTI as the preferred method for identifying students with learning disabilities is a reflection of the heightened role that evidence-based practice has taken in schools. RTI has emphasized the importance of teacher accountability for using evidence-based practices in reading and mathematics. In concept, RTI provides students increasingly explicit, intensive, and individually tailored instruction when achievement data suggests they are not making progress. Those who require the most intensive intervention are identified as learning disabled. Under this approach, general and special education teachers are required to employ evidence-based assessments and instructional strategies. At present, RTI has been applied mostly to reading during the primary grades, where a preponderance of research evidence for effective intervention and assessment exists. As states step up their capacity to implement RTI, its application to writing and mathematics should follow, as well as its application to content-area instruction in middle and secondary schools.

Research on teachers and teacher education has been used both to ratchet up expectations that students have access to highly qualified teachers, and to discredit formal teacher preparation. Large-scale analyses of student achievement data show that teachers are one of the strongest effects in the educational system. Value-added studies of teacher effects demonstrate that the most effective general education teachers can achieve student achievement gains that are as much as 50 percentile points greater than those secured by the weakest teachers. These findings, combined with evidence suggesting that teachers' subject matter knowledge has more impact on student achievement than teacher education courses have precipitated questions about the value of teacher education. Although these studies were conducted in the general education context, decisions about accountability based on policy makers' interpretations of them may apply to special education teachers as well.

As a result of accountability pressures and research findings pointing out students with disabilities' poor academic progress, IDEA and NCLB have mandated that students with disabilities be included in state assessments and meet annual yearly progress goals. IDEA also requires that students with disabilities have access to general education curriculum and receive individually designed instruction appropriate to their academic and behavioral needs. Both pieces of legislation also require that students with disabilities, particularly at middle and high school levels, have access to teachers who are highly qualified in both special education and the subjects they teach. At minimum, teachers can achieve highly qualified status by having a bachelor's degree and meeting state requirements for licensure in a content area and special education, which in some states simply means passing a state certification exam. Most special education professionals reject such a minimalist approach to preparing special education teachers, arguing that they will have no avenue for mastering the array of evidence-based practices they will need to teach students with disabilities.

Research on Teaching and Learning: Implications for Teacher Quality

Rapid advancements in technology and the increasing sophistication and accumulation of research on learning, disability, and teaching have contributed to a knowledge base that holds promise for improving the education of students with disabilities. These advances also demonstrate the sophisticated knowledge and skills teachers must have to educate students with disabilities successfully. Technological innovations (such as digitized text combined with scaffolds to assist comprehension) have enabled teachers to provide students with disabilities access to complex concepts and to engage them in higher order thinking. Technological advances also have helped students with disabilities compensate when performing certain academic tasks. For example, speech-to-print software has become increasingly accurate in its ability to record the human voice and subsequently enable students with significant spelling and writing problems to generate text independently. Universal design for learning provides a framework for curriculum design in which these technological innovations may be situated. Such innovations enable general and special education teachers to provide curricular access while individualizing instruction, making the lofty goals of IDEA attainable. . . .

In addition to advances in technology, research on learning and disability has grown in volume and sophistication. Researchers in neuropsychology, psychology, educational psychology, and special education are beginning to amass evidence about the brain and how it functions, how brain functioning might influence the information-processing capacity of some students with disabilities, and how intervention can be structured to improve the brain's capacity for processing information. . . . Although such research is more developed in decoding and spelling, research in mathematics also has begun to connect cognitive deficits and intervention strategies. This intervention research harkens back to scholarship undertaken in the categorical era; it represents a second generation of diagnostic/prescriptive research, done now with more sophisticated assessments, more well-established instructional practices, and stronger ties to academic curriculum. Findings from this research suggest that special education teachers need an understanding of how disability presents itself in an academic area and what must be done to intervene in academic processing deficits.

Findings from recent research on the cognitive processes underlying typical academic development demonstrate that students must receive instruction that engages them in deep processing of selected concepts so that discipline-specific information becomes well integrated in memory. As students progress from novice to expert learners, they abandon simple cognitive strategies, such as paraphrasing, and adopt deeper processing strategies, such as analyzing text to determine its credibility. DI and cognitive strategy instruction, routines known to be effective for special education students, cannot be applied universally across disciplines without careful consideration of how knowledge within a specific discipline will be acquired. For example, competent performance in algebra depends on a conceptual understanding of decimals, fractions, and percents; it also depends on efficiency in solving computational problems involving these concepts. To assist students with disabilities, teachers understand mathematical concepts and relationships among them and how procedural knowledge can support conceptual knowledge. Otherwise, they cannot diagnose how student understanding and procedural knowledge is breaking down and respond with the more intensive, carefully articulated math instruction that students with disabilities need.

Learners require a well-integrated knowledge base in a particular content area to be considered experts; it is reasonable to assume that expert teachers would also have well-integrated knowledge that allows them to recognize problems in their discipline and retrieve knowledge to solve them. Research over the past decade examining the knowledge and classroom practice of effective teachers suggests that such teachers have domain expertise and are able to demonstrate that expertise during instruction. *Domain expertise* refers to skill in teaching a subject and includes knowledge of how the discipline is structured and how students build knowledge within it. By contrast, some researchers and policy makers have touted the importance of subject matter mastery over domain expertise. However, although the portion of variance that subject matter knowledge contributes to between classroom gains in student achievement is statistically significant, it also is trivial in magnitude. This fact as well as findings from recent research on teacher knowledge and expert teacher practice have led some educational researchers to suggest that the domain expertise teachers possess is tied closely to the task of teaching. Several recent studies in both special and general education demonstrate linkages between the specialized domain knowledge needed for teaching and teachers' classroom practice in mathematics and reading. Observational studies reveal how effective teachers engage in content-rich instruction that is carefully crafted, well orchestrated, and responsive to students' diverse needs. Through their instruction, these teachers reveal a sophisticated understanding of knowledge needed to teach in a particular content area.

The research on teaching and learning suggests that special education teachers must have well-integrated knowledge bases, including an understanding of (a) content and how to teach it, (b) specific problems that students with disabilities may experience in a particular content area, (c) the role of technology in circumventing learning issues or supporting access to more sophisticated learning, and (d) the role of specific interventions and assessments in providing more intensive, explicit instruction within a broader curricular context. Taken together, several earlier assumptions about teacher quality support a more contemporary view of special education teacher quality and preservice preparation. Teachers will need disability-specific knowledge as they did in the categorical era; however, now they must understand how certain processing deficits affect academic learning. They also must be knowledgeable of evidence-based intervention strategies that address disability-specific needs. Further, their knowledge must fit within the framework of the general education curriculum, requiring collaboration with general education. Unlike we imagined in previous eras, the diagnostic and intervention knowledge of special education teachers must be well integrated with content domain knowledge. . . .

Using an RTI Framework to Rethink Special Education Teacher Preparation

The RTI movement holds potential to clarify and articulate special and general education teachers' instructional roles. During the integrated era, contributions that general education and special education teachers made to instruction were not well differentiated, in part because the boundaries between their roles had blurred. By contrast, RTI clarifies the roles that special and general education teachers play, and both roles require more sophisticated preparation. RTI . . . involves at least three tiers of instruction and intervention. At Tier 1, in addition to teaching the general curriculum, classroom teachers assume responsibility for monitoring student progress, developing and implementing instructional modifications when needed, and assessing the impact of those modifications on student performance. At Tier 2, classroom teachers retain primary responsibility for students who fail to thrive academically. However, at this point, they begin to work with a multidisciplinary team or other professionals (e.g., content-area specialists or special educators), to plan and evaluate more intensive intervention. Although students remain in the general education classroom, instruction is more intensive and monitoring more frequent and precise. Only when teams determine that students are not progressing satisfactorily in spite of Tier 2 accommodations and modifications are they referred for Tier 3 intervention. At Tier 3, students are provided intensive, explicit instruction to address their unremediated literacy and numeracy needs. Tier 3 instruction involves ongoing assessments and interventions based on those assessments. Many scholars recommend that, at Tier 3, instruction should be the purview of special education and special education teachers; we concur, as specially designed, individualized instruction is a defining feature of a free and appropriate education for students with disabilities.

RTI's ultimate success hinges not just on general and special education's ability to assign responsibility for who provides instruction at each tier but also on how instruction will be conceptualized at each tier. Although detailed explanations of tiered instruction lie beyond the scope of this article, we provide examples of how tiered literacy instruction might be enacted in elementary and secondary contexts. These illustrations are intended to serve as a foundation for discussing general and special education teachers' roles in an RTI framework and articulating how special education teachers can be prepared for those roles.

In the early elementary grades, research on how assessment and intervention can be used in the prevention of reading disabilities has demonstrated that increasingly explicit and intensive intervention in essential language and reading skills reduces the number of students requiring remedial reading services and mitigates the impact of learning disability. In the case of early reading instruction, then, Tier 1 would involve whole-class reading instruction that incorporates research-based practices focused on the essential components of reading (i.e., phonemic awareness, phonics, vocabulary knowledge, fluency, and comprehension). Tiers 2 and 3 instruction would target specific language deficits in reading and increasingly intensive ways of remediating them, with Tier 3 involving the most intensive instruction and frequent progress monitoring. Such intensive and responsive instruction requires deep knowledge of language, literacy, and potential processing deficits, and extensive experience with struggling learners.

Describing how tiered instruction operates in the later grades, however, is more challenging. In an article critiquing the feasibility and consequences of applying an RTI framework to content-area instruction, Mastropieri and Scruggs (2005) suggested that educators have not conceptualized what tiered instruction looks like in different content areas and caution that the field is a long way from doing so. Further, they suggest that poorly articulated frameworks for operationalizing tiered instruction do not help schools improve teaching quality. They argue that secondary instruction is fast-paced, lecture-based, and focused on abstract learning, and that it emphasizes memorizing content for high-stakes assessments. As a result, most secondary instruction in general education classrooms is not accessible to students with learning difficulties. Thus, little room is left for differentiating instruction or identifying areas of learning that could be remediated intensively within the general education curricular framework.

Although few would disagree with concerns about secondary instruction and its suitability for RTI, many educators—including school-based professionals already implementing RTI—would argue that the time is right for implementation. These educators posit that students' abilities to handle the literacy, language, and mathematics demands posed in content-area instruction are essential for genuine access to the general education curriculum. They assert that schools should move forward now with RTI, using the demands of content-area instruction and struggles that students with high-incidence disabilities experience as a way of describing how RTI works at the secondary level.

As students progress in school, the literacy and language skills they need to profit from content-area instruction change. The language and literacy skills students need to understand narrative texts differ from the skills required for reading and writing in different academic disciplines. For example, comprehension strategy instruction, an approach supported by the National Reading Panel, typically involves teaching students generic strategies, such as making graphic representations of text and summarizing text. Although both are important generic strategies that enable students to comprehend many genres of academic writing, they are insufficient for fully comprehending academic text. Each academic discipline has its own particular way of communicating ideas. In the area of science, to comprehend the natural world, students must be able to observe, measure, predict, and explain phenomena and relationships among them. Thus, comprehending and writing scientific texts require that students be able to activate prior knowledge, connect it with new knowledge, make predictions, question understandings of ideas being presented, raise questions about data, and summarize what they have learned from texts or experiments. By contrast, readers of historical text are less concerned with explaining phenomena and more focused on trying to determine the historical lens of the author and how an author's biases might influence the position he or she took when writing about a historical event or person. Students with high-incidence disabilities may experience difficulties acquiring the cognitive strategies as well as basic literacy and language skills needed to comprehend texts, and they are likely to struggle with adjusting their strategies to meet the demands of different disciplinary texts. . . .

Although the intricacies of RTI implementation are not well understood at this time, it is clear that successful RTI implementation demands greater teaching expertise and better preparation for the roles teachers will play at each tier. At Tiers 1 and 2, in addition to providing high-quality instruction in the general education curriculum, general education teachers must have knowledge of evidence-based remedial practices and be amenable to implementing them. Further, general education teachers need a solid grasp of CBM procedures. At Tier 2, special education teachers require solid understanding of the general education curriculum, and all teachers require collaborative skills to engage successfully in the multidisciplinary planning needed for cohesive instruction at this tier. Thus, integrating special and general teacher preparation is once again a top priority, as it was during the integrated era. However, preparation now must help general and special education teachers integrate evidence-based practices into content instruction.

Success at Tier 3 demands specialized expertise. Special education teachers must demonstrate, at minimum, a sophisticated knowledge base that extends beyond that of general education teachers, and this expertise must add value to the general education that students with disabilities receive. Research on expert learners and teachers and research on interventions for students with high-incidence disabilities can serve as a basis for identifying this expertise. Findings from this research strongly suggest that special education teachers will need domain knowledge in areas targeted for Tier 3 instruction as well as knowledge of interventions, technological adaptations, and assessments for high-risk learners. As students with disabilities are likely to need intensive assistance in reading, writing, and mathematics, special education teachers should have sufficient preparation in these content areas to enable them to teach students in elementary, middle, and high school. They also need to develop an instructional repertoire that integrates domain knowledge with knowledge of intensive interventions and assessments. Moreover, preparation should focus on either the elementary or the secondary level, as content literacy demands change depending on the grade level taught.

To develop such extensive expertise, special education teachers will require preparation in both general and special education. Research evidence has demonstrated that general education teachers with special education preparation are better prepared to meet the literacy and mathematics needs of students with disabilities than teachers who lack it. Feng and Sass also showed that special education teachers with special education preparation produced higher achievement scores for students in reading but not math. We believe that, after entering the field, special education teachers should undertake advanced preparation in special education focused on either elementary or secondary level. This advanced preparation would target knowledge and skills needed to (a) provide direct services to students receiving Tier 3 instruction, and (b) collaborate with general education colleagues to provide Tier 2 instruction. Such expertise is important for two reasons. First, according to the Feng and Sass's preliminary analyses, preparation in special education has a value-added effect on the achievement of students with disabilities. Also, expertise in how to assess, support, and remediate literacy and numeracy skills is essential for providing access to the general education curriculum. If special education teachers do not help students access the general education curriculum, then they fail to add value to their students' education.

Strategies for Improving Special Education Teacher Quality

To improve special education teacher quality and preparation, policy makers and educators must address long-standing concerns about shortages of special education teachers and the inadequate preparation of general education teachers. Special education teacher shortages continue to be severe, hovering around 10% since the passage of EHA. Licensure strategies have often been designed to remedy quantity issues with little attention paid to the impact on teacher quality. Noncategorical certification and, more recently, the emergence of fast-track, alternative routes to licensure reflect special education's emphasis on addressing shortages (as opposed to improving quality). Although concerns about remedying shortages are well justified, the problem with these licensure strategies is that they fail to articulate and support the concept of unique expertise. Moreover, many general education teachers are unprepared to cope with the diverse needs of students who fail to thrive in response to good classroom instruction. Studies of general education teachers demonstrate that they have difficulty differentiating instruction for students with disabilities and other at-risk learners, especially at the secondary level.

Attempts to improve teacher quality must meet these two powerful issues head on. There must be reform of general education preparation if Tier 1 and 2 instruction is to be responsive and provide a foundation that special education teachers can build on. Moreover, well-designed, effective Tier 2 and 3 instruction will be impossible unless special education teachers, particularly at the secondary level, have the expertise in content, language, literacy, and numeracy to engage in such instruction. To ensure that students with disabilities have access to high-quality teaching in both general and special education, policies and practices needed for supporting the RTI movement need to be integrated with those related to licensure, teacher education, and teacher salaries. The RTI movement must be supported by policy makers through legislation, policies, and public funding for implementation and teacher education. The strong push for RTI to be included in the reauthorization of NCLB is an example of how policy could be used to broaden support in general education. Many schools across the country are implementing RTI, and this trend is likely to hasten with passage of comprehensive federal legislation.

Public schools, acting alone, will be unsuccessful in responding to these pressures if general and special education teachers are not prepared for their designated roles. Colleges of education must embrace conceptions of preparing teachers that will ready them for their roles in RTI. Key changes in state teaching standards and licensure policies provide levers for changing the nature of preparation for both general and special education teachers. In light of emerging evidence on the importance of special education preparation for both classroom and special education teachers, states must require dual certification for all beginning teachers, advanced preparation in literacy and numeracy for all special education teachers, and content-area literacy for those working in secondary schools. At a minimum, however, states must implement standards and licensure systems that make clear the knowledge and skills general education teachers will need for teaching students with disabilities and the knowledge and skills special education teachers will need for providing both access to the general education curriculum and more intensive instruction at Tiers 2 and 3. Moreover, what special education teachers need to know to provide Tier 2 and 3 instruction in elementary schools should be differentiated from what they will need for secondary schools. . . .

Conclusion

The changes we propose for improving the quality and preparation of special education teachers are lofty and dramatic—and difficult to attain. However, the risks of failing to improve the quality of instruction are unacceptable. The ability of many students with disabilities to access the general education curriculum and make adequate annual yearly progress depends on the skill and motivation of their teachers. Students with disabilities continue to lag well behind their peers. Requiring special education teachers to become highly qualified in the subjects they teach prior to entering the classroom offers less promise as a solution to this problem than recruiting highly qualified general education teachers into special education. Good general education teachers know content and how to teach it, and they are skilled collaborators. They have a framework for understanding and integrating the specialized knowledge they acquire in preparing for RTI and so will be better positioned to meet the needs of students with disabilities. Of course, encouraging general education teachers to become special educators necessitates fundamental reform in school practice, incentives for teachers, and teacher education. Because RTI requires fundamental change in school practice, the time is right for undertaking this ambitious agenda.

The viability of special education as a profession rests on our capacity to be recognized as a legitimate contributor to RTI implementation. Special education teachers must be responsible for providing Tier 3 instruction, as well as collaboratively planning Tier 2 instruction with their general education colleagues. If special education teachers are not perceived as adding value to the education of students with disabilities in an RTI model, they may be marginalized in schools, and special education would risk losing its identity as a profession. . . . We can no longer afford to be unclear about who high-quality special education teachers are and how they should be prepared. . . .

Margaret J. McLaughlin

NO

Evolving Interpretations of Educational Equity and Students with Disabilities

The education of students with disabilities in today's schools is being shaped by two very powerful laws: the 2004 Individuals with Disabilities Education Improvement Act (IDEA) and the 2001 Title I of the Elementary and Secondary Education Act (ESEA) also known as the No Child Left Behind Act (NCLB). These laws are changing our conceptions about the meaning of special education and are the source of confusion and frustration among general and special educators as they attempt to implement the various provisions. Much of the frustration arises from the tension between the core policy goals and assumptions that underlie Title I and IDEA. . . .

The Tension

There is increasing recognition of a fundamental tension between the prevailing K–12 educational policy of universal standards, assessments, and accountability as defined through Title I and the entitlement to a Free Appropriate Public Education (FAPE) within IDEA. The possibility of such a conflict between the standards-driven reform model and special education policies was acknowledged more than a decade ago by a National Research Council (NRC) committee that concluded that the two policies were not incompatible; however, there were definite areas of misalignment. . . . The challenges that educators are confronting in aligning Title I and IDEA arise from differing interpretations of what constitutes educational equity. . . .

Educational Equity and K–12 Education

What constitutes an equitable education has been subject to much debate and discussion among educational policy makers over the years. . . . A recurrent theme in the debates is distinguishing between the ideals of educational equity and educational equality. As Green notes, equity is not the same as equality, "Inequity always implies injustice. . . . Persons may be treated unequally but also justly." (p. 324). Thus, equitable treatment in education may conflict with

From *Exceptional Children*, vol. 76, no. 3, Spring 2010, pp. 265–272, 273–276 (refs. omitted). Copyright © 2010 by Council for Exceptional Children. Reprinted by permission. www.cec. sped.org what constitutes equality depending on the particular interpretations as well as how we choose to measure it. At the core of the conflict between Title I and IDEA is the belief that students with disabilities may be treated unjustly in being held to universal standards. . . .

The Evolution of the Equity Concept

As noted earlier, the meaning of what constitutes educational equity shifted throughout the 19th and 20th centuries and has been confounded with interpretations of educational equality. However, the increase in publicly funded education in the United States in response to industrialization and increased immigration made visible issues related to equity. Coleman (1968) noted that, with the exception of the very poor children who did not go to school, children with disabilities, and Native American and African American children who did not have schools, educators' earliest interpretations of equity had three foci: (a) providing a free education up to the point that a child entered the workforce; (b) providing a common curriculum for all children regardless of background; and (c) providing that children of diverse backgrounds attend the same school within a specific locality.

Equity assumed society had an obligation to remove the economic barriers to education, that is, provide a free education in a geographically accessible area and provide exposure to a common or core curriculum. To be denied these things was to be treated inequitably. The need for the state to provide an opportunity for all students to have equal access to a public education grew out of an increasing recognition that education was linked to larger economic goals such as the need to create potential employees and reduce economic dependency. In this interpretation of equity, the state must only provide or make available specific educational opportunities; whether or not a child chooses to access education or benefits from this education is left up to the student and the family.

A number of events in the early part of the 20th century shaped the interpretations of the role of the state in providing publicly funded education, such as curricular reforms. Most of these, however, changed the opportunities that were provided but did not alter the fundamental notion that public education only needed to provide equal access to achieve equity. The 1954 *Brown v. Board of Education* decision altered this interpretation when it repudiated the notion that simply providing exposure to the same curriculum, regardless of location, constituted equity. Although the findings in the *Brown* decision were supported by the wide disparities in resources (i.e., funding, facilities, and teachers) existing in the segregated, all Black schools, the *Brown* decision began to link conceptions of equitable treatment to the effects or results of the education a child received. That is, giving the same to every child was not sufficient to determine equality without considering how the child benefited from the opportunity. Yet, following the *Brown* decision, equitable treatment as articulated in U.S. educational policy was measured in terms of reducing resource disparities between White and African American students. This focus on inputs remained grounded in the notion that states must provide equal opportunities but not equal benefit. Further, an important factor was the idea that measuring equitable treatment should be at the group and not at the individual student level primarily because measurement at the individual level would be infeasible and unproductive.

In 1966, the Equality of Educational Opportunity Study (EEOS), also known as the "Coleman Study," was commissioned by the U.S. Department of Health, Education, and Welfare to assess the availability of equal educational opportunities to children of different race, color, religion, and national origin. This study was conducted in response to provisions of the Civil Rights Act of 1964 and focused on inequities across schools in terms of facilities, staff, class size, and so forth and their connection to variation in student background and achievement. The assumption underlying this report was that two students attending schools with the same resources should have the same opportunities. The report also introduced the concept of equal access and used this phrase repeatedly and almost synonymously to mean equality in funds, facilities, teachers, and curriculum.

The findings of the Coleman Study documented the disparities among schools in terms of critical educational resources, but it is probably best known for its conclusion that a child's economic status accounted for more of the variation in achievement than did school resources. Subsequent to the publication of this report, Jencks and his colleagues reanalyzed the Coleman data and reached similar conclusions. However, whereas both studies documented that substantial inequalities in both educational resources and outcomes existed among children of different races and backgrounds, the reports differed in terms of what constituted evidence of equity. Jencks's (1972) concept of equity focused on providing individual students with, "as much schooling as he (sic) wants. [Noting that] equal opportunity in this sense guarantees unequal results" (p. 109). Equity was interpreted as equal claims to public resources while acknowledging the possibility of different or unequal outcomes. The Coleman study focused on establishing equal access for different groups of students (e.g., minority and poor students) to the same schools, same curriculum, and same expenditures. . . .

The shift toward a focus on measuring the outcomes of education was driven by the belief that larger societal and cultural forces may have limited opportunities for students from certain backgrounds. Thus, an African American student or a student living in poverty might not aspire to certain educational outcomes; therefore, it was the role of the state to promote the same outcomes. This notion of equity was embraced by liberal and progressive educators and became a driving theme in federal education policy. In this interpretation, equity is measured in terms of equality of outcomes as opposed to inputs and evolved into what Berne and Stiefel (1984) later defined as horizontal and vertical equity. Horizontal equity is interpreted as schools having equal or equivalent inputs such as funding or teacher-student ratios; whereas vertical equity assumes that different or unequal inputs may be required to attain equal outcomes—in short, that unequal students require unequal treatment. This version of equity requires a way to define and measure the desired universal educational outcomes of the standards-based model of education.

Spurred by events such as the release of the 1983 *A Nation at Risk . . .*, there were calls for greater curricular rigor and of state-imposed standards for what students must achieve. The passage of the Goals 2000: Educate America Act and the 1994 reauthorization of ESEA, Improving America's Schools Act, increasingly defined a state's responsibility in ensuring educational equity. That is, if states wished to access the federal funding associated with these programs, they were to be responsible for providing all school-age children access to the same rigorous content and be held accountable for ensuring that children reached, at a minimum, state-defined levels of proficiency in that content. Equity was to be measured in terms of student achievement on state assessments and the gap in performance between specific subgroups of students. The 2001 ESEA reauthorization built on the earlier versions of this law by adding provisions for assessing annually the performance of students in three key content areas and by specifying mandatory consequences for schools, districts, and states that fail to meet specific performance benchmarks. Notably, both the 1994 and 2001 ESEA reauthorizations revised the formula for distributing federal funds to states and schools. The formula began to shift resources toward the neediest schools consistent with the notion of vertical equity.

Educational Equity and IDEA

The quest for educational equity for children with disabilities paralleled to some extent the broader K–12 policies. Equal access to a free, public education for all children with disabilities—a major policy goal for much of the latter half of the 20th century—was achieved at the national level with the passage of the Education of All Handicapped Children Act of 1975 (EAHCA). Providing equal access followed the reasoning in the *Brown* decision that when a state provides an opportunity for an education in its public schools, such an opportunity is a right that must be made available to all on equal terms. . . . However, EAHCA was also deeply grounded in the policy goals of the emerging disability rights movement.

Disability Rights Goals

As conceptualized by Silverstein (2000), there are four major goals that guide all federal laws and other policies pertaining to children and adults with disabilities. These are (a) equality of opportunity, which encompasses individualization, integration, or inclusion; (b) full participation (i.e., self-determination); (c) economic self-sufficiency; and (d) independent living. These goals are expressed through various provisions within IDEA as well as Section 504 of the Rehabilitation Act of 1973 and the Americans with Disabilities Act (ADA).

Individualization is central to the concept of equality of opportunity in all disability policies and arises from the heterogeneous nature of disabilities as well as the impact of disabling conditions on functioning. The goal requires that each person with a disability be considered in terms of his or her strengths and needs. The latter includes considerations for accommodations, supports, and services. Adherence to the goal requires that educational programs and policies be flexible enough to respond to individual differences and not be based solely on categories, labels, preconceptions, or biases. As interpreted in IDEA, the concept of individualization is found in the core entitlement to a FAPE, which is operationalized through the individualized education program (IEP).

Another core element of equality of opportunity is the full integration or inclusion of persons with disabilities into all those activities and policies designed for persons without disabilities. Based on the principle of normalization, inclusion means making available to each person with a disability the opportunity to experience all of the conditions of everyday living in the same way and place as individuals without disabilities. Within IDEA, the goal of inclusion is expressed primarily through the least restrictive environment (LRE) provision. However, this principle also extends to ensuring that individuals with disabilities are considered in federal and state educational policies. . . .

Thus, a student with a disability who is being treated equitably is being considered as an individual, is given full access to those aspects of life available to persons without disabilities, has opportunities to make decisions about both mundane and important life events, and has opportunities to become independent and self-sustaining. As interpreted in IDEA, these goals are reflected in the provisions that govern the IEP process and content. The procedural requirements associated with the IEP ensure that each child is treated justly. There are also substantive requirements associated with the IEP that require that there be educational benefit to the child.

Educational Benefit

The notion of educational benefit is central to interpreting what constitutes an "appropriate" education for an individual student. The prevailing legal standard for determining an appropriate education comes from the very first U.S. Supreme Court case to consider IDEA and its provisions. The decision in this case established the precedent that the federal statute was not intended to maximize the potential of a student served under the law. Instead, the Court determined that the statute was intended to provide access to education that would allow the student to "benefit" from educational programs and services. . . .

Subsequent to the *Rowley* decision, lower federal court cases further established that the educational benefit due to students with disabilities must be "more than trivial."

Under current interpretation, a student with a disability served under IDEA has claims on public resources as required to meet what an IEP team determines will provide a level of educational benefit, determined on an individual basis. This is a somewhat Jencksian concept of equity in that a child may get as much as he or she needs to receive educational benefits determined by a team of professionals and the child and/or his parents. The concept of equity as determined by attainment of equal outcomes was not articulated in the 1975 EAHCA until the 1997 reauthorization of IDEA when the first adjustments to K–12 policy began to appear. The 1997 amendments required that states and local districts include students with disabilities in assessments with accommodations where appropriate, to report the performance of these students with the same frequency and in the same detail that they use to report the performance levels of students without disabilities and to develop alternate means of assessment for those students who are unable to participate in standard assessments. The 1997 amendments also required that IEP teams consider how a child's disability affects his or her involvement and progress in the general education curriculum and develop IEP goals that promote the child's progress in that curriculum.

The NCLB Influence

Of course, major changes occurred with the passage of the 2001 amendments to Title I of ESEA. The Act made a clear statement regarding the state's responsibility in providing an equitable education to all students, including those with disabilities. Students with disabilities are expected to participate in all aspects of the Title I provisions. . . . The regulations define how students with disabilities are to be assessed and how schools are to be accountable for their performance. Most notably, the accountability provisions require schools (and districts and states) to be held accountable for the performance of the *subgroup* of students with disabilities and for closing the achievement gap between this subgroup and all others. Two specific regulations deserve mention. In December 2003, the U.S. Department of Education (ED) issued regulations for the inclusion of students with "the most significant cognitive disabilities" in Title I assessments. These regulations grant states the flexibility to measure the achievement of the selected students against alternate achievement standards, but in terms of accountability, the proficient or advanced scores of not more than 1% of the student population tested may be counted. An alternate achievement standard is defined as "an expectation of performance that differs in complexity from a grade-level achievement standard." It is important to note that only the achievement standards and not the content standards are permitted to be altered. Thus, students' performance expectations are based on the same academic content as their peers without disabilities.

In April 2007, the ED issued another set of regulations permitting states to adopt "modified" achievement standards. These regulations make clear that modified academic achievement standards are intended for a small group of children, in addition to the "1% of students" whose disability precludes them from achieving grade-level proficiency and whose progress is such that they will not reach grade-level achievement standards in the same time frame as other students. The expectations for whether a student has mastered those standards, however, may be less difficult than grade-level academic achievement standards. Not more than 2% of proficient scores of students who are held to modified standards may be included in adequate yearly progress (AYP) calculations at any level. . . . Modified academic achievement standards must be based on a state's grade-level academic content standard and the student's IEP must include goals that are based on the academic content standards for the grade in which the student is enrolled. The 2004 IDEA amendments acknowledged these regulatory requirements and made several explicit references to ESEA in terms of requirements for such things as assessment, highly qualified special educators, and so forth. These changes signal the intent of Congress to better align if not merge the two major policies.

Standards-Based IEPs

As a result of the Title I regulations as well as the general move toward standards-based education, a new practice is emerging with respect to IEP development. Referred to as standards-based IEPs the practice directly links IEP goals to a state's grade-level content standards and assessments. Each child receives an individually designed plan of services and supports that are geared to moving the student toward attaining state-determined standards. The tensions between IDEA and Title I become quite evident in the implementation of standards-based IEPs. There is an assumption that all students with disabilities need or will benefit from the same educational outcomes (albeit some will be measured against different standards) and that the IEP team is to determine what resources the student may need to reach these common outcomes. From the perspective of IDEA, these IEPs can seem counter to the principle of individualization and subvert the procedural rights for determining what constitutes a FAPE for a student.

Considerations for Reconciling IDEA and Title I of the Elementary and Secondary Education Act

Including the group of children covered under IDEA within the basic policies of Title I of ESEA is consistent with the notion of equity that asserts that public education has a larger role in ensuring equity beyond providing whatever an individual student wants, or in the case of a student with a disability, what an IEP team decides he or she needs. This is tricky and contested territory because one needs to respond to the question "Needs to do what?" . . . The issue of whether all children may benefit from or need the same curriculum has long been debated as part of our nation's efforts to increase the achievement of children. Concerns about what happens to those who cannot or choose not to meet standards are not exclusive to students served under IDEA. However, for students served under IDEA the question of whether or not they are being treated unjustly when held to such standards becomes more potent given their entitlement to a FAPE.

The Purpose section of IDEA 2004 states that the goals of educating children with disabilities are: ensuring that all children with disabilities have available to them a free appropriate public education that emphasizes special education and related services designed to meet their unique needs and prepares them for further education, employment, and independent living. These goals are not dissimilar from those of all children; rather, it seems that the tension is as Green (1983) argues, that "We cannot [provide] an education that is uniquely suited . . . for each individual and at the same time give to each an education that is as good as that provided for everyone else" (p. 319). Yet, that is implicitly the intent of an appropriate education and also fuels the tension between standards and the determination of an appropriate education. However, at the same time that IDEA has accepted unequal, that is, individual treatment and unequal educational outcomes, there has been intense scrutiny and far less tolerance of inequalities in post-school employment and other functional outcomes. . . .

Employment, Further Education, and Independent Living

. . . The National Longitudinal Transition Study–2 (NLTS2) provides the most current national data on the postschool outcomes of students with disabilities who received special education services. The first wave of data was collected in 2003 from the first cohort of students within the sample to leave high school. Among this group, 31% of the sample had enrolled in some type of postsecondary institution, compared to 41% of students in the general population. . . .

About 40% of the youth were employed at the time of the first follow-up, which was substantially below the 63% employment rate among students without disabilities in the same age group. About 40% of the sample was working full time and about 40% of this group of former students was earning more than $7.00/hour, but only a third of all those employed were receiving any benefits with their employment. In terms of independent living, about three fourths of the youth were living with their parents 2 years after high school, which is similar to the general population. However, these outcomes varied by type of disability as well as by whether the student had received a high school diploma. Notably, students with more significant intellectual disabilities experienced lower rates of employment and independence. . . .

Clearly, receiving a high school diploma is an important outcome for students with disabilities, but also important is the rigor of graduation requirements. The National Center on Educational Outcomes (NCEO) conducted a survey of the 50 states and the District of Columbia in 2002 to 2003 to examine graduation requirements for students with and without disabilities. Results . . . indicated that 28 states had increased their requirements for all students, whereas two states increased requirements only for students without disabilities. However, in all but three of the 28 states, students with disabilities were allowed to obtain a standard diploma without completing all requirements. . . . At that time six states offered IEP/special education diplomas, 19 states granted certificates of attendance, 10 states granted certificates of achievement, and three states offered occupational diplomas. In addition, 32 states permitted IEP teams to make adjustments to graduation requirements. The unequal expectations for graduation may likely reflect an attempt to treat some students with disabilities differently in an effort to provide them an equitable opportunity to receive a diploma. Although such treatment may be fair, it may promote greater inequities if it results in loss of opportunity to gain knowledge and skills that are relevant and necessary for postschool success.

. . .

Concluding Thoughts About Educational Equity and Students with Disabilities

Obviously, there are some fundamental differences underlying the policy ideals expressed in NCLB and IDEA 2004. These are reflected to some degree in the policy goals. Although I would argue that the goals are less divergent than the means for reaching those goals. The stress of trying to implement standards-based IEPs, provide instruction in grade-level subject matter content while addressing the unique needs of an individual student with a disability can quickly obscure the ultimate goals of education for all students. Further, measuring progress in terms of aggregate versus individual measures of achievement creates a sense of unfairness. Yet, the data on employment and achievement inform us that, in the aggregate, students with disabilities are not receiving the same outcomes. The data also raise legitimate questions about the level of benefit the subgroup of students with disabilities are receiving from public education. But, do the data suggest inequities in the educational system? By that I mean, are students receiving equitable treatment in terms of access to curriculum, qualified teachers, and other inputs critical to the attainment of academic and educational outcomes important to their postschool success? . . .

The NLTS2 documented differences in course taking among students with disabilities. On average, more than half (59%) of the courses that secondary students with disabilities took were academic. However, the data also indicate that students with disabilities were less likely to be enrolled in higher level math and science courses. Not surprising, course taking differed by disability category, with more students identified as having mental retardation and other cognitive disabilities enrolled in vocational and special classes and more students identified as having specific learning disabilities enrolled in grade-level academic courses. In addition, a recent analysis of math achievement among secondary students with and without disabilities found that students with IEPs who attended schools that provided a range of math courses had significantly lower achievement than those in schools that provided only a more rigorous math curriculum. Are differences in access legitimate, meaning do they reflect the unique needs of a student even if they lead to unequal outcomes? As noted by Gelber (2007), prior discrimination or inequities can and do shape current inequalities in educational achievement. We can only speculate the extent to which preconceived and historic notions about students with disabilities as well as conceptions about their needs are reflected in their current educational outcomes. We also cannot know with certainty whether greater access to rigorous courses and higher expectations would make a difference to both in school and postschool outcomes. However, experience with the IEP has suggested that there are low expectations and lack of accountability suggesting that differences in access and outcomes between students with and without IEPs may result from a system that permits inequities as part of the individualization mandate and yet is vulnerable to preconceived and historic notions about students with disabilities. Without standards that guide the process, how are we to know if a student is being treated equitably?

The concepts of standards and individualization reflect different beliefs about equity. As noted by Brighouse and Swift (2008), it is not unusual for different values to conflict in political discourse, nor is it unusual to conclude that one value is more important than the other. However, they argue that in some instances, one has to make a judgment of whether Policy Y, which we believe to be so critical (e.g., IEPs with individually referenced outcomes), has a moral priority over Policy X (e.g., IEPs that are based on common standards). That is, does Y always trump X or only in some instances? For example, under what conditions might a parent of a child with a disability argue for individualized outcomes? Would a parent argue for lower standards for graduation if their child's diploma was not at risk? Would some educational outcomes matter more to some groups of students with disabilities? One cannot argue for individualizing outcomes only when it is convenient or beneficial. However, we must be explicit about if or when a comparative or relational concept of equity is called for and when certain inequities are tolerable.

In the case of students with disabilities, equity can be measured in terms of the procedural integrity of the IEP. These standards are consistent across individuals. Educational benefit, however, is relational. It must be determined in relation to something and this something must be consistent across some or all students with disabilities. The implications are that requiring each student with a disability to meet the same standards may, in fact, be inequitable. For instance, requiring all students with IEPs to pass the same exam in algebra in order to receive a high school diploma may not be just, particularly if this proficiency is unnecessary for independent living or certain jobs. However, who gets to decide? Is it truly equitable to allow the IEP team to determine that a specific child will not be provided access to algebra because they believe it will not be important to that student's future or because they believe the child will not be able to benefit? At what point can we accept as legitimate unequal outcomes among students with disabilities, and are the procedural requirements and safeguards of the law sufficient and reasonable for ensuring equitable treatment? I would argue that they are not and that we need to include in our measure of equity consideration of attainment of important educational outcomes. To go forward with a true alignment of the Title I and IDEA we must reconsider the structure, if not the purpose, of the IEP, which ultimately will affect what constitutes an appropriate education.

A New Way Forward

I believe that the concept of the IEP needs to reflect differential educational outcomes, based not on a case-by-case basis but on some rational grouping of students with disabilities. Although I believe that core procedural requirements can be maintained, the specific implementation of these may need to differ based on educational expectations measured in terms of attainment of certain levels of academic and, for some students, functional competence. Such a model was recently proposed by Gándara and Rumberger (2008) for linguistic minority students. They proposed defining four groups of students based on their educational goals: (a) English language proficiency, (b) English language proficiency and academic proficiency, (c) biliteracy, and (d) biliteracy and academic proficiency. Under their model, each group would have a defined set of educational outcomes based on the goal, and there would be different needs and resource implications for students as defined by the goals of their instruction.

A similar model could be applied to students with IEPs. I believe that IEPs could be differentiated for three groups of children and youth: those held to regular, modified, and alternate achievement standards. The first group, and certainly the largest of the groups, need IEPs that focus on accommodations and special education and related services that are tailored to their needs and directly related to enabling the students to fully *access instruction in grade-level subject matter content and to progress toward predetermined NCLB achievement goals.* Educational goals for these students should not differ from those of any other student, nor should the assessments used to determine educational needs or progress. After determining eligibility for services and that the student will be held to regular achievement standards, the IEP team can focus on meeting that student's needs, both in the academic as well as the social or behavioral areas as they impact access to the grade-level curriculum. The IEPs for these students should be simplified to reflect only the accommodations, services, and supports needed to progress toward proficiency on state standards. Progress should be monitored as it would be for students without IEPs. This approach to IEP development removes the risks of lowered expectations and denial of opportunity.

The IEPs for students held to modified achievement standards would also be based on grade-level content standards and would also focus on access to grade-level subject matter instruction and services to access and progress in that curriculum. However, the expected outcomes, benchmarks, and measures must reflect the modified achievement standards as established by the state. The IEPs for these children should reflect the more intensive and specialized services and supports required to enable them to meet the modified standards and progress toward proficiency on the regular state achievement standards. These students should not be permanently assigned to some sort of "modified" track, thus it is critical that progress measures be benchmarked to both the modified and regular achievement standards. It is difficult to know at this point what modified standards will look like as states are in the early stages of developing them along with the alternate assessments by which they will be measured. It is also unclear which students will be included in this group. Nonetheless, the role and function of IEP teams will be critical in identifying these students, designing educational interventions, and carefully monitoring progress.

The third and smallest group of students are those identified as having significant cognitive disabilities as defined by NCLB regulations. Alternate assessments based on alternate achievement standards must show a clear link to the content standards for the grade in which the student is enrolled, but the grade-level content may be reduced in complexity or modified, in some instances substantially, in order to meet the need of a student to develop skills. These alterations to curriculum will be reflected in the highly differentiated and individualized performance of the students in both academic and functional domains. Educational benefit must be measured in terms of differentiated outcomes, which will likely be individualized and should consider performance on alternate assessments and progress toward economic self-sufficiency and independent living. The IEPs of these students will contain goals and objectives that reflect the differentiated outcomes. Further, the claims on special education resources may be substantial and continue through age 21.

The differentiation in IEPs should in no way prohibit full and equal access to general education classrooms as determined on an individual basis. Decisions about least restrictive environment should be made after full consideration of the educational needs. However, regardless of where a student receives special education and related services, the regular, modified, or alternate achievement standards must establish the desired outcomes or benefits of education.

Just changing the IEP goals is really insufficient to address a fundamental shift in considering equity. A more radical suggestion is to consider what happens once a student with an IEP meets the regular education achievement standard. Should students who are at least proficient on the established achievement standards continue to have claims on special education resources? Under the notion of vertical equity, once a student has achieved the state-determined outcomes, the claims to unequal educational resources should cease. That is, these students would not be entitled to more than students who are similarly situated in terms of educational performance. As Green (1983) notes, "Some inequalities are fair and some are not" (p. 338). Just as it is inequitable to deny an individual student with an IEP access to the educational benefits as defined through state standards, it is also inequitable to provide resources to students beyond those required to achieve this "benefit." . . .

Changes to how one thinks about equity and students with disabilities affect much more than IEP decision making. The purpose of special education in the schools will also be altered. For the majority of students currently served under IDEA 2004, special education resources will support student progress toward regular state achievement standards and resources will be seamlessly blended into general education. For a lesser number of students with IEPs, special education will be more intensive and with more personalized goals. Resources and services will be more distinguishable from general education. The overall effect should be a more rational model of special education delivery that is more consistently applied across schools and districts.

This new policy model intentionally does not speak to the merits of the current standards, neither the subject matter content that is assessed nor how we are measuring students. These are political decisions and technical issues that affect all students and should be debated within that context. Nonetheless, interpretations of equity as seen in the national standards have reached the point where a significant reexamination of IDEA 2004 is required. It is in the best interests of the children and youth with disabilities in America's public schools for policy makers to come to terms with the conflicting beliefs and understandings of equity that underlie current policies and engage in serious debate of their relative merits. This will be necessary to truly align K–12 and special education in policy and practice.

POSTSCRIPT

Should Special Education and General Education Merge?

The Council for Exceptional Children (CEC), the largest international professional organization advocating for individuals with disabilities and/or gifts and talents, has developed a set of Policy Recommendations for Elementary and Secondary Education Act (ESEA) Reauthorization (www.cec.sped.org). Demonstrating how close the laws are, CEC's opening statements urge that ESEA be "carefully coordinated and balanced" with Individuals with Disabilities Education Act (IDEA). Their first recommendation urges Congress to "emphasize the importance of special education pedagogy that centers on the evidence-based expertise of special educators to alter instructional variables to individualize instruction for individuals with exceptional learning needs." The third recommendation encourages Congress to support special education teachers who "also possess a solid base of understanding of the general content area curriculum sufficiently to collaborate with general education" with stronger knowledge for each subject they teach directly. A later recommendation urges that Response to Intervention (RTI) be included in ESEA as well as IDEA.

This issue's authors agree on three key points. First, the current educational system prizes academic outcomes for each child. Second, special education is in transition, responding to changes in general education. Third, the two reauthorizations provide a rare opportunity to influence the future of both general education and special education. The authors differ on what that future should be.

Mary T. Brownell and colleagues see the future in RTI. General educators should have increased knowledge about disabilities, and special educators must utilize a solid content base as a foundation for specialized instruction. Tier 3 intervention should be virtually synonymous with special education. Avoiding this path will leave special education "marginalized" and adrift.

Margaret J. McLaughlin thinks that an "appropriate" education is not the same for every student. All educators must acknowledge that individuals have unique goals and needs. Insisting that all must pursue the same outcomes "can seem counter to the principle of individualization" and actually be unjust. There must be specialized education—perhaps a specialized curriculum—that is substantially different from that appropriate for typical learners.

Several authors describe how special education can fit "seamlessly" into general education. Discussing how special educators can be redefined as interventionists, Simonsen and colleagues (*Remedial and Special Education*, 2010) stated that special education "can be blended seamlessly" into a schoolwide

RTI model, with special educators contributing to each tier. Weber (*Phi Delta Kappan*, 2008) asks whether special education "has to be special," since all children deserve services and support. If these were provided, students would "fit seamlessly into the mainstream of public education." Even McLaughlin notes that, for most students, special education services could blend "seamlessly" into general education.

In sharp contrast, Zigmond, Kloo, and Volonino (2009) ask, "If a differentiated education is provided in the same place as everyone else, on the same content as everyone else, with adapted instruction that is not unique to the student with disabilities, is the student receiving special education?" (p. 201).

In the same thematic issue that included this issue's selections, Fuchs, Fuchs, and Stecker (*Exceptional Children*, 2010) consider the "blurring of special education." They view merger discussions as evidence that special education has veered from its original mission to teach students with the most severe educational challenges. The authors call teachers, administrators, and policy makers to remember the charge to special education and think carefully about how to use this specific knowledge in tomorrow's schools—in both RTI and specially designed instruction.

Doubtless, this discussion will continue for some time. Should general education and special education blend seamlessly into a continuum of in-class services to help all children? If IDEA is incorporated into ESEA, what will happen to its protections for parents and children? Will IDEA funding fold into ESEA and, if so, would that money be spent on students with disabilities? Will students with disabilities receive the most benefit by pursuing unified academic outcomes? Will differentiated outcomes lead to specialized instruction or return us to stereotypes and low expectations? Which path is the best for students with disabilities?

ISSUE 10

Can Scientifically Based Research Guide Instructional Practice?

YES: Samuel L. Odom, Ellen Brantlinger, Russell Gersten, Robert H. Horner, Bruce Thompson, and Karen R. Harris, from "Research in Special Education: Scientific Methods and Evidence-Based Practices," *Exceptional Children* (Winter 2005), pp. 137–148

NO: Frederick J. Brigham, William E. Gustashaw III, Andrew L. Wiley, and Michele St. Peter Brigham, from "Research in the Wake of the No Child Left Behind Act: Why the Controversies Will Continue and Some Suggestions for Controversial Research," *Behavioral Disorders* (May 2004), pp. 300–310

ISSUE SUMMARY

YES: Samuel L. Odom, Ellen Brantlinger, Russell Gersten, Robert H. Horner, Bruce Thompson, and Karen R. Harris, all college faculty members and educational researchers, begin their article with definitive support for research-based methodology. They herald proposals for quality indicators, to establish rigor in an array of research methods that can identify effective educational practices.

NO: Frederick J. Brigham, associate professor at the University of Virginia, Charlottesville, William E. Gustashaw III and Andrew L. Wiley, both doctoral candidates at the University of Virginia, Charlottesville, and Michele St. Peter Brigham, a special education practitioner, believe that disagreement, mistrust, and the shifting general education environment preclude the usefulness of scientifically based research to guide daily instruction.

Dismayed by decades of flat results on the National Assessment of Educational Progress, the framers of No Child Left Behind (NCLB) emphatically state that educators must use interventions based on scientifically based research "that involves the application of rigorous, systematic, and objective procedures to obtain reliable and valid knowledge" (NCLB, 2001). Interventions encompass educational practices, strategies, curriculum, and programs.

A profusion of educational materials now claim to be scientifically based. Close comparison with NCLB requirements may reveal that, although some may rely on the research done by others, they do not measure up to NCLB standards. This issue explores the controversy swirling around the application of these standards.

Two resources are available to assist educators in understanding the meaning and application of scientifically based research: *Identifying and Implementing Educational Practices Supported by Rigorous Evidence: A User Friendly Guide* (Institute of Educational Sciences, 2003) and the What Works Clearinghouse (http://www.whatworks.ed.gov). A third resource, the NICHCY's Research Center (http://research.nichcy.org) debuted in February 2006, focusing solely on special education.

Noting that many educational practices have been supported by "poorly-designed studies and/or advocacy-driven studies" (p. iii), the authors of *Identifying and Implementing* "seek(s) to provide educational practitioners with user-friendly tools to distinguish practices supported by rigorous evidence from those that are not" (p. iii).

This useful guide begins by defining NCLB's "gold standard" of evidence: randomized controlled trials (RCT), which are "studies that randomly assign individuals to an intervention group or to a control group, in order to measure the effects of the intervention" (p. 1). Briefly, students, similar on critical variables, are randomly assigned into two groups. One receives the intervention; the other does not. If the first group significantly outperforms the second, the intervention can be said to be effective. Similar students ensure that no other factors could account for the results. Random assignment of these students ensures that no bias differentiated the groups.

The What Works Clearinghouse (WWC), an online resource, "collects, screens, and identifies studies" on topic areas such as middle school mathematics, and reports "on the strengths and weaknesses of those studies against the WWC Evidence Standards so that you know what the best scientific evidence has to say." In addition to using RCT, the strongest evidence comes from studies that have lasted at least a semester, have outcome measures, and have been published in peer-reviewed journals.

Educational researchers have risen to this challenge. A number of prominent research-based journals have published thematic issues on the topic of scientifically based methodologies.

Our first selection is the lead article in one of these thematic issues. Odom, Brantlinger, Gersten, Horner, Thompson, and Harris review the considerable history of special education research. Embracing the use of scientific data to guide practice, Odom et al. discuss research stages, each of which requires specific methods to identify scientifically supported interventions.

In the second selection, Brigham, Gustashaw, Wiley, and Brigham argue that even gold-standard evidence will not resolve the controversies surrounding practices in special education. They believe competing motives, perspectives, and goals will not be eliminated by evidence. They also wonder if today's research findings will be relevant in the rapidly changing schools of tomorrow.

As you read these articles, ask yourself if the methods used in your school could stand up to gold-standard scrutiny. Can the assistance of *The User Friendly Guide* and WWC help you make better choices? Will parents, teachers, and administrators agree on the choices? What happens if they disagree?

YES

Samuel L. Odom et al.

Research in Special Education: Scientific Methods and Evidence-Based Practices

Should science guide practice in special education? Most individuals would say "Yes." However, the "devil is in the details." Major initiatives in other disciplines such as medicine, the allied health professions, and psychology are attempting to identify and disseminate practices that have scientific evidence of effectiveness. In education, national policies such as the No Child Left Behind Act (NCLB) require that teachers use scientifically proven practices in their classrooms. Yet, there is concern about the quality of scientific research in the field of education and disagreement about the type of scientific information that is acceptable as evidence. An oft-cited report from the National Research Council (NRC) states that science in education consists of different types of questions and that different methodologies are needed to address these questions. In contrast, other agencies and research synthesis organizations (e.g., the What Works Clearinghouse [WWC]) have focused primarily on the question of whether a practice is effective and proposed that the "gold standard" for addressing this question is a single type of research methodology—randomized experimental group designs (also called randomized clinical trials or RCTs).

In January 2003, the Council for Exceptional Children's (CEC) Division for Research established a task force to address these devilish details as they apply to special education. The operating assumptions of this task force were that different types of research questions are important for building and documenting the effectiveness of practices, and that different types of methodologies are essential in order to address these questions. The task force identified four types of research methodologies in special education: (a) experimental group, (b) correlational, (c) single subject, and (d) qualitative designs. The task force was to establish quality indicators for each methodology and to propose how evidence from each methodology could be used to identify and understand effective practices in special education. . . .

This article provides a context and rationale for this endeavor. We begin with a discussion of the importance of multiple scientific methodologies in special education research. Next, we examine efforts to identify high-quality research methodology and then examine initiatives in the fields of medicine and education to identify evidence-based practice. In conclusion, we propose

From *Exceptional Children*, vol. 71, no. 2, Winter 2005, pp. 137–148. Copyright © 2005 by Council for Exceptional Children. Reprinted by permission. www.cec.sped.org

that research and development on effective practices in special education exists on a continuum, with each methodology matched to questions arising from different points of the continuum. Also, it is important to acknowledge that although basic research serves as the foundation for the development of effective practices and is critically important for our work in special education, the issues addressed in this article will be most relevant for applied research.

Rationale for Multiple Scientific Research Methodologies in Special Education

The rationale for having different research methodologies in special education is based on the current conceptualization of research in education and the complexity of special education as a field. The history and tradition of special education research, when employing multiple methodologies, has resulted in the identification of effective practices.

Current Conceptualization of Research in Education

A primary emphasis in education policy today is to improve the quality of education for all of America's children. This policy, exemplified by NCLB, compels educators to use "teaching practices that have been proven to work." However, a general concern has been voiced about the quality of research in education. To address this concern, the National Academy of Sciences (NAS) created a committee to examine the status of scientific research in education. An operating assumption of this committee was that research questions must guide researchers' selections of scientific methods. The NAS committee proposed that most research questions in education could be grouped into three types: (a) description (what is happening?); (b) cause (is there a systematic effect?); and (c) process or mechanism (why or how is it happening?). The committee conveyed two important points about these types of research and their associated questions. First, each type of question is scientific. Second, the different types of questions require different types of methodologies. It follows that each type of methodology that empirically, rigorously, and appropriately addresses these questions is also legitimately scientific. Scientists and social philosophers as diverse as B. F. Skinner, John Dewey, and J. Habermas have emphasized that the appropriate match between question and methodology is an essential feature of scientific research.

Complexity of Special Education as a Field

In his commentary on the NAS report on scientific research in education and the policy emphasizing use of RCTs implied by NCLB, Berliner noted that such a conceptualization of science is based on hard sciences, such as physics, chemistry, and biology. He proposed that science in education is not a hard science but it is the "hardest-to-do science." Berliner stated,

> We [educational researchers] do our science under conditions that physical scientists find intolerable. We face particular problems and

must deal with local conditions that limit generalizations and theory building—problems that are different from those faced by the easier-to-do sciences [chemistry, biology, medicine].

Special education research, because of its complexity, may be the hardest of the hardest-to-do science. One feature of special education research that makes it more complex is the variability of the participants. The Individuals with Disabilities Education Act (IDEA) identifies 12 eligibility (or disability) categories in special education (Office of Special Education and Rehabilitation Services [OSERS]), and within these categories are several different identifiable conditions. For example, in addition to "typical" learning disabilities, attention deficit/hyperactive disorder is often subsumed under the Specific Learning Disabilities category. Autism is now widely conceptualized as a spectrum consisting of four disorders. Mental retardation varies on the range of severity. Emotional and behavioral disorders consist of externalizing and internalizing disorders. Visual and hearing impairments range in severity from mildly impaired to totally blind or profoundly deaf. Physical impairment can be exhibited as hypotonia or hypertonia. Other health impaired may incorporate health conditions as distinct and diverse as asthma, epilepsy, and diabetes. Adding to this variability is the greater ethnic and linguistic diversity that, unfortunately, occurs in special education because of overrepresentation of some minority groups.

A second dimension of complexity is the educational context. Special education extends beyond the traditional conceptualization of "schooling" for typical students. Certainly many students with disabilities attend general education classes. However, the continuum of special education contexts is broader than general education. At one end of the chronological continuum, infants, toddlers, and many preschoolers receive services in their home or in an inclusive child care setting outside of the public school settings (e.g., Head Start Centers). For school-age students with disabilities, placement sometimes occurs in special education classes or a combination of special education and general education classes. For adolescents and young adults with disabilities, special education may take place in community living or vocational settings in preparation for the transition out of high school and into the workplace.

Complexity in special education has several implications for research. Researchers cannot just address a simple question about whether a practice in special education is effective; they must specify clearly for whom the practice is effective and in what context. The heterogeneity of participant characteristics poses a significant challenge to research designs based on establishing equivalent groups, even when randomization and stratification is possible. Certain disabilities have a low prevalence, so methodologies that require a relatively large number of participants to build the power of the analysis may be very difficult or not feasible. In addition, because IDEA ensures the right to a free appropriate public education, some research and policy questions (e.g., Are IEPs effective in promoting student progress?) may not be addressable through research methodologies that require random assignment to a "nontreatment" group or condition. Last, in special education, students with disabilities are often "clustered" in classrooms, and in experimental group design, the classroom rather than the student becomes the unit on which researchers base random assignment, data analysis, and power estimates.

History of Special Education Research

Special education research has a long history in which different methodologies have been employed. In the early 19th century beginning with Itard's foundational work, *The Wild Boy of Aveyron*, there was a tradition of discovery, development, experimentation, and verification. Initially, the research methods employed in the field that was to become special education research were derived from medicine. Many of the early pioneers in services for individuals with disabilities (Itard, Seguin, Montessori, Fernald, Goldstein) were physicians. Similarly, early services for individuals with disabilities occurred in residential facilities and training schools, which were based on the medical tradition of care.

As psychology, sociology, and anthropology became academic disciplines, they provided methodological tools for research in special education. For example, Skeels's and Kirk's works, respectively, on early experiences and preschool education for infants and young children with mental retardation employed experimental and quasi-experimental group designs prominent in psychology. Edgerton's research on individuals with mental retardation who left institutions and moved to the community drew from methods in sociology and anthropology. In academic instructional studies, Lovitt and Haring based their methodology on the then newly created single-subject design methodology of the time. Farber's important early work on families of children with disabilities and continuing through work by Blacher and Dunst had its roots in family sociology. Many of the current special education research tools now frequently employed, such as sophisticated multivariate designs, qualitative research designs, and program evaluation designs, have their roots in general education and educational psychology. Today a range of methodological approaches are available to researchers in special education as a result of this rich history.

More than One Research Methodology Is Important in Special Education Research

A current initiative of the U.S. Department of Education is to improve the quality of research in the field of education, with the rationale that improved research will lead to improved practice. A major effort to improve quality has come through the establishment in 2003 of the Institute of Education Sciences (IES), whose mission is to expand fundamental knowledge about education. A central theme advocated by IES is to focus research on the questions of effectiveness and to employ high-quality research methods to address these questions. The gold standard for research methodology that addresses these issues is the use of RCT methodology. The IES acknowledges that different methodologies are important for addressing different questions.

The increased use of RCT methodology, when conducted well, will undoubtedly enhance the quality of research in education and special education. Rigorously conducted RCT studies have greater capacity to control for threats to internal validity than do quasi-experimental designs that are often used in special education. Because of this greater experimental control, Gersten et al. propose that random assignment to experimental groups is one indicator of high-quality group design research. The IES and Department of Education policy of encouraging RCT studies may well move the field closer to the goal of identifying evidence-based special education practices. But again, there are devilish details that challenge the near exclusive use of this methodology for investigating effective practices in special education.

In special education, other methodologies, such as single-subject designs, are experimental and may be a better fit for some research contexts and participant characteristics. Powerful correlational methodologies may suggest causal relationships by statistically controlling for competing hypotheses and may be essential for addressing causal-like questions when researchers are not able to conduct experimental group or single-subject design studies. The discovery and development of new effective practices may require researchers to work in naturalistic contexts where they may not be able to exert experimental control and/or in design experiments, or where they have the flexibility of changing certain elements of an intervention based on students' responses. Such descriptive and process-oriented research may require the use of qualitative methods. Educational researchers have acknowledged the value of mixing methodologies to provide a complementary set of information that would more effectively (than a single method) inform practice.

Quality Indicators of Research Methodology

Quality indicators are the feature of research that represents rigorous application of methodology to questions of interest. They may serve as guidelines for (a) researchers who design and conduct research, (b) reviewers who evaluate the "believability" of research findings, and (c) consumers who need to determine the "usability" of research findings. High-quality research is designed to rule out alternative explanations for both the results of the study and the conclusions that researchers draw. The higher the quality of research methodology, the more confidence the researcher and readers will have in the findings of the study.

Textbooks on educational research describe the methodology that investigators should follow, but they usually do not provide a succinct or understandable set of indicators that are useful for individuals who lack graduate training on research methodology. Several professional organizations have developed standards for describing and, in some cases, evaluating research. Division 16 of the American Psychological Association (APA) and the Society for the Study of School Psychology have established criteria for evaluating group design, single-subject design, and qualitative methodology used in research on practices in school psychology. Similarly, APA Division 12 Task Force on Psychological Interventions has established criteria primarily for experimental group designs studies used to provide support for therapies in clinical psychology and clinical child psychology. The CEC Division for Early Childhood (DEC) created procedures for describing research methodology for studies using group, single-subject, and qualitative research methodology, which they used to determine recommended practices for early intervention/ early childhood special education. These standards have been used to determine the quality of research methods employed; however, they have not been published as quality indicators that other researchers could use.

In their work on summarizing evidence for effective practices, which will be described in the next section, some research synthesis organizations have established evaluation criteria and methods for determining the quality of research. For example, the WWC created an evaluation instrument, called the Design and Implementation Assessment Device (DIAD), with which a rater could conduct an extremely detailed evaluation of a research article. At this writing, a DIAD has only been created for experimental and quasi-experimental group design, but the WWC reports that DIADs are also being constructed for single-subject and qualitative group designs. Other research synthesis organizations, such as the Campbell Collaboration and the Evidence for Policy and Practice Information Centre (EPPIC), have somewhat similar research evaluation procedures.

Efforts described here illustrate the progress that professional and governmental organizations have made toward establishing standards for quality in research. To date, however, such quality indicators have not been identified specifically for research in special education. As noted, the purpose of the work conducted by this task force was to establish a set of quality indicators that were clearly stated, understandable, and readily available for use as guides for identifying high-quality research in special education. These quality indicators are presented in the articles appearing in this special issue.

Evidence-Based Practice

The type and magnitude of evidence needed to verify a practice as evidence-based is a prominent issue in the discussion of scientific research and effective educational practices. These devilish details are critical for policymakers, practitioners, educational researchers, and consumers. Current endeavors to establish standards for evidence-based practice as well as to identify the evidence-based-practices themselves are occurring through two different, but related, initiatives. In this section, we describe briefly the history of identifying effective practices first in medicine and then other social science fields, efforts by professional organizations to identify effective practices, and similar efforts being conducted by research synthesis organizations.

Identifying Evidence-Based Practice

Like the evolution of special education research methods noted previously, the search for evidence-based practice originated in the field of medicine. Although the practice of evidence-based medicine extends back to the mid-19th century, the modern era of evidence-based practice emerged in the early 1970s and 1980s and came into fruition in Great Britain in the early 1990s. Cutspec tracked the evolution of evidence-based medicine from a movement that began with the intent to address the gap between research and practitioners' provision of medical care, moved to the use of the literature to inform practice decisions, and then became an approach to practicing medicine. Evidence-based practice is now a central part of medical education, education in allied health professions such as nursing, and counselor education.

General and special education have followed suit in adopting scientific evidence as the appropriate basis for selecting teaching practices. The impetus for the current evidence-based movement in education is similar to that in medicine: A concern that effective educational practices, as proven by research, are not being used in schools. This current concern reflects a long-standing discussion in the field of special education regarding the distance between research and practice. In response, a large number of initiatives have been established to identify practices that will generate positive outcomes for children. Two types of groups are sponsoring these initiatives: research synthesis organizations and professional associations that propose standards for practice.

Research Synthesis Organizations.   Research synthesis organizations systematically evaluate and aggregate findings from the research literature in order to inform practitioners. Perhaps the largest and longest standing synthesis organization is the Cochrane Collaboration . . . , located in Great Britain and founded in 1963. This organization, which focuses on medical and health research, consists of over 50 collaborative review groups and has completed over 1,300 reviews. Following this model, the Campbell Collaboration . . . was established in the United States in 1999 to assist individuals in education and the social sciences to make informed decisions about what works based on high-quality research and reviews. In Great Britain, EPPIC at the University of London Institute of Education . . . was created in 1993 to conduct systematic reviews of research on social interventions. This organization was recently funded to conduct reviews specifically on educational practices, which it plans to make available through their Research Evidence in Education Library. . . .

In the United States, the IES has established the WWC . . . , which is jointly managed by the Campbell Collaboration and the American Institutes for Research. WWC conducts reviews of educational practices supported by high-quality research and makes this information available to practitioners through Web-based databases. The U.S. Department of Education funds the Research and Training Center on Early Childhood Development (CED) . . . , which is conducting a set of practice-sensitive research syntheses on the effectiveness (and ineffectiveness) of practices for infants and young children with disabilities and their families. Whereas other organizational efforts primarily provide evidence that a practice is effective, the CED has created a more functional operational definition by stating that evidence-based practices are informed by research, in which the characteristics and consequences of environmental variables are empirically established and the relationship directly informs what a practitioner can do to produce the desired outcome.

To examine the effectiveness of programs for children with autism, a committee formed by NAS established guidelines for the strength of evidence provided by individual studies. The dimensions of the studies evaluated were internal validity, external validity, and generalization, with strength of evidence (i.e., from I to IV) evaluated for each.

A key feature in these research synthesis initiatives is the methodological criteria established to select or exclude research studies for the synthesis. Most organizations confined evidence of effectiveness to research studies that have employed RCT methodology or rigorously constructed quasi-experimental designs. The CED researchers took a broader view of the empirical linkage between a practice and an outcome and looked for descriptions of the process of the intervention practices that led to the outcome. The leadership of the WWC has noted that qualitative research may provide information about the ways in which interventions work and can be used to substantiate "promising practices" in education, although they proposed that clearly efficacious practices would require verification through RCTs. For the EPPIC, Oakley reported that they incorporated qualitative research in their reviews, but they had encountered multiple problems in their evaluation of qualitative studies.

Professional Associations.   Professional associations and groups have also examined the literature to determine effective practices. These groups have often established the level of evidence needed to identify a practice as effective. For example, the Child-Clinical Section of Division 12 of the APA established the Task Force on Empirically Supported Psychosocial Interventions for Children. They proposed the types and amount of evidence needed to identify a practice as (a) well-established (i.e., two well-conducted group design studies by different researchers or nine well-conducted single-subject designs); or (b) "probably efficacious" (i.e., two group design studies by same investigator or at least three single-subject design studies).

The Division for Early Childhood of CEC established a process for identifying recommended practices that incorporated evidence from the research literature. Mentioned previously, DEC conducted an extensive literature review to identify support for recommended practices and also to incorporate information from focus groups of experts, practitioners, and family members in the final identification of practices. The level or type of evidence needed to support a recommended practice was not identified.

The American Speech-Language-Hearing Association (ASHA) proposed that different types of evidence may be important for different clinical activities. For questions of treatment efficacy, they propose that different frameworks are available for evaluating the level of evidence that documents efficacy. They provide as an example one such framework developed by the Oxford Centre for Evidence-based Medicine. This system could be used to classify practices according to four levels of evidence:

- Level I evidence derives from meta-analyses including at least one randomized experimental design or well-designed randomized control studies.

- Level II evidence includes controlled studies without randomization and quasi-experimental designs.
- Level III consists of well-designed nonexperimental studies (i.e., correlational and case studies).
- Level IV includes expert committee report, consensus conference, and clinical experience of respected authorities.

The ASHA policy emphasizes that other frameworks are currently available or evolving and could be useful for specific questions related to treatment efficacy.

To date, the special education community has yet to develop systematic guidelines for specifying the types and levels of evidence needed to identify a practice as evidence-based and effective. The Division for Learning Disabilities (DLD) and the Division for Research (DR) jointly published a document entitled *Alerts,* in which an expert from the field reviews the literature relevant to a specific practice and describes the evidence or lack of evidence that underlies the practice. These alerts, however, have been based on individual authors' reviews of the literature and, although quite useful, different authors may well be using different criteria for the evidence they include. The second goal of the current DR Task Force, therefore, was to describe the types of results generated by each research methodology and to recommend guidelines for using the results as evidence of effectiveness, or lack of effectiveness, of practices in special education.

Where Do We Go from Here?

The Department of Education is under pressure to prove to Congress that there are educational practices that have evidence of effectiveness and that supporting educational research is a good investment of public funds. In specifying RCT methodology as the gold standard for research, the Department of Education is investing the bulk of research funding in addressing the question of effectiveness, which is clearly important. However, Berliner urges us to avoid confusing science with a specific method or technique. It is more important to look at the broader goal of using science to improve education for all children.

To accomplish such a goal, educational science might be more appropriately seen as a continuum rather than a fixed point. Levin, O'Donnell, and Kratochwill suggest that a program of educational research might be thought of as occurring in four stages. The first stage would involve observational, focused exploration and flexible methodology, which qualitative and correlational methods allow. Stage 2 would involve controlled laboratory or classroom experiments, observational studies of classrooms, and teacher-researcher collaborative experiments. Design experimentation involving qualitative methodology, single-subject designs, quasi-experimental and/or RCT design could be useful at this stage. Stage 3 research would then incorporate knowledge generated from these previous stages to design well-documented interventions and "prove" their effectiveness through well-controlled RCT studies implemented in classroom or naturalistic settings by the natural participants (e.g., teachers) in the settings. We propose that single-subject design studies could also accomplish this purpose.

If research ended here, however, the movement of effective, evidence-based research into practices that teachers use on Monday morning would likely fail. A further step in the development process (Stage 4) would be to determine the factors that lead to adoption of effective practices in typical school systems under naturally existing conditions. That last step would require research into organizational factors that facilitate or impede adoption of innovation in local contexts. The research methodologies that would generate this information are more likely qualitative, correlational, and mixed methods, as well as RCT and large-scale, single-case designs. Researchers may well draw from such disciplines as sociology, political science, economics, as well as education, in this research. Research at this stage may best occur though a partnership among researchers from education, researchers from other disciplines, local education agencies, and teachers. Indeed, an initiative is emerging from another panel convened by the NRC, which is proposing a broad federal initiative that would create just such a partnership.

Conclusion

If different methodologies are appropriate for addressing important questions in special education, then we, as a field, need to be clear about (a) the match between research questions and methodology, (b) the features of each methodology that represent high quality, (c) and the use of research findings for each methodology as scientific evidence for effective practices in special education. To date, we have numerous texts and papers that describe each methodology, but they are not a coordinated, clear index of how each contributes to the present research-to-practice challenge. . . .

Frederick J. Brigham et al.

Research in the Wake of the No Child Left Behind Act: Why the Controversies Will Continue and Some Suggestions for Controversial Research

The unique and sometimes competing interests of key stakeholders, which often drive the development of educational policy, may lead to misunderstanding and confusion. For example, policies espoused by educational advocates and the pragmatic management procedures of educational administrators are sometimes difficult to understand for educators who advocate the adoption of scientific practices. This is because science and advocacy have different traditions and purposes. Scientists begin from a position of doubt and collect evidence, whereas advocates are more likely to begin from a position of certainty. A different point of view yet is held by administrators and policymakers, who must work within the political system and deal with the realities of compromise and communication that affect policy development.

Given the differing perspectives and traditions of the stakeholders in educational reform, it is unlikely that any major educational policy will be without controversy. However, if a coherent educational policy is to be developed, controversial issues must be decided according to some framework. Failure to adopt a coherent position is likely to lead to a hodge-podge of competing initiatives rather than a broadened range of educational opportunities.

In 2001, the interests of various stakeholders were brought together in the passage of the No Child Left Behind (NCLB) Act. A crucial component of NCLB was the requirement that educators use practices that are validated through scientific research. This presents a useful opportunity for individuals concerned with the education of children with emotional or behavioral disorders (E/BD) to introduce scientifically validated practices into the classroom and collect data related to a number of important questions—mainly questions regarding better ways of providing instruction in academic skills. However, the history of educational practice suggests that consensus will be elusive at best, even with the soundest of scientific evidence. With this in mind, in this article we (a) describe reasons why educational practices will remain controversial

From *Behavioral Disorders*, 29(3) May 2004, pp. 300–310. Copyright © 2004 by CCBD Publications. Reprinted by permission.

even with the call for scientifically validated procedures and (b) suggest areas of research opportunities that NCLB may provide.

Policies, Science, Uncertainty, and Justification

To withstand debate, policies must often be crafted in such a way that people with different perceptions and purposes can recognize their interests in them. One way of creating such policies is to make the wording vague and, therefore, its meaning elusive. As a result, a variety of interpretations and actions are likely to follow from policy statements crafted into law. No Child Left Behind is no exception. For example, according to the U.S. Department of Education, "Under *No Child Left Behind,* states and school districts have unprecedented flexibility in how they use federal education funds, in exchange for greater accountability for results." Whether the flexibility provided by NCLB is real or illusory is debatable. It is clear, however, that this law, like most other policies, is open to a number of conflicting interpretations except for the bottom line—academic accountability.

One way of dealing with the uncertainty that accompanies large-scale policies is to analyze them with respect to a particular philosophical orientation. For example, the impetus for initiatives such as inclusion or whole language can be viewed as primarily philosophical rather than scientific because they are based not on data but on a sense of what should be. From this perspective, actions in violation of a philosophical orientation are irresponsible. Regrettably, acting according to philosophical principles has led to some unfortunate and ludicrous behaviors. For example, consider the behaviors exhibited by virtually any cult. The philosophic stances proclaimed by some cult leaders have led to mass suicides, killings, or other atrocities, often in the name of justice. In education, the whole language movement is probably the best known of the failed philosophies. However, movements such as facilitated communication and full inclusion are better seen as philosophical rather than scientific and empirical in their orientation. Although the evidence in support of these activities is lacking, proponents claim that they are worth implementing because they are consistent with their beliefs. However, in a zero-sum environment such as education, funds devoted to one thing are necessarily diverted from other options. Spending money on disproven programs such as facilitated communication is simply folly. A philosophical orientation, while important, is insufficient to protect the field from folly.

Scientists are more likely to endorse the position that it is foolish to act in a manner that fails to conform to the available data. This position is far from invulnerable to failure and unfortunate outcomes. Fortunately, science possesses a self-correcting mechanism that, over time, eliminates wishful thinking, self-serving bias, and erroneous beliefs from the body of accepted scientific belief. Although it has become fashionable in some circles to decry science as merely a sociopolitical activity, such a position drastically underestimates the power of science to serve society and, just as dramatically, overestimates the alternative approaches to guide decisionmaking.

The social aspects of scientific inquiry are actually a major part of science's self-correcting mechanism. The self-correcting mechanism is the major component that unifies all forms of scientific inquiry. This self-correcting mechanism limits the amount of effort expended on ideas that are unlikely to be productive and also limits the lifespan of ideas that do not produce consistent results. For example, through the self-correcting mechanism of science, strong genetic and environmental positions with regard to human behavior have given way to a more balanced interactionist perspective that accommodates both positions. In academic instruction, the idea that children would improve their spelling by drawing boxes around words and examining their shape has virtually disappeared from serious educational literature because the evidence failed to support it.

As Shermer put it:

> Science is a social process, where one is trained in a certain paradigm and works with others in the field. A community of scientists reads the same journals, goes to the same conferences, reviews one another's papers and books, and generally exchanges ideas about the facts, hypotheses, and theories in that field. Through vast experience they know, fairly quickly, which new ideas have a chance of succeeding and which are obviously wrong. Newcomers from other fields, who typically dive in with both feet without the requisite training and experience, proceed to generate new ideas that they think—because of their success in their own field—will be revolutionary. Instead, they are usually greeted with disdain (or more typically, ignored) by the professionals in the field. This is not because (as they usually think is the reason) insiders don't like outsiders (or that all great revolutionaries are persecuted or ignored), but because in most cases those ideas were considered years or decades before and rejected for perfectly good reasons.

Although the data are not always conclusive and the implications of data in social science are not always readily apparent, the absence of scientifically collected data fails to absolve policymakers and administrators from the need to act. In the absence of scientific advice, however, policymakers, administrators, practitioners, and other concerned parties often turn to influences such as tradition, currently popular ideas, ideas that are expedient at the moment, and various philosophical positions that they may hold. Sometimes the actions taken are counterproductive and actually undermine the responsible and ethical intentions of the policymakers.

If it were easy to undo these counterproductive actions and change course, we could chalk it up to learning through experience. When such policies are in place, however, they are very difficult to change even if they turn out to be unworkable. There are several reasons for this, including the following two: First, certain stakeholders have vested interests in keeping the policies intact. Second, people tend to develop justifications for their actions. Reasoning that has the appearance of rational scientific discourse is often used toward that end. In other words, it is common to find irrational actions supported by seemingly rational justifications. Thus, individuals are unlikely to engage in behavior that works contrary to their own interests (e.g., support a teacher licensing bill that would eliminate their jobs), and they are quite likely to develop elaborate ideational schemes to justify self-interested action as actually pursuant to larger and more noble motives.

Shermer provided an analysis of the ways in which people justify beliefs in "weird things." He defined weird things as

(1) a claim unaccepted by most people in that field of study,
(2) a claim that is either logically impossible or highly unlikely, and/or
(3) a claim for which the evidence is largely anecdotal and uncorroborated.

It is clear that people who are superstitious, foolish, or desperate are especially vulnerable to beliefs that fit these criteria. However, they are not the only people who fall victim to such beliefs. Smart people can also hold irrational beliefs and behave in a stupid manner. Shermer suggested that "smart people believe weird things because they are skilled at defending beliefs they arrived at for non-smart reasons." He proposed two forms of biased thinking—attribution bias and confirmation bias—that are primarily responsible for the maintenance of irrational beliefs by ostensibly rational individuals.

Attribution Bias

Attribution bias occurs when a behavior exhibited by both oneself and another person, even though identical, is suggested to have occurred for different reasons. Most often attribution bias is self-serving. That is, individuals perceive their own actions to have been for good and just reasons, whereas the same actions taken by others are dismissed as unjust and unjustifiable. Areas in which attribution bias have been noted include religious beliefs, vigilante behavior, interpersonal aggression, aggressive acts between nations, and even interpersonal relations among scientists. Ironically, even though science is described as having a major social component, Kramer found that scientists ascribed trustworthy and collegial intent to their own efforts to share resources, data, and the like with others but often believed that attempts to obtain resources, data, and the like by others were the result of untrustworthy and sinister motives.

Attribution bias in relation to NCLB is likely to result in proponents of any action being viewed with suspicion, even by others who support similar ideas. For example, suggestions that students should be excused from the statewide and district-wide assessment requirements of both NCLB and the 1997 reauthorization of the Individuals with Disabilities Education Act (IDEA) may be viewed as serving the interests of a child by one group and as an attempt to inflate a school's test scores by another. Whereas the extreme positions are easily identified, the likelihood is that the truth lies somewhere between these polar opposites.

We suggest that the production of scientific data is the best way to identify the most probable location of the truth between the self-serving poles of any debate. It must be noted, however, that scientific data can be determined as good or useful only in relation to a specific purpose or set of purposes. Therefore, the initial task facing producers of scientific research is to decide which goal or set of goals is most important to pursue. This is a difficult task that is far from being accomplished in education.

The implication of attribution bias is that, as individuals, we tend to attribute to ourselves greater nobility in purpose than we do our fellow citizens, and, as a nation, we are less than clear and unified about our educational goals. Thus, the call for scientifically based practices in education will probably do little to lessen the conflict surrounding any instructional method or decision.

Confirmation Bias

Confirmation bias, as it is commonly used in psychological literature, refers to the seeking or interpreting of evidence in ways that conform to existing beliefs, expectations, or a hypothesis in hand. According to Shermer, people often believe weird things because they have a "tendency to seek or interpret evidence favorable to already existing beliefs, and to ignore or reinterpret evidence unfavorable to already existing beliefs." As a result, people tend to find what they are looking for even if it is not there.

Confirmation bias is often the result of determining the truth by checking only positive and not negative instances. Although it is certainly more pleasant to examine the reasons for our successes, a full understanding can be reached only if we consider the reasons for our failures as well. Many of the controversial treatments for disabilities appear to be supported by confirmation bias. Rather than providing clear data obtained under replicable conditions, proponents of less-accepted treatments (and some popular but refuted treatments, e.g., modality-based instruction) use anecdotal evidence about how the treatment worked for them or a given child to assure decisionmakers that it will, therefore, work for others as well.

The evidence regarding the practice of coteaching appears to be one such product of confirmation bias. Weiss and Brigham pointed out that the studies that purportedly support coteaching were highly flawed in that they often failed to define coteaching, employed only teachers who were satisfied with their instructional arrangements, employed such vague outcome indicators as "improved" or "more accepted," and failed to describe what the teachers involved in coteaching did. Weiss concluded that coteaching was often used to meet the needs of students with disabilities despite the absence of supportive evidence. In addition, she pointed out that many examples of coteaching were actually outside of the recommendations found in the literature. Nevertheless, when we discuss this evidence with teachers and parents of students with disabilities, we are often informed that the evidence may say one thing but their experience or the experience of their friends is different.

One unfortunate outcome of confirmation bias is that by focusing on information that supports a given belief, an individual's views are rarely challenged. For example, the World Wide Web, although holding the potential to open unlimited stores of information to vast numbers of people, can also have the opposite effect. Rather than focusing on a variety of viewpoints, some users simply look for statements in agreement with a given predisposition and, through repetition, reinforce the predisposition. Still another form of confirmation bias results when individuals amass large stores of information that are unified around a given proposition. Such individuals can become so entrenched in a point of view or a way of doing things that it becomes hard to see things differently.

The Impact of Attribution Bias and Confirmation Bias on Educational Research

No Child Left Behind's step in the direction of clarifying educational goals by forcing attention on academic outcomes focuses on only one of the possible goals of a school—academic achievement. Whether or not the strength of the current emphasis on academics is desirable can only be answered by science with the response "It depends." It depends on the balance that is held between academics and other ostensible goals for any given community, school, or student. The exact nature of this balance is probably better analyzed politically or economically than scientifically. Once the goals are established, science can provide substantial assistance in reaching them. However, even if a unified set of goals could be established for all children in all U.S. schools, controversies would continue to erupt.

We have described two forms of bias, attribution bias and confirmation bias, that affect individual judgment regarding any source of data. Knowing that these forms of bias (and there are more that we have not discussed here) exist can help individuals guard against them. However, knowledge of the threat alone is a necessary but insufficient cure to the problems arising from bias. The self-correcting methods of scientific inquiry can, over time, mediate these forms of bias if decisionmakers and their constituents will trust data collected with due rigor and appropriate methods and expose their own beliefs to doubt and questioning. However, "issues of belief and doubt get into some very partisan ruts." Thus, NCLB may ask more of educational leaders, educators, and parents than it does of schoolchildren.

Suggestions for Research in the Wake of No Child Left Behind

Special education practice is highly dependent on the conditions present in general education. Moreover, influences such as statewide testing and budget constraints that affect general education personnel and program managers also affect special educators. Students with mild disabilities are most often called to the attention of school officials because they have been unsuccessful in meeting the demands of general education in some way. Many of the current special education regulations and initiatives have their roots in the past 3 or 4 decades in which general education programs were expanding the number of options available to students in U.S. schools. No Child Left Behind focuses attention squarely on academic achievement as the measure of educational accountability. It is a bottom-line, outcome-driven approach to educational decisionmaking. As such, it differs in many ways from earlier approaches to educational accountability. Furthermore, the unit of analysis applied by NCLB is actually the school and its disaggregated populations, rather than the individual, as was the case historically in special education.

The trend toward academic monitoring has already affected special education programs for many students. For example, educational programs for students with severe disabilities have moved from a developmental model to a functional model and subsequently to a model that attempts to link instructional activities to academic skills taught in the general education curriculum. Although such a trend can be viewed as opening up academic avenues that previously were closed to many students, it also closes off the opportunities for developmental and functional curricula by reallocating resources and attention to other issues. Whether or not this proves to be a positive step remains to be seen. However, the focus on academic outcomes is clearly related to enabling children to fit in to the general education environment in a more satisfactory manner. Similar trends can be seen relative to the educational programs of students with E/BD. With the emphasis on general education goals, it is difficult to imagine that programs or remediation and community-based or vocational education will receive the support necessary to serve the populations for which they were created. Rather than isolated developments in the special education community, such trends are better understood as responses to changes in the general education program.

The NCLB focus of accountability on the academic achievement of groups of students within schools will, in our opinion, call into question earlier research findings and policy decisions made relative to IDEA. This is because the nature and focus of the general education program under NCLB is different from the nature and focus under IDEA. How these differences will manifest themselves has yet to be settled. Nevertheless, changes in the general education program will, of necessity, prompt special educators to reevaluate the findings and recommendations made earlier if they wish their research findings to remain consistent with improving student performance relative to the general education curriculum. In the following sections, we suggest some specific areas of educational research that will benefit from additional scrutiny given the requirements of NCLB.

Planning and Service Delivery

Impact of Students with Disabilities on General Education

Inclusion of students with disabilities developed in an era of mostly expanding curriculum offerings and emphasis on tolerance of individual differences. The pressures to align resources with curricular areas that are measured in state- and district-wide tests appear to be narrowing the curriculum offerings of many schools in the United States. This reduction in the number of classes, coupled with the IDEA requirement of access to the general education curriculum and pressures for inclusion, suggests that more students with disabilities will be present in classes in which teachers are already experiencing increased pressure to raise their students' achievement. Students with E/BD will likely be seen as adding unnecessary impediments to the education of other students in the general education classroom. Rather than speaking of a special education student's right to receive an individualized program of special education and related services, researchers and advocates need to be able to respond with data examining the performance of students with E/BD in classes under these new pressures and curricular demands and to provide clear evidence that the education programs of other students are unaffected. Some evidence of this currently exists; however, the extent to which the conditions under which this evidence was collected reflect conditions in schools facing the bottom-line academic accountability of NCLB is unclear.

Individualized Education Programs

The backbone of a student's special education program is the individualized education program (IEP). In an era in which developmental and functional approaches prevailed, it made a great deal of sense to single out things that a given student would be learning that were different from the curriculum presented to most students. The result of the coupling of NCLB with IDEA's access to the general education curriculum clause appears to be that more students with disabilities are taking core academic classes and are to be measured by the same standards and at the same frequency as are students who have no disabilities. Under such conditions, the traditional IEP, with its detailed mapping of goals and objectives that form the curriculum for a particular student, seems redundant because the academic program delivered for students in a given classroom or course of study is dictated by the state curriculum standards. However, there may be specific benefits to this redundancy that would be better defended through data than through insistence that IEPs are clearly needed and beneficial. For example, rather than focusing on *what* a student with E/BD will do in a particular class, the IEP may still serve a useful function in describing *how* (e.g., the conditions and timelines) a student will fulfill the requirements. While it is certainly possible to craft an IEP focusing on such aspects of a student's educational program, there is little empirical evidence that educators currently know how to do so.

Another research issue related to IEPs is the extent to which they are actually individualized. Research conducted in the past several years has not been particularly supportive of the extent to which IEPs actually reflect students' educational needs or vary according to their characteristics. Indeed, our own experience with several school districts that pride themselves on the quality of their IEPs suggests that the "I" in IEP could more accurately stand for "interchangeable." Perhaps the interchangeability of IEPs is a necessary reflection of the movement to include students in the general education curriculum; perhaps it is the result of limited time, imagination, or training. Under the NCLB opportunities, it seems prudent to examine the functionality and uniqueness of the benefits of these documents relative to their costs.

Intervention

Appropriateness of a Standard Intervention Protocol for Students with Emotional or Behavioral Disorders

By *standard intervention protocol*, we mean a set of clearly defined and well-documented treatments that should be employed as a matter of course for students with behavior problems as well as for students whose problems are serious enough to warrant identifying them as having E/BD. Multiple gating procedures in E/BD, as well as "failure to respond to treatment" models for students with learning disabilities, are predicated on the proposition that children who fail to respond to interventions that would support most students are the students who are most likely in need of special education services. In that regard, it seems imperative to have a clear idea of what the word *treatment* means.

In regard to behavioral issues, treatment could mean anything from poorly executed and inconsistent reprimands to well-designed reinforcement or cognitive behavior management programs. For newly identified students, the efforts to manage problematic student behaviors are recorded in documents such as prereferral intervention plans, reports from teacher assistance teams, and other, similar reports. With proper assistance and support, teachers have been able to create useful and effective interventions for some students who otherwise would have been referred needlessly for special education evaluation. Most classroom teachers, however, are on their own in developing and maintaining behavior management programs for their classes and treatments for individual students. It is not at all clear that most school-based practitioners possess the expertise or the time and support to develop and implement unique behavior intervention programs for individual students. Furthermore, given the relatively consistent advice about general behavior management techniques provided by different tests in the field, it is not clear that unique treatments need to be developed as a first or even second step in dealing with problematic behavior.

Efforts at creating school-wide discipline programs have established baseline conditions that could be considered essential before individual treatments are implemented. Research data could be used to establish a "what to do next" category of treatment that would be recommended for students once general school-wide and class-wide efforts had failed. Such practices are commonly found in medical treatment models but have not yet taken hold in educational settings. The enormous advantage of such a system is that students would receive effective treatments more quickly and teachers would have additional guidance and assurance that they were, indeed, providing appropriate educational services to their students.

Preferred Target Domains

The obvious focus of intervention for students with E/BD is their behavior. However, behavior can serve a variety of functions, and the relationship of behavior to academic instruction is often underplayed in discussions of students with E/BD. One of the major functions of unacceptable behavior in classrooms is escape. We know that well-designed instruction is a mediator of students' behavior, yet we see little attention paid to the academic structure of the classrooms in which the misbehavior occurs.

Research on academic instruction as an antecedent is available to scholars and policymakers. It is clear that providing students with well-designed instruction that is within their ability to master reduces the incidence of behavior problems in the classroom. However, after NCLB's changes in academic emphasis, the extent to which teachers are able or believe that they are able to deviate substantially from state curriculum guides and timelines related to covering material before a certain test date is unknown. It is possible that little has changed since NCLB. It is also possible that the current emphasis on performance relative to test-linked standards makes general education teachers unwilling to make substantial curriculum adaptations.

The current popularity of coteaching as a service delivery model may also mediate the ability of special education teachers to provide instruction that is supportive of students with E/BD. Through coteaching arrangements, students with E/BD are considered to have their special education programs delivered to them in the general education classroom. However, as previously discussed, the model of coteaching is poorly supported for students with special education needs. In addition, the general education classroom may be a less hospitable place to deliver special education services after NCLB than it was prior to this legislation. One reason for this is the pressure exerted on teachers to cover specific content objectives regardless of student readiness or mastery of the material covered. Many special education teachers that we work with report that they and their general education colleagues experience great pressure from their district administrators to cover the content regardless of student mastery. While it is unlikely that many students will demonstrate mastery of content that has not been taught, content-coverage approaches are likely to result in incomplete teaching and partial mastery of material, particularly for nonperforming or disengaged students. As such, the NCLB standards may actually increase rather than decrease the range of achievement outcomes for students in diverse classrooms. We suggest that it is better to find out than to wonder whether this is the case.

Possible Research Outcomes

We have suggested that a number of the traditional elements of special education programming for students with E/BD should be reexamined in light of the requirements of NCLB and the changes in general education programs that are likely to evolve from implementation of that legislation. With regard to the relationship of general and special education, it is possible that the NCLB requirements place pressures on teachers that make the general education environment a less welcoming place than it was previously. It is also likely that such changes will make the general education environment a less desirable goal for students with E/BD. Another possible outcome is that NCLB actually will result in no detectable change in general education classrooms that will be relevant to the education of students with E/BD.

We also suggest that IEPs should be reexamined to determine their necessity, function, and actual ability to promote individualized treatment for students with E/BD. Related to this question, it is possible that researchers will document the necessity of the IEP for ensuring educational treatments for students with E/BD. Conversely, it is possible, given the pressure toward a standards-based curriculum and the previous evidence, that IEPs are rarely *individualized*—that they no longer serve their intended function. Another possible outcome might be documentation that the important functions of IEPs could be served by a much shorter document than is typically found in the folders of students with E/BD. If that were the case, researchers could turn their attention to the essential elements of IEPs that need to be maintained or new elements that need to be created, as well as those that are superfluous to effective intervention for students with E/BD.

Finally, we suggest that the traditional target domains of E/BD intervention may be affected by NCLB-prompted changes in the general education classroom. The flexibility of general education teachers or special education teachers working in inclusive settings or under coteaching models may be far more limited in NCLB-compliant classrooms than it was previously. It may be that teachers perceive their flexibility to be curtailed but that they would be able to offer flexible instruction with appropriate guidance. Researchers could provide a great service to the field by documenting what supports are most helpful to teachers under the pressures of test-linked standards.

We suggest that NCLB has the potential to make substantial changes in the educational landscape. The direct changes are clearly established in the legislation. Other changes may emerge as indirect effects of the legislation and will benefit from the attention of educational researchers to identify and describe them as well as to validate effective methods for dealing with these changes on behalf of students with E/BD.

Conclusion

No Child Left Behind offers a number of opportunities to the educational profession in return for a strong focus on academic accountability. One of the more commonly celebrated themes of NCLB is the call for educators to use practices that have been scientifically validated by research in their efforts to serve students with disabilities.

Although the call to use scientifically validated practices appears straightforward and within our grasp given the extant body of research, several factors suggest that it will be a more difficult and demanding task than many educators and policymakers believe. One of the difficulties affecting this enterprise is the impact of attribution and confirmation biases on the judgment of decisionmakers. Such biases work to maintain the status quo by allowing individuals to believe that their motives are somehow different from and more noble than the motives of those who disagree with them and by insulating them from evidence that contradicts or undermines personal beliefs. Furthermore, scientifically validated practices for students with disabilities are effective or ineffective in inclusive schools only relative to their interaction with the programs and expectations present in the general education curriculum. By altering the emphasis of educational programs to a predominant emphasis on performance on test-linked standards, NCLB will probably result in substantial changes in the actions, climate, and expectations of general education classrooms. How these changes will affect the service delivery, instructional, and behavioral options recommended for special education teachers has yet to be seen.

Whereas many of the findings of educational research may hold true after NCLB, others may not, and the way that they are used in the classroom may need adjustment. Components of effective special education practice interact with general education programs in much the same way that notes and scales interact with key changes in musical performance. When the rest of the orchestra changes key, it is in best interests of all the players to change at the same time. Those who do not wish to do so are better advised to be soloists or to write their own music. Special educators must respond to the key changes in general education. Transposing from one key to another can take a line of music from the comfortable range of an instrument or singing voice to a range that is impossible for the performer or vice versa. If the data suggest that the NCLB changes make general education a more productive and supportive place for students with E/BD, special educators should certainly play in the orchestra. If not, it may be time to reconsider "solo projects" and resurrect the dedicated service delivery models that have faded in recent years. In either case, we should let the data, rather than our biases, guide our actions.

POSTSCRIPT

Can Scientifically Based Research Guide Instructional Practice?

Odom and his colleagues identify "devilish details" complicating research efforts in special education: the heterogeneity of disability (consider the range within the autism spectrum alone) and the complexity of the contexts of special education (preschool to young adult; home, school, and work). To conquer these challenges, and continue the necessary pursuit of scientifically gathered data, they introduce articles that present quality indicators to establish rigor within a variety of research methods.

This range of acceptable methodology is actually encouraged by the Institute for Education Sciences, which agrees that "research designs and methods (must be) appropriate to the research question posed" (WWC, *What Is Scientifically Based Research?*). Still, to fully satisfy the gold standard, findings from other methodologies must be verified through RCT.

Originally skeptical about RCT, Forness (*Behavioral Disorders*, 2005) was convinced by its successful application in mental health. Agreeing with WWC standards, Forness believes that, despite their challenges, RCT studies are the only way to control variables and discover whether an intervention makes a critical difference.

Brigham and his coauthors maintain that controversies over instruction cannot be guided by scientific research until stakeholders agree on the purpose of education. Today's policymakers see academic achievement as the goal; special educators seek improved functioning and participation in society.

Consider inclusion, an educational practice supported by IDEA and a focus of many school interventions. Under NCLB, the efficacy of inclusion must be established through RCT studies. Could control groups be identified?

Every good study must begin with an agreement of the target phenomenon. A modest survey of preservice and practicing teachers revealed no universally agreed upon definition or model of inclusion (Snyder, Garriott, and Aylor, *Teacher Education and Special Education*, 2001). Variable definitions make conducting and analyzing research challenging indeed (Simpson, *Behavioral Disorders*, 2004).

In two districts involved in a project to increase inclusionary practices, models changed as teams developed and responded to student experience (Burstein, Sears, Wilcoxen, Cabello, and Spagna, *Remedial and Special Education*, 2004). Perhaps this change itself should be studied.

In *Improving Outcomes for Students with Disabilities* (National Council on Disability, 2004), a researcher asks, "Which is more valid, the work of an evidence-based research center or the experiences of families of children with disabilities? What is the basis for the criteria? Someone's [research] numbers or someone's real life experience?" (p. 4). For advocates, inclusion is a belief system, not a program or a research-based strategy (Villa and Thousand, 2005).

And yet, at least one researcher has devised a study of inclusionary practices within an RCT model. Russell Gersten (*Learning Disabilities Theory & Practice*, 2005) takes readers "behind the scenes," describing the complex, but rewarding, process of developing and conducting a gold-standard research project on inclusion. Other articles in this issue extend the discussion of this collaboration.

Intense partnerships with funded researchers are unavailable to most teachers. Networking through professional organizations, and the journals they publish, enables educators to become informed consumers in this evidence-driven era (Simpson, LaCava, and Graner, *Intervention in School and Clinic*, 2004). What is a teacher to do, though, when a resource such as WWC has not studied any special education methodologies?

Scientists seek evidence. Parents seek change and growth. Teachers want to use the best possible techniques to help students learn. Sometimes parents may want the school team to implement a promising treatment. Is the school compelled to reject the request if it has not been validated against a control group? Or, might the successes of one child stimulate a line of research inquiry that could identify a method that would help many?

If medicine and mental health use RCT, can education become more credible by doing the same? In this high-stakes time, can we afford not to do so? Can special education research be conducted in shifting school environments and be published fast enough to help teachers?

ISSUE 11

Does NCLB Leave Some Students Behind?

YES: Jennifer Booher-Jennings, from "Rationing Education in an Era of Accountability," *Phi Delta Kappan* (June 2006), pp. 756–761

NO: U.S. Department of Education, from "Working Together for Students with Disabilities: Individuals with Disabilities Education Act (IDEA) and No Child Left Behind Act (NCLB)," http://www.ed.gov/admins/lead/speced/toolkit/index.html (December 2005)

ISSUE SUMMARY

YES: Jennifer Booher-Jennings, a doctoral candidate at Columbia University, finds the accountability pressures of No Child Left Behind (NCLB) are leading some administrators to advise teachers to focus only on those children who will improve their school's scores; other students don't count much.

NO: The U.S. Department of Education FAQ Sheet on IDEA and NCLB advises readers that the link between these two statutes is sound, emphasizing how they work together to ensure that every student's performance and needs receive appropriate attention.

T he No Child Left Behind Act of 2001 (NCLB), a reauthorization of the Elementary and Secondary Education Act (ESEA), has changed the vocabulary and practice of educators in every publicly funded school in America.

More familiarly known as Title I, ESEA has long provided funds to districts to improve the educational performance of children from low-income families. In the reauthorization now known as NCLB, the U.S. federal government demands a return on its investment.

Four key principles form the foundation of NCLB:

- Schools must be accountable for student performance and teacher qualifications.
- States and districts must set growth targets and have the latitude to achieve them.
- Parents must have more information about their schools and broader educational options if their schools do not reach growth targets.
- Schools must use research-based instructional strategies.

The principle most on the minds of educators is accountability. States may set their own educational standards, but all students must be proficient in math and reading/language arts by 2013–2014. Some states designed high-level academic programs to meet world-class standards. Others preferred literacy standards, measuring the basic skills students will need to be successful in the world of work. Some have formulated separate sets of standards for students with severe disabilities.

States determine specific benchmark goals, staged to reach proficiency. Regular testing determines if a school is making Adequate Yearly Progress (AYP) toward the target: students must be assessed in reading/language arts and math annually in grades 3–8, and at least once in grades 9–10. Beginning in 2007–2008, students must be assessed in science at least once in grades 3–5, 6–9, and 10–12.

Some schools appear to be successful, but small groups within their walls do markedly less well than others. To hold schools accountable for the achievements of all students, NCLB identifies particular subgroups including students from low-income families, students from major racial and ethnic groups, those with limited English proficiency, and those with disabilities. Unless each subgroup makes AYP, a school is deemed not making total AYP.

Schools that do not make AYP are subject to an array of interventions. Their leadership must take actions to improve. Parents must be notified of the status and have the option of transferring to higher-performing schools. Supplemental educational services must be available. In the extreme, schools are subject to "corrective actions" under the guidance/supervision of external experts.

These expectations and consequences are taken seriously by all educators. While striving to meet goals, some wonder if all students will be part of the race or if some, especially students with disabilities, will be left behind.

Jennifer Booher-Jennings, after studying NCLB implementation in one Texas school, found teachers were encouraged to focus their attention on "the kids who count" because their improvement could increase school scores. Since students with disabilities didn't "count," or because they were "hopelessly" unlikely to do well, they were not deemed worthy of teachers' energy.

The U.S. Department of Education, in responses to frequently asked questions, maintains that NCLB and IDEA work in concert to ensure that every child with a disability reaches high standards. The FAQ notes that most children with disabilities are in general education placements. The information gleaned from frequent assessments should "shine a light on student needs and draw attention to how schools can better serve (them)."

As you read these articles, ask yourself how the schools in your neighborhood are implementing NCLB. Are all subgroups participating meaningfully or are some more important than others?

YES

Jennifer Booher-Jennings

Rationing Education in an Era of Accountability

Meet Mrs. Dewey, 46 years old and a veteran fourth-grade teacher at Marshall Elementary School. Mrs. Dewey entered the teaching profession in the wake of *A Nation at Risk* and has weathered the storm ever since. For the last 20 years, she has survived the continuous succession of faddish programs that have characterized American education reform. Year after year, administrators have asked Marshall teachers to alter their practice to conform to the latest theory. Mrs. Dewey's colleagues, frustrated by the implementation of such silver-bullet approaches, have often flouted the administrative directives and chosen instead to serve as the sole arbiters of their classroom practice.

But it is the newest of the new solutions that worries Mrs. Dewey most. The language of accountability is swift and uncompromising: hold educators responsible for results. Identify those teachers who, as President Bush says, "won't teach." Fair enough, Mrs. Dewey thinks. The consummate professional, Mrs. Dewey always looks for the silver lining.

Like other reforms, accountability requires teachers to embrace a new strategy. Data-driven decision making, a consultant told the faculty at a professional development session, is the philosophy Marshall teachers must adopt. The theory is simple. Give students regular benchmark assessments, use the data to identify individual students' weaknesses, [and] provide targeted instruction and support that addresses those areas. Mrs. Dewey remembers nodding approvingly. After all, this approach—gathering textured information on each student to guide instructional activities—was one she had been using for 22 years.

The consultant moved on. "Using the data, you can identify and focus on the kids who are close to passing. The bubble kids. And focus on the kids that count—the ones that show up at Marshall after October won't count toward the school's test scores this year. Because you don't have enough special education students to disaggregate scores for that group, don't worry about them either." To make this concept tangible for teachers, the consultant passed out markers in three colors: green, yellow, and red. Mrs. Dewey heard someone mutter, "What is this? The traffic light theory of education?"

"Take out your classes' latest benchmark scores," the consultant told them, "and divide your students into three groups. Color the 'safe cases,' or kids who

From *Phi Delta Kappan*, June 2006, pp. 756–761. Copyright © 2006 by Phi Delta Kappan. Reprinted by permission of Phi Delta Kappan and Jennifer Booher-Jennings.

will definitely pass, green. Now, here's the most important part: identify the kids who are 'suitable cases for treatment.' Those are the ones who can pass with a little extra help. Color them yellow. Then, color the kids who have no chance of passing this year and the kids that don't count—the 'hopeless cases'—red. You should focus your attention on the yellow kids, the bubble kids. They'll give you the biggest return on your investment."

As the bell tolls a final warning to the boisterous 9-year-olds bringing up the rear of her class line, Mrs. Dewey stares blankly into the hallway. Never did she believe that the advice offered by that consultant would become Marshall's educational mantra. Focus on the bubble kids. Tutor only these students. Pay more attention to them in class. Why? It's data-driven. Yet this is what her colleagues have been doing, and Marshall's scores are up. The community is proud, and the principal has been anointed one of the most promising educational leaders in the state. At every faculty meeting, the principal presents a "league table," ranking teachers by the percentage of their students passing the latest benchmark test. And the teachers talk, as they always do. The table makes perfect fodder for faculty room gossip: "Did you see who was at the bottom of the table this month?"

Mrs. Dewey has made compromises, both large and small, throughout her career. Every educator who's in it for the long haul must. But this institutionalized policy of educational triage weighs heavily and hurts more. Should she focus only on Brittney, Julian, Shennell, Tiffany, George, and Marlena—the so-called bubble kids—to the exclusion of the other 17 students in her class? Should Mrs. Dewey refuse to tutor Anthony, a persistent and eager little boy with no chance of passing the state test this year, so that she can spend time with students who have a better shot at passing? What should she tell Celine, a precocious student, whose mother wants Mrs. Dewey to review her entry for an essay contest? Celine will certainly pass the state test, so can Mrs. Dewey afford the time? What about the five students who moved into the school in the middle of the year? Since they don't count toward Marshall's scores, should Mrs. Dewey worry about their performance at all?

In her angrier moments, Mrs. Dewey pledges to ignore Marshall's approach and to teach as she always has, the best way she knows how. Yet, if she does, Mrs. Dewey risks being denounced as a traitor to the school's effort to increase scores—in short, a bad teacher. Given 22 years of sacrifices for her profession, it is this reality that stings the most.

Mulling over her choices, Mrs. Dewey shuts her classroom door and begins her class.

Unintended Consequences of Accountability Systems: Educational Triage

Test-based accountability systems aim to direct the behavior of educators toward the improvement of student achievement. The No Child Left Behind (NCLB) Act codified accountability as our national educational blueprint, requiring schools to increase test scores incrementally so that all students are proficient in reading and math by 2014. Yet, despite the stated intent of NCLB to improve outcomes for all students, particularly those who have been historically neglected, educators and others may adopt a series of "gaming" practices in order to artificially inflate schools' passing rates. Such practices include giving students a special education classification to exclude them from high-stakes tests, retaining students in grade to delay test-taking, diverting attention away from subjects not evaluated on high-stakes tests, teaching to the test, and cheating.

In what follows, I discuss two of the dilemmas presented by a less well-known gaming practice: educational triage. The insights offered here derive from an ethnographic study of an urban elementary school in Texas, to which I have assigned the pseudonym "Beck Elementary." Educational triage has become an increasingly widespread response to accountability systems and has been documented in Texas, California, Chicago, Philadelphia, New York, and even England. By educational triage, I mean the process through which teachers divide students into safe cases, cases suitable for treatment, and hopeless cases and ration resources to focus on those students most likely to improve a school's test scores. The idea of triage, a practice usually restricted to the direst of circumstances, like the battlefield or the emergency room, poignantly captures the dynamics of many schools' responses to NCLB. In the name of improving schools' scores, some students must inevitably be sacrificed. And the stakes are high—for schools, which face serious sanctions for failing to meet adequate yearly progress targets; for students, who increasingly face retention if they do not pass state tests; and for teachers, who are judged by the number of students they "save."

Dilemma 1. *Data can be used to improve student achievement, but they can also be used to target some students at the expense of others.* Data-driven decision making has become something of a sacrosanct term in education policy circles. Who could be against it? The public face of data-driven decision making—identifying the needs of each individual child and introducing interventions to remediate any learning difficulties—is sensible and beyond question.

But the Achilles' heel of education policy has always been implementation. When I listened closely to the conversations that educators at Beck Elementary School had about "being data-driven," the slippage between evaluating the individual needs of every student and deciding which students to target to maximize school performance quickly became evident. As I moved closer and closer to the classroom, the administrators' ideal version dissipated and gave way to a triage-based understanding of data-driven decision making. Teachers were most attuned to the chasm between administrators' theoretical proclamations and how the same administrators expected them to operate: teachers understood that the bottom line in this numbers game was the percentage of students who passed. Because of the unrelenting pressure to increase test scores, one mode of using data became dominant at Beck: the diversion of resources (e.g., additional time in class; enrichment sessions with the literacy teacher; and after-school, Saturday, and summer tutoring) to students on the threshold of passing the test, the "bubble kids."

All my questions about which students received extra help were met with the deferent maxim, "It's data-driven." When I asked one teacher how the school allocated additional services to students—for example, the reading specialist or after-school and Saturday tutoring—she provided the following response:

> It's all data-driven. . . . We do projections—how many of them do you think will pass, how many of them do you think will need more instruction, how many teachers do we have to work with, what time limit do we have? Based on that, who are we going to work with? It comes down to that. . . . We really worked with the bubble kids . . . that's the most realistic and time-efficient thing we can think of.

In this conception of data-driven practice, the choice to privilege one group of students over another is viewed as neutral and objective. The decision to distribute resources to those most advantageous to the school's pass rates is not understood as a moral or ethical decision. Instead, it is seen as a sterile management imperative. Protected by its scientific underpinnings, the data-driven focus on the bubble kids is difficult for teachers to attack. In sum, at Beck Elementary, the invocation of the phrase "data-driven" obscures, neutralizes, and legitimates a system of resource distribution that is designed to increase passing rates rather than to meet the needs of individual students.

The blunt vocabulary of triage infiltrated every corner of Beck. The tenor of the phrases used to describe students—"the ones who could make it" and "hopeless cases"—speaks not only to the perceived urgency to improve test scores but also to the destructive labeling of those children who find themselves below the bubble. Driven by the pressure to increase the passing rate, teachers turned their attention away from these students. As one teacher related in an interview:

> I guess there's supposed to be remediation for anything below 55%, but you have to figure out who to focus on in class, and I definitely focus more attention on the bubble kids. If you look at her score [pointing to a student's score on her class test-score summary sheet], she's got a 25%. What's the point in trying to get her to grade level? It would take two years to get her to pass the test, so there's really no hope for her. . . . I feel like we might as well focus on the ones that there's hope for.

To say that hope is absent for a 10-year-old child is a particularly telling comment on how dramatically the accountability system has altered the realm of imagined possibility in the classroom. Now, with an unforgiving bottom line for which to strive, teachers can retain hope only for those perceived as potential passers. To assert that students below the bubble are just too low-performing to help establishes that the only worthwhile improvement in this brave new world is one that converts a nonpasser to a passer.

The problem is that those students who arrive at school as the most disadvantaged are often the lowest scoring. And since the focus on the bubble kids at Beck Elementary begins not in the third grade—the first year that students take state tests—but the moment students enter kindergarten, they are branded as "hopeless cases" from the very first days of their schooling.

An important shift occurs in a system focused on the percentage of students above a particular threshold. When a low-performing student enters a teacher's classroom, he or she is seen as a liability rather than as an opportunity to promote individual student growth. As Michael Apple trenchantly wrote, the emphasis changes "from student needs to student performance, and from what the school does for the student to what the student does for the school."

Certainly one can imagine uses of data that could turn attention to the individual needs of each and every student. However, the current monolithic discourse on data-driven decision making begs for a discussion of unintended consequences. Data can be used to target some students at the expense of others, and it is happening today.

When we blindly defer to "the data," we abdicate responsibility for tough decisions, all the while claiming neutrality. But data are not actors and cannot do anything by themselves. Data do not make decisions; people make decisions that can be informed by data. Decisions about resource allocation are ethical decisions with which educators and communities must grapple and for which they must ultimately take responsibility.

What we need above all is a sustained discussion among educators and the broader polity about the very real tradeoffs involved in schools' responses to accountability systems. If schools adopt the practices of educational triage in response to NCLB, the consequence may be suboptimal outcomes for students "below the bubble," as well as for their peers who are mid-level and high-achieving students. And all of these unintended consequences can happen while official pass rates increase.

Dilemma 2. *It is unfair to hold schools accountable for new students or for subgroups that are too small to yield statistically reliable estimates of a school's effectiveness; however, the consequence of excluding some students may be to deny them access to scarce educational resources.* Educational triage does not end with the diversion of resources to the "bubble kids." Because of the fine print in NCLB, all students are not equally valuable to a school's test scores. Subgroups are not disaggregated if the number of test-takers does not meet a minimum size requirement, and students are not counted at all in a school's scores if they are not enrolled in a school for a full academic year. For example, in Texas, the scores of students who arrive at the school after the end of October do not count toward schools' scores. Such a definition is logical, for it attempts to isolate the impact of schools on students. Including students who have not attended the school for a reasonable period of time might bias estimates of the school's quality and unfairly penalize schools serving more mobile students.

However, if resources flow only toward those students who affect a school's outcomes, students who do not "count" may be denied access to scarce educational resources. I found that another pithy term, "the accountables"— those students who count toward a school's scores—was incorporated into the lexicon of Beck educators. Teachers engaged in a second kind of educational triage by focusing resources on the "accountables," to the virtual exclusion of students who "did not count." In accountability's ultimate contradiction, the protean word "accountable" retained only a semblance of its intended meaning—taking responsibility for each and every student.

How many students are affected by the mobility provisions of NCLB? Take the Houston Independent School District as an illustrative example. Serving 211,157 students, this district is the largest in Texas and the seventh largest in the nation. The average Houston school excludes 8% of its students from its "accountables." Almost one-third of Houston schools (31%) exclude more than 10% of their students from scores used for accountability. By any measure, this is not an insignificant number of students. Moreover, because mobility is not uniformly distributed across the population, some demographic groups have much higher numbers of mobile—and thus unaccountable—students. In Houston, an average of 16% of special education students and 11% of African American students are not counted in schools' scores because they have not been enrolled in a school for a full academic year. Ironically, the very students NCLB was designed to target are often those least likely to be counted.

A second way that students may "not count" stems from states' definitions of the subgroup size required for disaggregation. If states define subgroup size expediently, the scores of various subgroups will continue to be buried in schoolwide averages. Again, Texas is a good example of artful definition of subgroup size. Under the Texas state accountability system, subgroups must include at least 30 students and account for at least 10% of all students— or include 50 or more students—to be evaluated. Under Texas' NCLB implementation plan, subgroups must include at least 50 students and make up at least 10% of all students—or include 200 or more students—to be evaluated. Under the state system, 82% of Houston schools with African American test-takers disaggregate scores for African American students, while for the purposes of NCLB, only 66% do.

Though Texas does not include a special education subgroup in its state system, the impact of using the 50 and 10% or greater than 200 definition rather than the lower threshold is significant. Shifting the definition upward reduces the percentage of Houston schools that disaggregate scores for special education from 55% to 24%. Other states have similarly gamed the subgroup-size provision of the law. In 2005, the U.S. Department of Education allowed Florida to change its minimum subgroup size to 30 students who also make up 15% of test-takers. Because special education students rarely account for more than 15% of a school's population, very few schools in Florida will be required to disaggregate scores for these students.

There is an irreconcilable tension between accurately measuring school effects and forestalling the potential negative consequences of excluding some students from accountability calculations. If accuracy of measurement is privileged, some students will necessarily be excluded from accountability calculations. In order to best estimate school effects, a school should not be responsible for students who attend it for a short period of time. Similarly, small subgroups may yield statistically unreliable estimates of the school's efficacy with a particular group of students. Moreover, mainstream state tests may be inappropriate measures for some English-language learners or special education students. In other words, there are valid reasons, from a measurement perspective, for excluding students from schools' scores. On the other hand, the consequence of excluding these students may be to deny them access to scarce educational resources.

Better Choices?

So Mrs. Dewey can choose to teach all of her students, regardless of their potential contribution to her school's bottom line, or she can participate in educational triage. If she refuses to focus her time and attention on those students most likely to raise the school's scores, she risks not only the school's survival but her professional reputation as a good teacher and, potentially, her job.

Mrs. Dewey should not be asked to make such choices, and it is unconscionable to question her ethics when she does what she has little choice but to do. Systems of public policy cannot be designed solely for those with the moral certitude to qualify them for sainthood.

Educators will respond to systemic incentives, and NCLB's current incentives structurally induce behaviors that are inimical to broader notions of equity and fairness. In many cases, these perverse incentives turn educators' attention away from NCLB's intended beneficiaries. Until these issues are addressed, we can expect to see educational triage practices flourish across the country.

Working Together for Students with Disabilities: Individuals with Disabilities Education Act (IDEA) and No Child Left Behind Act (NCLB)

1. Are *NCLB* and *IDEA* in conflict with each other?

No. Both laws have the same goal of improving academic achievement through high expectations and high-quality education programs. *NCLB* works to achieve that goal by focusing on school accountability, teacher quality, parental involvement through access to information and choices about their children's education, and the use of evidence-based instruction. *IDEA* complements those efforts by focusing specifically on how best to help students with disabilities meet academic goals.

NCLB aims to improve the achievement of all students and recognizes that schools must ensure that all groups receive the support they need to achieve to high standards. That is why *NCLB* requires that schools look at the performance of specific subgroups of students, including students with disabilities, and holds schools accountable for their achievement. By including students with disabilities in the overall accountability system, the law makes their achievement everybody's business, not just the business of special education teachers. Shining the light on the needs of students with disabilities draws attention to the responsibility of states, districts, and schools to target resources to improve the achievement of students with disabilities and to monitor closely the quality of services provided under *IDEA*.

2. If *NCLB* focuses on school performance while IDEA focuses on individual students, how can a student's individual rights not be compromised under *NCLB*?

The requirements of *NCLB* do not infringe on the rights of students with disabilities under *IDEA*.

IDEA requires that schools provide special education and related services to meet the individual needs of each student with a disability. To provide these services, a team of educators and parents develop a plan (referred to as an "Individualized Education Program," or IEP) for each student with a disability that

From http://www.ed.gov/admins/lead/speced/toolkit/index.html, December 2005. Published by the U.S. Department of Education.

maps out what achievement is expected and what services are needed to help the student meet these expectations. With the appropriate supports and services, students with disabilities can and should be held to high standards.

NCLB is designed to ensure that schools are held accountable for educational results so that each and every student can achieve to high standards. Setting the bar high helps all students, including students with disabilities, reach those standards. The expectation of *NCLB* is that students with disabilities can achieve to high standards as other students, given the appropriate supports and services.

3. Was *NCLB* the first federal law to require states to include students with disabilities in the state's assessment system?

NCLB is the first law to hold schools accountable for ensuring that all students participate in the state assessment system, but it is built on earlier law. The 1997 amendments to the *IDEA* required that students with disabilities participate in state and district assessments and that their results be reported publicly in the same way and with the same frequency as those of other students. The federal law that preceded *NCLB*, the *Improving America's Schools Act of 1994*, required schools to include the assessment results of students with disabilities in accountability decisions for Title I schools. *NCLB* and the 2004 *IDEA* amendments strengthened a commitment to this requirement, and now all states are paying attention to testing students with disabilities and are using those results to hold schools accountable for the performance of these students.

Data indicate that participation and achievement levels are rising each year. Data from the National Council on Educational Outcomes (NCEO) show that in 2003, most states had 95 percent to 100 percent participation in state math and reading assessments by students with disabilities in elementary school, middle school, and high school. By including students with disabilities in the assessment and accountability systems, we raise our expectations for them while giving schools the data they need to help all of their students to be successful. *NCLB* is helping special education programs and each child's IEP team know what academic goals children need to achieve so that they are given the appropriate supports and services. *NCLB* tells us what we're working toward, while *IDEA* brings to bear multiple resources and services to help students attain the learning standards.

4. My school did not make Adequate Yearly Progress (AYP) because students with disabilities did not score well on the state test. Is that fair?

Only by holding schools accountable for *all* students will the spotlight of attention and necessary resources be directed to those children most in need of assistance and most often left behind academically.

Schools need to be accountable for all students. To achieve that goal, AYP is intentionally designed to identify those areas where schools need to improve the achievement of their students. What we are learning is that some schools perform well on average, but they may miss their AYP goals as a result of the student achievement of one or a few groups of students. The requirement for states, districts, and schools to disaggregate their data (i.e., separate their assessment data by the results of the different subgroups of students) is one of the fundamental principles of *NCLB*. This ensures that all schools and districts are held accountable for the performance of subgroups of students, not just the school as a whole.

The Department recognizes the challenges educators face in helping all children achieve to high standards. But allowing overall school performance to mask the lower performance of particular groups of students who need additional academic assistance would be *unfair* to those struggling groups of students.

5. Why should students with disabilities be tested and included in accountability systems?

Students with disabilities deserve the same high-quality education as their peers. Ever since Congress enacted the 1997 amendments to the *IDEA*, the nation has been working to improve the participation of students with disabilities in state assessments and provide students with disabilities access to the general education curriculum. Many states have been committed to this goal for an even longer period of time. The purpose of requiring participation in assessments is to improve achievement for students with disabilities. As Secretary Spellings has said on more than one occasion, "What gets measured gets done." Too often in the past, students with disabilities were excluded from assessments and accountability systems, and the consequence was that they did not receive the academic attention and resources they deserved.

Students with disabilities, including those with the most significant cognitive disabilities, benefit instructionally from such participation. One state explains the instructional benefits of including students with the most significant cognitive disabilities in its assessment system in the following way: "Some students with disabilities have never been taught academic skills and concepts, for example, reading, mathematics, science, and social studies, even at very basic levels. Yet all students are capable of learning at a level that engages and challenges them. Teachers who have incorporated learning standards into their instruction cite unanticipated gains in students' performance and understanding. Furthermore, some individualized social, communication, motor, and self-help skills can be practiced during activities based on the learning standards."

To ensure that adequate resources are dedicated to helping these students succeed, appropriate measurement of their achievement needs to be part of school and district accountability systems. Furthermore, when students with disabilities are part of the accountability system, educators' expectations for these students are more likely to increase. In such a system, educators realize that students with disabilities count and that they can learn to high standards, just like students without disabilities.

6. Is it fair to make students with disabilities take a test that they cannot pass?

For too long in this country, students with disabilities have been held to lower standards than their peers and unjustly routed through school systems that expected less of them than of other students. Several states have found that once students with disabilities are included in the assessment system and expected to achieve like other students, performance improves. In 2005, for example, 60 percent of fourth-graders with disabilities in Kansas were proficient in reading. This represented an increase over 2003, when 51 percent of students with disabilities were proficient.

Students with disabilities can achieve at high levels. That is why *NCLB* requires states and school districts to hold all students to the same challenging academic standards and have all students participate in annual state assessments. We test students to see what they are learning, identify academic needs, and address those needs. The purpose is not to frustrate children. Rather, it is to shine a light on student needs and draw attention to how schools can better serve their students.

If students are excluded from assessments, they are excluded from school improvement plans based on those assessment results. If all students are to benefit from education reforms, all students must be included. Only by measuring how well the system is doing will we clearly identify and then fill the gaps in instructional opportunities that leave some students behind.

We do, however, need to improve tests for students with disabilities. We need tests that measure what students know and can do without the interference of their disability. The Department is currently looking at ways to make tests more accessible and valid for a wider range of students so that all students can participate and receive meaningful scores. For more information about this work, please refer to item 13 of this document and to the proposed regulation that was released in December 2005. . . .

7. Why can't a student's Individualized Education Program (IEP), instead of the state assessment, be used to measure progress?

There are several reasons why IEPs are not appropriate for school accountability purposes. In general, IEP goals are individualized for each student and may cover a range of needs beyond reading/language arts and mathematics, such as behavior and social skills. They are not necessarily aligned with state standards, and they are not designed to ensure consistent judgments about schools—a fundamental requirement for AYP determinations. The IEP is used to provide parents with information about a student's progress and for making individualized decisions about the special education and related services a student needs to succeed. Assessments used for school accountability purposes must be aligned to state standards and have related achievement standards.

8. Students in special education get extra privileges in taking the state tests. Some of them get more time and get tested by themselves or in small groups. Isn't this unfair?

These "privileges" are called "accommodations." Accommodations are changes in testing materials or procedures, such as repeating directions or allowing extended time, that, by design, do not invalidate the student's test score. In other words, accommodations help students access the material but do not give students with disabilities an unfair advantage. These accommodations instead help level the playing field so that a test measures what the student knows and can do and not the effect of the child's disability. It is not unfair to allow valid accommodations during a test because these accommodations allow a test to measure the student's knowledge and skills rather than the student's disability.

The state is responsible for analyzing accommodations to determine which are acceptable on the basis of the test design. It is important for the state to make sure that students use only those accommodations that result in a valid score. For example, if the assessment is supposed to measure how well a student decodes text, reading the test aloud to the student would result in an invalid score.

9. **Isn't it unrealistic to expect *all* students with disabilities to meet grade-level standards? Students are in special education for a reason.**

Students receive special education services for a reason. They are in special education because a team of professionals has evaluated the child using a variety of assessment tools and strategies to gather relevant functional, developmental, and academic information about the child, including information provided by the parent, and determined that the child has a disability and needs special education services. Their achievement on grade-level standards is only part of the picture. It does not determine whether or not they need services. Assessments and other evaluation materials include those tailored to assess specific areas of education need. The child must be assessed in all areas related to the suspected disability including, if appropriate, health, vision, hearing, social and emotional status, general intelligence, academic performance, communicative status, and motor abilities. The impression that students are receiving special education services because they cannot pass a state test is a misunderstanding of what it means to be eligible for *IDEA* services.

Being in special education does not mean that a student cannot learn and reach grade-level standards. In fact, the majority of students with disabilities should be able to meet those standards. Special education provides the additional help and support that these students need to learn. This means designing instruction to meet their specific needs and providing supports, such as physical therapy, counseling services, or interpreting services, to help students learn alongside their peers and reach the same high standards as all other students.

10. **What about students with significant cognitive disabilities? Is it realistic to expect them to meet the same level of achievement as all other students?**

The expectation of *NCLB* is that the majority of students with disabilities can and should participate in and achieve proficiency on state assessments. We understand, however, that there is a small percentage of students with disabilities who may not reach grade-level standards, even with the best instruction. These are students with the most significant cognitive disabilities (about 10 percent of all special education students). The Title I regulations allow these students to take an alternate assessment based on alternate achievement standards that is less difficult and more tailored to their needs. Their proficient scores can be counted in the same way as any other student's proficient score on a state assessment. The Department has developed certain safeguards around this policy to help prevent students from being placed in an assessment and curricula that are inappropriately restricted in scope, thus limiting their educational opportunities (see item 11).

11. **It seems like the Department has said the following: "Only 1 percent of students with disabilities can take an alternate assessment based on alternate achievement standards." Is this true?**

The Department has not made such a statement. In fact, it reflects several common misunderstandings about federal education policy. Current Title I regulations permit a student's proficient score on assessments based on alternate achievement standards to count the same as any other student's proficient score on a state assessment, subject to a 1.0 percent cap at the district and state levels. If more than 1.0 percent of proficient scores come from such assessments, then the state must establish procedures to count those scores as nonproficient for the purposes of school accountability.

MYTH.   *The Department expects that only 1 percent of students with disabilities should take a test based on alternate achievement standards (1 percent cap).*

FACT.   The 1.0 percent cap reflects the following: 1 percent of *all* students represents about 10 percent of students with disabilities. While all children can learn challenging content, evaluating that learning through the use of alternate achievement standards is appropriate only for a small, limited percentage of students who are within one or more of the existing disability categories under the *IDEA* (e.g., autism, multiple disabilities, traumatic brain injury), and whose cognitive disability prevents them from attaining grade-level achievement standards, even with the very best instruction. The 1 percent cap (or approximately 10 percent of students with disabilities) is based on current incidence rates of students with the most significant cognitive disabilities, allowing for reasonable local variation in prevalence.

MYTH.   *IEP teams are limited in the number of students with disabilities that they may determine need an alternate assessment based on alternate achievement standards.*

FACT.   The cap is a limit on the number of proficient scores that may be included in AYP decisions at the district and state levels. The cap is not a limit on the number of students who may take such an alternate assessment based on alternate achievement standards.

FACT. IEP teams must make informed and appropriate decisions for each individual student, based on each student's unique needs. If more than 1 percent of all students in a district need to take an assessment based on alternate achievement standards, then all such students may take them. To protect students from inappropriate, low standards, however, districts and states are limited in the use of proficient scores based on alternate achievement standards in making AYP decisions.

FACT. Alternate assessments based on alternate achievement standards must only be given to students with the most significant cognitive disabilities. States must develop guidelines to help IEP teams determine which assessment is most appropriate for a student with a disability to take. If those guidelines are appropriately developed and implemented, IEP teams should be making the right decisions for their students.

12. Don't such "caps" interfere with IEP decisions?

No. The policies on including students with disabilities in assessment and accountability systems do not affect the IEP team's role in making specific individual decisions about how to best address the needs of children with disabilities. The policies do not restrict the number of students who can participate in an alternate assessment. Instead, the policy restricts, solely for purposes of calculating AYP for school accountability, the number of scores that can be counted as proficient or advanced based on alternate achievement standards on alternate assessments.

13. How will the Department's recent proposed regulations change the policy on assessing and including students with disabilities in school accountability?

Since the regulation permitting a state to develop alternate achievement standards for students with the most significant cognitive disabilities was issued, information and experience in states, as well as important recent research, indicate that there may be an additional number of students who, because of their disability, have significant difficulty achieving grade-level proficiency, even with the best instruction, within the same time frame as other students.

The best available research and data indicate that this group of students comprises about 2 percent of the school-age population (or approximately 20 percent of students with disabilities). The progress of these students with disabilities in response to high-quality instruction, including special education and related services designed to address the students' individual needs, is such that the students are not likely to achieve grade-level proficiency within the school year covered by the students' IEPs.

The Department is publishing proposed regulations to address how these students may be included in a state's assessment and accountability systems. The proposed regulations would permit a state to (1) develop modified achievement standards, that is, standards that are aligned with the state's academic content standards for the grade in which a student is enrolled, but may reflect reduced breadth or depth of grade-level content; (2) develop assessments to measure the achievement of students based on such modified achievement standards; and (3) include the proficient and advanced scores based on modified achievement standards in determining AYP for school accountability purposes only, subject to a cap of 2.0 percent at the district and state levels.

The goal of the proposed regulations is to recognize, based on research, the specific needs of an additional group of students with disabilities while ensuring that states continue to hold schools accountable for helping these students with disabilities meet challenging standards that enable the students to approach, and even meet, grade-level standards. The proposed regulations would require certain safeguards, such as requiring that modified achievement standards provide access for students with disabilities to grade-level curricula and do not preclude a student from earning a regular high school diploma. They would also require a state to develop clear and appropriate guidelines for IEP teams to apply in determining which students should be assessed based on modified achievement standards and to ensure that parents are informed that their child's achievement will be measured on those standards. The proposed regulations would also permit a state, in determining AYP for the students with disabilities subgroup, to include, for a period of up to two years, the scores of students who were previously identified as having a disability but who are no longer receiving special education services.

The proposed regulation affects both *IDEA* and *NCLB* by ensuring that the requirements for participation in state assessment systems are the same. With this proposed change, students with disabilities must participate in an assessment that results in a valid score.

14. How will *IDEA* and *NCLB* work together for students with disabilities in the future?

IDEA and *NCLB* reinforce and strengthen the goal of accountability for all children. Both laws require states to include students with disabilities in state assessments and to report publicly the achievement of students with disabilities. In addition, state performance goals under the *IDEA* must be aligned with the state's definition of AYP. Such consistency across these two laws will facilitate greater collaboration between special education and general education teachers and realize the goal of considering children with disabilities as general education students first. One of the ways that *IDEA* supports this effort is through new provisions added by the 2004 reauthorization of the *IDEA* that allow local education agencies (LEAs) to use federal special education funds to provide early intervention services for students who are at risk of later identification and placement in special education. (There is nothing precluding state funds from also being used for this purpose.) This provides an opportunity for educators to work together to implement scientifically based instructional practices like curriculum-based measurement to identify and address academic problems early.

POSTSCRIPT

Does NCLB Leave Some Students Behind?

"**M**rs. Dewey" dislikes being told to focus on students whose performance will lead to higher scores; this contradicts her professional ethics. Yet, she worries that teaching every child brands her as not contributing to the school's targets.

Secretary Spellings' words would puzzle "Mrs. Dewey":

> Special education is no longer a peripheral issue. IDEA and NCLB have put the needs of students with disabilities front and center. We've torn down the final barrier between special and general education. And now everyone in the system has a stake in ensuring students with disabilities achieve high standards. (Spellings, 2005)

If so, "Mrs. Dewey" might ask, "Why is my group of students with disabilities too small to matter?"

Subgroups and their sizes engender much discussion. Scores from a very small number of students may not be statistically valid or reliable. Additionally, with small subgroups, privacy can be compromised when scores become public. These issues are particularly relevant in small and/or rural schools (McLaughlin, Embler, Hernandez, & Caron, *Rural Special Education Quarterly*, 2005).

Under NCLB, states set their own minimum subgroup size. If a subgroup falls below the minimum size, it is considered as having met AYP, regardless of student scores.

An extensive study on subgroup size and confidence intervals (another statistical tool for evaluating scores) found minimum subgroup sizes vary widely nationwide, from 10 to at least 80 (Simpson, Gong, & Marion, http://www.nciea.org, 2005). Sometimes different subgroups had different minimum sizes. The authors noted that larger minimum subgroup sizes mask the performance of students with disabilities. Schools meet their targets without being accountable for these students.

Diverse groups have signified strong opposition to this practice (*Joint Organizational Statement on NCLB*, www.fairtest.org, 2004; National Conference of State Legislatures, 2005; Commission on No Child Left Behind, 2006). It continues. Does it lead to statistically accurate results or deny access to some students?

Authors of the Department of Education FAQ sheet might say schools who manipulate subgroup sizes violate the spirit of NCLB. The FAQ Sheet would advise "Mrs. Dewey's" administrators to believe their students with disabilities can meet high expectations and to use assessment results and services to pursue that target. In support, the Commission on No Child Left Behind (2006) found that disability subgroup scores were "very often not the sole reason a school is identified as not making AYP."

Yell, Katsiyannis, and Shiner (*TEACHING Exceptional Children*, 2006) express confidence that NCLB provides tools and guidance to meet its ambitious challenge. Inspired by its belief in students and educators, Faust (*In CASE*, 2006) finds "kernels of gold" in NCLB: opportunities for systemic change and growth.

Most people agree that students with disabilities should be included in education reform. Few would like to see these students relegated to shabby classrooms with outdated books. One quote strikes a jarring note:

> Nobody thinks kids with significant cognitive disabilities should be expected to reach the same standards as everyone else; it's hard if not impossible to find anyone in the Administration or on Capitol Hill who claims credit for the idea of including special education students as an NCLB subgroup in the first place. Once it was embedded in the law, however, special ed advocates seized on its potential, making it impossible to move. Spellings—and Secretary Paige before her—have been carefully walking federal policy back from this brink since the Act's ink was dry. (Petrilli, *The Education Gadfly*, 2005)

Is it possible that NCLB targets were painted with little thought of students with disabilities?

Is NCLB a leap forward, holding schools accountable for the performance of all students? Or, does NCLB represent a step backward, creating loopholes (varying subgroup sizes, alternate and modified standards, alternate assessments, safe harbor provisions) that exclude students whose parents and teachers trusted the promise that no child would be left behind?

ISSUE 12

Should Students with Cognitive Disabilities Be Expected to Demonstrate Academic Proficiency?

YES: Kevin S. McGrew and Jeffrey Evans, from *Expectations for Students with Cognitive Disabilities: Is the Cup Half Empty or Half Full? Can the Cup Flow Over?* (Synthesis Report 55) (National Center on Educational Outcomes, December 2004)

NO: James M. Kauffman, from *Education Deform: Bright People Sometimes Say Stupid Things About Education* (The Scarecrow Press, 2002), pp. 184–192, 247–252, 258–260

ISSUE SUMMARY

YES: Kevin S. McGrew, educational researcher and director of the Institute for Applied Psychometrics (IAP), and Jeffrey Evans, consultant and educational researcher for IAP, are wary that stereotypes of individuals with cognitive disabilities are used to form limited (and limiting) expectations and self-fulfilling prophecies.

NO: James M. Kauffman, professor emeritus of education at the University of Virginia, Charlottesville, and special education philosopher/researcher, believes that educators and parents must acknowledge that some students with cognitive disabilities cannot reach high academic standards and are best served by programs that develop other skills.

Beginning with Individuals with Disabilities Education Act (IDEA), 97, districts were required to include students with disabilities in all large-scale testing programs. The No Child Left Behind (NCLB) Act increased the stakes. Districts must report, and be held accountable for, the academic performance of students with disabilities.

Previously, the very fact that a student had a disability often meant they—and their performance—were excluded from testing programs. This was the case whether the student had a mild learning disability, moderate mental retardation, or a complex combination of sensory, physical, and cognitive issues. The existence of the disability was sufficient to preclude participation. Some thought this was the right thing to do; it spared students the frustration of testing on the general curriculum, which everyone knew they could not master.

To comply with IDEA and NCLB Act, Individualized Education Program (IEP) teams now decide not whether a student with a disability participates in district testing, but the way in which they can best demonstrate what they know and can do. Although parents may contest the manner of testing, they cannot ask for students to be exempt from the process. The following participation options are open:

- Regular assessment (that is administered to all students in that grade)
- Regular assessment with accommodations
- Alternate assessment based on grade-level achievement standards
- Alternate assessment based on alternate achievement standards
- Assessment based on modified achievement standards

States determine academic standards and assessment programs as well as their own method of alternate testing. In contrast to the familiar multiple choice test, some use portfolios; others select out-of-level testing, a method in which a test from a lower grade is used. All alternate assessments must be based on state academic standards.

Every school is held accountable for the adequate yearly progress of all students toward the goal of proficiency by 2013–2014. All children are expected to reach that target. States are permitted to count as "proficient" a limited number of students who take an alternate assessment based on modified or alternate achievement standards.

Should demanding standards really apply to all students? Educators generally agree that blanket exclusion of all students with disabilities was not wise and did not provide an accurate view of the accomplishments of all students. Now, some ask whether it is wise to expect all students to reach the same targets. Should students with cognitive or complex disabilities (e.g., mental retardation, traumatic brain injury, deaf-blindness) even participate if they are not expected to achieve these goals?

This issue's selections are somewhat longer than is typical for *Taking Sides*. Their length reflects the complexity of this critical controversy.

Kevin S. McGrew and Jeffrey Evans caution that there are dangers in relying on disability labels or IQ scores to anticipate what a student might achieve. They discuss the powerful impact expectations can have on accomplishments and worry that stereotypes will limit possibilities for students with cognitive disabilities.

James M. Kauffman maintains that some students, particularly those with cognitive disabilities, simply will not be able to reach high academic standards. He sees this as a reality that should be accepted and urges people to focus on what these individuals can do, and offering programs to develop their strengths.

As you read these articles, ask yourself if you believe all students can reach academic proficiency. Will students with cognitive disabilities surprise us all if only we raise our expectations? Or should we focus on functional, work-related areas for these students? Are lower academic expectations ever reasonable? Who decides?

YES

Kevin S. McGrew and
Jeffrey Evans

Expectations for Students with Cognitive Disabilities: Is the Cup Half Empty or Half Full? Can the Cup Flow Over?

Introduction

Over the past 30 years the United States has slowly and steadily clarified the meaning of access to a free and appropriate public education for students with disabilities. . . . Unfortunately, there is still limited consensus among educators regarding appropriate achievement expectations for students with disabilities, particularly those with cognitive disabilities.

A concern about low expectations and the need for high expectations was reflected in the IDEA's 1977 Preamble: "Over 20 years of research has demonstrated that the education of children with disabilities can be made more effective by . . . having high expectations for such children and ensuring their access to the general education curriculum to the maximum extent possible. . . ." IDEA 1997 clarified that all students with disabilities are to have access to instruction focused on the same skills and knowledge as all other students, and that their achievement is to be measured with the same district and statewide assessment programs as used for all students (and, adding an alternate assessment for those students unable to participate in the general assessment).

The *No Child Left Behind (NCLB) Act of 2001* further clarified that schools are to be held accountable for the adequate yearly progress (AYP) of all groups of students. NCLB specifically requires the disaggregation of assessment data for specified subgroups, including students with disabilities. The intended purpose of NCLB is "to ensure that all children have a fair, equal, and significant opportunity to obtain a high-quality education and reach, at a minimum, proficiency on challenging state academic achievement standards and state academic assessments." In other words, the expected educational outcomes for students with disabilities . . . are the same high expectations held for all students.

McGrew, K. S., Evans, J. *Expectations for Students with Cognitive Disabilities: Is the Cup Half Empty or Half Full? Can the Cup Flow Over?* (NCEO Synthesis Report 55, December 2004). Published by University of Minnesota, National Center for Educational Outcomes. http://education .umn.edu/NCEO/OnlinePubs/Synthesis55.html

Although data show that some students with disabilities are reaching the state-determined level of proficiency, many students with disabilities are still far from performing at this level. . . .

Many educators have grown increasingly concerned about the performance of students with cognitive disabilities who are appropriately working toward grade-level achievement standards, but whose current performance is far from a proficient level on grade-level achievement standards as measured by current statewide assessments. Considerable controversy surrounds the issue of what can and should be expected for these students. Some people argue that the vast majority of students with disabilities, when given appropriate access to high-quality curriculum and instruction, can meet or exceed the levels of proficiency currently specified. Many special education advocates believe that subscribing to the same high expectations and accountability for student progress will ultimately lead to improved instruction and learning for all students. Others argue that a student's disability will ultimately prevent the student from attaining grade-level achievement standards, even when provided appropriate instruction and accommodations. This latter group believes that it is unjust to punish schools when these students fail to perform at the proficient level.

The discrepant "expectations" arguments reflect very different perspectives regarding the nature of cognitive disabilities. These two perspectives have existed for many years. To make informed decisions about the best instruction and assessments for students with cognitive disabilities, several questions need to be answered. For instance, how many students with cognitive disabilities can be expected to achieve the same level of proficiency as other students? To what extent can we predict who these students are? Can we discern whether a student's failure to meet proficiency is due to the student's disabling condition or lack of appropriate instruction? Finally, what effects do teacher expectations have on student achievement?

This report was prepared to begin to address these issues. It includes an analysis of nationally representative cognitive and achievement data to illustrate the dangers in making blanket assumptions about appropriate achievement expectations for individuals based on their cognitive ability or diagnostic label. . . .

Overview

Few would argue that the concept of intelligence (IQ), and tests that measure the construct, has played a long and significant role in education, and special education in particular. The use of practical IQ tests is typically traced to the beginning of the century when Alfred Binet developed a battery of tasks to help identify children with learning difficulties. Binet's goal was to develop a means by which to identify struggling students who would then receive remediation via "mental orthopedics." Clearly, Binet did not believe that his measure of intelligence quantified an innate or "fixed" ability. Binet was an optimist who believed that the ability "glasses" of children with lower ability were half full, and that their vessels could be filled further.

In stark contrast to Binet's optimistic position was that of English psychologist Sir Cyril Burt, [whose] . . . work was based on the then popular view that intelligence was a genetically based fixed entity. Burt's ideas influenced the design of educational systems that segregated children in different educational tracks based on ability. According to Burt, "capacity must obviously limit content. It is impossible for a pint jug to hold more than a pint of milk; and it is equally impossible for a child's educational attainments to rise higher than his educable capacity permits." Clearly Binet and Burt viewed the proverbial half-filled glass differently.

A final view, based on the 1994 feel-good movie *Forrest Gump*, can be considered the "cup overflowing" perspective. Briefly, this movie portrayed the fictitious life history of Forrest Gump, an individual who was classified in the mental retardation range early in school. The exchange between the school principal and Forrest's mother clearly illustrated an educational approach grounded in the Burt philosophy:

School principal: "Your boy's . . . different, Miz Gump. His IQ's 75."

Ms. Gump: "Well, we're all different, Mr. Hancock. He might be a bit on the slow side. He's not going to a special school to retread tires!"

Ms. Gump's response, and the subsequent string of life achievements of her son Forrest (e.g., star football player in college, world-class ping-pong player, Vietnam war hero, CEO of successful shrimp company) reflects the "cup flowing over" perspective on IQ test scores. That is, Forrest's achievements were beyond his measured IQ (which was below the average sized "jug" according to Burt).

When faced with students whose classroom performances or achievement test scores surpass their measured . . . IQ scores by significant amounts, laypersons and professionals (e.g., educators and psychologists) frequently demonstrate an implicit subscription to a Burt philosophy that a person can achieve only up to his or her level of intelligence when they characterize Gump-like students as "overachievers." Ms. Gump's implicit intelligence conception, which was subsequently manifested in Forrest's accomplishments, would suggest that there is more to school learning than the size of a child's "IQ cup or jug"—other variables contribute to achievement.

Half-full or half-empty? Filled to-the-brim or the cup flowing over? Which intelligence-learning metaphor is correct? Burt versus Binet/Gump? Who should be believed during the current standards-driven educational reform fueled by the mantra that "no child shall be left behind" (NCLB), and that all children should reach grade-level standards. More importantly, which philosophy should guide educational expectations for students whose primary special education classification is tied closely to IQ scores below the normal range (i.e., students with mental retardation or cognitive disabilities)? Should educational expectations for students with cognitive disabilities be grounded in a Burt philosophy (i.e., expect academic performance and achievement no higher than the student's estimated cognitive ability), or should expectations be based on the more optimistic Gump philosophy (i.e., it is possible for students with cognitive disabilities to achieve higher than their IQ test score and at grade level)? . . .

Diversity within Disability Distributions

Probably no environment elicits individual differences sooner in life than formal education. In classrooms teachers strive to arrange conditions to elicit optimal performance among a diverse class of unique learners. However, due to the only true "law" in psychology (the law of individual differences), optimal learning conditions and techniques are not universal across learners.

This holds true for all learners—those with and without disabilities. It is important that students with disabilities not be saddled with group-based stereotyped low academic expectations. Just as the diversity of learning rates for students without disabilities is acknowledged, so it should be for students with disabilities. . . .

The federally funded *Special Education Elementary Longitudinal Study* (SEELS), the first ever nationally representative longitudinal investigation of elementary students with disabilities (ages 6 to 12), recently provided empirical support for the diversity of achievement levels of students with disabilities. According to the SEELS project director . . . the data indicate that "you can find kids with disabilities who are scoring right near the top—above the 80th percentile—and you'll find some in the middle . . . and then a lot more kids in the lowest quartile. So it's heavily weighted toward the low end but there's quite a bit of diversity." Although students with disabilities, as a group, tend to achieve in the lower half of the distribution of achievement, "individuals with disabilities can be found across the full range of academic performance." . . .

IQ and Disability: The Misunderstood Common Denominator

Despite their diversity of characteristics, the majority (58%) of students receiving special education services under IDEA share a common experience—most have been classified as having a learning disability or cognitive impairment (mental retardation) with the aid of an intelligence test. Despite many disputes over competing theoretical conceptualizations of intelligence and the utility of intelligence test scores, even the most ardent critics recognize that IQ tests "predict certain forms of achievement—especially school achievement—rather effectively."

Despite a defensible rationale for their early development and continued deployment in the schools, many people have developed . . . the inaccurate belief, often reinforced by court decisions, that measured intelligence is a genetically determined, largely fixed, global, and enduring trait that explains most of a student's success (or failure) in school learning. Such a Sir Cyril Burt conceptualization of intelligence can doom a student to low expectations if his or her IQ score is significantly below the norm. This fixed entity view of intelligence, summarized in the belief in the predictive power of the single global IQ score, represents the mental jug or cup being "half-empty" or "filled-to-the-brim" philosophy. According to this view, to expect more academic achievement than a person's estimated or measured IQ score is simply not possible.

A recent *Education Week* (2004) national survey (*Count me in: Special Education in an Era of Standards*) of 800 special and general education teachers suggests that most educators implicitly subscribe to the Burt IQ-potential philosophy. Eighty-four percent of surveyed teachers did not believe that students in special education should be expected to meet the same set of academic standards as students without disabilities. In addition, approximately 80% of the teachers felt that students with disabilities should not be included in the same state tests as students in general education, especially if the results are used for accountability purposes.

The surprising extent to which educators appear to hold alternative (and typically lower) standards and expectations for students with disabilities, although appropriate for many of these students, is troubling given the empirical reality of the predictive power of IQ test scores—scores that are often at the root of lowered expectations. Sir Cyril Burt's IQ-fixed potential legacy appears to be alive and well in America's schools (albeit not typically adopted maliciously or explicitly articulated).

Fortunately, decades of research on intelligence tests have repeatedly converged on a near unanimous consensus on the predictive accuracy of IQ test scores[;] it is time to "leave the Burt IQ-potential philosophy behind."

Reality of the IQ–Achievement Relationship: Statistics Made Simple

In an era of standards-driven educational reform, educators and policymakers must recognize the truth about IQ test scores and the resulting disability categories that are based on a continuum of IQ test scores. . . . The reality is simple. Given the best available theoretically and psychometrically sound, nationally standardized, individually administered intelligence test batteries, three statements hold true. Each of these can be explained in depth. . . . For greater conciseness here, the statements that hold true are:

- IQ test scores, under optimal test conditions, account for 40% to 50% of current expected achievement.
- Thus, 50% to 60% of student achievement is related to variables "beyond intelligence."
- For any given IQ test score, half of the students will obtain achievement scores at or below their IQ score. Conversely, and frequently not recognized, is that for any given IQ test score, half of the students will obtain achievement scores at or *above* their IQ score.

. . . Using the general IQ and Total Achievement (average across reading, math, and written language) scores for "real" norm subjects from the standardization of the *Woodcock-Johnson Battery Third Edition* (WJ III, . . . there is a strong linear relation between IQ and achievement, as evidenced by a strong correlation of .75. . . .

[However,] . . . even IQ tests that demonstrate some of the strongest correlations with achievement . . . cannot be used to provide perfect estimates of predicted achievement for *individual* students. . . . [For] subjects with IQs from 70–80, expected achievement scores range from a low of approximately 40 to a high of approximately 110. . . . [Half] of the individuals with IQs between 70–80 achieve at or below IQ-predicted achievement, and the other half . . . score at or *above* IQ-predicted achievement.

[These] data . . . suggest that the proper metaphor for the IQ-achievement prediction relationship is that the "cup can flow over." The carte blanche assumption that all students with disabilities should have an alternative set of educational standards and an assessment system is inconsistent with empirical data. . . .

The current reality is that despite being one of the flagship developments in all of psychology, intelligence tests are fallible predictors of academic achievement. IQ test scores (and associated IQ-based disability category labels) are adequate, but not nearly sufficient metrics, by which to make reasonably precise predictions about any particular *individual* student's future expected achievement progress. It simply cannot be done beyond a reasonable doubt.

The fallibility of IQ tests, coupled with the enduring presence of the ghost of Sir Cyril Burt's deterministic IQ-achievement educational philosophy, in the context of today's high-stakes educational accountability environment, raises the specter of many children with disabilities being denied the right to appropriate and demanding expectations. Stereotyping students with disabilities (often on the basis of disability label or test scores) as a group that should be excluded from general education standards and assessments is not supported by the best evidence from current science in the field of psychological and educational measurement. The potential soft bigotry of setting a priori IQ or disability label–based low academic expectations (for students with disabilities) needs to be recognized, understood, and minimized, if all children are not to be left behind.

Expectancy Effects: A Brief History and Literature Review

Since the 1970s, the notions of the "self-fulfilling prophecy" (SFP), the "Pygmalion Effect," . . . and more recently, "expectancy effects" (EE) have become commonplace in the educational psychology literature. In general, these terms refer to similar phenomena. . . .

Merton is recognized as the first to coin the term "self-fulfilling prophecy" which has now evolved into the more general phenomena of "expectancy effects." According to Merton, SFP occurs when an inaccurate definition of a situation elicits new behaviors which, in turn, make the originally inaccurate conception a reality. SFP is a compelling theory, largely because of its potential implications and elegant simplicity.

> The concept is simple enough: If we prophesy (expect) that something will happen, we behave (usually unconsciously) in a manner that will make it happen. We will, in other words, do what we can to realize our prophecy.

In most EE research, it is usually a person in a position of authority (e.g., an employer, medical professional, parent, teacher, . . .) who holds expectations about an individual (or group) under their supervision. According to the EE research, expectations expressed by an authority figure via verbal and non-verbal communication often influence the self-image and the behavior of the supervised person in such a way that the expectations held come to pass.

Origins of Expectancy Effects

. . . SFP is also often referred to as the "Pygmalion Effect" which was drawn from the title of the original book (Rosenthal & Jacobson, *Pygmalion in the Classroom*) that reported the phenomenon. SFP first appeared in early psychological research studies where it was demonstrated that experimenters could unwittingly influence the behavior of animal and human subjects during an experiment. In 1968, Rosenthal and Jacobson substituted teachers for experimenters in order to investigate the effects of teachers' expectancies on the intelligence test scores of their pupils. The Rosenthal and Jacobson study was designed to measure "whether those children for whom the teachers held especially favorable expectations would show greater intellectual growth than the remaining or control-group children" when evaluated . . . months later. Cotton provided a succinct summary of the original Pygmalion study:

> The Rosenthal/Jacobson study concluded that students' intellectual development is largely a response to what teachers expect and how those expectations are communicated. The original Pygmalion study involved giving teachers false information about the learning potential of certain students in grades one through six in a San Francisco elementary school. Teachers were told that these students had been tested and found to be on the brink of a period of rapid intellectual growth; in reality, the students had been selected at random. At the end of the experimental period, some of the targeted students—and particularly those in grades one and two—exhibited performance on IQ tests which was superior to the scores of other students of similar ability and superior to what would have been expected of the target students with no intervention.

The Rosenthal and Jacobson report suggested that teacher expectations could increase or decrease . . . IQ . . . test scores. Understandably, this report created a media sensation. The possibility that teachers could effect change (either positive or negative) in a student's IQ scores held considerable popular interest and appeal. . . .

Expectancy Effects and Intelligence

It would be an understatement to describe the EE research focused on the relations between teacher's expectations and intelligence as contentious. Post hoc re-analysis of the . . . Rosenthal and Jacobson investigation raised many questions about the study's methodology. Numerous attempts to replicate the Pygmalion effect . . . have proven unsuccessful. . . . In many of the subsequent follow-up studies the control groups often gained more IQ points than the experimental groups. . . .

Many . . . researchers have continued to examine the teacher–student expectancy effect. A clear connection between [EE] and IQ has not been established. However, *expectancy effects and academic achievement do appear to correlate positively.*

Expectancy Effects: How Large?

A frequently quoted estimate of the magnitude of Expectancy Effects (EE) in education is that 5% to 10% of student achievement performance might be ascribed to the influence of differential teacher expectations. More recently, average expectancy effect sizes from 0.1 to 0.3 have been reported. On first inspection, effect sizes of 0.1 to 0.3 appear to be of little practical import. This is wrong. According to Jussim et al., when discussing students who are the "targets" of EE, "a naturally occurring effect of 'only' .2 means, that on average, of all targets of high expectations, 10% show substantial improvement; and of all targets of low expectations, 10% show substantial decreases in performance." . . .

To reassure the reader of the importance of what appear to be significant, yet small correlations or effect sizes, one only needs to be reminded that many significant public and social policy decisions have been made on the strength of relations between variables that are of the same magnitude or lower than those reported for EE. . . . [A] special American Psychological Association . . . *Psychological Assessment Work Group* . . . provided the following examples:

- The reduction of the risk of dying from a heart attack by taking aspirin is based on $r = 0.02$
- The impact of chemotherapy on breast cancer survival; $r = .03$
- The value of antihistamines for reducing sneezes and a runny nose; $r = .11$
- The impact of Viagra on improved sexual functioning; $r = .38$

Furthermore, much like the long-term insidious effect of long-term exposure to subclinical levels of lead, asbestos, secondhand smoke, and other toxins, some research studies have suggested that even small EE can result in larger cumulative effects over time. Small EE could exert a substantial influence on student achievement, particularly for more vulnerable and "at risk" students.

Expectancy Effects and Student Characteristics

In the field of special education, EE was first investigated . . . with regard to the potential negative consequences of being labeled "mentally retarded." In general, this "stigma" research suggested that being labeled mentally retarded often led to changes in the behavior of adults who encouraged "learned helplessness." These studies reported that the attribution for success or failure for a mentally retarded person was more frequently assigned to the person's inherent low ability, while failure attribution for others was more frequently assigned to the person's effort.

Researchers have found that, in general, EE in classrooms are often related to a number of different student characteristics. "Teachers overestimate the achievement of high achievers, underestimate that of low achievers, and predict least accurately the responses of low achievers." Although low-achieving students have been found to receive more learning support, they also are communicated lower expectations via less pressure to achieve than high-achieving students. Additional student characteristics associated with teacher expectations include race, ethnicity, SES, physical appearance or attractiveness, . . . use of standard English . . . , prior negative comments or evaluations about a student by other teachers, readiness/maturity, and grouping/tracking effects. Similar to the early MR-stigma research, some teachers have been found to associate success to inherent ability in the case of high-achieving students and luck or chance for perceived low achievers. . . .

Expectancy Effects: Educator Behaviors

Although the claim that teacher expectancies can raise student intelligence has been effectively rebuked, most . . . critics have expressed the belief, supported by research, that expectancy effects do influence teacher-to-student performance and behavior. . . .

Expectancies can be expressed both verbally and non-verbally. Although most teachers report that they can fully control their behavioral affect and deceive students whenever necessary, at times the two primary modes of communication can send mixed signals. . . .

Even brief exposure to a teacher's face or body movements (e.g., differences in voice inflection) can provide a student with enough information to communicate expectancies. Teacher behaviors associated with the communication of low achievement expectancies to low achievement students have included:

- The provision of fewer opportunities to learn new material.
- Less "wait" time provided to answer questions.
- Providing answers or calling on someone else.
- Inappropriate feedback (more frequent and severe criticism for failure; insincere praise), limited reinforcement (e.g., giving reinforcement that is not contingent on performance), or rewarding more incorrect answers or inappropriate behavior.

- Providing less attention and more interaction in private settings.
- Providing differential treatment in grading (less frequently giving "the benefit of the doubt") and personal interactions (e.g., teachers less friendly or responsive; making less eye contact; giving fewer smiles).
- Providing briefer and less informative feedback.
- Providing less stimulating, and lower-level cognitive questions.
- Providing less effective (but time-consuming) instructional methods.

Expectancy Effects: Why Do They Occur?

Although the original research on [EE] was based primarily on studies where educators were provided false information regarding student potential, "most researchers have concluded that teacher expectations are not generally formed on the basis of 'false conceptions.'" Rather, they are based on the best information available about the students. Furthermore, even if the initial expectations a teacher forms for a student are realistic and appropriate, student learning and self-concept development can be limited as a result of *sustained expectation effects*. The adverse impact of sustained expectations can occur when teachers continue to engage in behaviors that result in the maintenance of previously formed low expectations (e.g., by giving low-expectation students only drill work). . . .

Attribution Theory

Certain beliefs about intelligence and learning may lead to lowered expectations for low-achieving students and students with cognitive disabilities . . . [Contemporary] social cognitive psychology research has suggested that *attribution theory* is a "useful framework for exploring teachers' response to children's academic outcomes, such as success or failure, in the general education classroom."

Briefly, attribution theory research has demonstrated that individuals (e.g., teachers) tend to attribute success or failure for an individual (e.g., students) to one of two different human characteristics—*ability* or *effort*. Graham and Weiner's studies found that the initial response of many classroom teachers to a negative student outcome is either anger or pity. Furthermore, the elicitation of anger or pity was differentially linked to the degree to which teachers perceived the student as responsible for his or her failure. Typically, when faced with student failure, a teacher pity response was elicited for students of low abilities while anger was the more frequent response to high-ability students (due to a perceived lack of effort or motivation). Furthermore, these researchers found that the anticipation of future failure for students was directly related to the perceived stability of the cause of the student failure. "Failure due to causes that are viewed as stable, such as low ability, will result in a high expectation that failure will recur, whereas failure due to unstable causes, such as effort or task difficulty, will result in a lower expectation of repeated failure. . . ."

Clark found . . . [that when] students use attribution information to make inferences about their own ability and effort, these inferences are manifest in the students' self-esteem, expectations for their own future successes and failures, and their classroom performance." . . .

Group Stereotyping

Expectancy effects may also reflect the differential treatment of an individual based on group membership stereotypes. Group-based self-fulfilling prophecies differ from individual-based self-fulfilling prophecies and are relevant to the educational practices of grouping, tracking, and institutionalized segregated instruction (e.g., separate special education classrooms). . . .

Researchers have reported the communication of differential expectations as a function of placement in different ability or tracked groups in classrooms. According to Cotton's research synthesis, "students in low groups and tracks have been found to get less exciting instruction, less emphasis upon meaning and conceptualization, and more rote drill and practice activities than those in high-reading groups and tracks." . . . In general, . . . tracking or ability grouping "may lead to the type of rigid teacher expectations that are most likely to evoke self-fulfilling prophecies and perceptual biases. Teachers often prepare more for and are more supportive toward students in high-ability groups."

Stereotype-based low expectations for "different" students . . . can beset anyone who belongs to a group with a specific reputation. When the stereotype or reputation is pejorative, . . . the effects can be significantly disruptive to individual development. Stereotypes have two salient characteristics: (1) they polarize perceptions and sharpen differences, and (2) they are rigidly held, readily fixated and resistant to change. Thus, the development of stereotypically based differential student academic expectations (based on group membership or label) can serve to fixate and exaggerate existing differences. . . .

Probably one of the more potentially insidious forms of stereotype-based expectation formation is that which results from the attachment of diagnostic labels (e.g., learning disabled, mentally retarded, emotionally disturbed, . . .) to students. Although all forms of social stereotypes (e.g., gender, social class, race, ethnicity, . . .) can produce harmful effects, diagnostic educational or medical disability labels almost always have the authoritative stamp of approval by a credible expert (e.g., psychologist, doctor). This major source of lowered teacher expectations has been repeatedly demonstrated in the special education research literature. Based on the previously summarized *Education Week* national survey of teachers, lowered expectations for all students with disabilities continue to be a latent force in many of America's classrooms, and may be exacerbated by the current wave of high-stakes educational accountability.

Beware of Silent, Shifting Standards

Research during the past decade has revealed that group-based stereotypes can be conceptualized as functioning as "standards against which individual members of stereotype groups are judged." Briefly, *stereotyping effects* occur when individual group members are evaluated in a direction consistent with group-based expectations or stereotypes. "For example, a man is judged a better leader than a woman; a physician is judged more intelligent than a hairdresser . . . these types of effects certainly indicate that stereotypes have been used to judge individuals and that the outcome is *assimilation*." The self-fulfilling prophesies previously described are examples of the commonly recognized assimilative stereotype effect.

Research on the "shifting standards model" suggests that assimilative effects alone fail to capture the complexity and extent to which stereotype-based expectations operate in group settings: "Less well recognized is the fact that stereotyping can also be manifested in other ways, most notably in counter-stereotypical or contrast effects."

Within-category standards are typically used when a person evaluates or judges an individual . . . of a stereotyped group . . . on stereotyped dimensions. For example, given the stereotype that students with mental retardation are "slower learners" than students of normal intelligence, one is likely to judge the learning capability of a particular student with mental retardation relative to (lower) standards for students with mental retardation and, the learning ability of a particular non-retarded student relative to (higher) standards of competence for non-retarded students. . . . "Good" does not mean the same thing for the student with mental retardation and the student of normal intelligence. . . .

Probably the most pernicious masked effect of the shifting standards model is that "evidentiary standards are lower for members of the group stereotyped as deficient on an attribute." When an individual . . . is a member of a group that is stereotyped as deficient on a trait or attribute (i.e., intelligence), evidentiary standards or expectations are often shifted in the direction of leniency, less challenge, and minimal competencies. [This] shift, . . . in turn, often produces behavior in the evaluator in the opposite direction of the stereotype. This shifting of standards "activates low (patronizing) minimizing standards that are more readily surpassed, producing a subjective sense of positivity—a 'wow' effect. That this positivity is not borne out in outcomes that matter for the target (getting a job or the key fielding position) suggests that the favorable treatment is more apparent and ephemeral than real." The essence of this phenomena is captured in the words of Alexa Pochowski, the assistant commissioner for learning services in the Kansas education department, . . . quoted in *Education Week* as saying:

> For too long, we held these students to lower standards . . . I hate to say it: I think we almost felt sorry for them."

. . . In summary, for students with cognitive disabilities, expectancy effects can be viewed as a form of **standards-based stereotyping.** This stereotyping can either produce direct . . . or indirect "hidden" stereotyping effects, both of which can exert negative influences on academic performance. The silent, subjective shifting (towards lower) evidentiary academic standards (for students with disabilities) represents a subtle, yet potentially potent force operating against the goal of "leaving no child behind."

Education Expectations: Caveats and Concerns

Teachers, like all humans, develop personal beliefs, opinions, and stereotypes. During most teacher preparation programs, educators are taught to become aware of potential expectancy effects and how to control their overt day-to-day teaching behavior to be more equitable, and to refrain from dispensing differential praise and criticism.

Given the popularity of the expectancy effects and self-fulfilling prophesies in the educational and psychological research and popular press, one could be led to believe that these negative influences are pandemic in school classrooms. This is not the case. Although some researchers have concluded that differential treatment of students is widespread, most researchers have concluded that the majority of educators (particularly experienced teachers and teachers who are very familiar with their students) form expectations based on the initial available information and "tweak" or adjust their expectations and instruction based on changes in student performance.

It is inappropriate to infer that the majority of educators are biased simply because they may hold differential expectations for some students. Often, differential treatment of students represents the appropriate implementation of individualized adaptive instruction responsive to the individual differences in a classroom. . . .

It is important to note that educators who may hold inappropriately low expectations for some students "are rarely acting out of malice; indeed, they are often not even aware that their low expectations have developed based on specious reasoning."

Nevertheless, the literature raises numerous issues that are directly relevant to today's educational context for students with disabilities in which both IDEA and NCLB are requiring improved performance. Particularly for those students with cognitive disabilities, the information on expectancy effects should cause us much concern. Is it possible that expectancy effects have been holding students back in the past? Are we under the influence of silently shifting standards—especially for students with cognitive disabilities? These and other questions are ones that states, districts, schools, administrators, and teachers need to ask themselves and others—as our nation strives to improve the performance of all of its students, including . . . those with cognitive disabilities.

James M. Kauffman

 **NO**

Education Deform: Bright People Sometimes Say Stupid Things about Education

Test Bashing Is Part of the "Progressive" Rhetoric That Thwarts Progress

Standardized testing has become the Great Satan of education in the minds of some, a "monster" that must be put out of schools. For example, Alfie Kohn condemns standardized testing—not just certain tests or the misuse of tests, but standardized tests as tools. . . . His suggestions for fighting standardized tests include not only civil disobedience by educators but printing bumper stickers with slogans such as "Standardized Testing Is Dumbing Down Our Schools." Like most slogans in education, this one, too, in my opinion, is vapid. Standardized testing can, indeed, be stupid or be used stupidly, but I doubt very seriously that it is the ogre responsible for dumbing down our schools. And rejecting standardized tests can only deprive parents, teachers, school officials, and governing bodies of an important tool in monitoring students' performance. . . .

Now it is undoubtedly true that some standardized tests are poorly made or misused, as are many teacher-made tests and other forms of "alternative assessment" such as portfolios. In fact, *any* form of assessment of which I'm aware can be (and has been) crudely made and badly used. So, why the seething hostility toward "standardized" testing? The answer is not simple, but I think much of the outrage over standardized tests is prompted by fears of comparisons of various individuals and groups who take the tests. Furthermore, educational theory has become, to some, a matter of religious conviction in which evidence doesn't matter. Too many educators—and, as well, too many people who are not educators—embrace "progressive" theory that relies on pet phrases and terminology for its defense of educational "quality" that tests are said not to be able to measure. These "reformers," who actually hold educational theories originated nearly a century ago, call for "real learning" that standardized tests are assumed not to be able to assess. . . .

Kohn and others who take a position against standardized tests also often raise the specter of uniformity across schools and states, which they

From *Education Deform: Bright People Sometimes Say Stupid Things About Education* (Scarecrow Press, 2002), pp.184–192, 247–252, 254–260. Copyright © 2002 by Rowman & Littlefield Education. Reprinted by permission.

see as being overly rigid. Even such politically conservative opinion writers as George F. Will suggest that America probably should not have a standard examination for high school graduation or a national curriculum. Perhaps it is inevitable that people of nearly all political persuasions will figure out some day that math and reading and much of what we need to know about science and geography and the United States government is not really different in different places. People might figure out that uniformity of expectations and curricula and testing might actually be beneficial in a society in which children move often to different localities or states. But it may take decades for people to arrive at these conclusions.

All the more reason, in my opinion, that standardized testing has a valuable role to play in measuring students' progress. . . . [One] argument against standardized testing is that comparisons of schools and states—perhaps of individuals as well—are insidious. No one is to be "left behind." . . . [Any] measure of progress—but most obviously a standardized measure—produces a distribution that by nature finds some to have performed better than others; for any measure that is not simply "yes/no" or "pass/fail" or in some other way a truncated range, there is a bottom fourth (first quartile) as well as a top fourth (or any other percentage of the sample one wishes to examine). So alternative assessment procedures that obscure if not obviate comparisons seem, to some, a godsend. Such alternative measures can help maintain the fiction that all students are excellent or give the misimpression that nobody is actually behind. The "progressive" idea seems to be that an "authentic" assessment will show that everyone and everything is cool—nobody can fail.

For some purposes there is no good substitute for the test that is standardized and can be failed—normed on a large sample of test takers by which we want to judge the achievement of individuals and groups. It is easier to shoot the messenger that brings unwelcome tidings than to confront the differences among individuals and groups that tests may reveal. . . . And it is easy to overlook the advantages of standardized tests while describing the tests themselves as monsters to be driven from our schools.

Some scholars have pointed out that the current popularity of standardized testing is really based on public concern about standards or accountability. The standards of performance that a state or school adopts are nearly always linked to a standardized test, and for this reason some writers refer to "test-linked standards." We do, I think, want to know how a student's performance compares to others' and to be able to compare average student performances across schools and states. It is only through such comparisons that we can address some problems, including the problem of how well we're doing and the problem of equity. Nevertheless, some people seem to be in favor of accountability—but without knowing how students are doing on any standardized test. To them, standardized tests seem to be a way of holding people responsible for teaching a standard curriculum, which they find anathema.

Mary Anne Raywid has voiced a familiar complaint: "One problem with the vast majority of tests, of course, is that they are curriculum-based." Well, it seems to me that we do want curriculum and testing to be aligned. That is, we want to teach what students are going to be tested on and to test what we teach.

In fact, curriculum-based assessment is what some of us are after. It makes no sense to test students on things they haven't been taught, and it makes good sense to base assessment on the curriculum. The curriculum could determine what is tested; the tests could determine what is taught. But, either way, it only makes sense for the two to be in sync. In fact, one is not likely to be developed without the other: Testing and curriculum *should* influence each other. To me, it makes little difference which comes first, as long as what is taught is really important stuff for students to learn. I suppose the question actually becomes what we think is important for students to know. Another way of putting it is to ask whether we think there is a common core of knowledge that most students should learn. I think there is this common content that most students should be expected to master, and I see no reason not to check up on how well we're doing it—to test it with a standardized instrument.

Others, particularly E. D. Hirsch, Jr., have described eloquently how having a core body of knowledge or core curriculum increases equity among groups of students differing in ethnicity or social privilege—or, at least, opportunities for achieving such equity. Standardized tests were invented, at least in part, to be fairer to students without social privileges—to focus on a student's performance rather than his or her genetic or social heritage that brought privilege in spite of what a student could do. Standardized tests *can* be used to increase equity if they measure important knowledge and if all schools and individuals are provided the resources needed to allow them to attain a reasonable standard. Standardized tests *can* be used to improve the clarity of schools' objectives and focus on instruction. Standardized tests *can* be used to allocate resources more efficiently, and they *can* be used as a common metric—a common, readily understood language of measurement—for communicating educational outcomes.

Please notice that I have *not* suggested that *all* students should learn exactly the same thing or be taught exactly the same way. I suggested that *most* students would benefit from a standard, core curriculum. . . . Some students are not going to be successful in the regular, general curriculum that may be right for the majority of students. I think it's essential that we provide alternatives for those students who cannot reasonably be expected to learn the core curriculum and be tested on it. . . . But, of course, here's the problem: Who should decide, and on what basis, that an alternative to the core curriculum is a better choice for a given student? Here are some givens, in my opinion: First, the decision should not be based on the student's ethnicity, gender, or social privilege. Second, the decision should be based on the student's estimated ability to learn the core curriculum. Third, there are no perfect decision makers. Any decision making scheme we can devise will produce some false positives (students thought to be able to learn the core curriculum but who cannot) and false negatives (students who are thought to be unable to learn the core curriculum but who can). The goals should be to make as few errors of judgment as possible in either direction and to correct errors as soon as they can be detected by changing the student's curriculum. But don't miss this given: Assuming that any core curriculum should be studied and mastered by *all* students simply guarantees a very large number of false positives. For a substantial number of kids and a significant percentage of the student population, it's not in the cards. The majority of the students I'm referring to have disabilities of one kind or another, although some of those with disabilities can and should learn the standard—general, core—curriculum.

Standardized tests, like every other human invention and some natural phenomena, will be abused. That is a given. We are well advised to recognize abuses without proscribing the use of the instruments that are abused, to use instruments responsibly. Obscuring or hiding differences on good standardized measures merely locks in place the social inequities that anti-testing forces say they oppose. We cannot address inequities that we will not admit are real and important. . . . [I] think we have yet to invent a better or more reliable way than standardized testing of finding out fairly what someone knows. The fact that some test questions are bad and that some people use scores unwisely should not be used as an excuse for bashing the very notion of standardized testing.

Every educational policy has a downside as far as I know, standardized testing and test-linked standards included. It is possible to narrow a curriculum unreasonably in efforts to prepare students for tests, and this is true for standardized tests or any other kind of assessment. It is possible to define good teaching simply as that which maximizes test performance—standardized tests or any other type of assessment. It is possible to use standardized test performance to devalue those who do not score well on them, but the same is true for any type of assessment—kids can be devalued because their performance is judged to be inferior, not up to expectations, not acceptable. And standardized tests or any other type of assessment can preclude certain opportunities for students who fail to meet expectations. Any kind of assessment of performance—standardized test or any alternative—can create anxiety in the person being assessed. Alternatives to standardized tests, such as "portfolio assessment" in which a student's work is judged in some way, have their downsides, too. They are cumbersome, extremely time-consuming, and present problems of reliability, validity, and comparisons across individuals and groups.

If our schools are being "dumbed down," I doubt that it's because of standardized tests. Much more likely, I think, is that the dumbing down is a result of fumbled thinking about issues in education, including mindless rhetoric that misleads people's thinking about the tools we use to assess educational progress. And make no mistake about this, either: *Standardized testing cannot take the place of the type of frequent teacher monitoring or assessment that is an essential part of good teaching.* Imagining that standardized testing provides sufficient early warning for failing students is similar to imagining that reporting tornado damage provides sufficient early warning of severe weather. Standardized tests can assess instructional success or failure long after the fact, and for that they're important, but they can't be relied upon to guide the instruction of individuals. . . .

Some who write about education policy see the advantages of good standardized testing but suggest "criterion-referenced" tests that set "benchmarks" of performance. Sometimes, these individuals even suggest that an advantage of such criterion-referencing is that the test does not rely on norms, that students' performance is simply compared to the criterion, not to other students' performance. This is quite a misleading interpretation of "criterion" or "benchmark." A reasonable person would, I think, have to ask something like this: How'd we come up with this criterion or benchmark?

A criterion or benchmark can be pulled out of the air or be based simply on someone's opinion of what a student should know at a particular age. But "pull-them-out-of-the-air" criteria are ultimately seen as arrogant and unworkable. Eventually, people come to their senses and inquire about what most students know at a given age. The criterion is then set based on a comparison to what most students can do. Otherwise, it is unreasonably high or unreasonably low.

People I think should know better than to refer to criterion-referenced tests as not comparative or non-normative. They're right in only a very restricted way—a student is judged to perform acceptably or not based only on comparison to the criterion or benchmark of performance. However, a reasonable person has to ask where the criterion comes from, and this inevitably takes us back to a normative sample or normative comparison. Witness the difficulties various states or school districts have in deciding on a "cut point" or benchmark on a standards of learning test. If the criterion is something that too few students can reach, then it's abandoned as unreasonable (and for good reason). If the criterion is something just about every student reaches without difficulty, then it's abandoned as too low (and with good reason). A criterion-referenced test does force the issue of manufacturing failure (just how much is enough, desirable, or too much?). But here's something I think you can go to the bank on: If a criterion is set that results in what is deemed a reasonable rate of failure and a few years down the road we find that nearly every child is passing it, we will see efforts to raise the bar because the benchmark is now judged too low.

Criterion-referencing might be a good idea. That is, it might be a good idea to set a standard that we think merits promotion to the next grade or graduation or the need for remediation. But nobody should be fooled into thinking that the criterion isn't based on some comparison to a normative group. And nobody should be fooled into thinking that every last student will reach whatever criterion is set. Some students will fail to reach the benchmark unless it is set at zero, and some will find reaching the benchmark ridiculously easy. That's one of the reasons we need special education. . . .

⌒◉⌒

Failure of Some Students with Disabilities to Reach a Standard Is Predictable

Why is the failure of some exceptional students to profit from standard educational programs utterly predictable? The answer seems obvious to me. It is because they differ significantly from the modal or typical student in instructionally relevant ways. Standard programs are designed for modal (most frequently occurring) students, not those at the extremes of a distribution. These standard educational programs simply cannot, and can't be expected to, accommodate extreme differences in instructionally relevant characteristics, like abilities to read, perceive, organize, store, retrieve, and apply information to the solution of particular problems. Some students with disabilities are going to fail to meet standard educational goals regardless of the instructional strategies a teacher uses.

Some students with disabilities can meet state testing standards, but not with the standard instructional program or in the standard amount of time or by the typical chronological age. And some students who are gifted will be bored out of their minds by having to repeat and by being expected to *appear* to learn things they learned long ago.

Pixie Holbrook described the futility and cruelty of requiring all students with disabilities to take state-mandated examinations that are appropriate for the majority of students. She describes the agony for herself and one of her pupils, Sarah, a fourth-grader with a learning disability. Sarah is a good and diligent student, but because of her learning disability she hasn't the skills required for the test.

> She knows she doesn't know. And she knows that I know she doesn't know. This is so very humiliating.
>
> Her eyes are wet now, but she's silent and stoic. I check in, and she re-assures me she's fine. She appears to be on the verge of weeping, but she will not be deterred. I cannot help her in any way; I can only sit nearby and return a false smile. I can offer a break, nothing more. Later, I calculated the reading level of this selection. Sarah reads like a second-grader, and the poem is at the high end of the fifth-grade scale. Her eyes are not just scanning the paragraphs. I know she has stopped reading and is just glancing and gazing. It's meaningless, and it hurts. Yet she attempts to answer every question.
>
> It is now 2 ½ hours, and my anger is growing. This is immoral and has become intolerable. And it's only the first day.

. . . Teachers and school administrators have, it seems to me, a moral obligation to recognize the fact that many special education students should not be required to take state competency exams.

Moreover, teachers have to be allowed, even encouraged, to recognize the limits of their instructional competence. Teachers should decline to teach students for whom their training is inadequate and decline to teach a curriculum that isn't right for their students. . . .

. . . [For] the life of me I can't figure out how someone . . . can . . . argue that teachers in elementary and secondary schools should just try to teach all students, regardless of students' characteristics. And, so some argue, if a teacher has a student that he or she can't seem to teach and manage or one who seriously interferes with teaching the rest of the class, then that teacher should just suck it up and learn to deal with it, never work to get the student taught in a special class or school. Maybe that teacher could ask for help, so the full-inclusion or merge-general-and-special-education argument goes, but not give up responsibility for the student and turn education of that student over to someone else.

I try to make this add up with any other profession's attitudes toward its clients, and I can't. What would we think of a dentist who said, "Well, no, I don't know what to do here, but I'm not going to refer you to someone else, because I am responsible for treating *all* of my patients? So I'll ask another dentist what to do and then do my best to follow the advice I get." Would we not want to wring the neck, if not sue, a mechanic or plumber or builder or lawyer who was in over his or her head—didn't have the skills demanded of the case and knew it—yet wouldn't give the job over to someone with the necessary skills?

Knowing the limits of one's knowledge and skill and being given the responsibility for refusing clients whose problems don't match one's training and skills are rather basic professional and moral responsibilities, it seems to me. Those who do not want teachers to decline to teach a child for whom they are not prepared believe one of two erroneous things, I think: (a) teachers shouldn't be professionals in any true sense or (b) students don't actually differ much in what's required to teach them. Teaching is teaching, they seem to believe, and if you can teach one student you can teach any student. I find that kind of denial maddening.

Students Who Fail at Certain Things Aren't Total Failures

Some people fail at few things, others at many. We have a tendency to write people off as failures if they fail at anything we think is important, regardless of the values or abilities of the person whose performance we judge to be failing. Much as we are too quick to judge someone who makes a vapid statement a stupid person, we overgeneralize. Surely, there are people whom failure seems to dog, and I believe there are people who could be described as *being* failures or as having failed generally at life. But those cases are, I think, rare. And, although some people may act like test scores are everything, we know that they're not—and we need to act like they're not.

Some people fail at something because of a disability, and their disability is then used against them in an unfair manner. True, we can't eliminate failure, and we can't and shouldn't "protect" people from confronting their own and other people's failures. But keeping failure at a particular thing or things in perspective is also important. Dan Hallahan and I, as well as many of our colleagues in special education, have noted that although people with disabilities can't do certain things (and, thus, could be said to fail in some respect) it is essential that we focus on what they *can* do, which for most people with disabilities is most of the things we consider normal or expected.

Failure at something doesn't make a person bad, nor does success make them a good person. Sometimes I think people misunderstand this and suppose that those who are gifted are better people and those who are disabled are not as good as others. Achievement or success at something doesn't make someone a better person, but it does enhance a person's opportunities. The more you know and are able to do, the more opportunities you have to learn and succeed. We do want to give students the greatest opportunity we can, and that means teaching them things that will open up new opportunities. I tried to make this clear in a previously published essay.

> Clearly, we do not want a human's worth to be measured simply by what he or she can do. That criterion would, for example, result in very little worth being attached to infants and young children. Yet, what someone can do is not a trivial matter. A just and humane society does not value people *for* what they can do, but it does unequivocally value peoples' ability to do certain things. If we do not value what people can do, then we have no reason to teach anyone anything. We value what people can do because of what accomplishment does for them, the additional opportunities it brings them—not because it makes them better people but because it makes them people who are better off.

Certainly, assuming that the test score is all that matters is perverse. It's the kind of perversion and stupidity we would be much better off without. We want kids to be happy and go to school excited about learning. Those objectives aren't incompatible with test scores unless we act as if, and teach kids that, test scores are all that matter. Still, avoiding test scores is just a way of evading reality.

One more thing here: It's important to note that failure once doesn't mean failure always. Most people can and do learn lots of things. Sometimes they have to try again, sometimes many times, before they learn a particular thing. Sometimes things just start to "click," and away they go. Sometimes people just seem to hit a "wall" and don't progress beyond it. Anyone who's practiced a musical instrument or sport knows the phenomenon most people call a learning "plateau," a point at which progress seems to stop. But persistence usually pays off, in that progress resumes with repeated practice—sometimes people experience a "breakthrough" in their progress, but not unless they're persistent. Yes, people differ in aptitudes for particular things and in skill in picking them up, but we have to be really careful not to assume that because a person is progressing only slowly (or rapidly) they'll always continue at that rate. . . .

꧁꧂

Exceptional Students Need Options for Curriculum, Instruction, and Placement

Because public education must serve all children's educational needs, the largest part of general education must be designed for the modal (most frequently occurring) characteristics of students and teachers. Public education is by definition a service designed for the masses. Any product or service intended for the public at large has to be designed around the typical characteristics of consumers. Economies of scale alone require this. The size, shape, and abilities of the typical citizen fall within a fairly narrow band of variability around the mean, and simple economics demand that things be designed with this in mind.

Surely, what some call "universal design" is important, and good design will accommodate a large range of individual characteristics. But, like "all," "universal" has its limits, often unspoken, sometimes not even recognized. If "universal" design can accommodate a larger segment of the population, that is all well and good. But remember that it is neither economically feasible nor necessary to eliminate all stair steps because some people can't use them or to design and equip every car so that a person with quadriplegia can drive it. Neither is it feasible or desirable to design a reading program for most children that will be appropriate for students with severe mental retardation.

Education has to be designed for what the average teacher and the average student can be expected to do, not what the exceptionally able or those with disabilities can accomplish. I'm not suggesting that the performance of the average teacher or student can't be improved, simply that expectations in the general education program can't outstrip what the average teacher can do with appropriate training or what the typical student can do with good instruction.

Because public education must address all children's educational needs, it must include explicit structures ensuring the accommodation of exceptional students. By definition, exceptional students require an extraordinary response from educators—something different from the ordinary, even if the ordinary is good. The standard educational program can serve most students very well, but it can't serve exceptional students without additional, explicit components—special structures that go beyond the normal or routine in such matters as goals, lines of authority, roles and responsibilities of personnel, budgets and purchases, allocation of time and space, modification of curriculum, evaluation of performance, and assignment of students to classes. Failure to create these explicit structures to accommodate students at the extremes of the performance distribution inevitably results in their neglect. They are forgotten. They don't just fail a little. They fail a lot, and their noses are rubbed in their failures.

The requirement of alternative educational goals and programs must be explicit for exceptional students. It's as simple as this, I think: When the interests of students with disabilities or those who are gifted are not explicitly mandated, they get lost in the shuffle. The implicit or explicit assumption that standard educational goals and programs will accommodate the needs of exceptional students is not just logically untenable. It also places the onus of proof that the program is inappropriate wholly on the student when questions arise about his or her performance. However, if there is an explicit requirement of alternative goals and programs for exceptional students, then the burden of proof is at least partly on the school to show that those alternatives are available to students for whom the typical program is unsatisfactory and in which an exceptional student cannot be expected to make satisfactory progress.

Alternative goals and programs must be expressed as alternative curricula and educational methods for exceptional students. It is not enough to have a separate place—a special class or school. Some exceptional learners need to learn something other than the standard curriculum, not just learn the standard curriculum in a different way or in a different place. And they may need instructional or behavior management procedures that are not needed by most students.

People not familiar with instruction may miss the distinctions of method that are important for exceptional students. For example, students with disabilities may require more trials, more examples, a different pace, smaller steps in a sequence, more reinforcement (praise, encouragement, or other rewarding consequences), more careful monitoring, more structure (e.g., higher predictability, more explicit instructions, more immediate consequences) than is desirable for typical students. There may be other distinctions that I have not listed here, but at least all of these are involved in more precise teaching. In short, the instruction of students with disabilities may need to be considerably more precise than the instruction that produces good results for typical students.

In many types of performance, it is the precision with which something is done that makes the difference, not the basic operation. This is true in driving, flying, playing music, shooting guns, and so on. Just consider the differences in level of performance of the same basic operations in the following comparisons: the typical drive to work versus driving in a high-speed race; flying from city *A* to city *B* versus flying with a stunt team; playing in a municipal band versus playing in one of the world's virtuoso combos; shooting targets in the backyard versus sharp-shooting for a SWAT team. Highly expert, precision performance requires extensive training. You don't give all soldiers the competence of the Special Forces by giving them a beret. You don't make every teacher a special educator by telling them good teaching of exceptional children is just good teaching because, after all, kids are more alike than they are different and good teachers use the same basic operations regardless who their students are.

POSTSCRIPT

Should Students with Cognitive Disabilities Be Expected to Demonstrate Academic Proficiency?

People sometimes live up to our expectations for them—or down to those same expectations. The power of positive thinking motivates many to unimagined levels of success. Kevin S. McGrew and Jeffrey Evans remind us not to let IQ scores limit the opportunities offered to children with cognitive disabilities.

Testifying at an NCLB Act hearing, Martha Thurlow (2004), a noted scholar of including students in large-scale testing, emphasized that the existence of a disability should not automatically mean students cannot reach high standards. Expectations must be raised.

Listen to the voices of teachers who have used alternate assessments to engage their students in academic standards. "My attitude [about her abilities] was denying her the opportunity to succeed." "Now I look at the possibilities instead of the limitations." "He is doing things I didn't realize he could do." These optimistic comments represent the findings of Moore-Lamminen and Olsen (Alliance for Systems Change, n.d.), who documented the positive experiences of teachers who have stretched their students to excel.

James M. Kauffman would likely be pleased that these teachers and their students had found success. Simultaneously, he would doubt that this increased academic focus will bring all students to proficiency.

A New Jersey high school teacher (Karp, *Rethinking Schools Online,* 2004) bemoans the fact that the proficiency hurdle masks significant student change. "On a test . . . where a passing score is 200, helping a bilingual, special education student from a low income household raise his/her test score from, say, a 50 to 199 counts for nothing. . . . Moving a student from 199 to 200 is success."

U.S. Secretary of Education Margaret Spellings appears to have acknowledged that holding all students to one standard may not be the best way to reflect a school's progress. Holding firm to the "bright-line principles" that all students must participate and reach proficiency targets, she has announced pilots for growth models of accountability.

These pilots, approved through a peer-reviewed process, will track the achievement of individual children from year to year. Schools receive credit for the progress of each child, instead of the number of students who reach targets. Such a model, first approved in Tennessee and North Carolina, would address Karp's concerns and also document the incremental growth of students with disabilities.

Growth models are receiving initial approval. Some are pleased that schools will be held accountable for steady progress of each student (Hershberg,

Phi Delta Kappan, 2005). The Council for Exceptional Children (CEC) (www
.cec.sped.org), an international professional association, has long advocated a
longitudinal growth model to document and validate the progress of students
who may not reach grade-level standards.

Even with growth models, can all students reach proficiency? The
Education Week study (Olson, 2004), cited by McGrew and Evans, noted
discrepant opinions among the participating teachers. The majority of special
education teachers surveyed were more optimistic about their students' content progress than were general education teachers. In addition, the special
education teachers felt more prepared to tackle the content challenge than
the general education teachers felt about teaching students with disabilities.
Which group is optimistic? Which is realistic? How will these different opinions affect student performance?

Do expectations hold students back, or do they set reasonable, reach-
able targets that make a productive adulthood more likely? Can higher academic standards for schools raise our expectations for students with cognitive
disabilities? Will growth models accurately reflect individual performance or
reinforce lower expectations?

ISSUE 13

Is Full Inclusion the Least Restrictive Environment?

YES: Rosalind Vargo and Joe Vargo, from "Voice of Inclusion: From My Friend Ro Vargo," in Richard A. Villa and Jacqueline S. Thousand, eds., *Creating an Inclusive School*, 2nd ed., pp. 27–40 (Association for Supervision and Curriculum Development, 2005)

NO: Amy Dockser Marcus, from "Eli's Choice," *The Wall Street Journal* (December 31, 2005)

ISSUE SUMMARY

YES: Rosalind and Joe Vargo, parents of Ro, use their voices to tell a powerful story of their daughter's success in fully inclusive educational programs, from kindergarten through college.

NO: Amy D. Marcus, staff reporter at *The Wall Street Journal,* records the voices of Eli's parents and teachers as they react to his message to leave a fully inclusive program in favor of a separate special education class.

Ask a group of people about the definition of "inclusion," and they will usually come up with a statement like "all children being educated in the same school." Ask again, "Do you mean *all* children?" The reply is likely to be a bit less certain, "Well, maybe not *all*." Probe a bit further and someone is likely to admit (with a bit of trepidation) that inclusion should mean all students except. . . . The words that follow might vary, but usually there are exceptions for students with severe cognitive challenges—those who have mental retardation or those who have disabilities in multiple areas and require complex and broad levels of support in order to communicate, move, and learn. So inclusion, for many people, really does not include *all* children.

Proponents of full inclusion have a very different answer. They say—and mean—*all* children being educated in the same school. Full inclusion advocates proclaim that all children, regardless of level of need, have a moral and legal right to attend their home school, be enrolled in general education classes, and receive all necessary supports within those classes. In a full inclusion environment, students don't need to fit into the school; the school needs to adapt to all students. Services are brought to the child; children are not sent out (or away) because what they need is not available or difficult to deliver.

Those who oppose full inclusion cite the difficulties of adapting instruction, meeting student needs, and acquiring material, training, and professional supports. Accustomed to traditional academic curriculum for some students and vocational, life-skills–based curriculum for others, they ask how the demands of both can be met.

The challenge of full inclusion is perhaps greatest at high schools, with their focus on distinct academic disciplines and college hopes. Communication between teachers is complicated by the increased number of people who interact with each student and the large number of students taught by each educator. The conversation has become even more intense with the advent of high-stakes testing, causing some to wonder if the needs of every child can be met within a typical classroom.

This issue presents the compelling voices and experiences of two sets of parents who have had much in common. They each had a child—now grown—with a significant disability. Both chose fully inclusive educational programs for their children. By their accounts, both children flourished. Then their experiences diverge.

Rosalind and Joe Vargo, parents of a young woman who communicates through sign language and uses a wheelchair, describe Ro's inclusive schooling experiences, from kindergarten through university. They share vivid illustrations of how Ro was recognized for her capabilities rather than judged by her appearance.

Amy D. Marcus communicates the reactions of Eli's parents, who were also strongly committed to inclusion. The selection relates their surprise when their son, who has Down syndrome, reaches high school and actively rejects inclusion to be with his friends with disabilities. Although Eli's parents abide by his choice, they have different questions about the outcome of the decision.

As you read these articles, consider the experiences of both these families. What successes and challenges did they experience? Why did their paths diverge? What would you think if you were in their shoes?

YES

Rosalind Vargo and
Joe Vargo

Voice of Inclusion: From My Friend, Ro Vargo

It was Tuesday, a beautiful autumn morning at Syracuse University. Ro had just finished her class "Topics in American Music—20th Century" in Bowne Hall and was walking back to the car (with my assistance) to go home. Joe, Ro's dad, was waiting in the car. He and I looked at each other and at Ro and wondered how we had gotten here. After all, it seemed like only yesterday. . . .

Kindergarten

Among our vivid memories is kindergarten and Ro's first invitation to a birthday party. Kristen's mother phoned to ask if she should make any special arrangements for Ro to attend. Fighting back tears, we responded, "No, but thanks for asking." Kristen's mom said her daughter was so looking forward to Ro coming. Then we said it: "We love Ro because she's our daughter. But do you know why other kids like her?"

The mom replied, "Well, I can speak only for my daughter, Kristen. She says she likes Ro's smile and that Ro is someone you can really talk to . . . and that she wears really neat clothes." Kristen's mom continued, "I think kids like Ro because she isn't a threat to them; they can just be themselves around her."

2nd Grade

In 2nd grade, we invited several kids to Ro's birthday party. Because we would be picking them up at school, we needed to know who would be coming. The night before the party, we called Eric's mom and politely asked, "Is Eric coming to Ro's party tomorrow?"

She said, "I'm sorry I didn't call you, but Eric said he just told Ro in school yesterday that he was coming. Was that all right?" It was more than all right! To Eric, the fact that Ro couldn't talk didn't mean that she couldn't understand him. . . .

From *Creating an Inclusive School*, 2nd ed. (ASCD, 2005), pp. 27–40. Copyright © 2005 by Association for Supervision & Curriculum Development. Reprinted by permission.

4th Grade

In 4th grade, a time when pressure to have the "right" clothes and hairstyles had already begun, Ro was voted "Best Friend" by her 25 "typical" 4th-grade classmates. Somehow, Ro's inclusion in the school life was making a tremendous difference in many kids as well. Her "giftedness" was recognized and celebrated.

We recall another night when a puzzling phone call came for Ro. Sharing the same nickname as my daughter, I thought the call was for me and I replied, "Speaking."

The young girl at the other end of the line clarified, "No, I'd like the Ro who goes to Ed Smith School."

I said, "Hold on," and exclaimed to Joe, "Someone wants to talk with Ro on the phone!" We got Ro from the dinner table and put the phone to her ear. Immediately recognizing the voice of her friend Ghadeer, Ro started laughing. She then nodded her head to indicate "yes" and followed with a head shake indicating "no." Curiosity got the best of me and I took the phone, reporting to Ghadeer, "Ro's listening and nodding her head."

Ghadeer said, "Great, I'm asking her advice about a birthday present for a friend. Now, did she nod 'yes' for the jewelry or 'yes' for the board game?"

Ro's 11th Birthday

We remember with pleasure Ro's 11th birthday party. Before the party, the mother of one of Ro's friends called to ask if the present she had picked out for Ro was OK. Apparently, her daughter hadn't been with her when she went shopping. She had just wrapped it and given it to her daughter to take to school that morning. She wasn't sure if the gift was the "in" thing and feared that her daughter would die of embarrassment if it weren't.

She had bought a jump rope for Ro—a deluxe model. Without hesitation, I said that it was a wonderful idea and a gift that Ro would love using with her sisters.

With a sigh of relief, the mom responded, "Well, I am glad. I was hoping that Ro was not handicapped or anything. Is she?"

For the life of me, I wanted to say "No" and save this mom obvious embarrassment. So I said, "Well, a little bit." After many of her apologies and my reassurances, we got off the phone as friends. She had made my day, my week, my life! The thought that an 11-year-old girl had received a birthday party invitation, wanted to go, and asked her mom to buy a present, *never thinking it important to mention that her friend had a disability*, still makes me cry with wonder and happiness. . . .

When Ro unwrapped the jump rope, all the girls were elated, shrieking, "I hope I get one of those for my birthday," and "Oh, cool." The girls immediately dragged Ro down the stairs and outside to the driveway, where they tied one end of the jump rope to her wrist. With the strength of her twirling partner, Ro was able to rotate the rope for her friends. It was Ro's best adaptive occupational therapy activity in months.

A Gift for Ghadeer

Probably the most profound testimony to inclusive education occurred in January 1993. Ghadeer, Ro's friend who had called to ask for advice on gift selection, suffered a cerebral hemorrhage, or severe stroke. At the age of 12, she was comatose for almost four weeks. . . . [After] weeks of having family, teachers, and friends read at her bedside, Ghadeer miraculously, although not completely, recovered. Her voice and articulation were so severely impaired that she could not communicate orally. To the amazement of the child's doctors and nurses, her disability did not stop her from communicating; she began to use sign language. An interpreter was quickly found who asked Ghadeer, "Where did you learn sign language?"

Ghadeer replied in sign, "From my friend, Ro Vargo!"

After four months of intensive rehabilitative therapy, Ghadeer returned to school, but now as a "special education" student requiring speech and language services plus physical and occupational therapy. Her family proudly reports that Ghadeer turned away the "special" bus and rode the regular school bus on her first day back to school. Furthermore, she advocated for herself to get a laptop computer to assist her with her schoolwork. Inclusive education enabled Ghadeer to get to know someone like Ro and to learn about augmentative communication systems and her rights, particularly her right to be part of her school, class, and friendship circle. She had learned that a person can still belong even if something unexpected—like a disability—happens.

What's Hard About Being Ro's Friend?

Ghadeer was one of many of Ro's friends who became quite capable of articulating for themselves what Ro meant to them and the kinds of things that they learned at school with her. That relationship became clear when Ro and a group of her friends responded to questions from parents and teachers in a session titled "Building Friendships in an Inclusive Classroom" at a national education conference that they attended.

Tiffany said, "I think Ro should be in class with all of us because how else is Ro going to learn the really important stuff? Besides, we can learn a lot from her."

Teachers asked Ro's friends some unusual questions, such as "Have you ever discussed her disability with her?"

Stacey replied, "No, I know she is different, but I never thought it important to ask. Like, for instance, I never thought to go up to a black kid in my class and say, 'You're black. How come you're different?'"

A "popular" question among teachers and parents—judging by their nods—was "What is the hardest thing about being Ro's friend?" As Ro's parents, we held our breath, waiting for responses such as "She drools," "She walks funny," or "She's a messy eater."

But again Stacey spoke up, saying, "The hardest thing about being Ro's friend is that she always has a parent or an adult with her." Ouch! That hurt. But Stacey's observation taught us, Ro's parents, an important lesson that will surely have a positive effect on our daughter's future.

Transition to Middle School

The transition from elementary to middle school was tough socially for Ro, as it can be for any adolescent. For Ro, the first months were spent in isolation, but her isolation was not one of physical proximity. Ro attended a regular 6th grade program and had to gain acceptance from her new middle school peers. Initially, she was ignored or stared at; a few classmates even teased her. When Ro was assigned to a work group, no group members complained out loud, but Ro noticed non-verbal signs of rejection. In those first months, we began to doubt our decision to include Ro in middle school. We recalled the comment a teacher from the previous year had made: "Middle school kids don't like themselves. How can you expect them to like your kid?"

Mauricha, a classmate, became Ro's closest new friend. It was Mauricha who broke the social barrier. Asked how the two became friends, Mauricha said, "I saw her. She saw me. We've just been friends ever since." One night when I was taking Mauricha home, she looked at me and touched my arm. "You know, Mrs. Vargo," Mauricha said, "lots of teachers think I'm friends with Ro cuz it gets me more attention. That isn't true. The truth is, I need her more than she needs me."

Ro's father and I would have to summarize Ro's middle school experience as fairly typical. When reflecting on our other daughters' experiences in middle school, we realized that there were many of the same issues: isolation at times, hot and cold friendships, recognition of and a growing interest in boys, physical changes, teasing, challenging class work, and parents who didn't know anything! Oh, yes. Ro went to her first dance and danced with Jermaine. . . .

Arrival at High School

. . . Ro and six other students with disabilities entered Henninger High School. Early on, Ro communicated, "I like . . . zoology . . ., and the kids and I have learned a lot. I have had some classes I didn't like. It is hard for me when classes have no small groups and no homework for me. Sometimes there is too much information. The worst is when neither the kids nor the teachers talk to me." . . .

Inclusive education in high school was offering Ro a whole new world of opportunities and choices. She joined the Key Club. . . . She accrued service hours through her volunteer job at a . . . fully inclusive day care. Ro was acting as a role model for many young students with disabilities, as well as for the whole class and her fellow workers.

During her early high school years, Ro communicated many things to us in various ways. . . . Her "voice" gave us a clearer vision of where and what Ro wanted to do with her life. . . .

On the afternoon of her first volunteer job, Ro had to fill out an application. Her teaching assistant completed it with Ro's input. However, 10 minutes later, Ro totally dissolved into a full-blown temper tantrum.

The panicked teaching assistant questioned Ro, "Does it have anything to do with the application?"

Ro nodded, "Yes."

"Was it #1, #2, #3 . . . ." until the question, "What has been your biggest challenge?"

Without consulting Ro, the teaching assistant had written "Rett syndrome." That was the one! Ro wanted it removed. Yes, the line about Rett syndrome.

Another time that Ro clearly expressed her thoughts was when she was nominated by her teachers for Student of the Month. She had to complete an information sheet for the committee who would select the winner. After much deliberation, Ro opted not to include any of her work with local university students and their numerous papers on her life experiences or any of her work with other girls with Rett syndrome. Basically, her nomination went in with just her name, age, and favorite teacher. Ro was making it clear that she didn't think that Rett syndrome was something important to share about herself. It wasn't really who she was, or what she did, or even what she wanted to have. . . .

The voice of Ro's peers was also becoming clearer and louder. While on the zoology trip to New York City, Ro and her dad struggled for three days to keep up with the fast pace of a very busy itinerary. Ro's classmates seemed oblivious to her tiring easily and to the locomotion problems that caused her to lag behind. It appeared that they hardly noticed her at all that weekend—at least that was Joe's observation. Ro still enjoyed the trip, and it was a wonderful bonding experience for her and dad.

Months later, we came to understand the ramifications and the benefits of Ro's participation in that trip. Students in the class began to vocalize, without our knowledge, concerns about Ro's support person in school. They complained to their teacher at first about how they thought the teaching assistant was disrespectful to Ro. When the teacher heard their complaints, she notified the principal. When there was no action, kids went to their parents and parents came to us. When the school administration failed to act, Ro's peers did!

The vision for inclusive education was a reality. We had hoped that the kids who sat in class with Ro would not seek to harm her now or in the days to come. We had hoped that they would protect her and take care of her, seek the social and legislative reforms to support the inclusive lifestyle that she had grown accustomed to, and gladly be her neighbors and her friends because they had shared the same space, the same hopes, and the same dreams. Ro and her peers in an inclusive high school setting were already living out the dream, and there was no going back for any of us.

After Ro's third year in high school, . . . Ro was clearly envious of the planning and choices that her sister Josie was engaging in. College visits, college applications, and senior pictures were taking place. We were unclear about what Ro's choices could be, and she communicated that the situation was not fair.

One night I read about an inclusive college setting in Kentucky. The ONCAMPUS program had been initiated as a collaborative effort between the Inclusive Elementary and Special Education Program of Syracuse University (SU) and the Syracuse City School District. . . . ONCAMPUS brought six high school students . . . with moderate to severe disabilities to the SU campus where they would participate with other SU students in . . . learning experiences.

Ro. . . . actively communicated her absolute delight with her peers that she was going to attend SU next year. She decided which courses to take, what clubs to belong to, and where she would eat lunch.

However, getting a handicapped parking permit proved to be no easy task. After much discussion and hassle, Ro was secured her permit. When I picked it up, the receptionist asked, "Oh, is this for Ro Vargo who went to Henninger High School?"

"Yes," I replied.

"Tell her I said 'Hi.'"

"You know Ro?" I asked.

"Yeah, I graduated with her from Henninger last year."

Inclusive education . . . another voice heard and in all the right places . . . another confirmation.

Syracuse University Students

Jacqueline[,] . . . is a sophomore at SU in the School of Social Work. She began to spend time with Ro on campus through her job as a residential habilitation counselor. She shared with Ro the names of all the good professors and the courses she should pass up! . . . Jackie was a member of SU's jazz and pep band, as well as the dance band. She would clue Ro in on any musical performances on campus. . . .

Justine had seen Ro on campus. . . . She was a senior in the Maxwell School of Communication at the time. As part of her final grade, Justine had to produce a short documentary. She approached Ro and asked if she would be willing to be part of a presentation highlighting the ONCAMPUS program. Ro agreed. A relationship developed that spanned a whole year. Justine introduced Ro to Gregg, another senior, who would be the codirector. They met frequently to talk and shoot videotape.

The final project culminated in a video titled *Ro*. Justine and Gregg's perspective was clearly evident in their work. It was respectful, serious, and funny, and Ro's hopes and dreams of being on a university campus were unfolded in the video. The images were searing and thought-provoking as Ro traversed the campus. Justine and Gregg's voice on this tape will last forever, and so will Ro's voice.

Ro's inclusion in high school and college settings has certainly caused my daughter some pain as she acknowledged her limitations and struggled to belong. Yet inclusion also prompted Ro's self-actualization, self-determination, and self-acceptance and her growing belief that there is nothing that she cannot do. Placing herself in a "regular" environment was a risk that Ro was willing to take.

Inclusive education has always been an emotional and physical risk for all of us, especially Ro. But it has clearly been worth it! . . . Today, Ro uses adult services, and we're starting all over again: justifying, rationalizing, sharing vision, relaying data, and information.

When parents of children with disabilities become lonely and fatigued, their voices can become silent. There are limited routes of appeal and no federal mandates to support Ro's inclusive lifestyle. Frankly, we are exhausted and frustrated. Nothing prepared us for this new fight to belong in a community outside of school. This adult, segregated mentality has taken its toll. We have been diligent advocates, articulate spokespersons. We've awakened—not only in Ro but also in many other students—the idea that inclusive education can mean college.

The impact of Ro's inclusive education is made clear by the relationships she forged along the way. Ghadeer called Ro to attend Ghadeer's high school graduation party. . . . Ro received a Christmas card from Mauricha, the middle school friend who broke the social barrier for Ro. The note began, "Hi, Ro. I know you probably don't remember me, but I have never forgotten you." Mauricha explained that she was working as a home health aide and taking a sign language course at night.

Kristen, Ro's teaching assistant, married Gavin. Ro was invited to the wedding, and she reminisced with the bridal party about the last time that they had all been in a limo together! . . . In a newspaper article highlighting the . . . high school graduations in the area, Kristen told a reporter that . . . "Ro was the sister I never had."

The Future?

Our "severely impaired" child has already accomplished more than we had ever thought possible, and she continues to grow. . . . We believe in those young adults who sat in class with Ro. They will not seek to harm her but will be her community—the ones who will protect and care for her. They will advocate social and legislative reform to support the inclusive lifestyle to which Ro and they have grown accustomed. They will gladly be her neighbors, caretakers, job coaches, and friends because they shared the same classes, space, hopes, and dreams.

Amy D. Marcus  **NO**

Eli's Choice

For years, Eli Lewis was the only student in his class with Down syndrome. The genetic condition, which causes a range of cognitive and physical impairments, made it harder for him to do his schoolwork. But his parents felt strongly that he could succeed. They hired a reading tutor. An aide worked with his teachers to modify tests and lessons so that he could be in the same classroom as everyone else. He participated in his middle school's award-winning chorus and was treated as a valued member.

But when all the other kids in his class were making plans to go to the local high school this fall, Eli, 14 years old, said he didn't want to go. He wanted to be in a small class with other students like him. "I don't want to get lost in a big crowd," Eli says.

Eli's declaration surprised his parents. Then his mother recalled the many times she stopped by the school to check on her son, only to find him eating by himself. Once, when she came to pick him up from a dinner that chorus members attended, she says she found Eli sitting with his aide, while the other students sat at a different table.

"The kids liked him, they knew him, they spoke to him," says his mother, Mary Ann Dawedeit. "They just didn't think of him as a peer." Eli, she says, was tired of "being the only kid who was different."

Federal law mandated in the 1970s that children with disabilities be offered a "free and appropriate public education" in the "least restrictive environment," rather than being separated only in special schools or institutions. Over the years, advocacy and additional laws resulted in efforts to get children with disabilities placed in regular classrooms, with proper support, whenever possible. The process, called "inclusion" or "mainstreaming," has largely been an academic success.

Studies have shown benefits for all children, not only those with disabilities, who study together. Many researchers argue this is one reason why people with Down syndrome have made such remarkable progress in recent decades. People with Down syndrome who learn in regular classrooms do much better academically, research has found. They also have significantly higher rates of employment after they graduate and earn more money than peers who studied mainly in self-contained classes.

And yet, Eli Lewis's experience poses a difficult dilemma, one that is only now starting to be recognized and addressed. With help, he had succeeded

From *The Wall Street Journal*, December 31, 2005. Copyright © 2005 by Dow Jones & Company, Inc. Reprinted by permission via Rightslink.

academically in a regular classroom. . . . [R]esearchers at the Center for Social Development and Education at the University of Massachusetts in Boston say that although people with intellectual disabilities made enormous gains academically due to inclusion, their social integration at school "remains stagnant."

In a survey of 5,600 seventh- and eighth-grade students from 70 schools across the country, more than half of the youths said they were willing to interact with students with intellectual disabilities at school. But only one-third said they would be willing to invite such students to their house or go to the movies with them, according to the survey done by the University of Massachusetts center and the Washington-based opinion firm, ORC Macro. "Student attitudes continue to remain the most formidable barrier to inclusion," the researchers concluded.

At first, Ms. Dawedeit and her husband, Howard Lewis, thought Eli might change his mind. The couple—who have two other sons who don't have Down syndrome—felt there were many advantages to Eli staying in a regular classroom, including greater independence and more interaction with the general student body. But eventually, Mr. Lewis says he began to recognize that having Eli in a regular classroom might not be "as important to Eli as it is to me."

Ms. Dawedeit remained reluctant. She talked with a friend who had a son with Down syndrome, who was also learning in a regular classroom. "I felt like I had let her down," Ms. Dawedeit says. "I had preached a mantra for so long to so many."

In May, at the science exposition at Eli's middle school, her feelings changed. The eighth-graders took over the school hallway and parents were invited to visit. Some students demonstrated elaborate experiments they had been working on. Eli worked with his aide to do research online about the chemical properties of silver. He learned where to find it on the periodic table. For the exposition, he printed out some of the documents he had found.

When his mother came to see his project, Eli again raised the subject of where he was going to high school. For Ms. Dawedeit, the contrast was sharp. Here was Eli, successfully participating in a science exposition with peers who didn't have disabilities—but still talking about wanting to be with other people with Down syndrome.

She says she realized she needed to try to accommodate her son's desire for a social group. "I really had to step back from my personal beliefs," she says.

In the fall, Eli enrolled in the ninth grade at Bethesda's Walter Johnson High School, a sprawling building of over 2,000 students. He is in a special program with 20 other students who have disabilities, including one who gets around in a wheelchair and has difficulty talking. Six of the students in the class have Down syndrome. Eli already knew some of the kids from various extracurricular activities, such as drama class and Special Olympics, where he participated in soccer, basketball, swimming, and bowling.

Getting out of the mainstream has meant trade-offs. His school is about 10 miles from Eli's house, farther than the local high school that his older brother attends. (The local high school doesn't have a separate special-education program.) A special-education bus now comes each day to pick up Eli, along with other students with disabilities.

"This was one of our big compromises," says his mother. In middle school, Eli walked to a bus stop and rode a regular school bus. "Other kids knew him," says Ms. Dawedeit. "Now he's a special-ed kid on a bus."

One evening in November, after a dinner of chicken burritos and salad, Eli helped his brothers, ages 12 and 17, clear the dishes. Then his parents watched him, as he started making his way through his homework—a worksheet to practice using nouns and verbs. Since Eli was born, they had fought to have him included in regular classrooms. Now it sometimes felt as if Eli might end up outside the world they had tried so hard to keep him in.

All along, they shared a similar goal: for their son to be able to live independently. But Mr. Lewis, a lawyer, began to worry that the academic gap between Eli and other classmates was getting wider in the regular classroom as he grew older, and might be too difficult to bridge in high school. "I'm not married to inclusion at the expense of Eli's getting the skills he needs," he says.

Ms. Dawedeit, a manager at a retail store, was less certain. She knew how much Eli, like all kids his age, wanted to belong. But without spending significant amounts of time in regular classrooms, how would he ever learn the skills he needed to reach the goal of living on his own? "The truth is he has to go out and get a job," she says. "If he's educated with his regular peers, then maybe a regular peer will hire him."

Eli finished his English worksheet, and got up to take a break. He came over and gave his father a hug. "Are you meeting any new kids at school, Eli?" his dad asked. "Not just yet, Dad," Eli answered. "Why are you hanging out only with the kids in your class?" his father queried. "Because I know them," Eli answered, and went into the kitchen to get some cookies.

At his new school, the Parent Teacher Student Association has put the issue of how to promote the inclusion of students with disabilities in extra curricular activities on the agenda for its January meeting. A student group that pairs students with disabilities with a buddy without disabilities has already scheduled several activities for the coming months, including ice skating and bowling.

Still, for most of his school day, Eli is now in a separate classroom from the general school population. Last month, ninth-graders in the general-education classes were reading the novel, "To Kill a Mockingbird." In the special-education classroom, the teacher was going over worksheets that had been adapted from the book, with some related questions.

Eli was signed up for a regular physical-education class, but asked his parents if he could switch to one with only special-education students. His mother was reluctant to change because it was one of his only chances to meet kids in the general-student population. She offered a compromise: He could switch to the special-education gym class with his friends if next semester he took weight-training as part of the regular class. Eli agreed.

Janan Slough, the assistant principal who oversees the special-education department at Eli's school, says the school has difficulty finding certified special-education teachers because of a national shortage.

The school tries to foster as many opportunities as possible for those with disabilities to be in general classrooms, she says. Still, she adds, "I feel caught" between juggling the need for socializing with the need to teach basic, crucial tasks, such as handling money. On one field trip, the special-education kids went to a grocery store; they were supposed to buy something their family might use at home, pay for it, and make sure they got correct change.

Most of the kids with disabilities need to focus on independent-living and job skills, rather than college preparation. "I'm charged with thinking about where they are going to be at 21," she says. "I don't want parents to come back and say, 'It's nice they were socially included and had parallel instruction, but you didn't prepare them for the world of work.'"

For now, Eli has only one class—ceramics—that he attends with the general school population. On a recent morning, Eli sat next to a boy assigned to help him. The students were designing tiles, and from time to time his peer assistant would look at what he was doing, or go with him to get more clay. For much of the class, the boy bantered with one of his friends, who had pulled up a chair next to him and was regaling him with a story. From time to time, Eli made a joke and the boys all laughed together.

But when they walked Eli back to the special-education classroom, there was no suggestion that they meet up again that day. When Eli was asked if he enjoyed spending time with his assigned partner, he shrugged and said, "It's OK."

Eli has a lot of ideas about what he wants to do after high school. In middle school, he took a media class and worked in the school's TV studio. Along with the other kids in the class, he was given a homework assignment to make a public-service announcement. Eli made one about the Special Olympics. "I want to be a director," he said, when asked about his plans after high school.

"Eli has serious career aspirations for himself that may not have anything to do with what the rest of the world sees for him after high school," said his mother, one afternoon last month, while waiting for him at a drama class he takes outside of school. The class, made up of students with and without disabilities, was planning a variety show, and Eli was excited about performing. Every night, he went to his room to work on a dance routine he had created to accompany a song from the soundtrack of the movie, "Holes."

His girlfriend, whom he met in elementary school and also has Down syndrome, had invited him to be her date to the upcoming Winter Ball at her private school. Next month, Eli will turn 15 and is planning a big party. The only kids he plans to invite also have disabilities, his mother says.

While she's glad he has found a social circle, she still wonders about what he's missing by going to special-education classes instead of staying in regular classes. "I go back and forth on it all the time," she says. For instance, his school has a state-of-the-art TV studio with editing facilities and a control room, where a class is given. Eli's parents wanted him to be in that class, but it's not possible right now because he needs to attend the special-education math class, which is held during the same period.

On a recent morning at school, Eli weaved around the teenagers lining the hallway. Some sprawled on the floor, catching up on homework. Others joked with each other by their lockers, or rushed to get to their next class.

Eli didn't talk to any of the students. He walked with purpose, heading to the special-education room.

When he got there, his face brightened when he saw one of his friends. "This is my best friend," he said, throwing his arm around the other boy, who also has Down syndrome. He pressed his face close to his friend's until their cheeks almost touched. Eli smiled. "What table are you sitting at lunch today?" he said as they walked together down the hall. "Come on, make sure you sit with me."

POSTSCRIPT

Is Full Inclusion the Least Restrictive Environment?

How can we not respond to the compelling narratives of these parents? Eli and Ro come alive in their words. The road was not always easy and branches into two different paths.

The inclusion literature abounds with stories that melt hearts and open eyes. Horowitz and Klein (*Educational Leadership*, 2003) describe their efforts to include a child with Down syndrome into their religious school kindergarten. They discovered that, through working to include Michael, they learned to see the potential in every child and the interconnectedness of us all.

Proponents of the wisdom of full inclusion, Villa and Thousand (2005) maintain that inclusionary programs acknowledge the right of each of us to belong. No one should have to "fit in" or prove their worthiness to be part of everyday life experiences.

Taking one step further, Sapon-Shevin (*Educational Leadership*, 2003) portrays inclusion as an opportunity to teach social justice. In her eyes, building successful inclusive schools challenges people to actively create the inclusive, democratic society we envision for our children.

Most writers acknowledge that successful full inclusion is far from easy to achieve. In two instructive articles, Villa and Thousand (*Educational Leadership*, 2003) and McLeskey and Waldron (*Phi Delta Kappan*, 2002) provide numerous examples of lessons learned through schools' efforts to become inclusive. Their practical suggestions emphasize that successful inclusive programs require collaborative, sustained partnerships between administrators, teachers, and parents.

Drawing on student voices, Chadsey and Han (*TEACHING Exceptional Children*, 2005) address the peer connections essential to successful inclusion. The students think "segregation is unfair" and urge educators to provide opportunities where friendships can flourish naturally, as they would between any students.

Another group of students (Moore and Keefe, *Issues in Teacher Education*, 2004) found friendships—and inclusion—less important than their educational environment. These high school students, asked about their educational experiences, favored separate programs. Although disliking the accompanying stigma, they felt special education classes offered a more responsive environment that attended to their learning requirements.

Teachers, too, are concerned about the full inclusion learning environment. Kavale and Mostert (*Exceptionality*, 2003) reviewed several studies that explored the "empirical evidence" of full inclusion. Teachers embraced the democratic, just goals of full inclusion, but were concerned about its responsibilities. Their enthusiasm often moderated as they struggled to meet daily challenges.

How are such divergent experiences possible? Zigmond (*The Journal of Special Education*, 2003) suggests the answer may lie in our questions. Instead of asking whether full inclusion is desirable for all, perhaps we should return to the individual focus that has been the hallmark of special education to ask: For whom is full inclusion the best course? What instructional goals are best served by full inclusion?

Ro's and Eli's parents regain common ground when they speak of the future. The Vargos believe Ro's typical peers "will be her community—the ones who will protect and care for her. They will advocate social and legislative reform to support the inclusive lifestyle." Eli's mother hopes "The truth is he has to go out and get a job. If he's educated with his regular peers, then maybe a regular peer will hire him."

All teachers seek to prepare students to be successful adults. In partnership with parents, we endeavor to support and guide the young people we share along this journey. Is there one road to this ultimate destination? If not, how can any of us know which is the path best taken?

ISSUE 14

Should Colleges Be More Accommodating to Students with Disabilities?

YES: Hazel Denhart, from "Deconstructing Barriers: Perceptions of Students Labeled With Learning Disabilities in Higher Education," *Journal of Learning Disabilities* (November/December 2008)

NO: Melana Z. Vickers, from "Accommodating College Students with Learning Disabilities: ADD, ADHD, and Dyslexia," *Pope Center Series on Higher Education* (The John W. Pope Center, March 2010)

ISSUE SUMMARY

YES: Hazel Denhart, who lectures at Portland State University, uses disability theory perspective to analyze the perceptions of students with learning disabilities about their experiences in higher education. Her interviewees identify social barriers that make college a less-than-welcome experience, and she recommends steps to reduce institutional intolerance.

NO: Melana Z. Vickers, an editorial writer for *USA Today*, uses information from interviews with on-campus experts, professors, and students to raise serious questions about the legitimacy of accommodations and disability services. Many of her interviewees think disabilities leading to accommodations can be purchased, to the detriment of everyone's experience.

Have you used a curb cut to ease the passage of your bike or a stroller or pushed the automatic door opener button when your arms were full? Did you know the now-ubiquitous food processor was for a one-handed cook?

All the above are accommodations, orginally designed to make the world more accessible for people with disabilities. Federal laws (Section 504, ADA) require that reasonable accommodations be provided so people with disabilities have fair and equal access to life's activities.

Most people would agree that Braille texts and ramps in buildings are reasonable accommodations making school more accessible.

What about scribes to transfer a student's into print? Extended time for exams? These can be accommodations as well—for people with disabilities affecting writing, processing material quickly, or sustaining attention. Some wonder whether these cross the line, making things too easy.

In schools, accommodations are adjustments to setting, timing, presentation mode, and/or response mode that allow students with disabilities to demonstrate what they know and can do. They are not intended to change the nature of a task, make it easier, or ensure that a student passes.

Accommodations achieved controversial status with the advent of high stakes testing and accountability. Federal laws require that schools provide appropriate accommodations so students with disabilities can participate fully in education and assessment.

Educators have become accustomed to regulatory rigor when selecting accommodations. Analyzing 12 years of research on accommodation policies, Lazarus, Thurlow, Lail, and Christensen (*The Journal of Special Education*, 2009) found that states have formalized regulations and guidelines. Despite some variability, there is general consensus that appropriate accommodations ensure that an assessment measures its intended content knowledge, rather than the effects of a disability.

Accommodations in postsecondary education are attracting attention. According to the National Longitudinal Transition Study-2 (NLTS2, 2009), 45% of students with disabilities pursue higher education. This increase might be attributable to successful use of accommodations throughout schools. Perhaps it is a consequence of Individuals with Disabilities Education Act (IDEA) 2004's emphasis on transition planning that can embrace postsecondary goals. The rise might also reflect the growing availability of college disability support centers (Sparks & Lovett, *Journal of Learning Disabilities*, 2009). This issue explores whether students with disabilities experience a welcoming learning environment when they make the move to college.

For her doctoral dissertation, Hazel Denhart, herself a person with a learning disability, interviewed students who were identified in college as having a learning disability. She sought to relate and summarize their perceptions and experiences. The voices of her participants speak of their significant struggle; despite their efforts, they feel they are often regarded as poor students. Once found eligible for accommodations, many did not want to use them, sensing disdain from their peers and professors.

Columnist Melana Z. Vickers offers a sharply contrasting view. Based on statistical reports and interviews with higher education administrators and professors, Vickers concludes that postsecondary schools have already made far too many concessions. She questions the legitimacy of the growing number of disability diagnoses, and the accommodations that accompany them, citing claims that both can be purchased. Hinting that faculty are reluctant to talk about their accommodations reservations, Vickers raises concerns about the possibility of a resultant student backlash at this special treatment.

As you read these articles, consider the differing perspectives of those interviewed. Are students with disabilities encountering bias and prejudice? Do colleges and universities differ that much from K-12 schools? Whose perspective has the strongest merit?

YES

Hazel Denhart

Deconstructing Barriers: Perceptions of Students Labeled With Learning Disabilities in Higher Education

Since the 1960s, intensive scientific inquiry into learning disabilities (LD) has yielded an immense body of excellent knowledge about its manifestation. . . . Medical researchers have identified physical differences in the brains of dyslexics altering visual perception, phonemic processing, semantic understanding, working memory, and muscle coordination. Brain researchers can see precisely where phonemic difficulties unfold when dyslexics wrestle the written word for meaning, and geneticists are tracking multiple entry points for the flow of dyslexia through the human genome. Meanwhile, social scientists from the relatively new field of disability studies are discovering how diversity in brain structure and brain function can be misunderstood as disability. From this perspective, LD is seen as socially created by values restricting how one's brain is permitted to function.

However, despite our vast knowledge of LD those who live with it still struggle for success. While their enrollments are up in postsecondary institutions the dropout rate of those labeled with LD remains high locking many into higher unemployment rates, more placement in lower prestige jobs, lower income from employment, and higher rates of poverty.

Since the early 1990s an expanding stream of qualitative research has invited the voice of those labeled with LD to illuminate the barriers facing them in higher education. That voice speaks to being silenced, misunderstood, and misrepresented by others.

The issue of being silenced is apparent in policy and practice where the voice of those labeled with LD has gone missing. Even to the present moment it continues to be nonlabeled researchers, policy makers, and practitioners debating the issues and setting agendas regarding services and accommodations for those who are labeled. . . . Few studies in LD research seek the voice of those labeled as to the impact of scientifically based interventions imposed on them or other possible solutions yet to be recognized by researchers who do not experience the phenomenon. It is puzzling that the voice of those labeled

From *Journal of Learning Disabilities*, vol. 41 no. 6, November/December 2008, pp. 483–488, 490–493, 494–495 (refs. omitted). Copyright © 2008 by Hammill Institute on Disabilities and Sage in association with American Rehabilitation Counseling Association (ARCA). Reprinted by permission via Rightslink.

LD is missing considering scientific research has provided them with adequate accommodations for equal participation, because federal civil rights law guarantees their inclusion in social and civic life. . . .

Theoretical Framework

This [doctoral] study was conducted through the lens of *disability theory* based in the emerging, interdisciplinary field of disability studies. The following interpretation of disability theory offers the reader a simple, common reference for understanding this particular study and is not given as theoretical currency or to canonize any particular elements of this dense body of literature.

Three foundational ideas form a rudimentary core of disability theory viewing disability as (a) socially constructed, (b) part of normal human variation, and (c) requiring voice to deconstruct it.

First, disability theory asserts that disability cannot be understood outside of the context where it arises because it is a *product of social interaction*. Indeed in the United States even the mere perception of disability is enough to disable as evidenced in the Americans with Disabilities Act (ADA) of 1990 giving federal protection to those not actually disabled according to societal norms but who are only regarded as such. Thus, one can be free of impairment and still be disabled.

Higgins, Raskind, Goldberg, and Herman (2002) illustrated the social construction of disability in *master status* where the label of disability spreads from a single-task incompetence across one's totality obliterating other quite sound abilities. For example, in societies where reading ability is considered a measure of intelligence, master status makes it inconceivable for a person who cannot read or write well to be regarded as an intellectual. Here, the dyslexic who cannot encode or decode print might have no difficulty comprehending an audio text or dictating into a recording device but this person will still be considered disabled or intellectually inferior because literacy through the eyes is privileged over literacy through the ears.

An example of *institutionally* held master status was found on an advertisement for a "therapeutic support group" at one university in the Pacific Northwest. A flyer posted across campus by the psychological services office depicted a large heading "A.D.H.D." with a subheading asking, "Do these describe you?" followed by a list of 18 negative attributes including "social misfit," "underachiever," and "undisciplined." Only one positive attribute, "creative," appeared near the bottom of the list. Here, the university's chief medical authority on attention-deficit/hyperactivity disorder (ADHD) publicly announced that students with an ADHD label necessarily belong to a stereotype invalidating their overall competence and capacity. . . .

Second, disability studies scholars argue impairments are a natural and productive part of *normal human variation* known to all at some point in the life span.

Finally, disability scholars posit that *voice* is necessary to deconstruct disability and to authentically understand it in research. Indeed the field of disability studies is characterized by action research comprised of scholars openly claiming their personal labels of disability, with the exception of scholars labeled with LD who largely remain missing from any research field.

Research on Students Labeled with LD in Higher Education

Three themes appear consistently in qualitative inquiry of students labeled with LD in higher education: (a) being misunderstood, (b) needing to work harder than nonlabeled others, and (c) seeking out strategies for success in education.

The theme of feeling misunderstood appears from the earliest ethnographies to more recent emancipatory research conducted as political action, and within autobiographical work. The voice of those labeled with LD speak of being regarded as intellectually inferior, incompetent, lacking effort, or attempting to cheat or use unfair advantages when requesting accommodations. The phenomenon of being misunderstood occurs both *intrapersonally* as well as interpersonally leading to devaluation and marginalization.

Intrapersonal (self) misunderstanding appears commonly in the use of the term "stupid" (or synonyms of this) by informants as a descriptor of themselves. Shessel and Reiff (1999) identified internalized master status in their use of the term *imposter phenomenon* to describe informants feeling they must have presented false impressions of themselves or somehow "cheated" the system by having been admitted to college as persons with LD traits. These informants feared being exposed as "frauds.". . .

Interpersonal misunderstanding with others is also common in the qualitative and autobiographical literature (as well as in some quantitative) where informants speak of being mistaken as intellectually inferior. Higgins et al. (2002) traced some issues of depression to informants' unhappy early school experiences of being bullied, teased, ridiculed, and hounded to a degree far exceeding the severity of their challenges. These qualitative findings might serve to illuminate those in clinical studies indicating high rates of loneliness, despair, depression, anxiety, and low self-esteem among LD subjects.

Feelings of being misunderstood have a direct impact on requesting accommodations. Studies found students labeled with LD feared they would be perceived as cheating if they tried to use accommodations. Hill's (1994) informants reported faculty members believed accommodations provided an unfair advantage. Hill's informants "were told certain modifications could not be made (e.g., extended time allowance on exams) because of the perceived 'advantage' it might give the student with a disability when compared to the non-disabled student . . ." (p. 11). In a study by Sarver (2000), one informant recalled "[some professors] have a really negative attitude towards me, even though they don't even know me" (p. 86). Elaqua, Rapaport, and Kruses's (1996) informants felt professors believed they "were trying to take advantage of the situation and attempted to 'pull a fast one' on them" (p. 6).

Abundant in the literature are tales of experiencing discrimination and even harassment after revealing LD to get accommodations. An engineering student in Barga's (1996) study was labeled a "dangerous engineer" (para. 18) by faculty after revealing her LD label to secure accommodations for an exam. Barga stated, "A meeting was held to have her removed from his class. Another meeting was held to have her removed from the department" (para. 18). Informants also speak of being advised to choose programs of study based on their disability rather than on their ability. Greenbaum, Graham, and Scales (1996) found fear of discrimination was a critical barrier for success among those labeled with LD. Not surprisingly, voice-based literature indicates a strong desire among informants for faculty and staff to undergo training about the nature of LD and how it is misunderstood.

The second major theme in the perceptions of students labeled with LD in higher education comes from the heavy workload they experience well beyond the scope of nonlabeled peers. Abundant in the literature are reports of students labeled with LD working themselves into a state of exhaustion even to the point of experiencing headaches and becoming physically ill from the workload. Ironically, these individuals are often judged as lazy or not trying hard enough as indicated in Lock and Layton's (2001) findings where some professors believed students use learning disabilities as an excuse to get out of work. Fearing stigma and misunderstanding, college students labeled with LD often avoid using their legally mandated accommodations that could ease their workload, fearing they would be misunderstood as cheating. . . .

Finally, the third theme from the perspective of students labeled with LD in the qualitative and autobiographical literature focuses on seeking empowerment strategies for practical as well as emotional needs.

Practical strategies include securing accommodations when possible such as audio texts, note takers, having exams read, demonstrating course mastery through alternative means, having extended time on exams, and receiving assistance from an LD specialist.

However, to receive these accommodations students must first be labeled with LD. From the perspective of students labeled with LD in higher education are emergent findings indicating the assessment experience can be oppressive. Most colleges implement a standard assessment process developed by the Association for Higher Education and Disability (AHEAD) for diagnosing LD in their college students. The AHEAD guidelines are based almost entirely on the original Individuals with Disabilities Education Act (IDEA) guidelines developed for children in public schools. The AHEAD guidelines call for intelligence testing as well as a battery of cognitive and psychological inventories and a complete diagnostic interview where clinicians gather from students detailed intricacies about their medical, developmental, social, and family history as well as probing into their psychological state and current social life. It is unquestionably an invasive experience. The interview is not limited to learning issues and can cover nearly any aspect of the student's being. . . . The testing for labeling is also expensive (equivalent to 6–8 weeks' pay for fulltime work at the minimum wage). Whereas some colleges subsidize the testing, others do not and not all colleges will accept the diagnosis granted free in K-12. Also, because current policy directs testing be repeated every 3 years, a K-12 diagnosis will expire and need to be redone before graduation with a bachelors degree.

Little is known from the perspective of college students labeled with LD as to the effectiveness and appropriateness of prescribed accommodations or what might work better. Studies indicate problems with accommodations such as recorded texts being inaudible or arriving too late—even long after the course concluded. While accommodations such as audio texts on tape will lighten the workload it cannot fully reduce it to the level of students with average reading skills. Taped texts use speech at a rate of 150 words per minute whereas the average reader reads at a rate of 300. Thus, reviewing audio texts take twice as long. Further, recorded texts cannot yet be highlighted or flagged as easily as printed texts. Trying to review a passage before an exam could require sorting through hours of audio recordings to find the correct passage, complicated when readers fail to note page numbers. However, technology is advancing quickly to remedy the highlighting issue. . . .

Purpose of the Study

The purpose of this phenomenological study was to identify commonly held structures of consciousness among a subset of college students labeled with LD as to their educational barriers and the ways they overcome them. . . .

Methodology

Where the anthropologist seeks to understand what a culture *looks* like from the position of an expert observer using an approach of "otherness," of "difference," of "not of us", the phenomenologist by contrast seeks to understand how it *feels* to be in a culture using an approach of "we," of "identification" between the informants and the reader. As a researcher labeled with LD, I was in the position of both expert and insider translating experience from the LD perspective to that of the scholarly, professional one.

Role of the Researcher

My capacity to learn remained largely invisible throughout the first quarter-century of my life when I lived in relative illiteracy with little promise of an adequate education. As a dyslexic with a visual perceptual disability I was misunderstood by those around me as being "slow," yet today I hold a doctorate in educational policy. Where my intellect was invisible to the educational institutions I encountered in my youth and young adulthood, it is now recognized and even given accolades. As a researcher I wanted to know what changed. It seemed unlikely that the neurophysiology of my brain changed that much. I am still dyslexic and struggle for the meaning of each printed word I encounter with my eyes. It seemed more likely that the dramatic change necessary for me to become literate and then to become a scholar occurred in the social environment around me. I embarked on this study seeking to understand the nature of the barriers I and others like me face and to identify the shared strategies we use to overcome them. This was a risky enterprise because education for me was oppressive, silencing, and marginalizing. This experience threatened to bias my study. The first step in addressing bias was to admit it will exist to some degree and that I cannot free myself of the strong emotion I feel at having my intellect—the most precious attribute of a human being—dismissed for the first two and a half decades of my history. It penetrates my life, saturating my every thought and move. The second step I took was to be as open as possible about my biases by telling my story to everyone concerned with this study; my doctoral committee, my informants, the gatekeepers associated with the study, and interested others watching it unfold. I sought criticism from everyone as to where I might be overlaying my story on the data. . . . Additionally, I guarded against personal experience by seeking informants who had very different histories from my own. I came from a working-class family, achieved literacy late, did not graduate from high school with my peers, attended community college for 5 years and then a public university (with minimal admission requirements) for another 9 years before earning a bachelor's degree. I had no LD specialist and no accommodations for the first 12 years of higher education. In contrast, my informants came from middle and upper-middle class families, some attended private grade schools and high schools, 10 of 11 graduated from high school on time, and all but one were attending an exclusive, private university with stringent admission requirements. . . . In other words, I intentionally looked for informants who had the opportunity for the best possible educational experience and the most resources to attain it. However, seeking to balance my experience with my informants' comes at the price of not being able to generalize these findings to the wider LD population. Still, the findings could offer something else; as an insider I established considerable trust with my informants and reached a level of candor and depth in the interviews unlikely to be attained by outsiders.

Participants

After receiving human subjects approval from my university, I approached informants through the offices of disability services at two colleges located in the Pacific Northwest; one an exclusive, private college (PC) with stringent admission requirements and the other a public, community college (CC) with no admission requirements. Criteria for participation required informants to be native speakers of English, have a diagnosis of LD determined by the [AHEAD] guidelines, and have no other physical or emotional impairments that could complicate the LD experience. . . .

Characteristics of Participants

Three male and eight female participants represented European American ancestry from the American middle and upper-middle class. All 10 of the PC students attended regular K-12 classes completing their schooling on time with their nonlabeled peers. Only one received accommodations (extra time on tests) in high school. These informants are not representative of the *identified* LD population in K-12, which might concern some readers. However, given that medical research indicates as much as 20% of the human population carries the genes for dyslexia and only about 5.5% are identified by the schools, one could argue that those moving through K-12 who could be identified with LD but who go unrecognized are actually more representative of the LD population than those who are identified. Some readers might also be concerned that if these informants were not identified with LD in K-12 they might be "faking" LD to seek advantage at a highly competitive school, an issue candidly discussed among professionals in the field. However, the informants in this study were labeled with LD by licensed clinical psychologists using the AHEAD guidelines for assessing LD in college students. This testing is rigorous and extensive taking about 8 hours to complete in the presence of a skilled clinician whose training is focused on screening out those who genuinely do not have the characteristics of LD. Also, considering the LD label leads to powerful and irrevocable stigma, it seems less likely that one would try to gain intellectual advantage by using a label that undermines one's intelligence. . . .

Findings

. . .

RQ I: What Are the Similarities in the Described Experiences of a Subset of College Students Labeled with LD?

The shared experiences of informants included (a) working harder than nonlabeled others, (b) having the workload unrecognized, (c) generating products incommensurate with the workload, (d) viewing the college LD specialist as crucial to success, and (e) experiencing rapport with others labeled with LD.

Nine of 11 informants spoke of working significantly longer hours than their nonlabeled peers on the same assignments. JJ commented, "People spent 2 or 3 hours on this paper. I spent 20 hours, easily." Porter observed, "I would turn in papers to my professors, papers I had spent, like, days on. And people around me were spending, like, hours."

Four informants indicated the workload went unrecognized. JJ said, "I think usually that I turn things in late and . . . they [professors] think I'm not good, that I'm just putzin' around." Rocky Top said, "I don't think my professors know how much, how hard I work."

Eight informants noted the excessive workload did not produce a commensurate product and feared the mediocre quality would reflect laziness. Bering noted, "I think that they might even think that I'm lazy, and that I don't spend time." Porter commented, "I have put so much into this and you can't even tell."

Eight of the 10 PC students spoke of the crucial role of the LD specialist in their success. This appears in part from her ability to see their perspective and recognize their workload. . . . Mac noted the professor's attitude toward him "totally turned around" when the LD specialist intervened and explained the situation to the professor who then allowed Mac to demonstrate his course mastery privately. The professor thus came to understand Mac as a dedicated student. Some regarded the LD specialist as a transformative figure. . . .

Finally, five of 11 informants experienced an *LD rapport* where communication flowed easily and without disability among them. Lea detailed a conversation style in the LD community at the PC, "We're all speaking in fragments at the exact same time, on top of one another . . . We are speaking this weird piece language, and everyone gets it." Porter said, "We're in the same zone, you know?" Beth said, "People who don't have learning disability can't understand what I'm doing."

RQ II: How Does This Subset of Students View Themselves Based on Their Experiences?

All these informants emphasized they had a healthy cognitive difference rather than a disability and 9 of 11 informants used the term learning difference at some point in the interviews to reference themselves. Only the CC informant used the term *learning disabled* to describe herself saying, "I say I have a learning disability which basically means that I learn differently than other people."

Ten of [11] informants spoke of being misunderstood by faculty. For example, Lea noted those labeled with LD were seen as "weird," "wacky," "not quite on the ball," and "not getting it together like they could if they really pushed the pedal to the metal." . . . When Sarah sought testing for dyslexia, one professor commented to her, "I think people just do it nowadays to get medicine for it." Beth's professor told her "Well, I don't know if you need to be taking this class if you have a learning disability." . . . Isaac and JJ viewed themselves as ideal students (hardworking, committed to scholarship, etc.) but argued the college could not accept them as such because the labels "LD" and "ideal" were incompatible. . . .

RQ III: What Has Been the Experience of This Subset of College Students . . . in the Process of Assessment and Accommodations?

. . . Five themes emerged . . . (a) positive and negative testing experiences, (b) surprise at the LD label, (c) validation of intelligence, (d) not receiving adequate information from the testing process, and (e) reluctance to use accommodations.

Three informants had positive experiences with the testing stemming from the novelty of first time testing and anticipating discovering what was "wrong." Positive experiences came with flattering remarks from the test administrator. For example, Sarah commented, "I was giving these really good stories and she [clinician] was just blown away by them." However, those who enjoyed testing indicated they would not want to repeat the process.

Five of 11 informants reported strong negative reactions to assessment testing. Negative experiences included emotional and physical pain (apparently related to cognitive exhaustion but this is not clear). Comments included, "It was so painful," "I felt awful and then I went home and cried," "It was horrible," and, "Oh, I hate them [assessment tests]. With a passion."

Some informants were surprised to be labeled with LD. Three had previously attributed their academic difficulties to being lazy or stupid before testing. Lea commented, "Well, I've learned about it that I'm not stupid."

All 11 participants felt pride at having their intellects clinically validated and often reminded themselves of their IQ scores or percentile ranking in times of alienation.

Eight participants reported not receiving enough information (or were not able to recall enough information) from the assessment to clearly understand how the LD impacted their daily living. For example, Sarah said, "I know that I have dyslexia, but I don't really understand what that means." . . .

Finally, 9 of the 10 informants who were granted accommodations expressed reluctance to ask for them. JJ said, "I feel like I can never ask for an extension because I feel like I don't . . . don't deserve it or something." Isaac commented, "I kind of feel like you're slacking, like you're failing in some way, which, [pause] for me, is one of the hardest things to get over . . . I'm not giving up, I'm not giving in . . . I'm just getting the help I deserve." . . . Kai was reluctant to ask for accommodations for fear "that they'll see me as different and not the same as the other students. Inferior almost."

In addition to their reluctance to ask for accommodations, five informants devalued the work accomplished with them. Lea said, "I feel like the less people utilize accommodations, the more valued their work is." . . .

RQ IV: What Does This Subset of College Students . . . See as Barriers to Their Access of Higher Education?

[O]ther barriers facing these informants included difficulties with (a) organizing concepts for reading and writing, (b) oral and written comprehension, (c) verbal communication, and (d) having a different way of thinking than nonlabeled peers.

Six informants spoke of difficulties with organizing concepts. Mac said, "I have trouble funneling all my concepts into sentences" adding, "I can get it out, but it takes forever. I write paragraph-long sentences. I cannot put periods in there." Rocky Top explained when it comes to organizing concepts, "I literally can't do it . . . I've never been explained how I can improve this." . . . Narrowing large texts and selecting key information to write papers was another source of organizing difficulties. JJ said, "The point is, is everything's important to me, so making an outline that's only supposed to be like two pages . . . I have no idea. It's all important . . ." . . .

Four informants also spoke of verbal communication challenges (potentially related to organizing concepts). For example, Mac said, "I don't talk much at all. And I definitely don't talk under pressure, in class . . . I just like, freeze up." Sarah said, "I had these great things to say, but they just never came out right."

Finally, six informants indicated they experienced a *different way of thinking* than nonlabeled peers. . . . Porter explained, "My brain is just like a pomegranate and they want it to be like an orange." Mac's different way of thinking drove him to contextualize new knowledge. Mac said, "I need to see the process, but they wanted you to just look at the equation and just associate the number, instead of seeing why."

RQ V: What Do This Subset of College Students . . . View as Their Accommodation Needs?

Participants indicated they needed: (a) self-understanding (including their different way of thinking), (b) traditional accommodations, (c) writing assistance, (d) organization strategies, and (e) visual strategies.

Ten of 11 informants felt self-understanding was a key strategy to overcome barriers. This understanding often came through the LD community group. For example, Lea said,

> Meeting other people and seeing myself in them and seeing, "oh, my god," that's the thing we share in common and it's not a flaw in me or something that I need to work out. It's like a way of being in the world. And when I see [it] in other people, it's like I like it in them.

Lea added, "It's not about how we fix ourselves with that group, it's like, how do we get this system to give us what we need. What do we need?". . .

Seven informants spoke of overcoming barriers with traditional accommodations, such as extra time on exams/papers, audio books, note takers, and tutors, whereas three benefited from medication for ADD/ADHD. Mac said, "Without the medication, like, I can get to the library and [pause] who knows what happens, it's like rolling the dice."

Five informants sought writing assistance. Rocky Top commented, "I work hard, I get tutors, I get note takers, I have an editor that does all of my papers for me." . . .

Five informants overcame barriers by using systems for organization. . . . Rocky Top commented that although she cannot learn to organize concepts she is otherwise an "organizational freak" commenting, "I make lists of everything and they are everywhere." Beth remarked, "I have to write everything down, and get everything organized, things have to be in little organized compartments."

Finally, five informants used visual strategies to overcome barriers such as multicolor highlighting, drawing outlines, and using visual imagery (metaphor) for organizing, learning, and remembering. Porter used the metaphor of a rug to narrow information for a paper saying, "When you write a paper you're not writing about the rug. You're writing about one, like, the cream in the rug. And pulling that out for people." . . .

Implications for Practice and Future Research

The issue of students labeled with LD being reluctant to ask for accommodations for fear of triggering discrimination is a serious matter. Adequate studies now demonstrate those labeled with LD in higher education do fear discrimination. But the degree to which it is present is not yet known. Larger scale quantitative studies need to be conducted to confirm if the discrimination is real and to what degree it might be experienced. These should be followed by qualitative studies exploring the nature and context of the discrimination and how those who experience it believe it should be addressed.

Universities might enhance educational success of their students labeled with LD through university-wide diversity training to raise awareness of LD, emphasize the importance of accommodations, and illuminate potential discrimination. Such training should be grounded in a basic disability theory where the social cause of the disability is identified, where normal human variation is recognized, and where the voice of those labeled with LD informs the training. Socially constructed disability can also be addressed in the development of democratic LD communities (not to be confused with therapy groups) on campuses where those labeled with LD can gather as citizens, identify problems, develop strategies, and speak on their own behalf. The role of the LD specialist could also be instrumental in both community building and diversity training. . . .

The issue of assessment testing also has implications. [F]uture studies need to investigate the psychological, emotional, and economic impact this testing might have on the population of those required to undergo it. It is not yet clear to what degree this testing has unrecognized, unintended consequences for those experiencing it especially in light of their needing to repeat it every 3 years. [F]uture studies need to investigate how well those undergoing testing are given beneficial information from it and to what degree they are invited to collaborate in determining accommodations. Finally, action research studies should inquire as to the feasibility of engaging disability theory to inform new policies and revise existing ones. Such studies could also inquire as to the possibility of replacing some aspects of diagnostic assessment and special accommodations with universal access. For example, if audio texts were available to any student paying the copyright fee and duplication costs then there would be no need for expensive diagnosis, labeling, and the resulting stigma. . . .

Conclusion

The finest accommodations based on the most sophisticated science will have no value if intolerance denies their use. I believe the most important change that can be made for students labeled with LD in education today is to grant them the agency to speak of the disabling force of discrimination. Those labeled with LD need the opportunity to gather of their own accord, share experience, discover an identity, and find a collective voice with which to turn outward and claim their place as equal citizens in the democracy. As it is for the birth of any newly recognized community this move will be a slow and arduous one. The journey to self-representation will be more complex than simply gathering into community and taking the floor for those whose intellect has gone unrecognized and whose true identity brings suspicion and stigma.

We must awaken to one another, to the essence of the phenomenon we share, and shatter the silence together. . . .

Melana Z. Vickers  **NO**

Accommodating College Students with Learning Disabilities: ADD, ADHD, and Dyslexia

Scan an undergraduate lecture hall at any U.S. college or university, and odds are that two out of every 100 students there will have Attention Deficit Disorder (ADD), Attention Deficit Hyperactivity Disorder (ADHD), or another learning disability such as dyslexia. These students are entitled to ask for special academic treatment under federal disability law. Such "accommodation" can include extra time to take exams, alternative exam formats such as oral or take-home, and classroom assistance such as the help of a note taker.

In the last decade, the proportion of undergraduates designated as learning disabled (LD) or as having ADD/ADHD has almost doubled, to reach more than 2 percent of the total U.S. undergraduate population, or 394,500 students. These figures do not include those disabled by mental retardation, autism, brain injuries, and other severe conditions, which are not considered in this paper. At colleges and universities that attract more affluent students, the numbers of LD and ADD/ADHD are even higher as a percentage of undergraduates. Most of the LD and ADD/ADHD (hereafter shortened to ADD) students are white males.

It would be natural for legally mandated special treatment of the LD and ADD students to rise along with their numbers. But the special treatment appears to be rising even more rapidly than the number of students. [At] the University of North Carolina at Chapel Hill, the number of LD and ADD students seeking eligibility for accommodations has almost doubled since 2002 and has grown eightfold since the 1980s. what's more, the rate of growth is still accelerating.

The diagnosis and accommodation of cognitive disabilities have helped some students a great deal. Students who in the past were unable to perform well now have the opportunity to achieve their true potential. Yet the accommodation of LD and ADD college students is becoming controversial, because neither all the diagnoses, nor all the accommodations, are perceived as legitimate. Some professors have spoken out against accommodating students whose condition doesn't warrant the special treatment, and many others have complained privately about the power and secrecy of the disabilities offices that decide whether students are to be accommodated.

The American Association of University Professors (AAUP) has published calls for reform. Organizations that administer national, standardized

From *Pope Center Series on Higher Education,* March 2010, excerpts (notes omitted). Copyright © 2010 by John William Pope Center for Higher Education Policy. Reprinted by permission.

entrance exams such as the College Board have been criticized in the media and by scholars for their accommodation policies. And as the news reports of well-to-do students obtaining unwarranted LD or ADD diagnoses for the sole purpose of obtaining academic accommodations multiply, other students are likely to speak out against the practice.

The issue will gain new attention . . . when the U.S. District Court for the Western Division of Kentucky will reconsider a case called *Jenkins v. National Board of Medical Examiners*. The case involves a medical student (Jenkins) with a reading disability who has received accommodations on exams in his past schooling and now seeks accommodations, including extra time, on his medical school exams. A lower court denied the accommodations, but a federal appeals court . . . ordered the court to reconsider its decision and to re-evaluate whether the student is disabled under new, looser definitions of learning disability signed into law in . . . 2008 as amendments to the Americans with Disabilities Act.

If the lower court reverses itself, accommodations in colleges nationwide are likely to expand. There is, however, an "out." Postsecondary institutions may seek exemptions under the new amendments to the Americans with Disabilities Act. Besides redefining disability more loosely, the amendments state that postsecondary institutions may be exempted from the new language if they can show that it would cause them to fundamentally alter the nature of the academic services involved. Such an exemption could keep schools from having to accommodate students under the new standards. Even so, some professors see the current accommodations as an infringement on their freedom to set academic standards for their students. . . .

This paper will review the controversy over ADD and LD accommodations and suggest how schools might better address this growing problem. Until now, the issue has had a low profile, both because of federal laws that keep the details of a student's accommodation private and because faculty members have avoided discussing a problem affecting disabled students for fear of being viewed as politically incorrect. Indeed, few faculty members were willing to be interviewed on the record for this paper. . . .

Background

No other disability has seen as dramatic a rise in numbers of diagnoses in recent decades as have LD and ADD. In 2006, fully 5.6 percent of all Americans aged 3–21 and enrolled in public education (preschool through high school) were diagnosed with LD or ADD, up from 3.6 percent of that population in 1981. By contrast, the proportion of Americans aged 3–21 with hearing, visual, orthopedic, and other impairments has stayed steady over the same period, at about 0.1 percent apiece. Speech and language impairments rose slightly from 2.9 percent to 3 percent, and mental retardation has been cut in half from 2 percent to 1 percent of this population. Autism has grown to 0.5 percent of this school-age population, up from 0.1 percent in 1995–96, the frst year it was measured.

The National Institutes of Health (NIH) define ADD/ADHD as a disorder whose symptoms include difficulty in staying focused and paying attention, difficulty in controlling behavior, and hyperactivity. NIH defines learning disabilities, including dyslexia, as disorders that affect the ability to understand or use spoken or written language, do mathematical calculations, coordinate movements, or direct attention. School-aged children are diagnosed with these disorders by licensed psychologists or doctors who use as their guide the *Diagnostic and Statistical Manual of Mental Disorders* of the American Psychiatric Association. . . .

Since there is no single test to determine whether a child has such a disorder, there can be—and there is—great variance in the diagnoses from specialist to specialist and from demographic group to demographic group.

The LD and ADD diagnoses are not randomly distributed, either in the school-age population or in the postsecondary population. An undergraduate student with ADD or LD is exponentially more likely to be white, male, and from a family with high income and college-educated parents, than female, nonwhite, or with parents with lower income or level of education. There are no recorded Asian undergraduates disabled by ADD, and only 0.7 percent of Asian students have a learning disability, according to government data. Only 1.6 percent of disabled Latinos are disabled by ADD, 5.8 percent by learning disabilities, or 7.4 percent in total. In contrast, white undergraduates with ADD represent 7.7 percent of the white disabled population, and 5.8 percent of the LD population. For black, disabled undergraduates, the numbers are 3.8 percent ADD, and 1.2 percent LD.

The diagnosis numbers suggest several possibilities. For one, white male undergraduates from upper-income, high-education families may be disproportionately afflicted by ADD and LD. Alternatively, they may be overdiagnosed. Other possibilities are that nonwhites and lower-income, lower-educated undergraduates are underdiagnosed or that they are not predisposed to ADD and LD. whatever the case, the unevenness of the distribution of the diagnosis—and thus of accommodations that can be acquired with the diagnosis—adds contentiousness in an area of mental health that has seen a high degree of controversy in recent years. . . .

Regional distinctions in the proportions of ADD and LD diagnoses are evident as well. The disabled undergraduate population in New England colleges and universities is 22.8 percent LD or ADD. By contrast, in the Plains region, it is 15.1 percent. The variations aren't huge, but they raise questions about the reliability of the diagnoses. . . .

Perhaps the biggest changes driving the diagnoses were the Americans with Disabilities Act of 1990 (ADA), the Individuals with Disabilities Education Improvement Act of 1997 (IDEA), and its reauthorization and revision in 2004. Along with the Rehabilitation Act of 1973, these federal laws mandate that disabled students from age 3 to 21 (but to a lesser degree college-age) must be provided with services, monitoring, assessment, and other aspects of treatment in publicly funded education. By mandating services and treatment, the laws have driven up the number of school mental health professionals and raised the level of awareness of teachers. Many actively seek to identify and assist students who they suspect should have their learning abilities assessed.

The rise in LD and ADD diagnoses has stirred controversy. One reason is evidence that some diagnoses are illegitimate. Various news organizations including *ABC News* and *USA Today* have reported that for a price it's possible to secure an illegitimate ADD diagnosis in order to obtain academic advantage. Scholarly journals have also studied the topic of what one termed the "undesirable incentives to seek diagnosis"—in order to obtain extra time for taking exams, for instance. A psychologist in California advertises his diagnostic services online at testaccommodations.com, with his principal message being that an ADD or LD diagnosis can provide extra time for testing for the SAT as well as professional programs such as medical school or law school. . . .

The director of disability services at UNC-Chapel Hill, Jim Kessler, says that "oh yes, you can" buy an LD diagnosis, and that one can therefore buy accommodations as well. He adds, however, that it would require "a lot of work" for an otherwise nonqualifying student to buy the diagnosis and the accommodation, and that those who do it are "going to be such a small, small group of people." He says that this concern is tiny in the greater scheme of issues facing the disabled and that professors or other observers who are concerned about such illegitimate accommodations "need to get a life."

How to Obtain Accommodations

To obtain accommodations, students must apply to college disabilities offices. To use typical language from a disabilities office website, an LD or ADD student may request accommodations to "overcome limitations that keep him or her from meeting the demands of college or university life."

Such accommodations can include providing note takers or scribes who write what the student dictates, converting textbooks or course packs into accessible mediums such as audio recordings, giving extended time on tests, alternative forms of tests (i.e., using scribes, tape recorders, computers, or oral administration of the test) or alternative locations for tests (such as a quiet room for one person), a lessened load of courses while having full-time status, and course substitutions.

In order to qualify for such accommodations, the student must provide the college's disabilities services office with evidence of the disability and how it limits the student. The University of North Carolina-Chapel Hill requires a "description of *current substantial limitations* as they relate to meeting the various demands of University life" and a documented discussion (typically from a medical professional and a school professional) of academic achievement in the last two to three years and how it has been affected by the disability.

College disabilities websites typically make clear that the threshold for special treatment in college is higher than it was in elementary and high school, and that accommodations aren't automatic for students who had received them in K-12. The UNC-Chapel Hill site notes that the medical documentation must address the student's current level of functioning. Having had IEPs (Individualized Education Plans, mandated by law for disabled students in grade school), 504 Plans (mandated by the Rehabilitation Act of 1973), and Summary of Performance plans (which discuss the student's readiness for postsecondary education, and are described in the IDEA Act of 2004), provides historical evidence of accommodations but these are generally not considered sufficient to make a student eligible for services. . . .

The student identifies himself or herself to the disabilities office voluntarily, then follows up with the documentation. A single administrator or a committee then decides if the student can qualify for disability services. If so, a disabilities expert meets with the student to determine what services, including accommodations, are warranted. The office then sends the student's relevant professor(s) a note on the need for the accommodation on such-and-such a date or over such-and-such a period. The paperwork does not describe the disability, only the requirement for accommodation.

Of all disabled students on a campus (orthopedically disabled, vision-impaired, hearing-impaired, depressed, etc.) statistics show that the LD and ADD students are the most likely to receive disability-related services. Nationally, 51.1 percent of LD and ADD students receive services (most likely accommodations) on campus, compared with 19 percent of mobility-impaired students, and 22 percent of visually or hearing-impaired students.

These data suggest several things. First, the ADD and LD population is more inclined than any other disabled group to request special services and also to receive them. The reason may be that the adjustments made for, say, physically or visually impaired populations—ramps, Braille signs, and the like— exist as permanent structures whose presence doesn't need to be requested by a disabled group; they're part of the campus universal design. By contrast, the academic accommodations have to be requested student-by-student. . . .

The Rules for Higher Education

Because of the different federal laws under which colleges and K-12 schools operate, some students who were eligible for accommodations/special treatment and services in K-12, and even when taking their SAT exam, find that they are not eligible for accommodations or services in college. Postsecondary institutions are not governed by the Individuals with Disabilities Education Improvement Act of 2004, which mandates services and intervention for students with special needs and disabilities in K-12 education.

Rather, higher education is governed by Section 504 of the Rehabilitation Act of 1973 and also the Americans with Disabilities Act. These are civil rights statutes, as opposed to education statutes, requiring that all postsecondary institutions make reasonable and necessary modifications to rules, policies, and practices to prevent discrimination and ensure access and opportunity for students with disabilities. "Equal access and opportunity" means the same access and opportunity available to the general population. Disability is defined under the ADA as "a physical or mental impairment that substantially limits one or more of the major life activities of such individual" who is disabled.

The requirement for "equal access and opportunity" is more uncertain and difficult to put into practice with respect to academic services than with, say, getting a physically disabled student to the second story of a building or to view a film. Until the ADA was amended in 2008, the threshold for providing accommodation for LD or ADD was that the student must prove not only that the disability exists but also that the disability prevents functioning in a given academic setting (say, a lecture, lab, or exam) at a level equal to that of the general population.

Some campuses appear more willing to grant accommodations than others. UNC-Chapel Hill turned down only one applicant for disability services, including accommodations, last year. By contrast, the University of North Alabama turns down half its applicants for disability services. . . . If more data were available on accommodations at various colleges, their differing rates of refusal would be easier to measure.

The difference from one college to the next also has to do with the different application processes. As noted, UNC-Chapel Hill has a committee that reviews the initial applications for services, but the decision whether to grant an accommodation is made by an individual disabilities expert. Other North Carolina colleges use individual administrators, not committees, to review disabilities cases.

Leaving the decision to a single administrator is the prevailing practice across the country. Yet that is where some of the trouble begins. A 2007 report by a coalition of LD and ADD advocacy groups and mental health professionals found that the disability experts in these offices do not always apply a consistent or legally rigorous standard in judging eligibility for accommodations. The report from the National Joint Committee on Learning Disabilities says that:

> at the postsecondary level, there is a lack of uniformity in determining whether an individual is eligible as a person with a disability and in identifying needed supplemental services and accommodations for access. There are no consistent or agreed upon principles related to interpretation of data and information to determine student eligibility, access to services, and appropriate accommodations.

This report, *The Documentation Disconnect for Students with Learning Disabilities: Improving Access to Postsecondary Disability Services*, also notes that "[s]econdary and postsecondary institutions differ in their programs and expectations . . . [and] educational decisions are made by postsecondary personnel with varying qualifications.". . .

Among the kinds of documentation sought is evidence that the applicant's level of intelligence and level of academic achievement are several standard deviations apart. This "discrepancy model" type of documentation demonstrates that the applicant's ability to achieve the level of academic performance typically associated with his or her level of intelligence would be impaired if the applicant's disability were not accommodated. . . .

On the majority of campuses where individuals, not committees, decide whether to grant accommodations, there remains concern about their fairness and legitimacy. Transparent, committee-based processes would ensure greater uniformity in decision making. A committee process would also provide a sturdier base from which to defend a decision to refuse a request for accommodation, if the refusal were appealed.

Faculty Views of Accommodation

For the most part, professors accept and cooperate with the accommodations system, this author's interviews suggest. Indeed, UNC-Chapel Hill disabilities administrators could think of only a handful of cases in the last two decades where professors disputed an accommodations request. The coordinator of UNC-Chapel Hill's Academic Success Program for Students with LD and ADHD, Theresa Maitland, explains that "[i]t's very rare to meet someone who isn't cooperative because in today's world these disabilities touch everyone. Often these professors have children or a grandchild who has these conditions, or they may have them themselves."

The experience of UNC-Chapel Hill history professor Richard Kohn is consistent with that assessment: In his 18 years at UNC, Kohn has found the staff of the disabilities services offices "reasonable in their recommendations, requirements, and behavior." He says that the offices "have extraordinary power, or at least used to: they can and probably occasionally do compel faculty to abide by their ruling." But he adds that "the bother to us faculty is truly minor."

But whether professors' cooperation comes about because all professors agree with an institution's LD and ADD accommodations policy or because some choose not to oppose it publicly for fear of the consequences of their opposition is far less clear.

A 2008 survey of 192 professors at a large Midwestern university on the subject of accommodations for LD students shows that some professors are ambivalent about whether testing and other accommodations of LD students are fair to students without accommodations. . . . Moreover, . . . professors were somewhat unwilling to provide major accommodations to students, including extra credit assignments, fewer assignments, reduced reading, or a different grading curve. [P]rofessors were somewhat willing to provide test accommodations. . . .

This author's interviews found similar results, albeit from a smaller sample. Few professors interviewed by this author were willing to have their names associated with criticism of the accommodations system, or even to be quoted anonymously on the subject. The criticism itself was forthcoming, however. Faculty members said that they thought that criticism of current accommodation practices was widely shared but unlikely to surface publicly. In the prevailing inclusive and egalitarian context of most colleges, their colleagues would want to avoid being associated with a position that may be construed as being anti-disabled. Several professors also noted that disabilities services offices are very powerful and that when the professors had had occasion to choose between trying to oppose their decisions or backing down, they had chosen simply to back down.

The role faculty members play in the accommodations process is one of implementation, not of judging the validity of the request. Their role is to agree to give the student the extra exam time or other accommodation, produce an exam several days early and submit it to the disabilities office, or prepare written lecture notes for the student, and the like.

To illustrate with a typical example involving exams, a student whose request for an accommodation has been granted by the disabilities office takes a paper form to his or her professor and requests extra time on an exam or a noise-free exam room, or, in the case of UNC-Chapel Hill, has a letter from the disabilities office e-mailed directly to the professor. The professor signs the paperwork, and then must plan accordingly. The professor must prepare a copy of the exam several days early to be sent to the disabilities office. Then, the student may start the exam, say, two hours earlier than the rest of the class, isolated from the other students so as not to share the exam's contents to those who are starting at the scheduled exam time. Or, if the accommodation relates to distractability, the student may start at the scheduled exam time but in a noise-free room. Other requests might include giving a disabled student advance notice of a pop quiz, providing extra time for submitting assignments, or submitting written lecture notes for the student.

It's easy to see how such requests might raise concerns among professors about cheating. UNC-Chapel Hill's Kessler recounts that one student's accommodation, which allowed the student to take an exam home to complete, led to questions about whether the student would cheat. Also, professors noted in interviews that when accommodated students don't begin the exam at the same time as the remaining students, or are not sequestered for the full duration of the other students' exam, they fear that the student could compromise its contents.

Other concerns were more minor, including the fact that sometimes professors must respond to students who bring in their accommodations forms a day or two before the accommodation is needed, requiring a scramble to produce an exam at the required deadline. It was also noted that students overall, in recent years, appear to have a sense of entitlement—albeit expressed politely—that students in the past did not. . . .

A final aspect of accommodations that raises concerns among professors is the accommodation's secrecy, or the accommodated student's right to privacy. For a start, under the federal Family Educational Rights and Privacy Act of 1974, the student's type of disability is kept secret from the professor and is not noted on the accommodations paperwork. Theoretically, a professor could request that the disabilities office supply more information about the student's disability—for example, by sharing the educational and medical documentation supporting the student's request for accommodations. The professor could do this on the grounds that he or she has a "legitimate educational interest" in understanding the disability's effects, according to an interpretation of the law provided by the U.S. Department of Education after some confusion was reported. But the department adds that a university or college would be free to deny such requests by having a policy against them.

Some professors chafe at this secrecy, objecting to changing their academic standards for one student in response to an assertion that is backed by secret evidence known only to the disabilities office, and not by verifiable fact. (Other professors said they have no interest in knowing about the student's condition, because they have no qualifications for assessing it.)

The wider problem with the secrecy surrounding the student's disability, however, is that professors must in turn keep the accommodation secret as well. Richard L. Stroup, an economics professor at North Carolina State University in Raleigh, says that professors are told by the disabilities office not to discuss accommodations with anyone. He and other professors interpret that to mean that if someone asks for an assessment of the student—in the form of a graduate school or job recommendation, for instance—the professor is obligated to withhold the information that the student had, say, twice as much time on exams as other students did. Stroup questions the propriety of drawing a professor into that sort of evasion. He also says that the accommodations process may not ultimately be beneficial to disabled students, because they acquire a false sense that they will be accommodated in the workplace, for instance by being given extra time to complete a task that is time-sensitive.

To be sure, a more open process for granting accommodations won't address all professors' concerns. But a review of accommodations policies could lead to explicit policy changes that would address the sense some professors have that they are being required to mislead third parties on the student's behalf. In addition, a committee system for granting accommodations in which professors could participate would tamp down the latent criticism that the accommodations process can be unfair. Such reforms wouldn't address all the controversy surrounding accommodations, however. Legal issues, questions about legitimacy of the diagnoses, as well as students' questions about fairness, would remain. . . .

ADA Amendments

A second legal development is likely to have a great infuence as well. In the fall of 2008, Congress amended the Americans with Disabilities Act, lowering the standard for assessing whether a person is "substantially limited in performing a major life activity" (to use ADA language), and therefore disabled. Congress's amendment, signed into law by President George W. Bush, states that its purpose is "to reject the standards enunciated by the Supreme Court in *Toyota Motor Manufacturing, Kentucky, Inc. v. Williams* . . . (2002)." Specifcally, Congress rejected the finding that

> the terms "substantially" and "major" in the definition of disability under the ADA "need to be interpreted strictly to create a **demanding** standard for qualifying as disabled," and that to be substantially limited in performing a major life activity under the ADA "an individual must have an impairment that prevents or severely restricts the individual from doing activities that are of central importance to most people's daily lives."

In practice, this change has significantly lowered the threshold for accommodation. . . .

As if that language in the amendment weren't enough to keep lawyers at postsecondary institutions busy, the amendment also states that "reasonable modifications in policies, practices, or procedures shall be required" to comply with its language—with a key exception. That exception occurs when "an entity can demonstrate that making such modifications in policies, practices, or procedures, including academic requirements in postsecondary education, would fundamentally alter the nature of the goods, services, facilities, privileges, advantages, or accommodations involved."

In other words, colleges and universities may be exempt from the new, looser definition of disability if they can show that applying it would alter the nature of their academic program and standards. Certainly, some professors might argue that the looser definition would indeed affect their academic freedom to assess their students fairly and according to their existing standards. . . .

Unless the institutions successfully use the loophole provided by the amended ADA, this legal trend may facilitate more eligibility for accommodations in college and university and bring with it associated costs in terms of personnel needed to administer the requests, faculty time in providing the additional required materials, and legal work required to comply with the new standards. At a time when both education budgets and budgets for disabilities programs are being cut by state governments, it's difficult to see how the changes to accommodations policy mandated by new federal law can be implemented with any ease.

Fairness Questions

Disabilities services experts on campus recognize that there is a risk that the accommodations they offer may be perceived by non-disabled students as unfair, particularly if the accommodations are granted too freely or subjectively, or if the requests come from students who are improperly qualified for them. The website of the disabilities services office at the University of Mississippi has gone so far as to post an article saying that over-accommodation of students who aren't entitled to them "may contribute to prejudices, lower academic standards, and fuel backlash by students and faculty that cannot be easily dispelled.". . .

[T]his author was unable to find students who were willing to talk about the fairness issue for this study. It would seem unlikely that the reason for the silence is full agreement with the policies. The director of disability services at UNC-Chapel Hill, Jim Kessler, said he hadn't heard of any overt student backlash against accommodations and attributed that to the fact that the accommodations such as extra time for exams are arranged privately, without other students knowing about them. He did note, though, that disabled students who do not participate in exams with the rest of the class face the risk of being asked by fellow students about their perennial absence during tests. . . .

One can see how controversy could arise over the demographic imbalance in ADD and LD diagnoses—as indicated earlier, the preponderance of these diagnoses are for white males from high-income families. Some minority and economically disadvantaged students may be entitled to disabilities diagnoses but don't receive them, either because their high schools didn't offer them the services that would have led to their diagnosis or because their parents couldn't afford private diagnoses or weren't aware of the issue to begin with. Thus, they might perceive the demographic imbalance as unfair. It's also worth recalling here that experts ranging from the UNC-Chapel Hill disability services director to administrators at the College Board say that students can and do buy diagnoses and accommodations. . . .

Recommendations and Conclusion

Learning disabilities and ADD are an important issue in campus life, if only because of the growing number of students diagnosed with these disabilities. The accommodation of these students through extra time on exams and other such provisions is increasing. Yet it is not widely discussed in public, for a variety of reasons including fear of being seen as anti-disabled.

But the issue is evoking controversy. As newspaper reports, scholarly publications, legal battles, and a handful of writings by professors imply, not everyone is in agreement about the degree to which LD and ADD students are accommodated, or should be accommodated, in higher education.

The controversy won't end anytime soon—indeed, there's a high probability it will grow if a less stringent disabilities law and upcoming legal decisions trigger more LD and ADD accommodations on campuses. Meanwhile, well-meaning administrators will be caught between a desire to serve the genuine needs of their disabled students and the need to avoid unfairness by granting accommodations to students who don't really deserve them.

At the very least or as an initial step, administrators should . . . open up their accommodations processes for closer scrutiny. They should include faculty members on panels that consider initial applications for accommodations—not just for appeals—so that legitimate concerns about academic quality and fairness can be addressed. Schools should have strict standards for determining eligibility and produce data on the numbers of accommodations granted, refused, and appealed per year.

Reporting on the numbers of requests for accommodation that are granted will reveal inconsistencies in ADA enforcement across campuses. It will also force openness on the subject while preserving the individual privacy of disabled students. It's surprising that the federal government doesn't require such reporting already.

A radical alternative would be to open up the accommodations to every student, where practicable. The idea has been floated among some testing and disabilities experts recently. It would follow the principle—attractive among disabilities experts—of universal design. For example, postsecondary institutions could let all students decide whether to have extra time (time-and-a-half, or double-time, say) on an exam, but make their extra time publicly known by flagging it on their grade reports. Thus, disabled students would have equal opportunity to do well on exams and would be able to avail themselves of accommodations without having to go through the ordeal of applying for them and being accepted or rejected. And other students who want the extra time could have it just by asking. This might help their performance, leveling the academic playing field for all, rather than only for those with a diagnosis, and undercutting any argument that the extra time is unfair. Flagging the grade reports would be a measure of extra time only, rather than a measure of disability, and thus would not be discriminatory.

To be sure, some professors may see time-and-a-half or double-time as unreasonable or impractical. In some fields, such as emergency medicine, it would indeed be unreasonable, because speedy completion of a task is of central importance. but that would not be the case in all areas of study. As accommodations rise, this "universal design" solution may be the greatest leveler of the playing field.

Accommodations of LD and ADD students are here to stay as long as there is an Americans with Disabilities Act and Section 504 of the Rehabilitation Act—and as long as there are students who suffer from impediments to learning. Unfortunately, the potential for abuse of LD and ADD diagnoses, as well as the accommodations process, is here to stay as well. Wise administrators would do well to report more fully on their accommodations process and make it more transparent and rigorous. Only that way can any latent perception of unfairness or compromised standards, whether from faculty or students, be done away with. Such openness would be to the benefit of the campus as a whole and disabled students in particular.

POSTSCRIPT

Should Colleges Be More Accommodating to Students with Disabilities?

Individuals with Disabilities Education Act (IDEA) entitlements to special education expire when a student turns 22 or receives a high school diploma. IDEA includes disability categories, which states enhance with specific regulations. In elementary and secondary schools, accommodations are seen as leveling the playing field, so individuals with disabilities have equal access to education. Multidisciplinary teams, including the student, convey information about accommodations and their direct relationship to a disability.

Postsecondary education is governed by the Americans with Disabilities Act and Section 504. No specific disability categories are listed in either. To be eligible for reasonable accommodations, individuals must have (or be regarded to have) a major physical or mental impairment that substantially limits one or more major life activities. Individuals must self-disclose their disability and accommodation status.

Hazel Denhart conveys the voices of college students diagnosed with learning disabilities who feel they are silenced, and limited by intolerance at the college level. Reluctant to use accommodations because of the stigma they encounter, the students develop advocacy skills through the support of specialists. The perceptions Denhart shares are underscored by Egan and Giuliano (*North American Journal of Psychology*, 2009) who found students with disabilities to be in a no-win situation. The undergraduates they interviewed expressed negative views of those who did well using accommodations. Without the accommodations, the students may not have equal access. The National Longitudinal Transition Study-2 (NLTS2) found that only 24% of students who received disability-related accommodations in high school did so in postsecondary settings.

Complicating the situation, Denhart's participants were not identified as needing disability-related accommodations during their K-12 education. Not having been part of IDEA's transition process, they would be coming fresh to the complexities of discussing a disability and identifying accommodations.

Melana Z. Vickers raises a key point when she notes that evaluations at the college level are inconsistent as are procedures for determining eligibility and assigning accommodations. In many colleges, a single individual determines a student's status. Faculty receive notices of accommodations and have limited avenues to learn about disabilities and their impact on learning. Describing postsecondary identification as a "heterogeneous mess," Sparks and Lovett (2009) find "the sheer number of criteria . . . is dizzying and the range of criteria is depressing" (p. 507).

The Association on Higher Education and Disability (AHEAD), a rich source of information, offers best practice advice in disability documentation (www.ahead.org). AHEAD notes that accurate information is necessary to establish protection from discrimination/harassment as well as to select accommodations and recommends that groups of stakeholders establish policies and practices that are consistent, individualized, and informative. Using existing information, knowledgeable examiners, and clear communication, colleges can design a disability support system that is consistent and not masked in mystery.

The current emphasis on preparing students to be college and/or career ready signals that the time is right to address this situation for the benefit of all. Are college students with disabilities increasing in number or are we seeing a new population venturing into college? Acknowledging the difference in laws, what consistent practices can higher education adopt from the K-12 systems and IDEA? Most importantly, how can we address the strong sentiments expressed by all the people interviewed by this issue's authors? Would their concerns be lessened if procedures were more consistent and transparent? Colleges cannot be more accommodating until these questions are solved.

Internet References . . .

Council for Exceptional Children

The Council for Exceptional Children (CEC) is the largest international professional organization addressing issues surrounding education of students with disabilities, as well as those who are gifted and talented. CEC's site introduces you to current events in the field, recent legislative developments, and an array of specialized divisions focused on particular aspects of special education.

http://www.cec.sped.org

IRIS Center for Faculty Enhancement

This joint project of researchers at Vanderbilt University and the Claremont Graduate University is funded by the U.S. Department of Education, Office of Special Education Programs. Signing up for the IRIS Web site brings you notices of various case study units addressing current topics. Resources are interactive and free of charge.

http://iris.peabody.vanderbilt.edu

Children and Adults with Attention-Deficit/ Hyperactivity Disorder

Children and Adults with Attention-Deficit/Hyperactivity Disorder (CHADD), founded in 1987 by families seeking information about this disorder, is now a national organization linked to a variety of activities. The CHADD Web site contains extensive information on ADHD and ADD and is helpful to anyone who wants to learn more about these conditions.

http://www.chadd.org

Autism Society of America

The mission of the Autism Society of America is to promote lifelong access and opportunity for all individuals within the autism spectrum, and their families, to be fully participating, included members of their community. Education, advocacy at state and federal levels, active public awareness, and the promotion of research form the cornerstones of ASA's efforts.

http://www.autism-society.org

National Institute of Mental Health

A branch of the National Institutes of Health, the National Institute of Mental Health (NIMH) is focused on generating and disseminating information regarding mental health conditions.

http://www.nimh.nih.gov

National Association for Gifted Children

The National Association for Gifted Children is a professional association dedicated to increasing public awareness about gifted learners, their needs, and appropriate services.

http://www.nagc.org

UNIT 3

Exceptionalities

*E*arlier sections of this book focus on global issues regarding the education of children who learn differently than their peers. In addition to the arenas of law, policy, and practice, controversies exist about the reality of particular exceptionalities and the efficacy of unique methodologies. The fervent desire of parents and educators to help children nurtures the development of approaches that promise success. The challenge of evaluating new ways of thinking will be with us as long as there are children who need extra support to realize their potential. We will face that challenge best when we work collaboratively.

- Do Gifted and Talented Students Need Special Schools?
- Can RTI Reduce the Number of Children Identified with Specific Learning Disability (SLD)?
- Is Mental Health Screening an Unwarranted Intrusion?
- Is ADHD a Real Disorder?
- Are There Scientifically Effective Treatments for Autism?
- Does Working with Parents Have to Be Contentious?

ISSUE 15

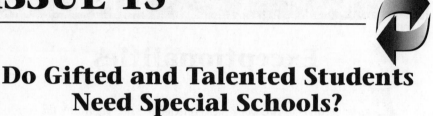

Do Gifted and Talented Students Need Special Schools?

YES: **John Cloud**, from "Are We Failing Our Geniuses?" *Time Magazine* (August 27, 2007)

NO: **Susan Winebrenner and Dina Brulles**, from *The Cluster Grouping Handbook* (Introduction) (Free Spirit Publishing, 2008)

ISSUE SUMMARY

YES: John Cloud, a staff writer for *Time Magazine* since 1997, profiles a number of extraordinarily gifted young people challenged for the first time in a specialized school that pushes them to reach their potential in a way that public schools could not.

NO: Susan Winebrenner and Dina Brulles work with educators to design and deliver cluster-based programs that address the needs of the gifted within their neighborhood school and provide options for a range of students to reach their potential.

T his *Taking Sides* focuses on individuals who have disabilities and require 504 plans or special education services. These students struggle the most with learning, requiring supplemental supports and services to make the progress that comes easily to others.

Another group of exceptional learners also require specialized programming and services. These students are at the other end of the bell curve—gifted and/or talented far beyond most of their age-mates.

No Child Left Behind (NCLB) defines the gifted and talented as "students, children, or youth who give evidence of high achievement capability in areas such as intellectual, creative, artistic, or leadership capacity, or in specific academic fields, and who need services and activities not ordinarily provided by the school in order to fully develop those capabilities" *(Title IX, Part A, Section 9101(22), p. 544)*.

The unique educational needs of gifted/talented students are not addressed by any federal mandates. Despite their need for programming "not ordinarily provided by the school," they are not covered by special education law because they do not have disabilities. There is no federal requirement to identify, or develop programs for, students who have unique gifts and/or talents.

The National Association for Gifted Children (NAGC) monitors the status of gifted/talented education. Programs are completely dependent on individual state policies and funding. "(In 2006–07), although 27 states mandate the identification of gifted students and 24 states mandate services, only five states provide funds to all districts by mandate; 10 by discretionary funding based on applications" (www.nagc.org). The sole source of federal funding is a grant competition funded by the Jacob K. Javits Gifted and Talented Student Education Program.

Extraordinarily gifted/talented minds have long fascinated psychologists, teachers, and parents. We each know our own children are brilliant, but who exactly is gifted? NAGC publishes a comprehensive reference evaluating existing research and indicating pressing needs in a range of topics, from policy to identification to instructional strategies (Plucker & Callahan, *Critical Issues and Practices in Gifted Education* [P&K], 2008).

One key chapter (Miller, P&K, 2008) reviews several ways giftedness is conceptualized. There is no universal definition. Proponents of Terman look for an IQ score more than two standard deviations above average. Gardner finds giftedness in one or more of eight independent multiple intelligences, ranging from linguistic to musical to intrapersonal. Renzulli differentiates between the schoolhouse-gifted and those who create/produce original products that impact society.

Educational options vary with the conceptualization of giftedness. A sampling includes early school admission, curriculum acceleration in small classes, acceleration through grade skipping, enrichment activities based on the standard curriculum, home schooling, mentoring (by professionals or older students), correspondence courses, summer institutes, and advanced coursework.

John Cloud believes the United States is failing our geniuses, stifling them in a bureaucratic system that lacks the knowledge or creativity to support challenging programs. Cloud presents compelling profiles of young learners who have outgrown their neighborhood schools and will wither and fade unless their talents are nurtured and guided. Cloud's students find room to grow at a unique private school.

Susan Winebrenner and Dina Brulles present the Schoolwide Cluster Grouping Model (SCGM): "an inclusion model in which students with exceptional learning needs are integrated into mixed-ability classrooms and teachers are expected to provide appropriate differentiation opportunities for any students who need them." By careful clustering, and attention to teacher professional development, SCGM stimulates the full range of students to flourish without having to leave home.

As you read these selections, ask yourself whether your state acknowledges the needs of gifted students. How does your district conceptualize giftedness? What model do you think works best?

YES

John Cloud

Are We Failing Our Geniuses?

In U.S. Schools, the Highest Achievers Are Too Often Challenged the Least. Why That's Hurting America—and How to Fix It

Any sensible culture would know what to do with Annalisee Brasil. The 14-year-old not only has the looks of a South American model but is also one of the brightest kids of her generation. When Annalisee was 3, her mother Angi Brasil noticed that she was stringing together word cards composed not simply into short phrases but into complete, grammatically correct sentences. After the girl turned 6, her mother took her for an IQ test. Annalisee found the exercises so easy that she played jokes on the testers—in one case she not only put blocks in the correct order but did it backward too. Angi doesn't want her daughter's IQ published, but it is comfortably above 145, placing the girl in the top 0.1% of the population. Annalisee is also a gifted singer: last year, although just 13, she won a regional high school competition conducted by the National Association of Teachers of Singing.

Annalisee should be the star pupil at a school in her hometown of Longview, Texas. While it would be too much to ask for a smart kid to be popular too, Annalisee is witty and pretty, and it's easy to imagine she would get along well at school. But until last year, Annalisee's parents—Angi, a 53-year-old university assistant, and Marcelo, 63, who recently retired from his job at a Caterpillar dealership—couldn't find a school willing to take their daughter unless she enrolled with her age-mates. None of the schools in Longview—and even as far away as the Dallas area—were willing to let Annalisee skip more than two grades. She needed to skip at least three—she was doing sixth-grade work at age 7. Many school systems are wary of grade skipping even though research shows that it usually works well both academically and socially for gifted students—and that holding them back can lead to isolation and underachievement. So Angi home schooled Annalisee.

But Angi felt something was missing in her daughter's life. Annalisee, whose three siblings are grown, didn't have a rich social network of other kids. By 13, she had moved beyond her mother's ability to meaningfully teach her. The family talked about sending her to college, but everyone was hesitant. Annalisee needed to mature socially. By the time I met her in February, she

From *Time Magazine*, August 27, 2007, pp. 41–47. Copyright © 2007 by Time Inc. Reprinted by permission via Rightslink.

had been having trouble getting along with others. "People are, I must admit it, a lot of times intimidated by me," she told me; modesty isn't among her many talents. She described herself as "perfectionistic" and said other students sometimes had "jealousy issues" regarding her.

The system failed Annalisee, but could any system be designed to accommodate her rare gifts? Actually, it would have been fairly simple (and virtually cost-free) to let her skip grades, but the lack of awareness about the benefits of grade skipping is emblematic of a larger problem: our education system has little idea how to cultivate its most promising students. Since well before the Bush Administration began using the impossibly sunny term "no child left behind," those who write education policy in the U.S. have worried most about kids at the bottom, stragglers of impoverished means or IQs. But surprisingly, gifted students drop out at the same rates as nongifted kids—about 5% of both populations leave school early. Later in life, according to the scholarly *Handbook of Gifted Education,* up to one-fifth of dropouts test in the gifted range. Earlier this year, Patrick Gonzales of the U.S. Department of Education presented a paper showing that the highest-achieving students in six other countries, including Japan, Hungary and Singapore, scored significantly higher in math than their bright U.S. counterparts, who scored about the same as the Estonians. Which all suggests we may be squandering a national resource: our best young minds.

In 2004–05, the most recent academic year for which the National Opinion Research Center (NORC) has data, U.S. universities awarded 43,354 doctorates— more than ever during the 50 years NORC has gathered the data. But the rate of increase in the number of U.S. doctorates has fallen dramatically since 1970, when it hit nearly 15% for the year; for more than a decade, the number of doctorates has grown less than 3.5% a year. The staggering late-1960s growth in Ph.D.s followed a period of increased attention on gifted kids after Sputnik. Now we're coasting.

To some extent, complacency is built into the system. American schools spend more than $8 billion a year educating the mentally retarded. Spending on the gifted isn't even tabulated in some states, but by the most generous calculation, we spend no more than $800 million on gifted programs. But it can't make sense to spend 10 times as much to try to bring low-achieving students to mere proficiency as we do to nurture those with the greatest potential.

We take for granted that those with IQs at least three standard deviations below the mean (those who score 55 or lower on IQ tests) require "special" education. But students with IQs that are at least three standard deviations above the mean (145 or higher) often have just as much trouble interacting with average kids and learning at an average pace. Shouldn't we do something special for them as well? True, these are IQs at the extremes. Of the 62 million school-age kids in the U.S., only about 62,000 have IQs above 145. (A similar number have IQs below 55.) That's a small number, but they appear in every demographic, in every community. What to do with them? Squandered potential is always unfortunate, but presumably it is these powerful young minds that, if nourished, could one day cure leukemia or stop global warming or become the next James Joyce—or at least J.K. Rowling.

In a no-child-left-behind conception of public education, lifting everyone up to a minimum level is more important than allowing students to excel to their limit. It has become more important for schools to identify deficiencies than to cultivate gifts. Odd though it seems for a law written and enacted during a Republican Administration, the social impulse behind No Child Left Behind is radically egalitarian. It has forced schools to deeply subsidize the education of the least gifted, and gifted programs have suffered. The year after the President signed the law in 2002, Illinois cut $16 million from gifted education; Michigan cut funding from $5 million to $500,000. Federal spending declined from $11.3 million in 2002 to $7.6 million this year.

What's needed is a new model for gifted education, an urgent sense that prodigious intellectual talents are a threatened resource. That's the idea behind the Davidson Academy of Nevada, in Reno, which was founded by a wealthy couple, Janice and Robert Davidson, but chartered by the state legislature as a public, tuition-free school. The academy will begin its second year Aug. 27, and while it will have just 45 students, they are 45 of the nation's smartest children. They are kids from age 11 to 16 who are taking classes at least three years beyond their grade level (and in some cases much more; two of the school's prodigies have virtually exhausted the undergraduate math curriculum at the University of Nevada, Reno, whose campus hosts the academy). Among Davidson's students are a former state chess champion, a girl who was a semifinalist in the Discovery Channel Young Scientist Challenge at age 11 (the competition is open to kids as old as 14) and a boy who placed fourth in both the Nevada spelling and geography bees even though he was a 12-year-old competing against kids as old as 15. And last year the school enrolled another talented kid from a town 1,700 miles (some 2,700 km) away: Annalisee Brasil, whose mother moved with her to Reno so Annalisee could attend the school (her father was working in Longview at the time).

The academy is being watched closely in education circles. The Davidsons are well-connected philanthropists who made their fortune in the education-software business—Jan and a friend conceived the hit Math Blaster program in the early 1980s. She and her husband sold Davidson & Associates for roughly $1.1 billion in 1996. They have given millions of dollars to universities and tens of thousands to Republican politicians like George W. Bush and Senator John Ensign of Nevada. Gifted kids often draw only flickering interest from government officials, but Secretary of Education Margaret Spellings attended the Davidson Academy's opening.

At the academy, the battered concept of IQ—complicated in recent years by the idea of multiple intelligences, including artistic and emotional acuity—is accepted there without the encumbrances of politics. The school is a rejection of the thoroughly American notion that if most just try hard enough, we could all be talented. Many school administrators oppose ability grouping on the theory that it can perpetuate social inequalities, but at the Davidson Academy, even the 45 élite students are grouped by ability into easier and harder English, math, and science classes. The school poses blunt questions about American education: Has the drive to ensure equity over excellence gone too far? If so, is the answer to segregate the brightest kids?

How We See Them

As a culture, we feel deeply ambiguous about genius. We venerate Einstein, but there is no more detested creature than the know-it-all. In one 1996 study from *Gifted Education Press Quarterly*, 3,514 high school students were asked whether they would rather be the best-looking, smartest, or most athletic kids. A solid 54% wanted to be smartest (37% wanted to be most athletic, and 9% wanted to be best looking). But only 0.3% said the reason to be smartest was to gain popularity. We like athletic prodigies like Tiger Woods or young Academy Award winners like Anna Paquin. But the mercurial, aloof, annoying nerd has been a trope of our culture, from Bartleby the Scrivener to the dorky PC guy in the Apple ads. Intellectual precocity fascinates but repels.

Educators have long debated what to do with highly gifted children. As early as 1926, Columbia education professor Leta Hollingworth noted that kids who score between 125 and 155 on IQ tests have the "socially optimal" level of intelligence; those with IQs over 160 are often socially isolated because they are so different from peers—more mini-adults than kids. Reading Hollingworth, I was reminded of Annalisee, who at 13 spoke in clear, well-modulated paragraphs, as though she were a TV commentator or college professor. For an adult, the effect is quite pleasant, but I imagine other kids find Annalisee's precision a bit strange.

In Hollingworth's day, when we were a little less sensitive to snobbery, it wasn't as difficult for high-ability kids to skip grades. But since at least the mid-1980s, schools have often forced gifted students to stay in age-assigned grades—even though a 160-IQ kid trying to learn at the pace of average, 100-IQ kids is akin to an average girl trying to learn at the pace of a retarded girl with an IQ of 40. Advocates for gifted kids consider one of the most pernicious results to be "cooperative learning" arrangements in which high-ability students are paired with struggling kids on projects. Education professor Miraca Gross of the University of New South Wales in Sydney has called the current system a "lockstep curriculum . . . in what is euphemistically termed the 'inclusion' classroom." The gifted students, she notes, don't feel included.

We tend to assume that the highly gifted will eventually find their way—they're smart, right? The misapprehension that genius simply emerges unbidden is related to our mixed feelings about intelligence: we know Alex Rodriguez had to practice to become a great baseball player, and we don't think of special schools for gymnasts or tennis prodigies as élitist—a charge already leveled against the Davidson Academy. But giftedness on the playing field and giftedness in, say, a lab aren't so different. As Columbia education professor Abraham Tannenbaum has written, "Giftedness requires social context that enables it." Like a muscle, raw intelligence can't build if it's not exercised.

People often wonder how to tell if their child is gifted. Truly gifted kids are almost always autodidacts. Take Max Oswald-Selis. He moved to Reno from Sydney with his mother Gael Oswald so that he could attend Davidson. Max is 12. The first time I saw him at the academy, he was reading an article about the Supreme Court. He likes to fence. He loves Latin because "it's a very regimented language. . . . There's probably at least 28 different endings for any given verb, because there's first-, second- and third-person singular and plural for each tense. . . ." He went on like this for some time. Max didn't get along especially well with classmates in Sydney and later Kent, England, where his mother first moved him in search of an appropriate school—and where she says he was beaten on the playground.

Max is Gael's only child, so when he taught himself to read at 3—she says she hadn't even taught him the alphabet—she wasn't sure it was so unusual. Then around age 4, he read aloud from a medical book in the doctor's office, and the doctor recommended intelligence testing. At 4, Max had the verbal skills of a 13-year-old. He skipped kindergarten, but he was still bored, and his mother despaired. No system is going to be able to keep up, she thought.

Gael, a math teacher, began to research giftedness and found that high-IQ kids can become isolated adults. "They end up often as depressed adults . . . who don't have friends or who find it difficult to function," she says. Actually, research shows that gifted kids given appropriately challenging environments—even when that means being placed in classes of much older students—usually turn out fine. At the University of New South Wales, Gross conducted a longitudinal study of 60 Australians who scored at least 160 on IQ tests beginning in the late '80s. Today most of the 33 students who were not allowed to skip grades have jaded views of education, and at least three are dropouts. "These young people find it very difficult to sustain friendships because, having been to a large extent socially isolated at school, they have had much less practice . . . in developing and maintaining social relationships," Gross has written. "A number have had counseling. Two have been treated for severe depression." By contrast, the 17 kids who were able to skip at least three grades have mostly received Ph.D.s, and all have good friends.

At the Davidson Academy, all the kids are skipping ahead quickly—in some cases they completed more than two years of material last year. There's no sixth grade or ninth grade or any grade at the academy, just three tracks ("core," "college prep," and "college prep with research"). The curriculums are individualized and fluid—some students take college-prep English but core-level math. I sat in on the Algebra II class one day, but it wasn't so much a traditional class as a study session guided by the teacher, Darren Ripley. Kids worked from different parts of the textbook. (One 11-year-old was already halfway through; most Americans who take Algebra II do so at 15 or 16.) Occasionally Ripley would show a small group how to solve a problem on the whiteboard, but there was no lecture.

The Founders

Ultimately the academy's most important gift to its students is social, not academic. One of the main reasons Jan and Bob Davidson founded the school was to provide a nurturing social setting for the highly gifted. Through another project of theirs, the Davidson Institute for Talent Development, each year the Davidsons assist 1,200 highly gifted students around the U.S. who need help persuading their schools to let them skip a grade or who want to meet other kids like them. Often the kids are wasting away in average classes, something that drives Bob Davidson crazy: "I mean, that's criminal to send a kid [who already reads well] to kindergarten. . . . Somebody should go to jail for that! That is emotional torture!"

Davidson, 64, carries an air of peremptory self-assurance. He unself-consciously enjoys his place in the plutocracy. During a tour of the Lake Tahoe manse he and Jan, 63, call Glen Eagle, he showed me his red Ferrari, his private theater, and the two 32-ft. totem poles just inside the entry. They are made from cedar at least 750 years old and feature carvings of the Davidsons and their three kids, who are now grown. Bob sees his work for the gifted as akin to the patronage that sustained the artists and inventors of the Renaissance. His view of giftedness is expressed through simple analogies: Educators often "want people to have equal results. But that's not likely in our world. You know, I would love to be equal to Michael Jordan in my basketball talents, but somehow I never will be."

But such an uncomplicated view of intelligence—one that esteems IQ scores and raw mental power—has had at least one awkward consequence for the Davidson Academy: it doesn't mirror America. Twenty-six of the 45 students are boys; only two are black. (A total of 16 are minorities.) The school is unlikely ever to represent girls and African Americans proportionately because of a reality about IQ tests: more boys score at the high end of the IQ scale (and, it should be said, more score at the low end; girls' IQ variance is smaller). And for reasons that no one understands, African Americans' IQ scores have tended to cluster about a standard deviation below the average—evidence for some that the tests themselves are biased.

Not everyone at the academy embraces a strict IQ-based definition of giftedness. Its curriculum director, Robert Schultz, emphasizes the importance of interpersonal skills, passion, and tenacity in long-term success. Still, the Davidsons point out, correctly, that they are serving an underserved population, kids whose high IQs can make them outcasts. The academy provides a home for them and also functions to check their self-regard since they finally compete day to day with kids who are just as bright. Because everyone at Davidson performs so well, says Claire Evans, 12, "other kids can't say, 'Well, I'm better than you because I did this good.' I did that good too!" (Of course, being labeled prodigies in stories like this one probably inflates them, but researchers have found that outside labeling has less effect on your self-concept than where you fit in with peers you see every day.) Going to Davidson has been an adjustment for kids used to "being on the top of the pile," in the words of Colleen Harsin, 36, the academy's director. Harsin has heard Davidsonians arrive at difficult realizations: "I'm not as smart as I thought I was." "Somebody's better at math than I am. That's never happened."

A New Isolation?

No matter their IQs, these are still kids on the rocky promontory of adolescence. Hormones crackle; tempers rise. The boys shove; the girls gossip; a kid hits another kid during volleyball. "They are O.K. with the team sports, but this is a group that really loves the individual sports—the rock climbing was a big hit," says Kathy Dohr, the gym teacher. You do get the sense sometimes that the Davidson students are alone together. An older boy who says he was beaten up at other schools told me, "I can't say I have many friends here, but I'm not hated. . . . The school does tend to be pretty much sort of cliquish."

The academy has been good for Annalisee Brasil, even though dividing into two households has been expensive and stressful for the Brasils. She has made friends at the academy and at the university, where this summer she completed a precalculus course so that she can take college calculus in the fall. She has also developed an interest in biochemistry. Socially, Annalisee is finally learning to get along with others in a close-knit setting. "It's been interesting having to deal with that and getting used to, you know, the judgments of other kids," she told me in February. "We get into arguments a lot, because we're all really smart people with opinions, and it doesn't always turn out that great. Sometimes I take things a little too personally. You know, I'm the typical sensitive artist, unfortunately."

The Davidson kids feel less isolated, but have the Davidsons simply created another kind of isolation for their students? When I asked curriculum director Schultz this question, he replied in an e-mail that schools can nurture traits like "civic virtue and community development." And he warned of the alternative: "Essentially these individuals are left to their own devices [in regular schools] and really struggle to find a space for themselves. . . . Some successfully traverse society's pitfalls (for instance, Albert Einstein); others are less successful (for instance, Theodore Kaczynski). In either case, unless performance was noted as deficient (in Einstein's case, he was believed to be a mute) via school personnel, schools did nothing to provide services. This continues today."

But there is something to be said for being left to one's own devices and learning to cope in difficult surroundings. Einstein is a good example: it's a myth that Einstein failed math, but he hated his Munich school, the Luitpold Gymnasium. Like many other gifted kids, he chafed at authority. "The teachers at the elementary school seemed to me like drill sergeants, and the teachers at the gymnasium are like lieutenants," he later said. Einstein was encouraged to leave the school, and he did so at 15. He didn't need a coddling academy to do O.K. later on.

That's not to say the best approach is a cold Dickensian bed. But Einstein's experience does suggest a middle course between moving to Reno for an élite new school and striking out alone at age 15. Currently, gifted programs too often admit marginal, hardworking kids and then mostly assign field trips and extra essays, not truly accelerated course work pegged to a student's abilities. Ideally, school systems should strive to keep their most talented students through a combination of grade skipping and other approaches (dual enrollment in community colleges, telescoping classwork without grade skipping) that ensure they won't drop out or feel driven away to Nevada. The best way to treat the Annalisee Brasils of the world is to let them grow up in their own communities—by allowing them to skip ahead at their own pace. We shouldn't be so wary of those who can move a lot faster than the rest of us.

Susan Winebrenner
and Dina Brulles

 **NO**

The Cluster Grouping Handbook

Within the current politics of education, the focus of most educators is on the learning needs of students who score below grade-level standards. There is a general assumption that students who can score well on standardized tests must be learning. When we speak of children being "left behind," we are usually referring to those students who are scoring below desired levels. The need for students performing below grade level to be supported so they can meet and even exceed standards is not in dispute. Equally indisputable are the consequences faced by students, teachers, parents, administrators, and schools when students do not reach these standards. But in our efforts to reach and teach struggling students in order to bring all students to grade-level performance standards, are some students being overlooked or underserved? What attention is focused on learners who readily master the content and are ready to move forward even though many of their classmates are not? Or on those exceptional students who walk in the classroom on the first day of school already able to pass state grade-level tests with exemplary scores? If learning can be described as forward progress from the entry point at the beginning of a school year, then the students who are most likely to be "left behind" when it comes to individual academic growth may be the students with exceptionally high ability—those we call gifted learners.

The field of gifted education is currently experiencing its lowest level of political support since the early 1960s. The launching of *Sputnik I* by the Soviet Union had created intense interest in nurturing America's most capable students so they could help the United States compete with the Soviets in the space race. Now, decades later, attention to No Child Left Behind (NCLB) has significantly reduced political interest in challenging gifted students in our school. Budget cuts have led to the reduction or elimination of gifted-education positions in many school districts. This affects not only gifted students but also high-performing students not necessarily categorized as gifted. Fewer students in the United States are majoring in science and mathematics than in past years. At the present time, more than 90 percent of the scientists in the world are being educated in Asia.

The United States' position as a world leader may be at greater risk from the challenges to its educational system than from any other factor. Egalitarian issues and budget concerns have led to the elimination of ability grouping in favor of heterogeneous grouping practices. The absence of ability grouping

From *The Cluster Grouping Handbook* by Susan Winebrenner and Dina Brulles (Free Spirit Publishing, 2008), pp. 1–8 (excerpts). Copyright © 2008. Reprinted by permission of Free Spirit Publishing, Inc., Minneapolis, MN. All rights reserved. www.freespirit.com

practices has led to the loss of attention to the differentiated learning needs of gifted and high-achieving students. As a consequence, many highly able students are leaving their established public schools in favor of charter schools and homeschooling, taking away from their school districts valuable talent along with considerable tax dollars.

Without visible and continuous support for gifted students, forces now present in the field of gifted education are being impacted. Some state legislatures have abandoned the practice of earmarking funds specifically for gifted education, which leaves the decision of funding gifted services to the discretion of each school or district. Fewer jobs are available for educators who want to specialize in teaching gifted students. Little state or national attention is directed toward the fact that gifted students may be consistently denied regular opportunities to experience at least one year's academic growth for each year they are in school. Most importantly, many parents are being told that their gifted children will experience differentiation in the regular classroom, while the reality is that very little of classroom teachers' efforts at differentiation are being addressed to gifted learners. It takes specialized training for classroom teachers to know how to challenge gifted students. Effective differentiation for the gifted will generally not take place until teachers have noticeable numbers of those students in their classes and until they have received training in how to effectively motivate and challenge them.

Why Meet the Learning Needs of High-Ability Students?

On a day-to-day basis, the highest-ability students usually receive the least amount of the teacher's time. Based on their high test scores and grades, these students are expected to make it on their own or with a minimal amount of guidance.

Looking at students on a bell curve provides a striking illustration of the inequity of this situation, and of what can be lost as a result. While the bell curve has the potential to create unease among some educators, we use it for one purpose only: to demonstrate that the learning needs of students at both ends of the learning continuum are identical.

. . . To teach a class of students, effective teachers usually plan the content, pacing, and quantity of instruction based on what is known about typical students of the age and grade for that class. In a mixed-ability classroom, these are the students in the middle of a heterogeneous group—those students of average abilities on the bell curve. In this same classroom, there will be a number of students who come to the grade level missing many of the basic understandings that typically would have been acquired in earlier grades. These are the students to the left on the bell curve. A third group of students will also be part of this classroom: those who are ahead of their grade-level peers in what they know and can do. These are the students to the right on the bell curve.

When teachers discover struggling students in their class—those below or left of average on the bell curve—they make instant adjustments to their methods of teaching. They may change the pace by moving a bit slower. They may lessen the amount of work for some students. They may change the methods they use to accommodate the learning styles of struggling students. They may change the way in which they interact with the students and try to pair them up with partners who can work well with them. They may adjust the content to reinforce prerequisite concepts that were not learned in earlier grades.

Teachers make these necessary adjustments because the students' learning needs *differ from the average.* Now imagine folding that bell curve in half, left to right. You will clearly see that gifted students are *as far removed from average* on the right side of the curve as are struggling students on the left side. While there are myriad reasons for supporting gifted children's educational growth, this fact alone provides a clear justification for exactly the same intervention to accommodate their needs—an adjustment of pacing, content, workload, and approach to teaching and learning. Gifted students need a faster pace, a smaller amount of practice with grade-level standards, an understanding of their independent work style, a teacher who is comfortable acting as a guide and coach, and opportunities to work with partners who are similar in learning ability, style, and preferences. They need this not because they are gifted, but because they are *not average.*

Gifted students are no more "special" than any others. However, grade-level standards describe what typical students should be able to learn at a certain age. When we accept the fact that gifted children are able to learn at levels that exceed their chronological age expectations, we immediately understand why grade-level standards must be adjusted for them. We do this because, like those students who struggle to meet the standards, gifted students are equally divergent from the "norm."

Meeting the Needs of All Students: The Schoolwide Cluster Grouping Model (SCGM)

We present a unique approach to help schools meet the needs of all students, including those who are gifted. It is called the Schoolwide Cluster Grouping Model (SCGM). The practice of cluster grouping students is gaining popularity in many states since the method can provide full-time academic services to gifted students without major budget implications and it has the potential to raise achievement for all students in the grade levels that are clustered. With the SCGM, gifted students are grouped into classrooms based on their abilities, while all other students are placed according to their achievement levels. Cluster grouping with the SCGM is different from other cluster grouping methods because the classroom compositions are carefully structured with two main goals: (1) to ensure a balance of abilities throughout the grade level *without returning to the practice of tracking* and (2) to reduce the learning range found in every classroom.

. . . These two goals can be accomplished by dividing the students at a given grade level into five groups. Group 1 represents the identified gifted students who will be in the gifted cluster. Group 2 represents high-achieving students who are not gifted but are very capable learners. These students will be clustered and placed in the classes that do not have the gifted-cluster group. (Clustering gifted students and high-achieving students not identified as gifted in separate classrooms is a key component of the SCGM, which has been shown to expand academic growth for both groups.) Group 3 represents students with average academic performance. Group 4 represents students whose performance is below average, and Group 5 represents students who produce work that falls considerably below grade-level expectations, or those with significant learning challenges. Students who are identified as "twice-exceptional"—those who are gifted and also have a learning challenge—are placed in Group 1, as are identified gifted students who are not fluent in English. . . . Typical gifted-cluster classrooms will include students from Groups 1, 3, and 4; the other classrooms at the grade level will include students from Groups 2, 3, 4, and 5. Ideally, no classroom will include both gifted students *and* students who perform far below average, so the achievement range in all classrooms will be narrower than that of a randomly heterogeneous classroom.

How does this type of clustering differ from tracking? The two main differences are that, in the SCGM, all classes are heterogeneous and all students are provided a varied curriculum. Opportunities for moving faster or going deeper into the curriculum are consistently offered to the entire class, which means there are times when some students in the gifted-cluster group (Group 1) will be experiencing differentiation and times when they won't. There are also times when students not identified as gifted can benefit from available differentiated learning opportunities.

This is different from a tracking system, in which all students are grouped by ability for much of the school day and are rarely exposed to learning experiences that extend their expected achievement ranges. In a tracking system, students are assigned a set curriculum based on their ability level, and they generally do not veer from that curriculum. With schoolwide cluster grouping, every class in the grade level has students with a range of learning abilities and levels. In order to reach that range, the teachers naturally have to modify or extend the grade-level standards.

In the SCGM . . ., all classes have high-performing students. While one or two classes have a cluster of gifted students, all other classes have a cluster of high-achieving students who, while not identified as gifted, can easily serve as positive academic role models. In a cluster model, learning opportunities are open to all students in the class, and teachers use their students' entry points, or readiness, to determine levels and pace of curriculum. Teachers are trained in differentiation and curriculum compacting, students receive ongoing assessment, and the results of schoolwide cluster grouping are continually evaluated.

What the Research Says About Cluster Grouping

Research documenting the benefits of keeping gifted students together in their areas of greatest strength for at least part of the school day supports the philosophy behind schoolwide cluster grouping. Moreover, the research suggests that all students, including those categorized as average and below-average students, thrive when gifted students are placed in their own cluster groups within heterogeneous classes.

The SCGM is an inclusion model in which students with exceptional learning needs are integrated into mixed-ability classrooms and teachers are expected to provide appropriate differentiation opportunities for any students who need them. An inclusion model has already been in use for many years as a method for providing special education services to students who have been identified as having exceptional educational needs. However, it is only when a class has a noticeable group of gifted students—a cluster—that teachers will be most likely to accommodate *their* exceptional educational needs. When there are only one or two gifted students in a class, teachers often tend to assume the students are learning as long as they are getting high grades and, as a result, minimize or overlook their need for expanded learning opportunities. Teachers are also likely to count on these students to help other students with their learning, a practice that robs the gifted students of opportunities to move forward in academic areas.

Clustering requires that teachers differentiate instruction. Differentiation occurs when teachers modify the curriculum and their instructional methods in response to the needs, strengths, learning styles, and interests of individual students so that *all* students have an opportunity to learn at their full potential. To be successful, the gifted-cluster teacher must have ongoing training in how to teach high-ability students in the cluster model. The SCGM creates a setting for providing appropriate instruction that is feasible for teachers and for enhancing the likelihood that differentiation will take place.

The SCGM: Who Benefits, and How?

The SCGM offers a win-win educational approach that benefits all stakeholders in the school community—students, teachers, administrators, and parents. Grouping gifted children in a regular classroom can provide academic, social, and emotional advantages to the students and make teaching gifted students more manageable for teachers. Gifted students feel more comfortable when there are other students like them in the class. They are more likely to choose challenging tasks when they can do that work in the company of other students. Teachers attuned to differentiating instruction are more likely to provide appropriate learning opportunities for gifted students and for other students as well. The school is able to provide a full-time, cost-effective program for gifted students since their learning needs are being met every day. Parents who are satisfied that their children are experiencing consistent challenge at school are more ready to work cooperatively with the school and the teachers and less likely to remove their children from public education.

Impact of the SCGM on Gifted Students

Gifted students who are clustered demonstrate high achievement because they experience more consistent challenge in their learning activities. Their scores on achievement tests show forward progress—rather than lost ground, as has been the case in some schools where gifted students are not placed in clusters or are not consistently challenged in other ways.

When gifted students are purposefully clustered in otherwise heterogeneous classes, rather than split up so that each class has one or two gifted students, their learning needs are much more likely to be noticed by the teacher. They also enjoy more attention to their social and emotional needs because of the specialized training the teacher receives.

Cluster grouping also makes it more likely that gifted kids will work to their full potential and take advantage of available differentiated learning opportunities because they will have other students to work with on these advanced learning tasks. Having serious competition from other students like themselves, they begin to develop more realistic perceptions of their abilities and to better understand and accept their learning differences. With so many opportunities to work and learn together, gifted students become more comfortable working at extended levels of complexity and depth in a given subject or topic. Their willingness to take risks in learning experiences increases when they spend time with others who share the same interests, have similar abilities, and can also benefit from the available differentiation opportunities.

Impact of the SCGM on English Language Learners

Cluster grouping offers exciting opportunities for schools to meet the needs of gifted English language learners (ELL students). When gifted students are served only in a pull-out model, gifted students who are not proficient in English are frequently kept out of services because of their inability to work at the same pace and level as the gifted students already proficient in English. With cluster grouping, extended learning opportunities are available in the regular classroom. When ELL students with high learning potential are present in classes where consistent challenge is available, they make faster progress in attaining English fluency and academic achievement.

A significant increase in achievement in students of different ethnic groups can also be expected from using cluster grouping. These findings result from classes in which teachers can be more focused and effective in their teaching. Another reason for the achievement gains is that gifted-education training required for cluster teachers helps the teachers set high expectations for *all* students—expectations to which students respond positively.

Impact of the SCGM on All Students

It has already been noted that students at all ability levels benefit from this model because teachers have more training in how to differentiate the curriculum and the pacing for all types of students, ensuring that learning success can be within the reach of all. A further benefit results from the fact that gifted and high-achieving students are motivated, work more independently and are allowed to spend more learning time on activities that interest and challenge them, opening up more time for teachers to spend with those who need additional assistance.

As teachers become more adept at recognizing giftedness in their students, the number of students they nominate for gifted testing increases yearly in schools that use the SCGM. This is especially noticeable in classes that do *not* have the gifted cluster, demonstrating the benefit of clustering high-achieving children who are *not* identified as gifted in separate classrooms. These classroom structures provide opportunities for the high-achieving students to thrive and emerge as new academic leaders.

Impact of the SCGM on Teachers

Student achievement is positively correlated with effective teaching. The SCGM allows teachers to be more effective because they are teaching a class with a smaller range of learning levels. The system provides opportunities for teachers to more readily respond to the needs of all their students, to challenge gifted students clustered together in mixed-ability classes, and to engage in practices that lead to improved academic achievement for students not identified as gifted, working at or above grade level. As a result, over time with the SCGM, more students in a school are identified as high achievers and fewer as low achievers.

For a school that already has a pull-out program for gifted students, the cluster model makes scheduling out-of-class activities easier. The resource (pull-out) teacher has to work with only one classroom teacher's schedule per grade level instead of the schedules of all the teachers at a particular grade level. The gifted-cluster teacher, whose gifted students venture to another classroom for pull-out services, understands that while they are gone, students who remain should be experiencing activities that reinforce standards the gifted students have already mastered. Therefore, when the students return from the pull-out program, they do not have any "missed" classroom work to "make up," and the teacher does not have the added layer of planning and record keeping that typically comes with makeup work.

When the SCGM is implemented with the goal that all teachers will eventually receive the related staff development, over time it is possible to ensure that all teachers who wish to teach a classroom with a gifted cluster will have the opportunity. At the same time, teachers, students in all classrooms benefit from the teachers' facility with differentiating the curriculum to meet students' varied learning needs.

Impact of the SCGM on Administrators

Schools that use the SCGM find that they can still offer valuable services for their gifted students even in the presence of reduced budgets or lack of political support. This helps administrators assure parents of gifted students that their children's learning needs will be served. Cluster grouping actually provides full-time placement and service for gifted students in the schools *without* the cost of creating and maintaining a separate gifted-education program. Gifted students are retained in the public school system and, moreover, gifted education becomes part of the school culture.

When schools take the time to implement the SCGM strategically, carefully planning the groups for cluster classrooms, training as many teachers as possible to implement gifted-education strategies, educating parents about how their children's school experience will be affected, and conducting ongoing student assessments and program evaluations, the result can be a cohesive and budget-friendly schoolwide approach to gifted education that brings the school community together as it raises student achievement levels.

Impact of the SCGM on Parents

Providing a cluster grouping model announces to the community that the school is committed to recognizing and serving its gifted students and enhancing achievement opportunities for all students. As parents of gifted students come to understand how clustering impacts their children's learning opportunities, they see that the schools are providing full-time gifted services, that teachers are responding to their children's needs, and that their gifted children spend time learning with other students of similar ability. Parents of students *not* identified as gifted are also likely to appreciate the opportunities the clustering arrangements and differentiation strategies afford their children. When these parents become familiar with the research that shows how the SCGM facilitates the emergence of new leaders in classes that do not have a gifted cluster, they may realize that, for the first time, their children have more opportunities to demonstrate academic leadership roles. Many students have had this very positive experience as a result of schoolwide cluster grouping.

POSTSCRIPT

Do Gifted and Talented Students Need Special Schools?

The authors describe two very different worlds. The students at Davidson Academy learn how to use the full range of their abilities, stretching each day. Ruf (*Losing Our Minds*, 2005) identifies five levels of giftedness, emphasizing the critical need for specialized programming. Without this, students become frustrated with the boredom of everyday work and can appear to have behavior problems.

Susan Winebrenner and Dina Brulles present a model that provides the benefits of ability grouping without the isolation of tracking. Educators maintain high levels of professional skill, which benefits all learners. Carol Ann Tomlinson, who writes extensively about differentiated instruction, underscores the need to support teachers through the hard work of continuous differentiation.

Efficacy research is not conclusive, partially due to the inability to use control groups, but Schroth (P&K, 2008) finds one absolute: any service is better than none. As described, cluster models benefit a range of students, and more students are identified as high achievers. They are, indeed, "financially friendly." On the other hand, students in public special schools with a disciplinary focus outperform gifted peers in all other learning environments. The logistics of residential schools, however, are frequently impractical.

Two other aspects of gifted education demand consideration: underrepresentation of minorities and of those who are twice exceptional. Both must be considered.

The underrepresentation of ethnically diverse students in gifted programs is a long-acknowledged fact (Gentry, Hu, & Thomas, P&K, 2008). This is especially the case with African American boys and Latino children. Although Asians are frequently described as "overrepresented" in gifted education, a finer breakdown reveals that this is not uniformly so of all Asian groups. Ford (*Journal for the Education of the Gifted*, 2003) is concerned that the effects of poverty can mask the strengths of a gifted child. She advises a move away from traditional, normed IQ tests to alternative measures that take into consideration the complex contexts of student lives.

Context is also critical for twice-exceptional children—those who are both gifted and have a disability. An illuminating study by the National Education Association (www.nea.org.specialed, 2006) found three basic categories of twice-exceptional children. First are those who have been formally identified as gifted, but not as having a disability: their giftedness masks the disability (think of a very bright child with a learning disability). Second are those

331

formally identified as having a disability, but not as gifted: the disability masks the giftedness (consider someone's first impression of Helen Keller). The third group of children may not have been formally identified under either category: the characteristics combine to present the appearance of an average student.

Concern for gifted education has another dimension given NCLB's target of universal proficiency by 2013–14. Especially in working class schools, Carnevale (*Education Week,* 2007) warns that gifted students are left behind as the majority struggle to get to "average." In more affluent districts, parents may focus more on college entrance standards, raising the standards beyond the basic.

Each of these issues becomes more compelling when funds are in short supply. John Cloud challenges us to explain why society's commitment to the gifted should not be at least as large its commitment to athletes, or to those with disabilities. And yet, according to the Javits Web site (www.ed.gov/programs/javits/awards.html), "In 2007, the Javits appropriation was cut substantially. As a result, a new competition . . . will not be held. Future competitions are contingent upon future appropriations." What is the future for our gifted children? Can we afford to wait to find out? Can they?

ISSUE 16

Can RTI Reduce the Number of Children Identified with Specific Learning Disability (SLD)?

YES: Lynn S. Fuchs, from *NRCLD Update on Responsiveness to Intervention: Research to Practice* (National Research Center on Learning Disabilities, Winter 2007)

NO: Cathy G. Litty and J. Amos Hatch, from "Hurry Up and Wait: Rethinking Special Education Identification in Kindergarten," *Early Childhood Education Journal* (February 2006)

ISSUE SUMMARY

YES: Lynn S. Fuchs, a prolific scholar in the area of learning disabilities and one of the several researchers in the National Research Center for Learning Disabilities, explains how Research to Intervention (RTI) strategies can separate a struggling learner from one with specific learning disability (SLD).

NO: Cathy G. Litty (Western Carolina University) and J. Amos Hatch (University of Tennessee) discuss the increasing academic pressures for kindergarten children; they believe special education services should be provided as soon as possible to students who will eventually be found eligible.

Specific learning disability (SLD), is the disability designation for the majority of students covered by IDEA. It is the only disability specifically defined in IDEA, and the only one for which assessment methodology is addressed.

Students with SLD encounter substantial learning difficulties not attributable to other disabilities, such as mental retardation or a sensory impairment. They have not experienced environmental, cultural, or economic disadvantage. They have received quality instruction. In other words, all the conditions for learning are present, but learning is not occurring at a developmentally typical rate.

Assessment to determine SLD has traditionally focused on the concept of severe discrepancy. Educators and psychologists looked for a significant difference between the student's ability (usually measured by an IQ test) and academic achievement. Many complain that this process requires students to "wait to fail," since the discrepancy often does not become significant during the earliest years of school.

Prevalence rates for SLD vary from under 3% of all students in Georgia to 7% in Rhode Island (LD Summit Consensus, 2001). This variation likely reflects inconsistent approaches to identification, using SLD as "the sociological sponge that wipes up the spills of general education" (Gresham, LD Summit, 2001).

Courts have found a lack of evidence in favor of the discrepancy model as well as documented standardized test bias against minority children and English language learners (Zirkel, *CEC*, 2006). These challenges, along with concern for the sheer number of students in this category, led Congress to address SLD identification directly.

IDEA 2004 signaled a dramatic shift in the way schools could identify students as having SLD. Districts are now directed not to require that teams rely solely on finding an ability/achievement gap. Instead, teams "may use a process which determines if a student responds to scientific, research-based intervention." Schools can use the approaches in combination.

Briefly, assessment through RTI involves gathering student progress information on a consistent basis, beginning with universal screening. All students are to experience research-based classroom instruction (Tier 1). Students whose regular in-class assessments show an unsatisfactory rate of growth would receive more intense general education services and progress monitoring (Tier 2). Those who do not respond to this level of assistance move on to Tier 3 or higher. If formal evaluation rules out the exclusionary factors listed above, the student could be identified with SLD and be considered for special education.

Diagnosis through RTI accomplishes two ends. RTI acts as a prevention tool, focusing teacher attention on students who are progressing slowly. Interventions address difficulties before they become large enough to warrant disability status. Students and teachers no longer need wait for the discrepancy to reach significance.

Lynn S. Fuchs, whose research identifies both benefits and risks in using RTI, believes the number of students found to have SLD will be reduced by effective general education intervention. Checking student progress on a regular basis, and providing data-based help as soon as it seems needed, will help many children learn successfully without resorting to special education.

In the second selection, Cathy G. Litty and J. Amos Hatch, university faculty members, describe the hurried academic pace of today's kindergartens. Even though teachers can monitor student progress, and adjust teaching strategies, Litty and Hatch fear this just delays necessary special education services for students who need them.

As you read these articles, consider the viewpoints they present. Will RTI be the key to reducing SLD numbers? Or will it merely postpone the inevitable?

YES

Lynn S. Fuchs

NRCLD Update on Responsiveness to Intervention: Research to Practice

What RTI Is

Students with SLD make up the majority of school-age individuals with disabilities. The number of students with SLD has increased (from 1.2 million in 1979–1980 to 2.9 million in 2003–2004). Many policymakers and school administrators are concerned about the increasing numbers of students with SLD. The concern is that some of these students may be capable of learning without special education if they are provided effective general education.

The usual method for identifying SLD relies on the difference between IQ and achievement. Research now shows that this method has many problems. For example, children who read poorly have similar characteristics, regardless of whether they have a discrepancy between IQ and achievement. Also, the size of discrepancy does not indicate the severity of the SLD. Moreover, data obtained through an assessment of the IQ-achievement discrepancy do not inform instruction in important ways.

RTI is a promising model for a new way to identify SLD as a student's failure to respond to teaching methods that research has shown to work well for most students.

Here is one example of an RTI process.

STEP 1: All students in a school are given short tests. The aim is to identify those students whose scores are low and so seem to be at risk of developing a learning disability.

STEP 2: The progress of these at-risk students is checked for five to eight weeks. A short test is given each week. Students whose progress is low in response to *general education instruction (Tier 1)* are identified.

STEP 3: These students receive *small-group instruction (Tier 2 and Beyond intervention)* for nine to 20 weeks. This instruction usually consists of three to four sessions per week. Each instructional session lasts 30 to 40 minutes. Each week, a short test measures the student's progress. They also are tested at the end of instruction. *Students who respond well to the intervention return to Tier 1 (general education) instruction.* Responding well means the student has improved each week

From *National Resource Center on Learning Disabilities,* Winter 2007. Published in 2007 by U.S. Office of Special Education Programs/Department of Education. www.nrcld.org

during instruction and has a satisfactory achievement score at the end of the intervention. Student progress continues to be checked to catch any student who is not able to keep up a good rate of learning while back in general instruction.

STEP 4: *Students whose response to small-group instruction is poor are given a comprehensive evaluation.* A poor response is a low rate of improvement each week and a low achievement score at the end of the intervention.

STEP 5: To answer questions that arose during Tier 2 and Beyond, a *comprehensive evaluation* is conducted using valid and reliable data collection measures that are targeted specifically to student needs. The aim is to determine whether it is correct to identify the student as having a learning disability. A student may be identified as having some other disability—for example, mental retardation, speech/language delay, or emotional or behavioral disorder.

STEP 6: *Special education is delivered with a more intensive instructional program.* Progress continues to be checked each week. If at any time data indicate that the student is not progressing adequately with the instructional program, the special educator changes the program. *Once a student has a strong rate of learning and reaches a satisfactory performance level, the student exits special education and returns to Tier 1 general education instruction.* The student's progress in Tier 1 instruction continues to be checked so that corrective action may be taken as needed.

The reasoning behind this RTI method of identifying learning disabilities is this: When a student does not respond to generally effective interventions both at Tier 1 and at Tier 2 and Beyond, the quality of instruction is not a likely reason for poor academic progress and, instead, may provide evidence of a disability.

Benefits

An RTI model may offer several benefits. First, an RTI model for identifying students with SLD has the benefit of *early identification and intervention.* Students at risk for SLD can be screened as early as January of kindergarten or September of first grade. This decreases the likelihood that students will slip through the system without detection of their learning problems.

A second potential benefit of an RTI model of SLD identification is *systematic screening, which reduces screening bias.* Systematic screening, which involves testing all students, decreases reliance on teacher-based referral. This reduces possible teacher bias and reduces the variability in SLD identification practices. Referral and identification for SLD vary in part because teachers differ in their views about how students perform and why they may be learning poorly. This variability in teachers' views and attributes results in missed opportunities to serve students with SLD.

A final potential benefit of RTI is *linking identification assessment with instructional planning.* Presently, the assessment process for documenting a discrepancy between IQ and achievement takes a lot of resources. At the same time, the resulting test scores have little connection with planning effective instruction. Many special and general education teachers find results from traditional tests are not much help in designing instruction. Using RTI to identify students as having SLD keeps the assessment focus on the student's learning. The RTI model switches the emphasis from assessment for identification to instructionally relevant assessment. It involves monitoring student progress and systematic testing of changes in instruction.

Risks

Despite the promise of an RTI model for identifying learning disabilities, key conceptual issues need to be sharpened. RTI methods need to be further specified and studied.

One potential pitfall of RTI is *whether strong intervention models and measures are available to produce strong learning outcomes.* For schools and teachers to be able to use RTI, instructional procedures that are shown to be effective across teachers and schools must be available. In addition, measures are required to follow learning over time. These tools are available for some, but not all, academic areas. They are better developed at some grade levels. For example, a fair amount of work has been accomplished in beginning reading to provide the groundwork for both RTI intervention and measurement procedures. By contrast, in math, spelling, and writing, measurement procedures for tracking growth are well established, but more research is needed on validated intervention methods for testing responsiveness to instruction. More information is available at the early grades than for older students.

A second potential pitfall concerns *having enough trained professionals available.* To use an RTI model in the thousands of school districts in this country, large numbers of trained professionals are required. They will need the knowledge and skills to put in place defined tutoring methods or to solve problems through research. They also will need the knowledge and skills to monitor student learning, to interpret the assessment results, and to make decisions about eligibility. Moreover, using RTI requires a new way of thinking about assessment and instruction for many professionals, including school psychologists, special and general educators, and principals. To date, RTI models have been implemented only on a small scale by highly trained personnel in research settings. Using RTI on a large scale, in many school systems and many states, has not yet been tested. It will require developing and carrying out an ambitious training agenda for school professionals.

Finally, *RTI practitioners will need to determine when to begin due process and parental involvement.* Does due process begin with problem-solving adaptations to general education or with the intensive short-term preventive instruction? Is it delayed until the student is found to be unresponsive to instruction and a special education classification is imminent? On the one hand, due process early in the identification process may be essential to protect against students getting caught in a cycle in which they linger between general education and some layer of services short of special education, without parents being aware or having input. On the other hand, initiating due process early in identification will be costly and will add considerable time and personnel requirements to identification. Clearly, discussions are needed about due process in such a changed identification system.

How NRCLD's Research Is Helping Schools Implement RTI

Two large studies have been conducted, one in *reading* and the other in *math,* in which students were followed over time.

Reading

NRCLD worked in 42 classrooms across 10 schools. Some schools had large numbers of high-poverty families, and other schools had large numbers of middle-class families. Students from these classrooms were selected for taking part based on low scores on brief reading measures given at the beginning of first grade. These 252 students were randomly assigned to receive the instruction or not at the beginning of January, depending on how they actually improved during the fall.

Instruction Group

Students who had been randomly assigned to receive small-group instruction (and who did not improve much in reading during the fall) continued to receive reading instruction in the general education classroom. They also took part in Tier 2 small-group instruction for nine weeks. Small-group instruction consisted of three, 45-minute sessions per week.

Control Group

By contrast, students who had been randomly assigned to the control group (and who did not improve much in reading during the fall) continued to receive all of their reading instruction in the general education classroom. They did not receive small-group instruction.

Findings

At the end of first grade, students who had received small-group instruction read substantially better than students who did not receive small-group instruction. Many fewer students qualified as SLD given the various methods we used to define SLD. The alternative ways of defining SLD at the end of first grade, some based on traditional methods of discrepancy between IQ and achievement and others based on RTI approaches, designated different students as having a learning disability.

Math

We conducted a study similar to the reading study but not identical. We worked in 41 classrooms across 10 schools. Some schools had large numbers of high-poverty families, and other schools had large numbers of middle-class families. Based on their math scores near the beginning of first grade, students from these classrooms were designated as not at risk for SLD in math (127 children) or as at risk for SLD in math (569 children). The at-risk children were randomly assigned to receive small-group instruction or not beginning in November.

Instruction Group
Students who had been randomly assigned to receive small-group instruction continued to receive math instruction in the general education classroom. They also took part in Tier 2 small-group instruction for 20 weeks. This instruction consisted of three, 30-minute sessions per week.

Control Group
By contrast, students who had been randomly assigned to the control group continued to receive all of their math instruction in the general education classroom. They did not receive small-group instruction.

Findings
At the end of first grade, students who had received small-group instruction computed and understood math concepts substantially better than students who did not receive small-group instruction. Many fewer students qualified as SLD given the various methods we used to define SLD. The alternative ways of defining SLD at the end of first grade, some based on traditional methods of discrepancy between IQ and achievement and others based on RTI approaches, designated different students as having a learning disorder.

Conclusions

From these studies, we draw several conclusions that should influence how schools conduct RTI.

1. One-time testing at the beginning of the year does not provide an adequate basis for identifying children who need Tier 2 and Beyond small-group instruction intervention. Instead, one-time testing can be used to identify a pool of students whose progress then needs to be monitored, using brief weekly tests, for five to eight weeks. Then, a slope of improvement (that is weekly rate of gain) can be calculated to determine which children have progressed nicely in response to the Tier 1 general education program and which children require Tier 2 and Beyond intervention.
2. Tier 2 and Beyond small-group instruction can be effective in promoting better achievement. It also can be effective for sorting out children who will learn well with well-designed instruction versus children who require more intensive special education. With Tier 2 and Beyond small-group instruction, fewer children finish first grade with the kinds of academic deficits that make them appropriate for disability certification.
3. This RTI process can provide a sound basis for identifying students to receive a comprehensive special education evaluation.

4. Tier 2 and Beyond instructors need to be well trained and supervised for Tier 2 and Beyond benefits to accrue. With training and supervision, formal teaching certification is not necessary. Continuing problem solving to address the learning needs and behavioral challenges of individual students needs to be provided by a licensed teacher who has a strong teaching background.
5. Different methods for quantifying "response" to Tier 2 and Beyond small-group instruction will result in different numbers of students being identified for comprehensive special education evaluation. Some methods work better than others at identifying students with severe academic deficits. One method that appears to work well is to define adequate response as students demonstrating (a) a strong rate of improvement during small-group instruction as well as (b) adequate final performance at the end of small-group instruction.
6. Some students who demonstrate adequate response to small-group instruction will fall behind again when they return to Tier 1 general education without the continuing support of small-group instruction. For this reason, it is important that schools continue to monitor the progress of these students with brief weekly assessments so that corrective actions may be taken when needed, including returning to Tier 2 and Beyond small-group instruction.

Frequently Asked Questions about RTI

Will this process delay identification?   The RTI process takes longer than a traditional one-step comprehensive evaluation. However, beginning at Tier 2, students are receiving services designed to remediate their learning problems—a prevention strategy. The aim is that the prevention built into RTI will reduce the number of students incorrectly identified as having a disability because they have not received strong instruction. It may help many students get on an upward track toward successful academic outcomes. Also, RTI facilitates prevention and identification early in the primary grades. In contrast, the traditional method of identifying a discrepancy between IQ and achievement often occurs later in schooling since it may be many grades before a sizeable discrepancy accrues.

Does each child have to go through RTI or can a child have a traditional assessment?   Schools honor parent requests for a traditional one-step comprehensive evaluation, in lieu of the RTI process. Legislation suggests that the evaluation of a child suspected of having a disability must include a variety of assessment tools and must not rely on any single measure.

What does "research-based intervention" mean?   A research-based intervention constitutes a set of practices. Each of those practices is tested and evaluated in controlled studies. Each practice must be shown to be effective. In a controlled study, students are matched (found to be similar) according to the criteria important to the study. Students are randomly assigned to a treatment or no treatment group. The outcomes for students in both groups are compared.

Who initiates an RTI process?   Typically, children are identified to take part in Tier 2 and Beyond interventions based on their universal screening scores, when students are tested once, at the beginning of the school year. Many times, such universal screening is supplemented with short-term progress monitoring (for example, over five weeks) to determine the student's response to general education.

What will be required for professional development?   An RTI process of SLD identification will require professional development to prepare school staffs to do the following activities:

- Collect and interpret screening scores using existing data or individually administered brief assessments on all students
- Ensure the quality of general education by selecting strong curricula and by conducting observations to document that those strong curricula have been used well. This requires examining class-wide patterns of response to determine when teachers require assistance to improve the quality of their instructional programs and then providing that assistance
- Collect continuing progress-monitoring data and interpret the data
- Design Tier 2 and Beyond programs that incorporate validated intervention protocols
- Implement those Tier 2 and Beyond programs with fidelity.

Who is responsible for the various activities required to implement RTI as a method of SLD identification?   Faculty in a school building must work collaboratively to implement RTI as a method of SLD identification. In some schools, the work is distributed as shown in the table on the next page.

How long will the comprehensive evaluation be and what professional is likely to give the Step 4 assessment?   The comprehensive evaluation should be specifically targeted to answer questions that arise during Tier 2 and Beyond instruction. It should be done in collaboration with the perspective of the student's general education teacher. Typically, answering these relevant questions involves only a small number of relatively brief tests. For example, if mental retardation is suspected as the disability category, school psychologists might administer the Vineland Adaptive Behavior Scale along with a two-subtest Wechsler Abbreviated Scale of Intelligence instead of giving a full-blown intelligence test to rule out mental retardation.

What proportion of students is likely to be identified as at risk (for Tier 1 monitoring) and for the Tier 2 and Beyond diagnostic trial?   The proportion of students identified for different steps in the RTI process depends largely on the quality of general education. When general education instruction is of questionable quality, research suggests that 20 percent to 25 percent of a school population is likely to be identified as at risk and demonstrate unresponsiveness to Tier 1. Of course, providing the Tier 2 and Beyond diagnostic instructional trial to 25 percent of a school population challenges a school's resources. In contrast, research also suggests that with high-quality general education, only

Task	Responsibility
Collecting screening data using existing data or individually administered brief assessments on all students	Teachers & trained aides
Interpreting screening data	Special educators & school psychologists
Ensuring the quality of general education	Curriculum specialists at the school or district level, school psychologists, teachers, & parents
Collecting continuing progress-monitoring data	Teachers & trained aides
Interpreting progress-monitoring data	Special educators & school psychologists
Designing Tier 2 and Beyond programs that incorporate validated intervention protocols	Special educators & school psychologists
Implementing Tier 2 and Beyond programs with fidelity	Trained aides under the supervision of special educators & school psychologists
Conducting the Step 4 evaluation	Special educators & school psychologists

9 percent to 10 percent of students will be identified as at risk and respond inadequately to Tier 1, with approximately half of those students responding to high-quality Tier 2 and Beyond instruction. Clearly, a need exists to ensure high-quality general education. In a similar way, integrity of the RTI process requires a strong Tier 2 and Beyond diagnostic instructional trial.

Are there schools currently carrying out RTI as a method of SLD identification and, if so, how can I learn more about their methods?   Yes, some schools are implementing RTI as a method of SLD identification. . . .

Cathy G. Litty and
J. Amos Hatch

 **NO**

Hurry Up and Wait:
Rethinking Special Education
Identification in Kindergarten

Introduction

The nature of kindergarten is changing, and the needs of young children with disabilities are often being ignored as these changes take place. Kindergarten teachers are being asked to implement standards-based curricula that many believe "hurry" the academic development of even the most able children. The tradition of most school systems and the policy of some is to delay doing evaluations for special education identification until after the kindergarten year. This traps children who will eventually qualify for special education services into waiting at least an extra year before their special learning needs will be addressed. It also places kindergarten teachers in a difficult position. They face all the complexity associated with teaching children with disabilities, but get none of the support. Although some teachers have the experience, expertise, and confidence to accommodate the needs of children with special learning needs, the system is set up to create a difficult year for many kindergartners and their teachers. In effect, the system is saying to young children with disabilities that are as yet unidentified: *Hurry up* and fit into an academically driven school setting *and wait* a year for the services you need to be successful. To kindergarten teachers, the message is: *You are on your own.*

Today's Kindergarten

The nature and purposes of kindergarten have changed over the past decade. Factors that have influenced these changes include (a) the experience of being a child is vastly different than it was just a generation ago, (b) advances in knowledge about what young children are capable of learning have challenged traditional perspectives on appropriate practice in kindergarten classrooms, and (c) the standards-based accountability movement has worked its way down into early childhood classrooms. Although many teachers and others interested in early childhood would like to preserve kindergarten's traditional role of providing a buffer to help smooth young children's transition from

From *Early Childhood Education Journal*, 33(4), February 2006, pp. 203–207 (refs. omitted). Copyright © 2006 by Springer Science and Business Media. Reprinted by permission via Rightslink.

home to school, it is a fact of life that kindergartens are becoming more like the first and second grades of the recent past.

Children entering contemporary kindergartens are assumed to bring with them academic knowledge and skills that not long ago were considered appropriate instructional objectives for first grade. Five-year-olds are now assumed to have already acquired social understandings and capacities that used to comprise a central place in the kindergarten curriculum. Kindergartners are now routinely tested and evaluated on the mastery of academic standards that were previously thought to be beyond their developmental understanding. So, what teachers and students spend their time doing in the new kindergarten looks quite different than what they did a few years ago. The curriculum is more rigorous, teaching methods are more direct, and expectations for academic achievement are much higher. While these changes have implications for all children, we are particularly interested in what they mean for young children who may be at risk, especially the thousands of young children with undiagnosed disabilities who enter kindergarten each year.

Special Education Identification

Federal law dictates that teachers refer children about whom they have concerns for special education evaluation, but they must intervene in some way with modified strategies before this can occur. We know that great variability exists across schools and systems regarding how interventions and referrals are carried out, but we believe that current policy and practice concerning the identification of young children for special education services continues to be dominated by the assumption that it is better to wait until first grade than to start the special education identification processes in kindergarten. The basic logic has been that because the administration of standardized instruments is central to the identification process and young children are not developmentally ready for standardized testing experiences, then kindergartners should not be placed in special education programs based on unreliable psychometric data. Further, because kindergarten-aged children are maturing so rapidly, it is hard to make distinctions between normal delays in development and the presence of certain long-term disabilities. Even further, since kindergarten has traditionally been a place where children were gently socialized into the world of school, not much was lost by allowing children who may eventually qualify for special education services to play out the kindergarten year receiving the same program as their age-mates.

In cases where developmental delays are dramatic or behavior in the classroom is uncontrollable, the "wait till next year" rule is sometimes waived. But, these cases are rare. The mode is much more likely to be that teachers who have concerns about their kindergartners' capacities to be successful because of disabilities are put on hold and told to see if they "grow out of it" or "learn how to act in school."

The United States Department of Education (2003) reports that over 13% of children between the ages of three and 21 qualify for special education services. While we recognize that some disabilities may be difficult to identify in early childhood, it is reasonable to assume that a similar percentage of kindergartners qualify for services. We know that thousands of children in kindergartens across the United States will eventually be assessed and receive special services for an identified disability, so the question becomes: *Why wait?*

Why Wait?

The point we are trying to make is simple on its face. If 5- and 6-year-old children are ready for the academic emphasis that defines current kindergarten practice, then they are also ready for the special education identification system. You can't have it both ways. Either young children are cognitively and emotionally mature enough for both or neither. The same arguments that have been used for years to make the case for developmental as opposed to academic approaches in kindergarten form the basis for arguing against assessing children for special education placement during kindergarten. Those arguments have failed to convince policy makers of the efficacy of developmental approaches. As a result, kindergarten curricula and teaching methods are decidedly academic in nature. Given the state of contemporary kindergarten programs, it no longer makes good sense to argue that kindergartners are not developmentally ready for special education assessment.

Kindergartners and their teachers are part of the accountability system that drives almost everything that happens in contemporary education settings, including preschool and kindergarten classrooms. National, state, and local accountability initiatives mandate standards-based curricula, prescribed instructional approaches, and standardized testing for younger and younger children. Schools and teachers have no choice but to reconstitute kindergarten curricular, instructional, and assessment practices in an effort to meet increasing accountability requirements. Kindergarten children at all ability and maturity levels face the challenges of meeting the expectations of "accountability shove-down" (Hatch, 2002). Since these expectations do not go away because a child may experience difficulties that significantly reduce his or her chances for school success, we believe waiting an extra year for the special education system to begin providing support is no longer justified.

Inadequate Choices

How should teachers and schools deal with the difficulties of working within a system that expects academic performance of all children while delaying extra support for those who will have the most difficulty meeting expectations? We see inadequate options and better options for dealing with the difficulties inherent in the current situation. Among the inadequate choices are ignoring, delaying, retaining, and redshirting.

It is always a bad choice to act like nothing is wrong when children in our care are put at risk. Pretending that the current climate in early childhood education is a temporary anomaly and that traditional kindergarten programs will reemerge as standard practice is wishful thinking at best. Hoping that the needs of kindergarten children with disabilities will be met in programs with no provision of special education services also ignores reality. This issue is real for children, teachers, and families. Imagining that it will go away only increases the risk for all involved.

Delaying has been institutionalized by the system. However, teachers, schools, and parents make a bad choice when disabilities are suspected and action is delayed. It is understandable that teachers faced with all the complexity of teaching in contemporary kindergarten classrooms rely on the prevailing ethos of waiting until next year when considering options for addressing the needs of their students who struggle most. Many are concerned that some young children might be labeled prematurely by the system simply because their rate of development differs from their peers. We share this concern but believe that teachers and other educators responsible for special education referral and evaluation processes can be equipped to make sound judgments based on solid information gathered from a variety of sources (see discussion of monitoring below). Great care should be taken when making decisions about special education referral, but waiting to act on behalf of children for whom special education services are designed denies those children of help that will have more effect the sooner it is provided.

Another inadequate choice for dealing with this situation is retaining children in kindergarten. Unfortunately, this is the unspoken policy of many schools and school systems. Kindergartners who demonstrate clear delays in their academic progress, in effect, "fail" kindergarten and are retained. This approach may have its roots in nativist early childhood perspectives that assume that maturation is the primary determinant of children's readiness for school, but the literature on the effects of retention (and this includes placement in so-called developmental kindergartens or transition classes) consistently shows that it is a bad idea. What retention means for kindergartners with undiagnosed disabilities is that they are set up to receive a "double dose of the same medicine," when what they actually need is special education intervention.

Retention happens after an unsuccessful kindergarten year, [and] redshirting happens in anticipation of a difficult year. Neither is a good choice for the children we are talking about here. Redshirting is a term used to describe the practice of waiting for an extra year before starting a child in kindergarten. Many parents and some teachers have come to believe that giving children an extra year (to grow, learn, mature) helps children who might otherwise struggle. Just as athletes are held out of the action during their redshirt season, age-eligible kindergartners wait on the sidelines, then start formal schooling one year older than their peers. Like retention, redshirting has failed to demonstrate significant benefits for children. For children with disabilities that are as yet unidentified, redshirting may provide an escape from inadequate choices discussed earlier. But, if the better choices to follow were implemented, holding a child out of kindergarten for a year would be a bad option.

Better Choices

We have discussed what schools, teachers, and parents should not do, but what should they do in response to a situation in which 5- and 6-year-old children with potential disabilities are denied access to special education services during their kindergarten year? It seems to us that the best choice is to stop delaying the process of identifying eligible children for special services. Where it is formal policy to not assess kindergartners for possible disabilities, a reexamination of that policy is needed. Where informal practices are in place that severely limit special education assessments during kindergarten, honest and open deliberations about the effects of those practices on the life chances of young children with disabilities are essential. Kindergarten has changed, and expectations for kindergartners have escalated. Placing young children with unidentified disabilities in contemporary kindergartens while denying them access to services for which they will become eligible 1 year later seems indefensible. The span of "lost" time when services could be provided is significant in the life of a young child. Parents, educators, and advocates for young children should do everything they can to change policies and practices that perpetuate this flawed approach.

Beyond trying to change the system, what should teachers and schools be doing now? Three better choices are balancing, monitoring, and adjusting. The balancing we are talking about is good practice in any early childhood classroom. It goes beyond providing equal parts of teacher-directed lessons and child-centered activities. It is more than covering the state-mandated skills in a developmentally appropriate way. The balancing we advocate is about teachers having a strong grasp of the curricular expectations where they work, an in-depth knowledge of the children in their classrooms, and a broad repertoire of teaching strategies for helping kindergartners be successful. Contemporary kindergarten teaching is complex, and teachers make countless decisions that demand special knowledge of curriculum, children, and teaching.

Balancing means making decisions about what will be taught, to whom, and how. In virtually any public school kindergarten, the "what to teach" part will be strongly influenced by district, state, and national curriculum guidelines. Most teachers will have more autonomy in deciding who will work on what parts of the curriculum at a given time. And, most teachers retain some control over the selection of teaching strategies through which children learn the content. Effective kindergarten teachers deal with this array of factors by applying a model of decision making that involves them in drawing on instructional strategies from direct to incidental teaching, and everything in between. Some strategies will work for the whole group, and some will have to be tailored for individuals or small groups. Children who are struggling in kindergarten should be learning every day, just like their peers. Those likely to be identified for special education services in first or second grade may require more creativity and support, but the model is the same. Kindergarten teachers are responsible for balancing curriculum expectations, individual differences among children, and teaching strategies for all their students. Leaving children with potential disabilities out of the balance is wrong and unnecessary.

By monitoring, we mean gathering and using information that helps teachers keep an appropriate balance for every child, including those who are struggling in kindergarten. We include elements of evaluation and assessment in the monitoring construct, but the principal aim is for teachers to collect information that will allow them to better address the needs of all their children. Monitoring begins as soon as information is available. Most systems now administer screening instruments before or soon after kindergarten entry. The information generated by these standardized screening tools can be a valuable source of information for kindergarten teachers as they set up classrooms and make curricular and instructional plans. But early monitoring should include the collection of data that go beyond the screening results. Gathering insights from parents, preschool teachers, and caregivers is another important avenue for finding out what children are like, what they need to be successful, and what dimensions of their development may need a closer look. These insights can be gathered using information checklists, questionnaires, and direct contact with those who know the children best. Having this information right away will help kindergarten teachers adjust the experiences they provide for children from the beginning of the year, rather than waiting to see what problems arise for which children.

Teachers should continue to monitor throughout the school year. Systematic observation and documentation of the children's behavior within the classroom environment is the best way to keep track of what's going on, what works, and what needs to be changed. Data in the form of anecdotal records, checklists, or rating scales that reflect children's performance on daily classroom tasks are essential elements of monitoring. Young children should be assessed with tasks that are functional and meaningful, and examples of work that the child has completed are excellent sources of information. Work samples and portfolios can be useful tools to aid the teacher in monitoring a child's skill level and conceptual development. As systematic monitoring processes unfold, careful records should be maintained because these will provide the best evidence available for making sound decisions about referring kindergartners for special education evaluation. This type of assessment can help early childhood professionals to verify the severity of difficulties a child may be having or rule out other possible explanations for performance that is below that of the other children in the class.

Direct evidence of children's activity in the classroom is among the best information for making adjustments to meet the needs of kindergartners, especially those who are struggling. Adjusting means adapting curriculum and modifying instruction so that every child is learning in kindergarten. Based on the understandings gained through the monitoring processes described above, adjusting should be a natural consequence of seeing what children can do and what they need more help to accomplish. Adapting the curriculum may mean changing the pace for some children, starting them at a place farther down on the curriculum skills' hierarchy than where most kindergartners are operating, then moving them forward at a pace that accommodates their capacities.

Modifying instruction is about calling on a wide repertoire of teaching strategies that improve children's chances of being successful. It means putting aside beliefs that a single approach to delivering instruction is best in any and all situations. Modifying instruction includes being strategic and tactical about how to teach particular content to particular children. For example, Hatch (2005) describes teaching strategies that include incidental teaching, thematic teaching, and direct teaching, along with instructional tactics such as grouping, modeling, demonstrating, coaching, tutoring, discussing, practicing, and individualizing. Adjusting curriculum and teaching to address children's strengths and needs is a vehicle for meeting the expectation that teachers will intervene with modifications before referring children for special education evaluation. More importantly, it would go a long way toward ensuring that children who will eventually be identified for special education services learn all they can in kindergarten. It is certainly a better choice than allowing them to languish for a year waiting for the special education system to kick in.

Summary

We believe the complex version of a balanced approach described above is good practice in any kindergarten. By providing children who will eventually be identified for special services with a balanced program based on careful monitoring and adjusting, schools can do a lot to change the status quo. This approach is much preferred over the ignoring, delaying, retaining, and redshirting that dominate current practice for (not) dealing with the issue of what to do with children with disabilities that are not identified in kindergarten.

Yes, balancing, monitoring, and adjusting are necessary in kindergarten classrooms that include children with special needs, identified or not. But, no, they are not sufficient for addressing the needs of children with disabilities during their kindergarten year. In response to the changing nature of early experiences, our expanded knowledge base about how children learn and develop, and especially the impact of the accountability movement, kindergartens have changed. Curricula have expanded, expectations for performance have escalated, and definitions of appropriate teaching approaches have broadened. In the face of these changes, all kindergarten children are being forced to "hurry." But, some of these kindergartners (an average of two or three in each class of 20) are at a distinct disadvantage. These children are currently being asked to "wait" for services for which they will qualify once they enter the special education system. It is time to rethink special education identification in kindergarten. It's not fair to the children, their families, or their teachers to continue policies and practices that force young children with disabilities to hurry up and face the consequences of operating in a newly defined kindergarten, but wait at least a year for the support they need to be successful.

POSTSCRIPT

Can RTI Reduce the Number of Children Identified with Specific Learning Disability (SLD)?

Compton (2006) *Journal of Learning Disabilities* talks about "the nudges" necessary to help children learn. Everyone needs little nudges from time to time. A need for stronger and longer nudges might signify a disability. RTI is designed as a system of progressively more intense nudges, within the general education environment, enabling students to receive supplementary instruction without a disability label, which some find stigmatizing (Brown-Chidsey, *Educational Leadership,* 2007).

The SLD definition stipulates that the child must have had the opportunity to learn through solid teaching strategies. Lynn S. Fuchs notes that the strong instruction mandated by RTI might reduce the number of students who are inappropriately placed in special education, usually with an SLD diagnosis.

Emerging proficiency in English can contribute to low standardized test scores, which might be misinterpreted as a disability (Klingner, Artiles, & Barletta, *Journal of Learning Disabilities,* 2006). Careful attention to student progress might also reduce inappropriate SLD determinations in English language learners.

Several supports exist to help educators track student growth over time. The National Center on Student Progress Monitoring (www.studentprogress.org) provides an abundance of resources on using Curriculum Based Measurement (CBM) to project student progress. The Research Institute on Progress Monitoring (RIPM) at the University of Minnesota focuses on developing seamless and flexible assessment-tracking strategies. A themed issue of *The Journal of Special Education* (2007) presented RIPM analyses of the CBM research base.

Litty and Amos approve of interventions and monitoring, but are concerned about how long interventions take. Children with disabilities need the big nudge of special education, not delaying tactics that waste valuable time. Chandler (*The Washington Post,* December 31, 2007) predicts a backlash from parents who see RTI as a strategy to contain special education costs at the expense of providing needed services to their children.

Late in 2007, several federal agencies jointly hosted an invitational RTI Summit for over 700 stakeholder representatives. Teams of key state educators and parents learned about RTI models and began to develop implementation plans, accessing available federal and state resources.

Written proceedings for the RTI Summit are available at the website for the new National Center on Response to Intervention (www.rti4success.org). The Council for Exceptional Children (2008) related highlights of the lively breakout session on using RTI to identify learning disabilities. Nonresponsiveness may occur for many reasons, one of which might be the quality of the intervention (D. Mellard). RTI data are important, but only as one part of a comprehensive evaluation, which requires multiple measurements and a team decision (D. Deshler). Both speakers, Mellard and Deshler, are noted researchers in the SLD field. CEC also reported concerns about the validity of RTI procedures, which have been focused primarily on younger grades and on literacy.

RTI procedures are written into IDEA, yet the majority of RTI teaching and data collection are the responsibilities of general education teachers, delivering a mixed message to educators and to parents. The success of this initiative may rest heavily in the arena of general education (Baskette, Ulmer, & Bender, *Journal of the American Academy of Special Education Professionals*, 2006; Bradley, Danielson, & Doolittle, *Journal of Learning Disabilities*, 2005).

Will RTI procedures supplant traditional testing to determine SLD? Will the number of students identified with SLD diminish as general education options develop? Or, will parents decide to bypass RTI intervention periods in favor of special education evaluations, hoping for even more intense services?

ISSUE 17

Is Mental Health Screening an Unwarranted Intrusion?

YES: Nathaniel S. Lehrman, from "The Dangers of Mental Health Screening," *Journal of American Physicians and Surgeons* (vol. 11, no. 3, pp. 80–82, Fall 2006)

NO: Mark D. Weist, Marcia Rubin, Elizabeth Moore, Steven Adelsheim, and Gordon Wrobel, from "Mental Health Screening in Schools," *Journal of School Health* (vol. 77, pp. 53–58, February 2007)

ISSUE SUMMARY

YES: Nathaniel S. Lehrman, clinical director (retired) of the Kingsboro (NY) Psychiatric Center, warns that new mental health screening requirements, heralded as a way to increase the health of the nation, will intrude on basic freedoms, lead to inappropriate labels, and increase revenue for pharmaceutical companies.

NO: Mark D. Weist, Marcia Rubin, Elizabeth Moore, Steven Adelsheim, and Gordon Wrobel, consultants and researchers in mental health, see this screening as a way to identify those who need early intervention in order to prevent the development of debilitating mental illnesses.

Virginia Tech, Northern Illinois, and Columbine: These three schools and countless now-silent adolescents remind us how fragile our existence can be. Three schools that make us wonder about the students we teach. How many friends, teachers, and parents have worried whether they missed a clue that could have saved a life?

Researchers at the National Institute of Mental Health (*NASET News Alert*, www.naset.org) announced the ability to predict the future development of psychosis by assessing an individual's risk factors. Intervention during a *critical window* could prevent the development of serious mental illness. Who would not want to intervene?

Noting that between 5 percent and 7 percent of all adults and children have a serious mental illness, the President's New Freedom Commission on Mental Health (NFC) observed "(m)ental health ranks first among illnesses that cause disability in the United States, Canada, and Western Europe. This serious public health challenge is underrecognized as a public health burden. In addition, one of the most distressing and preventable consequences of undiagnosed, untreated, or undertreated mental illnesses is suicide" (www. mentalhealthcommission.gov, 2003).

The NFC final report lists six goals for an improved quality of mental health in the United States. Goal 4, Early Mental Health Screening, Assessment, and Referral to Services Are Common Practice, includes a recommendation to screen for mental health disorders. This goal would be achieved through regular screenings of children and youth. The intent is to identify those in need and deliver intervention to prevent the development of a mental illness. Seemingly benign, this call for regular screening has engendered much controversy.

In the first selection, psychiatrist Nathaniel S. Lehrman describes mental health screening as an unwarranted intrusion into individual and family privacy. Acknowledging the good intentions of the NFC, Lehrman is concerned that inadequate screening tools will stigmatize people with unfounded diagnoses. Only the pharmaceutical companies will benefit.

In the second selection, Mark D. Weist and colleagues, who practice and conduct research in psychiatry, support systematic mental health screening. They emphasize the effectiveness of early intervention, especially through school mental health services. Weist and colleagues maintain that, delivered in a timely fashion, mental health interventions can reduce the stigma of mental illness.

Representative Ron Paul (TX), a contender for the Republican presidential nomination, is one of several legislators who introduced a bill (H.R. 2387) prohibiting the use of federal funds for any universal mental health screening. As support for this measure to limit government intrusion into private lives, the authors cite efforts to formalize a diagnosis of "extreme intolerance" as well as the suggestion of one federally funded program that children who share their parents' traditional values may instigate school violence. Like Lehrman, these legislators see such claims as leading to stigmatizing labels that result in pressure for pharmaceutical treatment.

Responding to an earlier version of H.R. 2387, and in support of screening, the National Alliance on Mental Illness (NAMI) (www.nami.org) appealed to Congress to reject the misinformation provided by antiscreening advocates. To NAMI, the tone of proposed legislation engenders fear, enhances stigma, and keeps people away from needed help. Screening merely identifies those who need more intensive evaluation. This, and any medical treatment, can only happen with full parental involvement and consent.

As you read these articles, consider the powerful issues they raise. What is the best way to balance cherished individual rights and freedoms with the desire to avert a tragedy? Who decides where the line should be drawn?

YES
Nathaniel S. Lehrman

The Dangers of Mental Health Screening

The New Freedom Commission on Mental Health

According to the President's New Freedom Commission on Mental Health (NFC), all American parents will receive notice from their youngsters' schools of the new screening program during the 2005–2006 school year. It will test for mental illness in the 52 million students and 6 million adults working in schools, and expects to find at least 6 million in need of treatment. The force of government will then urge or compel them to receive that treatment.

But children aren't the only targets. The commission's final report looks forward to having both children and adults screened for mental illnesses during their routine physical examinations.

The sale of psychiatric medications—antipsychotics and antidepressants—rose from $500 million to $20 billion between 1987 and 2004, a 40-fold increase. A pharmaceutical stock analyst recently predicted that continuing to widen our definitions of illness will result in increased sales of medications. This amounts to corporate-sponsored creation of illness, to enhance revenue. With the new screening program, the government-sponsored "discovery" of illness will augment the already existing corporate "promotion of undiscovered illness"—which means even more medication sales. And by allowing experts to define peaceful, law-abiding citizens as ill and in need of treatment (which increasingly is becoming involuntary), the program comes to resemble the witchhunts of 16th-century Europe.

Screening and Its Victims

This is how the program works. In December 2004, as part of the TeenScreen program created to implement the NFC blueprint, Chelsea Rhoades and her Indiana public high school classmates were given a 10-minute, yes-or-no computer test, which had no room for alternate answers or explanations. A few students were not given the test because their parents had opted them out, an option the Rhoades family had not known about in advance.

From *Journal of American Physicians and Surgeons*, 11(3) Fall 2006, pp. 80–82 (refs. omitted). Copyright © 2006 by Association of American Physicians and Surgeons. Reprinted by permission. http://www.jpands.org/

Shortly after Chelsea took the test, a local mental health center employee told her that she was suffering from obsessive-compulsive disorder because she liked to help clean the house, and from social anxiety disorder because she didn't party much. The worker then suggested that if her condition worsened, her mother should bring her to the center for treatment. Chelsea says all her friends were also told they had something mentally wrong with them. The only youngsters not supposed to be suffering from some mental disorder were those with opt-out slips.

Furious at this intrusion into their privacy and parental rights, the Rhoadeses sounded the alarm. With the help of the Rutherford Institute, they have filed a lawsuit against the school district for failing to inform them about the test or to obtain permission for Chelsea to take it.

Even more frightening was the experience of 13-year-old, black Aliah Gleason, an average, but rather obstreperous seventh-grade student in an Austin, Texas, suburb. After her class was screened for mental illness, her parents were told that she needed further evaluation because she scored high on a suicide rating. She was referred to a university consulting psychiatrist, and thence to an emergency clinic. Six weeks later, a child protection worker appeared at her school, interviewed her, summoned her father to the school, and ordered him to take the girl at once to Austin State (psychiatric) Hospital. When he refused, she took Aliah into emergency custody and had a police officer drive her to the hospital.

During Aliah's five terrible months in the hospital, her parents were forbidden to see or speak to her. While there, she was placed in restraints more than 26 times and given at least 12 different psychiatric medications, many of them simultaneously. After that, she spent four more months in a residential facility, where she received even more psychotropic medications.

Despite her caretakers' uncertainty about her clinical diagnosis (and whether she even had a psychiatric illness), her parents had to go to court to have her released. The professionals they chose for her then tapered her off all medication and successfully addressed problems—both hers and the family's. She is now doing well in school, participating in extracurricular activities, and according to her psychologist, Dr. John Breeding of Austin, recovering her high spirits.

At a Colorado homeless shelter, 50 percent of the 350 young people given the TeenScreen were found to be suicidal risks, and 71 percent screened positive for psychiatric disorders. Although such youngsters are certainly suffering from residential and social instability, and probably from not eating or sleeping properly, the TeenScreen diagnoses lead to medications instead of appropriate interventions.

The particular purpose of children's mental health screening is supposedly to prevent suicide. But the Columbia University TeenScreen program acknowledged that 84 percent of the teens who tested positive were found to be not really at risk. And, as Sharav points out, an evaluation by the authoritative U.S. Preventive Services Task Force (USPSTF) concluded that screening for suicide failed to demonstrate any benefit at reducing suicide. The report noted that the screening instruments have not been validated. Moreover, there is insufficient evidence that treatment of those identified as high risk reduces either suicide attempts or mortality.

What Is Mental Illness?

What is the mental illness for which we are now screening? Years ago, the term "mental illness" referred only to the insane: people with bizarre ideas who were unable to function socially. Such disabled individuals were social annoyances who might also be dangerous to themselves, others, or both. Other maladaptive psychological patterns such as nervousness or sadness have also been called mental illness, but these produce distress rather than disability. Over the past several decades, however, the term has been expanded to include increasingly more of the thousand natural ills to which the flesh is heir. A recent report from Harvard and the National Institute of Mental Health, for example, says that 46 percent of Americans will at some point in their lives develop a mental disorder.

Many of those thousand natural ills are included among the 400-odd disorders listed in the latest edition of the American Psychiatric Association's (APA) *Diagnostic and Statistical Manual of Mental Disorders,* the DSM. Calling it the psychiatric bible, Herb Kutchins, professor of social welfare at California State University, Sacramento, and Stuart A. Kirk, professor of social welfare at the University of California at Los Angeles (UCLA) point out that since there are no biological tests, markers, or known causes for most mental illnesses, psychiatric diagnosis is based almost entirely on symptomatology—depression, anxiety, disorganization, obsessive thinking, compulsive behavior, and other subjective symptoms.

Depression, for example, has as many causes as there are people suffering from it: job difficulties, failure to attain expectations, and problems in relationships are but a few. Basing psychiatric diagnosis entirely on symptoms can be compared to making fever a definitive diagnosis; symptoms are not disorders in themselves, but products of other psychological and/or physiological phenomena. The cure of depression—a term rarely used today although a common occurrence yesterday—requires that an individual's particular problems be addressed. Psychiatry's dependence on symptom-based diagnostics is a major reason for the specialty's mounting pessimism.

One reason for higher estimates of the prevalence of mental disorders is that the APA keeps adding new disorders and more behaviors to the manual, as Kutchins and Kirk point out. The increase in the number of these disorders, along with the greatly increased use of new medications to treat them, parallels the increase in individuals disabled by these disorders. Rates for psychiatric disability in America have risen from 3.38 per thousand in 1954; to 13.75 in 1987, when the atypical anti psychotics and SSRI antidepressants were introduced; to 19.69 in 2003. The number of patient care episodes—the amount of care given, as measured by the number of people treated each year for mental illness at psychiatric hospitals, residential facilities for the mentally ill, and ambulatory care facilities—rose similarly: from 1,028 per 100,000 population in 1955; to 3,295 in 1987; and to 3,806 in 2000. Since the start of the "medication era," the number of mentally disabled people has risen nearly sixfold.

How the History of ADHD Predicts the Effects of Screening

Kutchins and Kirk point out that children are considered to exhibit signs of attention deficit hyperactivity disorder (ADHD) when they are deceitful, break rules, can't sit still or wait in lines, have trouble with math, don't pay attention to details, don't listen, don't like to do homework, lose their school assignments or pencils, or speak out of turn. This common childhood behavior is defined as a disorder by the psychiatry department of the New York University (NYU) School of Medicine. ADHD is now diagnosed in 6 to 9 percent of school-age children and 4 percent of adults. Its "symptoms"—acting impulsively; easy distractibility; interrupting others; constant fidgeting or moving; and difficulty in paying attention, waiting one's turn, planning ahead, following instructions, or meeting deadlines—can be found in any of us. With diagnosis and treatment, the department contends, ADHD symptoms can be substantially decreased.

The process through which ADHD became accepted is important, but little recognized. In 1980, the list of symptoms then called ADD (attention deficit disorder) was first accepted into the DSM. Seven years later, hyperactivity was added, thus making ADHD. Within a year, 500,000 youngsters were assigned this diagnosis.

A few years later, ADHD was classified as a disability, and a cash incentive program was initiated for low-income families with children diagnosed with ADHD. A family could get $450 a month for each child so labeled, and the cost of treatment and medication for low-income children would be covered by Medicaid. Then in 1991, schools began receiving educational grants of $400 annually for each ADHD child. The same year, the U.S. Department of Education classified the disorder as a handicap, which required special services to be provided to each disabled child.

By 1996, close to $15 billion was spent annually on the diagnosis, treatment, and study of this supposed neuropsychiatric disorder. Recently, public health officials in the United States, Canada, and the United Kingdom have issued warnings about previously known, but undisclosed risks associated with the stimulant medications used to treat ADHD.

What has happened with ADHD presages what can be expected from government-sponsored mental health screening. One example is the case of the first-grade son of Patricia Weathers. After a school psychologist diagnosed the "disorder," she was pressured into medicating him.

"The medication eventually made him psychotic," she said. But when she stopped giving it to him, the school reported her to state child protection officials for "child abuse." Weathers cofounded AbleChild . . . and filed a lawsuit against school officials.

"We have 1,000 stories like this," she states. Meanwhile, her son is now 15 and "doing fine."

Rep. Ron Paul, M.D., (R-TX) a congressman who has been a physician for more than 30 years, has criticized government agencies for charging parents with child abuse if they refuse to drug their children. Some parents have even had their children taken from them for refusing to give them medications.

Mrs. Weathers's experience is far from unique. According to Dr. Andrew Mosholder of the FDA's Office of Drug Safety, about 2.5 million children in this country between ages 4 and 17 currently take ADHD drugs, 9.3 percent of 12-year-old boys, and 3.7 percent of 11-year-old girls. And although these medications have been used for years, the harm they can cause to the heart and circulatory system, and the psychiatric difficulties they can produce, is only now being publicly discussed.

No matter how we define mental illness in children or adults, it cannot be diagnosed by simple screening. Nobody can, by merely looking at someone else, or even on the basis of a questionnaire, differentiate the transient emotional disturbances we all have from those that last longer.

The ephemeral nature of suicidal ideation and depressive feelings among teens is specifically mentioned by the Columbia TeenScreen report. Screenings won't prevent suicide because those who are contemplating it usually won't tell. Indeed, the screening process itself can produce significant anxiety among those in whom mental illness is being "diagnosed." Such efforts to find their troubles by frightening people, and thus aggravating those troubles, are misdirected. Only when gross insanity exists can mental illness be recognized on inspection, and then we need neither experts nor screening.

Troubled people can indeed benefit from good mental health care. But good treatment requires that a physician actually examine a patient and address that individual's unique problems, with the patient's knowledge and consent. This requires time, and busy practitioners are often under severe time constraints. Thus, they are pressured to quickly prescribe medications to relieve symptoms that are often transient even if untreated.

In my opinion, relying on medication as the definitive treatment of psychiatric complaints, rather than addressing their real causes in patients' lives, is responsible for the gross overuse of psychiatric medications, especially among children, but also among seniors:

- Twenty-nine million prescriptions were written last year in the United States for Ritalin and similar medications to treat ADHD, 23 million of them for children.
- From 60 to 70 percent of children in foster care in Massachusetts are now being given psychiatric medications.
- About 40 to 50 percent of students arrive at some colleges with psychiatric prescriptions.
- Approximately 41 percent of prescriptions for one group of 765,000 people over 65 were for psychotropics.
- As many as 75 percent of elderly, long-term-care nursing home residents in another study were being given psychotropics.

The screening program will aggravate this already unfortunate situation.

Conclusions

Good intentions notwithstanding, the mental health screening program created by the president's NFC probably will harm thousands of Americans by
giving them stigmatizing diagnoses that can follow them for the rest of their
lives. The program's government-sponsored promotion of long-term medications will compound the harm, as the experience with ADHD has shown.

As Sharav points out, screening for mental illness serves no medical or
societal purpose. Screening will, however, do much to increase the benefits to
the drug manufacturers and to the mental health provider industry. Good psychiatric care is voluntary, and based on trust between patient and physician.
The involuntary government-sponsored mental health screening program, as
demonstrated by the cases of Aliah Gleason and Chelsea Rhoades, represents
psychiatric malpractice.

Their cases also demonstrate how the program undermines basic American freedoms, as parents are coerced to medicate their children, sometimes
with severe adverse effects.

We need to start to undo psychiatry's 50 years of overdependence on psy-
chopharmacology, rather than expanding it through mental health screening.

Mark D. Weist, Marcia Rubin, Elizabeth Moore,
Steven Adelsheim, and Gordon Wrobel

NO

Mental Health Screening in Schools

Background

A significant gap between the mental health needs of children and adolescents and the available services has been well documented. For example, between 12% and 27% of youth might have acting-out behavioral problems, depression, and anxiety; yet, as few as one sixth to one third of these youth receive any mental health treatment. In this context, school mental health (SMH) programs have grown progressively. This growth reflects increasing recognition of the need to address the mental health needs of children and youth and the many advantages of SMH programs. These include reducing barriers to student learning, unmatched access to youth, and ability to engage youth in an array of strategies that can simultaneously address their educational, emotional, behavioral, and developmental needs. In fact, for youth who do receive mental health services, most receive them in schools. In addition, SMH programs can reduce stigma, enhance the generalization and maintenance of interventions, increase opportunities for preventive services, and promote efficiency and productivity of staff and programs. Program evaluation data and early research suggest that *when done well*, SMH services are associated with satisfaction by a number of different stakeholder groups including students and contribute to achieving outcomes valued by families and schools.

Strong federal support for SMH programs and services is found in the US Surgeon General's reports on mental health and child and adolescent mental health; large federal initiatives such as the Safe Schools/Healthy Students Program and the Child and Adolescent Service System Program. *Achieving the Promise: Transforming Mental Health Care in America,* the report issued by the President's New Freedom Commission on Mental Health in 2003, emphasized the large gap between needs and effective services and the lack of a national priority on child and adolescent mental health. The 6 goals and 19 recommendations of the report strongly support SMH, including recommendation 4.2 to "improve and expand school mental health programs" and a related recommendation 4.3 to "screen for co-occurring mental and substance use disorders and link with integrated treatment strategies."

From *Journal of School Health*, 77(2) February 2007, pp. 53–57 (refs. omitted). Copyright ©
2007 by American School Health Association. Reprinted by permission of Wiley-Blackwell
via Rightslink.

Achieving the Promise calls for an approach that connects policy, training, practice, and research on mental health services and that improves behavioral, emotional, and academic functioning of youth. This approach is reflected in a pyramid of programs and services. The foundation aims to improve school environments and broadly promotes health as well as academic success. The second tier encompasses targeted prevention programs and early identification practices that help recognize and refer students with unmet mental health needs. Providing access to effective treatment services for serious and/or chronic disorders occupies the top of the pyramid. This model is congruent with a public health approach to disease prevention and detection. It incorporates a continuum of educational messages that promote health and prevention and incorporates early identification practices that ensure cost-effective treatment for disabling health conditions. This pyramid model for health and mental health promotion has been embraced by the World Health Organization and other groups but unfortunately does not reflect the way programs and services are delivered to children and youth in the United States.

Although historically, school-based mental health services were provided primarily to students qualified for special education services, more recently, schools have expanded mental health and social services for all students as part of their coordinated school health program. Today, there are a number of different models for offering these services in schools, with an array of service components ranging from alcohol and other drug use treatment, case management, individual and group counseling, and referrals to community mental health systems and providers. Despite this, there remain numerous barriers including

- insufficient funding
- inadequate training and supervision of staff
- difficulty coordinating a full continuum of prevention and intervention services
- maintenance of quality and empirical support of services
- limited evaluation of outcomes of services to improve programs and contribute to policy improvement.

Providing treatment services within school buildings is often challenging for additional reasons, including

- environmental characteristics (poor office spaces, crowded classrooms)
- frequent changes in personnel (high teacher and administrator turnover)
- distinctive knowledge bases and cultures (education and mental health)
- difficulties in fully engaging families
- academic demands stemming from the No Child Left Behind educational reforms.

These issues are increasingly documented in the published literature, especially in relation to research-based interventions.

Mental Health Screening in Schools

Youth with internalizing disorders such as depression, anxiety, or suicide ideation are not as easily identified as those with acting-out or externalizing disorders. Individuals with internalizing conditions comprise a significant population; the 2003 Youth Risk Behavior Survey, a nationally representative sample of more than 15,000 high school students throughout the United States, found that in the 12-month period preceding the survey 16.9% had seriously considered attempting suicide, 16.5% had made a plan for attempting suicide, 8.5% had attempted suicide one or more times, and 2.9% had made an attempt requiring medical attention. In addition, studies have shown that students contemplating suicide or even those who had previous attempts were not known or detected by school personnel. Furthermore, 90% of teens who commit suicide have a mental health issue at the time of their death but are usually not receiving treatment.

For these reasons, formal screening programs that detect depression and suicide ideation are recommended. The New Freedom Commission on Mental Health recommended screening in multiple settings as a critical component of a public health approach to prevention and early intervention for mental health issues in youth. The Commission went so far as to name the Columbia University TeenScreen program as a model program for identifying at-risk youth and linking them to critical intervention services. TeenScreen is currently implemented in 460 sites in 42 states and involves systematic and supported assessment of youth mental health needs in schools along with technical assistance and guidance on addressing identified needs. Other effective programs such as Dominic and the Signs of Suicide program are also widely available. These recommendations have led to increasing discussion among mental health providers of the need to advance mental health screening in schools. A few states, such as Ohio, Illinois, and New Mexico, have moved to expand screening in multiple settings as part of their efforts to transform their child's mental health system.

However, screening in schools is not without controversy. Some perceive screening as government intrusion, and others describe it as a violation of the family's right to privacy. These concerns appear to be based on the erroneous belief that screening programs in schools require all students to be screened against their wishes or against those of the parents. In fact, "mandatory universal screening" for behavioral health issues does not exist anywhere and has never been recommended by any federal agency or community screening program. All existing mental health screening programs are voluntary and require active informed consent of the family and the assent of the student. It is likely that another factor contributing to the misunderstanding surrounding screening is stigma. The President's Commission acknowledged the pervasive nature of stigma and the need to actively address it.

While there are no currently agreed-upon national standards for mental health screening in schools, a number of federal agencies, professional organizations, and advocacy groups have issued helpful resources. Both the Substance Abuse and Mental Health Services Administration and the National

Alliance for the Mentally III recently released documents confirming the importance of screening as part of a public health approach to early identification and intervention for behavioral health problems and offering guidelines for the appropriate use of screening. Well-established screening programs such as TeenScreen generally have experientially based recommendations for implementation and strongly recommend active parental consent for any screening in schools. Another helpful resource on screening and assessing mental health and substance use disorders was issued by the Office of Juvenile Justice and Delinquency Prevention of the US Department of Justice, which includes a set of criteria for selecting screening methods. The American Medical Association's Guidelines for Adolescent Preventive Services includes recommendations for screening behavioral and emotional conditions, such as substance abuse, eating disorders, depression, suicide risk, and school or learning problems. All these guidelines and criteria for mental health screening can provide a foundation for developing standards for the school setting.

Other Issues

In trying to decide whether to implement a screening program, there are other factors that districts will need to consider. For example, strategic planning should attempt to gauge the needs of individual schools in relation to the school/community's abilities to respond to those needs. This will require a self-assessment process. In addition, prior to advancing the agenda related to mental health screening in schools, the community should consider:

1. Availability of trained staff and other resources to conduct screening.
2. Availability of mental health providers with training in evaluating and treating those children and youth identified by screening.
3. Need for technical assistance in system development for ensuring parental consent and student assent for participation in screening.
4. Selection of age-appropriate screening measures.
5. Logistics including when to do the screening, finding the right confidential space for screening, and provision of alternative activities for youth who do not have parental permission for screening.
6. Resolution of liability concerns.

First Steps

Once a district has addressed the issues outlined above and decided to move toward implementing a formal screening program, five additional elements will need to be considered: inclusive planning, collaborative relationships, logistics, training and supervision, and integration.

Inclusive Planning
Planning should involve all significant stakeholders including families, education professionals, primary care providers, mental health professionals, and other representatives from the community. Once configured, the planning body might begin with a policy review to ensure that sufficient safeguards are in place to protect privacy and confidentiality. Districts can also benefit from

ongoing technical expertise from community agencies that respond to related mental health issues such as substance abuse, child welfare, law enforcement, or other specialty systems.

Collaborative Relationships

To promote collaboration, the sharing of resources, and to address liability concerns, memoranda of agreement should be established between schools and collaborating community agencies to ensure adequate clarification of responsibility. Ideally, local initiatives and agreements between child serving systems should be approved of and supported by state systems, such as state departments of education, mental health, juvenile justice, and child welfare.

Logistics

The time to conduct screening must be determined. Some have recommended transitional years such as sixth and seventh and ninth and 10th grades as critical times when clinical symptoms often linked to increased suicide risk sometimes develop. However, screening efforts at these ages should ideally be part of broader efforts within communities to promote wellness, mental health, and learning success for youth from preschool through young adulthood. Locally collected data such as emergency room data can assist in identifying age groups at particular risk. In the absence of locally available data, state and national data such as the Youth Risk Behavior Survey . . . can be helpful. However, if the planning group determines that there are inadequate resources to provide adequate follow-up to the screen, the screening process should be delayed until adequate resources are marshaled and confidence of adequate follow-up is increased.

Training, Supervision, and Support

Staff that participate in screening will require adequate training and supervision. Personnel will be needed who can coordinate the work; select age-appropriate and culturally sensitive measurement tools; manage associated technology for administering, scoring, and interpreting the data; and establish and sustain relationships with school and community providers.

Regardless of whether a school implements a systematic screening program, all schools should enhance their capacity to identify youth who present signs of emotional/behavioral disturbance. These disturbances represent barriers to learning and are indicative of the development of serious mental health concerns. Schools should connect these youth to appropriate resources and services. Professional development will be required to raise awareness and increase knowledge of child and adolescent mental health needs, the factors that promote healthy youth development and those that contribute to mental health problems, specific signs of distress, and strategies to assist distressed youth in obtaining help. All staff should have a clear understanding of referral procedures and know how to determine when a youth is in crisis and needs an immediate intervention.

Integration

Mental health screening should be one aspect of a full continuum of effective mental health programs and services in schools. Such programs can only exist when there is a full partnership between families, schools, and child serving systems, particularly the mental health system. There must be strong emphases on quality assessment and improvement, empirically supported practice, and evaluating outcomes of services. Findings from outcome evaluations should be used to continuously improve services and should connect to advocacy and policy agendas.

Conclusion

The President's New Freedom Commission on Mental Health provides specific recommendations to improve and expand school mental health programs and to screen for co-occurring mental and substance use disorders and link with integrated treatment strategies. The New Freedom Initiative and its 19 specific recommendations represent a call to action for communities and states to move beyond fragmented and ineffective approaches to illness care for a small percentage of those in need toward a true public mental health promotion system that ensures quality and effectiveness along a full continuum of services. Consideration of the issues outlined in this article should help schools and communities determine whether they are ready to include screening in schools as part of their SMH program.

When implemented with appropriate family, school, and community involvement, mental health screening in schools has the potential to be a cornerstone of a transformed mental health system that identifies youth in need, links them to effective services, and contributes to positive health and educational outcomes valued by families, schools, and communities.

POSTSCRIPT

Is Mental Health Screening an Unwarranted Intrusion?

The Executive Summary of the NFC's final report, *Achieving the Promise*, begins with this statement: "We envision a future when everyone with a mental illness will recover, a future when mental illnesses can be prevented or cured, a future when mental illnesses are detected early, and a future when everyone with a mental illness at any state of life has access to effective treatment and supports—essentials for living, working, learning, and participating fully in the community." As the outcome of its work, the NFC anticipates transforming the current complex fragmented system of mental health into a more integrated system of care for all.

Four compelling stories illustrate this controversy: Aliah, Rosie, Chelsea, and Courtney. Lehrman sees Aliah's and Chelsea's experiences as examples of the intrusive consequences of screening; Weist et al. would cite Rosie and Courtney as solid reasons to screen.

Lehrman tells Aliah's story: on the basis of an in-school screening and against the wishes of her parents, Aliah was hospitalized, isolated from her parents, and subjected to heavy medication. Compare Aliah to Rosie, the lead named plaintiff in a class action suit against the state of Massachusetts. The suit charged that nine children were hospitalized, or at risk for hospitalization, because Massachusetts did not provide Medicaid-mandated screenings and necessary home-based mental health services. The court ruled in Rosie's favor, reinforcing the need for these services in hopes that no other children would get "lost in the system" (Kenny, www.massmedicaid.org/briefs_16.html, 2007).

Lehrman also shares the experiences of Chelsea Rhoades, said to have mental health problems as a result of a brief in-school screening. Angered that they had not been notified of this intrusion into their lives, Chelsea's parents filed a lawsuit against her school (www.rutherford.org). Contrast this to Courtney, whose experience with in-school screening, and resultant mental health services, led her to say, "I'm not sure where I would be today if I didn't get screened. I'm not even sure I would be here at all" (Friedman, *The New England Journal of Medicine*, 2006).

One key element of this debate focuses on the type of parental permission requested. Methods of participation in any activity can be mandatory or voluntary; granting permission can be either active or passive. A mandatory activity is just that; everyone must participate. Statewide assessment systems are mandatory activities. Active voluntary permission requires a parent/guardian to sign a paper supporting their child's participation. Because permission slips can get lost—in transmission or on the kitchen table—passive/opt-out permission is sometimes employed. In this method, an informational permission note indicates that the student will participate in the stated activity unless the parent/guardian sends an objection to the school. *Achieving the Promise* is clear that screening is to be voluntary and that "parents should be included in the process of making choices and decisions for minor children" (Executive Summary). Some suggest a more active permission process would result in fewer children being screened (Effrem, www.edaction.org/2005/021405.htm).

Few would deny the benefits of providing help to those in need, especially to avoid a tragic event. It is harder to find agreement on how to identify those in need of services. Does mental health screening pry into personal thoughts and make value judgments about family choices or is it a valuable opportunity to deliver services that can make a life difference?

ISSUE 18

Is ADHD a Real Disorder?

YES: Evelyn B. Kelly, from *Encyclopedia of Attention Deficit Hyperactivity Disorders* (Greenwood Press, 2009)

NO: Hara E. Marano, from *Nation of Wimps: The High Cost of Invasive Parenting* (Broadway Books, 2008)

ISSUE SUMMARY

YES: Evelyn B. Kelly, a science writer, journalist, and adjunct professor at the College of Education, St. Leo University, presents an encyclopedia of characteristics, causes, and interventions for the several conditions that are all very real attention deficit hyperactivity disorders.

NO: Hara E. Marano, also an author and journalist, frequently writing for *Psychology Today* and other popular publications, believes that "hothouse parenting" and "overparenting" have created children who overreact to life events because they have not been allowed to develop naturally.

$\mathbf{A}$DHD, evokes a person who moves incessantly, has difficulty concentrating, and is distracted by environmental stimuli. Three types of ADHD are identified: predominantly inattentive, predominantly hyperactive-impulsive, and combined. Here are the official diagnostic criteria for ADHD:

A. Either (1) or (2):

    (1) Six (or more) of the following symptoms of inattention have persisted for at least 6 months to a degree that is maladaptive and inconsistent with developmental level:
- often fails to give close attention to details or makes careless mistakes
- often has difficulty sustaining attention in tasks or play
- often does not seem to listen when spoken to directly
- often does not follow through on instructions and fails to finish chores or duties (not due to oppositional behavior or failure to understand)
- often has difficulty organizing tasks and activities
- often avoids, dislikes, or is reluctant to engage in tasks that require sustained mental effort
- often loses things necessary for tasks or activities
- often forgetful

(2) Six (or more) of the following symptoms of hyperactivity–impulsivity have persisted for at least 6 months to a degree that is maladaptive and inconsistent with developmental level:
- often fidgets with hands or feet or squirms in seat
- often leaves seat unacceptably
- often runs about or climbs excessively when inappropriate (in adolescents or adults, may feel restless)
- often has difficulty playing quietly
- often talks excessively
- often blurts out answers before questions completed
- often has difficulty awaiting turn
- often interrupts or intrudes on others.

B. Some symptoms present before age 7
C. Present in two or more settings
D. Clear evidence of clinically significant impairment
E. Symptoms are not due to another disorder
(Adapted from DSM-IV-TR, 2000)

A developmental condition, ADHD is often considered when a child experiences difficulty focusing or behaving. Mention of ADHD is routinely accompanied by the name of a frequently used prescriptive medication.

The Centers for Disease Control and Prevention (CDC) indicate, 3% to 7% of school-aged children were reported to have an ADHD diagnosis as of 2006 (www.cdc.gov), about two children in every classroom of 25. This diagnosis occurs more frequently in boys who are non-Hispanic, primarily English-speaking, and covered by health insurance.

The U. S. Department of Education, Office of Special Education and Rehabilitative Services regularly updates two companion documents on ADHD. One addresses identification and treatment; the other contains an extensive array of strategies for instruction and behavior management (http://www2.ed.gov).

This issue's selections are excerpted from books that address the existence of ADHD from contrasting perspectives. Each author offers evidence to support her point of view and hopefully convince readers.

Evelyn Kelly's *Encyclopedia of Attention Deficit Disorders* is a comprehensive volume containing over 150 entries. Our selection focuses on the history of ADHD-like behaviors, their diagnosis, and their appearance in adults. Kelly discusses the serious consequences ADHD can have on schooling and life. She cautions readers not to view every active moment as convincing evidence of ADHD, but neither to ignore behavior that could signal this condition.

Hara E. Marano discusses ADHD in her book, *A Nation of Wimps*, which addresses how today's competitive environment leads parents to see every childhood event as crucial to future status and financial well-being. Marano describes "invasive" parents who structure every moment, "cheating" their children from the opportunity to engage in "simple" play. Discussing research findings that support how play fosters self-control and creativity. ADHD develops as a reaction to forced academic pressure and deprivation of unstructured playtime.

As you read these selections, ask yourself how often you have wondered if you or someone you know has ADHD. Are you experiencing long-term challenges, short-term pressures, or another condition that affects your attention and focus?

YES

Evelyn B. Kelly

Encyclopedia of Attention Deficit Hyperactivity Disorders

Introduction

Frazzled and befuddled, the mother of 5-year-old John brought him to the specialist's office. His teacher said he was the terror of the kindergarten, and his parents were concerned about his nonstop destructive behavior at home. In the doctor's office he jumped from chair to chair, climbed under a table, and flailed his arms like an animated rag doll. He picked up the tape and stapler from the receptionist's desk and then began to flip the light switch off and on, to everyone's annoyance. He ambled over to a group of children and butted into a game they were playing. They complained about his bossiness and moved away from him. The doctor immediately suspected John had attention-deficit hyperactivity disorder (ADHD). Is it really ADHD or is it something else?

The words "attention-deficit hyperactivity disorder" or ADHD are on the lips of many teachers, parents, and physicians. Generally, the child displays a persistent pattern of inattention and/or hyperactivity and impulsivity, which developed in the early years. When other symptoms such as forget-fulness, poor impulse control, and distractibility begin to interfere with the child's performance in the classroom or at home, parents become concerned. Unfortunately, the condition may persist into adulthood.

In 1998, the American Medical Association stated that ADHD is one of the best researched disorders in medicine. It is also one of the most controversial. Yet, with all the interest and research, no one knows what causes ADHD or how to cure it.

ADHD is considered to be a developmental disorder largely neurological in origin. The term "developmental" means that certain traits such as impulse control are slower to develop in these children than in the general population. That degree of lag appears to relate to the degree of severity of the disease. The compound terms "neurobehavioral" or "neurodevelopmental" disorders are frequently used to describe the disorder. The Greek root *neuro* means "nerve." ADHD is not thought to be a disorder relating to the brain and nervous system. However, the origin, causes, and treatments are subjects of debate and controversy.

From *Encyclopedia of Attention Deficit Disorders* by Evelyn B. Kelly, Greenwood Press, 2009, pp. ix–xi, 85–87, 91, 92, 9–11, 12. Copyright © 2009 by Evelyn B. Kelly. Reprinted by permission of Greenwood Publishing Group (ABC-CLIO).

ADHD is not just a fad that has been created in the latter half of the 20th century. It is documented in history. In 493 B.C. Hippocrates, the great physician on the Greek island of Cos, described a condition in patients who had quick sensory experience and their souls moved quickly on to the next impression. Believing that an imbalance of the four humors—water, fire, earth, and air—causes all diseases, Hippocrates attributed this condition to an overbalance of fire over water. He recommended a diet of barley rather than wheat bread and fish rather than meat; he also recommended adding water drinks and natural and diverse physical activities. Even Shakespeare referred to a serious malady of attention in King Henry VIII.

In 1845 a German, Dr. Heinrich Hoffman, wrote an illustrated book of children's poetry that described a boy named Fidgety Phillip, who obviously had all the symptoms of ADHD and who met a tragic end when he pulled all the food on the table over on top of him. Dr. Hoffman attributed the problem to bad behavior and certainly never considered it could be inherited from parents.

ADHD was first observed clinically in 1902. Sir George F. Still described a group of impulsive children who had behavioral problems. He added the idea that the problems of these children could be traced to a genetic disorder and not poor parenting. Still called the condition a "morbid defect of moral control." Others studied the condition and found the condition to be one that had identifiable symptoms.

Twentieth century scientists began to look for the causes of ADHD. In 1918, a terrible influenza epidemic left many survivors with neurological dysfunctions; some survivors exhibited behaviors that corresponded to ADHD. Dr. Bradley made a chance discovery in 1937; he found that a group of children with behavioral problems in Providence, Rhode Island, improved after receiving stimulant medication. In 1957, the stimulant methylphenidate (Ritalin) became available and in various forms and is still one of the most prescribed medications. . . .

Although it does affect 3–5 percent of school-age children, no simple test exists for ADHD. According to the American Psychiatric Association (2004), the condition is more common in boys with a ratio of two to one. Girls may hide the condition by sitting back and refusing to participate and consequently go undiagnosed. An estimated 60 percent of children diagnosed with ADHD retain the disorder as adults.

In a classroom not paying attention, losing things, making careless mistakes, and forgetting to turn in homework are normal to some degree, and taken individually may not indicate anything problematic. However, the child with ADHD may have a constellation of symptoms that interfere with school, home, and friends. Many of these children will carry the disorder into adulthood, when it will also cause tremendous problems. . . .

Diagnosis of ADHD

Diagnosis of ADHD is not an all-or-nothing concept. If one has food poisoning or measles, the diagnostician can point to an absolute cause based on symptoms and behavior. However, there are no concrete medical tests to diagnose ADHD, which therefore makes the diagnosis of ADHD subjective.

Although the diagnosis is not like other medical conditions, several strategies for determining ADHD are in play. These strategies lie in careful observation and analysis of the behaviors of the individual from many sources. Because many conditions can mimic ADHD, a thorough physical examination is essential. ADHD may be diagnosed by excluding many other possible conditions.

There are four important reasons for the proper diagnosis of ADHD:

1. Diagnosis gives information regarding treatment planning and the long-term course.
2. Diagnosis is necessary to obtain special services.
3. It is necessary for medical and legal reasons.
4. Diagnosis guidelines are important for consensus on who is included and how many are treated in research projects.

To the physician or psychologist, diagnosing ADHD is much more like trying to determine if the person has clinical depression. Everyone feels sad from time to time, but clinical depression will significantly impair the function of the person over a sustained period of time. Thus, the ADD/ADHD diagnosis is not for people who have occasional symptoms but for those whose function over a period of time is affected.

Making the problem even more perplexing is that some people will demonstrate proficiency at times. For example, a high school student is the star of the football team; he can remember and execute complex plays to perfection and concentrate to catch the ball with efficiency. He is bright, with an IQ in the superior range, but is in constant trouble with his teachers for not doing work, not paying attention in class, and making inappropriate comments in class. His teachers might ask, "If you can pay such attention on the football field, why can't you pay attention in class?" It may not just be the field where the person may concentrate; some may be involved in playing video games, drawing, building with Legos, or completing mechanical tasks. Yet, these same people may have trouble preparing for a major exam.

To diagnose ADHD, several types of professionals are involved: pediatricians, clinical psychologists, educational psychologists, teachers and school staff, and neurologists. Guidelines in the United States are provided in a manual known as the *Diagnostic and Statistical Manual*, 4th ed., revised, usually referred to as DSM-IV-R, which gives direction for diagnosis of recognized mental illnesses. To begin the diagnosis of ADHD, DSM-IV-R lists six essential steps:

1. The parent interview. This should include discussing problems, developmental history, and family history. Parents are encouraged to recount specific situations and instances and try not to make general statements about behavior, such as "he is bad" or "he just won't pay attention."
2. Interviewing the child about home, school, and social functioning.
3. Teachers and parent complete behavior-rating scales describing home and school functioning.

4. Obtaining data from the school. The data should include grades, achievement test scores, current placement, and other pertinent information.
5. The psychological testing for IQ and screening for a learning disability. This step may have been completed previously but is pertinent here for completing the picture of ADHD.
6. Physical and/or neurological exams.

DSM-IV states that these steps are only suggested and are not universally followed. The diagnosing professional should always consider other possibilities and rule them out before making a diagnosis of ADHD. . . .

[N]ot all may have specific training in the disorder. It is important to look for a professional who does have special interest and training for the disorder.

Knowing the differences in the qualifications and services may help the family choose the health care provider who can best meet their needs. Child psychiatrists are doctors who specialize in diagnosing and treating childhood mental and behavioral disorders. Pediatricians and psychiatrists can provide therapy and prescribe medications. Child psychologists can diagnose and help the family in many ways with the disorder, but they are not medical doctors and must rely on the child's physician to do medical exams and prescribe medication. Neurologists are medical doctors who work with disorders of the brain and nervous system; they can diagnose ADHD and prescribe medicine. However, unlike psychiatrists and psychologists, neurologists usually do not provide therapy for the emotional aspects of the disorder.

What Are the Subtypes of ADHD?

Although DSM-III used the term Attention Deficit Disorder (ADD), DSM-IV uses only the term Attention Deficit/Hyperactivity Disorder (ADHD) but classifies it into three different subtypes: ADHD predominantly hyperactive, ADHD inattentive, and a combined type.

Dr. Thomas Brown of Yale University has championed the recognition of children who have ADHD without hyperactivity. He believes these children are underdiagnosed because they are not the restless, intrusive, driven as if by a motor, Dennis-the-Menace stereotype. He notes these children are more like the stereotypes of "space cadet" or "couch potato" rather than the "whirling dervish" that one depicts as being the person with ADHD. Brown believes that even publications about ADHD offer little guidance about this disorder without hyperactivity.

Adults tend to overlook three specific groups of people with ADHD:

- Bright students. Adults think these people who underachieve are lazy and choosing not to do their work. However, individuals with ADD are found at all IQ levels.
- Females. Girls with ADD do not tend to stand out in the crowd and usually do not draw attention to themselves with dramatic disruptive behavior.

- Students under stress. When a student is daydreaming, the adult may explain away such behavior with family circumstances, such as divorce, unemployment, poverty, or multiple moves. What may be forgotten is that ADD is common in families under psychosocial distress. . . .

The **Centers for Disease Control and Prevention (CDC)** believes that only trained health care professionals should make a diagnosis of ADHD. This position is held because the symptoms may be part of other physical conditions, such as hyperthyroidism. Some normal individuals may exhibit some of these conditions from time to time. It is the pervasiveness of the symptoms that keep the person from functioning in school, work, and social relationships that form the strength of the factors in diagnosis. . . .

The diagnosis and evaluation of ADHD actually currently has no reliable objective tests. Because several of the symptoms overlap with other conditions, even a skilled clinician can have difficulty in determining differences. An astute clinician must perform a thorough medical and psychiatric evaluation. Useful tests include urine drug screening, serum thyroid-stimulating hormone, complete blood count, chemistry panel, a and a history of central neurologic illness, infection, or trauma. Many common medications may contribute to psychiatric symptoms. One of the main factors in diagnosis is the presence of chronic ADHD symptoms since childhood, without a major depressive episode. Several other scales have been developed for diagnosis. . . .

Adult ADHD

The idea of adult ADHD is fairly new and somewhat controversial. Papers dealing with an adult equivalent of childhood hyperactivity/minimal brain dysfunction were found in the late 1960s and 1970s, but they did not get widespread acceptance of the adult equivalents in the fields of psychiatry and clinical psychology. In 1994 Edward Hallowell and John Ratey wrote *Driven to Distraction,* which became a best seller and brought adult ADHD to the public's attention. Scientists, such as S. Goldstein (1997), K. Nadeau (1995), and Paul Wender (1995), conducted serious and rigorous scientific research on adults with ADHD. During the 1990s, more and more scientists began to consider the disorder as a real condition worthy of diagnosis and treatment. . . .

Several other popular books, as well as the media, also called attention to ADHD in adults. Internet chat rooms, Web pages, and bulletin boards were dedicated to this topic, and support groups such as ADDA and CHADD began to include adults with ADHD in their discussions. Adults with the disorder began to ask questions that challenged the old idea of the 1960s that they would outgrow the condition. The adult form of ADHD was found to share many of the attributes of childhood ADHD and was found to respond to similar medications and treatments. The acceptance of ADHD in adults continues at the present time and is likely to increase in the decades ahead.

Many adults realize they have ADHD when they seek diagnosis for a son or daughter. Up to 65 percent of children diagnosed with ADHD will continue to manifest symptoms of the disorder in adulthood. . . .

Adults are diagnosed under the same criteria as young people, including the fact that the symptoms began prior to age 7. Adults with ADHD may face challenges in self-control, self-motivation, executive functions, and inattention. They usually exhibit fewer of the impulsive and hyperactive tendencies that children have. However, they exhibit secondary symptoms such as disorganization, lack of follow-through, thrill-seeking, and impatience. These attributes may cause numerous problems in the work world.

Joseph Biederman, professor of psychiatry, Harvard Medical School, in a 2004 AMA briefing, observed that adults with ADHD had significant problems in the quality of their lives. According to Biederman, eight million adult Americans are estimated to struggle with inattention, impulsivity, and hyperactivity. He referred to his study of a large-scale survey that estimates yearly loss of household earning potential due to ADHD in the United States to be $77 billion. In the study he matched patients by educational levels. ADHD patients with high school education earn significantly less than their non-ADHD counterparts. On the average those with ADHD had household incomes $10,000 lower for high school graduates and $4,334 lower for college graduates. About 50 percent of those with ADHD reported they have lost or changed jobs because of the disorder. . . .

Although the existence and burden of ADHD have previously been questioned, ample data now support the validity of ADHD as diagnosis. Many successful people proclaim their struggle with ADHD as children and adults. . . .

Hara E. Marano

 **NO**

A Nation of Wimps: The High Cost of Invasive Parenting

Play, it seems, has an image problem. The public thinks it's . . . child's play. Child's play! Do we have a more dismissive locution in the English language? The importance of play is thoroughly counterintuitive. Play looks like a waste of time—*looks like*—because it is not goal directed. That is the very essence of play, activity that's not goal directed. And we adults are goal directed. So we trivialize kids' play. It gets in the way of other things we want to do on our way to achievement, a goal we also very much want for our children and are very worried about these days—counterproductively, the evidence indicates.

Few things in life are as ambiguous as play. Suspended between reality and unreality, it both is and isn't what it appears to be. Is the act of chasing in a game of tag real or is it make-believe? Is it serious or is it antic? Is the running intended or pretend? Inhabiting a fine and fleeting line between the substantive and the simulated, play compels constant shifts of perspective along with attention to the elements of communication just for players to decipher the meaning of an action. Like art, play is an experience that is almost impossible to define—because it encompasses infinite variety—and is as elusive as an image in the Versailles Hall of Mirrors. Is it an activity or a state of mind? Spontaneous or rule-bound?

. . . By its very ambiguous nature [play] gives brains a workout. It is cognitively challenging. It requires attention, and so it sharpens senses. It both demands and inspires mental dexterity and flexibility. It thrives on complexity, uncertainty, and possibility. That makes play just about the perfect preparation for life in the twenty-first century.

The big question is why we bother to play at all. After all, play is by definition mental and physical activity not related to survival. What distinguishes it from all other activity is that it has no goal whatsoever, which is not to say that people have not tried to put play to work to serve other goals—which immediately makes it not play at all. Play is always strictly voluntary, which is the source of enjoyment and underlies the sense of freedom it generates. In a classic 1938 study, *Homo Ludens* (Man the Player), the Dutch anthropologist Johan Huizinga insisted that play is, like art, "a primary category of life," a unique state that is absorbing and involves uncertainty and often a sense of illusion or exaggeration, though it has its own rules and boundaries. And as

From *A Nation of Wimps: The High Cost of Invasive Parenting* by Hara Estroff Marano, (Broadway Books, 2008, pp. 85–88, 90–95, 99, 100–101). Copyright © 2008 by Hara Estroff Marano. Reprinted by permission of The Stuart Agency for Hara Estroff Marano.

with art, perhaps we can't define it, but we know it when we see it. But above all, play exists outside ordinary life; even though they are absorbed in play, players are always aware that the play is not "real," that its consequences do not carry over into everyday life. Play defines a place apart, a safe and protected space where the rules of normal life are suspended.

It is a basic tenet of evolutionary psychology that useless behaviors—and worse, deleterious ones, which play can seem to be since it erodes energy, wastes time that could be spent searching for food or studying for SATs, and opens players to injury—pretty quickly get drummed out of behavioral repertoires. Yet in the animal kingdom, play increases, rather than decreases, with increasing brain complexity.

If play is more prominent in advanced species, could it be that play itself plays a major role in advancing the species? "We need play to become fully human," says the groundbreaking neuroscientist Jaak Panksepp, of Washington State University, who has studied play extensively in animals and humans. Play is the signature mammalian behavior, he contends. The very essence of play, . . . is to exercise and expand human variability and flexibility. We play because we can, we play because we need to, we play because it gives us a shot at keeping up with a world of unpredictably changing environments. Given the accelerating rate of cultural change, who can foretell what the world is going to be like in ten years and what information and skills will be most in demand in our information economy?

Play makes us nimble—neurobiologically, mentally, behaviorally—capable of adapting to a rapidly evolving world. Play cajoles us toward our human potential. It preserves alternatives—all the possibilities our nervous system tends to otherwise prune away as we specialize in what become our own quirks of behavior. It's no accident that all the predicaments of play—the challenges, the dares, the double dares, the chases—model the struggle for survival. . . . Play is our free connection to pure possibility, a prime pathway to transcendence precisely because it is so mercurial. Play is the future with sneakers on.

And that is probably why it spurs creativity. In making our brain circuits more flexible, play prompts us to see the world in new ways, says Robert Root-Bernstein, a professor of life sciences at Michigan State University, MacArthur "genius award" grantee, and longtime researcher of creativity. We can make new connections. Play encourages people to synthesize knowledge across different domains. The capacity to invent is intimately wrapped up in the freedom to play. Root-Bernstein has found that genius inventors and scientists are accomplished at playing—as musicians, in the visual arts, with writing and poetry. And many had created imaginary worlds as children, engaging in the activity known in the psych biz as "world-play."

In a study he conducted of MacArthur fellows, two-thirds of the grantees cited a connection between their childhood play world and their adult work. Even among those who didn't engage in childhood world-play, half still felt that play of some kind prepared them for their adult careers. Perhaps it's the attitude and experimental freedom of play itself that stay with them and shape their working lives. Play safely allows us to take risks. As Huizinga saw it, play is by its very nature conducive to experimentation, providing an opportunity for trying on new roles and attempting tasks that might be avoided in "real" life as too difficult or unpleasant. As the highest expression of our humanity, play benefits not only individuals but society as a whole. The instinct for play is a central element in the creation of human culture. "Civilization arises and unfolds in and as play," Huizinga insisted. . . .

The End of Play

In the hothouse that child raising has become, play is all but dead. Thanks to achievement pressures, kids' play is going the way of the hula hoop. Under pressure to create an atmosphere of achievement, schools are doing away with recess in the belief that less time for play leaves more time for study. Deemed extraneous and expendable, play, like art classes, has been sacrificed to the mistaken, mechanistic belief that the path to educational efficiency is straight and narrow and runs strictly through reading, math, and science. This is a Taliban-like approach to education, a kind of academic fundamentalism no more congruent with the richness of human nature, curiosity, and development than the religious kind.

Even in preschool, play is under assault; desks and work sheets are increasingly replacing blocks and make-believe, the play that emanates from children's free-flowing mental activity. The percentage of time that preschool kids spend in play decreased from 40 percent in 1981 to 25 percent in 1997. At the same time, a four-billion-dollar tutoring industry has sprung up—with a whopping 26 percent of it lavished on two- to six-year-olds.

What play there is has been corrupted. The organized sports many kids participate in are managed by adults according to their rules; difficulties that arise are not worked out by kids but adjudicated by adult referees. Kids' play is professionalized; team sports are fixed on building skills and on winning and losing, not on having a good time. There's nothing light-hearted about a soccer game when children are paid by their parents every time they play in a winning game. . . .

In the push to prepare kids for a radically changed world, it seems so very intuitive to remove play in favor of more time for schoolwork and testing—what educators themselves call "drill and kill." We're in an extended cultural moment where leaders think that getting tough with education is better than overhauling an educational system that is increasingly out of step with children's learning needs and informational opportunities; a system that increasingly requires clinical diagnosis and pharmaceutical support to hold kids in their seats seems more suited to the industrial age than the information age, where creative problem solving is the key to innovation. The current disdain for recess has echoes of our Puritan past, which may be something familiar enough to fall back on in the face of fear and uncertainty. Our Puritan forebears knew that work, not play, was the key to their success and saw labor as a way of glorifying God. Play, according to this view, threatens to undermine both our success and our salvation. The achievement pressures on kids reflect nothing so much as New Puritanism. But what no one has yet publicly reckoned with is that play has extraordinary intellectual and developmental value and it is almost all completely counterintuitive.

Play: Practice for Adulthood

Contrary to the widely held belief that only intellectual activities build a sharp brain, it's in play that the cognitive skills are most acutely developed. By play I'm referring not to adult-coached and adult-monitored sports but to true play: free, unstructured play, where the kids invent the activities, the activities reflect their own curiosity and interests—and they can find their own ways to be with each other. Anxious parents may regard play as trivial, but studies of children around the world demonstrate that the social engagement of play actually sharpens intellectual skills. Child's play fosters decision making, memory, thinking, and speed of mental processing. This shouldn't come as a surprise. After all, the human mind is believed to have evolved to deal with social problems.

There's no question that today's parents want the best for the kids. They especially want them to be prepared to thrive in a fast-changing world for which they themselves did not feel at all prepared. But in removing play from childhood, they have it precisely backward. . . . At its heat, play is rule-bound activities in which the outcome is unknown. It's the way we learn to handle the unexpected. Play sharpens wits and makes mental processes nimble— resilient and ready for whatever life throws our way. . . .

Nature's Spitball

Play turns out to be critical neurologically. That is the great hidden secret of play. Panksepp's research reveals that play turns on hundreds of genes in the brain and it acts in specific areas. It generates the production of a nerve growth factor called BDNF (brain-derived neurotrophic factor), and it does it in the frontal cortex of the brain, the executive control center.

BDNF is well recognized as the key modulator of nerve cell development, the creation of new nerve cells, called neurogenesis, and the branching of nerve cells that literally gives us behavioral flexibility, and survival itself. It is helpful to know that other things that turn on BDNF production are learning and vigorous exercise. One thing that turns off production of BDNF is stress. Further, BDNF is what's missing in depression. All of the therapies that work in relieving depression stimulate production of BDNF. Right there is a potentially critical connection, with lack of play setting the stage for psychopathology.

What play does, by stimulating neurogenesis, is hasten the development of the frontal cortex and program it. It solidifies the executive functions of the brain. In other words, it fosters the maturation of the very centers of the brain that allow us to exert control over attention, regulate our emotions, and control our behavior. Here is the very subtle trick that nature plays: it uses something that's *not* goal directed to create the very mental machinery for people to *be* goal directed. It creates the inhibitory circuitry of self-regulation and attention.

In other words, says Panksepp, social play "helps program higher brain areas that will be required later in life." You've got to admire it—the ability of play to stimulate the maturation and transformation of the brain is concealed under the fun. The subtlety and subversiveness of the transaction probably constitute the major reason why we haven't caught on to the importance of play.

But today's parental pressure obscures the value of play and makes it seem like a waste of time, a distraction from the true goal of academic and vocational success. Such a dismissive attitude toward play leads kids themselves to view any activity that is not explicitly goal directed as worthless and dilatory. Unfortunately, human development just doesn't unfold in a beeline.

ADHD—Have We Got It Backward?

In a direct challenge to current cultural dogma, Panksepp has gathered new evidence that play, neurobiologically constructive, helps build the brain in ways that encourage kids to control themselves and learn. The "learning disorder" known as attention deficit hyperactivity disorder, or ADHD, may result not from faulty brain wiring or chemistry gone awry, as conventional medical thinking holds, but from restriction of the urge to play. Further, vigorous bouts of unstructured social play, especially in preschoolers—the kind of play that adults often put a stop to—may be the best "therapy" for reducing the impulsive behaviors that characterize the disorder, the most common childhood psychiatric problem in America.

In fact, abundant social play in animals activates genes for neural growth factors in the executive portion of the brain. The neural tendrils that sprout in the brain in the wake of vigorous play supply raw material for the development of the circuitry of self-regulation that may ultimately tame impulses such as inappropriate play urges, suggests Panksepp.

Play—could it really be the cure for ADHD? Could so many smart people have badly misinterpreted the symptoms of inattention as the disease itself and failed to see how blatantly those symptoms suggest their own remedy? Panksepp is no stranger to upending orthodoxy. His extensive studies of neural systems among mammals suggest that, like us, animals have a range of emotions. A much-talked-about 2005 article in the prestigious journal *Science* proposed that a 50-kilohertz chirp emitted by rats in response to playful tickling (by him and the graduate students in his lab) and during their own "rambunctious shenanigans" is evidence of "an ancestral form of human laughter" and joy. It's worth noting that those tickled creatures also learn tasks faster, play more, and are more socially responsive.

Panksepp's studies also furnish evidence . . . that we are wired to play, innately constituted to seek the stimulation and mental activity that play produces. Play is an activity both of intellect-driven humans and of instinct-driven animals, its universality suggesting that its roots lie deep in our brains and may well be embedded in our genes. The urge to play is a fundamental neurological "drive"—it is powerful and arises spontaneously, without any learning. Thwarted or left unfulfilled, it creates symptoms of ADHD. The 6 to 16 percent of American children diagnosed with ADHD may be normal kids who simply have a strong desire to play or who encounter greater restrictions of activity.

It may be that the way American schools and parents are pushing for academic achievement is causing the very problem that makes learning so difficult for so many. Says Panksepp: "We need to worry about the social environments we have created that do not allow enough play and that seem to be leading to a dramatic increase in the diagnosis of ADHD."

Working with newborn rats, Panksepp and colleagues have created lesions in the brain's frontal cortex that lead to ADHD-like behavior. The damaged animals are especially prone to excessive playfulness. But when they were given one hour per day of access to play during their first week of life, the extra play alleviated the impulsive symptoms. The findings imply that the fundamental disorder in ADHD is not a deficit of attention at all but the inability to control the impulse to play—a deficit of behavioral inhibition. This makes great sense in the upside-down universe of brain disorders. "Most psychiatric problems ultimately reflect difficulties individuals encounter in regulating their feelings," notes Panksepp. Not in having the feelings, but in controlling them.

Panksepp has shown that the positive social engagement of play, though it originates in lower, instinctual regions of the brain, stimulates significant cortical activity in the frontal lobes. "The more cortical activity, the more it's possible to pay attention to the outside world—you can do what teachers want," he explains. Not only does the nervous system need play to fully mature; it appears to need a sufficient amount at a specific time.

The evidence so far points to liberal amounts of rough-and-tumble play from ages three to six. Panksepp told a recent neuroscience conference in New York that he's ready "to take to the human laboratory" the evidence from his animals studies. To lay the groundwork for a play intervention program, he conducted a feasibility study of vigorous play among pre-kindergarteners in the Bowling Green, Ohio, public school system. "The kids liked it very much, even if some of the teachers did not," he reports. One of his findings: girls seem to engage in rough-and-tumble play as much as boys do; there is no gender difference in play preference at that age.

"What really needs to be done now is to identify children who are on the ADHD track and give half of them very intense and persistent natural play activity twice a day every day, like food and water, for at least half an hour each session," he says. The double dose is a direct suggestion from studies and observations of baboons in the wild, indicating that there are circadian patterns to play. Animals seem to naturally experience two periods of extended play per day, although they also enjoy shorter romps at frequent intervals.

Play's effects on the brain are not limited to the frontal lobes. During play, deep dopamine reward circuits swing into action—the same channels of motivation and attention that get hijacked by drugs of abuse and all addictive activities. Further, play stimulates the joy chemicals known as opioids; they help mediate social reward in the brain. That's what makes romping around so much fun—and so hard to stop doing just because Mom issues a call to come in from outside. "Play is a tool of nature for social learning to construct the fully social brain," Panksepp says. "It prompts the frontal lobes to mature."

Unfortunately, the drugs commonly used to treat ADHD dramatically reduce the impulse to play in animals, Panksepp has found. "Might it be that so many American children are given Ritalin partly because it reduces disorderly behaviors that arise from poorly regulated playful urges? These molecules are highly effective in the classroom—but they would be comparably effective for the kids who don't need it. They would attend and perform better, too. That's the nature of the brain."

Chemically thwarting the drive to play—particularly with potential drugs of abuse such as Ritalin and other psychostimulants—might not just undermine self-regulation. It appears to be a bad idea for other reasons as well. Studies show that especially in young animals, psychostimulants can sensitize the opioid system so that later drug use may be especially attractive. Further, the drugs can have long-lasting personality effects. "To put it bluntly," says Panksepp, "they make our animals more urgently materialistic—more eager for external rewards." Play is a natural way to induce the chemistry for euphoria, at the same time that it helps organize the brain in social ways—and boosts the motivation to learn in the social environment of school.

Parents of ADHD kids often seek Panksepp out. If the child is very young, he always asks the father whether he rough-and-tumble plays with his child. "If he says no, we recommend doing it every day, religiously, if there's time in the morning—and if the child doesn't have a playmate, again in the evening for a while, an hour or so before bedtime. We have parents who say that Johnny is better. We have anecdotal data, but no more than that—nor does anyone else." Not yet, and probably not anytime soon; the climate for a federally funded study of play is not quite favorable. . . .

Not to be underestimated: the role of play in creating an environment everyone enjoys. . . . In a study done in Austria, children were given unlimited access to toys—provided they did their work first. Whenever their work was done, they could play with toys the rest of the day. The kids who got the chance to play performed as well academically as the kids in other classrooms—*but they wanted to go to school more*. The teachers liked the classrooms, and the parents liked the school. Similarly, a study done in the United States looked at kids coming into first grade with a reading background versus those coming in with a more old-fashioned play background, where there was talk and singing and make-believe. The kids who came in having been taught reading performed better during the first grade—but they were no better by the end of first grade. And they were much more depressed. "The opposite of play is not work," insisted Sutton-Smith. "It's depression."

That makes play essential not just for motivation but for all of mental health. Psychologists and psychiatrists have long known that emotionally disturbed children play only in very limited ways. Their play is rigid and obsessive; they enact the same scenarios over and over again. Play is often a primary therapy for children who have experienced trauma of some kind. . . . Through play therapy, traumatized children get to imagine new outcomes to their dire experience. They get to exert control over their world. And in fact, if traumatized children are not given the opportunity to find a way out through play, they will enact their experience in play over and over again. . . .

In the final analysis, child's play seems tethered to a pendulum that swings between two opposing beliefs about the nature of children and their development—one positive, expansive, and optimistic, one darker, mechanical, and deterministic. At one extreme, children are seen as cognitive beings that must be programmed much like computers—emphasis on the *cog* in *cog*nitive. Preschools eliminate play corners to make room for academic training in letters and numbers and color naming. It's never too soon to start cramming in information. And kids need external reinforcement to be motivated to do anything. In this scheme, play becomes the enemy of literacy activities such as reading. It's a very conservative view of children, assumes they are more or less blank slates bringing nothing to the table—and lags behind the evidence by at least half a century, in some estimates. . . .

POSTSCRIPT

Is ADHD a Real Disorder?

Attention Deficit Hyperactivity Disorder (ADHD) is firmly established in our society. Information about the disorder and its treatments is readily available. The National Institute of Mental Health (NIMH) offers the online booklet *Attention Deficit Hyperactivity Disorder* (www.nimh.nih.gov, 2008) accompanied by extensive references. NIMH describes ADHD as a neurobiological condition with genetic linkages. Environmental toxins can also be contributors.

ADHD is acknowledged by Individuals with Disabilities Education Act (IDEA) and referenced under Other Health Impairment, although some mistakenly refer to it as a learning disability. Organizations, Web sites, clinics, and medications attest to its existence. But is it real?

While supporting the existence of ADHD, Kelly often mentions that there are "no concrete medical tests" for ADHD, making diagnosis "subjective." Simultaneously, the *Encyclopedia's* section on the diagnosis of ADHD describes a complex set of procedures to rule out other conditions. In fact, the *Encyclopedia* closes with an appendix of close to 50 "conditions that may be confused with ADHD." These range from emotional disturbances to hearing problems to food allergies.

Careful evaluation of ADHD-like behavior is urged by Smith, Barkley, and Shapiro (2007), who describe three levels of diagnostic procedures. Checklists and brief interviews are minimally sufficient. An extensive "ADHD Checkup" combines assessment (including consideration of the effects of motivation, time of day, and fatigue) and some intervention. The third, and best, type considers the Checkup with the way the child responds to a series of interventions. Barkley feels medication helps, but sometimes reduces the motivation to try more complex approaches.

Studying three groups of children over time, Rabiner, Murray, Rosen, Hardy, Skinner, and Underwood (*Journal of Developmental and Behavioral Pediatrics,* 2010) found instability in teacher ratings of student attention. Many children rated as inattentive in 1 year were not rated that way the next school year. Rabiner and colleagues suggest that maturity, improved nutrition, or changed classroom situations may affect students' attention in school. They suggest annual evaluations to confirm whether the condition really exists.

The scientific community has not identified a specific cause or universally effective interventions; few believe ADHD can be cured. Standard treatments include medication, behavioral supports, and counseling. A combination of these is usually found to achieve the most significant and long-lasting change.

Hara E. Marano prescribes more unstructured play. Far from time-wasting, she believes children will use this opportunity to develop focus, resilience, and creativity. Similarly, Wiener (*Educational Leadership,* 2006) felt the deficit thinking often found in urban schools might be attributed to reduced opportunities for recess and playing. Evelyn B. Kelly's selection notes that Hippocrates recommended "diverse physical activities" to improve imbalanced humors.

Writing in the *Wall Street Journal* (2008, April 17), Shellenbarger explores "the silver lining" of ADHD. Interviewing the founders of Jet Blue and Kinko's, she sees signs that their ADHD masked remarkable creativity and ingenuity. Although the negative messages from school could be overwhelming, the outcome was much different because supportive parents reinforced what their child did right.

Deciding whether ADHD exists, and what to do about it, is our challenge. Have we lost our ability to tolerate anything other than total compliance and predictability, especially from little boys? Or, are we becoming increasingly aware of powerful biomedical conditions that affect our ability to attend, learn, and work? Are we running to ADHD (and medication) to make life easier or just beginning to understand its prevalence and implications? Does the remedy lie in a pill—or a playground, or in accepting children as individuals?

ISSUE 19

Are There Scientifically Effective Treatments for Autism?

YES: James B. Adams, Stephen M. Edelson, Temple Grandin, and Bernard Rimland, from "Advice for Parents of Young Autistic Children," Autism Research Institute, www.autism.org (Spring 2004)

NO: Committee on Educational Interventions for Children with Autism, Division of Behavioral and Social Sciences and Education, National Research Council, from *Educating Children with Autism* (National Academy Press, 2001)

ISSUE SUMMARY

YES: James B. Adams (Arizona State University), Stephen Edelson (Center for the Study of Autism), Temple Grandin (Colorado State University), and Bernard Rimland (Director of the Autism Research Institute) recommend to parents of young children with autism an array of effective treatment options, many of them biomedical based.

NO: The Committee on Educational Interventions, chaired by Catherine Lord, director of the University of Michigan's Autism and Communication Disorders Center, summarizing their examination of research studies of educational treatments for children with autism, found little consistent evidence to support the efficacy claims made by their proponents.

In 1943, Leo Kanner described a puzzling type of young child who preferred "aloneness" to the company of others. Kanner identified a combination of social isolation, significant delays in language development, and a tendency to engage in repetitive behavior and resist change; he named this group of behaviors infantile autism.

Early in the recognition of autism, Bruno Bettelheim and other psychoanalytically oriented psychologists posited that autism stemmed from unloving "refrigerator mothers" who failed to provide warm, responsive parenting. His theory was disproved by other researchers who found no difference between parents of children with autism and those with typical children.

Autism occurs with varying levels of severity. Children with high-functioning autism (termed Asperger's syndrome) display defining characteristics to a moderate degree. More significant challenges are experienced by children diagnosed with autism, Rett's syndrome, and/or PDD/NOS (pervasive developmental disability/otherwise not specified). Collectively, these are referred to as autism spectrum disorders (ASDs). The Autism Society of America (www.autism-society.org) Web site contains abundant information on many aspects of ASDs.

For the first 30 years of its recognition, autism occurred two to five times per 10,000 births. Prevalence figures have skyrocketed. The Centers for Disease Control and Prevention reports 1 in every 110 children was classified as having an ASD in 2006, an increase of 57% since 2002 (*Morbidity and Mortality Weekly Report*, December 2009).

Considerable dispute exists about the cause(s) of autism and the reason(s) behind the sudden rise in its occurrence. Many speculated that vaccines cause autism. Most (but not all) believe this issue has been resolved in the negative, especially since thimerisol, the mercury-containing vaccine preservative, has been removed from most childhood vaccines. Brown, author of *Babies 411*, provides a concise review of this controversy (www.immunize.org/catg.d/p2068.pdf) from the perspective of a pediatrician who advocates vaccinating children.

There is little disagreement about parental reaction to a diagnosis of autism: "Our boy, our beautiful boy, was floating away from us, and there was nothing we could do" (Isaacson, *The Horse Boy*, 2009) Or about a parent's drive to take positive action: "I was on a race against time to set him on a developmental path that would lead to independent living. The urgency to help him was almost primal" (Lytel, Washingtonpost.com, 2008).

Selecting an intervention is another matter entirely. A recent Amazon search for books on autism yielded 5,826 results. Some claim to describe medical facts about autism. Many speak powerfully about children "cured" by a specific method, medical treatment, or diet.

The authors of the first selection have personal and professional connections with this field. A number are parents of children with autism. Bernard Rimland is a pioneering researcher in autism. The life of Temple Grandin, an adult diagnosed with autism, is the subject of an Emmy-award winning film. Offering advice to parents of young children with autism, these authors review a number of methodologies they believe helpful and supported by research.

At the request of the federal Office of Special Education Programs, the Committee on Educational Interventions for Children with Autism integrated information from existing research, theory, and policy. This group of skilled researchers concludes that no one method has been substantiated as irrefutably effective.

As you read these articles, consider that almost everyone speaks to the urgency of beginning services early, sometimes before 2 years of age. Reeling from the diagnosis of their child, parents feel compelled to make a rapid choice. Powerful narratives of how an unusual methodology led to a cure may influence them. Educators want to respond to parents, but also to use research-based methods. How can each group make informed decisions? What happens when they disagree?

YES ◀ James B. Adams, Stephen M. Edelson, Temple Grandin, and Bernard Rimland

Advice for Parents of Young Autistic Children

Introduction

This paper is geared toward parents of newly diagnosed autistic children and parents of young autistic children who are not acquainted with many of the basic issues of autism. Our discussion is based on a large body of scientific research. Because of limited time and space, detailed explanations and references are not included.

Receiving a diagnosis of autism can be devastating to some parents, but for others it can be a relief to have a label for their child's symptoms. Many parents can be overwhelmed by fear and grief for the loss of the future they had hoped for their child. No one expects to have a child with a developmental disability. A diagnosis of autism can be very upsetting. Joining parent support groups may help. However, these strong emotions also motivate parents to find effective help for their children. The diagnosis is important because it can open the doors to many services, and help parents learn about treatments that have benefited similar children.

The most important point we want to make is that autistic individuals have the potential to grow and improve. Contrary to what you may hear from outmoded professionals or read in outmoded books, *autism is treatable.* It is important to find effective services, treatments, and education for autistic children as soon as possible. The earlier these children receive appropriate treatment, the better their prognosis. Their progress through life will likely be slower than others, but they can still live happy and productive lives.

What Is Autism?

Autism is a developmental disability that typically involves delays and impairment in social skills, language, and behavior. Autism is a spectrum disorder, meaning that it affects people differently. Some children may have speech, whereas others may have little or no speech. Less severe cases may be diagnosed with Pervasive Developmental Disorder (PDD) or with Asperger's Syndrome (these children typically have normal speech, but they have many "autistic" social and behavioral problems).

From www.autism.org, Spring 2004. Copyright © 2004 by Autism Research Institute. Reprinted by permission.

Left untreated, many autistic children will not develop effective social skills and may not learn to talk or behave appropriately. Very few individuals recover completely from autism without any intervention. *The good news is that there are a wide variety of treatment options which can be very helpful.* Some treatments may lead to great improvement, whereas other treatments may have little or no effect. No treatment helps everyone. A variety of effective treatment options will be discussed below.

Onset of Autism: Early Onset vs. Regression

Autism develops sometime during pregnancy and the first 3 years of life. Some parents report that their child seemed different at birth. These children are referred to as early-onset autism. Other parents report that their child seemed to develop normally and then had a major regression resulting in autism, usually around 12–24 months. These children are referred as late-onset or regressive autism. Some researchers argue that the regression is not real or the autism was simply unnoticed by the child's parents. However, many parents report that their children were completely normal (e.g., speech, behavior, social) until sometime between 1 and 2 years of age. The possible causative role of vaccinations, many of which were added to the vaccination schedule in the 1980s, is a matter of considerable controversy at present . . .

Prior to 1990, approximately two-thirds of autistic children were autistic from birth and one-third regressed sometime after age 1 year. Starting in the 1980s, the trend has reversed—fewer than one-third are now autistic from birth and two-thirds become autistic in their second year. The following results are based on the responses to ARI's [Autism Research Institute's] E-2 checklist, which has been completed by thousands of autism families. These results suggest that something happened, such as increased exposure to an environmental insult, possibly vaccine damage, between ages 1 and 2 years.

Several brain autopsy studies have indicated that brain damage occurred sometime during the first trimester of pregnancy, but many of these studies involved individuals who were born prior to 1990. Thus, these findings may not apply to what appears to be the new population of regressive autism.

Speech Development

One of the most common questions parents ask is: Will my child develop speech? An analysis of ARI's data involving 30,145 cases indicated that 9% never develop speech. Of those who develop speech, 43% begin to talk by the end of their first year, 35% begin to talk sometime between their first and second year, and 22% begin to talk in their third year and after. A smaller, more recent survey conducted by the first author found that only 12% were totally nonverbal by age 5. So, with appropriate interventions, there is reason to hope that children with autism can learn to talk, at least to some extent.

There are several ways to help autistic children learn to talk, including:

- Teaching speech with sign language; it is easy for parents to learn a few simple signs and use them when talking to their child. This is referred to as "simultaneous communication" or "signed speech." Research suggests that the use of sign language increases the chance of children learning spoken language.

- Teaching with the Picture Exchange Communication System (PECS), which involves pointing to a set of pictures or symbols on a board. As with sign language, it can also be effective in teaching speech.
- Applied Behavior Analysis: described in more detail later.
- Encouraging child to sing with a videotape or audiotape.
- Vestibular stimulation, such as swinging on a swing, while teaching speech.
- Several nutritional/biomedical approaches have been associated with dramatic improvements in speech production including dimethyigly-cine (DMG), vitamin B6 with magnesium, and the gluten-/casein-free diet to be discussed further below.

Genetics of Autism

Genetics appear to play an important role in causing some cases of autism. Several studies have shown that when one identical twin has autism, the other co-twin often has autism. In contrast, when one fraternal twin has autism, the co-twin is rarely autistic. Studies trying to identify specific genes associated with autism have been inconclusive. Currently, it appears that 20 or more genes may be associated with autism. This is in contrast to other disorders, such as Fragile X or Rett's syndrome, in which single genes have been identified.

A large number of studies have found that autistic individuals often have compromised immune systems. In fact, autism is sometimes described as an autoimmune system disorder. One working hypothesis of autism is that the child's immune system is compromised genetically and/or environmentally (e.g., exposure to chemicals). This may predispose the child to autism. Then, exposure to an (additional) environmental insult may lead to autism (e.g., the MMR vaccine) or mercury-containing vaccine preservatives (i.e., thimerosal).

If parents have a child with autism, there is an increased likelihood, estimated at 5% to 8%, that their future children will also develop autism. Many studies have identified cognitive disabilities, which sometimes go undetected, in siblings of autistic children. Siblings should be evaluated for possible developmental delays and learning disabilities, such as dyslexia.

Possible Environmental Causes of Autism

Although genetics play an important role in autism, environmental factors are also involved. There is no general consensus on what those environmental factors are at this point in time. Since the word "autism" is only a label for people who have a certain set of symptoms, there are likely to be a number of factors that could cause those symptoms. Some of the suspected environmental causes for which there is some scientific evidence include:

- Childhood vaccinations: The increasing number of vaccines given to young children might compromise their immune system. Many parents report their child was normal until vaccinations.

- MMR vaccine: Evidence of measles virus [has] been detected in the gut, spinal fluid, and blood. Also, the incidence of autism began rising significantly when the MMR was introduced in the [United States] (1978) and in the United Kingdom (1988).
- Thimerosal (a mercury-based preservative) in childhood vaccines. The number of vaccines given to children has risen over the last two decades, and most of those vaccines contained thimerosal, which is 50% mercury. The symptoms of mercury poisoning in children are very similar to the symptoms of autism.
- Excessive use of oral antibiotics can cause gut problems, such as yeast/bacterial overgrowth and prevents mercury excretion.
- Maternal exposure to mercury (e.g., consumption of seafood high in mercury, mercury dental fillings, thimerosal in RhoGam shots).
- Lack of essential minerals: zinc, magnesium, iodine, lithium, and potassium may be especially important.
- Pesticides and other environmental toxins.
- Other unknown environmental factors.

Prevalence of Autism

There has been a rapid increase in the number of children diagnosed with autism. The most accurate statistics on the prevalence of autism come from California, which has an accurate and systematic centralized reporting system of all diagnoses of autism. The California data show that autism is rising rapidly, from 1 per 2,500 in 1970 to 1 per 285 in 1999. Similar results have been reported for other states by the US Department of Education. Whereas autism once accounted for 3% of all developmental disabilities, in California it now accounts for 45% of all new developmental disabilities. Other countries report similar increases.

We do not know why there has been a dramatic increase in autism over the past 15 years, but there are several reasonable hypotheses. Since there is more than one cause of autism, there may be more than one reason for the increase. A small portion of the increase of autism where speech is delayed may be due to improved diagnosis and awareness, but the report from California reveals that this only explains a minute part of the increase. However, the increase in the milder variant called Asperger's Syndrome may be due to increased diagnosis. In Asperger's Syndrome, there is no significant speech delay and early childhood behavior is much more normal. The major reason for the increase is certainly due to environmental factors, not genetics, since there is no such thing as a "genetic epidemic." Some *possible* environmental factors were discussed in the previous section, and an increased occurrence of one or several of those factors probably accounts for the rapid increase in autism. . . .

What Is the Difference Between Asperger's Syndrome and Autism?

Asperger syndrome is usually considered a subtype of high-functioning autism. Most of the individuals with Asperger syndrome are described as "social but awkward." That is, they want to have friends, but they do not have the social skills to begin and/or maintain a friendship. While high-functioning autistic individuals may also be "social but awkward," they are typically less interested in having friends. In addition, high-functioning autistic individuals are often delayed in developing speech/language. Those with Asperger syndrome tend not to have speech/language delays, but their speech is usually described as peculiar, such as being stilted and perseverating on unusual topics.

Medical Testing and Treatments

A small but growing number of physicians (many of whom are themselves parents of autistic children) are involved in trying safe and innovative methods for treating the underlying biomedical basis of autism—the Defeat Autism Now! (DAN!) program. . . .

Routine medical tests are usually performed by traditional pediatricians, but they rarely reveal problems in autism that can be treated. Genetic testing for Fragile X syndrome can help identify one possible cause, and this testing is typically recommended when there is mental retardation in the family history. Many physicians do not conduct extensive medical testing for autism because they believe, incorrectly, that the only useful medical treatments are psychiatric medications to reduce seizures and behavioral problems.

Some of the major interventions suggested by DAN! practitioners include:

- Nutritional supplements, including certain vitamins, minerals, amino acids, and essential fatty acids
- Special diets totally free of gluten (from wheat, barley, rye, and possibly oats) and free of dairy (milk, ice cream, yogurt, etc.)
- Testing for hidden food allergies, and avoidance of allergenic foods
- Treatment of intestinal bacterial/yeast overgrowth
- Detoxification of heavy metals.

Psychiatric Medications

The various topics covered in this overview paper for parents of young autistic children represent, for the most part, a consensus of the views, based on research and personal experience, of all four authors. However, the authors differ in their opinions on the role of psychoactive drugs should play. . . .

Grandin has a relatively accepting position on the use of psychiatric medications in older autistic children and adults. She feels that it is worthwhile to consider drugs as a viable and useful treatment. Rimland and Edelson, on the other hand, are strongly opposed to the use of drugs except as a possible last resort, . . .— [t]hey feel the risks are great and consistently outweigh the benefits. Adams has an intermediate view. . . .

Educational/Behavioral Approaches

Educational/behavioral therapies are often effective in children with autism, with Applied Behavioral Analysis (ABA) usually being the most effective. These methods can and should be used together with biomedical interventions as together they offer the best chance for improvement.

Parents, siblings, and friends may play an important role in assisting the development of children with autism. Typical pre-school children learn primarily by play, and the importance of play in teaching language and social skills cannot be overemphasized. Ideally, many of the techniques used in ABA, sensory integration, and other therapies can be extended throughout the day by family and friends.

Applied Behavior Analysis Many different behavioral interventions have been developed for children with autism, and they mostly fall under the category of Applied Behavioral Analysis (ABA). This approach generally involves therapists who work intensely, one-on-one with a child for 20 to 40 hours/week. Children are taught skills in a simple step-by-step manner, such as teaching colors one at a time. The sessions usually begin with formal, structured drills, such as learning to point to a color when its name is given; and then, after some time, there is a shift towards generalizing skills to other situations and environments.

A study published by Dr. Ivar Lovaas at UCLA in 1987 involved 2 years of intensive, 40-hour/week behavioral intervention by trained graduate students working with 19 young autistic children ranging from 35 to 41 months of age. Almost half of the children improved so much that they were indistinguishable from typical children, and these children went on to lead fairly normal lives. Of the other half, most had significant improvements, but a few did not improve much.

ABA programs are most effective when started early (before age 5 years), but they can also be helpful to older children. They are especially effective in teaching non-verbal children how to talk.

There is general agreement that

- behavioral interventions involving one-on-one interactions are usually beneficial, sometimes with very positive results
- the interventions are most beneficial with the youngest children, but older children can benefit
- the interventions should involve a substantial amount of time each week, between 20 and 40 hours depending on whether the child is in school
- prompting as much as necessary to achieve a high level of success, with a gradual fading of prompts
- proper training of therapists and ongoing supervision
- regular team meetings to maintain consistency between therapists and check for problems
- most importantly, keeping the sessions fun for the children is necessary to maintain their interest and motivation.

Parents are encouraged to obtain training in ABA, so that they provide it themselves and possibly hire other people to assist. Qualified behavior consultants are often available, and there are often workshops on how to provide ABA therapy.

Sensory Integration   Many autistic individuals have sensory problems, which can range from mild to severe. These problems involve either hypersensitivity or hyposensitivity to stimulation. Sensory integration focuses primarily on three senses—vestibular (i.e., motion, balance), tactile (i.e., touch), and proprioception (e.g., joints, ligaments). Many techniques are used to stimulate these senses in order to normalize them.

Speech Therapy   This may be beneficial to many autistic children, but often only 1–2 hours/week is available, so it probably has only modest benefit unless integrated with other home and school programs. As mentioned earlier, sign language and PECS may also be very helpful in developing speech. Speech therapists should work on helping the child to hear hard consonant sounds such as the "c" in cup. It is often helpful if the therapist stretches out and enunciates the consonant sounds.

Occupational Therapy   Can be beneficial for the sensory needs of these children, who often have hypo- and/or hypersensitivities to sound, sight, smell, touch, and taste. May include sensory integration (above).

Physical Therapy   Often children with autism have limited gross and fine motor skills, so physical therapy can be helpful. May also include sensory integration (above).

Auditory Interventions   There are several types of auditory interventions. The only one with significant scientific backing is Berard Auditory Integration Training (called Berard AIT or AIT) which involves listening to processed music for a total of 10 hours (two half-hour sessions per day, over a period of 10 to 12 days). There are many studies supporting its effectiveness. Research has shown that AIT improves auditory processing, decreases or eliminates sound sensitivity, and reduces behavioral problems in some autistic children.

Other auditory interventions include the Tomatis approach, the Listening Program, and the SAMONAS method. There is limited amount of empirical evidence to support their efficacy. . . .

Computer-based auditory interventions have also received some empirical support. They include Earobics . . . and Fast ForWord. . . . These programs have been shown to help children who have delays in language and have difficulty discriminating speech sounds. Earobics is less much expensive (less than $100) but appears to be less powerful than the Fast ForWord program (usually over $1,000). Some families use the Earobics program first and then later use Fast ForWord.

Computer Software   There are many educational programs available for typical children, and some of those may be of benefit for autistic children. There is also some computer software designed specifically for children with developmental disabilities. One major provider is Laureate. . . .

Vision Training and Irlen Lenses   Many autistic individuals have difficulty attending to their visual environment and/or perceiving themselves in relation to their surroundings. These problems have been associated with a short attention span, being easily distracted, excessive eye movements, difficulty scanning or tracking movements, inability to catch a ball, being cautious when walking up- or downstairs, bumping into furniture, and even toe walking. A 1- to 2-year vision training program involving ambient prism lenses and performing visual-motor exercises can reduce or eliminate many of these problems. . . . More information on vision training can be found on Internet Web site of the College of Optometrists in Vision Development. . . .

Another visual/perceptual program involves wearing Irlen lenses. Irlen lenses are colored (tinted) lenses. Individuals who benefit from these lenses are often hypersensitive to certain types of lighting, such as fluorescent lights and bright sunlight; hypersensitive to certain colors or color contrasts; and/ or have difficulty reading printed text. Irlen lenses can reduce one's sensitivity to these lighting and color problems as well as improve reading skills and increase attention span. . . .

Relationship Development Intervention (RDI) This is a new method for teaching children how to develop relationships, first with their parents and later with their peers. It directly addresses a core issue in autism, namely, the development of social skills and friendships. . . .

Preparing for the Future

Temple Grandin: "As a person with autism I want to emphasize the importance of developing the child's talents. Skills are often uneven in autism, and a child may be good at one thing and poor at another. I had talents in drawing, and these talents later developed into a career in designing cattle handling systems for major beef companies. Too often there is too much emphasis on the deficits and not enough emphasis on the talents. Abilities in children with autism will vary greatly, and many individuals will function at a lower level than me. However, developing talents and improving skills will benefit all. If a child becomes fixated on trains, then use the great motivation of that to teach reading, use calculating the speed of a train to teach math, and encourage an interest in history by studying the history of the railroads."

Developing Friendships

Although young children with autism may seem to prefer to be by themselves, one of the most important issues for older children and adults is the development of friendships with peers. It can take a great deal of time and effort for them to develop the social skills needed to be able to interact successfully with other children, but it is important to start early. In addition, bullying in middle and high school can be a major problem for students with autism, and the development of friendships is one of the best ways to prevent this problem.

Friendships can be encouraged informally by inviting other children to the home to play. In school, recess can be a valuable time for teachers to encourage play with other children. Furthermore, time can be set aside in school for formal "play time" between children with autism and volunteer peers—typical children usually think that play time is much more fun than regular school, and it can help develop lasting friendships. This is probably one of the most important issues to include in a student's Individualized Education Program (IEP, or education plan for the child). Children with autism often develop friendships through shared interests, such as computers, school clubs, model airplanes, etc. Encourage activities that the autistic individual can share with others.

School Programs

For children younger than 3 years old, there are early intervention programs. For children over 3 years of age, there are pre-school and school programs available. Parents should contact their local school district for information on their local programs. In some cases a separate program for special-needs children may be best, but for higher-functioning children integration into a regular school setting may be more appropriate, provided that there is enough support (a part- or full-time aide, or other accommodations as needed). It is important that parents work with their child's teacher on an Individual[ized] Education Plan (IEP), which outlines in great detail the child's educational program. Additionally, meeting with the child's classmates and/or their parents can be helpful in encouraging other students to interact positively with the autistic child.

In some states, home therapy programs (such as ABA and speech therapy) may be funded by the school district, rather than through the state. However, it may take considerable effort to convince the school district to provide those services. Check with your local ASA chapter and other parents about how services are usually provided in your state. . . .

Long-Term Prognosis

Today, most adults with autism are either living at home with their parents or living in a group home. Some higher-functioning people live in a supported-living situation, with modest assistance, and a very few are able to live independently. Some are able to work, either in volunteer work, sheltered workshops, or private employment, but many do not. Adults with PDD/NOS (not otherwise specified) and Asperger's generally are more likely to live independently, and they are more likely to work. Unfortunately, they often have difficulty finding and then maintaining a job. The major reason for chronic unemployment is not a lack of job skills, but rather due to their limited social skills. Thus, it is important to encourage appropriate social skills early on, so [that] they are able to live and work independently as much as possible.

Some of the most successful people on the autism spectrum who have good jobs have developed expertise in a specialized skill that often people value. If a person makes him/herself very good at something, this can help make up for some difficulties with social skills. Good fields for higher functioning people on the spectrum are architectural drafting, computer programming, language translator, special educator, librarian, and scientist. It is likely that some brilliant scientists and musicians have a mild form of Asperger's Syndrome (Ledgin, 2002). The individuals who are most successful often have mentor teachers either in high school, college, or at a place of employment. Mentors can help channel interests into careers. Untreated sensory oversensitivity can severely limit a person's ability to tolerate a workplace environment. Eliminating fluorescent lights will often help, but untreated sound sensitivity has caused some individuals on the spectrum to quit good jobs because ringing telephones hurt their ears. Sensory sensitivities can be reduced by auditory integration training, diets, Irlen lenses, conventional psychiatric medications, and vitamin supplementation. Magnesium often helps hypersensitive hearing.

It should also be pointed out that the educational, therapy, and biomedical options available today are much better than in past decades, and they should be much better in the future. However, it is often up to parents to find those services, determine which are the most appropriate for their child, and ensure that they are properly implemented. *Parents are a child's most powerful advocates and teachers*. With the right mix of interventions, most children with autism will be able to improve. As we learn more, children with autism will have a better chance to lead happy and fulfilling lives.

Committee on Educational Interventions
for Children with Autism, Division of
Behavioral and Social Sciences and Education,
National Research Council

 **NO**

Educating Children with Autism

Conclusions and Recommendations

This [selection] summarizes the committee's conclusions about the state of the science in early intervention for children with autistic spectrum disorders and its recommendations for future intervention strategies, programs, policy, and research. The [selection] is organized around seven key areas pertaining to educational interventions for young children with autistic spectrum disorders: how the disorders are diagnosed and assessed and how prevalent they are, the effect on and role of families, appropriate goals for educational services, characteristics of effective interventions and educational programs, public policy approaches to ensuring access to appropriate education, the preparation of educational personnel, and needs for future research.

Diagnosis, Assessment, and Prevalence

Conclusions

Autism is a developmental disorder of neurobiologic origin that is defined on the basis of behavioral and developmental features. Autism is best characterized as a spectrum of disorders that vary in severity of symptoms, age of onset, and association with other disorders (e.g., mental retardation, specific language delay, epilepsy). The manifestations of autism vary considerably across children and within an individual child over time. There is no single behavior that is always typical of autism and no behavior that would automatically exclude an individual child from a diagnosis of autism, even though there are strong and consistent commonalities, especially relative to social deficits.

The large constellation of behaviors that define autistic spectrum disorders—generally representing deficits in social interaction, verbal and nonverbal communication, and restricted patterns of interest or behaviors—are clearly and reliably identifiable in very young children to experienced clinicians and educators. However, distinctions among classical autism and atypical autism, pervasive developmental disorder—not otherwise specified (PDD-NOS), and Asperger's disorder can be arbitrary and are often associated with

From *Educating Children with Autism* by Committee on Educational Interventions for Children with Autism, pp. 211–227. Copyright © 2001 by National Academies Press. Reprinted by permission.

the presence or severity of handicaps, such as mental retardation and severe language impairment.

Identifying narrow categories within autism is necessary for some research purposes; however, the clinical or educational benefit to subclassifying autistic spectrum disorders purely by diagnosis is debated. In contrast, individual differences in language development, verbal and nonverbal communication, sensory or motor skills, adaptive behavior, and cognitive abilities have significant effects on behavioral presentation and outcome, and, consequently, have specific implications for educational goals and strategies. Thus, the most important considerations in programming have to do with the strengths and weaknesses of the individual child, the age at diagnosis, and early intervention.

With adequate time and training, the diagnosis of autistic spectrum disorders can be made reliably in 2-year-olds by professionals experienced in the diagnostic assessment of young children with autistic spectrum disorders. Many families report becoming concerned about their children's behavior and expressing this concern, usually to health professionals, even before this time. Research is under way to develop reliable methods of identification for even younger ages. Children with autistic spectrum disorders, like children with vision or hearing problems, require early identification and diagnosis to equip them with the skills (e.g., imitation, communication) to benefit from educational services, with some evidence that earlier initiation of specific services for autistic spectrum disorders is associated with greater response to treatment. Thus, well-meaning attempts not to label children with formal diagnoses can deprive children of specialized services. There are clear reasons for early identification of children, even as young as 2 years of age, within the autism spectrum.

Epidemiological studies and service-based reports indicate that the prevalence of autistic spectrum disorders has increased in the last 10 years, in part due to better identification and broader categorization by educators, physicians, and other professionals. There is little doubt that more children are being identified as requiring specific educational interventions for autistic spectrum disorders. This has implications for the provision of services at many levels. Analysis of data from the Office of Special Education Programs, gathered for school-age children since the autism category was recognized in 1991, would support investigation of whether the dramatic increases in the numbers of children served with autistic spectrum disorders are offset by commensurate decreases in other categories in which children with autistic spectrum disorders might have previously been misclassified or whether these dramatic increases have come about for other reasons.

Although children with autistic spectrum disorders share some characteristics with children who have other developmental disorders and may benefit from many of the same educational techniques, they offer unique challenges to families, teachers, and others who work with them. Their deficits in nonverbal and verbal communication require intense effort and skill even in the teaching of basic information. The unique difficulties in social interaction (e.g., in joint attention) may require more individual guidance than for other children in order to attract and sustain their children's attention. Moreover, ordinary social exchanges between peers do not usually occur without deliberate planning and ongoing structuring by the adults in the child's environment. The absence of typical friendships and peer relationships affects children's motivation systems and the meaning of experiences. Appropriate social inter-actions may be some of the most difficult and important lessons a child with autistic spectrum disorders will learn.

In addition, the frequency of behavior problems, such as tantrums and self-stimulatory and aggressive behavior, is high. The need for systematic selec-tion of rewards for many children with autistic spectrum disorders, whose motivation or interests can be limited, requires creativity and continued effort from teachers and parents to maximize the child's potential. Although general principles of learning and behavior analysis apply to autistic spectrum dis-orders, familiarity with the specific nature of the disorder should contribute to analysis of the contexts (e.g., communicative and social) of behaviors for individual children and result in more effective programming. For example, conducting a functional assessment that considers contexts, and then replac-ing problem behaviors with more appropriate ways to communicate can be an effective method for reducing problem behaviors. . . .

Role of Families

Conclusions

Having a child with an autistic spectrum disorder is a challenge for any family. Involvement of families in the education of young children with autistic spectrum disorders can occur at multiple levels, including advocacy, parents as participating partners in and agents of education or behavior change, and family-centered consideration of the needs and strengths of the family as a unit. Nearly all empirically supported treatments reviewed by the com-mittee included a parent component, and most research programs used a parent-training approach. More information is needed about the benefits of a family-centered orientation or combined family-centered and formalized parent training in helping parents.

It is well established that parents can learn and successfully apply skills to changing the behavior of their children with autistic spectrum disorders, though little is known about the effects of cultural differences, such as race, ethnicity, and social class, nor about the interactions among family factors, child characteristics, and features of educational intervention. For most fami-lies, having a child with an autistic spectrum disorder creates added stress. Parents' use of effective teaching methods can have a significant effect on that stress, as can support from within the family and the community. Parents need access to balanced information about autistic spectrum disorders and the range of appropriate services and technologies in order to carry out their responsibilities. They also need timely information about assessments, educa-tional plans, and the available resources for their children. This information needs to be conveyed to them in a meaningful way that gives them time to prepare to fulfill their roles and responsibilities.

In the last 10 years the widespread availability of the Internet and media attention to autistic spectrum disorders have increased parents' knowledge but often conveyed perspectives that were not balanced nor well-supported scientifically. Of crucial importance is the question of how to make information available to parents and to ensure their active role in advocacy for their children's education. . . .

Goals for Educational Services

Conclusions
At the root of questions about the most appropriate educational interventions lie differences in assumptions about what is possible and what is important to give students with autistic spectrum disorders through education. The appropriate goals for educational services are the same as those for other children: personal independence and social responsibility. These goals imply continuous progress in social and cognitive abilities, verbal and nonverbal communication skills, adaptive skills, amelioration or behavioral difficulties, and generalization of abilities across multiple environments. In some cases, reports have suggested that particular treatments can foster permanent "recovery." However, as with other developmental disabilities, the core deficits of autistic spectrum disorders have generally been found to persist, to some degree, in most individuals.

Research concerning outcomes can be characterized by whether the goal of intervention is broadly defined (e.g., "recovery" or "best outcome") or more specifically defined (e.g., increasing vocabulary or peer-directed social behavior); whether the design involves reporting results in terms of group or individual changes; and whether the goals are short term (i.e., to be achieved in a few weeks or months) or longer term (i.e., over years). A large body of single-subject research has demonstrated substantial progress in individual responses to specific intervention techniques in relatively short periods of times (e.g., several months) in many specific areas, including gains in social skills, language acquisition, nonverbal communication, and reductions in challenging behaviors. Studies over longer periods of time have documented joint attention, symbolic play, early language skills, and imitation as core deficits and hallmarks of the disorder that are predictive of longer term outcome in the domains of language, adaptive behaviors, and academic skills.

Many treatment studies report postintervention placement as an outcome measure. While successful participation in regular classrooms is an important goal for some children with autistic spectrum disorders, the usefulness of placement in regular education classes as an outcome measure is limited because placement may be related to many variables other than the characteristics of the child (e.g., prevailing trends in inclusion, availability of other services). The most commonly reported outcome measure in group treatment studies of children with autistic spectrum disorders has been changes in IQ scores, which also have many limitations.

Studies have reported substantial changes in large numbers of children in intervention studies and longitudinal studies in which children received a variety of interventions. Even in the treatment studies that have shown the strongest gains, children's outcomes are variable, with some children making substantial progress and others showing very slow gains. The needs and

strengths of young children with autistic spectrum disorders are very heterogeneous. Although there is evidence that many interventions lead to improvements and that some children shift in specific diagnosis along the autism
spectrum during the preschool years, there does not appear to be a simple
relationship between any particular intervention and "recovery" from autistic
spectrum disorders. Thus, while substantial evidence exists that treatments
can reach short-term specific goals in many areas, gaps remain in addressing
larger questions of the relationships between particular techniques, child characteristics, and outcomes. . .

Characteristics of Effective Interventions

Conclusions

In general, there is consistent agreement across comprehensive intervention programs about a number of features, though practical and, sometimes,
ethical considerations have made well-controlled studies with random assignment very difficult to conduct without direct evaluation. Characteristics of the
most appropriate intervention for a given child must be tied to that child's
and family's needs. However, without direct evaluation, it is difficult to know
which features are of greatest importance in a program. Across primarily preschool programs, there is a very strong consensus that the following features
are critical:

- Entry into intervention programs as soon as an autism spectrum diagnosis is seriously considered;
- Active engagement in intensive instructional programming for a minimum of the equivalent of a full school day, 5 days (at least 25 hours)
  a week, with full year programming varied according to the child's
  choronological age and developmental level;
- Repeated, planned teaching opportunities generally organized around
  relatively brief periods of time for the youngest children (e.g., 15–20
  minute intervals), including sufficient amounts of adult attention in
  one-to-one and very small group instruction to meet individualized
  goals;
- Inclusion of a family component, including parent training;
- Low student/teacher ratios (no more than two young children with
  autistic spectrum disorders per adult in the classroom); and
- Mechanisms for ongoing program evaluation and assessments of individual children's progress, with results translated into adjustments in
  programming.

Curricula across different programs differ in a number of ways.
They include the ways in which goals are prioritized, affecting the relative
time spent on verbal and nonverbal communication, social activities,
behavioral, academic, motor, and other domains. Strategies from various programs represent a range of techniques, including discrete trials, incidental
teaching, structured teaching, "floor time," and individualized modifications
of the environment, including schedules. Some programs adopt a unilateral
use of one set of procedures, and others use a combination of approaches.

Programs also differ in the relative amount of time spent in homes, centers, or schools, when children are considered ready for inclusion into regular classrooms, how the role of peers as intervention agents is supported, and in the use of distraction-free or natural environments. Programs also differ in the credentials that are required of direct support and supervisory staff and the formal and informal roles of collateral staff, such as speech language pathologists and occupational therapists.

Overall, many of the programs are more similar than different in terms of levels of organization, staffing, ongoing monitoring, and the use of certain techniques, such as discrete trials, incidental learning, and structured teaching. However, there are real differences in philosophy and practice that provide a range of alternatives for parents and school systems considering various approaches. The key to any child's educational program lies in the objectives specified in the IEP and the ways they are addressed. Much more important than the name of the program attended is how the environment and educational strategies allow implementation of the goals for a child and family. Thus, effective services will and should vary considerably across individual children, depending on a child's age, cognitive and language levels, behavioral needs, and family priorities. . . .

Public Policies

Conclusions

The Individuals with Disabilities Education Act (IDEA) contains the necessary provisions for ensuring rights to appropriate education for children with autistic spectrum disorders. However, the implementation and specification of these services are variable. Early intervention for young children with autistic spectrum disorders is expensive, and most local schools need financial help from the state and federal programs to provide appropriate services.

The large number of court cases is a symptom of the tension between families and school systems. Case law has yielded an inconsistent pattern of findings that vary according to the characteristics of the individual cases. The number of challenges to decision-making for programming within school systems reflects parents' concerns about the adequacy of knowledge and the expertise of school systems in determining their children's education and implementing appropriate techniques.

The treatment of autistic spectrum disorders often involves many disciplines and agencies. This confuses lines of financial and intellectual responsibility and complicates assessment and educational planning. When communication between families and school systems goes awry, it can directly affect children's programming and the energy and financial resources that are put into education rather than litigation. Support systems are not generally adequate in undergirding local service delivery programs and maximizing the usefulness of different disciplines and agencies, and transitions between service delivery agencies are often problematic.

A number of states have successful models for providing services to children with autism, and mechanisms are becoming increasingly efficient and flexible in some states. In most cases, existing agencies at state and federal levels can develop appropriate programs without restructuring—with the possible addition of special task forces or committees designed to deal with issues particular to children with autistic spectrum disorders. . . .

Personnel Preparation

Conclusions

The nature of autistic spectrum disorders and other disabilities that frequently accompany them has significant implications for approaches to education and intervention at school, in the home and in the community. Approaches that emphasize the use of specific "packages" of materials and methods associated with comprehensive intervention programs may understate the multiple immediate and long-term needs of children for behavior support and for instruction across areas.

Teachers are faced with a huge task. They must be familiar with theory and research concerning best practices for children with autistic spectrum disorders, including methods of applied behavior analysis, naturalistic learning, assistive technology, socialization, communication, inclusion, adaptation of the environment, language interventions, assessment, and the effective use of data collection systems. Specific problems in generalization and maintenance of behaviors also affect the need for training in methods of teaching children with autistic spectrum disorders. The wide range of IQ scores and verbal skills associated with autistic spectrum disorders, from profound mental retardation and severe language impairments to superior intelligence, intensify the need for personnel training. To enable teachers to adequately work with parents and with other professionals to set appropriate goals, teachers need familiarity with the course of autistic spectrum disorders and the range of possible outcomes.

Teachers learn according to the same principles as their students. Multiple exposures, opportunities to practice, and active involvement in learning are all important aspects of learning for teachers, as well as students. Many states and community organizations have invested substantial funds in teacher preparation through workshops and large-audience lectures by well-known speakers. While such presentations can stimulate enthusiasm, they do not substitute for ongoing consultation and hands-on opportunities to observe and practice skills working with children with autistic spectrum disorders.

Personnel preparation remains one of the weakest elements of effective programming for children with autistic spectrum disorders and their families. Ways of building on the knowledge of teachers as they acquire experience with children with autistic spectrum disorders, and ways of keeping skilled personnel within the field, are critical. This is particularly true given recent trends for dependence on relatively inexperienced assistants for in-home programs. Providing knowledge about autistic spectrum disorders to special education and regular education administrators, as well as to specialized providers with major roles in early intervention (e.g., speech language pathologists), will be critical in effecting change that is proactive. Findings concerning change in educational and other opportunities suggest that administrative attitudes and support are critical in improving schools. . . .

Needed Research

Conclusions

There are several distinct and substantial bodies of research relevant to young children with autistic spectrum disorders. One body identifies neurological, behavioral, and developmental characteristics. Another body of research addresses diagnostic practices and related issues of prevalence. Another has examined the effects of comprehensive early treatment programs on the immediate and long-term outcomes of children and their families. These treatment studies tended to use some form of group experimental design. An additional body of research has addressed individual instructional or intervention approaches, with many studies in this literature using single-subject experimental methodology. Altogether, a large research base exists, but with relatively little integration across bodies of literature. Highly knowledgeable researchers in one area of autistic spectrum disorders may have minimal information from other perspectives, even about studies with direct bearing on their findings.

Most researchers have not used randomized group comparison designs because of the practical and ethical difficulties in randomly assigning children and families to treatment groups. In addition, there have been significant controversies over the type of control or contrast group to use and the conditions necessary for demonstrating effectiveness. Although a number of comprehensive programs have provided data on their effectiveness, and, in some cases, claims have been made that certain treatments are superior to others, there have been virtually no comparisons of different comprehensive interventions of equal intensity.

Across several of the bodies of literature, the children and families who have participated in studies are often inadequately described. Standardized diagnoses, descriptions of ethnicity, the social class, and associated features of the children (such as mental retardation and language level) are often not specified. Fidelity of treatment implementation has not been consistently assessed. Generalization, particularly across settings, and maintenance of treatment effects are not always measured. Though there is little evidence concerning the effectiveness of discipline-specific therapies, there is substantial research supporting the effectiveness of many specific therapeutic techniques.

POSTSCRIPT

Are There Scientifically Effective Treatments for Autism?

Authors of the two selections agree on some points. Autism is a serious disability that can have disastrous consequences. Intensive, early intervention is critical. There are many methods from which to choose. Here is where agreement lessens.

James B. Adams and his colleagues believe strongly in a biomedical cause for autism. Our environment is hurting children. Although educational interventions are important, they advocate medical treatment as well.

The Committee on Interventions holds that autism's increasing prevalence is due to changes in diagnostic practices. As the field learns about autism, more children are given this diagnosis instead of another, such as mental retardation or language/communication disability. Noting the wide range of characteristics in children with ASDs, the Committee says much more systematic research is needed to find the best educational interventions.

One of the most widely used treatments is applied behavioral analysis (ABA). An intensive therapy based on the work of Lovaas and colleagues, ABA methods require many daily hours of 1:1 work, reinforcing children for increasingly complex behaviors. This approach begins with an emphasis on eye contact and basic attention and moves on to academic and social interactions. Supporters assert ABA has *cured* their child. Detractors maintain that existing research studies are flawed and that learned behavior does not generalize to new settings.

Claiming that her son is her science, actress Jenny McCarthy adopted a combination of behavioral therapy, diet, and supplements that "became the key to saving Evan from autism" (*Mother Warriors*, 2008). Doctors don't have an answer but she, and the mothers she quotes, knows what they have seen and who they believe.

Paul Offit (*Autism's False Prophets*, 2008) empathizes with the helpless feelings of parents and acknowledges that the "glacial pace of research," combined with a child's slow progress, can lead to frustration and a demand for a solution. Despite inspiring anecdotal claims, Offit cautions that proponents of alternative therapies such as stringent diets, chelation, and anti-yeast medications offer false hope, wasting time and money. He shares the words of parents who feel betrayed by misleading promises of recovery.

Writing to parents, Rader (*EP*, 2008) reminds readers that the phrase "there is presently no cure for this condition" is simply not acceptable to people seeking to help their child. Many currently accepted methods began as nontraditional therapies before they were validated by extensive research; every intervention began with one person's observations of change.

Endeavoring to determine which treatments parents are using and which are seen as effective, the Interactive Autism Network (www.iancommunity.org) has identified more than 300 different therapies, many delivered simultaneously. Harchik and Ladew (*EP*, 2008) caution parents that employing several approaches at once could dilute the effectiveness of each, making it difficult to identify the effects of any.

But not everyone wants a cure for autism. Web sites and blogs reveal diverse perspectives. Consider three. The banner for DAN! (www.defeatautismnow .com) proclaims "Autism is Treatable. Recovery is Possible," and links readers to DAN! doctors. The UC Davis MIND Institute (www.ucdmc.ucdavis.edu/ MINDInstitute), begun as a collaboration between families and doctors with the desire to "fight back," is "committed to the awareness, understanding, prevention, care and cure of neurodevelopmental disorders." In contrast, The Autistic Self-Advocacy Network (www.autisticadvocacy.org) "seeks to advance the idea of neurological diversity, putting forward the concept that the goal of autism advocacy should not be a world without Autistic people. Instead, it should be a world in which Autistic people enjoy the same access, rights and opportunities as all other citizens."

A child of two is diagnosed with autism. Intervention is essential. Time is of the essence. There is no uniformly successful intervention, but there are plenty of heartfelt testimonials. What's a parent to do? If each child is unique, can research prove the worth of any method? How does anyone decide?

ISSUE 20

Does Working with Parents Have to Be Contentious?

YES: Jenna Goudreau, from "Parenting Through Special Education," *Forbes* (August 5, 2009)

NO: Jennifer Krumins, from "Choose Your Advocates Wisely: Getting the Best for Your Child," *EP Magazine* (August/September 2009)

ISSUE SUMMARY

YES: Jenna Goudreau relates the compelling story of parents who have to fight with school systems and battle legal complexities to get the free appropriate public education they feel is right for their children with disabilities.

NO: Jennifer Krumins, a special education teacher and mother of a child with autism, advises parents to ease tension, stress, and pressure by finding an advocate who can serve as an "interpreter" in a complex educational system and teach them how to secure the necessary supports with a positive approach.

The meeting is to be convened in 5 minutes. In attendance are 10 educators and Mr. and Mrs. Jones. The group will be discussing a recent evaluation of Jessie Jones, a third grader, to consider eligibility for special education. This is the middle of a very long process. Everyone looks ready for a serious conversation.

Let's take a few steps back to see what led to this meeting. Jessie is a sociable child who enjoys sports, videogames, and family time. School is another matter for discussion. Unlike others in the class, Jessie began kindergarten with no preschool experience. Although most classmates had mastered the basics of numbers, letters, and school routines, it was all new to Jessie, who has been struggling ever since.

This year, Jessie's teachers decided it was time to formally explore the reasons behind these struggles. Mr. and Mrs. Jones reluctantly agreed to an evaluation to determine whether Jessie qualified for special education. They were not happy with the possibility that Jessie could have a disability, but everyone agreed Jessie might need more than a classroom teacher could provide.

Along with the form asking written permission for a battery of unfamiliar tests came a dense brochure explaining parental rights within the special education process. The Jones' learned that no evaluation could be conducted without their written consent. They would meet with school staff to discuss the evaluation results, after they had received a copy of all reports. If this team established that Jessie had a disability requiring specially designed instruction, it would formulate an Individualized Education Plan (IEP) specifying recommended services and projecting goals to be reached in 1 year. The brochure repeated what Jessie's teachers had said: No special education services could be provided (or changed) without written parental approval on that IEP.

There was also a lengthy section on due process: What could happen if the parents and the schools disagreed, now or in the future. If they disagreed with the school's evaluation, the Jones' might be eligible for a second opinion at school expense. If they disagreed with the school's proposals, they could ask for a resolution meeting to discuss their concerns. In their state, the Jones' could also ask for mediation, where a neutral third person would attempt to find common ground between the school and parents. If that did not work, the brochure outlined increasing levels of appeal, where other neutral parties would decide whether the school's IEP met the letter of the law. Parents could even go to state or federal courts.

Mr. and Mrs. Jones knew parents with good experiences in the special education process, but had spoken to others who were frustrated and unhappy. At the beginning of this meeting, they were anxious and uncertain. So many people were sitting on *the other side* of the table. They felt concerned and alone. The reports they received had been full of unfamiliar information about Jessie. They worried they would not understand; they would not ask the right questions; they would not make the right decisions. They had known Jessie's teachers for a long time, but could they trust them now?

Jenna Goudreau and Jay Mathews, both professional journalists, relate the experiences of several parents who have fought their way through "the maze of education laws" to ensure their child with disabilities was well-served. Each presents a story of unending frustration, battling school personnel about the type, location, and amount of services needed.

Jennifer Krumins, a teacher, an author, and a parent of a child with autism, acknowledges the isolation felt by parents who are entrusting their vulnerable child to a suddenly legalistic bureaucracy. Krumins counsels that a knowledgeable, objective advocate can be a guide through this unfamiliar territory. She encourages parents to choose an advocate who focuses on solutions and options rather than blame and arguments.

Returning to the meeting with Mr. and Mrs. Jones, think of the possibilities. Like some, their experience may be positive. They might feel part of a mutually respectful collaborative team that crafts a strong plan for Jessie (Fish, *Preventing School Failure*, 2008). Then again, the Jones might feel unheard and lose the trust they had in teachers to do the best for Jessie (Angell, Stoner, and Sheldon, *Remedial and Special Education*, 2009).

As you read these articles, consider your own school experiences. Did you feel anger about the surprising stiff-necked rigidity of teachers and administrators who seemed so nice before this lengthy process began? Did you feel anger about the surprising stiff-necked rigidity of parents who seemed so nice before this lengthy process began? What did parents and teachers do to keep communication open and consider alternative points of view? How did each handle disagreement?

YES

Jenna Goudreau

Parenting Through Special Education

It's a typical summer morning for Maureen Blasko, an associate director at Ernst & Young's Washington, D.C., office. While she helps her 8-year-old twins get ready for the day, her husband makes their lunches and shuffles them out the door—one is off to golf camp; the other to figure skating.

Katie, her eldest, is 15. From birth, she's suffered a host of medical issues and now attends a special education school for her epilepsy, learning disabilities and ADD. Blasko still gets her dressed, ties her shoes and reminds her to brush her teeth and hair after she finishes breakfast. She will stay and see that Katie gets safely on the summer school bus (at 7:30 a.m., it's late again), but her mind is already jumping ahead to her packed work schedule. When the bus rumbles in, it's one kiss on Katie's cheek and she's off to the office.

Working moms are expert jugglers. While many are putting in long hours to grow their careers, they are also striving to get their kids in the best schools or classrooms, and watching over homework and after-school activities. Having children with special needs complicates things exponentially. And it's not just a small few dealing with disabilities. According to the U.S. Department of Education, 13.6% of students have disabilities and 6.5 million children are enrolled in special education.

There are federal laws in place to help parents and their special needs kids, but the education system can be difficult to navigate. Parents have to be constant advocates, adding a whole other layer to the familiar working mother balancing act.

The Basics

The Individuals with Disabilities Education Act (IDEA) is a federal requirement, enacted in 1975 and still evolving, that ensures children with disabilities receive a "free appropriate public education" from ages 3 to 22. Each state must provide the minimum requirements, though some provide more, and all interpret the law differently and on a child-by-child basis.

Every child confirmed to have one of 13 disabilities—ranging from autism or learning disabilities like dyslexia to physical or sensory impairments—is administered an Individualized Education Plan (IEP) catered to his or her

From *Forbes*, August 5, 2009. Copyright © 2009 by Forbes Media. Reprinted by permission of Forbes Media LLC.

specific needs. An IEP team that includes the child's parent, a general education teacher, a special education teacher, a school representative and others with special knowledge of the child or disability creates the plan and meets annually (or more, if needed) to discuss the student's progress.

What the Laws Lack

Taking care of her now 23-year-old son, who has several physical and learning disabilities, consumed much of Carol Berman's time—so much so that the former market researcher at a large brokerage firm had to give up her job. His disabilities, and the attendant physical therapy, fights with health insurance companies and "the maze of education laws" had to take precedent. It was a financial blow to her family on top of everything else.

"The basic tenet of the law, that each child is entitled to a 'free appropriate education in the least restrictive environment' becomes tricky," she says. "To a parent, 'appropriate' means 'best,' which is not necessarily the case for the school districts."

She hit several roadblocks. The general policy of inclusion, when special needs children and mainstream kids share a classroom, made it difficult for her son to keep up with the advancing curriculum. She also felt that the advisers who recommended services did so based more on funding and statistics than to the specific strengths and weaknesses of her son.

Ellen Notbohm, author of the best-selling *Ten Things Every Child with Autism Wishes You Knew,* agrees that there are "100,000 interpretations of the law." She tells parents that constant communication with the school is their best bet and suggests they "look for a school that will see the child as a whole child and not as a baggie of broken parts." But the power—and ultimate responsibility—lies with the parent.

A Second Job

Marilyn Haese, mother of two sons, ages 19 and 17, both diagnosed with dyslexia and AD/HD, runs her own PR agency, Haese & Wood, in Century City, Calif. She is the first to admit a working mom with special needs kids must devote a Herculean amount of time to their education. It becomes a second job.

Every school year she has had to reintroduce her children's ever-changing needs to the school—classroom teachers, yes, but also the librarian, gym teacher and even the principal. Their report cards had measurements that changed and became harder to decipher as the boys aged. But her biggest obstacle has been her battles against her children's IEP teams.

Haese discovered that she had to champion what *she* knew was in the best interests of her boys. When her older son was in elementary school, for example, he was moved from a mainstream school to a special ed school. Concerned about the social and educational ramifications of extracting him from a "normal" setting, she moved him back to public school—after much ado and against adviser recommendations. He's now in college and she believes the transfer made all the difference. She now tells other parents to be proactive, address problems early and to be the voice your child doesn't have.

Early on Chantai Snellgrove of Vero Beach, Fla., realized she was naive to blindly trust the school system and has been battling it ever since. "It's very frustrating," she says. "If you don't know the right questions, you won't get very far." As the mother of a 12-year-old daughter with language and learning disabilities, she's had to immerse herself in the research, keep meticulous records and negotiate fervently with an "intimidating" team of professionals to ensure her daughter gets what she needs.

Advocating for her child was so complicated and time consuming that, once Snellgrove learned the ropes, she found a new career—helping others embarking on the same path. Last year, she founded the online magazine, *Parenting Special Needs,* a resource she says she wished she had from the start.

Ernst & Young's Blasko admits that she has also applied her business acumen to IEP meetings. "Everything is a negotiation, just like work," she says. She got into a boardroom-style broil recently. When Katie, her 15-year-old, was placed in three job skills training classes and had no time in her schedule for science, Blasko refused. Katie will be taking biology in the fall.

What's Next

Rich Robinson, executive director of the Federation for Children with Special Needs, a services and support organization for parents, says he keeps an eye on the controversial issues surrounding special education. Full federal funding, he says, is the "politically hot debate."

[In 2009, p]rograms falling under the Individuals with Disabilities Education Act (IDEA) are set to receive $12.2 billion as part of the American Recovery and Reinvestment Act (ARRA). Half was given out in April and the other $6.1 billion will be released in September. The funds, in part, will go toward retraining displaced teachers to specialize in special education.

In other words, it appears that the federal government is looking at special education to help stimulate the economy. To many of these working mothers, shifting funds sounds like a sigh of relief.

Choose Your Advocates Wisely:
Getting the Best for Your Child

Imagine . . . after months of waiting and anticipation, the moment has finally arrived! Your beautiful baby enters the world and life is the fullest it has ever been! As the nurse gently places your newborn in your arms she slips a book into your hands. "This is your child's manual," she explains. "Be sure to read it as soon as possible. Oh, and pay close attention to the section regarding special needs."

A crazy scenario. I know, but at times I wish that I had been given that manual! Navigating the parenting role is tricky at the best of times but, finding your way with a child that has special needs is even more demanding and difficult. This is a path that may not have been traveled by family and friends. Loneliness, disappointment, frustration, and a sense of failure can make the journey miserable. The challenges can become overwhelming once your child reaches school age. It is at that time that you enter a whole world of professionals that will have your precious child for six hours out of the day! It is a world that is a culture unto itself with its own language and its own set of rules. You may feel like an outsider. You may feel that you need help. You may need someone to act as an interpreter in this new land.

You begin the investigation . . . look on the Internet and the Yellow Pages . . . can someone out there help me do the best for my child in school? Before you choose the person who will be your guide and advocate for your child, you must do some homework, for the sake of your child and for your own sanity. There are many people who call themselves advocates, but it is up to you—the parent—to make an informed decision as to whether the person is truly qualified to advocate for a student with special needs and whether this person is a "good fit" with you, your child, and your goals. Take the time to do your research. The decision you make can literally affect your own and your child's life in ways that you never dreamed possible. The person that you choose will impact your relationship with school personnel, your spouse, your child, and the members of your family. The advocate will have a direct effect on your marriage, your personal relationships and your family. You are inviting someone to enter into your world. Be very careful to whom you give this precious gift.

From *Exceptional Parent (EP) Magazine*, vol. 39, no. 8/9, pp. 34–36, August/September 2009. Copyright © 2009 by EP Global Communications, Inc. Reprinted by permission.

What Role Can an Advocate Play?

- Assist parents in finding supports and resources that are available
- Model effective relationship building and problem solving skills
- Listen to all parties in a genuine and non-judgmental manner
- Clarify issues
- Suggest options and possible solutions
- Document meetings or help parents to understand documents such as psychological assessments
- Locate and provide information
- Speak on the parent/child's behalf when they cannot speak for themselves
- Help the family with written correspondence, documentation or phone calls
- Attend meetings
- Follow up on decisions made and actions taken

The following are a few points to ponder before deciding whom you will choose:

Advocates Should Have the Qualifications to Be Able to Speak with Integrity and Knowledge about Exceptionalities in Learning

A high level of qualification brings a level of respect to the table. Humans are far more likely to listen to someone who has "walked in their shoes" and has experience in education and special needs. It is probably safe to say that very few people are willing to modify their own expertise and professional methods based on the ideas and opinions of someone who has little or no experience and credentials in the field. As an educator, sitting in meetings with someone who has no special education qualifications and having them point out your deficiencies is a waste of time and money. Any parent who has experienced being lectured on the best methods of raising children by a person who has no children may know how frustrating this can be. Teachers are more likely to be open to the opinions and suggestions of someone who is at least qualified to make such statements. It makes sense that if you want to cultivate the best education for your child, you would expect an advocate that had the special education credentials and experience that would enhance your role as parent. Maintaining professional development by attending conferences, keeping up to date on current policy documents and procedures are important qualifications to have. Special education is a constantly evolving science and an advocate must be up to date. A solid knowledge of local resources, services providers, and community programs facilitates problem solving. It is equally important that the advocate you choose have the interpersonal skills necessary to work collaboratively with others to create solutions. As a parent, expect the person that you hire to be qualified to help you to work with the school.

Advocates Should Know Your Child

People who are chosen to represent your child need to read assessments, report cards, interact and spend time with the child in order to really know who they are working for. Then the role of advocacy is authentic and not a matter of fighting for a cause or for an ego boost. When an advocate knows the parent and the child well, he or she can help to uncover the common ground between school and home. The advocate should be able to explain how your child's disability may impact their learning and then work with you to help prioritize your child's needs. A wise advocate is someone who will look for solutions and not blame. Advocates should see the child in the context of his classroom. A child's program on paper can never tell the whole story. There is no way that a teacher can put into words all of the supports, plans, visuals, tools and strategies that are employed to make the child successful. The child's world tells far more than any documentation could ever describe. It important to note that entering a classroom is opening a "sacred trust." Just as you would not let someone that you do not trust into your home, teachers must be wary to whom they open their classrooms. If someone is entering the room to "observe" and then report back to the parent all of the things that they think are being done incorrectly and to "build a case" against the school, the relationship has then been destroyed. Would you want someone coming into your home to "observe and critique" you as you carry out the daily functions of parenthood?

Advocates Should Be Objective and Solution Minded

While interviewing an advocate, listen carefully for language that promotes solutions rather than vengeance. The advocate's personal experience with a school district, board, or previous personal history has no place in the discussion. This is about YOUR child. The advocate may utilize background knowledge of the people and resources to facilitate a workable plan for your child. In order to secure a positive proactive response from the people that are in relationship with your child, the advocate is best to be respectful, courteous, considerate, and open minded. Of course, this is true of every member of a team.

Can the advocate help your child access the best education possible without putting undue stress on the resources and personnel involved? Sometimes in the hopes of helping a parent, promises are made that are overly taxing on a personal or financial level . . . the school must educate all students, not just yours. Parents may disagree and say that it is really their child that they care about. While that is very true, schools cannot operate on this premise. Educational institutions have a duty to look after the collective while at the same time ensuring that each individual receives what is needed. It is not fair to assume that school staff should take from one child in order to provide for another. Imagine someone suggesting that a parent take away resources from one of their children in order to give to another. There are solutions that can work for everyone. We need to be searching for them as a team.

Advocates Should Be Facilitators, not Dictators

Listen and observe an advocate carefully. Are they talking as if they are going into battle? Using words like "them" and "us?" Watch for an ego that is using your child to feed itself! Egos look out for egos, not children. Red flags should wave wildly when an advocate sees only negatives in a child's education, or when promises of specific outcomes for your child are made. An advocate that speaks with an "I'll show them" attitude is not going to effectively negotiate a plan that makes everyone want to do their part. Problems are not solved that way. Children do not win in these scenarios.

Humans need to be acknowledged for the effort that they invest; we need to feel supported and respected. We are more open to solutions when we are not feeling defensive. No person, neither educator nor parent, should leave a discussion feeling that they have been ignored, rejected or discounted if they were genuinely promoting a child's needs and not their own. When the disagreement lowers itself to the level of acting like children who are demanding that everyone play by their rules, the child with special needs is no longer the center of the discussion. An advocate is worth their weight in gold when they can objectively look at a situation without an emotional charge and create solutions that work for the child.

Each member of a team has a perspective on how to best help a child: a principal, community agency member, speech pathologist, teacher and a parent have ideas that stem from their training and experience. A skilled advocate is able to listen to each member's ideas and see solutions that draw on the strengths of each person at the table.

Ultimatums, threats, and accusations drive a wedge between parents and teachers that is extremely damaging to the child because the message that the parent is giving is that they trust this person more than the teacher.

The End of the Road

As a parent, it can be intensely frustrating when you feel that a system is failing your child. At times, the anger and resentment can be too much to bear. It is easy to fall into the trap of vengeance and revenge. Going to the press or calling a lawyer should never be done without serious thought of the repercussions. These actions should never be born from an emotional reaction. The cost will be high. Before taking any action, the question that should be front and center is: "How will this benefit the child? How could this hurt the child?" It is all too easy to get caught up in the feeling of retribution. When we feel helpless it is almost intoxicating to gain a sense of power. We need to be honest with ourselves about what is driving our course of action. Before taking such steps, consider that your child may have many years in school ahead of him. Your child's siblings may have many years in the educational system. The damage caused by legal action and/or public humiliation cannot help but affect your relationships with the very people that you will rely on to give your children the best, I am speaking of the deep-seated hurt, mistrust and fear that sinks into the soul of anyone that has been affected by litigation and bad press. Public humiliation and bad press may make a school system give in to your demands but it does nothing to draw out the best of any human being or relationship.

This is not to say that legal action is not necessary at times but, it is a LAST resort. Advocates may or may not be affiliated with an attorney but they are not lawyers and they should not be giving legal advice.

Final Thoughts

Hiring an advocate does not take away the parent's role in decision-making. Advocates make sense of the documents, technical language and educational jargon. They may explain options or the requirements of special programs, attend meetings and ask clarifying questions but, as the child's parents, you make the decision. Your child needs YOU to be in charge: your role is long term!

Educators need to listen, really listen to what it is that parents are asking for. We may have to sort through layers of hurt, anger, resentment and fear to see the authentic concern for their child. I believe that most times we can meet the requests of the parent at some level. Look for common ground.

The relationship between parent and school can be difficult because a child's life is at stake and emotions run high but, with hard work, respectful dialogue and child-centered problem solving, it is possible to work as a team to make the most of a child's education. It is up to the adults to make it work for the sake of the children.

POSTSCRIPT

Does Working with Parents Have to Be Contentious?

$\mathbf{F}$riction can arise when teams discuss appropriate services. Berlin (*Phi Delta Kappan,* 2009) explains that the Supreme Court has ruled that schools are required to provide the "floor of educational opportunity," not maximize the potential of each child. In words sure to strike an emotional cord, Berlin notes that some courts refer to appropriate services as a Chevrolet, not a Lexus, even though every parent wants the very best for their child.

The cost of special education is often criticized, particularly when budgets are tight and cuts must be made. A review of the special education "spending spiral" in Massachusetts (Mohl and Sullivan,www.massin.org, 2009) complained that state efforts to "tighten the rules" for eligibility and "narrow the standards for services" had not put "the brakes" on spending. Increased special education costs were bemoaned, without comparative analysis of general education spending. This viewpoint could motivate anyone to fight hard to secure scarce resources for their child. It also demoralizes educators trying to collaborate with parents.

Each of this issue's selections mentions financial pressures. Jennifer Krumins says that a wise advocate can discover the array of available supports and strategies and help parents understand that schools have a responsibility to all children.

Regardless of finances, educators and parents alike should advocate for appropriate educational programs, but parents can focus solely on their own child. After interviewing an array of parents involved in special education, Trainor (*Remedial and Special Education,* 2010) identified four advocacy styles. "Intuitive advocates" rely on personal knowledge of their children, whereas "disability experts" add information gathered from specialists and independent research. "Strategists" use more sophisticated awareness of IDEA, including the powerful role parents should play. "Change agents" move beyond the school, using their knowledge to help other parents. Different styles lead to different results. Trainor found parents were more successful at achieving their ends as they moved beyond the intuitive style.

Other circumstances can affect parental participation. Trainor alerts educators to be sensitive to the impact of cultural and linguistic differences. Parents who feel marginalized may need support to believe they are equal partners in this process. Studying Chinese families, Lo (*Preventing School Failure,* 2008) learned the parents thought educators who left meetings early were rude, especially when the parents had taken time off from work, resulting in a loss of income. Lo also discovered the words of interpreters frequently did not match those of the speaker.

Special education is based on laws written to ensure an appropriate education for children with disabilities. Teachers and administrators are professionally bound to uphold these laws and implement strong programs. Brochures designed to inform often sound more like legal contracts than guides for parents trying to plan an education for their child with a disability. Pressures to identify the right educational option are intense.

Facilitated IEPs represent an emerging practice utilized when parent/school interaction has been contentious, or less than productive (Mueller, *TEACHING Exceptional Children*, 2009). This process is designed to avoid more litigious routes, which are costly in time, money, and relationships. A neutral, expert facilitator maintains focus and order while parents and educators attend to the content of the meeting. The facilitator helps both identify key concerns, respond respectfully, and stay on topic.

In any special education meeting, parents must realize that well-meaning people might disagree about what is best. Educators must listen actively, speak clearly, and involve parents as partners. Wouldn't all of us want this for our own child? Can we reach this goal?

Contributors to This Volume

EDITOR

DR. MARYANN BYRNES is an associate professor in the Graduate School of Education at the University of Massachusetts–Boston. Dr. Byrnes consults with schools and districts on issues of policy, the implementation of IDEA, program evaluation, and professional development. Dr. Byrnes served as a special education administrator for 18 years, having taught at elementary, middle, and high school levels. She is past president of the Massachusetts Federation of the Council for Exceptional Children and past president of the Massachusetts Association of Administrators of Special Education (ASE). Dr. Byrnes earned her undergraduate degree at the University of Chicago, her masters degree at Northwestern University, and her doctorate at Rutgers University. Dr. Byrnes' current research focuses on the use of explicit, unambiguous accommodations for students with disabilities.

AUTHORS

JAMES B. ADAMS is the father of a young girl with autism, diagnosed in 1994, and that is what led him to shift much of his research emphasis to autism, focusing on biological causes and treatments. He is currently a full professor in the Department of Chemical and Materials Engineering at Arizona State University. He created and teaches a course on heavy metal toxicity, focused on lead and mercury toxicity.

HOWARD S. ADELMAN is professor of psychology and codirector of the School Mental Health Project and the National Center for Mental Health in Schools at UCLA. He began his professional career as a remedial classroom teacher in 1960 and received his Ph.D. in psychology from UCLA in 1966. He directed the Fernald School and Laboratory at UCLA from 1973 to 1986 and has codirected the School Mental Health Project since 1986.

STEVEN ADELSHEIM is the director of New Mexico School Mental Health Programs.

JENNIFER BOOHER-JENNINGS is a doctoral candidate in the Department of Sociology at Columbia University in New York City. Her research focuses on accountability, school organization, and school choice.

ELLEN BRANTLINGER is a professor emeritus of the School of Education at Indiana University. She earned her B.S. at Antioch College in 1963 and her Ed.D. at Indiana University in 1977. She is an expert on how parents, educators, and caregivers view the sexuality of the mentally handicapped and on the sterilization of people with mental disabilities. She is the author of *Fighting for Darla* (1994) and *The Politics of Social Class in Secondary School* (1993).

RACHEL BROWN-CHIDSEY is an associate professor of school psychology at the University of Southern Maine. Her research areas include curriculum-based measurement, response to intervention, and scientifically based reading instruction methods.

FREDERICK J. BRIGHAM is Associate Professor of Special Education, University of Virginia, Charlottesville.

MICHELE ST. PETER BRIGHAM is the choral music director and special education instructor at Western Albemarle High School and adjunct faculty in the School of Continuing Education and Professional Studies at the University of Virginia.

MARY T. BROWNELL is a professor of Special Education at the University of Florida as well as the Irving and Rose Fien Endowed Professor and director of the National Comprehensive Center to Improve Policy and Practice in Special Education Professional Development. Her research efforts focus on improving the reading instruction of both general and special education teachers and improving the induction of beginning special education teachers into the classroom.

DINA BRULLES is director of the Gifted Education Department in the Paradise Valley Unified School District in Arizona and a faculty associate of the

College of Education at Arizona State University, where she teaches graduate courses in gifted education. Dina currently serves as president of the Arizona Association for Gifted and Talented (AAGT), and vice president of the national gifted organization, Supporting Emotional Needs of the Gifted (SENG).

VICTORIA CRAIG BUNCE is the director of Research and Policy for the Council for Affordable Health Insurance. She has been an active advocate for market-oriented solutions to the problems in America's health care system.

JOHN CLOUD is a staff writer for *Time Magazine*, where he has worked since 1997.

CHRISTOPHER T. CROSS is a senior fellow at the Center for Education Policy and a distinguished senior fellow at the Education Commission of the States. During his 32 years in Washington, D.C., he served in both the executive and the legislative branches as an assistant secretary at the U.S. Department of Education, the Republican staff director of the House Committee on Education and Labor, and as deputy assistant secretary in the old Department of Health, Education and Welfare.

LOUIS C. DANIELSON is currently a statistician in the Division of Innovation and Development at the Bureau of Education for the Handicapped.

HAZEL DENHART is experienced in Service Learning development and implementation that started in 1994 when she worked on the design of Portland State University's Service Learning Program where she taught until 2008. This program was recently named to the U.S. President's Higher Education Community Service Honor Roll with Distinction, one of the highest federal recognitions a college or university can receive for its commitment to volunteering, service-learning, and civic engagement.

DONALD D. DESHLER is a professor of special education and the director of the Center for Research on Learning at the University of Kansas. He also serves as the codirector of the National Research Center on Learning Disabilities, funded by the Office of Special Education Programs in the U.S. Department of Education.

M. SUZANNE DONOVAN is a senior program officer at the National Research Council's Commission on Behavioral and Social Sciences and Education and study director for the Committee on Minority Representation in Special Education. Her interests span issues of education and public policy. She has a Ph.D. from the Richard & Rhoda Goldman School of Public Policy, University of California, Berkeley, and was previously on the faculty of Columbia University's School of Public and International Affairs.

STEPHEN M. EDELSON has practiced medicine for more than 20 years. As an autoimmune specialist and founder of the Edelson Center for Environmental and Preventive Medicine in Atlanta, he has successfully treated thousands of patients using innovative and effective alternative therapies. Dr. Edelson lives and works in Atlanta, Georgia.

JEFFREY EVANS does research with the Institute for Applied Psychometrics (IAP) and the Woodcock-Johnson development team. He has published in the area of reading achievement. Jeff is currently working on educational test development and writing projects with IAP. He also serves on the volunteer board of directors of United Cerebral Palsy (UCP) of Central Minnesota. Jeff holds a master's in communications disorders from St. Cloud State University.

SUSAN C. FAIRCLOTH is an assistant professor at Pennsylvania State University. Dr. Faircloth's publications and research interests center on leadership, special education, higher education, cultural diversity, and the education of American Indians and Alaska Natives.

WILLIAM C. FRICK is an assistant professor at the University of Oklahoma.

DOUGLAS FUCHS is a professor of special education at Peabody College of Vanderbilt University. He also serves as the codirector of the National Research Center on Learning Disabilities, funded by the Office of Special Education Programs in the U.S. Department of Education.

LYNN S. FUCHS is the Nicholas Hobbs Professor of Special Education and Human Development at Vanderbilt University, where she also codirects the Kennedy Center Reading Clinic. She has conducted research on assessment methods for enhancing instructional planning and on instructional methods for improving reading and math outcomes for students with learning disabilities.

PAUL J. GERBER is a professor in the Department of Foundations of Education and the Department of Special Education and Disability Policy, as well as a clinical professor of psychiatry at Virginia Commonwealth University.

RUSSELL GERSTEN is the executive director of Instructional Research Group. Currently, he directs the mathematics component of the Center on Instruction, a comprehensive technical assistance center for No Child Left Behind. He is also a professor emeritus in the College of Education at the University of Oregon. He received his Ph.D. in special education from the University of Oregon in 1978.

JENNA GOUDREAU is an editorial assistant at *Forbes* magazine.

TEMPLE GRANDIN is a designer of livestock handling facilities and a professor of animal science at Colorado State University. Facilities she has designed are located in the United States, Canada, Europe, Mexico, Australia, New Zealand, and other countries. In North America, almost half of the cattle are handled in a center track restrainer system that she designed for meat plants. She obtained her B.A. at Franklin Pierce College and her M.S. in animal science at Arizona State University. Dr. Grandin received her Ph.D. in animal science from the University of Illinois in 1989.

WILLIAM E. GUSTASHAW III is an assistant professor in the College of Education, Special Education and Rehabilitation Counseling at the University of Virginia. His research interests include effective instructional practices for students with disabilities, teacher education, and special education policy.

KAREN R. HARRIS is the Currey-Ingram Professor of Special Education and Literacy at Vanderbilt University, Nashville, Tennessee. Dr. Harris' research focuses on the theoretical and intervention issues in the development of academic and self-regulation strategies among students who are at risk and those with severe learning challenges such as learning disabilities and attention deficit hyperactivity disorder.

J. AMOS HATCH is a professor of early childhood education at the University of Tennessee, Knoxville. Dr. Hatch has written/edited three books on qualitative methods and served a 4-year term as editor of the *International Journal of Qualitative Studies in Education.*

THOMAS HEHIR served as director of the U.S. Department of Education's Office of Special Education Programs from 1993 to 1999. As director, he was responsible for federal leadership in implementing the Individuals with Disabilities Education Act (IDEA). Hehir played a leading role in developing the Clinton administration's proposal for the 1997 reauthorization of the IDEA.

JOHN HOCKENBERRY is an award-winning television commentator, a radio host, and a foreign correspondent who became a paraplegic in an auto accident when he was 19. He lives in Brooklyn, New York, with his wife, Alison, and their two sets of twins—Zoe and Olivia, and Zachary and Regan.

ROBERT H. HORNER is a professor in the Department of Special Education at the University of Oregon, Eugene. Dr. Horner has published over 150 professional papers and six texts. He currently codirects the OSEP Technical Assistance Center on Positive Behavioral Interventions and Supports and the OSEP Research and Demonstration Center on School-wide Behavior Support. Dr. Horner also codirects the Positive Behavior Research and Support research unit at the University of Oregon.

JAMES M. KAUFFMAN is the Charles S. Robb Professor of Education at the University of Virginia in Charlottesville, Virginia, where he also serves as director of the doctoral program in special education. His primary areas of interest in special education are emotional and behavioral disorders and learning disabilities. He is coeditor of *Behavioral Disorders*, the journal of the Council for Children with Behavioral Disorders, and he is coprincipal investigator of the Center of Minority Research in Special Education (COMRISE). Among his many publications are *Characteristics of Emotional and Behavioral Disorders of Children and Youth*, 7th ed. (Prentice Hall PTR, 2000) and *The Least Restrictive Environment: Its Origins and Interpretations in Special Education*, coauthored with Jean B. Crockett (Lawrence Erlbaum, 1999). He received his M.Ed. in teaching in the elementary school from Washburn University in 1966 and his Ed.D. in special education from the University of Kansas in 1969.

EVELYN B. KELLY has been an independent writer, speaker, and educator. Her books include *Encyclopedia of Attention Deficit Hyperactivity Disorders* (Greenwood, 2009) and *Gene Therapy* (Greenwood, 2007).

JENNIFER KRUMINS has been a teacher in Ontario, Canada, for 20 years. She earned her Special Education Specialist and undertook extensive training from Queen's University in Kingston, Ontario, and the Geneva Centre for Autism in Toronto, Ontario.

NATHANIEL S. LEHRMAN is clinical director (retired) at the Kingsboro Psychiatric Center in Brooklyn, New York.

CATHY G. LITTY is an associate professor in the Department of Special Education/Human Services at Western Carolina University.

DANIEL J. LOSEN is a research associate with the Civil Rights Project at Harvard University and the principal investigator for the Conference on Minority Issues in Special Education in Public Schools. He is presently developing research and policy fact sheets for members of Congress on the topics of dropouts and Title I of the Elementary and Secondary School Act. Before becoming an attorney, he taught in public schools for nearly 10 years and founded an alternative public school.

HARA E. MARANO is Editor-at-Large of *Psychology Today* and has been writing about psychological issues for more than 20 years. She lives in Brooklyn, New York.

AMY DOCKSER MARCUS is a Boston-based staff reporter for the New York bureau of *The Wall Street Journal*. Born in Boston, Massachusetts, Marcus earned a bachelor's degree from Harvard University.

KEVIN S. McGREW is the director of the Institute on Applied Psychometrics (IAP) and is currently a visiting professor in the Department of Educational Psychology at the University of Minnesota. Dr. McGrew has extensive experience in both clinical (1:1) and large-scale assessment, and in data management and analysis. Dr. McGrew has published over 60 journal articles, books, or book chapters covering many areas of special education.

MARGARET J. McLAUGHLIN has been involved in special education all of her professional career, beginning as a teacher of students with serious emotional and behavior disorders. Currently she is the associate director of the Institute for the Study of Exceptional Children, a research institute within the College of Education at the University of Maryland.

ELIZABETH MOORE is a research coordinator at the Center for School Mental Health Analysis and Action, University of Maryland School of Medicine.

ROBERT MULLIGAN is the director of special education and counseling in the Point Pleasant Beach Public Schools (New Jersey).

SAMUEL L. ODOM is an assistant professor of education and Otting Professor of Special Education in the School of Education, Indiana University, Bloomington.

GARY ORFIELD is a professor at the Harvard Graduate School of Education and director of its Project on School Desegregation. His report, "The Growth of Segregation in American Schools: Changing Patterns of Separation and Poverty since 1968," was recently issued to the National School Board Association.

LYNDA A. PRICE is an associate professor of special education at Temple University. She received her M.A. from the University of Minnesota in 1979 and her Ph.D. in 1995. Her professional interests include qualitative research methods and design in special education.

BERNARD RIMLAND is a research psychologist (Ph.D.) and a director of the Autism Research Institute, which he founded in 1967. He is also the founder of the Autism Society of America (1965) and the editor of the *Autism Research Review International*. His book, *Infantile Autism: The Syndrome and Its Implication for a Neural Theory of Behavior* (1964), is widely credited with changing the view that autism is an emotional illness, caused by destructive mothers, to the current recognition in the field of psychiatry that autism is a biological disorder.

MARCIA RUBIN is the director of Research and Sponsored Programs at the American School Health Association.

GWYN W. SENOKOSSOFF is an instructor at the College of Education, University of South Florida, St. Petersburg.

SCOTT M. SHANNON is a pediatric psychiatrist who is board-certified in general psychiatry, child/adolescent psychiatry, and holistic medicine. He currently has a private practice in holistic child psychiatry and serves as medical director of four residential treatment centers for children in Northern Colorado.

PAUL T. SINDELAR, is a professor of special education and the co-director of the Special Education Department at the University of Florida. Research interests are instructional methods for students with educational disabilities.

TOM E.C. SMITH is a professor of special education and department head of the Department of Curriculum and Instruction at the University of Arkansas. His research interests include disability law and inclusion.

MARK W. STEEGE is a professor and clinical coordinator in the School Psychology Program at the University of Southern Maine. Dr. Steege earned his doctorate at the University of Iowa and completed postdoctoral work as a pediatric psychologist at the University of Iowa College of Medicine.

KIM STODDARD is an associate professor in the College of Education at the University of South Florida, St. Petersburg. Her research interests include the development of school–university partnerships, the implementation of inclusive practices, teacher education, and implementation of thematic units.

LINDA TAYLOR is codirector of the School Mental Health Project and the National Center for Mental Health in Schools at UCLA. Throughout her career, she has been concerned with a wide range of psychosocial and educational problems experienced by children and adolescents. Her early experiences included community agency work.

BRUCE THOMPSON is a professor and a distinguished research fellow in the department of educational psychology at Texas A&M University, College Station.

H. RUTHERFORD TURNBULL III is the cofounder and codirector of the Beach Center on Disability at the University of Kansas. He is a professor of special education and former courtesy professor of law there, and his research interests include special education law and policy, disability policy generally, and, most recently, the effects of federal policy on treatment issues raised by the Schiavo cases.

U.S. DEPARTMENT OF EDUCATION (USDE) promotes educational excellence for all Americans. Created in 1980 by combining offices from several federal agencies, the USDE remains true to its original directive to ensure equal access to education and to promote educational excellence throughout the nation.

ROSALIND AND JOE VARGO, mother and father of Ro Vargo, use their voices to tell a powerful story of their daughter's success in fully inclusive educational programs, from kindergarten through college.

MELANA ZYLA VICKERS is a widely published journalist who writes editorials on education and public policy for *USA Today*. She also is a regular contributor to *The Weekly Standard* and *National Review Online* and has appeared on the PBS show *Newshour*, CNN, Fox, and other news channels.

MARK D. WEIST is a professor and director of the Division of Child and Adolescent Psychiatry in the Center for School Mental Health Analysis and Action, University of Maryland School of Medicine.

J.P. WIESKE is the director of state affairs for the Council for Affordable Health Insurance (CAHI).

ANDREW L. WILEY joined the Center for Social Development and Education (CSDE) in 2005. Mr. Wiley has completed his doctoral coursework in special education at the University of Virginia and is currently completing his dissertation. Mr. Wiley has a bachelor's degree and a master of teaching degree from the University of Virginia. He has worked as a behavior resource teacher in an intensive center program for elementary students with emotional/behavioral disorders, as an autism resource teacher, and as a behavior specialist in Fairfax County, Virginia. Mr. Wiley has taught graduate courses in behavior management and methods for teaching exceptional children.

SUSAN WINEBRENNER is a full-time consultant who works with school districts to help them translate current educational research into classroom practice. She received her B.S. in education and her master's degree in curriculum and instruction from the University of Wisconsin.

GORDON WROBEL has worked as a psychologist for Minneapolis Public Schools and the state of Minnesota.